The Politics of Regulation

THE

POLITICS

OF

REGULATION

James Q. Wilson

EDITOR

Basic Books, Inc., Publishers

NEW YORK

Library of Congress Cataloging in Publication Data
  Main entry under title:

  The Politics of regulation.

  Includes bibliographical references and index.
1. Industry and state—United States—Addresses,
essays, lectures. 2. Trade regulation—United States
—Addresses, essays, lectures. I. Wilson, James Q.
HD3616.U47P64   338.973   79–2751
ISBN: 0–465–05967–8

CONTENTS

v

Contents

PART IV

Conclusions

INTRODUCTION

JAMES Q. WILSON

These essays were written out of a common interest in discovering the relationship between private power and public purpose. This relationship is of special importance in a liberal regime such as that of the United States. Liberalism now means many things, but in the beginning it signified a commitment to liberty and, properly understood, it still refers at least to that. A liberal democracy erects, between the public and the private sectors, barriers that, though often porous and always changing, require the government to respect certain matters as private and to impose legal controls on private action only for publicly agreed-to purposes and in accordance with due process of law. That aspect of liberalism is well understood by conservatives.

By the same token, a liberal democracy can only formulate public purpose and protect constitutional procedures if the government itself is not the instrument of some private faction that seeks to use public powers for narrow or self-seeking ends. No large government such as ours can hope to act only in accordance with the "will of the majority." The majority of citizens do not have a "will" on most political matters, and if they did—and could always insist on it—the resulting policies might be as tyrannical as those of a single despot. But if the majority cannot always rule, then it is important to make certain that narrow interests do not rule in their stead. This aspect of liberalism has been generally understood by liberals.

Finding arrangements that would permit a democratic republic to avoid rule by either impassioned majorities that were heedless of the barriers between public and private life or by self-seeking factions that ignored the distinctions between private and public power was the central problem confronting the Founders. James Madison and his colleagues were at pains to devise a constitutional order that would minimize the possibility of either kind of tyranny. Their solution, of course, was to make "ambition counteract ambition," so that the many factions found in a large nation, operating through a constitutional system that required the sharing of powers and the fragmentation of authority, would make it impossible for one faction to capture the government or for the government to dominate society. They hoped that policy would be enacted only by means of a "coalition of the majority" acting on the principles of "justice and the general good."[1]

This system may have worked well during the century and a half of limited government when Washington was content to operate the post office, issue the currency, devise a tariff, distribute the public lands, and fight the Indians. From time to time some private interest group might dominate one or the other of these policy areas, but a government that did little was but little feared. Federal politics were essentially legislative politics, dominated by political parties and carried out more or less in an arena of clearly competing interests.

Today the federal government is active with respect to virtually the full range of human affairs; much of its power is exercised, and many of its purposes are defined, by a large bureaucratic apparatus. We are aware that the government affects almost every aspect of our lives; moreover, we worry that the agencies that have this effect operate, not in an arena of competing interests to which all affected parties have reasonable access, but in a shadowy world of powerful lobbyists, high-priced attorneys, and manipulative "experts." Many persons believe, in short, that ambition no longer counteracts ambition, but rather that the ambitions of bureaucrats are reinforced by the electoral needs of congressmen and the private claims of interest groups.

This concern is certainly shared by citizens who today complain of the "oil companies" or "the unions" or "the intellectuals" and their alleged grip on the reins of political power. The oft-remarked decline in popular confidence in government has been accompanied by—indeed, it is in part measured by—a rise in the belief that government

Introduction

works for the benefit of a few large interests. Citizens disagree over the identity of those interests, but not over their power.

Younger, more critically disposed scholars and journalists have sharpened this fear of large interests by asserting that the political order will in large measure reflect underlying economic interests and by directing their inquiries to the discovery of exactly what these interests are and how they operate. Some write in a traditional Marxist perspective; others simply are restless with the formulation, suggested by some older scholars, that the United States is a pluralistic political system in which continuous bargaining among all relevant interests ensures the development of politically, if not philosophically, optimal policies.

The language of these critics has entered the everyday vocabulary of citizens and writers. One cannot mention regulatory agencies without adding the observation that, of course, such agencies are likely to be "captured" by the interests they are supposed to regulate. To suggest that matters are any different from this is to mark oneself as hopelessly naïve, or even disingenuous.

If one believes that regulatory agencies are captured, one must explain why business firms so often complain of their decisions. One possibility is that business is lying—pretending to be hurt to disguise the benefits it receives. Another is that complaints are sincere, but they are addressed chiefly to the minutiae of regulatory irritants or to specific decisions affecting a single firm, and not to the pattern of industry protection created by the existence of competition-reducing regulations. Still another possibility is that different regulatory agencies have different effects: those that fix prices or control entry may confer advantages on an industry while those that enforce standards governing the quality of a product or the conditions of its manufacture may impose significant costs. Finally, business may be correct—it *is* hurt—but of course that leaves open the question of whether the hurts endured by industry are worth the benefits created for citizens.

But if the "capture" theory is correct—at least in some cases—it is unreasonable to assume that only business firms would be able to capture an agency. As government regulates more aspects of our lives, a greater variety of interests—occupations, professions, institutions, associations—acquire a stake in influencing the behavior of the regulatory agencies. If we assume that the airline companies will try to capture the Civil Aeronautics Board, it makes sense to assume that professors will try to capture the National Science Foundation, teachers to capture the Department of Education, environmentalists to capture the Council on Environmental Quality, and civil rights activists to capture the Office for Civil Rights. The plausibility of this assumption is sometimes obscured by calling agency-interest relations of which we approve "citizen participation" and agency-interest relations of which we disapprove "capture," but the issue is very much the same whatever rhetorical label we choose to employ.

If we accept the largest implications of the capture theory, we are forced to the unhappy conclusion that the more the government attempts to do, the more its various parts will fall under the control of specific and self-seeking groups in society. An activist government will become—at least under existing constitutional arrangements—a government of cartels and clients. That this has already occurred is one of the arguments of Theodore J. Lowi's influential book, *The End of Liberalism.* [2] If he is right, then only two remedies are available. One, favored by liberals, is new constitutional or legislative devices that will allow the government to be both active and uncaptured (these proposals include "clear standards," "sunset laws," widened court review of agency decisions, and "consumer advocacy"). The second, favored by conservatives, is to have the government do less, thus leaving a greater variety of decisions to the market or to private lawsuits.

The empirical question is whether capture—or clientelism—has become so pervasive and so immune to change that either a very different, or a very much smaller, government is necessary. The essays in this book cannot give a full answer to that question, but they can shed light on agency-interest relations in a variety of important policy areas. It will not be giving away too much of the argument of these chapters to say that, when one examines matters closely, they appear to be a good deal more complicated than is assumed by either liberal or conservative critics of clientelism.

Many people find complexity dull: simple statements are easier to remember; dramatic arguments are more interesting to read. Persons who found the various Ralph Nader books on regulatory agencies memorable will be disappointed by what follows here. Naderite accounts of the Federal Trade Commission and the Antitrust Division are catalogs of real and imagined horror stories, written in the best muckraker tradition and useful precisely because they stimulated many people to take an interest in the shadowy but significant world of the regulatory bureaucracy. But if matters are left where Mr. Nader and his young colleagues left them, we acquire little more than a sense of an antinomian struggle between Good and Evil that can be resolved only by the advent of a new Savonarola who, by preaching and punishment, will expunge the Devil.

Introduction

This book is an effort to go beyond an account of the newsworthy scandal to an exposition of how various regulatory agencies ordinarily operate. People—and groups—are affected more by routine performance than by the occasional crisis. The behavior of the Antitrust Division cannot be inferred from what one believes did or did not happen in the ITT case during the Nixon administration any more than the behavior of state public utility commissions can be inferred from the fact that Samuel Insull, the utility magnate, was instrumental in their creation.

The agencies covered by this book were selected by no particular plan: at various times over the last several years, students of mine have expressed an interest in studying regulatory politics and they chose, on the basis of their own inclinations, what agency interested them. The results, however unintended, comprise a reasonably comprehensive selection of such agencies. There are some traditional rate-setting or entry-controlling agencies (the Federal Maritime Commission, the Civil Aeronautics Board, and the state public utility commissions); there are also some major examples of the "new" product- or process-oriented agencies (the Occupational Safety and Health Administration and the Environmental Protection Agency.) There are agencies that deal with only a few industries (the Food and Drug Administration) and agencies that deal with all industries (the Federal Trade Commission and the Antitrust Division of the Department of Justice.) And there is one study of an agency that regulates nonbusiness organizations—the Office for Civil Rights in the Department of Health, Education, and Welfare. Some of these agencies have scarcely changed at all (the Federal Maritime Commission); others have changed greatly (the Civil Aeronautics Board).

The authors of these chapters did not approach their work on the basis of a common methodology or a shared set of political convictions. They were interested in the *politics* of regulation: in how goals were determined, conflict resolved or managed, standards set, and policy enforced. All the chapters were written by people whose principal academic training was in political science. For the most part, they neglected, except in passing, the economics of regulation—the costs and benefits of one or another regulatory policy. But, in a larger sense, the authors were very interested in the extent to which economic theory might explain the behavior of these agencies—interested, that is to say, in whether, or to what degree, agency actions could be accounted for by the rational pursuit of self-interest narrowly defined on the part of persons in and out of a given agency. Beyond these common concerns, however, each piece of research was designed by the author involved without reference to the work of others.

Nor do the authors agree on the value of the regulatory programs they have studied, or on the general value of government intervention in market transactions. Some are skeptical of the worth of the agency, others believe that the agency is necessary but could do a better or more efficient job, and still others feel that their agencies are doing as well as could be expected. Except by implication, however, these chapters were not written to make a case for or against a particular policy or agency, but rather to explain how and why government acts the ways it does.

Five of the nine chapters are drawn from completed doctoral dissertations, some of which have been or soon will be published. Two (Mansfield and Behrman) were originally written as senior honors' theses at Harvard and one (Rabkin) draws from ongoing graduate research. Another (Quirk) is based on postdoctoral research. Before any chapters were written, however, the authors conferred on the scope, organization, and style of the essays to ensure that they would address some common issues: how the agency was created and its fundamental legislation passed; what the agency normally does (how it defines its task); what major controversies have erupted over its rule-making or rule-enforcing procedures; and how one might best explain the agencies' preference for one course of action rather than another. All these agencies exercise discretionary authority, some under statutes so vague as to provide little more than a general hunting license. The authors are interested in competing theories about why an agency uses its discretion in one way rather than another. The last chapter, by the editor, offers his summary version of what his nine colleagues have found. Though each author has had an opportunity to comment on it, it should be taken as a personal statement and not a collective conclusion.

The entire enterprise, now several years old, was made possible by the generous support of the Sloan Foundation. Its grant to Harvard University to support research and writing on issues in public management provided the resources for the field research in almost every case and for the final writing (and rewriting) in every case. We express our great appreciation to Sloan and especially to Arthur Singer and Stephen White, whose light touch is appreciated almost as much as their deep pockets. As editor, I am especially grateful for the advice of Christopher DeMuth and Richard Caves and for the editorial assistance of Leslie Cornfeld.

PART I

TRADITIONAL REGULATION: RATES AND ENTRY

CHAPTER 1

State Regulation of Electric Utilities

DOUGLAS D. ANDERSON

During the past decade, the lives of few public officials have been more harried than those of state commissioners charged with the responsibility of regulating electric utilities. Caught between the demands of utilities to raise rates, of consumers to keep them down, and of environmentalists and others to "do something" about conservation and the energy crisis, commissions have been asked to mediate some of the most rancorous of recent domestic political disputes and to take on planning and pricing tasks that are historically unfamiliar to them. Explaining how state commissions have coped with these competing demands, especially in California and New York, will be a chief purpose of this chapter. Some perspective on recent changes can be gained through an evaluation of the forces that led to the establishment of electric utility regulation by the states.

DOUGLAS D. ANDERSON

Origin of State Utility Commissions, 1898–1907

The most widely held view on the origin of state laws regulating public utilities is that these laws were passed over the strenuous objection of the utilities; and that, once established, regulatory commissions had to contend with the sniping utilities which were forever striving to restrict their jurisdiction. This interpretation was expressed in one of the earliest textbooks on public utility regulation, published in 1933, and has remained a part of the folklore of regulation ever since.[1]

In fact, state regulation received the public support of leaders in the electric power industry as early as 1898; after the movement for regulation was successful in establishing commissions in nearly every state, the electric utilities vigorously defended the jurisdiction of the commissions against encroachment by local and federal authorities. If other utilities saw state regulation as inimical to their interests, electric utilities in the leading states did not.[2] That the utilities sought to preserve their autonomy is uncontested; they did this not by opposing state regulation, but by seeking it.

In 1907 there were essentially four possibilities for the future of the electric power industry: (1) control by the industry, with utility systems operated as private monopolies; (2) government ownership; (3) private ownership subject to state regulation; (4) private ownership subject to municipal regulation. Although the first possibility doubtless had the support of some businessmen, it was not a viable alternative. As electric utilities began to touch the lives of more and more people, there was nearly universal recognition that its development must be subject to some public influence. For different reasons three disparate groups— the electric utilities, the National Civic Federation, and a number of reform governors—joined forces in support of the concept of state regulation in place of either of the other alternatives. Since the motivation for regulation differed among these groups as well as within them, it is important to examine the role of each.

The Utilities

It is impossible to render an adequate description of the contributions of electric utilities to the movement for state regulation without discussing the important role played by Samuel Insull, an immigrant to the United States from Great Britain who had served for a time as Thomas

Edison's secretary and would later head Commonwealth Edison, Chicago's huge electric power system. In 1892, at the age of thirty-one, Insull arrived in Chicago to take control of Chicago Edison, which was then only one of the city's more than thirty electric companies.[3] Insull immediately set out to expand the business and fashion a monopoly of service in the city. He purchased and then retired from production the assets of competitors and obtained exclusive rights to buy the electrical equipment of every American manufacturer. The potential for growth was enormous. In 1892 only 5,000 customers in a city of 1,000,000 used electric lights. With his success in raising capital, expanding capacity, and consolidating competitors, Insull soon became the city's most important electric utility executive. But plans for further expansion were threatened five years after Insull arrived in Chicago by a group of boodlers on the city council known as the Gray Wolves.

In 1897 the Wolves had succeeded in devouring Charles Tyson Yerkes, the city's powerful traction magnate. Under state law, Chicago's public utilities were franchised by the city council for a maximum of twenty years. Because Yerkes's transportation system was a conglomerate of many smaller companies, he had to go to the city council for a renewal of his franchise every few years. This made it difficult for Yerkes to sell the long-term bonds that were necessary for his system's further development, and it meant that the Gray Wolves had repeated opportunities to harass Yerkes into making payments for favorable votes. In 1896 Yerkes devised a bold scheme to rid himself of the menace of the city council by encouraging the legislature to establish a state regulatory commission that would take control of local transportation companies away from city councils and to pass a bill that would extend the franchise to a period of fifty years. Yerkes apparently made $500,000 available to secure the votes of members of the 1897 legislature, but his bribery attempt was exposed, and his plan to remove utilities from local control was ultimately defeated by an odd coalition of boodlers and reformers.[4]

Yerkes's bill to extend the franchise period to fifty years passed, but city councils retained the power to grant the franchises. Within a year even this law was repealed, but during the time it was on the books, it gave the Gray Wolves a new opportunity to focus their special skills on Samuel Insull. A few days after the franchise bill passed, the Wolves sent emissaries to Insull to inform him of their plan to franchise a new competitor—the Commonwealth Electric Company—which they would own. The Wolves had no intention for the company to be anything but a dummy corporation—their sole purpose was to shake loose a considerable offer from Insull to buy the franchise. Insull flatly refused their first offer to sell, so the Wolves took steps to turn the paper corporation into an active competitor. It was then that they learned of Insull's exclusive rights to the purchase of electrical equipment. Without equipment Commonwealth Electric could scarcely compete. Four months later, the Wolves agreed to sell the franchise to Insull for $50,-000—a mere fraction of what they had hoped to get out of him.[5]

Insull's experience must certainly have affected his attitude toward local control of utilities, for in the following year (1898), as president of the National Electric Light Association (NELA), the industry's trade association, he advocated the elimination of competitive franchises and the establishment of a system of legislative controls of rates and service.[6] Competition, he argued, had not served to lower the price of electricity, but only to make investments riskier and costs higher. To acquire capital at low interest rates, utilities needed to be protected from competition; but in return for exclusive franchises, they must be willing to accept public control. Alluding to the European experience, Insull said:

The more certain this protection is made, the lower the rate of interest and the lower the total cost of operation will be, and consequently, the lower the price of the service to public users. If the conditions of our particular branch of public service are studied in places where there is a definite control, whether by commission or otherwise, it will be found that the industry is in an extremely healthy condition, and that users and taxpayers are correspondingly well served.[7]

Despite his standing in the industry, Insull's position was still too far advanced for the association to endorse. He did manage to establish a Committee on Legislative Policy and appointed himself to it, but it had little impact during the next six years.[8]

Insull had initially proposed state regulation as an alternative to local competition and the political bargaining that was associated with it, and as a means for reducing risk and lowering the cost of capital to the industry. But it was a different threat that ultimately made supporters of state regulation out of his fellow utility executives: the spread of municipal ownership. Insull himself had no real fear of municipal ownership; indeed, he had advocated a government-owned system for England and had even spoken for municipal ownership in the United States on occasion.[9] Other electric utility executives were not so sanguine about municipal ownership. They were terrified that the movement would wrest from them control of their businesses. Insull saw in this fear the basis for a new campaign for state regulation. With others, in 1904 he formed the Committee on Municipal Ownership under the auspices of the NELA with a view to presenting regulation as the only alternative to government ownership. Two years later, the committee was transformed into the Committee on Public Policy.

The report of the Committee on Public Policy which was read at the Washington, D.C. convention of the NELA in June 1907 is the most important statement on the role of government and utilities ever issued by the industry; it has since served as the basis of the industry's position on the subject. It was particularly timely because in that same year the first modern public utility commissions were established in New York and Wisconsin. The report's acceptance by the convention was due in large measure to the prestige of its authors—the Committee on Public Policy.[10]

The members of the committee were under no illusions that the industry could escape the demand for public scrutiny of operations and rates. Their report stated, in part:

That which is now uppermost in the public mind is public supervision and control. In the judgment of your committee some form of such supervision and control is inevitable in many if not all of the important states of the Union, and we believe it should be welcomed by the parties in interest, provided it is put, as we believe it can be, in such form as to preserve the rights and properties of the companies as well as to promote the interests of the public. The practical question is not whether there is to be such regulation and control as it is what the nature and form of them are to be.[11]

In the view of the committee, if municipal ownership were to be avoided, the form of control needed to be public regulation. In introducing reports on "Municipal Ownership" and "Public Regulation and Control" the committee wrote:

The [two] subjects . . . are intimately connected with each other. Neither can be adequately discussed without reference to the other. Indeed, one is the alternative of the other. Municipal ownership is demanded largely because of the absence of proper regulation and control. Public regulation and control, if efficient, removes the necessity or excuse for municipal ownership by securing fair treatment for the public.[12]

The subcommittee report on Municipal Ownership, written by Alex Dow (head of Detroit Edison) and Samuel Insull, developed this theme,

Douglas D. Anderson

noting that "the propaganda in favor of municipal ownership is losing its vitality . . . to a large extent because of the rapidly-approaching culmination of the idea of public regulation." The general public, Dow and Insull argued, is not so interested in the form of ownership or control, as it is in good service at reasonable rates. If public regulation could secure fair treatment, the public would accept it as an alternative to government ownership. But in a warning that rang of prophecy, Dow and Insull stressed:

> Municipal ownership is not discredited; it is merely forgotten. It would be a serious error to assume that the present movement of public sentiment toward public regulation signifies that municipal ownership is now or is soon going to be consigned to the limbo of discredited theories, along with such crazes as free coinage of silver at a ratio 16 to 1. If public regulation shall fail to establish a good understanding between the corporations operating public utilities and the customers of those corporations, we shall inevitably have a revival of the cry for municipal ownership.[13]

Having established municipal ownership as the only alternative to public regulation, and having made the case for the latter, the full committee sounded the following precautionary note:

> While agreement may be reached upon the general principle that public regulation and control of public service corporations is desirable in the public interest, and is not necessarily inimical to the safety and value of corporate investments, it is another and much more difficult matter to agree upon the nature and scope of it.[14]

A review of legislation pending in New York and other states to create utility commissions prompted the committee to express admiration for the provision of staggered terms for the sake of continuity, but to express concern over the breadth of discretion granted to regulatory commissions. Much would depend on the quality of men appointed to the commissions. Undesirable commissioners could inflict "tremendous harm" on the companies. "Indeed, it is difficult to suggest any other political machine which would be anything like as effective in its operations and as baneful in its consequences."[15] Every effort should be made to obtain good men as commissioners, the committee urged. "To that end we would advocate long terms and secure tenure of office, with adequate salaries, sufficient as far as possible to remove the element of self-sacrifice in the acceptance and incumbency of the offices." Interest-

8

ingly, the committee went on record as supporting the proposal that the regulated companies be assessed for the salaries of the commissioners.[16]

The reports of the Committee on Public Policy and its subcommittees on regulation and municipal control are a gold mine for early industry attitudes on the role of government in the utility business. Its authors were as certain that the movement for government control was unstoppable as they were that it was linked to larger forces, including the demand for more stringent control of railroads.[17] They were equally convinced that they needed to support the movement for state commissions in order to protect their businesses. "The wise course would seem to consist, not in an attempt to stem the tide of public opinion, but rather in seeking to evolve and define that method of public supervision and measure of control which will permit . . . the companies [to] conduct their business in the most progressive and enterprising manner," wrote Samuel Scovil and Joseph B. McCall.

The Subcommittee on Public Regulation and Control summarized its position in the following three conclusions:

First—That the National Electric Light Association should favor properly constituted general supervision and regulation of the electric light industry.

Second—That if state commissions be constituted, they should be appointed in that manner which will give them the greatest freedom from local and political influences to the end that their rulings shall be without bias.

Third—That state commissions should be clothed with ample powers to control the granting of franchises, to protect users of services against unreasonable charges or improper discrimination, to enforce a uniform system of accounting and to provide for publicity. If the state provides for publicity on the one hand, on the other hand it should safeguard investments. Regulation and publicity would be a grievous wrong unless accompanied by protection.[18]

Although the subcommittee reports were not voted on separately, they received the general approval of the full committee, and when a resolution calling for the acceptance and adoption of the report of the Committee on Public Policy was placed before the association, it received a unanimous vote of approval.[19]

Even before the convention, a number of electric utility executives were at work in their states supporting the concept of regulation. Their support was not everywhere uniform, nor effective, but the widespread historical impression that the most important leaders of all public utilities were dragged kicking and screaming into a system of state regulation is simply wrong. In Wisconsin, for example, the state which together with New York shares the distinction of having the first public utility commission, Henry C. Payne, the vitriolic, antiprogressive, Republican boss, who happened also to be the vice-president of the Milwaukee Electric Railway and Light Company, actively lobbied for a state regulatory commission.[20]

In California, where the effort to regulate electric utilities was greatly influenced by public discontent over the affairs of the railroads, the largest utilities were in "the vanguard of those clamoring for its passage."[21] In 1909 the president of the Pacific Coast Gas Association urged utilities to work for the adoption of state regulation, "on account of the growing desire on the part of our city governments to regulate our affairs."[22] A legislative committee composed of representatives of the Pacific Gas and Electric Company, the Los Angeles Gas and Electric Company, and the Pacific Lighting Company was appointed by the same convention to work on behalf of state regulation. The next year, the association's president came out in even stronger terms in favor of regulation by the state government: "Local men are not capable of fixing rates for public service corporations without prejudice." He then asserted that state regulation would provide "a much more settled condition as to competition."[23]

When the bill to enlarge the railroad commission's jurisdiction to cover all of the utilities was before the state legislature in 1911, the affected utilities sent their representatives to speak in support of its passage. John Britton of PG&E and Tiery Ford of the Sierra and San Francisco Light and Power Company told the *San Francisco Examiner,* "we are glad to be regulated for our own sake."[24] Had the utilities opposed the Public Utilities Act, it would not have passed both houses of the legislature as easily as it did. The month the law went into effect, a high official of the Southern California Edison Company voiced his conviction that the new commission would provide "absolute stability of our securities and protection from unnecessary competition."[25]

The National Civic Federation

The success of the movement for state regulatory commissions was aided by the managers of leading electric power companies and other utilities, but it was by no means the result of their efforts alone. Of similar importance was a group of civic reformers and corporate liberals, some of whom were organized in the National Civic Federation.[26]

If utilities sought regulation to protect themselves from competition and municipal ownership, the National Civic Federation and other participants in the coalition for state commissions had different motivations and correspondingly different views of the proper role of government regulation.

State Regulation of Electric Utilities

Noting that no "impartial" or "scientific" study had ever addressed the relative merits of private and public ownership and operation of public utilities, the National Civic Federation announced its intention, in September 1905, to conduct such an investigation on both sides of the Atlantic. A general commission of 150 widely known corporation heads, labor leaders, and "publicists" was formed to raise money for the study; its executive committee included men like Samuel Insull, John Mitchell, president of the United Mine Workers, and Louis Brandeis, who at the time was practicing law in Boston. A separate "Committee on Investigation," consisting of twenty-one members, was formed and charged with the duty of carrying out the actual study. In order to ensure "the greatest possible degree of impartiality," the committee was divided equally among persons who had expressed opinions in favor, against, or not at all on the question of municipal ownership.[27] Insull's friend, Charles L. Edgar, president of Boston Edison, was a member of the committee, as were Frank Parson, president of the National Public Ownership League, and John R. Commons, professor of economics at the University of Wisconsin.

That so diverse a group should be able to issue a consensus report at all is remarkable. Nonetheless, after two years of study, the committee released its findings in the summer of 1907, with nineteen out of the original twenty-one members agreeing to its majority report. The following principle had the unanimous support of the committee:

Public utilities are so constituted that it is impossible for them to be regulated by competition. Therefore, they must be controlled and regulated by the government; or they must be left to do as they please; or they must be operated by the public. There is no other course. None of us is in favor of leaving them to their own will, and the question is whether it is better to regulate or to operate.[28]

As to the question of private or public ownership, the committee's majority concluded that it could not take a general position. But it did agree on two points:

(1) Public utilities, whether in public or in private hands, are best conducted under a system of legalized and regulated monopoly;
(2) Private companies operating public utilities should be subject to public regulation and examination under a system of uniform records and accounts and of full publicity.[29]

Perhaps even more interesting are the reasons the committee gave for being "unable to recommend municipal ownership as a political

11

panacea." Their chief concern appears to have been a fear that municipal ownership would perpetuate the power of urban political machines by increasing the number of city jobs available for patronage. The committee did not find political machines operating in British local governments.[30] Instead, in England and Scotland, "we found a high type of municipal government, which is the result of many years of struggle and improvement. Businessmen seem to take a pride in serving as city councillors or aldermen, and the government of such cities as Glasgow, Manchester, Birmingham and others includes many of the best citizens of the city." Such conditions were "distinctly favorable to municipal operation."[31]

By contrast, many American cities did not enjoy such favorable conditions, in large part because of the corrupting influence of the public service corporations which pandered to politicians. "There seems to be an idea with many people," the committee wrote, "that the mere taking by the city of all its public utilities for municipal operation will at once result in ideal municipal government. . . . We do not believe that this of itself will accomplish municipal reform."[32] Successful municipal operation of public utilities "depends upon the existence in the city of a high capacity for municipal government." Until that capacity develops, it is better to reassert control over the private operation of the utilities through regulation. "With the regulations we have advised, with the publication of accounts and records and systematic control, the danger of the corruption of public officials is very much reduced."[33]

The report of the National Civic Federation proved to be an important stimulus for state regulation, not only because of the wide publicity the investigation and findings generated, but also because its conclusions served as the general outline for state legislation, even before they were formally published. In Wisconsin John R. Commons was asked by former Governor Robert M. La Follette and Assembly Speaker Herman L. Ekern to draft a law extending state regulation to municipal and interurban public utilities. La Follette knew that Commons was at work on the NCF's investigation, and that his recommendations would closely resemble those of the National Civic Federation. They did, and the draft bill that Commons produced became the Wisconsin law which later served as a model for many other states. Of the influence of the NCF, Commons wrote:

It was in the midst of winding up [the] Civic Federation's report that I worked during six months on the public utility law. . . . I adopted nearly the whole of the recommendations signed by 19 of the 21 members of the investigating committee of the Civic Federation. I did not, on my own initiative, introduce anything new in drafting the bill.[34]

The Reform Governors

In addition to the utilities and the National Civic Federation, the movement for state regulation of electric utilities had the support of leading progressive governors; indeed, a number of them used regulatory issues as a catapult to national prominence. Four governors in particular—Charles Evans Hughes of New York, Robert M. La Follette of Wisconsin, Hiram Johnson of California, and Woodrow Wilson of New Jersey—established the reputations which made them serious contenders for the presidency on the bedrock of government control of private enterprise. Each of these men was governor of his respective state when the key battles creating state commissions to regulate utilities were fought.[35] Although the four governors differed in many ways and eventually opposed one another for the nation's highest office, they tended to share a similar view on the regulation of public utilities when the movement for state commissions was in its infancy.

The story of the early political career of Charles Evans Hughes, in particular, merits closer attention than others because it was Hughes who sponsored the legislation in New York that created the first modern state utility commissions and because his success provided a powerful example for scores of political entrepreneurs anxious to curry favorable public opinion in launching careers of their own.

At the turn of the century, New York City was in the midst of a battle over utility rates and service. In 1902 Mayor Seth Low rejected all bids for public lighting, charging that the companies were gouging the people and that they had an obligation to provide adequate service at a reasonable price. The utilities disputed this, claiming that the seller alone had the right to set the price.[36] Low was defeated for reelection in 1903, but his successor, George B. McClellan, continued to tilt against the utilities and talk about setting up a municipal lighting plant. Meanwhile, the City Club and the Merchants Association began agitating for an investigation into the rates of gas and electricity. Tammany Hall stood solidly against an investigation, but mounting pressure finally succeeded in prompting the state legislature to authorize an inquiry.

The press remained skeptical. Hughes would lead the investigation, but he belonged to the same church as John D. Rockefeller, who supposedly controlled the gas monopoly. (He even taught Rockefeller's son in his Sunday school class.) Furthermore, he was a friend and former law partner of the attorney retained by the utilities to represent their inter-

13

ests in the investigation. There were not many journalists who thought the investigation would be anything other than a "whitewash expedition," as were so many earlier legislative investigations.[37]

For most, the spate of revelations prompted by Hughes's methodical examination came as a complete surprise. Hughes's public image changed overnight. Whereas the press had castigated him as a "trust lawyer," they now celebrated him as a major new public figure. The New York *Evening Mail* described Hughes as "a large man, not burly, but with the appearance of one who is built on big, strong lines. He looks strong. His shoulders are square, his limbs solid, his teeth big and white and his whiskers thick and somewhat aggressive."[38] Newspapers had a field day with Hughes's whiskers. Cartoonists depicted the whiskers as the straws of a broom, sweeping corruption out and good government in.[39] The *World* confided to its readers that "in real life [the whiskers] are broader, braver, bigger, bushier" than they appeared in photographs, and that "when in action they flare and wave about triumphantly like the battle flag of a pirate chief."[40]

Among other revelations, Hughes succeeded in proving: (1) that Consolidated Gas Company had charged the city $80,000 for the same amount of electric current for which private customers paid $25,000; (2) that the monopoly was selling electricity to the city for 4.86 cents per kilowatt hour, while earning a profit of 2.44 cents per kilowatt hour; (3) that the New York Gas and Electric Light Company sold current to residential customers at an average rate of 8.042 cents per kilowatt hour, but produced it at a cost of 3.664 cents, and that some customers paid as much as 15 cents for this electricity; (4) that Consolidated had sought to keep rates up and taxes down by reporting its taxable property to be only 75 percent of what it valued the same property at for rate making purposes.[41]

Hughes completed the investigation in three weeks and with remarkable energy produced his report a week later, in time to take it and his proposals to Albany before the close of the legislative session. Hughes made two recommendations for the price of electricity and gas that won immediate applause from the public: that the maximum price of electricity be dropped by one-third, from 15 cents to 10 cents, and that the price of 1,000 cubic feet of gas be dropped by one-quarter, from $1 to 75 cents.

More importantly, Hughes rejected the concept of controlling the corporations by franchise provisions and general laws and called instead for a public service commission to supervise the activities of gas and electric utilities in the state:

State Regulation of Electric Utilities

The gross abuse of legal privilege in overcapitalization and in the manipulation of securities, for the purpose of unifying control and eliminating all possible competition shows clearly that there can be no effective remedy by general legislation or through ordinary legal proceedings, and that for the protection of the public there should be created a commission with inquisitorial authority, competent to make summary investigations of complaints, to supervise issues of securities and investment in the stocks or bonds of other companies, to regulate rates and to secure adequate inspection or otherwise enforce the provisions of the law.[42]

Although the 1905 legislature responded by creating a State Commission of Gas and Electricity, the commission's rate setting powers were few and quickly constrained by a court challenge that blocked the recommended reduction in the price of gas.[43]

A little over a year later, after an investigation into the insurance industry succeeded in making him a national figure, Hughes was elected governor of New York. The day after his inauguration, he submitted his legislative program, the most important component of which was the proposal to abolish the state's Board of Railroad Commissioners, the Commission of Gas and Electricity, and the Rapid Transit Board of New York City, and to create in their place two comprehensive state public service commissions; one for New York City and one for the rest of the state. The governor was to appoint the members of both commissions and be able to remove any commissioner at will. Hughes deeply felt that unless the governor retained strict control over the appointments and removal process, the commission that regulated utilities in New York City, especially, would come under the influence of the machine and antiprogressive politicians he had struggled against.

The legislature was not so eager to curb the machine's power as Hughes was, however, and picked up his gauntlet. But they were no match for the governor. Hughes carried his campaign for the public service commissions bill to gatherings of citizens throughout the state. He used every possible occasion to win support for his bill. To an audience of businessmen he ridiculed the charge that the regulatory movement would wreak havoc on industry. He called for their support:

It is a revolt against all the influences which have grown out of an unlicensed freedom, and of a failure to recognize that these great privileges, so necessary for public welfare, have been created by the public for the public benefit and not primarily for private advantage.[44]

Hughes's appearance, his rhetoric, and his program received such favorable press attention that the legislature was cowed and gave the governor the sought-after commissions without compromise on May 22, 1907. A little more than a month later, the Wisconsin legislature followed suit with its own bill authorizing the state's Railroad Commission to regulate financial activities, establish service standards, and fix the rates of heat, light, water, power, and telephone companies.[45]

Anxious to "do something about the public utility problem," spurred on by the example of New York and Wisconsin, and supported by the favorable opinion of a wide assortment of interests, the legislatures of nearly two-thirds of the states passed laws creating comprehensive state commissions to regulate electric and other utilities in the half-dozen years that followed 1907. Vermont was the first after New York and Wisconsin, and established its commission in 1908. Maryland followed in 1910. The next year nine more states enacted public utility laws creating commissions: California, Connecticut, Georgia, Kansas, Nevada, New Hampshire, New Jersey, Oregon, and Washington. In 1912 only one state—Arizona—created a state commission, but the next year saw a spate of new commissions before the movement temporarily petered out: Colorado, Idaho, Illinois, Indiana, Maine, Massachusetts, Missouri, Montana, North Carolina, Ohio, Oklahoma, Pennsylvania, Rhode Island, Virginia, and West Virginia.[46]

Regulatory Tasks

The one element common to all of the supporters of electric utility regulation was defensive: the desire to be protected. Consumers sought protection from high rates; progressives sought protection from political machines and monopoly power; electric utilities sought protection from municipal ownership. From its inception, utility regulation has reflected this defensive posture. Its functions have been largely negative—aimed at preventing the worst abuses rather than at promoting the optimal use of economic resources.[47]

This attitude has had two important effects. First, it has meant that small consumers of electricity have ignored the regulatory process unless some scandal or political entrepreneur succeeded in making real or imagined abuses highly visible. Second, it has meant that throughout most of the seventy-year history of electric utility regulation, the utilities themselves have been free to make virtually all of the important decisions regarding the production and marketing of electricity as long as commissions judged their rates to be "fair and reasonable."[48]

The "mature" regulatory process can be thought of as a series of phases, the most important of which are the day-to-day activities of the staff; the formal regulatory process, consisting of a triallike hearing, presided over by the commission or an administrative law judge, in which evidence is presented and challenged; and the informal regulatory process, consisting of the interaction among commissioners, their staff, the regulated utilities, various intervenor groups, and the political leadership of the state.[49]

Day-to-Day Activities of the Staff

The day-to-day activities of commission staffs include processing the data on operations and finances which are submitted at regular intervals by utilities, inspecting meters and plant facilities for accuracy and safety, auditing accounts either continuously or intermittently, and recording and investigating consumer complaints. For many customers, the complaint process is the essence of regulation. Invoking the name of the local department of public utilities along with the threat of filing a complaint is about the only recourse an upset customer has when, for example, the gas company fails to turn on his service promptly.

These complaints together with the scheduled reports and the results of on-site investigations serve as the early warning system of the commission. Complaints and spot checks by commission investigators are primarily useful in identifying problems of service quality or safety, since the rates which utilities charge, once approved by the commission, are assumed to be "just and reasonable." In New York and California, monthly, quarterly, and annual financial reports on operating expenses and revenues are closely followed by the staff in order to track the earnings of the utilities. If the staff thinks the companies are earning excessive rates of return, it may recommend that the commission institute a formal hearing on its own motion to investigate the level of earnings, or it may recommend that the commission informally seek to negotiate a reduction in rates.[50]

Rate reductions are not common in today's inflationary world; rate increases are. (As we shall see, however, this is a recent development —rate *reductions* were the historic rule.) When a utility decides that its rates are too low to allow it to earn a reasonable return on investors' equity, it files a proposed increase in its tariffs, or rates. Typically, the new rates are immediately suspended for a period of from three to ten months, while the commission institutes a formal rate proceeding to determine whether the new rates are "fair."

The Formal Regulatory Process

The elements of the formal regulatory process used to set rates for electric utilities have been well developed in the last seventy years, and have become known as "cost of service rate making."[51] There are five key steps in cost of service rate making: the first four together determine the total revenue which a utility may earn—its "revenue requirement"—and the fifth is devoted to a consideration of how rates will be designed to yield the authorized revenue—"the rate structure." The process of determining the revenue requirement is easy to describe. First, a test year is selected for the firm. (Usually this is the most recent twelve-month period for which data exist.) Next, the firm's operating costs, depreciation, and taxes for the test year are added up. This amount, together with the total profit figure that regulators think is reasonable for the utility to earn, constitutes the revenue requirement. (Regulators arrive at what they consider to be a reasonable profit in the third and fourth steps of the process by determining the utility's total net investment, its rate base, and by multiplying that by a commission-determined rate of return.)[52]

Once the revenue requirement has been established, the only remaining step is determining how the rates will be structured—which classes of customers will be charged how much. Until recently, this step has been left almost entirely to the discretion of utility management with the only requirement being that rates not be "unduly discriminatory." Once approved, it is these *rates*—not the total revenue or earnings of the company—which are fixed and which may not be changed without commission authorization. As long as a certain tariff schedule is in effect, any excess profits which a company may earn by charging such rates is not subject to refund.

In part, this absence of control over rate structures has been due to a lack of commission expertise, time, and access to data; but there are two other, more important reasons. First, regulators have always conceived their function to be the prevention of excess profits rather than the promotion of economic efficiency. Consequently, whatever resources have been available to the commissions have been devoted to strengthening their ability to challenge the utilities' revenue requirement case. Second, from the end of World War II until the late 1960s, the price of electricity was of no great concern to the average residential consumer. Monthly bills were stable and relatively small. In the two decades from 1951 to 1971, the real price of energy actually dropped 43 percent.[53] As long as rates were falling, consumers were simply indifferent as to how utilities structured their rates. In the absence of customer complaints, state commissions, even the largest and most skilled ones, had no incentive to exert systematic control over utility rate structures.

From this description of regulatory tasks, it can be seen that regulators were seldom required to engage in much planning or to take much responsibility for the economic effects of utility rate structures. That has changed dramatically in the last ten years. State commissions have been challenged as never before to assume responsibility for key decisions regarding both the production and pricing of electricity. To place these changes in the proper context, it is necessary to digress briefly for a description of the economics of electric power production and the general practice of setting rates.

Electric Power Production and Pricing

The production of electric power is subject to a special condition that the production of other commodities is not: it cannot be stored. Since electricity must either be used or wasted the moment it is produced, there is no inventory that can be drawn upon when demand is especially heavy. As a consequence, power plant facilities have to be large enough to meet a system's *peak* demands. Peak periods vary by time of day and by season. From an efficiency standpoint, users who take power "on-peak" should pay the added or marginal cost of providing the extra capacity needed to serve them during that time. "Off-peak" users—those customers who take power when much of the system's capacity is idle—should not be charged at all for power plant capacity, but only for the extra costs for fuel, labor, and materials required for the satisfaction of their demands. Since investment in electric plants is large and overhead costs are high, this difference between what is charged for electricity taken on-peak and that which is used off-peak can be substantial.[54]

Contrary to what is indicated by economic theory, the basic pattern of rates charged by most electric utilities takes into account volume but not time of use. It is often referred to as a "declining block" tariff or "promotional" rate design because the cost per kilowatt hour of electricity declines with increased usage. Large users may pay only half as much per kilowatt hour as small users.[55] Promotional rates were instituted in this country largely through the efforts of Samuel Insull, who first learned of their use in England in 1894.[56] During the development of the industry, when economies of scale could be realized by the construction of larger and larger plants, promotional rates made a good deal of sense. By promoting use, larger plants were built and the price per kilowatt hour lowered. With the maturing of the industry, such opportunities were depleted, and promotional rates have become more difficult to justify. Utilities which still cling to a system that gives lower rates to industrial and large-volume users do so in large part because they are discriminating in price in accordance with elasticity of demand, and not because they are fostering efficiency.[57]

Although economists have long talked and written about the importance of restructuring electric utility rates to be in greater conformity with marginal costs, few of them had much hope that their advice would be acted upon.[58] Yet, precisely those things that economists said would not happen, are happening in the leading states, and they will likely be followed elsewhere, as well. The reason for this dramatic new interest in subjecting rate structures to closer regulatory supervision is not that utility commissions have suddenly "seen the light." They have changed their behavior in response to alterations in the economic and political environment in which they operate. It is to these changes in the political economy of regulation that we next turn.[59]

Structural Change in the Process of Regulation

From the end of World War II until the late 1960s, promotional campaigns urged people to "live better electrically" by purchasing new electric appliances and building "all-electric homes." The declining block structure that utilities used to price electricity stimulated this growth in demand. The more consumers used, the less per unit they paid. Everyone—utility executives, investors, state regulators, and consumers—seemed satisfied with promotional pricing because the growth in demand meant that larger generating plants could be constructed and greater economies of scale realized. Investors liked the larger plants because they promised increased profits. Utility managers were attracted to the opportunities for growth in sales. Regulators had the happy task of watching the industry become more efficient and, on occasion, of negotiating rate reductions.

In the absence of conflict, newspapers ignored the utilities, except for

State Regulation of Electric Utilities

an occasional story on the financial page noting the issuance of bonds to finance new construction. Planning and pricing decisions—how many new plants, of what type, where and when they should be built, and who should be charged for them—were made largely by the industry itself, with little supervision by the government regulators. As long as rates were stable or declining and service was reliable, about the only people who paid any attention to state utility commissions were utility executives. In most instances, this meant that commissions were in the backwater of state politics. Appointments were often political payoffs and largely went unnoticed. It was not uncommon for commissioners to treat their office as "no-show" jobs. Many were poorly trained and were even less interested in the technical affairs of utility regulation.

In New York an influential commission source offered the following analysis:

> I think that if you look closely at the composition of the commissions in the sixties and the fifties—which I have—it's not too difficult to see that they weren't very good. The commissioners were almost all political appointees—either defeated candidates or retiring politicians who were basically in need of a job. And it's evident in the performance of the companies. First of all there were very few rate cases—with Con Ed being about the only exception—and they were small. . . . Companies were earning well in excess of [a reasonable] amount and there seems to be evidence that they were expanding capacity at a greater than optimal rate.[60]

Another long-time observer of state commissions remarked: "You can put your brother-in-law who needs a job in as earthquake commissioner . . . and he'll do fine—as long as there is no earthquake."[61]

For many state commissions, the earthquake hit in October 1973 in the form of the Arab oil embargo. As a direct result of the embargo, fuel costs skyrocketed to nearly four times their 1972 levels. These costs were soon reflected in increased electricity rates. Nationwide, rates rose 90 percent in the five years after 1970. In New York the increase was even sharper: some customers were paying nearly twice as much per kilowatt-hour in 1974 as they had in 1972.[62] People who had been induced to buy "all-electric" homes were especially hard hit. Consolidated Edison, New York's giant utility, reported that the typical monthly bill for residential electric heat in Westchester County was about $250 in March 1974, which was up from around $130 one year earlier.[63]

But rising fuel costs were only one source of the rise in electricity rates. By 1967 the economies of scale and other technological advances which had caused electricity prices to fall from World War II levels had largely been achieved.[64] The effect of inflation in the cost of capital and construction wages soon swamped the savings associated with larger size. From 1972 to 1975 the cost per kilowatt of new nuclear capacity rose 80 percent while the cost of new coal-fired power plants doubled.

Utility Rate Cases

These dramatic increases seriously threatened the financial position of the utilities, which deluged regulatory authorities with requests for permission to raise rates. The increase in regulatory activity is reflected in the number of general rate reviews conducted by state utility commissions. In 1963 only 3 cases were being reviewed nationwide. By 1969 the number had increased to 19, and by 1975 it had shot up to 114.[65]

From the point of view of the utilities, the problem with general rate cases is that they take so long to be decided. In some of the larger cases in the mid-1970s, it was not unusual for the process to take eighteen months or even longer. To counteract the effect of "regulatory lag," it became common for utilities to file a new request for permission to raise rates immediately upon completion of a previous rate case and to urge regulators to adopt or to extend the use of "fuel cost adjustment clauses" which allowed them to increase rates to cover escalating fuel costs without first going through a lengthy hearing process.

Helpful as the fuel cost adjustment clauses were to the utilities, they did not solve the companies' financing problems. In one case in particular, that of Consolidated Edison in New York, the 1973 oil embargo hit with such fury that even the fuel clause was unable to save it from near financial disaster. In 1974, 75 percent of Con Ed's electricity was produced by burning foreign oil.[66]

> Con Ed was immediately affected by the embargo. . . . A black market for oil developed with Con Ed buying oil on the high seas at $23 to $24 per barrel— up from $4 to $5 per barrel earlier. . . . Even though the New York State Public Service Commission authorized a temporary increase of something like $75 million in February, 1974, in April the company was on the brink of bankruptcy because it couldn't raise working capital. . . . Working capital is maintained on hand to tide them over between outflow for fuel costs and operating expenses and wages, and inflow of revenue. . . . Banks were refusing to loan, and people weren't buying its bonds. When the commission refused to allow the company to use working capital to pay [common stock] dividends, the company had to pass on its dividends in April. The stock stopped trading for a while.[67]

It was the first time in eighty-nine years that the giant utility had failed to pay quarterly dividends on its common stock. In a desperate attempt to raise cash, the utility's chairman, Charles F. Luce, proposed that the Power Authority of the State of New York (PASNY) buy two of Con Ed's unfinished generating plants for $450 million.

The shock of Con Ed's actions reverberated throughout the industry. The common stock of Boston Edison fell from over $25 on April 22 to about $15 on May 14. Duke Power's stock dropped over 12 percent. Financial analysts worried about the industry's ability to raise capital. Said one: "Con Ed lost the institutions long ago, but its dividend allowed it to count on the little old lady in tennis shoes. Now it has lost her, too. And lost her for a lot of other utilities." Said another: "Utilities . . . have long been considered the best stocks for widows and orphans, and now we have the largest of them in trouble and passing its dividend. This throws the viability of the entire industry in doubt. It makes it more difficult for us to sell securities at a time when we need to sell them more than ever." Some executives began reexamining ambitious construction plans in light of the new fuel and capital costs. Toledo Edison cut a stock offering in half, while Detroit Edison hesitated before offering an issue of $150 million and then slashed it by a third to get it sold. The American Electric Power Company (AEP) reported its intention to make drastic cutbacks in its construction program—at least $250 million in two years.[68] In the bond market, financial analysts downgraded the bonds of many electric utilities, which meant that the utilities and ultimately the consumer would have to pay more to borrow money for new construction. From 1974 through June 1977 there were 184 changes in the ratings of electric utility debt by Moody's and Standard and Poor's, the two major rating services. Thirty-five issues were upgraded and 150 were downgraded.[69] It soon became common for utility executives like Lelan Sillin Jr., the chairman and president of Northeast Utilities, the largest power supplier in Connecticut, to contend that the regulation of electric utilities had "broken down."[70]

Consumer Response

Utility executives were not the only ones to question the efficacy of state regulation. The enormous rate hikes and fuel cost increases that were authorized in order to preserve the utilities' financial standing soon shocked consumers out of their state of indifference. Organizations mushroomed across the country as irate consumers crowded into the once-sleepy hearing rooms of state public utility commissions to voice their opposition to further rate increases. In close pursuit of the consumers came television and newspaper reporters, ever eager to broadcast a confrontation. Regulators, who a few years before had enjoyed the relative obscurity of technical debates over such arcane matters as the proper valuation of a utility's rate base and the correct treatment of depreciation, now saw those same debates recast in emotional terms before a wide audience.

Commissioners were caught in a double bind. If they failed to grant rate requests, the utilities would threaten that they were faced with insolvency, at worst, or much higher prices for new capital, at best. On the other hand, approval of rate increases made the commission appear to be rubberstamping industry requests, and that resulted in more and more consumer representatives appearing at rate hearings, which in turn attracted even more attention from the press.[71]

Environmental Representation

Coinciding with the awakened interest of consumers, a second new, and more ideologically motivated group of intervenors began showing up at commission hearings in the early seventies: the environmentalists. Groups such as the Sierra Club and the Environmental Defense Fund (EDF) identified the electric power industry as a major source of environmental degradation. The industry's progrowth ethos and pricing policies were especially suspect. Where the industry's engineers looked and saw modern, technically efficient generating units, environmentalists looked and saw foul air, scarred landscape, and polluted streams. They argued that utilities failed to "internalize" these social costs in their pricing structure and so encouraged their users to consume more electricity than was optimal. Moreover, because the price of electricity did not vary by time of use, they claimed that utilities built more power plants than were needed in order to meet their peak demands. Starting in 1973, the EDF and other groups began making appearances in rate cases in Wisconsin, Michigan, New York, and California to urge regulators to pay more attention to the environmental effects of the industry's building and pricing plans.

As a result of these two new participants, the scope of conflict over the regulation of electric utilities changed dramatically. Decision making no longer was the sole province of the industry with the mild supervision of the regulators. Politicians, the press, and the environmental and consumer groups, all clamored for a role.

The interests of these new participants were by no means identical. Environmentalists wanted to stop pollution; consumers wanted to stop rate increases; regulators wanted a way out; politicians wanted a way up. At about the same time that environmentalists discovered that they could not stop all new power plant construction, consumers found themselves unable to prevent all rate increases. The formal hearing process greatly advantages those who can present a positive alternative or who have the resources to cast serious doubt on someone else's proposal. In 1972 environmentalists and consumers could do neither. They found themselves objecting to new construction or new rate hikes with no effective means to counter the utilities' presentations. The antiindustry groups searched for an opening that would give them access to industry decision-making before plans were submitted to regulatory authorities. The focus of this search soon became the rate structures of the regulated firms.

For both environmentalists and consumers, the reform of rate structures was a way to achieve indirectly what they might fail to get directly. Both saw the key element of utility rate structures—the declining block method of pricing—as inimical to their concerns. Environmentalists were convinced that under another pricing scheme —one that did not promote high-volume usage—there would be less need to build new generating facilities. Consumers opposed the declining block structure because it appeared to favor the large user—especially industrial and commercial users—at the expense of the smaller, residential consumer. Together they urged utility regulators to hold "generic" hearings on rate structure reform and to force utilities to abandon the declining block method of pricing.[72]

The Issues

Of the many proposals advanced to reform rate structures, the two that have received the most attention are "peak-load pricing" and "lifeline" rates. Environmentalists prefer peak-load pricing based on marginal costs, which differentiates rates according to time of use. Residential consumer advocates, on the other hand, favor lifeline rates, which are designed to price the first several hundred kilowatt-hours of electricity below cost. Logically, the two differ fundamentally, although it is possible to combine elements of both in practice.

In addition to environmentalists, peak-load pricing advocates include Federal Energy Administration experts and an impressive list of academic and consulting economists who have appeared before state commissions on behalf of the concept. They base their arguments on economic theory: society's resources will be optimally allocated only if rates reflect the true marginal costs of production. Their appeal, therefore, is to the value of efficiency; although, in the case of the environmentalists, it is not efficiency for its own sake, but rather for the purpose of raising prices, discouraging demand, and preventing the growth of the industry.

Residential consumer groups are willing to allow prices to rise only if it is the price paid by someone else, such as industrial and commercial users. To this end they advocate "inverting" the rate structure whereby the cost per kilowatt-hour rises rather than falls with increased volume. Coupled with this is usually the proposal that a "subsistence" quantity of electricity (usually 250 or 300 kilowatt-hours per month) be provided at a subsidized rate—a "lifeline" guarantee.[73]

Both of these proposals emanated from outside of state regulatory commissions, but where they have received serious consideration, they have succeeded primarily because regulators saw in them the means for coping with the competing demands that they "do something" about electric rates, the environment, and "the energy crisis."

The two largest states, California and New York, have been the states (in addition to Wisconsin) in which reform proposals have made the most headway. The two states are alike in that their respective public service commissions have large and well-trained staffs which regulate some of the largest investor-owned utilities in the nation. Yet they have taken different approaches in dealing with the new demands for public accountability and responsiveness in the pricing of electricity. California has adopted *both* lifeline and time-of-day rates; New York has eschewed lifeline in favor of peak-load pricing.

Lifeline in California: The Politics of Pricing

It is putting it mildly to suggest that the California Public Utilities Commission (PUC) does not enjoy the esteem of the industrial and utility interests it regulates. The state commission is one of a half dozen often mentioned by financial analysts as fostering an "unfavorable regulatory climate." In 1978 *The Wall Street Journal* editorialized that the commission's majority "has made it a positive villain to utility executives and shareholders."[74] But the agency has not always been viewed as such. Indeed, under Governor Ronald Reagan, the PUC was characterized in the press as the "give-away" commission, run by inept political hacks and staffed by demoralized bureaucrats. So favorable toward industry and the utilities was the commission that one California utility executive conceded that the PUC was "like a friendly bear in a china shop" and was causing the company public-relations problems.[75]

The negative publicity reached a head in 1974 when the state's largest daily newspapers and at least one television station featured lengthy exposes of the PUC's personnel and procedures.[76] Much—though not all—of this adverse publicity was due to the enormity of rate increases authorized under the state's fuel cost adjustment clause. In 1973–74 the PUC authorized $608 million in pass-through rate increases to electric utilities without public hearings, while authorizing $96 million in general rate increases which required public hearings and intensive scrutiny.[77] The result was monthly increases in electricity rates throughout most of 1974.

Indeed, 1974 was a propitious year for mounting a campaign to alter the structure of electric utility rates in California. Governor Reagan had announced that he would not seek another term in the November elections, and a host of potential successors were eager to develop issues to run on. The controversy surrounding the PUC and its approval of rate increases exerted a magnetic force on these would-be heirs. Jerry Brown, his rivals, and half of the California legislature eventually included sharply worded attacks on the PUC in their campaign rhetoric. And the established politicians were not the only ones seeking to exploit the PUC's problems. The commission provided a valuable "enemy" around which consumer advocates could develop organizational strategies and a stable incentive base. The most successful of these was a group that came to be known as the Citizens Action League (CAL). CAL's campaign against a proposed $233 million general rate increase for Pacific Gas and Electric (PG&E) quickly evolved into a campaign for lifeline rates that was cleverly christened "Electricity and Gas for People" (E&GP).

The CAL campaign was born in January 1974 when a group of about 100 people who had been active in civil rights and the antiwar movement met at a conference in the San Francisco Bay area sponsored by "Organize, Inc.," a training center built around the ideas of the late Chicago activist, Saul Alinsky. The conference had the purpose of "reviewing the lessons of social activism learned in the sixties and devising organizational strategies for the seventies."[78]

The meeting was organized by Mike Miller, who had trained with Alinsky and had led a successful neighborhood group in San Francisco called the Mission Coalition. Miller was aided by Tim Sampson, an instructor in social work at San Francisco State College. A key purpose of the meeting was to identify an issue which would be useful in building a coalition of low- and middle-income people. The leaders wanted to build an organization which could eventually be used "to change the basis of power and work for economic justice."[79]

A number of different issues were considered. The OPEC price increases made the oil companies a natural choice, but the leaders worried over how to organize an anti-oil company campaign. The Pacific Gas and Electric Company seemed to be a good alternative. As Tim Sampson was later to remark:

> If we had had a handle on the oil companies, we would have gone after them. Instead we settled for the "mom and pop" store of the oil industry which was the electric and gas utility. Someone had brought to the meeting a clipping from the newspaper, announcing that PG&E was asking for the largest rate increase in history on top of huge rate increases for fuel offsets. We looked at the possibility of fighting PG&E as an organizing issue. It got us into the energy field, which was good. It gave us a chance to fight a large corporation which was a monopoly. Plus it had its headquarters in San Francisco, where most of our support was, as did the PUC which regulated it. It just looked good all the way around.[80]

Shortly after the January conference, a smaller group met to draft a platform for the E&GP campaign. Since the group's primary purpose was to build an organization by using the utility as an adversary to work against, its leaders were much more flexible on the definition of issues than they would have been if the campaign had been approached from a different perspective. Wrote Mike Miller:

> Lifeline cannot be understood other than in its context of building what "new populists" call majority constituency organizations. Our fundamental purpose in the campaign was not only to win a victory that would provide important benefits to low and mid-line income consumers, but to build an organization in which these consumers became active citizens. We see ourselves as organizers whose primary job is to build people power. The basic thing we wanted to do was build an organization that could challenge big business, make bureaucracy more accountable to the public, and force the political parties and elected officials to take stands on issues that we defined by organizing the people.[81]

Lifeline rates proved to be the issue on which the utilities, the PUC, and the politicians were most vulnerable, but that was not immediately apparent to the CAL leaders. Sampson, who was chairman of the E&GP campaign and later president of CAL, said the group "initially zeroed in on stopping the rate hike."[82] Blocking all rate increases seemed to be too difficult in the face of rapidly rising costs, however, so E&GP shifted focus to the structure of rates:

We actually picked lifeline to focus on after we were well into our utility campaign. From the beginning, both lifeline and fair share rates were part of our platform, which also included stopping the rate hike, a fair chance for public power, and an end to price fixing and profiteering. Our focusing in on lifeline had an immediate organizing value. As we experimented with it, it was apparent that everyone was really responsive to the notion—particularly to the notion that lifeline would be for everybody.[83]

On February 5, 1974, less than a month after CAL's January organizing conference, over 400 people converged on the PUC hearing dealing with the proposed $233 million rate increase. With them came the news media. After a brief statement attacking the utility and the PUC's failure to regulate it, the group left the state building to march about one mile to PG&E's corporate headquarters on Market Street. The news media followed them to hear a company public-relations spokesman refuse to accept E&GP's demands that the rate request be withdrawn and a new one drafted that would include lifeline rates. Finally, the company security guards locked the building to keep the E&GP crowd out of doors. The evening news reported this all in great detail, and the E&GP campaign was launched.[84]

The E&GP leaders recognized from the start that they could not win lifeline through the PUC's normal decision-making process as long as the Reagan appointees controlled the five-member board. The majority could be counted on to oppose the measure steadfastly. After its initial confrontations with the PUC and PG&E, the group concentrated on making the issue of rate reform an important part of the legislative and gubernatorial campaigns.

Throughout the summer and fall of 1974, E&GP sought pledges of support for a legislatively mandated lifeline rate from candidates for the legislature. An early, important ally was Speaker of the Assembly Leo McCarthy, who next to the governor is probably the most powerful elected official in Sacramento. McCarthy wrote Mike Miller on September 20, 1974 to indicate his support for the lifeline concept in PG&E rate schedules.[85] Privately, he worked with E&GP on a draft of a bill which he had agreed to introduce in the assembly.

The PUC Lifeline Decision

Despite the pressure of the legislative campaign, as late as January 1975, the PUC—commissioners and staff—was solidly opposed to the lifeline concept. Commissioner Vernon L. Sturgeon, president of the PUC, said bluntly:

Lifeline is a fraud. No one gets lifeline because it causes higher rates for business and they pass on more than that cost of business to consumers. It's good for PR and nothing else. They tried to push it as conservation, but that's pure unadulterated b—— s——.[86]

Most members of the staff agreed with the Reagan commissioners on lifeline. A senior staff examiner confided that in his opinion, lifeline is "misguided compassion." Engineers dismissed it as "an attempt to sell a 'free lunch.' "[87] On February 25, 1975 the commission secretary wrote Assemblyman Miller to express the PUC's opposition to the proposed bill.[88]

The PUC's solid wall of opposition to lifeline began to crumble in February 1975, when newly elected Governor Brown made his first appointment to the commission. Brown had promised to appoint commissioners who would "open up the process of regulation and be more accountable to public opinion." His first choice for the job was Leonard Ross, a twenty-nine-year-old former assistant professor. Ross had a law degree and an economics degree from Yale and the reputation of being a "whiz kid." (As an eleven-year-old, Ross had actually won The $32,000 Dollar Question on television.)

From the start, Ross took exception to the position of his colleagues on lifeline. On March 6, 1975, he directed the commission secretary to write Assemblyman Miller to inform him that he had not been appointed to the PUC when the commission decided to oppose the bill.[89] In the same month, he further indicated his support for the lifeline concept by choosing Jim Cherry as his legal assistant. Cherry was a close friend of Tim Sampson of E&GP and had represented consumer groups in favor of lifeline at commission hearings on the PG&E case.[90] Together with Cherry, Ross worked out a strategy to "sell" lifeline. The two decided to define the issue as a "basic human right" and an aid to "conservation," rather than as an income redistribution measure.

Ross's first target was Governor Brown's next appointment to the Public Utilities Commission, Robert Batinovich. When Batinovich was appointed in March 1975, he was known to the public chiefly as an "enemy of Richard Nixon." He had earned his place on the former president's list by contributing heavily to the campaigns of George McGovern and Paul McCloskey, in addition to that of Jerry Brown.[91]

Batinovich had some initial reservations about lowering the rate on the lifeline block from its original level (which was the proposal in the bill before the legislature at the time), but he was favorable to the notion of doing away with the declining block rate structure. Batinovich and Ross hit upon a compromise which allowed a lifeline rate prospectively: the rates for the lifeline quantity of electricity would remain frozen at the current level. Further rate increases would be allocated to the utility's tail blocks until the rate structure was inverted.

Once the compromise was reached, Ross and Batinovich spoke out publicly in favor of a lifeline rate. Surprisingly, within a month, David W. Holmes, the new commission president and a Reagan appointee, agreed to back the lifeline position of Ross and Batinovich, and secured the majority support of the commission for the concept. On August 25 the PUC secretary wrote Assemblyman Miller, this time to indicate commission support for the lifeline bill.[92] Ten days later, the bill passed the senate and went to the governor for his signature. The law left it to the PUC to designate "a lifeline quantity of electricity which is necessary to supply the minimum energy needs of the average residential user for . . . space and water heating, lighting, cooking and food refrigeration."[93]

The fact that Commissioner Holmes had agreed to support Ross and Batinovich on lifeline meant that the commission could issue its own decision in favor of lifeline in advance of the effective date of the legislation, an option that the PUC exercised in the PG&E case that had stirred up the initial controversy.[94]

Implementing the Lifeline Law

Despite overwhelming staff opposition to lifeline, the decision was relatively easy to implement. In response to the legislative mandate, hearings were held to determine lifeline quantities of gas and electricity. The task of preparing estimates of the minimum needs of the average residential consumer by climatic zone and by use required some judgment, but after the decision was made, little coordination was needed to implement the rate. The "basic" lifeline quantity for the use of lighting, cooking, and food refrigeration was set at 240 kwh per month. An additional 250 kwh per month was allowed for consumers with electric water heating and up to 1,420 kwh per month above that was allowed for residential users who relied on electric space heating in the mountainous areas of the state. Slightly lower allowances were approved for residential consumers living in master-metered apartments.[95]

In February 1977 the PUC filed a report to the legislature on the effects of the lifeline rates on California customers. While the price of the lifeline quantity of electricity remained unchanged, PG&E's average charge on all other sales had risen 16.77 percent.[96] A later report showed that some PG&E industrial rates had actually increased as much as 94.8 percent.[97] In 1976, 97 percent of PG&E's residential users had bill reductions as a result of lifeline. The lifeline mandate had resulted in shifting the burden of rate increases to commercial and industrial users, which is exactly what its proponents had hoped it would do.

Peak-Load Pricing in New York: The Politics of Efficiency

Less than a year after the California lifeline decision, the New York Public Service Commission (PSC) unanimously concluded that "marginal costs ... provide a reasonable basis for electric rate structures" and ordered each of the electric utilities within its jurisdiction to develop studies "sufficient to translate marginal cost analyses into rates."[98] Within six months the commission had examined and found reasonable the state's first mandatory time-of-day rate based on marginal cost. It was offered by the Long Island Lighting Company (LILCO) and was to apply to the utility's 175 largest commercial and industrial customers. The rate became effective February 1, 1977.[99]

The principal force behind these decisions and the "generic" rate investigation that led the commission to embrace the principles of marginal cost was Alfred E. Kahn.[100] Kahn was appointed chairman of the PSC in July 1974—he would later serve under President Carter as chairman of both the Civil Aeronautics Board and the Council on Wage and Price Stability. He had been professor of economics at Cornell and the dean of the university's College of Arts and Sciences. From the day he was made chairman, Kahn had a clear understanding of the principles that would guide his regulatory efforts. He had spent more than twenty-five years teaching such courses as "Private Enterprise and Public Policy" and in 1970 had published *The Economics of Regulation: Principles and Institutions,* a highly regarded, two-volume treatise.[101] For Kahn, the value of marginalist principles for guiding pricing decisions was unquestioned. However, he arrived on the scene with an open mind as to the feasibility of marginal cost pricing in regulated industries, with a recognition that certain notions may not be politically or administratively attainable, but also with an enthusiasm to pursue the topic until those constraints become clear. It was for that purpose that he urged the commission to institute the generic rate hearing. Kahn was not acting entirely on his own initiative; the immediate impetus for the generic hearing came from separate petitions filed by two unlikely cosponsors: the Environmental Defense Fund and the state's seven major investor-owned utilities.

The Environmental Defense Fund

The EDF's interest in rate reform as an alternative to growth dates from its intervention in 1973 in a Wisconsin case. Five months before the New York commission ordered the generic hearing, the Wisconsin Public Service Commission, acting largely on a record developed by the EDF, became the first commission to embrace long-run incremental cost as a basis for designing electric rate structures.[102] New York was the EDF's next move after Wisconsin. The organization tried intervening in a Niagara Mohawk case in early 1974 with only partial success. Kahn's subsequent appointment as chairman encouraged them to seek a generic hearing.

Edward Berlin, who was the EDF's counsel in these rate cases and would later be appointed by Governor Hugh Carey to the New York Public Service Commission, explained that Wisconsin was chosen as the trial state partly out of convenience, and partly because of its reputation for progressive regulation which dates back to La Follette:

We looked around and it just seemed to be the best place to make our case at the time . . . primarily because that was where Charley Cicchetti was [the EDF's economist who at the time was an associate professor at the University of Wisconsin] and also Wisconsin had a chairman who was a young attorney who had a reputation as a progressive. Then, too, Wisconsin was small enough—the utility was small enough—and we thought that was important.[103]

By the time they petitioned for the generic proceeding in New York, the Environmental Defense Fund had had considerable experience in promoting regulatory reform. The organization was quickly developing a national reputation for sponsoring responsible testimony. Its initial efforts caught the attention of other consumer and environmental groups interested in the possibilities of rate structure reform. EDF simultaneously intervened in rate cases in other states, notably California, and was soon joined in its advocacy of marginal cost by witnesses from the Federal Energy Administration.

DOUGLAS D. ANDERSON

The Utilities

New York's seven major investor-owned utilities joined EDF in petitioning for a generic hearing, but for quite different reasons. Actually, the utilities were divided among themselves as to the merits of marginal cost. Some, like Long Island Lighting Company (LILCO) and Con Ed, which were faced with huge capital needs and deteriorating load factors, were interested in the concept. Others, like Niagara Mohawk, which still wanted to expand and grow, were decidedly against abandoning the declining block rate.

That the utilities should enter a similar petition so soon after EDF was a surprise to many of the commission's staff members, some of whom speculated freely as to their motivations. The best insight came from a source close to the chairman. When asked whether the utilities were invited to petition for the hearing, the informant said:

> In so many words, yes. Shortly after Chairman Kahn came on the scene, he had a meeting with the chief executive officers of all of the utilities in his office in which he explained his commitment to marginal principles in rate design and his belief in the immediacy of the problem. He also sought to convince the utilities that the effort was worthy of their support and that the chairman recognized his need to rely on the assistance of the utilities—however reluctantly they would consent—for success. After due consideration, the utilities agreed that it was in their best interest to seek a generic hearing, so all of them petitioned together.[104]

For some of the utilities, the generic proceeding represented a means of slowing down the progress of rate structure reform, rather than speeding it up. Together the utilities engaged National Economic Research Associates, a consulting firm, to present the affirmative case for marginal cost-based rates, but individual utilities hoped the hearing would drag on without the commission's taking action.[105]

Once it was decided that marginal cost provided a reasonable basis upon which to base rates, the commission counted the yeas and nays which had been entered in the proceeding. In strong support of the concept were the Long Island Lighting Company, the Environmental Defense Fund, the Federal Energy Administration, New York City, and Chemung County Neighborhood Legal Services. In support, albeit less forcefully, were Consolidated Edison, Central Hudson, New York State Electric and Gas, Orange and Rockland Utilities, the staff of the New York Public Service Commission, and the New York State Consumer Protection Board. In strenuous opposition were Niagara Mohawk,

Airco, the General Services Administration, the Industrial Power Consumers Conference, the Multiple Intervenors (an industrial customer group), and the Rockland County Industrial Energy Users Association.[106]

Implementing Marginal Cost in LILCO Rates

The first utility to petition the commission for permission to restructure its electric rates in accordance with principles of marginal cost was the Long Island Lighting Company (LILCO). At the time the utility had an exceptionally poor load factor—45 percent. Its summer peak had been growing at a rapid clip. Its capital needs were huge, and it was unable to meet the interest coverage necessary to preserve the rating of its bonds.[107] LILCO's managers hoped that incremental pricing would help improve the company's load factor by inducing off-peak consumption, so they asked the commission to consider their proposals in the context of the utility's 1975 general rate case. In deference to the other utilities, the commission agreed to postpone such consideration until after the decision on marginal cost had been reached in the generic hearing. Within six months of that decision, LILCO had its new rate structure. But first the commission had to fashion a policy for a number of the issues raised in the generic proceeding, particularly with regard to the disposition of any excess revenues that might be generated by pricing electricity at marginal cost.

Excess revenues create a problem. Rate structures based on marginal costs are designed independently of the process which sets a utility's overall revenue requirement. Only by chance will marginal cost-based rates return to the utility precisely the amount of revenue deemed reasonable for it to earn. It is much more likely that, in an inflationary world, marginal cost-based rates will generate revenues in excess of those the utility is allowed to earn by traditional ratemaking rules. (Regulators in most states value a utility's physical assets at their "original cost"—the price paid by the utility to purchase the assets in the first place, or at their "fair value"—a cost that is typically higher than original cost, but less than the cost of replacing the assets.) The question then becomes: what to do with the excess revenues if the utility is not to be allowed to keep them? Some means must be found for reducing electric rates without distorting the price signals which are the raison d'être of marginal cost.

The economic principle that would guide the disposition of such revenues is the so-called "inverse elasticity rule": the extra revenues should be rebated to consumers in inverse relationship to their elasticity of demand. The less responsive to price changes are customers, the greater should be their reduction in rates—and vice versa.

While the inverse elasticity rule is a simple and noncontroversial proposition in the abstract, its application is both difficult and controversial. In the first instance, the rule requires a great amount of information about customer responsiveness to price changes. While much recent empirical research has been directed to this issue, the question has not been settled.[108] Second, despite the primitive quality of demand elasticity estimates, industrial and commercial users fear that regulators will operate on a "best hunch" that the demand of residential consumers is more inelastic than their own and use the inverse elasticity rule to shift to these big users greater responsibility for utility revenue requirements. Lifeline proponents are quick to make this assessment as well, and so have been wholehearted advocates of the inverse elasticity concept. They argue that their proposals are compatible with economically efficient rates, even if that is not their primary purpose, because residential demand for the first block of electricity must surely be most inelastic.[109]

Unlike the large users and to some extent the utilities who opposed lifeline rates on purely materialistic grounds, the engineers of the Public Service Commission objected to lifeline because it offended their sense of mission. At the time of the generic hearing, the chief of the staff's rates and valuation section said:

Lifeline is still being considered and the commission hasn't had a recommended decision—but the staff's position in anticipation of those hearings is that lifeline is an explicit effort to build in subsidies into electricity rates which we don't think is justified; that is to say, is not our role to pass on.

This is social policy and properly the role of the legislature. The mandate that the PSC has is to get out of the business of subsidies that characterized rates in the teens and twenties and begin to base rates more closely in line with costs. To the extent that lifeline deviates from that, it was not part of our mission.[110]

The commission's director of research, an economist, expressed his concern that rebate proposals in keeping with "inverse elasticity" might threaten even modest hopes for basing rates on marginal cost:

One of the problems is that lifeline adherents seize upon incremental rates as a possibility for redistributing income. I'm opposed to that. . . . These proposals just scare industrial and commercial users into opposition because they are afraid they'll end up footing the bill—and thereby jeopardize the whole move toward marginal cost.[111]

Breaking Up the Opposition

With support from the governor and the legislature for his rate initiatives, and with at least some of the utilities favorably inclined, the only unified opposition that Kahn faced in implementing a marginal cost-based rate structure came from the large users who were afraid they would end up paying more. In response to this pressure Kahn devised a compromise (first suggested by LILCO) that shattered the unity of opposition, answered the charge that the new rate would be discriminatory and secured the success of marginal cost, even though it muted its impact. The strategy was as simple as it was effective: no consumer class as a class would be required to pay more under marginal cost-based rates than it had under traditional rate-setting methods; it might pay less.

In effect, the policy meant that no excess revenues would be rebated to residential customers even if justified by virtue of "inverse elasticity" or because industrial users took a greater percentage of their electricity "on-peak" rather than "off-peak." Furthermore, it suggested that if the load factor of those users who were metered for time-of-day rates improved, their contribution to the utility's overall revenue requirement might be reduced. Even more important, it meant that if some large users ended up paying more under the new rates, others would necessarily end up paying less.

The LILCO Decision

Having fashioned a policy that shattered opposition to a new marginal cost-based rate structure, and having won the support of key people in the executive branch and in the legislature, the commission was able to dispose of the remaining issues and dispel further opposition by adopting a policy of "gradualism." The tariffs approved in the LILCO case applied to only the largest customers—those whose monthly recorded demand exceeded 750 kilowatts in any two months of the previous year. The daily peak period was broadly defined (from 10:00 A.M. to 10:00 P.M.) to avoid the problem of shifting peaks, as was the seasonal peak (June through September).[112]

It was in defining marginal costs that perhaps the greatest compromises were made. Using a methodology developed by Ralph Turvey, a British economist, LILCO rate engineers had identified three periods: peak, intermediate (or shoulder peak), and off-peak. No capacity charge at all would be assigned to the off-peak period on the assumption that there was a zero probability that that period would eventually become

37

the peak. Upon the first application of the methodology, the ratio between peak and intermediate periods was in the range of 18:1 to 20:1.[113]
LILCO felt that this was too abrupt a change from its traditional rate
and would cause hardship to its peak customers, so it recommended
that the commission approve, instead, an 8:1 differential for these
charges. On advice from its staff, the commission accepted the spirit of
this recommendation, and went the utility one step further. It authorized a demand charge of $6.40 per kilowatt for peak use and $1.60 per
kilowatt for shoulder peak use—a ratio of only 4:1, and a far cry from
strict marginal cost assessment.

The Effects

These compromises, and that of keeping customer revenue responsibilities unchanged by class, had the effect of creating a new rate
structure that does not differ greatly from a peak-load pricing scheme
based on average historical costs—a fact that distresses some historical-
cost proponents, who wish people would stop calling the LILCO decision a "milestone for marginal cost." But staff engineers think the compromises were necessary to take the first step toward marginal cost, and
they are perfectly willing to admit that LILCO's is not the "ideal" rate
structure.

A year after the new rates went into effect, LILCO's preliminary
studies showed that the rate structure was having exactly the effect that
Kahn had told the industrial users it would have. Of 173 accounts for
which the PSC staff had figures, only 11 users paid more under the new
structure of rates than they would have under traditional rates. All of
these increases were less than 2 percent, while among those who received decreases, the savings ranged up to 21.3 percent. As a class, these
173 large users saved over $1.5 million, about 4 percent.[114]

Conclusion

The effort by the New York State Public Service Commission under
Chairman Alfred Kahn to adopt and implement a new rate structure
for electricity based on the principles of marginal cost is a landmark
case. Other state commissions have and will look to New York for
leadership in reforming their own rate structures. Many will face the

same issues that were raised in New York: whom to meter; whether to use and how to define marginal costs; what to do about excess revenues; and especially, whether to adopt lifeline rates. Unlike California, New York did not choose to adopt lifeline rates for residential consumers.

The failure of lifeline in New York could have been due to the opposition of important groups, or to the inability of prolifeline groups to generate needed support, or to both. A comparison of the two states suggests that lifeline failed in New York primarily because prolifeline groups failed to organize as much support for the concept as their California counterparts did. There are several reasons for this. First, although the New York commission under Kahn's predecessor, Joseph Swidler, had its share of public relations problems, it did not appear to be as blatantly probusiness as did the California Public Utilities Commission at the time of Governor Reagan. Swidler had the reputation of being a professional, fair-minded regulator, who had demonstrated his independence throughout a lifetime of service on the Tennessee Valley Authority and, under Democratic presidents, on the Federal Power Commission. The Reagan PUC, on the other hand, was perceived even by business executives as reckless and "too much in favor of business for business' own good." Mike Miller and Tim Sampson found that the California PUC was a useful "devil" in organizing the Citizen's Action League. Perhaps because the New York commission did not appear to be as "evil" as its California counterpart, organizing effective groups was more difficult there.

Second, Kahn, another professional, replaced Swidler as chairman of the commission in June 1974, before the gubernatorial race in New York had heated up. Kahn's credentials, plus the reputation of Swidler before him, safeguarded the commission from some attacks to which it might otherwise have been subject. In California, by contrast, the commission became a lightning rod for opposition from left-liberal political entrepreneurs who made the commission a major issue in that state's gubernatorial campaign. One of Governor Jerry Brown's campaign promises was to "open up" the PUC and "make it more responsive"—a pledge he followed up on by appointing Leonard Ross to the commission.

Finally, the New York lifeline supporters failed to create the coalition of environmental groups, consumer groups, and labor that was formed in California. The California coalition organized around "inverted rates" which promised conservation for the environmentalists and low prices for the residential user and which neutralized the opposition of labor. Although it began to weaken toward the end of its campaign, the California coalition lasted long enough for the legislature to stamp its

39

proposal into law. No comparable coalition was formed in New York.

Taken together, the California and New York experiences with electric utility rate reform illustrate a simple, yet often overlooked fact. Far more than is commonly recognized, regulatory politics depends upon dynamic factors in the economic and technological environment of regulation. Most studies—even those that purport to be based on "life-cycle theories"—offer a static snapshot of an agency coping with "industry," but with little sense of the way in which technology and market forces alter that industry and thus create new problems for the agency.

In the case of electric utility regulation by the states, major controversies involving "cost of service" rate making procedures were resolved by the end of World War II. Commissions were charged with the obligation of assuring "just and reasonable" rates, good-quality service, and the avoidance of "undue discrimination." While these terms remain vague to the layman, they are terms of art, given content by a long history of judicial interpretation. In practice they came to mean that the task of regulators was to protect consumers against excessive rates and to protect investors against loss of property, while utilities were granted the right to structure rates in a way that would yield the commission-determined "revenue requirement." As long as technological opportunities promised lower costs through increased usage, utilities were given a free hand to adopt rate structures that promoted consumption. Large users clearly benefited from this policy, but so did consumers, investors, and as a result, regulators.

When in the late 1960s and early 1970s these technological opportunities were largely exploited, the practice of allowing utilities to structure their own rates ceased to be noncontroversial. As the cost of construction and debt escalated, the savings achieved through larger-scale plants diminished. For utilities that suffered from a deteriorating load factor, it no longer was economical to encourage high-volume usage—especially if taken "on-peak." These trends reached crisis proportions following the OPEC oil embargo of October 1973. Fuel cost adjustment clauses helped utilities raise large amounts of working capital, but the devices did not solve the utilities' longer-term production problems.

These technological and economic changes completely altered the political context of state utility commissions. Enormous rate increases stimulated the organizational efforts of angry residential consumers, who rediscovered the regulatory process at the same time environmentalists began pressuring both utilities and regulators to reexamine the industry's progrowth ethos. Where once had existed a sort of tacit coalition between large and small users, there was now open hostility. Instead of having the happy task of presiding over a process that seemed to bestow benefits upon everyone, regulators in the 1970s were faced with the unpleasant duty of allocating misery among rival and intensely vocal groups.

The regulatory response to these new requirements has not been predetermined. There is an element of choice in regulatory behavior. How this choice is exercised depends on a number of factors. One is accidental—who happens to be in charge and when. Alfred Kahn's efforts on the New York Public Service Commission illustrate the impact one person can have on the regulatory process. Were it not for Kahn, New York would probably not have emerged as the leading state on the matter of peak-load pricing. But just as important, had Kahn been chairman in 1964 instead of 1974, he probably would not have been able to move the commission and the utilities to adopt marginal cost-based rates. Another factor explaining regulatory behavior is more patterned: the emergence of a new political career for policy entrepreneurs in the regulatory field. The positions of Ross, Batinovich, and Holmes in the California lifeline case were all motivated by what they considered to be opportunities for political advancement created by the controversy surrounding the commission.

Certainly in California and New York, commissions have not responded to the changed industrial and political environment as if they were "captured" by the utilities or their largest users. Old notions of regulatory "capture" were based on the assumption—perhaps valid in the case of electric utilities during the 1950s and 1960s—that industry exercised exclusive control over the relevent incentives for regulators. Now industry obviously does not. Either there are no external incentives (Kahn, at the peak of his career, was much more concerned that his actions conformed to the norms of his profession than whether they happened to please some special interest), or the incentives are under the shared control of industry, the media, and the political process. The experience of California utilities at the time Leonard Ross and his associates directed the Public Utility Commission suggests that industry's share of control may even approach zero.

CHAPTER 2

Federal Maritime

Commission

EDWARD MANSFIELD

All oceangoing common carriers engaged in United States foreign commerce come under the jurisdiction of the Federal Maritime Commission (FMC), which uses two principal tools to regulate these carriers: the power to approve or disapprove price-fixing agreements and the power to reject discriminatory rate schedules.* Five commissioners preside over the FMC, which was established in 1961 to administer a statute that dates back to 1916. With a budget of approximately $8 million and a staff of only 314, the FMC is one of the smallest independent regulatory commissions.

Among those who are familiar with its operations, the FMC has a reputation for poor performance. The Senate Governmental Affairs Committee recently ranked it at the bottom of the seventeen regulatory agencies it investigated.[1] A briefing paper prepared for the Carter administration in 1977 concluded: "With rare exceptions, the FMC has been unable to regulate effectively the ocean common carriers operating in the foreign commerce of the United States. . . . Our foreign commerce would be better served if the FMC were abolished."[2] Even the FMC's current chairman has confessed: "Some of my friends hinted

---

*The FMC also has authority to regulate offshore domestic commerce (i.e., shipping between Alaska, Guam, Hawaii, etc., and the continental United States). This area of the FMC's responsibilities will not be considered in this chapter.

that nomination to the Maritime Commission was an event that any sensible man would scrupulously avoid."[3]

Origins: Conferences and Regulation

During the 1890s, steamship lines began to operate price-fixing cartels in open defiance of the Sherman Antitrust Act. Within a short time, these cartels or "conferences" were prevalent in most of the U.S. trades. In 1912 Congress appointed an ad hoc committee to investigate the situation. In the words of its chairman, Congressman Joshua Alexander of Missouri, the purpose of the committee was "to determine whether or not [Congress] should recognize the agreements existing between carriers by water or recommend that the Sherman antitrust law be enforced against them and those combinations be broken up."[4] In its final recommendation the Alexander Committee (as it came to be called) struck a compromise. It decided that "agreements should be permitted," but only if they were brought under "effective government supervision."[5] This recommendation became the basis for the Shipping Act of 1916, which ever since has been the cornerstone of American regulatory policy in the area of ocean shipping.

Some commentators have suggested that the Shipping Act was a wolf in sheep's clothing; that Congress's real aim was not to regulate liner shipping, but to promote the U.S. merchant marine. But this interpretation is almost certainly incorrect. Specifically, it does not explain why the program that was enacted was the one that the shippers rather than the carriers had advocated in their appearances before the Alexander Committee or why the Shipping Act had to be passed *over the opposition* of the carriers.* The truth is that Congress had a genuine—if dim —regulatory intent when it established the FMC's predecessor agency.

When the Alexander Committee concluded in its report to Congress that "agreements should be permitted," it was reiterating a position that almost all shippers held. Since many of them had refused to testify in person—they evidently feared retaliation from the conferences—the committee sent out a circular letter eliciting replies which it promised to keep confidential. A total of 227 replies were received; only 10 of

*"Shippers"are firms that send goods by sea, "carriers" are owners of merchant ships who sell space to shippers.

them recommended that "existing combinations be dissolved and free and unrestrained competition be restored.[6] As the committee later put it:

A vast majority of the leading American exporting and importing firms who expressed their view on the subject . . . contended that shipping agreements, conference relations, or oral understandings . . . are necessary if shippers are at all times to enjoy ample tonnage and efficient, frequent, and regular service at reasonable rates.[7]

Both the shippers and the Alexander Committee accepted the argument that conferences are not merely functionally desirable, but also economically indispensable. This argument runs as follows: Ocean shipping is a natural monopoly because of high fixed costs (overhead and vessel operation, which amount to 70–75 percent of the total) and low variable costs (the costs of loading and discharging cargo, which amount to 25–30 percent of the total). Once a voyage has been scheduled, fixed costs have been accounted for. Therefore a carrier has an incentive to take any cargo that pays more than variable cost in order to fill up his ship. However, this policy causes him to lose money in the long run because he never recovers all of his fixed costs. Eventually he will have to withdraw from the trade, as will many other carriers, until only one firm remains. Then the shippers on that route will be at the mercy of a monopolist.[8] This argument is of dubious merit; because it rests on a presumption that there is excess shipping capacity in the ocean trades, which forces carriers to compete for an inadequate supply of cargo (rather than the other way around). Such an overcapacity cannot exist unless carriers consistently overestimate the total demand for shipping. There is no evidence that the carriers do overestimate, but even if they do, why should shippers be forced to pay for someone else's lack of foresight?[9] (Chronic overcapacity, to the extent that it exists today, results from the artificially high rates that conferences are able to maintain.) Nevertheless, the Alexander Committee was not persuaded by such criticisms. The following oft-quoted passage summarizes its position:

It is the view of the Committee that open competition cannot be assured for any length of time by ordering existing agreements terminated. The entire history of steamship agreements shows that in ocean commerce there is no happy medium between war and peace when several lines engage in the same trade. Most of the numerous agreements and conference arrangements discussed in the foregoing report were the outcome of rate wars, and represent a truce between the contending lines. To terminate existing agreements would necessarily bring about one of two results: the lines would either engage in rate wars which would mean the elimination of the weak and the survival of the strong, or, to avoid a costly struggle, they would consolidate through common ownership. Neither result can be prevented by legislation, and either would mean a monopoly fully as effective, and it is believed more so, than can exist by virtue of an agreement.[10]

Although the committee may have relied on a spurious economic argument, it was not so shortsighted as to believe that the conference system had no attendant risks for the shipper. Many shippers who testified in person raised objections to specific conference practices— and the committee listened. For example, grain exporters from Baltimore complained that the conference was holding their port up for ransom:

We are not only the last ones served, but we only get our proportion of the business by having the rate we do. It is a fact that we have the highest outward rate of any Atlantic port. That is the only thing which gives us any business at all.[11]

Indeed, 44 of the 227 anonymous respondents registered complaints about discriminatory rates. One of them told the committee that the conferences' contention that they treat all shippers alike "makes those of us who are in the business smile." Another made the following remarks:

We are quite certain that special privileges and advantages are given to some and denied to others. We find that in the English trade the steamship lines will give a better freight rate on the same commodity to one firm than they will give to another, excusing themselves on the ground that their rate is based according to the quantity contracted for. We believe that this is an extremely bad practice.[12]

Shippers also voiced concern about inadequate cargo space (in 42 of the 227 replies) and exorbitant rates (in 73 of the replies). All of these concerns were embodied in the committee report. The so-called "Alexander Report" lists seven hazards of the conference system, most of which amount to a restatement of the obvious proposition that price-fixing cartels can charge whatever price they want. Although the Alexander Committee saw many advantages in the current system, it had to admit that carriers were "under no legal obligation to continue these advantages."[13]

Not only did Congress share the concerns voiced by shippers, it also adopted the solutions proposed by them. Sixty-eight of the 110 anonymous replies that were "unfavorable to steamship agreements and conferences as now conducted" contained recommendations for legislation. Thirty-five of these respondents endorsed "a comprehensive system of Government supervision, sufficiently broad to embrace the regulation of rates, the approval of contracts and agreements, and the general supervision of all conditions of water transportation which vitally affect the shipper.[14] The Alexander Committee, evidently agreeing with these shippers, asked Congress to enact a program of "effective government control." Agreements would have to be filed with the Interstate Commerce Commission (ICC) for approval; they would be disapproved if they were "unjustly discriminatory" or "detrimental to commerce." The ICC would also have the power to look into the freight rates of oceangoing foreign commerce, and "could order such rates changed" if it found them to be unreasonably high or unjustly discriminatory between ports or shippers.[15]

For the most part, the Shipping Act of 1916 incorporated the Alexander Committee's recommendations. Two changes were made, neither of critical importance. First, instead of expanding the authority of the ICC, Congress created an entirely new agency—the United States Shipping Board. Second, Congress decided to restrict the agency's rate authority to questions of discrimination and not have it look into the reasonableness of rates. The latter change was not as significant as one might think. The Alexander Committee and the shippers who submitted testimony had never contemplated giving the ICC the power to fix rates; they wanted it only to be able to disapprove unreasonable ones. Thus it would be fair to say that Congress's aim when it passed the Shipping Act was no different from the Alexander Committee's goal when it investigated the conference system. To quote one commentator: "The multifarious provisions of the Shipping Law . . . are tightly bound together by a consistent thread of deliberate national policy. . . . The law, in language and spirit, is intended as a shipper-protection statute."[16]

It is true that the Shipping Act contained an important nonregulatory provision: it authorized the Shipping Board to acquire and operate a fleet of approximately fifty vessels. Some observers say that this measure was designed to promote the U.S. merchant marine and that it gave the new agency "an inherent conflict of interest problem."[17] If they are correct, we would have reason to doubt the seriousness of Congress's intentions regarding the regulatory portions of the act. However, these commentators have misread the legislative history.

Significantly, the merchant marine's strongest supporters in Congress *opposed* the Shipping Act. They favored government subsidies for the shipping industry, not a government-owned merchant marine. Senator Jacob Gallinger, the minority leader and a well-known defender of the U.S.-flag fleet, called the bill "a virtual declaration of war on the American shipbuilding industry" and "a scheme for discouragement and destruction" of the U.S. merchant marine. Another outraged senator exclaimed, "This board will put the shipping interests in a straight-jacket."[18] As one writer remarks, the carriers themselves "were opposed bitterly to Government entry into the shipping industry and considered the regulatory proposals almost equally as undesirable." P. A. S. Franklin, president of the International Mercantile Marine Co. and a noted spokesman for shipping interests, characterized the bill as "a club to be held over the heads of shipping," both in that ships owned by the Board would compete with private industry and in that the Board would regulate industry practice. Another steamship company executive put it succinctly: "Less legislation and not more is necessary for the continued development of our merchant marine." The *New York Times,* in one of many editorials against the bill, commented that "The measure will never be enacted, if the trade's protest is observed as any guide to what ought to be done."[19]

Given that a powerful lobby opposed the Shipping Act, it may seem puzzling that it ever passed. The conventional wisdom is that our legislative system gives organized opponents numerous opportunities to defeat unfavorable legislation. However, as James Q. Wilson notes, there have been exceptions to this rule, such as the Pure Food and Drug Act, the highway safety act and the clean air and water acts. Wilson offers an explanation for these phenomena:

Each [of these bills] represented, not the triumph of an organization, but rather the successful mobilization of a new, usually temporary, political constituency. On occasion this was made easier by a dramatic crisis that put the opponents at a hopeless disadvantage—for example, the thalidomide disaster, or the investigation of Nader.

The creation of the Shipping Board followed this pattern. There was a particular crisis that enabled the Shipping Act to pass under conditions of "majoritarian" rather than "coalitional" politics.[20]

That crisis was World War I. At the outbreak of the war, Great Britain, France and Germany had withdrawn most of their ships from U.S. foreign commerce. As a result, shipping services declined and the rates soared. Between June 1914 and March 1916, rates from the United States to Britain on grain went from 5 cents a bushel to 50 cents a bushel, on cotton from 20 cents per 100 pounds to $2.50 per 100 pounds, and on tobacco from $3.00 per 100 pounds to $30.00 per 100 pounds. By July 1916, *The Washington Post* could say: "Ocean freight rates are absurdly high."[21]

For two years the shipping interests had been able to prevent Congress from enacting the Alexander Committee's recommendations.[22] But in 1916 the escalation of ocean freight rates offered a compelling justification for regulating the conferences. The Shipping Act was presented as a twofold solution to the problem: freight rates would be lowered by increasing the number of ships afloat and by reducing the instances and impact of collusion among carriers.

Naturally, the bill's supporters tried to heighten the sense of crisis. Committee reports prepared by supporters of the legislation in the House and Senate extensively documented the rise in freight rates. In April 1916 Congressman Alexander told a New York audience: "If we do not pass this legislation at this session of Congress, I shall consider it not less than a national calamity." Even such opponents of the Shipping Act as the *New York Times* conceded that it was "the most important bill of the session." They argued, however, that the real crisis was not the level of freight rates but the possibility of "state socialism."[23]

In September the bill swept through Congress on highly partisan votes. In the Senate no Republican voted for the bill and no Democrat voted against it; in the House only eight Republicans voted for it and only two Democrats voted against it. Majoritarian politics had replaced coalitional politics. As one contemporary journal noted:

The adoption of this measure has undoubtedly been stimulated by the continued difficulty of transportation growing out of the European war, and there are many who believe that without the existence of the war and the exigencies growing out of it, no such act would have been adopted, or perhaps seriously considered, by Congress.[24]

The Office of Tariffs

The Shipping Act requires every carrier and conference operating in the foreign commerce of the United States to file a "tariff" with the commission.[25] This "tariff" is a looseleaf volume containing "rules"

The Federal Maritime Commission

(statements regarding the type of service provided) and a schedule of commodity rates in back. In order to alter a rule or rate, a carrier (or conference) must file a tariff amendment. Rate *increases* cannot go into effect until they have been in the commission's hands for thirty days. The commission keeps its updated tariff volumes open to the interested public (which consists mainly of a number of commercial tariff-watching services), and any carrier who charges anything other than his published rates subjects himself to a civil penalty of not more than $1,000 a day.

The FMC is supposed to insure that the tariffs it has on file are in accord with sections 16, 17 and 18(b)(5) of the Shipping Act. Section 16 makes it unlawful for a common carrier to "give any undue or unreasonable preference," while section 17 forbids common carriers from charging "any rate, fare, or charge which is unjustly discriminatory between shippers or ports." The distinction between section 16 and section 17 is an elusive one; in most discrimination cases, a violation of both sections is alleged.

For forty-five years, these essentially identical provisions were the entire substantive law on tariffs. However, in the late 1950s, Representative Emmanuel Celler's Antitrust Subcommittee of the House Judiciary Committee conducted an investigation into the ocean freight industry. Revelations in the hearings led Celler to exclaim that the FMC's predecessor agency had an "unparalleled" record of "regulatory neglect." Celler concluded that the problem was not Congress's mandate, which contained "a veritable arsenal of weapons," but rather the FMC's administration of that mandate.[26] Even so, in 1961 Celler's subcommittee cooperated with the House Merchant Marine Committee in drafting amendments to the Shipping Act. The principal amendment in the area of tariff regulation was section 18(b)(5), which gave the agency the power to

disapprove any rate or charge filed by a common carrier by water in the foreign commerce of the United States or conference of carriers which, after hearing, it finds to be so unreasonably low or high as to be detrimental to the commerce of the United States.

This amendment restored the language that the Alexander Committee had sought to include in the original shipping act.

To enforce sections 16, 17 and 18(b)(5), the FMC has an Office of Tariffs and Intermodalism with thirty-seven employees, approximately twenty-eight of whom are tariff analysts. Essentially, the analysts in the

Office do three things. First, they generate statistics. A recent annual report states that in fiscal 1976, 339,893 new tariff pages were filed, of which 336,551 were accepted and 3,342 were rejected.[27] Thus, the Office disapproved about 1 percent of the tariff pages it received. This makes it sound as if the Office is doing a creditable job of rate regulation, but that is not the case. As one tariff analyst explained to an interviewer, "The biggest reason [for rejection] is the permanent filing not agreeing with the temporary. [In addition] I'd say that 20 percent of the rejections are for less than thirty days' notice."*

A statistical analysis of FMC records roughly confirms these estimates. Out of 3,591 tariff pages rejected in calendar year 1976, 1,124—or 31 percent—were rejected for violating the thirty-day notice provisions. Also, 879—or 25 percent—were rejected because they violated "46 CFR 536.3," the FMC's regulations that cover such technicalities as the width of the margins, the quality of the paper, and the numbering of the tariff pages. Finally, 461—or 13 percent—were rejected because a permanent tariff filing did not match a temporary one. (Because of the thirty-day rule, a carrier will often file a rate increase by Telex so that he does not have to wait for an official tariff amendment to be printed up. FMC regulations permit this, but require that the temporary filing be followed by an identical permanent one.[28]) One analyst, who handles the tariffs of conferences that use professional tariff printing services, confessed that he has only "four to five rejections a year." The typical analyst, on the other hand, has about twenty-three rejections a year (each rejection averages about 5.6 pages). This discrepancy would seem to support the conclusion we derived from the statistics—namely, most of the FMC's tariff rejections are for "technical things, trivia," as one lawyer put it.

In fairness to the commission, there are good reasons why the analysts do not attempt to evaluate the reasonableness of rates. For one thing, the statutes—as almost any lawyer who practices before the commission will tell you—"do not have teeth in them." Before it can reject a rate under section 18(b)(5), the FMC must (1) hold a hearing, (2) show that the rate is unreasonable, and (3) show that it is so unreasonable as to be "detrimental to commerce." Because of this difficult threefold burden, no one (neither the commission nor a shipper) has ever successfully invoked section 18(b)(5) alone. Section 18(b)(5) has been successfully invoked in combination with sections 16 and 17, but this means that this section essentially adds nothing to the commission's powers. The Ralph

*All quoted material not otherwise referenced is drawn from interviews conducted by the author.

The Federal Maritime Commission

Nader Study Group has castigated the commission for not disapproving "exorbitant rates."[29] Such criticism is plainly unfair. Even the FMC's bitterest enemy, the Justice Department, admits that the commission has "only minimal ratemaking powers over foreign commerce."[30] Indeed, one tariff analyst confessed that he does not even look at individual rates. This is understandable, though it leaves unanswered the question of just how the analysts do spend their time.

This brings us to the second and third tasks that the analysts perform. A procedure has been established within the Office of Tariffs to handle what are known as "informal rate cases." Suppose a shipper comes to the Commission with a complaint that the rates charged him are too high. This complaint is forwarded to the Office of Tariffs, where one of the analysts writes the shipper a letter. The letter either advises the shipper to plead his case before the carriers, or (if he has already tried that) it tells him in delicate language that there is nothing the commission can do. If the shipper has not yet contacted the carriers, the analyst will also write a letter to them requesting a copy of their reply to the shipper's complaint. As one analyst explained, the rationale for this procedure is that the carriers will be "less likely to throw the [shipper's] request in the trashcan."

In its report on the FMC, the Ralph Nader Study Group describes a case involving the Weis-Fricker Mahogany Co., an importer of lumber from South America. Weis-Fricker had complained to the commission that its rates were too high. The commission told it to seek redress from the conference. These efforts failed, so Weis-Fricker came back to the commission. This time the FMC replied, "We are writing the conference requesting that the matter receive prompt attention." Meanwhile the FMC allowed new conference rates to go into effect "offering no relief to the company."[31] What the author of this report seems not to realize is that Weis-Fricker's experience is the accepted way of doing business at the commission. Even the analysts acknowledge as much:

There's not much we can do. Usually they [the shippers] come to us first. Then basically we tell them that the commission has very little power over rates, and they should try to get redress from the conference.

This guy imported retanned furniture from Hong Kong and the New York Freight Bureau [the conference covering the inbound Hong Kong–U.S. East Coast trade] had a rate increase. His competitors were importing from the Philippines but when there was a general rate increase there they exempted retanned furniture since it's a major product of the Philippines. What can we tell the guy? We wrote him a letter telling him to write the conference. And they reduced the rate. Not much, but they reduced the rate.

Besides generating meaningless statistics and answering informal complaints with toothless letters to the carriers, the analysts also uphold the pretense of regulation in a third way: by requiring "justifications" for general rate increases. When a carrier or conference raises the rates on 50 percent of its items by 3 percent or more, this is known as a general rate increase. The Office of Tariffs handles such increases in the following manner:

They have a program they call "regulation by letter-writing." Say our client files a 5 percent rate increase. Sure as night and day they'll write a letter to the carriers and say they need some justification. The carriers write back some general bull——. They'll write back and say it's not definite enough. Then they'll drop it. Every one of these takes two or three letters. It permits them to go before Congress and say they're exercising surveillance. But it's just a pain in the ass, and they're not going to do anything because they don't have the authority.

The commission has an informal requirement that carriers provide economic data in support of all general rate increases. The analysts enforce this requirement by writing a letter to the perpetrators whenever they detect such an increase. This author was not permitted to see one of these letters, but FMC officials indicated that they typically consist of a series of questions covering seven different factors (rising fuel costs, higher labor costs, etc.) that might make it necessary for a carrier to raise his rates in order to preserve his profit margin. However, as the preceding quotation suggests, the commission is not likely to do anything even if the carrier ignores the letter. One tariff analyst put it bluntly: "We're at their mercy. We get only what they want to give us." Even the FMC's current chairman admits that this justification requirement is not especially useful, since the analysts are "looking at tariffs from the perspective of an area where they don't have any power." Nevertheless, the letter writing continues.

Branch chiefs in the Office of Tariffs estimate that their subordinates spend about half their time filing and examining tariff pages and about half their time answering letters. Does the Office of Tariffs have the legal authority to do anything more? So far all we have shown is largely wasted motion: the analysts uphold a pretense of regulation while neglecting the substance of it. Yet perhaps that is all one can expect. We know that Congress intended the FMC to exercise serious regulation of freight rates, at least in the area of shipper discrimination; we must now ask whether Congress gave the agency the legal tools to carry out this mandate.

The Federal Maritime Commission

For the most part, the tariffs that the FMC has on file do not even meet the Commission's *formal* standards for approval as set out in 46 CFR 536. A former FMC employee claims that he had "a standing offer of $100 for anyone who could find a tariff that didn't have anything unlawful in the first ten pages." For instance, 46 CFR 536.5 (f) says that

> A commodity item may, by use of a generic term, provide rates on a number of articles without naming such articles, provided such item contains a reference to an item in the tariff which clearly defines the types of commodities contained in such generic term.

Nevertheless, approved tariffs frequently contain generic terms like "snack foods," "gas station equipment" and "Chinese merchandise"—without any subsequent definition. "Publication of rates which duplicate or conflict with the rates published in the same or any other tariff" is also forbidden, according to 536.5 (I). Yet one shipper says he once saw a tariff in the U.S.-Venezuela trade that had separate rates for "weedkillers," "compounds, weedkilling," "herbicides" and "killers, weed." (The last rate was the lowest).

Cargo classifications have become a way for carriers to give hidden (and illegal) discounts to large shippers. Most tariffs are organized as follows: There are rates for classes of commodities, such as "frozen meat" or "furniture." Each class rate is then followed by a series of special rates for single commodities within that class, such as "frozen veal cut in three-inch cubes" or "frozen filets mignons cut one-inch thick." The special rates are invariably lower than the class rates—because individual shippers have negotiated them. An economist within the FMC described to an interviewer a typical case of "how rates are made":

> You want to sell screwdrivers in Austria. You tell the [carrier] to reduce the rate because otherwise you cannot move the cargo. But he can't because of other screwdrivers he's carrying. So he finds [i.e., creates] another rate for screwdrivers greater than six inches long.

However, such discounts are only available to large shippers. A small shipper cannot threaten to take his cargo elsewhere (i.e., to a contract carrier, a mini-landbridge operator,* or another conference). Therefore

*"Mini-landbridge" refers to a particular kind of service between two ports in which the carrier's ships do not actually stop at both ports. For example, a carrier whose ships operate between Europe and the U.S. Atlantic Coast could offer "mini-landbridge" to the Gulf Coast by dropping off cargo in Savannah, Georgia, say, and paying to have it shipped overland by rail to Gulf Coast ports. As far as the receivers of the cargo are concerned, it would be as if the carrier offered direct service to the Gulf.

his request for a special rate will be ignored. A recent FMC study revealed that citrus fruit was the largest single commodity passing through Canadian Atlantic ports. California citrus growers had chartered Swedish ships out of Montreal in order to escape the high rates demanded by the U.S. Atlantic conferences. As one economist remarked, "This is evidence of the alternatives open to the large shipper."[32]

Discrimination against small shippers aside, there seems to be no logical reason for commodity pricing. Many U.S. trades are almost completely containerized. And one container costs just as much to ship as any other. An FMC branch chief put it this way to an interviewer:

Explain to me the difference in cost between one container which is full of groceries and another which is full of paper. There are exceptions: Some cargo is subject to risk (such as booze, which might get stolen). But from a transportation standpoint, there is no point in maintaining the fiction of commodity rates . . .

So this is an example of where we've got to get our ass into the twentieth century. Other modes of transportation don't have this problem because they don't have the tradition. The tradition has had an effect on the cerebral matter of these executives. Rigor mortis of the brain has set in.

An economist, however, would argue that commodity pricing has survived not because it is a traditional practice but because it is a profitable one. In essence, commodity pricing means charging more for those cargoes,—usually higher-valued—that can bear a higher rate. (Of course, carriers can do this only in a situation of imperfect competition.)

Even if the FMC chose not to issue a rule requiring containerized carriers to offer only an "f.a.k." (freight all kinds) rate for consolidated shipments, other less drastic steps within existing rules could be taken to protect the small shipper. For example, the tariff analysts could reject rates that have obviously been tailored for single shippers (and therefore obviously violate sections 16 and 17, as even a few FMC officials will admit). Or they could refuse to accept tariffs that contain vague or duplicate generics like "gas station equipment" or "killers, weed" which allow identical commodities to go under different rates, depending on the economic leverage that the particular shipper wields. By thus restricting the ability of carriers to discriminate among clients, the FMC might end up reducing the average level of rates, since any preferential rate that a carrier offered to attract a large shipper would have to apply to small shippers of that product as well. (And, perhaps more important, the FMC would be giving large shippers the same *incentive* as small shippers to oppose anticompetitive carrier practices.) Unfortunately, the analysts have a narrower view of their proper role. In a later section we shall consider various explanations for this view. First, however, the other major FMC task—reviewing conference agreements—will be discussed.

The Office of Agreements

The FMC's power to regulate agreements comes from section 15. Its relevant portion reads:

Every common carrier by water, or other person subject to this Act, shall file immediately with the Commission a true copy of every agreement with another such person subject to this Act, or modification or cancellation thereof. . . .

The Commission shall by order, after notice and hearing, disapprove cancel or modify any agreement, or any modification or cancellation thereof, whether or not previously approved by it, that it finds to be unjustly discriminatory or unfair as between carriers, shippers, exporters, importers, or ports, or between exporters from the United States and their foreign competitors, or to operate to the detriment of the commerce of the United States, or to be contrary to the public interest, or to be in violation of this Act, and shall approve all other agreements, modifications, or cancellations.

Thus an agreement, in order to be approved, must not fall into any of four enumerated categories. Once approval has been granted, the parties receive an exemption from the antitrust laws; carriers who cooperate without FMC permission to do so subject themselves to a civil penalty of not more than $1,000 a day in addition to the threat of antitrust prosecution. Approvals are not intended to be permanent; some observers have even argued that section 15 gives the FMC the power to regulate rates by disapproving the basic agreement of any conference that sets its prices too high.[33] But in fact the FMC never reviews previously approved agreements and almost never disapproves a new agreement—unless there is a formal protest.

After a proposed agreement has been filed with the commission, it is forwarded to the branch of the Office of Agreements that has geographic responsibility for that section of the trade. (In FMC parlance, "agreement" refers to anything that comes under section 15. The law requires that even trivial amendments to previously approved agreements be submitted for approval.) The branch chief reviews the agreement, perhaps makes a preliminary recommendation, and then assigns it to one of his analysts. The analyst "notices" the agreement—that is, he puts an official notice of it in *The Federal Register,* inviting interested parties to respond.

If the agreement is a per se violation of the antitrust laws (as all conference agreements and many amendments to conference agreements are), then the proponents must file a statement of justification. That is because the Supreme Court, in *FMC* v. *Aktiebolaget Svenska Amerika Linien,* [34] ruled that anticompetitive agreements should be approved only if the proponents "bring forth such facts as would demonstrate that the [agreement] was required by a serious transportation need, necessary to secure important public benefits or in furtherance of a valid regulatory purpose of the Shipping Act." In this 1968 decision, the Court reasoned that "by its very nature, an illegal restraint of trade is in some ways 'contrary to the public interest.' " Therefore, it concluded, anticompetitive agreements are presumptively invalid under the Shipping Act—unless the carriers show otherwise. The *Svenska* decision, as it came to be known, forced the commission to modify its earlier methods of review, which one analyst characterized to an interviewer as follows:

I joined in '61. At that time all we looked for was grammar and punctuation. Those of us conversant with the problem thought there ought to be some justification. Something sophisticated like a pooling agreement would come in and we'd say, "What do you want it for?" The carriers would say, "None of your f——ing business."

At least on the surface, the approach is different now. Most agreements must be accompanied by a statement of justification. The statement of justification and the text of the agreement are evaluated by an analyst, who recommends either that the agreement be approved or that it be made the subject of an investigation and hearing. The commissioners themselves make the final ruling, though in most cases they accept the staff's recommendation.

It is difficult to describe the standards of review that the analysts in the Office of Agreements apply, largely because the analysts themselves do not know what standards they are using. Their verbalizations of the *Svenska* requirement sound confusing and even contradictory:

The Federal Maritime Commission

I'll go along with [anything] assuming it's within the bounds of "unduly."

The most reliable test is still the fact [that] if someone's being gored, they scream.

It's not cut and dried. ——— assigns it to an analyst. As soon as we can, we review that agreement to see that it complies as nearly as it should with General Order 24 [the FMC's regulation interpreting section 15].

As one lawyer put it, "Since the staff operates in the gray, the filing parties are obviously in the dark."[35] All of this confusion conceals a simple fact: *Svenska* has been converted from a substantive requirement to a formal one. Instead of insisting that the letter of justification establish certain propositions, the analysts merely insist that it be a letter of justification. The analysts do not examine the content of a claim, but only whether a claim has been made. Or, to put it in another way, not only are there no substantive standards, there is also no substantive scrutiny.

This is not to say that anything is acceptable as a justification. Often one of the analysts will decide that a particular letter of justification is inadequate. In that case he will write the proponents (using a form letter that the Office provides) and request another. If the second statement is also inadequate, he will request a third. In fact it is not unusual to see three or more letters of justification filed on behalf of a single agreement. Obviously such a process, in the words of one attorney, "moves with glacial speed." Proposed agreements can vegetate at the staff level for a year or more.[36]

The delays might be excusable were it not for the nature of the analysts' objections. For example, according to the FMC's internal guidelines, justifications are supposed to be in the form of affidavits of fact. Sometimes an analyst will reject a statement because it is not an affidavit or because it does not allege enough facts, even though accepted affidavits may contain only irrelevant facts and the lay opinions of counsel. Or, as another example, occasionally an analyst will reject a statement because he has received "comments" from a shipper or competing carrier. "Comments"—as opposed to a formal protest—are generally filed when some party dislikes an agreement but does not want to endure the time and expense of a formal hearing. The analyst will not examine the substance of these "comments"; instead he will merely forward them to the proponents and seek a rebuttal—i.e., another statement of justification. Once the rebuttal has been filed, the comments are put aside. The analyst thus takes the position that the adequacy of the statement of justification depends upon whether there

57

are outstanding comments, not upon the merit of those comments or of the proponents' replies. Even the steamship conference attorneys, who have a stake in preserving this process, admit that the FMC's review of justifications is more show than substance. One attorney termed it "a pure paper-shuffling operation." Another remarked to an interviewer:

I don't think the strong justification has been shown. And I'm talking about a lot of our own agreements. A lot of times there's no serious public need and the only justification is that the parties want the agreement.

Recently the Thailand Pacific Freight Conference applied to the FMC to have its basic agreement extended to cover the joint fixing of "mini-landbridge" rates. Members of the conference had been competing in this area of service. The seven-page affidavit that the conference filed, from which the following excerpts are taken, is typical of the justifications that the agreement analysts accept:

I, S.S. Marr, being duly sworn under oath, depose and say:

1. I am Secretary to the Thailand Pacific Freight Conference (Thaipacon), a position I have held since 1951. . . .

4. Agreement No. 9474-3, as filed for approval, would extend the scope of the Conference Agreement to include what is commonly referred to as "mini-landbridge" cargo. Such cargo would originate at ports in Thailand and move under joint rates on through bills of lading to U.S. Pacific Coast ports, thence transcontinentally by inland rail carriers to destinations on the U.S. Atlantic and Gulf Coasts. At present, this cargo is moving exclusively in containers under the individual mini-landbridge tariffs of the carriers elsewhere referred to in this affidavit. . . .

10. An important reason for adopting and filing our application is the real and present threat to stability that now exists in our trade. With four of the carriers who already have their own tariffs on file, a significant amount of containerized cargo is now moving outside the Conference's jurisdiction. Although the Conference does not maintain regular mini-landbridge cargo figures, we estimate that approximately 6–7,000 revenue tons of cargo moved under the mini-landbridge tariffs of these four carriers in 1976, about 15–20 percent of the 1976 Thaipacon port-to-port total of 40,000 revenue tons. I am of the view such intermodal movements are increasing by leaps and bounds.

11. Among these carriers (as their tariffs on file with the Commission show), there are numerous discrepancies, not only in actual rate levels and charges, but also in such important areas as free time and demurrage, CFS receiving charges, equipment detention charges, destination charges, minimum bill of lading charges and minimum container charges. Each of these areas directly affects total shipper cost and each is highly competitive among carriers.

12. In order, therefore, to remain on an equal footing with others, shippers must keep up with and constantly review the mini-landbridge tariffs of four different Conference members, as well as those who operate outside the Conference. This is an expensive, costly and wasteful exercise which would be largely eliminated by approval of our application. . . .

16. Finally, I have been made aware of no opposition to this Agreement here in Thailand and, I have been informed there were no adverse comments or protests to the Agreement received by the Federal Maritime Commission. Therefore, on behalf of all the members of the Conference, I urge the expeditious consideration of this Agreement and approval at the earliest time.[37]

To cite a recent study of the FMC: "The presumption against the restraint on competition is overcome by showing the existence of competition."[38]

Justifications become irrelevant if the agreement is formally protested, thanks to another court decision. In 1969 the FMC approved a leasing arrangement between New York City and the New York Port Authority without a hearing. The terms of the lease would have given the New York Port Authority the sole right to operate ship passenger terminals in New York City for at least seventy years. Marine Space Enclosures, a company "identifying itself as interested in operation of a different terminal," took the FMC to court, arguing that its protest of the agreement had not been granted a fair hearing. The court of appeals agreed and further held that the commission could not make approvals without a hearing whenever there was a nonfrivolous protest and the agreement would have "a significant impact on commerce." Basically this decision has meant that the commission must hold a hearing on any formally protested agreement that is a per se violation of the antitrust laws.[39]

For this reason, one should be skeptical of claims that the FMC is getting "tougher" on agreements. It is true that there has recently been a substantial increase in the number of docketed agreements, as shown in table 2–1.[40] However, ten of the fourteen investigations ordered during 1977 were due to protests. The FMC took the initiative only four times—twice with proposed pooling agreements in the Peruvian trade (the commission characterizes pooling agreements as "the ultimate in anticompetitive arrangements"[41]), once with a request for intermodal authority, and once with a proposed interconference agreement between two South Seas conferences. In the latter case, the counsel for the proponents filed a bizarre motion for reconsideration of the commission's order of investigation, arguing that the commission's arbitrary behavior (i.e., its decision to order an investigation despite an absence of protests) justified this "highly unusual and possibly unprecedented" request.[42]

The increase in the number of docketed agreements is the result of an increase in the number of formal protests. In January 1977 the Justice Department established a Regulated Industries Section within the Antitrust Division. Since then, it has played the role of consumer advocate in ocean shipping by filing a large number of protests. As one of its attorneys explained to an interviewer in August 1977:

I'd say since January we've commented on [read: protested] fourteen or fifteen agreements, and I think the commission has ordered investigations and hearings in about five of them so far.
[Q. How many did you oppose before last January?]
We opposed things now and then, but not with regularity. We opposed the North Atlantic Pool Agreement and the Superconference, and we also opposed the Sea-Land–U.S. Lines merger.

Sources within the maritime industry claim that the Justice Department has been trying to "cripple" the conference system indirectly by "clogging up virtually all the regulatory channels through which shipping has to pass."[43] This complaint has a touch of irony, since several steamship lines, evidently encouraged by the Justice Department's success at delaying approvals, have begun to protest their competitors' proposals. U.S. Lines, for example, filed at least three protests during the first eight months of 1977. These new tactics—and not a new approach on the part of the FMC's regulators—account for the sudden rise

TABLE 2–1
FMC Hearings on Agreements (1970–77)

Year	1970	1971	1972	1973	1974	1975	1976	1977
Number of Docketed Proceedings Dealing with Agreements	6	8	5	2	9	4	5	14
Number of Docketed Agreements*	8	8	7	2	12	7	9	28†

*There is a discrepancy between the figures in the two rows because one investigation sometimes covers more than one agreement.

†By comparison, 103 agreements were approved without hearing during the first eight months of 1977.

The Federal Maritime Commission

in the number of investigations. As one administrative law judge at the FMC asserted (though with some exaggeration):

[Q. Why are there so many docketed agreements?]
Because the Justice Department has taken it upon itself to protest every agreement that's filed. The Justice Department would like to see us abolished. . . .
  Don't confuse what I have said with some of the public pronouncements. Publicly we have stated that the standards are stricter, or that the standards set forth are now going to be applied.

On the whole, the FMC appears to have essentially a letter-writing mission—a mission, in other words, that is really a nonmission. To quote one attorney's summary opinion:

They [the shippers] are very disillusioned. They think the commission is in the carriers' pocket. As lawyers the conference asks us, 'What shall we do?' and we'll tell them the likelihood of the commission doing anything is very low.

Economists today are divided on the theoretical merits of a regulated ocean shipping industry. Some share the Alexander Committee's view that government control is a necessity because liner shipping is a natural monopoly; others feel that free competition would work and urge Congress to rescind the antitrust exemption. But both groups agree that either alternative—effective regulation or free competition—would be vastly preferable to the FMC's totally ineffective regulation. Notice, for example, the similarities in the conclusions reached by two recent studies—one of which accepts the Alexander Committee's premises and the other of which does not. The judgment of the first study was that FMC regulation "assists carriers in controlling the forces of competition." "The performance of the ocean freight industry can be no worse than it is now," the author added.[44] Likewise, those who conducted the second, more empirical, study decided there was ample evidence from trends in market shares and price levels to indicate that carriers operate in "an unconstrained conference system." From 1968 to 1975 the U.S. North Atlantic/Europe trade went from 54.2 percent conference inbound and 60.2 percent conference outbound to 74.5 percent conference inbound and 79.6 percent conference outbound. (These percentages do not include nominally independent carriers who had formed rate agreements with the conferences.) Also, for representative conferences on that trade, there was a *real* price increase during that time of 149 percent.[45]

What's Wrong with the FMC?

One former FMC official claims: "The biggest failure of the agency is that the top people just aren't qualified people." Many who are close to the agency offer this explanation of FMC conduct. In a recent survey of lawyers and administrative law judges on the performance of eight regulatory agencies (conducted at the request of Senator Abraham Ribicoff's Committee on Governmental Affairs), the FMC placed at the top of the list for having "unqualified Commissioners" as "one of [its] three most important problems." The commissioners of the FMC were judged to have less "understanding of the laws they administer," to exhibit less "interest and commitment to their work as regulators," and to be less deserving of reappointment when their terms expire than the commissioners of any of the other regulatory agencies.[46] Indeed, the low caliber of FMC Commissioners has become a popular joke among Washington lawyers, as the following comments, related to an interviewer reveal:

They have had two commissioners on that for sixteen years about whom the nicest thing you can say is that they're semistupid. We represent a lot of foreign clients. Many times they come to Washington and they want to meet the commissioners and, as a citizen, I'm embarrassed.

There are two inherent problems. One is if you appoint a guy who doesn't know anything, you're likely to get an ignoramus; and if you appoint someone who does know something, you're likely to get a crook. But apart from those inherent problems, there has simply arisen a tradition of making these agencies [the FMC and its predecessors] a dumping ground for the human dregs.

The average time that they devote to their work is about a half hour a day. Sometimes they go abroad. You can imagine what the foreign nations think of these jerks.

Similar criticisms have been voiced by the analysts themselves:

You may have heard that some of the commissioners aren't playing with a full deck. Well, they may have started with a full deck, but they certainly left some cards behind when they came to the commission.

For a typical example of a commissioner, consider Ashton Barrett. "Ashcan," as he has sometimes been called, was first appointed by President Kennedy in 1961 and recently retired after having served sixteen years on the commission, a number of them as vice-chairman. According to his official biography, Barrett's experience for the job consisted of the fact that he had "invested in the essential services of building construction, laundering and dry cleaning."[47]

Other commissioners have arrived with equally dubious qualifications. James V. Day, who was first appointed in the same year as Barrett and whose current term expires in 1979, had been a director of public relations for the American Legion. Another forgettable FMC appointee was James Fanseen, whom one lawyer characterized as "a Baltimore playboy who had never seen a ship in his life." Technically this remark was incorrect, since discussion at Fanseen's confirmation hearing had centered on his extensive yachting background in the Baltimore area.[48]

It is not surprising that such commissioners have spent more time "grandstanding" (as one tariff analyst put it) than formulating policy. For example, recent oversight hearings revealed that no digests of cases or policy guides have ever been prepared to assist the agreement analysts in interpreting section 15. Yet the same hearings revealed that in fiscal 1976, the chairman of the FMC was away from the agency for 148 days.[49] A legislative liaison for the FMC put it this way: "Historically, the role of the commissioners is to serve in the agency and not get involved in the policy."

But when an agency has an unbroken record of regulatory failure, one suspects that something more is at fault than the leadership. Either the agency had good leaders at one time who were unable to reform the agency (because the fundamental problem lay elsewhere); or else the agency never had good leaders, in which case one might reasonably infer that incompetent leadership is less a cause than a consequence of poor performance. The FMC—on account of its unsavory reputation—seems to have had trouble attracting capable executives. As one lawyer who criticized the Ribicoff study for its superficiality remarked to an interviewer:

You just have problems: Where are you going to get someone who's really smart and aggressive to become chairman of the Maritime Commission?

First of all, the jobs are more desirable at the SEC, the NLRB. There are people at the Maritime Commission who if they didn't have those jobs they wouldn't have a job at all.

One senior administrative law judge emphasized that commissioners are not especially well paid, derive few intangible benefits from their service, and are continually being pressured by the shipping industry. "Do you think I'd take that job?" he asked.

While low prestige may have made the FMC less appealing to a talented executive, it has made the agency more appealing to Congress and the president when political debts have to be repaid. "Ashcan" Barrett was originally appointed because his college friend, Senator James Eastland, "took particular interest in the matter." James V. Day got his job because the Maine congressional delegation, assisted by presidential adviser Larry O'Brien, lobbied on his behalf.[50] To quote a former managing director of the FMC: "Commissioner is a political job. It's as simple as that."

A better explanation for the FMC's inability to regulate ineffectively is that the agency must administer a vaguely worded statute in a political environment dominated by the carriers. Section 15 is so broad that, according to one of the FMC's administrative law judges, "theoretically any agreement can be justified." Nor have the courts given the agency any substantive guidance: "serious transportation need" is no less ambiguous than "in the public interest." As a result, the analysts have no idea which agreements they should be approving. Therefore they behave as one might expect them to: they simply respond to outside demands. In the words of a briefing paper prepared for the Carter administration:

There would appear to be no discernible pattern of operations [at the FMC] other than reacting to pressure from Congress, the White House, other Government departments, foreign-flag interests, or U.S.-flag interests.[51]

One agreement analyst remarked, "What we're doing now is completely reactive. There's no policy." Another agreement analyst commented that his office "acts like an amoeba in an ionized solution. When it hits an ion, it jumps."

In the vicinity of the FMC, there are more carrier ions than shipper ions. As one attorney put it in an interview:

All the guys you talked to represent carriers. There are practically no lawyers who represent shipper interests. Nobody. If you go back to other guys you'll find one or two guys outside of myself [representing shippers] in one hearing [apiece]. . . .

The shippers don't have a coherent voice. And the commission doesn't go out and drum them up. I handle these reparations cases because I'm retired and it doesn't bother me if I don't make a living on it. The shippers can't afford to pay, most of the time.

One analyst said he knew of approximately thirty law firms that represent carriers, but only one that represents shippers. Even the chairman of the FMC recently admitted to the House Merchant Marine Subcommittee that shippers' voices "have not frequently been heard at the Commission."[52] One shipper estimated in an interview that the ratio of carrier input to shipper input in formal and informal proceedings was 1,000 to 1. Another made the following comments:

The major shortcoming [of the FMC] is that the carriers have had an overwhelming input. That's a problem with all regulatory bodies, but with the Federal Maritime Commission especially, the carriers have had an overwhelming voice.

When the analysts hear only demands for approval, and the statute is broad enough to permit the analysts to recommend approval in good conscience, the inevitable result is that all agreements are approved. Senator Paul Douglas, who led the Joint Economic Committee into an investigation of the FMC's administration of the Shipping Act in 1965, was perceptive enough to recognize this problem:

In the absence of general standards based on national policy, the tendency became irresistible [for the FMC] to permit what was on the one hand adroitly advocated by special interest, and on the other hand was not condemned under articulated guidelines. As a result, a quite unintended negative principle emerged. Steamship operators came to believe that they had prescriptive rights to engage in monopolistic practices, which were to be deemed lawful unless individually disapproved. This is a far cry from the philosophy of the Shipping Act that only in particular circumstances, and only when strictly supervised by the Government, should steamship lines be granted antitrust immunity.[53]

"The general policy is that if nobody protests, it's okay" an attorney for several conferences remarked. An agreement analyst confessed in an interview that because the analysts themselves are "not so sure" what the standards are, they "pay more attention" to the carriers, who "do tend to get more out of the agency." A shipper was more specific: "Unless someone says, 'There's no serious transportation need,' I don't think the commission is willing to make that judgment on their own." An attorney for the Justice Department is probably not far from the truth in his claim that "absent any impact from any other sources, the commission would approve any agreement."

Tariff regulation must be considered a separate case—to some extent. Because of the sheer volume of rates that have to be examined, and—perhaps more important—because tariffs, unlike agreements, go into effect automatically unless disapproved, tariff examiners have had to routinize their responsibilities. To satisfy this need for routinization, the analysts have chosen the role of "publishing tariffs." One branch chief explained, "Our job is to get the tariffs into the binders so that the public has access to them." An analyst remarked that "it's like a menu. Shippers can come in and find out what rates are charged." In practice, "publishing tariffs" involves not only stuffing the pages into the binders but also checking for certain technical problems—such as page margins being an improper width—and for changes in the overall price level (i.e., temporary surcharges and general rate increases). Performing this role enables the analysts to feel much less frustrated than their counterparts in the Office of Agreements—they are more certain what their job is. It also permits the analysts the satisfaction of knowing they are not just a rubber stamp for the shipping industry's requests. One attorney noted: "A tariff examiner gets to feel very low if he thinks he's not doing anything more than shuffling pages. He feels much more important if he can stop the wheels of commerce."

But this pattern of review totally excludes questions of shipper discrimination. That is why the law on discrimination goes substantially unenforced, even when it is reasonably clear—as in 46 CFR 536.6 (1), which prohibits duplicate tariffs like "weedkillers" and "killers, weed." Since the tariff analysts cannot plead that all of their standards in their prime area of regulatory responsibility are ambiguous, it would seem that the two offices present different case studies. Nevertheless, if we ask why the tariff analysts selected the particular routine that they did, we can see that both offices share the same underlying problem. The basic law on tariff discrimination—sections 16 and 17 of the Shipping Act —contains impossibly vague phrases like "undue or unreasonable preference." When shippers bring tariff complaints to the Commission, they always object to absolute price levels (over which the FMC has little power) rather than relative price levels. As one shipper put it, "In arcane matters like evaluating discriminatory rate structures you don't have a great deal of shipper input." As a result, the analysts come to believe that there is no such thing as illegal discrimination *in* tariffs. In their view, special rates are legitimate "discounts based on volume"; "undue preference" occurs when a carrier charges *something other than* a published rate. An attorney from the Justice Department went so far as to tell an interviewer that tariff analysts "belong to the school of thought that big shippers are entitled to whatever concessions they can get [in tariffs]." This explains why they routinely "publish tariffs" where a more sensible approach would focus on abuses of the commodity classification system.

It would not be accurate to say that the FMC has been "captured" in any sinister way; indeed, the FMC performs a number of tasks, such as rejecting tariff pages for trivial reasons and requiring multiple justifications for garden-variety agreements, that drive carriers to distraction. "They do not regulate, but they annoy" is how one attorney put it. In general, a shipper can delay approval of an agreement for several months merely by filing "comments" on it; one organization (the National Association of Alcoholic Beverage Importers, known affectionately within the FMC as "the booze people") specializes in filing one-shot comments for that very purpose. If a shipper persists in "commenting" on an agreement (which almost never happens), he can usually force the proponents to withdraw it. To quote a shipper representative:

When [the FMC] hears from shippers, it's been responsive. —— has been fortunate in that when it has something to say, the Federal Maritime Commission has not only been willing to listen but has acted on it.

The root of the problem is not corruption in the FMC, but a reluctance of shippers to come forward.

There are several reasons why shippers, for the most part, do not appear before the commission. Shippers are often competing among themselves; a major exporter or importer may find that it is more profitable to negotiate with the conference directly in order to secure a special rate than to try to prevent an agreement (or tariff) from being approved. In the first case, he will be benefiting only himself; in the second case, he will be benefiting other shippers as well, some of whom may be his competitors. At least one senior official of the FMC believes that big shippers pursue this strategy. He told an interviewer:

We very rarely hear from Dow or GM or any of the conglomerates because they always get the rate they want. Our big problem is that the little shipper has no voice. First of all, he has no representation in Washington. And it costs a lot of dough.

After all, a big shipper has much less to fear from an unregulated conference system, and therefore much less to fear from a docile FMC. As one of the FMC's analysts commented, "It's sort of like Master Charge. The big shipper has clout." Two economists found that on conference-dominated routes, major export commodities account for a smaller share of the freight bill than of aggregate value or aggregate tonnage.[54] The real purpose of the Commission, an FMC official observed, is "to keep the small shipper from being screwed."

If it is obvious why big shippers lack a motive to challenge FMC actions, it is not obvious why small shippers lack the resources for such challenges. Small shippers, for example, could pool their resources. Why are there no trade associations that emulate the Justice Department by protesting anticompetitive agreements? First, there are certain built-in disincentives. Many exporters and importers do not deal with carriers directly, but hire a freight forwarder to arrange the transportation. Freight forwarders earn a commission that is a fixed percentage (usually 1 1/4 percent) of the freight rate; they have no incentive to complain about exorbitant shipping costs or the restrictive practices that create such costs. Also, even when a firm arranges its own transportation, this task is generally assigned to a traffic manager, an official who has low standing in the corporate hierarchy. The traffic manager may prefer an absence of competition (even if his ultimate boss does not), because a traffic manager's job is made easier when rates and services do not have to be compared. Finally, many firms are genuinely unaware of the potential benefits of going to the commission, because they assume that the FMC has no power simply because it has no authority to set reasonable rates.

But shipper ignorance and archaic industry practices can only survive so long as the cost of freight is not very important. While there is a shortage of data (which in itself suggests a lack of shipper concern), an informed view is that most freight rates are between 5 and 15 percent of the delivered price of the cargo.[55] In its study of the trade between the United States and Hawaii, the FMC found that freight costs average 7 percent of the retail price of fresh tomatoes, 6 percent of the retail price of canned peas, and 2 percent of the retail price of ground roast coffee. Between the United States and Puerto Rico (according to another FMC trade study), freight rates are less than 5 percent of the cost of washing machines, less than 3 percent of the cost of gas stoves, and less than 1 percent of the cost of portable TV sets.[56] Although these domestic routes are shorter than most international routes, the length of the voyage generally has little impact on the freight rate; thus, the percentages in foreign and domestic commerce should be roughly similar. Largely because freight rates are but a small portion of a typical shipper's expenses, the demand for shipping services tends to be very inelastic. One recent study gave a figure of –0.13, which means that if freight rates went up 10 percent, the amount of cargo being shipped would decline by only a little more than 1 percent.[57]

The Federal Maritime Commission

Congress and the FMC

If the FMC's problem is a combination of an ambiguously worded statute and a one-sided political environment, then apathetic shippers are only partly to blame for the agency's misfortunes. Part of the blame must rest with Congress for not having clarified the FMC's mandate either formally or informally. Indeed, for the most part, Congress's attitude toward the FMC has been one of indifference. The commission has been criticized on a number of occasions—the Celler hearings of 1959–62, the Douglas hearings of 1965, the Ribicoff investigation of 1977. But this criticism tends to be followed by long periods of neglect. From the start of the Ninety-first Congress to the start of the Ninety-fifth Congress, only one bill was passed relating to the FMC's regulation of foreign commerce: PL 92–416, converting certain criminal penalties to civil penalties for violations of the Shipping Act. Congress seems to be more concerned with renaming the agency that administers the Shipping Act than with improving the Act itself. (Since 1916 we have had the Shipping Board, the Shipping Board Bureau, the U.S. Maritime Commission, the Federal Maritime Board, and finally the Federal Maritime Commission.)

Congressional staff members take the attitude that the FMC is at fault for not proposing legislation:

I don't think the FMC has exercised leadership in actually presenting legislation.

[Q. They claim it's not their job.]

For Christ's sakes! They can claim whatever they want, but I read the statute and it's their responsibility. Section 208 [of the Merchant Marine Act, 1936]: "Recommendations for legislation." No one's really held them to that, but I think they should be held to that very strongly.

In fact, the FMC does make proposals; the problem is that those proposals seldom reach Capitol Hill because the Office of Management and Budget refuses to grant them clearance. "Normally the structured legislative program is bottlenecked on an annual basis," an official in the FMC's Office of Legislative Counsel explains. Congress, however, is fully aware of OMB's role and (as one former congressional staff member admits) it could obtain the FMC's legislative proposals if it wanted to.

Congress has not shown any inclination to redirect the agency's progress by informal methods, either. As Richard J. Daschbach, the current chairman of the FMC relates: "[For] eight years I was on the Senate committee [the Merchant Marine and Tourism Subcommittee of the Senate Commerce Committee]. I think we had a hearing on the FMC at the very most four times." The House Merchant Marine and Fisheries Committee has been somewhat more active than its Senate counterpart. During the Ninety-fourth Congress, it held hearings on "third flag" carriers and intermodalism. However, these hearings were basically forums for considering special-interest legislation. The so-called "Third Flag Bill," which would have forced foreign-flag lines to set their rates no lower than the cheapest rates offered by American lines, had been introduced at the behest of several American carriers and shipping unions. These shipping interests claimed that the bill was needed to deal with the "Russian threat": state-supported Soviet lines operating as independents in the U.S. trades, offering rates 10 to 15 percent below those of the conferences in order to capture a significant portion of America's oceangoing commerce (and thereby undermine its national security). But since the Soviets carry only 3 percent of U.S. liner imports and 4 percent of U.S. liner exports (and their rates, moreover, are no lower than those of other independents), it is difficult to take the threat of Soviet rate-cutting seriously.[58] One suspects that the real aim of the bill's supporters was to reduce competition in general; the Soviets were merely a convenient political excuse.

The second hearing dealt with a bill which would have given the FMC exclusive authority over intermodal tariffs, thereby settling its jurisdictional dispute with the ICC. This legislation had also been requested by the shipping interests, who wanted the FMC and not the relatively more active ICC to regulate these combined land-sea voyages.

Nor has Congress taken advantage of the opportunities for oversight inherent in the confirmation process. Even "Ashcan" Barrett had little trouble getting reconfirmed. His last appearance before the Senate was a brief, pro forma affair: Senator Eastland opened the hearing by delivering a speech to the effect that Barrett was "a damn good man." Senator J. Glenn Beall asked Barrett two questions which had to be repeated because the commissioner could not hear them. Then the hearing ended with the following exchange:

The Federal Maritime Commission

Senator Hollings: Commissioner Barrett, you have been with the Commission for quite a while. Isn't that correct?

Mr. Barrett: Yes, sir; I was sworn in on October 12, 1961.

Senator Hollings: If something was wrong with you, we would have already heard it. (Laughter)

Mr. Barrett: Well, I work underground. (Laughter)

Senator Hollings: We don't have any questions in addition to what Senator Beall has asked. We appreciate your appearance here this afternoon. We will move as promptly as we can within the committee for your confirmation.[59]

In the Ribicoff survey of lawyers and administrative law judges, the FMC finished second only to the Federal Trade Commission for having "insufficient congressional oversight" as "one of [its] three most important problems."[60] As we have seen, Congress did not originally intend to set up an agency dominated by the shipping interests; nevertheless, Congress is helping to perpetuate one. Why is this so? Why does Congress appear to have renounced its original intention?

Part of the answer lies in the structure of Congress itself. As Harold Seidman says, "It is highly misleading to speak of *the Congress* as if it were a collective identity."[61] The "Congress" that passed the Shipping Act is not the same as the "Congress" that currently oversees administration of that Act. The latter consists in effect of one committee and one subcommittee: the House Committee on Merchant Marine and Fisheries and the Subcommittee on Merchant Marine and Tourism of the Senate Committee on Commerce, Science and Transportation. Richard Fenno would probably classify these committees as "reelection" committees rather than "public policy" or "internal influence" committees.[62] Like the House Post Office and Civil Service Committee, which is Fenno's "reelection" committee par excellence, they have a jurisdiction that largely consists of one handout—in this case, the $388 million maritime subsidy program (fiscal 1976 appropriation). Since the subsidies (which are administered by the Maritime Administration, not the FMC) can only go to American-flag ships and American-flag ships must employ a 75 percent American crew (100 percent if the ship is receiving an operating differential subsidy), the program has two key constituencies: shipowners and labor unions. These two groups frequently join in their lobbying efforts. One example is the Labor-Management Maritime Committee, organized in 1950 by six carriers and the National Maritime Union,[63] that testified extensively in support of the Third Flag Bill and that recently mounted a television advertising campaign on behalf of oil cargo preference. The two constituencies form an impressive power bloc. One official of the FMC put it: "You've got to remember it says something about the industry's strength that a Merchant Marine Committee still exists."

The two committees resemble Fenno's Post Office Committee in member goals as well as environmental constraints. As David Price has said, "There is no area of its jurisdiction where the [Senate Commerce] Committee has responded more faithfully and less imaginatively to the expressed interests of a powerful lobby than it has in relation to the United States merchant marine."[64] During the ninety-fifth Congress, four of the five members of the Merchant Marine Subcommittee came from states with an obvious proshipping interest: Ted Stevens (Alaska), Daniel Inouye (Hawaii), Russell Long (Louisiana), and Warren Magnuson (Washington). Similarly, the House Merchant Marine Committee historically has had about twice as many members from coastal districts as one would predict from random selection.[65] The committee's current chairman John Murphy (New York) is a favorite with the maritime industry because, as one lobbyist remarked, "His district [Staten Island and Manhattan] makes him concerned." An FMC branch chief was willing to generalize: "No one's representing the public interest. They [the members of the two committees] are all representing private interests." The oversight committees view their role as one of promoting the U.S. merchant marine. It would be self-defeating for them to help the FMC do a better job of regulating it. It is worth noting that none of the congressional investigations that we have discussed were conducted by the merchant marine committees.

As we have seen, the origin of ocean shipping regulation was politically similar to the origin of the Pure Food and Drug Act of 1906, the National Traffic and Motor Vehicle Safety Act of 1966, and the various clean air and clean water acts of the early 1970s. All of these policies, to use Wilson's terminology, imposed "concentrated costs" and provided "distributed benefits." (It is incorrect to consider the antitrust exemption a "benefit," since conferences had been operating without hindrance for twenty years.) Wilson's analysis suggests that while such policies may occasionally be adopted, they are less likely to be successfully implemented. Once the legislation has passed, client politics will resume. Unorganized supporters of the policy may turn their attention elsewhere while organized opponents turn their attention to the agency so they can constrain its policy.[66]

Such client politics soon characterized the Shipping Board and its successors. Once the Shipping Act had passed, the steamship lines set out to undermine its purposes. Their efforts achieved almost immediate success. Approvals of conference agreements became a routine matter.

The only time that the Shipping Board took an interest in regulation was when it went before Congress at the urging of the conferences to request authority to set minimum rates—so that it could eliminate rate cutting by independents. According to one contemporary commentator, it did not take long for the Shipping Board to be "dominated by the very interests which it had been organized to regulate."[67]

Meanwhile, Congress lost interest in shipping regulation. In 1920 it gave the Shipping Board its first promotional responsibilities. Eventually, under a variety of merchant marine acts that authorized direct and indirect subsidies to American shipbuilders, the Shipping Board and its successors acquired a dual mandate of regulating U.S. commerce and fostering the U.S. merchant marine.[68] As one might expect, the latter goal took precedence over the former. After Celler's investigation created a public uproar, all promotional responsibilities were transferred to the Maritime Administration. But Congress, on the whole, has remained inattentive to the fate of the FMC. And until another crisis occurs or can be manufactured, it seems unlikely that this attitude will change. Even then, it is probable that the change will only be temporary, and that within a short time the FMC will come to be viewed as a "political dumping-ground" (to use one FMC official's phrase) once again.

Conclusion

The Alexander Committee probably relied on faulty economic reasoning when it urged Congress to regulate the ocean shipping industry in 1914. Many would argue that the benefits the Alexander Committee alleged for a regulated conference system—stable rates, frequent service, equal treatment for all shippers—could be attained more easily and more cheaply in the free market. But the *political* error that advocates of shipping regulation made was even more significant. When it passed the Shipping Act, Congress was trying to set boundaries on what seemed to be an unfair competitive situation. However, the boundaries were so vague that the effect was simply to substitute political for economic competition. And Congress should have realized that any political competition was bound to be unfavorable to the shippers, because what matters in politics is the intensity of one's concern and shippers have much less of a stake in the level of freight rates than do carriers.

But there must be a reason why Congress did not write a narrower law in 1916 and why Congress has not clarified the agency's mandate since then. The reason is this: When public attention is focused on the abuses or needs of the shipping industry, as was the case in 1916, narrow statutes seem unnecessary; there is no imbalance in interest representation to worry about. The need for clear standards occurs only later, when public attention is diverted; but then it is impossible to enact those standards into law. This problem seems to be inherent in any attempt to regulate an industry as obscure as ocean shipping.

CHAPTER 3

Civil Aeronautics Board

BRADLEY BEHRMAN

Few regulatory agencies—if any—have ever altered their policies as rapidly or radically as did the Civil Aeronautics Board (CAB) between 1974 and 1978. In 1974 the CAB was striving vigorously to protect the airline industry from competition and was regarded by many critics as the epitome of an agency "captured" by the industry it regulates. In 1976 the agency unanimously endorsed legislation that would have substantially reduced its powers to restrain competition—legislation strongly opposed by the airline industry. By 1978 the CAB not only was supporting deregulatory legislation but also was doing everything it could (within legal and political constraints) to deregulate without even waiting for new legislation. When Congress passed the Airline Deregulation Act of 1978[1]—which will make the CAB the first major federal regulatory agency ever to be abolished[2]—it did not so much *impose* reforms on the CAB as it *affirmed* policies that the CAB had been trying to implement for almost a year. In fact, the CAB's pursuit of deregulation played a prominent role in diminishing congressional opposition to the new legislation.

New appointments to the CAB were crucially important to the agency's policy shift between 1974 and 1978. One new member was appointed in 1975, one in 1976, and two in 1977. From these new members, a new chairman was designated in 1975 and another in 1977. Each new member—and each new chairman—was known from the beginning to be more favorably disposed toward airline deregulation than his predecessor had been. The leadership provided by the new chairmen —John Robson from 1975 to 1977, and Alfred Kahn from 1977 to 1978 —was vital to the CAB's espousal of deregulation.

But to explain the policy shift solely as a product of new appointments would be to overlook other factors that were also fundamentally important to the shift. First, arguments for airline deregulation gained ascendency at the CAB because of increasing support not only from the newly appointed members, but also from the veteran members who remained. From the time the shift began until shortly before Congress passed the Airline Deregulation Act, never more than two of the CAB's five memberships were held by people appointed after 1973.[3] Obviously, the new members would have been powerless to redirect CAB policies if not for cooperation from veteran members.

Furthermore, the external political environment with which the CAB must contend in making policy—and with which the president and his advisers must contend when selecting appointees—became increasingly amenable to deregulation between 1974 and 1978. Had the political environment remained hostile to deregulation, as it had always been before 1974, pro-deregulation individuals almost certainly would not have been appointed to the agency, and it would have had both less political incentive and less ideological inclination to change its policies.

The change in the external political environment stemmed from changes in the nation's economic condition, from shifts in CAB policy, and from a few influential political leaders' endorsements of airline deregulation. The inflation and recession that simultaneously beset the nation in the early 1970s squeezed profits for airlines in general and caused severe financial problems for several airlines in particular. Attempting to restore the airlines' financial health, the CAB adopted unprecedentedly anticompetitive policies during the early 1970s. These policies prompted both liberals and conservatives to complain that the CAB was more concerned with protecting the airlines than with protecting the general public. These policies also prompted certain influential politicians to pay close attention to arguments that CAB regulation was inherently flawed and should be eliminated—arguments that had been made for many years, primarily by academic economists, but that previously had been virtually ignored both at the CAB and in Congress. In 1975 Senator Edward Kennedy and President Gerald Ford established airline deregulation as a prominent political issue when they began pressing for legislation to reduce the CAB's powers. During the next three years, airline deregulation gained important new supporters. Among them was Jimmy Carter, who announced his endorsement shortly after succeeding Ford into the presidency.

The nation's general economic expansion between 1975 and 1978 augmented both the economic suitability and the political feasibility of reducing CAB restraints on competition. Not only economically but also politically, the gravest short-run risk involved in promoting greater competition among the airlines was the prospect that airlines already in financial difficulty would be pushed into bankruptcy; any bankruptcy attributable to "too much" competition would almost certainly have provoked a congressional backlash against the CAB's procompetitive shift and undoubtedly would have killed pending legislative proposals for reducing CAB regulation. The nation's economic upturn significantly increased demand for air travel and thereby boosted the airline industry's financial health. Consequently, even the financially weakest carriers were prosperous enough to withstand a substantial increase in competition. This reduction in the economic risks of airline deregulation substantially increased the political tenability of deregulation.

Economists often complain that regulatory agencies downplay or even ignore available economic theory on how market incentives can be used to achieve policy goals. They complain that many agencies effectively insulate themselves from pertinent theory, seemingly blinded by external political pressures, by lack of understanding of basic economic principles, and by tradition. They insist that regulatory policies would be less costly and more effective at overcoming breakdowns in the free market if the various agencies—and Congress—would rely more on government incentives that work *through* the market and less on "command-and-control" rules that suppress the market.[4]

As of the early 1970s, the CAB was certainly a leading example of an agency that downplayed the views of market-oriented economists. Although economists have a much-deserved reputation for disagreeing among themselves, they agreed almost unanimously that Congress should deregulate the airlines and that in the meantime the CAB should sharply reduce regulatory restraints on competition.[5] But the CAB moved in the opposite direction during the early 1970s.

After 1974, however, the CAB increasingly heeded economists' arguments that it previously had dismissed. In a sense, the story of the CAB's shift from a philosophy of protectionism to a philosophy of deregulation is the story of how long-ignored economic theory became the foundation of CAB policy.

The History of the CAB

The CAB's Principal Functions: Route Licensing and Rate Regulation[6]

Since 1938 the Civil Aeronautics Board has wielded absolute authority over entry and pricing in all commercial interstate air transportation. Except in cases where the CAB has explicitly exempted airlines from regulation, each airline that crosses state lines has needed to obtain a "certificate of public convenience and necessity" from the CAB before starting operations, and it has needed the CAB to amend its certificate in order to expand operations to any new route.[7] All fares of certificated carriers have been subject to CAB approval: the CAB has been empowered to disallow fares that it has considered too low as well as those it has considered too high.[8]

Through the device of mandatory authority, the CAB has exercised control over airlines' exit from particular communities. Until late 1977, the CAB customarily made its route awards mandatory—at least in a loose sense—by attaching a minimum-service requirement (the requirement for specified routes has commonly been as low as one round trip per day) to route certificates. Airlines have needed to have the CAB's permission to abandon any mandatory authority.[9] Mandatory authority has signified a guarantee of service to individual communities rather than to specific routes, insofar as any airline certificated to fly between two points could, without seeking CAB approval, substitute indirect service in place of direct service. Thus any airline mandatorily certificated to fly between A and B could fulfill its service obligation merely by retaining both points in its route network and providing some combination of flights, no matter how circuitous, to link the two points.

By virtue of its authority over entry and pricing, the CAB has been placed in the role of managing what at least one critic of the CAB has characterized as an "imperfect cartel":[10] the CAB could keep newcomers out of the industry and could prop prices higher than they would otherwise be, but it could not prevent airlines serving the same routes from competing with respect to various aspects of service quality—for example, free liquor, meals, stereo headsets, amount of legroom between seats, and frequency and timing of flights.[11] By driving up per-passenger operating costs, service competition can squeeze profit margins as thinly as competitive price-cutting can. Thus, except on monopoly routes, high prices have never guaranteed large profits for airlines even when demand for air travel has been high.[12]

The Creation of the CAB

Congress created the CAB by passing the Civil Aeronautics Act of 1938.[13] The legislation was avowedly intended to aid the airline industry: the declaration of policy in the act included such objectives as "regulation to . . . foster sound economic conditions" among the airlines and "the promotion, encouragement, and development of civil aeronautics."[14] In establishing federal control over entry and pricing in the industry, the act imitated legislation that Congress had already enacted for two other transportation industries—the railroads and the motor carriers (trucks and buses), which were regulated by the Interstate Commerce Commission. However, unlike the previous legislation, the act directly linked federal control over rates and entry to a federal subsidy program. Although the subsidy program is now of negligible importance to the industry—it accounted for about 0.3 percent of the industry's total operating revenues in 1978[15]—it was the principal short-term concern of the airline industry and of Congress throughout the 1930s.

The airline industry of the 1930s was an "infant industry" that had always been heavily dependent on mail pay from the federal government. The $23.4 million in domestic passenger revenues collected by the airlines in 1938 was about 0.7 percent of the amount collected in 1978 (in constant dollars),[16] and the 533 million revenue passenger-miles carried on scheduled flights in 1938 was an even smaller fraction of the number carried in 1978.[17] The commercial airline industry had been virtually nonexistent until Congress passed the Air Mail Act of 1925 (commonly called the Kelly Act), which established a federal air-mail-contract program for private carriers.[18] (Between 1918 and 1925, the army had carried airmail.[19]) Until the mid-1930s, air-passenger travel was light, and airlines derived most of their revenues from mail pay. In 1931, for example, mail pay accounted for over 91 percent and passenger revenues for only 8.1 percent of the airmail carriers' $18.5 million in total revenues. The year 1935 was the first year that the airline industry's passenger revenues exceeded mail pay; passenger revenues accounted for 56.8 percent and mail pay for 40.8 percent of the airmail carriers' $21.6 million in total revenues. In 1938 passenger revenues made up 58.2 percent and mail pay 36.7 percent of the airlines' $40.1 million in total revenues.[20]

Before the passage of the Civil Aeronautics Act, the airmail-contract program functioned both as a subsidy program and as a de facto regulator of entry into the airline industry. By design, mail pay was only loosely based on actual costs of carrying airmail and almost always exceeded those costs substantially, thereby providing airmail carriers a hefty surplus that subsidized growth of scheduled passenger service. Almost everywhere, flying costs were too high and demand too low for such service to be profitable without mail pay, so virtually no one other than holders of airmail contracts provided that service. Although there were no legal barriers to entry in the airline industry (aside from meeting safety standards established by the Department of Commerce[21]), failure to obtain airmail contracts meant being effectively barred from the industry.

The airline industry received close attention from Congress during the 1930s primarily because of problems detected in the airmail-contract program. Postmaster General Walter Brown's administration of the program between 1929 and 1933 aroused charges that Brown had consistently given special treatment to a few large carriers in awarding contracts; more specifically, Brown was accused of violating legal requirements for competitive-bidding procedures and of overpaying carriers for their services. At the recommendation of Postmaster General James Farley, Brown's successor, in February 1934 President Franklin Roosevelt canceled all airmail contracts and ordered the army to carry airmail. However, an alarming rash of accidents—sixty-two crashes and twelve fatalities in less than three months of the army's airmail operations—soon prompted the president to suspend army carriage of airmail. While Congress considered new legislation for airmail contracts, in April and May, Roosevelt directed the Post Office to solicit bids from private carriers for temporary contracts.[22]

In June 1934 Congress passed the Air Mail Act of 1934.[23] The act strengthened requirements for competitive-bidding procedures in the awarding of contracts and divided jurisdiction over airmail contracts between the Post Office and the Interstate Commerce Commission. As before, the Post Office was vested with responsibility for awarding contracts and determining routes and schedules. The ICC was directed to review the pay rates for each contractor and, when necessary, to reduce rates to prevent contractors from collecting unreasonably high profits. The act also created a Federal Aviation Commission, consisting of five members appointed by the president, to study aviation and to make recommendations for new legislation.[24]

The commission issued its report in January 1935. It proposed that an independent commission be created to regulate entry, pricing, and other aspects of the airline industry. President Roosevelt promptly endorsed all of the commission's recommendations except that of establishing a new agency. Believing that all transportation regulation should be administered by a single agency, he favored vesting the Interstate Commerce Commission with all regulatory authority over the airlines.[25]

Between 1935 and 1938, Congress considered proposals for reforming the airmail-contract program and for subjecting the airline industry to comprehensive federal regulation of entry and pricing. Throughout this time, Senator Patrick McCarran (Democrat, Nevada) and Representative Clarence Lea (Democrat, California) were indisputably the leading congressional spokesmen for legislation to regulate the airlines.[26]

Proponents of regulating pricing and entry typically focused on the alleged threat of "destructive competition." They argued that in the absence of regulation, more airlines would enter the industry than the available traffic could support. Because of this excessive entry as well as the appearance of "cut-rate fly-by-night" operators, competition would push prices dangerously close to cost or even below cost, thereby causing severe financial instability in the airline industry. Consequently, service would be unreliable in terms of both scheduling and safety. Bankruptcies would be frequent. The surviving airlines, fighting to survive on perilously thin profit margins, might try to reduce costs by intermittently canceling flights, by terminating service to various points, and by scrimping on safety precautions.[27]

These arguments reflected the nation's widespread ambivalence toward competition in the wake of the depression. Having experienced a disastrous breakdown of the free market—a breakdown highlighted by severe deflation of prices—the nation was leery of relying on unrestrained competition to spur firms to satisfy the public's needs. It was especially nervous about industries which provided essential public services—for example, transportation, communications systems, and electricity.

The arguments about the dangers of destructive competition also served as a public-interest rationale for airlines to use in trying to convince Congress to protect them from *all* competition. Over the short run, holders of airmail contracts were interested primarily in getting rid of the competitive-bidding process. They disliked having to place low bids and thus to squeeze profit margins when trying to secure renewal of contracts and to win new contracts. Over the longer run, they were also concerned about facing new competition from unsubsidized carriers. Owing to growing public receptiveness to air travel, and, more important, to technological advances that reduced airlines' per-passenger and per-mile operating costs, scheduled air-passenger service was becoming increasingly economical. By the late 1930s, there was reason to believe that, at least on a few of the nation's most heavily traveled routes, airlines not holding mail contracts would soon be able to earn a profit as scheduled passenger carriers;[28] failure to obtain a mail contract was ceasing to be an insuperable barrier to entry. Thus, contract holders were concerned not only about competition that was already taking place, but also about prospects that competition would markedly intensify in the future.

Between 1935 and 1938, the airmail-contract program produced what many congressmen interpreted as proof of the airline industry's intrinsic susceptibility to destructive competition. A 1935 amendment to the Air Mail Act of 1934 gave the Interstate Commerce Commission authority to raise pay rates (up to a statutory maximum) for carriers found to be earning less than a reasonable return from their contracts.[29] This provision gave airlines competing for contracts a strong incentive to place bids that were lower than their actual costs of carrying mail: if an airline placed a below-cost bid and won the contract, it could hope for the ICC subsequently to raise the pay rate above cost and thereby to make the contract—and the corresponding route—profitable; but if the airline did not place such a bid, it probably would lose the contract and thus the financial incentive for serving the route.[30] The effects of this incentive reached a pinnacle of absurdity in 1938, when Braniff Airways bid about $.00002 per airplane mile for a contract to carry mail between Houston and San Antonio, only to be underpriced by Eastern Airlines's bid of $.000 per mile.[31]

Meanwhile, the airline industry grew rapidly but incurred substantial financial losses. Between 1935 and 1938, domestic airline operations grew 46 percent in plane-miles flown and more than doubled in available seat-miles and revenue passenger-miles. Passenger revenues grew more than 80 percent and total revenues almost 75 percent. However, revenues lagged behind expenses. In fiscal year 1935 (July 1934 through June 1935), airlines lost almost $3.3 million (14.3 percent of the amount of total revenues). Their losses fell to $750,000 (2.3 percent) in 1936 and to $150,000 (0.4 percent) in 1937, but rose to $1.5 million in 1938 (3.7 percent).[32] Edgar Gorrell, president of the Air Transport Association (the trade association of airlines holding mail contracts), testified at congressional hearings in 1938 that of the $120 million of private capital that had been invested in the existing air-transport system, $60 million had been lost.[33] In view of the available data on yearly operating losses,

Gorrell's estimate of lost investment seems highly exaggerated (perhaps Gorrell counted normal capital depreciation in his estimate). Nevertheless, the airline industry's financial condition in the late 1930s was clearly unhealthy and seemed to be getting worse rather than better.

In Congress, disputes over airline regulation centered principally on organizational and administrative issues rather than on the question of whether regulation was desirable. There was widespread agreement in Congress that, for the sake of improving the airlines' financial health and of promoting orderly growth of air service throughout the nation, the airmail-contract program should be made less competitive and the federal government should regulate entry and pricing for the entire airline industry. The main reason Congress did not pass regulatory legislation earlier than 1938 was controversy over the question of whether regulation of pricing and entry in the airline industry should be conducted by the Interstate Commerce Commission or by a new agency.

The most prominent opposition to regulation came from the Post Office and the Department of Commerce. They argued that pending regulatory proposals would unduly protect existing airlines from having to compete with new airlines or with each other and would thereby reduce incentives for efficiency and innovation.[34] However, few congressmen took this view very seriously. In fact, it is likely that many congressmen dismissed the positions of the Post Office and the Department of Commerce as being based on self-interest rather than principle. All the leading airline-regulation proposals between 1935 and 1938 provided for a consolidation of aviation policy-making and regulation in either the Interstate Commerce Commission or a new agency. Thus, in a sense, the proposals constituted repudiations of the Post Office and the Department of Commerce, and it would have been surprising if either department had supported them. (As previously noted, existing legislation empowered the Post Office to specify routes and schedules for airmail carriers and empowered the Department of Commerce to regulate airline safety.)[35]

With Senator McCarran and Representative Lea serving as the principal sponsors of the bill, both houses of Congress passed the Civil Aeronautics Act by an unrecorded but almost certainly overwhelming margins in June 1938. President Roosevelt signed the act that same month, and it became effective in August.[36]

The act aided holders of airmail contracts by changing the mail-contract program and by erecting a new barrier against competition. It abolished the competitive-bidding system and, in effect, converted the airmail-contract program into a need-based subsidy program. The act directed the CAB to set mail rates, and the criteria to be used in rate-setting included "the need of each ... carrier for compensation."[37] The "grandfather" provision of the act granted route certificates with perpetual eligibility for mail pay to all airlines that held mail contracts and had provided regular service during the four months preceding the effective date of the act.[38] Thus, the act built permanent open-ended mail contracts into the new certificates. In giving the CAB the power to set price floors and to limit entry, the act imposed restraints on competition among existing carriers as well as on competition from new entrants to the industry—restraints whose stringency would depend on how the CAB administered the act.

To a certain extent, the Civil Aeronautics Act could be characterized both as a narrow "industry bill" and as a reflection of economic beliefs generally prevalent during the 1930s. Aside from the act's congressional sponsors, airlines were its most enthusiastic and most visible supporters. Their spokesmen were prominent participants both in public hearings on airline legislation and in behind-the-scenes drafting; there was little that airlines wanted to have in the new legislation but did not get. Few interest groups have ever been as overtly and uncontestably preeminent in legislative proceedings as the airline industry was during the congressional deliberations that led to passage of the act.

However, the Civil Aeronautics Act also showed signs of being a "consensus bill" that might have passed even in the absence of strong industry backing. The concept of regulating entry and pricing in the airline industry received widespread support from people lacking any financial or political ties with the industry. In September 1932, at which time few if any industry leaders had even thought about the desirability of comprehensive regulation, presidential candidate Franklin Roosevelt became one of the first public figures to endorse that concept. In a campaign speech delivered in Salt Lake City, Roosevelt advocated extending controls of entry and pricing to all modes of transportation; at that time, such controls applied only to railroads. (Roosevelt presented this proposal as part of a package of reforms for bolstering the railroad industry, which then was in the midst of a severe financial crisis.) In brief, the rationale behind Roosevelt's proposal was that (1) the federal government, in regulating railroads without placing any restrictions on the various transportation industries that vie with the railroads for traffic, had harmed railroads by imposing an unfair competitive disadvantage on them; (2) this disadvantage could be rectified only by equalizing regulation for all modes of transportation; (3) equalizing regulation by diminishing regulation of the railroad industry would, due to structural instability of the industry, unleash destructive competition among railroads and thereby worsen their plight;[39] and (4) due to the impracticality of deregulating the railroads, federal regulation of transportation should be equalized through the extension of regulation to all of the railroads' competitors—motor carriers, airlines, and water carriers.[40]

Subsequently, the idea of equalizing transportation in the manner proposed by Roosevelt attracted substantial support and little opposition from the nation's academic community and from the various "blue-ribbon" panels that studied the issue.[41] In view of the fact that the vast majority of economists during the 1970s supported the elimination of price controls and entry controls over the airline industry, it is ironic that during the 1930s the vast majority of them supported the creation of those controls.[42]

Depending on whether we are prone to defend or deride Congress's reasoning in forming the CAB, the Civil Aeronautics Act was a masterwork of either flexibility or ambiguity—"flexibility" to make extreme shifts in policy as needed to deal with changing conditions in the airline industry, or "ambiguity" to enable the CAB to argue that it was faithfully carrying out congressional intent no matter what policy goals it pursued. The act's policy statement listed a number of vague, potentially contradictory objectives—for example, "foster[ing] sound economic conditions in [air] transportation," the "promotion of adequate, economical, and efficient service," and "competition to the extent necessary to assure the sound development of an air-transportation system properly adapted to the needs of the foreign and domestic commerce of the United States, of the Postal Service, and of the national defense."[43] Meanwhile, the statement failed to single out any of the goals as having priority over the others.

The act's specific provisions guiding CAB control over entry and pricing were similarly open to subjective interpretation. The act directed the CAB to adjudicate airlines' applications for new routes in the following manner:

The Board shall issue a certificate . . . if it finds that the applicant is *fit, willing, and able* to perform such transportation properly . . . and that such transportation is *required by the public convenience and necessity;* otherwise such application shall be denied. [emphasis added][44]

The act directed the CAB to judge the legitimacy of an air fare by considering

(1)   The effect of such rates upon the movement of traffic;

(2)   The need in the public interest of adequate and efficient transportation . . . at the *lowest cost consistent with the furnishing of such service;*

(3)   Such standards respecting the character and quality of service to be rendered by air carriers . . .;

(4)   The inherent advantages of transportation by aircraft; and

(5)   The *need of each air carrier for revenue* sufficient to enable such air carrier, under honest, economical, and efficient management, to provide *adequate and efficient air carrier service.* [emphasis added][45]

Clearly, these broad directives could be used to justify a wide range of policies: from ardently anticompetitive to vigorously procompetitive. For example, the CAB could stifle new competition by deeming it harmful to "sound economic conditions" or superfluous to "the public convenience and necessity," or by declaring applicants unfit, unwilling, or unable. Conversely, the CAB could encourage new competitors to enter various routes by judging such competition "necessary to assure the sound development of an air-transportation system" and "required by the public convenience and necessity," and by judging applicants for new routes "fit, willing, and able." As it turned out, the CAB tended toward the first approach for most of the period 1938 to 1974. Afterward, it became increasingly receptive to the second approach, until its advocacy of competition became advocacy for deregulation.

The CAB's Interpretation of Its Mandate, 1938—1974: An Overview

Between 1938 and 1974, the CAB generally placed its primary emphasis on sustaining "sound financial conditions" for each of the certificated airlines providing scheduled passenger service. It refused to allow new airlines to enter the industry or existing carriers to enter each other's routes when it appeared that new entry would harm the financial interests of an existing carrier. The CAB's attitude toward fare reductions— which were most often proposed by new airlines trying to enter the industry—was much the same. The CAB confined entry of new carriers almost exclusively to fringe markets that were served minimally or not at all by existing carriers and it did not encourage or even allow fare reductions except when all the airlines were prospering and could easily withstand greater price competition.

The CAB took a dim view of new entry almost from the beginning. In two of the first route cases to be decided, the agency admitted two new airlines into the industry on a very small scale—one to serve what had previously been a monopoly route, and the other to operate a "pick-up" device that eliminated the necessity of landing to load airmail.[46] Soon afterward, however, the CAB stated that the number of existing airlines was "sufficient to insure against monopoly in the average route case" and enunciated a policy of denying route applications of new airlines except in "peculiar circumstances presenting an affirmative reason for a new carrier."[47]

The only area in which the CAB adopted a liberal attitude toward new entry into air-passenger carriage was in nonscheduled operations, which the agency totally exempted from route controls and rate controls in 1938.[48] The CAB's motivation for granting this exemption was threefold: there were many "fixed-base" operators who functioned essentially as air taxis, flying on a contract basis to various points from a single airport rather than over a fixed route; the CAB could not have regulated these operators without imposing onerous financial burdens on them or without expending substantial time and resources of its own; and insofar as these operators were small, unsubsidized, and constituted no competitive threat to the certificated carriers, there was virtually nothing for anyone to gain from having the CAB regulate them.[49]

However, after the end of World War II, carriers operating under the exemption began to compete more and more directly with the certificated airlines. With war-surplus aircraft much less expensive than standard passenger aircraft, hundreds of former military pilots took advantage of the exemption and of the high postwar demand for air travel by forming new airlines. By charging fares 35 to 40 percent lower than those of the certificated carriers and often by providing a close approximation of scheduled service (despite the terms of the exemption), these "nonscheduled" airlines secured significant shares of traffic on some of the most heavily traveled routes. By 1951 they were carrying almost 7 percent of the nation's air-passenger traffic and posing a formidable competitive challenge to the certificated carriers.[50]

In response, the CAB began restricting the scope of the exemption. In May 1949 it withdrew the blanket exemption from the "large irregulars"—nonscheduled carriers that exceeded CAB specifications for size and take-off weight of aircraft[51]—and required that they reapply for exemptions on an individual basis. In May 1950 the CAB announced that large irregulars could remain eligible for exemptions only by offering three or fewer flights per month on the eleven most heavily traveled routes and eight or fewer flights per month on the others. Subsequently, the CAB rejected a large majority of the ninety-seven applications submitted for large-irregular-carrier exemptions; in passing judgment on the applications, it was especially quick to turn down carriers that had previously violated the terms of their exemptions.[52]

After some minor modifications in the terms of exemptions, the CAB in January 1959 decided to certificate twenty-three of the large irregulars as "supplemental" airlines. However, despite numerous applications, the CAB declined to certificate any irregulars as scheduled carriers. Thereafter, confined by the terms of their certificates to charter-type operations, the supplementals continued to provide service at fares much lower than those of the scheduled carriers but were prevented from posing a significant competitive threat to the scheduled carriers.[53]

In gradually narrowing the exemption and then certificating some irregulars for providing a limited sort of "specialty" service, the Board demonstrated a fundamental theme of its 1938–1974 entry policies: to allow new airlines to enter the industry only if their operations would not constitute significant or direct competition with airlines already certificated to provide scheduled passenger service. Between 1950 and 1974, for example, the Board turned down all ninety-four of the applications that would-be entrants to the industry submitted in pursuit of domestic "trunkline" authority—authority to fly between major cities.[54] The only new entry the CAB permitted aside from the irregulars was restricted to all-cargo service, to small-community service that was uneconomical for the existing certificated carriers to provide, or to service using small planes with limited seating capacity and short flight ranges.[55]

As suggested by the CAB's ruling in the *Transcontinental Coach-Type Service Case*,[56] the agency's propensity to protect the certificated scheduled carriers from competition stemmed in part from concurrent desires to hold down subsidies *and* to maintain service on lightly traveled, unprofitable routes. In this case, four irregular carriers had applied for certification to provide scheduled service between the east and west coasts at fares substantially lower than the incumbent carriers' lowest fares.[57] While acknowledging the past importance of the irregulars in making new low-fare services available to the public and implicitly acknowledging the fitness of the four applicants to provide reliable scheduled service, the CAB denied the applications. It justified this decision using the principle of "cross-subsidy," whereby profits from an airline's heavily traveled, long-haul routes would enable the airline to sustain unprofitable service elsewhere while drawing little or no subsidy from the government.[58]

Even if this policy was unsound on economic grounds, as many economists have argued, it was almost a political necessity. Throughout its history and especially during the 1950s, the CAB was under strong, broad-based congressional pressure to prevent the government subsidy bill from rising very high or very fast;[59] thus it was leery of permitting new competition that threatened to increase carriers' need for subsidy by squeezing their profit margins. However, when the CAB tried to save money by allowing discontinuation of subsidized service to particular towns, the affected congressional delegations almost invariably complained bitterly, few if any congressmen openly defended the CAB's action, and the CAB was often forced to continue the service. Indeed, after the CAB in the late 1940s and early 1950s granted *tempo-rary* certificates to a new class of airlines (the local-service carriers) to provide subsidized service on an *experimental* basis to small, previously unserved communities, Congress intervened in 1955 to prevent the CAB from suspending this service: it passed legislation making all of the local-service carriers' certificates permanent.[60]

Aside from considerations of holding down subsidies and preventing large-scale abandonment of routes, there were other factors that certainly contributed to the CAB's consistent refusal to permit new airlines to compete directly with the certificated scheduled carriers—or to permit the existing carriers to engage in vigorous price competition among themselves. First, the existing airlines were well-situated to influence CAB policy-making. Obviously, they all had a high stake in the outcomes of CAB policies. As a result, it was worthwhile for them to expend substantial resources—often cooperating as a group—trying to shape CAB policies through such means as direct lobbying before CAB members and congressmen, rewards to sympathetic congressmen in the form of campaign contributions and votes, and punishments of hostile congressmen through the channeling of funds and votes to opposing candidates. Meanwhile, virtually no one else had a large sustained financial or ideological interest in CAB policy. Almost by default, most of the information that congressmen and CAB members received as well as the political pressure directed at them strongly favored anticompetitive policies. (This situation changed radically after 1974 as airline deregulation became a visible political issue.)

Second, airlines going out of business have always been much more visible to Congress and the public than have lost opportunities for fare reductions. If the CAB triggered the financial failure of an airline by allowing "too much" competition, it would provoke widespread criticism; but if it fostered inefficiency and unnecessarily high prices by permitting "too little" competition, few members of Congress or the public would notice unless the CAB's methods of suppressing competition were especially flagrant.[61] Thus, even if not for the airlines' political strength, the CAB has always had a political incentive to bias its policy in an anticompetitive direction.

Third, after one or two decades of operation, the CAB's practice of protectionism was solidly grounded in precedent (as established by written decisions) and had become an almost unchallenged way of life in the agency. Indeed, the force of the precedent was so strong that most CAB members and staff accepted the argument that to endanger the financial health of an incumbent carrier by letting other airlines enter its routes or by letting its competitors reduce fares would not be merely a matter of *reinterpreting* the Civil Aeronautics Act (which in 1958 was reenacted as the Federal Aviation Act[62]) but of *violating* both the act and the principles of due process (especially as set down in the Administrative Procedure Act[63]). Furthermore, the CAB was always concerned over the likelihood that any decision significantly departing from precedent would be reversed—embarrassingly so—on judicial review. Moreover, the CAB apparently had no members and virtually no staffers who even attempted to stay abreast of economists' analyses of airline regulation. Thus the CAB effectively blinded itself to economists' development of arguments favoring less regulation and more competition in the airline industry.

At first glance, the contentions that CAB policy before the mid-1970s continuously reflected protectionist principles may seem to be belied by the CAB's very visible—and substantial—shifts between extreme anticompetitiveness and moderate procompetitiveness with regard to rivalry between existing carriers. Indeed, whereas the CAB granted few new route certificates and discouraged price reductions during the late 1940s, early 1960s, and early 1970s, it increased the number of carriers on many routes already being served and forcefully encouraged discount fares during the mid-1950s and late 1960s.[64]

Although changes in CAB membership and accompanying changes in CAB ideology probably contributed to these fluctuations in policy and although congressional and presidential pressure also contributed at times,[65] another variable was much more important: airline profits, which commonly rose or fell along with the condition of the economy. The CAB usually was vigorously anticompetitive when the airlines were suffering financially, and it was relatively procompetitive when the airlines were prospering. Thus, to a large extent, CAB policies between 1938 and 1974 were a result of applying stable protectionist principles to changing economic conditions.

The Road to Deregulation

Pre-1975 Evaluations of CAB Regulation

Although Congress voted nearly unanimously in 1978 to deregulate the airlines, before 1975 the case for airline deregulation was taken seriously by virtually no one other than academic economists. Pre-1975 criticisms of CAB regulation concentrated more on alleged flaws in the CAB's procedures and organizational structure than on any need for making the airlines more competitive.[66] The only congressmen who pressed for more competition advocated *maintaining* CAB regulation in a more procompetitive form and, although they sometimes attracted considerable attention, they had little impact on CAB policy.[67] The certificated airlines frequently complained about the CAB's handling of particular cases, but none of them ever suggested that the CAB should be abolished; indeed, all were vehement defenders of the principle of CAB regulation. Before 1975 economists stood virtually alone in favoring full-fledged deregulation, and their arguments were never taken seriously by policy makers.

Economists Develop a Case for Deregulation Before the mid-1960s, even the economic literature contained few arguments on the desirability of reducing CAB regulation.[68] What little it did contain was inspired largely by the CAB's restrictive treatment of the irregulars and presented theoretical arguments that giving the irregulars more freedom to compete would reduce fares without seriously disrupting the financial health of the industry. The most serious weakness of these arguments—and one of the major reasons why they attracted little more than passing attention even among economists—was that they had little empirical support.

The first clear-cut empirical evidence that CAB regulation was working against the interests of the traveling public appeared on routes served by non-CAB-regulated, low-fare airlines in California and later in Texas. During the late 1950s and early 1960s, Pacific Southwest Airlines (PSA), which was not subject to CAB controls on routes and prices, pioneered low-fare air-passenger service in California. In 1961 and 1962, before CAB-certificated carriers began to adjust their fares to more competitive levels, PSA charged $13.50 for its Los Angeles–San Francisco flights. Meanwhile, the cheapest fare available on any CAB-certificated carrier ranged between $16.45 and $16.95, or 22 to 25 percent greater than PSA's fare.[69] While CAB-regulated carriers responded to price competition in California, these airlines and the CAB maintained relatively high prices elsewhere in the country. In 1965, for example, the jet coach fare on all airlines was $13.50 for the 340-mile trip between San Francisco and Los Angeles but was $24.95 for the 400-mile flight between Boston and Washington, D.C.;[70] the fare per mile between Boston and Washington was 57 percent higher. By 1974, the one-way coach fare was $18.75 between Los Angeles and San Francisco but was $41.67 between Boston and Washington;[71] the fare per mile was 62 percent higher between Boston and Washington than between Los Angeles and San Francisco.

After beginning intrastate operations in Texas in 1971, Southwest Airlines also charged much lower fares than those of the CAB-regulated carriers. On the 239-mile Dallas-Houston route in 1975, for example, Southwest charged peak and off-peak fares of $25.00 and $15.00, respectively. On the same route, CAB-certificated carriers charged an "economy fare" of $32.00.[72] Meanwhile, CAB-regulated carriers' cheapest available fares on other routes of comparable length, such as Las Vegas–Los Angeles and Chicago–St. Louis, ranged between $28 and $30.[73]

Although their fares were low, the intrastate carriers earned healthy profits, typically equaling or exceeding the CAB-certificated carriers' average rates of return on operating investment. Indeed, from 1972 through 1974, Air California, an intrastate carrier which began operating in 1967, consistently earned an annual rate of return of over 24 percent—higher than any CAB-certificated airlines. In 1974, after suffering some losses while establishing itself in Texas, Southwest Airlines attained a 12.6 percent rate of return. Meanwhile, the average rates of return for the trunk airlines between 1972 and 1974 ranged between 5.5 percent and 6.8 percent, and the average return for local-service airlines ranged between 9.5 percent and 12.2 percent.[74]

The intrastate carriers were able to earn higher profits despite charging lower fares than the CAB-certificated carriers because they used denser seating configurations (more seats on any given model of aircraft) and also attained a higher load factor (the percentage of seats that is filled). In 1975, for example, PSA and Southwest both put an average of 13 percent more seats on Boeing 727s than did the CAB-certificated carriers.[75] In addition, they both attained a 64 percent load factor, while the average was 57 percent for the CAB-certificated trunk lines and 54 percent for the CAB-certificated local-service carriers (whose operations are similar to the intrastates' in terms of size and average trip length).[76]

For economists interested in improving economic efficiency, the intrastate carriers were not intrinsically better or more competitive than the CAB-regulated carriers. They were, however, distinctive for offering a new trade-off between price and service quality—a combination of lower fares and lower-quality service that much of the public preferred. To put more people on each plane, they had to hold flight frequencies below what they otherwise would have been for any given level of traffic. They also had to give passengers smaller seats, less legroom, and less chance of enjoying a luxury many travelers value highly: sitting next to an empty seat. Aside from putting more people on each plane, the intrastate carriers reduced per-passenger costs even further by cutting back on meal service and other "frills" offered by the interstate carriers.[77] Thus, travelers who chose intrastate carriers over interstate carriers typically had to sacrifice some conveniences in order to pay lower fares; but the rapid growth in intrastate carriers' traffic demonstrated that many people were glad to make this trade-off. Largely—though perhaps not entirely—because of the low fares, passenger traffic on the California intrastate carriers increased by an average of over 23 percent per year between 1965 and 1971, compared to an aggregate annual average of only 4.7 percent for all domestic routes under 500 miles.[78] Similarly, traffic on Southwest Airlines grew at annual rates of over 20 percent in both the Dallas-Houston and the Dallas–San Antonio markets between 1970 and 1974. Meanwhile, traffic grew less than half as fast on CAB-regulated interstate routes of comparable length and passenger volume.[79] The intrastate carriers attracted so much new traffic that they were able to *increase* flight frequency rapidly even while holding load factors high and prices low.

Economists argued that CAB regulation was responsible for the absence of lower-fare, low-frills service in interstate markets. In reconciling their contention that interstate fares were "too high" with the fact that CAB-regulated airlines' profits were, on average, low to moderate, they argued that the CAB's restraints on price competition did not stop the airlines from being competitive (except on monopoly routes) but instead increased their incentives to compete in service. Prevented from lowering prices toward the level of per-passenger costs, airlines sought to lure passengers by outperforming each other in terms of flight frequency, legroom, free liquor, and other aspects of service quality, thereby raising costs toward the level of prices.[80] Economists claimed that by freeing airlines to compete with regard to price as well as service, deregulation would expand the range of price-quality options available to consumers. Those travelers who placed a high value on frills could pay extra for them, and those who placed a low value on them could forgo them and fly more cheaply.

While favoring deregulation, economists stressed that lower price floors and freer entry were both prerequisites for any substantial and long-lasting reduction in price competition; by itself, lowering or even eliminating price floors would not give airlines much incentive to reduce prices. The fewer firms there are in a market and the lower the probability that a new firm will enter in the event that the incumbent firms make their profit margins "too large," the easier it is for the incumbent firms to develop a "live-and-let-live" attitude and thus for the firms as a group to collude tacitly to abstain from competition—especially from price competition.[81] Recognizing that almost all airline routes have no more than three carriers—and may not ever be able to sustain any more than that at one time—and that nonregulatory barriers to entering the industry are not large,[82] economists concluded that regulatory policy on entry was the crucial determinant of whether eliminating the CAB price floor would encourage vigorous competition over the long run. If CAB controls on entry were lifted, then a new airline or two could and would enter routes whenever the incumbent carriers' prices became "too high." This threat of entry would compel the incumbents to keep their prices low. On the other hand, if the CAB's restrictive policies on entry were continued, then the incumbents could maintain high prices with relative impunity (and if a price war of any sort ever pushed fares down, the protected incumbents would, over the long run, be able to push fares back up).

By 1974 economists had produced a formidable literature on the desirability of airline deregulation, but their arguments had no political clout. Policy makers at the CAB and in the congressional committees with direct jurisdiction over the CAB almost universally dismissed pro-deregulation economists as "ivory-tower theorists" who knew nothing about the realities of running an airline. In doing so, they noted that everyone who was directly involved in the airline industry—airline labor, airline financiers, and the CAB-regulated airlines themselves—vigorously opposed any major reductions in CAB regulation.

The Airline Industry's Motive for Opposing Deregulation   The airline industry has always been ambivalent toward CAB regulation. Airlines have continually criticized the CAB for deciding route cases too slowly or simply incorrectly, for approving rate increases too slowly to cover rising costs, and for burdening them in other ways. However, the airlines have also highly valued the financial stability created by CAB protection from competition. Because they perceived this stability as being well worth the various costs imposed by CAB regulation, they all stood ready in 1974 to defend the CAB against proponents of deregulation.

As described previously (pp. 98–103,) the CAB's most obvious method of promoting financial stability was to prevent new entry and fare reductions whenever they seemed likely to cause a significant squeeze in incumbent carriers' profits. Indeed, in its written opinions rejecting route applications, the CAB commonly focused on risks that new entry would cause undue diversion of traffic from incumbent carriers.[83] Similarly, in opinions disallowing fare reductions, it commonly focused on risks that lower fares would cause undue "dilution" of airline revenues.[84]

The CAB also promoted financial stability in the airline industry by giving preferential treatment to financially weak carriers in route proceedings. When deciding which of the competing applicants should be allowed into lucrative markets, before 1974 the CAB often chose financially troubled carriers over other carriers purely to aid the weaker carriers.[85]

Perhaps the least obvious—but certainly the most important—of the CAB's contributions to financial stability was the regulation-created value of route certificates. Because the CAB issued very little route authority relative to the various airlines' demand for it, route certificates had a high market value. Because the CAB barred airlines from selling routes and rarely allowed them to exchange routes, an airline could obtain an extensive addition to its route system in a short period of time only by merging with another airline. Consequently, any time a weak, money-losing carrier had to go out of business, it was able to do so by merging rather than going bankrupt; other airlines, anxious for extensive new route authority, advanced generous merger offers— offers many times greater than the value of the carrier's personnel, planes, and other assets.[86] As a result, banks and other financiers typically lent money readily even to airlines that were losing money; they knew they were protected against default. Indeed, though many CAB-certificated airlines have been merged, none holding authority to provide scheduled service has ever gone bankrupt.[87]

Thus, CAB regulation meant security for everyone connected with the airline industry: job security for airline managers, whose companies were cushioned against the sort of financial crises that precipitate firings of management; job security as well as higher wages for airline workers, who retained full seniority when their employers were absorbed through mergers and who therefore had little to lose by making large profit-squeezing demands at contract-negotiation time;[88] stability in stock-market values for airline stockholders, whose holdings might occasionally fall in value but would never suffer a bankruptcy-induced collapse; and security from loan defaults for airline lenders.

If policy makers before the mid-1970s ignored the arguments for deregulation, they did so not only because no one in the airline industry wanted deregulation, but also because there were no clear signs that CAB restraints on competition had hurt either the industry or the public. Indeed, before the 1970s, the CAB seemed to be doing a good job of harmonizing the interests of airlines and consumers. Between 1938 and 1970, the industry grew rapidly; industry profits were consistently healthy but reasonable (large enough to support continued expansion but small enough to escape charges of "excessive" rates of return); airlines paid their employees exceptionally well; and air fares generally fell or remained steady—even when prices for most other goods and services rose.[89] In the early 1970s, when the airline industry began having financial problems, most industry observers—regardless of whether they had ties to any airlines—believed that reducing regulation to increase competition would only exacerbate the problems. With profit margins disconcertingly thin, they reasoned that, notwithstanding economists' arguments for deregulation, prices could not possibly fall without putting at least a few airlines out of business.

Insofar as the airline industry was content with CAB regulation and most of the public was apathetic, supporters of airline deregulation could expect to continue being ignored or even scoffed at until some sort of crisis befell the airline industry or some sort of scandal occurred at the CAB; only then could they expect to get a serious hearing from policy makers. Indeed, crisis and scandal during the early 1970s were both important to the rise of airline deregulation as a prominent political issue.

Aviation Regulatory Reform Ripens as a Political Issue, 1969–1975

Between 1969 and 1974, the CAB adopted policies that were zealously anticompetitive—perhaps unprecedentedly so. The agency thereby made itself vulnerable to charges that it was protecting the airlines at the expense of the traveling public. In the process, it unwittingly provided proponents of deregulation with valuable political leverage. By 1975 airline deregulation or "aviation regulatory reform"[90] had received strong endorsements from both Senator Edward Kennedy and President Gerald Ford—a rare and formidable bipartisan combination.

The CAB's anticompetitive shift was triggered by the onset of a national economic recession in 1969. Since the early 1960s, the airlines had benefited from the nation's rising economic prosperity, which had kindled increasing demand for air travel, and from significant declines in per-passenger and per-mile operating costs, achieved through the conversion from turboprop aircraft to jets (a conversion which began in 1958).[91] The annual average rate of growth in domestic air traffic was over 20 percent between 1965 and 1968, and the airline industry's annual rate of return on investment averaged over 8 percent.[92] In hopes of spurring further growth and in recognition of the industry's enhanced ability to cope with increased competition during periods of high profits, during the middle and late 1960s the CAB maintained liberal entry policies and, while not pushing for reductions of regular fares, vigorously urged the expansion of discount fares.[93] Expecting continued rapid traffic growth in the 1970s and continued liberal grants of new route authority from the CAB, between 1966 and 1968 many airlines bought large numbers of Boeing 747s and DC-10s—newly developed wide-body "jumbo" jets that offered carriers an opportunity for further reducing their per-passenger costs by carrying large numbers of people. But by the time manufacturers began delivering these new jets to the airlines, the recession had begun and traffic growth had slowed substantially. With the inflationary wage-price spiral pushing airlines' operating costs up, with airlines needing money to pay for their new planes, and with traffic and revenues growing much more slowly than expected, the airlines found their profits being squeezed very thin.[94] In response, several airlines (principally the larger ones) requested—and the CAB instituted—a markedly anticompetitive shift in its policies.

Under ever-present congressional and public pressure to restrain price increases, the CAB accomplished this shift principally through efforts to restrain scheduling competition among airlines and thus to improve profits by raising load factors. Upon becoming CAB chairman in October 1969, Secor Browne unofficially began what later became known as the "route moratorium." Under the moratorium, the CAB disapproved almost all new route applications by refusing to hold hearings on them; the only formal rulings the CAB issued on such applications were their dismissals as "moot" or "stale" after they had been pending for years. The best-publicized victim of this procedure was World Airways, a supplemental carrier that in 1967 had applied for authority to provide scheduled service between the east and west coasts for one-way fares of between $75 and $79—less than half the lowest coast-to-coast scheduled fare then available. The CAB essentially ignored World's application until 1973, when it dismissed the application as stale.[95] The only new route applications that the CAB approved during the route moratorium, which lasted until 1975, were those that were uncontested plus a few that previously had been set down for hearing.[96]

In 1971 the CAB authorized several major airlines to meet with their competitors to negotiate capacity-limitation agreements. Soon afterward, the CAB approved an agreement that reduced flight frequencies on four major transcontinental routes by between 6 percent and 38 percent (varying according to season). Consequently, load factors and profits rose for all three airlines serving those routes. This agreement was originally approved to last for six months, but the CAB later approved extension of the agreement to eighteen months and also approved additional capacity-limitation agreements on two other routes.[97]

Meanwhile, the CAB modified its fare policies to reduce scheduling competition even further and also to reduce price competition. As part of its Domestic Passenger-Fare Investigation (DPFI),[98] which lasted from 1970 to 1974, in 1971 the CAB announced that all subsequent proposals for fare adjustments would be evaluated according to whether airlines would earn a reasonable return if they attained an average load factor of 55 percent.[99] Thus, the CAB would no longer let airlines use price increases to pay for scheduling competition that increased the number of flights so far out of proportion to passenger demand as to cause load factors to fall below 55 percent. In a later phase of the DPFI, the CAB announced that for rate-making purposes it would henceforth treat discount fares as though they were full fares: it would not let airlines rely on increases in regular fares to make up for losses incurred through discounting.[100] In yet another phase of the DPFI, the Board established a rigid pricing formula that required each airline's fares throughout its system to be proportional to flight mileage —even where actual costs markedly diverge from being proportional to mileage.[101] While these and other Board decisions made during the DPFI helped to restrain increases in regular fares, they also made the airlines even less competitive in pricing than they traditionally had been under CAB regulation.

By early 1973, passenger traffic was reviving and inflation was subsiding so that the airlines' profits and their ability to withstand competition began to rise toward normal levels.[102] However, two events diverted the CAB from returning to more competitive policies. First, Secor Browne resigned in March 1973 and was replaced as CAB chairman by Robert Timm. Whereas Browne had endorsed the route moratorium and capacity limitations only as temporary emergency measures to ameliorate overcapacity during an economic downturn, Timm felt such measures were appropriate as permanent elements of CAB policy: Timm wanted the CAB to control not just price competition but all competition—at all times. Indeed, at least one observer noted that capacity agreements could serve as the means for turning the airline industry into a "perfect cartel."[103]

Second, in October 1973, the Arab oil embargo began. As fuel prices rose during the ensuing shortage, the airlines' financial problems returned. While traffic growth faltered again, the airlines' operating costs rose substantially. As the president's Energy Policy Office adopted a mandatory fuel-allocation program, the CAB encouraged airlines to reduce their flight frequencies in order to save fuel and granted blanket antitrust immunity to any capacity-limitation agreements that airlines might want to propose. By November 1974 twenty-six routes were covered by capacity-limitation agreements.[104]

Largely because of the sharp increase in fuel prices, the CAB let air fares rise rapidly. It approved general fare increases of 5 percent in December 1973 and 6 percent in April 1974. During the same period, it also phased out several discount fares, thereby raising average fares another 5.4 percent.[105]

By spring 1974 the profit margins of most airlines had returned to healthy levels, but Chairman Timm still desired to minimize competition among the airlines. As he had done ever since becoming a CAB member in 1971, Timm openly expounded a proindustry ideology, contending that the best way to protect the interests of travelers was to protect the airline industry's profit margin.[106] In the process, Timm made himself and the CAB an easy target for critics who charged that they were protecting the airlines at the expense of the traveling public.

In June 1974 Senator Edward Kennedy decided to hold oversight hearings on the CAB. During the spring of 1974, Kennedy, the chairman of the Senate Subcommittee on Administrative Practice and Procedure, had been looking for a new general counsel to direct the subcommittee staff and for a topic on which he and his subcommittee could hold hearings. Kennedy offered the job to Stephen Breyer, a Harvard

Law School professor specializing in economic regulation and administrative law, and also asked Breyer for advice on choosing a topic.[107]

Breyer recommended that Kennedy hold hearings either on the CAB or on procedural reforms proposed in the wake of the Watergate scandal (for example, creation of a permanent special-prosecutor's office modeled after the temporary Watergate Special Prosecution Force). Breyer noted that the CAB, which was his choice, had both advantages and disadvantages as a topic. On one hand, arguments for airline deregulation—arguments to which hearings on the CAB would draw attention—had been well developed by economists and were likely to attract support from a broad range of people: to consumers, airline deregulation could offer the promise of lower prices (a promise especially timely in view of the nation's problem with inflation); to disillusioned liberals, it could present an opportunity to strike at what was perceived as business-government complicity; and to conservatives, it could provide an opportunity for a cutback in "big government." Because of this broad appeal and the current vulnerability of the CAB to attack, there seemed to be a reasonable chance that hearings on the CAB would lead to passage of significant reform legislation. Furthermore, studying CAB regulation would give the subcommittee valuable background for future investigations into the effects of CAB-type regulation (in particular, control of pricing and entry) on other industries—trucking and energy, for example. Thus, unlike post-Watergate reform, airline deregulation was not a dead-end issue, but was part of a cluster of issues that Kennedy and the subcommittee could develop.

On the other hand, due to the complex, technical nature of airline-regulation issues, hearings on the CAB would require extensive, time-consuming preparation by the subcommittee staff and probably would not attract much public attention; indeed, among the general public, there was currently little if any interest in the issue of reforming airline regulation. Relative to hearings on the CAB, hearings on reform proposals inspired by Watergate certainly would, owing to the simplicity and timeliness of the issues involved, require less staff preparation and attract much more attention from the press and the general public. But if there was less chance of hearings on post-Watergate reforms being ignored, there was also little reason to believe that they would prod Congress into enacting any significant new legislation.

Telling Breyer that he was more concerned about achieving a legislative success than getting short-term publicity, Kennedy selected the CAB as his topic. He planned to hold the hearings early in 1975, with Breyer heading the subcommittee staff's preparation for them.[108]

Between June 1974 and the start of the Kennedy hearings in February 1975, several developments reinforced the CAB's reputation as a "servant" of the scheduled airlines. In July, newspaper stories revealed that CAB Chairman Timm had gone on an expense-paid trip to Bermuda with executives from an aircraft manufacturer and several airlines.[109] Representative Harley Staggers, chairman of the House Committee on Interstate and Foreign Commerce, bitterly denounced Timm's conduct.[110] For critics of the CAB, the "Timm scandal" was a symbol of the CAB's anticompetitive policies being more a product of Chairman Timm's close friendships with airline executives than of impartial conviction.

In October the CAB advanced proposals that would have drastically limited the ability of charter airlines—the "supplementals," which were the nation's leading source of low-fare air travel—to compete with the scheduled carriers. The proposals included establishment of a rate floor that would substantially have reduced the freedom of charter carriers to undercut the fares of scheduled carriers. The proposals also would have prevented charter carriers from carrying more than 1/4 of 1 percent of the number of passengers carried by scheduled airlines and would have limited each charter airline on major routes such as New York-Las Vegas to only one flight every three months. (The immediate purpose of these proposals was to bolster the finances of Pan Am and TWA, both of which were losing money and were facing strong competition from charter carriers on various international routes.)[111]

In November, over a vigorous dissent by two Board members, the CAB approved a 4 percent fare increase. Insofar as the CAB had already disallowed discount fares and enacted two other general fare increases since December 1973, this action meant that the average fare had risen more than 20 percent in less than a year. Coming so soon after Timm's Bermuda trip, this latest fare increase aroused especially harsh criticism of the CAB.[112]

Convened in February 1975, the Kennedy hearings made two major contributions to the political advance of airline deregulation. First, they provided a valuable public forum—with extensive press coverage—in which critics of CAB regulation could present their arguments and refute those of the CAB's defenders. The hearings—and especially the summary report on the hearings[113]—closely examined the anticompetitive effects of the CAB's policies. In particular, they gave extensive attention to the large differential between CAB-regulated fares on interstate routes and non-CAB-regulated fares on intrastate routes in California and Texas. They also developed a new rebuttal to the longstanding argument that stringent controls on entry were needed to maintain a system of cross-subsidy preserving small-community service without resorting to large increases in government subsidy: they uncovered empirical evidence that claims made by airlines on the magnitude of cross-subsidy in the nation's airline network were grossly exaggerated.[114] For many years, economists had attacked cross-subsidy for causing inefficient allocations of resources and for surreptitiously "taxing" travelers on profitable routes to pay for unprofitable service elsewhere.[115] Thus the hearings and the report enabled proponents of deregulation to begin arguing that cross-subsidy was not only undesirable, but also insignificant. Overall, the hearings and report were significant for giving the case for deregulation—or at least for procompetitive reform of the CAB—substantial visibility that it had previously lacked and that would help it gain new political support. This visibility would not only aid the advance of reform legislation, but would also give the CAB an incentive to conduct a thorough reexamination of its policies.

Second, the hearings prodded the Ford administration to press for reform significantly sooner and more vigorously than it otherwise would have. By 1974 the idea of airline deregulation had already received serious attention in parts of the executive branch. For several years, economists at the Council of Economic Advisers as well as economists and lawyers in the Antitrust Division of the Department of Justice had contended that competition-limiting regulation of airlines and other industries encouraged inefficiency and typically raised prices significantly higher than they would otherwise be.[116] Sharing this view, economists at the Department of Transportation meanwhile had developed legislative proposals for reducing regulation of entry and pricing in various areas of transportation, including aviation. However, these and other proponents of reducing competition-limiting regulation had little effect on administration policy until the fall of 1974. Indeed, from spring until November 1974, the administration had favored the establishment of a rate floor for charter airlines (as a means of helping to cure Pan Am's and TWA's financial troubles without resorting to direct subsidy).[117]

Inflation helped to make the administration more receptive to arguments for airline deregulation. In August 1974, when Gerald Ford succeeded Richard Nixon to the presidency, inflation was running at about 12 percent per year, and most Americans viewed it as the nation's most serious problem.[118] In the process of developing a new antiinflation program, in September, Ford convened a "summit conference on inflation," attended by economists, business leaders, labor leaders, consumer advocates, and others. While there was much disagreement at the conference on the merits of various methods of fighting inflation, there was a virtual consensus that government regulation often raises prices. Twenty-one of the twenty-three economists at the conference signed a resolution favoring reduction or elimination of twenty-two "sacred-cow" programs—including CAB regulation—that reduce competition and efficiency.[119] Partly due to the lack of attractive policy options for fighting inflation and partly due to the high compatibility between the idea of trimming government regulation and Ford's conservative dislike of big government, in early October, Ford designated regulatory reform as a major element in his antiinflation program.[120]

The Kennedy hearings prompted the Ford administration to treat airline deregulation as a top priority in its regulatory-reform efforts. They set a de facto deadline by which the administration had to testify in detail about its attitude toward *aviation* regulatory reform and thus either to reaffirm or to downplay its October pronouncements on the *general* merits of trimming regulation. This situation gave great leverage to administration officials who wanted the administration to move ahead quickly and forcefully in supporting airline deregulation. They achieved a major breakthrough: presenting the administration's official position at the first day of the hearings, Acting Secretary of Transportation John Barnum labeled the existing regulatory structure for airlines "outdated, inequitable, inefficient, uneconomical, and sadly irrational" and announced that the administration was currently developing major reform legislation that would be released soon.[121]

The Ford administration's early endorsement of aviation regulatory reform was important in redirecting CAB policy because it was translated into not only a new legislative proposal but also the appointment to the CAB of a new, reform-minded chairman. Disapproving of Robert Timm's personal conduct—as in the Bermuda-trip scandal—and of his policies, President Ford declined to reappoint Timm as CAB chairman when Timm's term expired at the end of 1974. (However, Timm remained at the CAB for a time because his term as a member did not expire. Ultimately, he resigned under pressure from Ford's staff.[122]) In March 1975 Ford appointed John Robson to join the Board and to become chairman. As chairman, Robson would lead the CAB into an era of an unprecedented and thorough reassessment of its policies.

BRADLEY BEHRMAN

The CAB Decides to Endorse Fundamental Regulatory Reform, 1975–1976

On April 8, 1976, testifying on the Ford administration's proposal on aviation regulatory reform, CAB Chairman Robson startled his audience by announcing that the agency had *unanimously* agreed that Congress should pass legislation which would substantially reduce the CAB's powers and would thus reduce restraints on competition in the airline industry. Robson's announcement was surprising for at least three reasons. First, it made the CAB the first federal regulatory agency ever to endorse a significant curtailment of its authority. Second, it came a mere thirteen months after the Kennedy hearings, at which the CAB had staunchly defended its past efforts to restrict competition. Third, only two new members had taken office since 1974; the other three had all been members since 1973 or earlier.[123]

The reexamination that led to this "conversion" began at the CAB several months before Robson became chairman. It was prompted by outside pressure from both the Ford administration and the imminent Kennedy hearings. Late in 1974, after President Ford announced that his administration would launch a general push for regulatory reform, the Office of Management and Budget (OMB) began pressing various regulatory agencies to conduct fundamental reexaminations of their policies and procedures—reexaminations for which OMB would arrange funding.[124] For obvious reasons, self-assessments by government agencies typically concentrate more on defending current policies against outside criticisms than on identifying means for self-improvement. However, perhaps sensing that frank self-criticism was the only way the CAB could defuse charges of pro-industry bias, in January 1975 the CAB organized an internal task force to conduct a forthright reappraisal of the fundamental assumptions underlying CAB regulation. Even former chairman Timm endorsed the intent of the project. Indeed, in a January 15 memo to Acting Chairman Richard O'Melia, Timm stated that the task force's study "must go far beyond administrative or housekeeping concerns," and should

explore afresh all the areas into which our regulation reaches and to determine, without preconception or prejudice, whether deregulation, or the regulatory status quo, would be in the best interest of the consumer and the industry. . . . [The study] should question the continuing viability of the Federal Aviation Act and specifically whether the mandate to "promote" an infant industry is necessary or advisable in the changed circumstances of the present day. Perhaps new objectives should be articulated to supplant others which have already been met.

104

If deregulation by function (rates, routes, etc.) seems indicated, they should further examine how and in what time span the phasing out should occur.[125]

Going beyond mere rhetoric, the CAB made special arrangements to ensure the objectivity of the task force. It appointed Roy Pulsifer—a CAB lawyer and self-taught economist known to be critical of many CAB policies—to head the task force, and it allowed Pulsifer to choose the other four members of the task force. Furthermore, the CAB gave the task force freedom to work independently, without any obligation to reveal any of its findings or conclusions until its final report was published.

After becoming CAB chairman late in April 1975, John Robson made reappraisal a major priority of the CAB. At the outset, Robson was not sure what types of reforms would be appropriate for the CAB and certainly was not committed to deregulation,[126] but he felt strongly that the CAB should become a leader in exploring various options for reform; he did not want the CAB to confine itself exclusively to responding to reform proposals from outside critics. Immediately upon taking office, Robson commissioned an outside research firm to study the feasibility of experimenting with deregulation on several major airline routes. On July 7, after the study was completed, Robson publicly proposed an experiment in deregulation and invited all interested parties to send the CAB comments supporting or opposing the experiment.[127] As virtually all respondents argued, the experiment itself was misconceived; it probably would not have produced dependable information on the likely effects of total deregulation, and it could well have been illegal.[128] Nevertheless, the proposed experiment was important insofar as it unambiguously signaled that the CAB was seriously ready to consider reform.

Ironically, the proreform conversion of Robson's fellow members of the CAB arose largely from persuasion by CAB staffers who had been at the agency before Robson arrived. Robson never seemed to wield much direct influence over the policy views of the other members. Indeed, at least two of the other members seemed to resent Robson, frequently criticizing him for trying to impose "one-man rule" at the CAB. Robson facilitated the CAB's conversion mainly by harnessing proreform sentiment in the CAB staff to influence the other members.

The first major staff endorsement of reform came from the Pulsifer task force, which released its final report in July 1975. While refraining from criticizing the CAB's past interpretations of its statutory mandate, the report straightforwardly endorsed airline deregulation:

The general conclusion of the Special Staff on Regulatory Reform is that protective entry control, exit control, and public utility-type price regulation under the Federal Aviation Act are not justified by the underlying cost and demand characteristics of commercial air transportation. . . .

The present system of regulation causes higher than necessary costs and prices (which in turn suppress demand), weakens the ability of carriers to respond to market demand and other constantly changing conditions, narrows the range of price/quality choice to the user, and thus produces a misallocation of the nation's economic resources. . . .

Accordingly, the Special Staff recommends that protective entry, exit, and public utility-type price control in air transportation be eliminated within three to five years by statutory amendment to the Federal Aviation Act.[129]

In September the CAB assembled many of its top staff people into a new task force to review Chairman Robson's proposed deregulation experiment as well as the comments various groups had sent in on the experiment. In doing so, the task force began exploring ways besides the experiment for the CAB to address reform. In October 1975 the Ford administration introduced the reform proposal that John Barnum had promised at the Kennedy hearings, and the task force began evaluating this proposal; once the administration had introduced the proposal, it was almost inevitable that the CAB would eventually be called to testify on it before Congress.[130] Perhaps influenced by the Pulsifer Report and certainly believing that the CAB's policies under Robert Timm's chairmanship had been overly anticompetitive, the task force reached virtual unanimity in rejecting Robson's deregulation experiment and in endorsing a significant reduction of CAB power over entry and pricing. The same was true of a steering committee of CAB bureau directors and members' assistants who reviewed the task force's recommendations and passed them on to the CAB in January 1976.[131]

These displays of strong staff support for reform probably should not be credited with converting any heretofore closed minds on the CAB to reform but at the very least they were important in assuaging CAB members' doubts about reform. The recommendations made the idea of reducing CAB regulation seem much more sensible than had the various outside economists who previously had argued for deregulation. Their influence was most obvious in the case of members Joseph Minetti and Lee West. They had frequently dissented from CAB policies in 1973 and 1974 as unduly anticompetitive and had long been ready for a significant procompetitive adjustment in CAB policy, but they had not previously endorsed a reduction in the CAB's powers and had frequently been at odds with Robson.[132]

Three weeks before the staff steering committee delivered its proreform recommendations to the CAB, the prospects for a unanimous CAB endorsement of reform had already been improved by the resignation of former chairman Timm. Although Timm had favored a slight pro-competitive adjustment of CAB policy after being stripped of his chairmanship, he had never renounced his belief in a philosophy of protectionism. (Both before and after leaving the CAB, he frequently criticized the concept of reducing CAB regulation.) Timm's replacement, R. Tenney Johnson, took office in late March 1976, only two weeks before the upcoming hearings. Johnson was a former CAB general counsel who had been dismissed by Timm in 1973 for opposing capacity-limitation agreements, and he returned to the agency as an immediate supporter of reform.

In April 1976, when the Senate Aviation Subcommittee convened hearings on aviation regulatory reform, the prospects for new reform legislation seemed weak, at best. Although Senator Kennedy and the Ford administration had advanced separate but similar legislative proposals and had forged a formidable bipartisan coalition for reform, there was no groundswell of public or congressional support for reform.[133] Senator Howard Cannon of Nevada, the chairman of the Senate Aviation Subcommittee, was widely regarded as a "friend of the industry" and was known to be hostile to Kennedy's and the Ford administration's proposals. Unless he decided to endorse reform—and unless his counterpart in the House did the same[134]—aviation regulatory reform would stagnate; because of their positions, each man wielded virtual veto power over reform legislation.

Robson's April 1976 testimony before the Senate Aviation Subcommittee was especially significant as a new type of argument for airline regulatory reform: Robson's and the CAB's position was that CAB regulation of pricing and entry not only had encouraged inefficiency and higher fares but in the long run was likely to destroy the financial health of the airlines.[135] Robson pointed out that traffic growth and technology-based reductions in per-passenger costs since 1938 had been huge. He argued that these factors were largely responsible for the airlines' being able to reap healthy profits, to grant their workers significantly higher wage increases than workers in other industries received, and, especially in the 1960s, to refrain from increasing fares—all at the same time. Conditions for the industry were so good during that period that "any mistakes by the board or the industry could be and were absorbed by the expansion of the economy and the industry."[136]

As Robson observed, this remarkable combination of rising traffic and falling costs had not continued into the 1970s and was not likely to resume. He noted that a number of air transport forecasts had estimated traffic growth rates for the next decade to be only one-half of the pre-1970 averages. While traffic growth slowed, costs could rise substantially due to the energy crisis, increasingly stringent consumer protection and environmental requirements, and general inflation. Consequently, the airline industry could suffer from a chronically serious profit squeeze.[137]

Robson and the CAB predicted that this problem could have serious ramifications for the airlines' long-run capital financing. He observed that low profits had already given the airlines serious difficulty in raising money through the sale of stock, thereby forcing them to borrow more money to pay for capital investments. As airlines' debt-equity ratios rise, they become increasingly vulnerable to downswings in the economy and increasingly undesirable credit risks for lenders. Robson warned that under the current system of CAB regulation, this problem could become so severe that some airlines might be unable to raise capital funding even through borrowing, in which case the federal government would be pressured to insure loans made to airlines. As the government's financial involvement with the airlines increased, so would the government's need to protect taxpayers by demanding greater influence over how the airlines spend their money. To prevent defaults on the loans, the government might need to impose increasingly restrictive, anticompetitive policies, much like those that former CAB Chairman Robert Timm had advocated: large, frequent fare increases; and reductions in service on individual routes through such measures as capacity-limitation agreements and cuts in the number of airlines serving each route.[138]

Asserting that "there are substantial dangers in continued, uncritical reliance upon the regulatory framework established in 1938," Robson and the CAB therefore concluded that there are "two fundamental options" for the nation's future aviation regulatory policy: a "progressively stricter utility-type scheme," such as that just described; or "a system which minimizes governmental interference to the greatest extent possible and emphasizes greater management freedoms in entry, exit, and pricing." Acknowledging that "uncertainties and risks attach to any decisions Congress might make with respect to the basic direction for air transport," Robson and the CAB favored the option of reduced regulation.[139]

The CAB's *unanimous* endorsement of aviation regulatory reform as *necessary for the financial health of the airline industry* profoundly affected Senator Cannon. It was a compelling argument from an organization that, if anything, appeared to have political and material interests in *opposing* reform rather than supporting it. As Robson finished his presentation, Cannon was visibly shaken: several observers who attended the hearings reported that "his jaw dropped." Antireform airlines had recently lost credibility in Cannon's eyes by arguing that a weak charter-liberalization proposed by Cannon would seriously disrupt scheduled carriers' financial stability.[140] Thus, suspecting that the airline industry might be "crying wolf" in opposing deregulation, Cannon was especially receptive to the CAB's argument for reform and later began to echo it. In a speech on June 22, 1976, Cannon denounced the "zealous economists" and the "ivory tower specialists" who had led President Ford and Senator Kennedy to endorse reform, but then announced that he would soon introduce a reform proposal of his own:

> I am honestly convinced that President Ford, Senator Kennedy and others are *dead wrong* when they say that the cure to the current malaise facing the government, the industry, and the public today is free and open entry into the airline system for all comers. . . .[141]
> But . . . most assuredly our airline system is in trouble and continued regulation as practiced by the CAB over the past five years, as Mr. Robson has recognized, is not in the public interest or in the interest of the carriers. *We need more competition, but not unlimited competitors.* . . . I plan to introduce legislation to revitalize the airline industry with new competition, with more freedom to set fares and with procedures designed to force the CAB to make decisions in a timely and responsible fashion.[142]
>
> [Emphasis added]

Cannon's insistence that "we need more competition but not unlimited competitors" pinpointed a significant philosophical difference between Ford and Kennedy, on one hand, and Cannon and the CAB on the other. Ford and Kennedy had accepted economists' arguments that entry and pricing in the airline industry should be completely *deregulated.* They stopped short of deregulation in their legislative proposals and promoted the proposals as *aviation regulatory reform* because endorsing deregulation was then a politically untenable position.[143] In contrast, Cannon and at least three of the CAB's five members were unequivocally opposed to deregulation and openly said so.[144] They designed their proposals with the idea that CAB regulation should be continued, but with a more procompetitive mandate from Congress. Unlike Ford and Kennedy, they wanted to repudiate CAB regulation as practiced between 1969 and 1974 rather than CAB regulation per se.

In view of this philosophical difference, the CAB's endorsement of reform should be viewed as having been crucially important in persuading Senator Cannon to support reform and thereby keeping the issue alive in Congress. To Cannon, Kennedy's and the Ford administration's arguments for reform lacked credibility, but the CAB's arguments were convincing. Rather than blocking reform, Cannon made it his top personal priority for new legislation. Furthermore, rather than trying to prevent President Carter's appointments of two pro-deregulation economists to the CAB in 1977, he supported the appointments. These appointments led to even more momentous policy changes at the CAB than had taken place under Chairman Robson.

The CAB Embraces Deregulation, 1977–1978

The CAB's post-1974 renunciation of anticompetitive protectionism entered a new stage in 1977, when President Carter (who within two months of being inaugurated had publicly endorsed airline deregulation) appointed to the Board Alfred Kahn, as chairman, and Elizabeth Bailey. Kahn and Bailey were the first professional economists ever to serve on the CAB and they favored deregulation when they took office. Under Kahn's leadership, the CAB went beyond merely endorsing new legislation and began trying to deregulate the airlines without waiting for new legislation to pass.

Before summer 1977, when Kahn and Bailey arrived at the CAB, the agency had not only endorsed reform legislation but also had already made its policies significantly more procompetitive than they had been during the several years leading up to the Kennedy hearings. At those hearings, Acting Chairman O'Melia had announced the end of the route moratorium.[145] Early in April 1975, shortly after the end of the hearings, the CAB had proposed a significant reduction in operating restrictions on charter carriers, whose fares were typically about half those of the scheduled carriers.[146]

After late April 1975, when John Robson became chairman, the CAB's policies on routes and rates had continued moving in a procompetitive direction. In July 1975, the CAB had canceled the capacity-limitation agreements.[147] In August, it had adopted its April proposals for relaxing restrictions on charter carriers.[148] Especially after finishing developing its position on regulatory reform legislation (a project that diverted substantial staff time from other matters), Robson took steps toward making some significant, competition-promoting route awards. As the year 1976 ended and 1977 began, the Board opened two particularly important route cases involving low-fare applicants: the *Transcontinental Low-Fare Route Proceeding,* in which World Airways resumed its efforts to fly between the east and west coasts, this time for $99 one-way, 44 percent cheaper than the current coast-to-coast coach fare;[149] and the *Chicago-Midway Low-Fare Route Proceeding,* in which two entirely new airlines were proposing to fly on routes linking Midway Airport in Chicago with six other major Midwestern cities, at fares 30 to 50 percent below current levels.[150] In an unanimous decision issued in June, (after Robson had left the Board and before Kahn arrived), the CAB had recommended that Laker Airways (Freddie Laker's "Skytrain") be permitted (by the president and the British government) to provide scheduled service between New York and London; Laker had proposed to charge a one-way fare of $135, or 45 percent less than the lowest fare then available between New York and London, and the present carriers had objected vigorously.[151]

Along with adopting a more liberal attitude toward entry, the CAB had become willing and even eager to approve the expansion of low-fare service by present carriers. In September 1976 the CAB had substantially liberalized its charter rules and had thereby given the supplemental airlines unprecedented freedom to compete with the scheduled airlines.[152] In January 1977 the CAB had approved Texas International Airlines's "Peanuts Fare," a 50 percent discount offered on selected flights over five medium-length routes in the Southwest.[153] In March 1977 the CAB had approved proposals by American Airlines and two other airlines to offer a new "Super-Saver" discount fare between New York and California.[154] This discount, which had been initiated by American Airlines largely as a response to competition unleashed by the recent charter liberalization, offered savings of up to 50 percent to passengers meeting certain travel requirements.[155]

The policies Kahn inherited were certainly a far cry from deregulation, but they offered great promise for achieving a dramatic and rapid increase in price competition. The new discount fares and the Super-Saver fares, in particular, set off a powerful "ripple effect" that shook the industry's fare structure nationwide: people traveling between a point A near New York and a point B near California found that they could save money by flying an *indirect* route—A-New York–California-B, taking advantage of the Super-Saver between New York and California—rather than the direct one. Consequently, airlines serving the direct routes lost business and were increasingly obliged to institute Super-Savers or other new discounts on those routes to reverse the trend. Thus the seeds of a proliferation of discount fares in domestic air travel had already been planted by June 1977, when Kahn became chairman. Because of Laker Airways, which expected to begin operations in September 1977, a similar proliferation was also likely to take place in transatlantic air travel.

When Kahn took office, he was anxious to reduce regulatory restraints on competition as rapidly and completely as possible, but he could not have immediately committed the CAB to anything even resembling a vigorous pursuit of deregulation. The three noneconomist CAB members who remained after Bailey was appointed (in August) all favored reducing regulation but had vigorously opposed total deregulation;[156] Kahn and Bailey's pro-deregulation view was in the minority. Furthermore, since many congressmen were highly skeptical of the pending reform legislation and most apparently were steadfastly opposed to deregulation,[157] the CAB could not even propose drastic or rapid moves toward deregulation without risking a vigorous backlash from Congress.

Mindful of these limitations, Kahn spent the remainder of 1977 pursuing deregulation by encouraging CAB members and staff to formulate policy decisions according to economic principles—principles that almost unequivocally argued for deregulation—and by endorsing cautious gradualism as the best means of unleashing new competition in the airline industry. Kahn filled key CAB staff positions with people who had already endorsed the economists' case for deregulation and had been actively promoting regulatory reform from posts outside the agency.[158] (The chief motivation for these people to work for the CAB was the same as for Kahn and Bailey: expectations that they could do more for deregulation by working from within the CAB than by attacking it from the outside.) In addition, Kahn consciously attempted to run CAB meetings as seminars that sought to identify the most economically efficient policy and *then* to consider how such a policy could be implemented without violating the law; he believed that the CAB's traditional tendency toward protectionism had stemmed largely from its failing even to consider economic efficiency in shaping policy and in deciding cases, from its unspoken perception of route certificates as property rights that would be violated if excessive new competition were permitted, and from its faithfulness to precedent. Kahn was especially successful in "educating" fellow CAB members through his wit, his articulateness, and his ability to make the other members feel he was open-mindedly listening to their concerns rather than trying to force his views on them.

While seeking to transform the CAB from a proponent of reform into a proponent of deregulation, Kahn publicly stressed his belief that the airline industry should not be subjected to sudden or drastic increases in competition. His reasons for this belief included not only the political considerations just described, but also a politically sensitive economic consideration: the desirability of avoiding any major disruptions, such as an airline bankruptcy.[159] For the rest of the year, the CAB's endorsement of pending reform legislation and its policies on routes and rates remained quite similar to those that had been adopted under Robson: ready approval of new discount fares and treatment of route cases involving low-fare applicants as a top priority.

By late 1977 these policies had yielded impressive results. Discount fares had proliferated dramatically, both domestically and on transatlantic routes. Super-Saver discounts, which had originally been available on only two routes, were now available in almost twenty transcontinental markets and seemed likely to spread much further.[160] In response to Laker's low fares, the other airlines that had preceded Laker in serving New York–London and other U.S.–European routes had instituted a wide range of new discount fares very similar to the Super-Savers.[161] Millions of travelers who had previously been unable to afford air travel scrambled to take advantage of the new discounts. Meanwhile, improvement in the general health of the economy brought a general increase in consumer demand for goods and services. This increase reinforced the travel-inducing effects of the discounts. Thanks to both factors, airlines' passenger traffic surged to record levels, airlines' load factors jumped upward, and airlines began earning record profits.[162]

The main shortcoming of the 1977 price competition was its limited scope. Domestically, the only fare reductions involved promotional discounts that, like Super-Saver, involved advance-reservation requirements, length-of-stay restrictions, and other conditions; there had been no reductions in any "regular" fares—the fares that require no such preconditions.[163] Except for the Laker fares, the same was true in the transatlantic markets. Furthermore, so long as regulatory barriers to entry remained strong, there was a lingering danger that the recent burst of price competition would subside and that airlines would stop offering the discounts.

In late 1977, with the idea of remedying this situation, Kahn began to use CAB route policies to encourage price competition with intensified aggressiveness. In December 1977 the CAB formally specified low fares as one of its official criteria for evaluating competing route applications.[164] In addition, the CAB began to dispense new route authority that was permissive rather than mandatory.[165] This innovation would allow airline managements to be more responsive to market conditions than the CAB's previous route policies had allowed: carriers with permissive authority to serve a particular point could enter it or exit from it at will, as warranted by fluctuations in traffic or the competitiveness of other carriers.

By the spring of 1978 the economic and political limitations on Kahn's pursuit of deregulation had receded substantially, relative to what they had been when Kahn became chairman. The airlines were setting new profit records every month,[166] and there was little chance that even a rapid increase in competition would jeopardize any airline's financial health. Indeed, a few airlines had started to contend that rapid deregulation would cause less financial disruption than gradual deregulation.[167] More important, Kahn had succeeded in persuading his fellow CAB members to be increasingly receptive to deregulation. Meanwhile, the airlines' falling fares and rising profits—together with Kahn's exceptional persuasiveness as a public speaker[168]—had aroused enthusiastic public and congressional support for Kahn and the CAB's policies. Hence, the agency was becoming increasingly free politically to pursue deregulation.

However, the CAB's authority to retract regulatory restraints, especially those governing entry, appeared to be strictly limited by existing law. In applying the Federal Aviation Act to route cases, the CAB traditionally had assessed whether an additional carrier was "required by the public convenience and necessity" on the route in question and then, if the answer was yes, had awarded mandatory authority to a limited number—usually only one—of the competing applicants. This procedure had compelled the CAB to conduct an extensive comparative analysis of competing applications in each case. Since the Administrative Procedure Act required that the CAB present justification for approving some applications to the exclusion of others[169] and since giving "too many" carriers mandatory authority to enter a route could inflict severe financial harm on airlines already serving the route, the Board had traditionally given all applicants and all incumbents—as well as parties from the cities served—extensive opportunity to file statements on the various applications, to make oral presentations, and even to cross-examine witnesses; these practices were all considered indispensable elements of due process. Thus CAB route cases rivaled full-dress judicial proceedings for their procedural complexity—and, as a result, for their susceptibility to court-like delays. Between 1965 and 1974, for example, the average route case took about two years to proceed from the initial filing of the application to the final decision.[170] Accordingly, Kahn and the CAB did not expect to be able to issue final rulings on either the *Transcontinental Low-Fare* case or the *Chicago-Midway Low-Fare* case until March 1979—even though these cases were the CAB's highest-priority route cases.[171] Thus, until the Board could find a legal justification for breaking away from the traditions of comparative selection, of mandatory authority, and of strictly defined due process, its ability to let new low-fare carriers spread to routes throughout the nation would be extremely limited—and therefore so would its ability to prod incumbent carriers with the continuous threat of entry that is so essential for sustaining price competition over the long run.

In the spring of 1978, taking advantage of the favorable political and economic conditions, Kahn and the CAB embarked on an extremely aggressive drive to vitiate all anticompetitive aspects of CAB regulation—a drive that involved an abrupt departure from legal precedent. The cornerstone of this drive was a new policy of "multiple permissive entry." This policy, which the CAB tentatively adopted on April 14 in opening the *Oakland Service Case,* provided that permissive route authority would be granted to *all* "fit, willing, and able" applicants in a case, with "fit, willing, and able" being defined liberally.[172] This policy signified a near equivalent of deregulation on a route-by-route (or city-by-city) basis: the CAB was promising virtually all carriers free entry and exit from specific routes. On April 18 the CAB tentatively agreed to decide the *Chicago-Midway Low-Fare Rate Proceeding* according to the new policy;[173] when the decision was rendered final in July, it was the first to implement the policy.[174] Considered even by much of the CAB's own staff to be of questionable legality, the policy provoked a court suit by Delta Airlines.[175] (The case was rendered moot by the passage of the Airline Deregulation Act in October.[176])

The CAB advanced deregulatory initiatives not only on entry but also on charter restrictions and on pricing. In March 1978, the CAB proposed an extensive liberalization of the operating guidelines for charter carriers.[177] This proposal, which the CAB in August formally adopted as a new policy,[178] rendered the charter restrictions so slight and gave the charters so much freedom to compete with scheduled carriers that it substantially blurred the long-standing distinction between supplemental and scheduled airlines. On April 14, the CAB proposed to give airlines blanket approval to reduce fares as much as 50 percent below the previously designated standard fare, except in unusual circumstances;[179] in September the CAB formally implemented this policy, after having given quick and enthusiastic approval to all discounts that airlines proposed during the intervening months.[180] As in the case of the multiple–permissive–entry policy, the Board's new policies on charters and pricing both triggered lawsuits.

Although this aggressive pursuit of deregulation was in a sense a continuation of the procompetitive shift begun at the CAB before Kahn became chairman, it was at the same time a sharp break from the pre-Kahn approach to regulatory reform. While the CAB under Robson had endorsed regulatory reform and, in the process, had decisively rejected the agency's traditional stance on how procompetitively it *should* regulate the airlines, it had retained a traditional interpretation of how procompetitively it *could* regulate under existing law. Indeed, while favoring the idea of low-fare transportation, in January 1976 the CAB had struck down on purely legal grounds World Airways' second application to provide cut-rate coast-to-coast scheduled service (the first application had been filed in 1967 and dismissed in 1973); it had unanimously ruled that it could not certificate World to provide scheduled service because World was already certificated as a supplemental carrier.[181] (This legal interpretation was subsequently overturned by a U.S. Circuit Court of Appeals.[182]) Because of this ruling and others, Robson and the CAB had aroused criticism for allegedly understating the procompetitive flexibility of the Federal Aviation Act in an effort to "prove" the need for new reform legislation. Whereas the Robson-led agency had been hesitant to depart from legal precedent in order to reduce regulation, the Kahn-led CAB set out to test thoroughly the deregulatory limits of the existing law. By the spring of 1978, the Kahn-led agency had apparently decided to concentrate on applying economic theory to the airlines—and thereby trying vigorously to deregulate them—without worrying much about traditionally accepted legal constraints.[183]

By embarking on deregulation under the existing law, Kahn's CAB played an important role in bringing about congressional passage of deregulatory legislation. Indeed, the CAB's bold deregulatory initiatives perhaps gave more of a boost to deregulatory legislation than did the CAB's continuing endorsement of such legislation.

As of February 1978, opponents and proponents alike considered the prospect of Congress's passing regulation-reducing legislation to be highly uncertain, and virtually all observers agreed that there was no chance Congress would pass legislation mandating full-fledged deregulation.[184] The previous year's proliferation of discount fares and the accompanying surge in airline profits seemed to have done less to help the cause of deregulatory legislation than to hurt it. They had demonstrated that, contrary to what most airline executives apparently believed when the first Super-Saver fare was introduced, large-scale price cutting could be a useful, profit-boosting marketing tactic and that greater-than-traditional tolerance on the part of the CAB toward price competition could benefit consumers and airlines alike. Certainly the success of the Super-Savers and other discounts strongly suggested that legislation substantially relaxing or even eliminating CAB price floors would not cause the sky to fall in on the airline industry.

Yet, as opponents of reform legislation were quick to point out, Super-Savers and other discounts were not the product of deregulation, but had been spreading *under the existing law without any major departures by the CAB from legal precedents.* Opponents argued that deregulation could not possibly push fares much lower than they had already fallen and that adopting deregulatory legislation—especially legislation removing entry controls—would create great risks in pursuit of benefits that were already being achieved. Judging from the trouble that reform legislation was experiencing in Congress, these arguments seem to have rendered the recent growth in discount fares a noncontributor—if not a liability—to the political advance of deregulation.

By February 1978 a few CAB-regulated airlines had endorsed the idea of substantially reducing CAB restraints on competition, but none had endorsed complete deregulation, and most remained strongly opposed to the passage of any procompetitive reform legislation. Meanwhile, airline labor had remained vehemently opposed—almost unanimously so. The proreform "defections" in the airline industry had certainly given deregulation a big boost in Congress, but the industry's antireform bloc had remained highly influential with a large number of congressmen.

The four CAB-regulated airlines that supported regulation-reducing legislation all did so because they believed that CAB protection from price competition benefited them less than would freedom to expand and to raise prices without waiting for CAB approval. For example, in explaining a proreform position first announced in the spring of 1976, United complained bitterly that while the CAB had frequently allowed other airlines to enter United's routes, it had not given United a major route award in many years; and that the CAB during the 1970s had failed to let fares rise rapidly enough to cover increases in operating costs.[185]

For a variety of reasons, the other fourteen CAB-regulated airlines maintained their traditional positions defending the maintenance of CAB regulation. Delta, which had relied heavily on CAB-protected monopoly routes in achieving the highest rate of return in the industry, perceived that its profits were so high that they definitely would not rise and probably would fall in the event of deregulation. TWA and Eastern, which were among the largest airlines but since the mid-1970s had consistently been among the weakest financially, intensely feared the heightened price competition certain to result from deregulation; indeed, before the recent surge in airline profits, many industry observers had regarded TWA and Eastern as possible bankrupts in the event of deregulation. The smaller carriers opposing reform legislation generally feared that deregulation would clear the way for larger carriers to use their superior financial resources to overwhelm them.[186]

By vigorously pursuing deregulation during and after the spring of 1978, the CAB acted in two ways to soften congressional opposition to deregulatory legislation. First, its initiatives helped to convince many congressmen that, contrary to anti-deregulatory airline rhetoric of the previous few years, airline deregulation was *not* a dangerously risky policy. With fares still falling *and* profits still rising after the CAB began to eliminate entry controls and price floors, many congressmen—and much of the general public—began perceiving falling fares and rising profits as results not of flexibility in the traditional regulatory framework but of *deregulation.*[187] Whereas many congressmen had previously viewed Super-Saver fares as a demonstration that a lot of price competition could be achieved without deregulation, they now began viewing them instead as signs that deregulation, as pursued by Kahn's CAB, was desirable and should be encouraged.

Second, the CAB's efforts gave airlines a growing sense that deregulation of entry and elimination of price floors were inevitable and therefore that trying to prevent the passage of deregulatory legislation was futile if not counterproductive. Before the spring of 1978, anti-deregulation airlines had perceived that the threat of deregulation would completely disappear if they could stop new legislation from passing. But as it became clear that the CAB would pursue deregulation without waiting for new legislation, airlines increasingly realized that they had little chance of stopping deregulation—at least not before the CAB had implemented it substantially. The airlines could not expect Congress to pass a resolution against the CAB's policies because the policies were overwhelmingly popular. There was some chance that a court would strike down the CAB's deregulatory policies as contrary to the agency's legal mandate to regulate, but there was almost no chance any such ruling would be issued soon enough to do the anti-deregulation airlines much good. Once a lawsuit was filed against the CAB, it would take at least nine months and perhaps as long as eighteen months for a court to reach a verdict.[188] After such a long time, the CAB's policy of deregulation might be so well established and popular that Congress would quickly respond to any court ruling against the CAB by passing new legislation to reinstate the policy. Moreover, after a year or so under CAB-administered deregulation, many if not most airlines would have gone so far toward adapting themselves to deregulation that they might well suffer greater disruption from having strict controls on entry and pricing restored than from finishing the transition to deregulation.

For airlines, one of the most vexing aspects of the transition taking place in the spring and summer of 1978 was that all the ground rules were still tentative. In particular, they did not know how fast or in what order the CAB would apply its new policy of multiple permissive entry to various routes. They did not know whether the CAB's deregulatory initiatives, particularly multiple permissive entry, would be upheld in court. They did not know whether Congress would pass deregulatory legislation or, if it did, what its terms would be. This uncertainty interfered with airlines' market planning; it made aircraft purchasing especially difficult. Not knowing how much opportunity they would have to expand or how they would be affected by new competition on various routes, airlines had trouble determining the size and number of aircraft to buy. Moreover, banks and other financial institutions were reluctant to give airlines favorable terms on loans because the uncertainty surrounding deregulation cast doubt upon the industry's long-term financial stability.[189]

Thus, as airlines began to sense that the CAB had to some extent made deregulation a foregone conclusion and that blocking deregulatory legislation would only prolong uncertainty about the terms of deregulation, the airline industry's antireform bloc eroded. In March 1978 (before the CAB had formally announced that it would try to implement multiple permissive entry or proposed to give automatic approval to fare reductions, but after its ardently deregulationist intentions had become clear), Western and Braniff publicly endorsed a moderate regulation-reducing bill then pending in the House.[190] Insofar as both carriers previously had been among the most vehement opponents of the passage of any regulation-reducing bill, their new positions were significant even though they remained opposed to full-fledged deregulation.[191] In April, American Airlines endorsed the idea of rapid and total deregulation and in May announced support for the CAB's policy of multiple permissive entry.[192] Previously, American not only had opposed deregulation but also had advocated giving the CAB *additional* regulatory power—power to regulate service competition in addition to price competition.[193] After the spring of 1978, other airlines toned down or even discontinued their anti-deregulation activities. In

June, at a meeting of members of the Air Transport Association (the airline industry's principal trade association), airline representatives approved a statement seeking the "earliest possible resolution of the question of regulatory reform legislation." In addition, while failing to agree on a resolution calling for total deregulation, they endorsed the "principle of eliminating to the maximum extent possible federal economic regulation of the airlines and pre-empting substitute state regulation in the interest of assuring operation of free market forces in air transportation."[194] By September 1978 only a handful of airlines still actively opposed deregulation.

As the CAB's deregulatory policies became more popular and as airline opposition to deregulatory legislation declined, congressional opposition to deregulation evaporated. In October 1978 both houses of Congress passed almost unanimously the Airline Deregulation Act of 1978.[195] The act removed the CAB's deregulatory policies from legal challenge and provides for the CAB's authority over domestic routes to be terminated at the end of 1981, for its authority over domestic fares to expire at the end of 1982, and for the CAB to be abolished at the end of 1984.[196]

Of course, we can only speculate on which individuals and events were truly indispensable to the advance of airline deregulation and which were not. There is no way of knowing whether the fate of airline deregulation would have been different if, for example, general upturns and downturns in the economy had been timed differently than they actually were; if in 1975 President Ford had appointed someone other than John Robson to be CAB chairman; or if in 1977 President Carter had appointed someone other than Alfred Kahn to succeed Robson. But it seems clear that one of the biggest lessons to be learned from the story of airline deregulation is that despite the unquestionably formidable strength of tradition, bureaucratic inertia, and other seemingly impersonal forces in resisting change, the efforts of a handful of individuals *can* make a big difference in altering policy. Indeed, a handful of individuals at the CAB made a big difference in changing not only CAB policy but congressional legislation as well.

PART II

REGULATION OF COMPETITIVE PRACTICES

CHAPTER 4*

Antitrust Division of the Department of Justice

S U Z A N N E   W E A V E R

The Antitrust Division of the United States Department of Justice is the nation's oldest example of a major federal effort to use the courts to regulate business activity. Rather than relying on a commission or administrative agency to oversee some particular industry, Congress, in creating the division, sought to restrain certain business malpractices wherever they occurred by challenging them through the adversary system. Presumably, the industry-wide scope of the division and the involvement of the courts would minimize any tendency toward business "capture;"[1] but, as we shall see, these methods created problems of their own.

The Antitrust Division has a budget of $29.8 million and is made up of 462 attorneys and 59 economists. It enforces a number of antitrust-related statutes and seeks in various ways to promote the idea of competition within the federal government. But the bulk of the division's time is spent enforcing the country's two major antitrust statutes, the Sherman Act and the Clayton Act. The Sherman Act, passed in 1890, declares illegal "every combination, contract or conspiracy . . . in restraint of trade," and further forbids monopolization or attempts to monopo-

---

*The material in this chapter is adapted from Suzanne Weaver, *Decision to Prosecute: Organization and Public Policy in the Antitrust Division* (Cambridge, Mass.: MIT Press, 1977). Reprinted by permission.

lize a market.[2] The Clayton Act, passed in 1914 and amended by the Celler-Kefauver Act in 1950, has as its main provision a ban on corporate mergers that may significantly threaten competition in any line of commerce."[3]

To enforce these laws, the division is organized in a number of sections, most of them made up of attorneys and defined along industry lines. A section will have a list of the forms of commerce over which it has jurisdiction (though the industries on the list may not all be related to one another in any easily discernible way); over the years sections have also been organized and reorganized according to other principles. Assistant attorneys general heading the division have sometimes established special sections to deal with problems high on the national agenda, as with energy. They have organized sections around particular legal problems, as with patents. They have decided that one or another geographic area of the country needs more attention and have therefore added to the list of the division's field offices around the country. Thus the jurisdictions of the division's various sections sometimes overlap.

The attorneys in these sections investigate cases of possible antitrust violations. When the division thinks it has found such a violation, it can take the suspected offender to court. Last year the organization prosecuted fifty-eight such cases. The prosecutors can ask the court to impose civil penalties or, most notably with the Sherman Act, criminal ones. If only civil penalties are being considered, the division may also enter into negotiations with the companies it is suing to try to find a mutually agreeable settlement for a case without having to go to trial. Last year thirty-four cases were settled by consent decrees that emerged from this type of negotiation.

Recent critics of government regulation of business have given mixed reviews to this system of antitrust enforcement.[4] Regulation through antitrust, they have said, is certainly more acceptable than regulation through the commissions: it is better to give an agency a relatively specific mandate and have it take corporate America to court than to make it responsible for an industry's overall health and welfare and thus open the way for an indulgent (and perhaps corrupt) solicitude towards businessmen. But, this view continues, precisely because of antitrust's large potential for keeping the corporations in check, the politicians— the politically appointed attorney general who heads the Justice Department, the White House itself, the congressional committees that control the Antitrust Division's budget—have entered into a sort of conspiracy (explicit or tacit) to keep the agency harmless and tethered.

Antitrust Division of the Department of Justice

Its budget is too small, its investigative powers too circumscribed, and its penalties too light.

Whether this was ever a fair picture of antitrust enforcement was always doubtful. But in the years since these criticisms first gained currency, times have changed. It would be difficult for anyone to deny that the general political atmosphere surrounding the division today is permitting a substantial growth in the agency's powers and activities. The division has launched and is carrying on massive monopolization cases against IBM and AT&T. The demands of these cases have prompted the division to ask for larger budget and personnel increases than it has received in the past, and Congress—sometimes over the reluctance of the president's budget overseers at the Office of Management and Budget—has been forthcoming. The Senate antitrust subcommittee that for years lent the division substantial support under the chairmanship of Senator Philip Hart has become even more supportive under his successor, Senator Edward M. Kennedy. Moreover, in 1976 Congress passed an Antitrust Improvements Act that increased the division's power to get information out of corporations and increased the penalties it could impose for antitrust violations.

But if the power of the Antitrust Division is in some sense at its highest point in history, its reputation is not. The great monopolization cases that the division has brought are setting new records for length, complexity, and confusion; indeed, a presidential commission has just finished investigating the puzzle of what can be done about the antitrust prosecutors' elephantine cases.[5] This commission of inquiry had a variety of practical suggestions to offer, but also concluded that perhaps the only way to really shorten the proceedings is to amend the Sherman Act itself and make it easier for the government to win cases under it.

The sense of frustration is evident in other places as well. After years of endorsing almost every extension of antitrust doctrine that the division proposed in the cases it brought, the Supreme Court has begun ruling against the Division.[6] Finally, there has begun to accumulate a substantial body of scholarship arguing that vigorous antitrust enforcement, at least as the division has been defining and pursuing it over the years, is not good for the economy but exactly the opposite: a perversion of Senator John Sherman's goals and a drag on our economy's progress.[7] In short, antitrust organization and policy have, at this time of their success, become subject to more fundamental debate than ever. This paradox, it will be argued, has relevance to some of the dilemmas that plague the issue of business regulation as a whole.

SUZANNE WEAVER

Origins

As with the study of regulatory agencies in general, discussion of antitrust policy must begin with its legislative history. There is somewhat more agreement about the Sherman Act's origins than about other early regulatory statutes. The Sherman Act was a response not to industry's desire to obtain federal protection from the uncertainties of competition, but rather to a popular sentiment that large corporate organizations were gaining too much power over the lives of individual citizens.[8]

The record is somewhat less clear about just what kind of corporate power the citizenry so resented and thus what kind of abuse the Sherman Act was meant to extirpate. The story of the rising discontent with big business in post–Civil War America is usually taken to begin with the Patrons of Husbandry, also known as the Grange, a farm organization that starting in the 1870s publicized farmers' complaints against the businesses that supplied them—farm machinery manufacturers and banks—and against the railroads that they had to pay to transport their products.

The Grange wanted public regulation of railroad rates and practices; they got what they wanted in the "Granger laws" passed by several states. But the Grangers had no specific policy to propose for dealing with their other oppressors. Their platform called for the elimination of the monopolies that were unjustly increasing the farmer's costs. But they used the word "monopoly" loosely. Some Grange pronouncements seem to have referred to monopoly proper, in the modern economists' sense of the word. Some seem to have been about concentrated industries in general. Still others concerned unacceptable business conduct that could occur without any significant market concentration. Moreover, the Grange never was able to say just what should be done about these abuses and structural flaws. Though such distinctions and elaborations were not the Grange's chief worry, they have become the source of considerable debate and confusion among modern antitrust policymakers.[9]

There was another source of public pressure that prompted the Sherman Act: the antitrust sentiments that began to appear in general-audience books and periodicals in the 1880s. Here again, one can clearly see an influence on the legislators who finally passed the Sherman Act, but it is hard to detect in these writings any particular policy prescription. The daily press often condemned the "trusts" and carried articles exposing various business abuses. But these newspapers specialized in striking examples, not in systematic arguments or fine distinctions. The years just before the Sherman Act also saw the appearance of some of the most famous antibusiness books ever written in America, but they did not have anything very concrete to suggest about framing an actual antitrust policy. Henry George's *Progress and Poverty* argued that the maldistribution of land was the source of all the country's social and economic ills, while Edward Bellamy, in his book *Looking Backward*, found free-market competition so unpalatable that he actually preferred private monopoly.[10]

Nor are the writings of economists of the time any definitive guide to the meaning of antitrust. Most orthodox economists of the day did not think that government action was the proper cure for monopoly-induced inefficiencies; they thought high monopoly profits would attract new competitors to an industry and thus provide the cure for their own disease in the long run. Economists of the time who were comfortable with the idea of government intervention in the marketplace were not so sure that competition was the chief value that the government should promote.[11]

If this account were to follow the form we have come to expect from histories of regulation, it would now proceed to describe the special-interest groups that organized and used the public, journalistic, and professional discontent with the trusts to obtain specific, concrete benefits from the federal government in the form of the Sherman Act. Certainly this is the pattern, revisionist historians have argued, most typical of regulatory agency births: measures that on the surface look as if they were meant to assert public supremacy and control over a business sector were actually passed with the enthusiastic connivance —and even at the initiative—of businessmen seeking to become regulated and thus acquire federal protection from their competitors or from the varied whims of the state governments.

But with the Sherman Act, though there were surely relatively small competitors who welcomed it, this does not seem to have been the case. Historians have not found the secret interest engineering the proceedings from behind the scenes. In fact, in its combination of public sentiment, journalistic attention, and congressional politics, the account of the Sherman Act's passage seems distinctly modern.

Public sentiment on the trust question was intense in the late 1880s: by 1890 ten states had passed some kind of antitrust statutes, and six state supreme courts had declared trusts illegal. The Democrats adopted an antitrust plank in their presidential platform of 1888. Such a stand was especially congenial to them since it fit nicely with the Democrats' low-tariff position, appealed to farmers and laborers who might otherwise defect to third parties already promising relief from monopolies, and might make up for President Cleveland's refusal to advocate the coinage of silver. The Republicans, concerned about their reputation as the party of the rich, likewise adopted an antitrust plank for their 1888 platform.

It was Senator John Sherman who first brought an antitrust bill to the floor of Congress in 1888. He had been defeated for his party's presidential nomination and wanted to build himself one more legislative memorial in a long career. In July 1888 he engineered a Senate resolution directing all antitrust bills to his Senate Committee on Finance. He then brought a bill out of committee which, by January 1889, had been debated and amended enough to be taken as a serious effort. The Fiftieth Congress ended without definitive action on the bill but Sherman introduced it again in the Fifty-first. This bill came to the Senate floor in February 1890. It was attacked, as it had been the previous year, mainly on the grounds that Congress's power over interstate commerce did not give it the authority to produce an antitrust statute both constitutional and effective.

For a time the bill seemed stalled, but in March—whether because House Republicans had dropped plans for competing bills, or because Congress began to feel the public's impatience, or because Sherman grew impatient and made his attitude felt—the Senate gave the bill five days of debate. By the end of the debate, the bill had acquired many amendments; one of Sherman's opponents had actually succeeded in having it sent back to the Judiciary Committee to resolve outstanding legal issues.

But, contrary to general expectations,[12] the Judiciary Committee produced a bill of its own similar to Sherman's. Even the man who had been the bill's chief opponent on the floor voted for it in the Judiciary Committee. The bill then passed the Senate by a vote of 52 to 1 and was given Senator Sherman's name as a courtesy. After brief debate, the House passed the bill with one amendment but was persuaded in conference to withdraw the amendment. President Benjamin Harrison signed the bill, which became law on July 2, 1890. Throughout the process, there was little evidence that Congress was acting in response to pressures from specific economic interests on the outside.

To understand the legislative intent of the Sherman Act, one must rely heavily on the congressional debates that actually attended the bill's passage, and even more particularly—since the debate did not deal extensively with questions of fundamental purpose—on the speeches of Senator John Sherman himself.

"The popular mind," Senator Sherman explained himself in a famous comment on his bill's purpose,

is agitated with problems that may disturb the social order, and among them all none is more threatening than the inequality of condition, of wealth and opportunity that has grown within a single generation out of the concentration of vast combinations of capital to control production and trade and to break down competition. These combinations already defy or control powerful transportation corporations and reach state authorities. They reach out their Briarean arms to every part of our country. They are imported from abroad. Congress alone can deal with them, and if we are unwilling or unable there will soon be a trust for every production and a master to fix the price of every necessity of life.[13]

At another point, he denounced the operation of "the law of selfishness, uncontrolled by competition":

If we will not endure a king as a political power we should not endure a king over the production, transportation, and sale of any of the necessaries of life. If we would not submit to an emperor we should not submit to an autocrat of trade, with power to prevent competition and to fix the price of any commodity.[14]

Sherman was speaking about a phenomenon familiar to us: market power, and the tendency it has to restrict output and raise prices in ways that harm consumer welfare. But he was also speaking as something other than a free-market economist—no great surprise from the man whose own protectionist tariff position led one opponent of his to accuse him during the Sherman Act debates of being, in effect, a "father of the trusts."[15] Sherman was speaking the language of politics: he was appealing not simply to "consumer welfare" in a purely economic sense but also to fears about inequalities of wealth and opportunity, fears about the relationship between private and public power, and the more general anxieties in which the issue of the trusts had become enmeshed. Moreover, he was speaking not simply about the imperatives of market structure but about "selfishness" and "defiance," attributes of willfulness and of bad faith.

The attitude toward antitrust that such speeches reveal is both broader than a strictly economic approach in the sense that it mistrusts private corporate power for reasons in addition to those of economics, and narrower because it emphasizes purposiveness as a crucial sign of the existence of this power.

In the years that followed the passage of the Sherman Act, judges have ascribed to it every purpose from lowering prices to ensuring the survival of the mom-and-pop grocery store and fostering political decentralization. Just recently a presidential commission on antitrust trials made a typical contribution to the discussion of the law when it asserted that antitrust's purposes included "economic efficiency, consumer welfare, and the decentralization of economic, social, and political power."[16] Some of these goals are not only considerably different from the promotion of consumer welfare in the economic sense but can in many cases contradict it: the friendly, socially constructive mom-and-pop grocery store may not be—indeed, in many cases demonstrably is not—the cheapest way of getting the groceries to the consumer.

In the last few years, there has been a strong attack on this persistent incoherence. Robert Bork, in particular, has argued that insofar as Senator Sherman had any operational intention in his lawmaking, it was to maximize consumer welfare as an economist would understand that welfare. Moreover, Bork says, there is no evidence that Sherman intended any of his other phrases to be taken as goals that should be pursued if they contradicted Sherman's major welfare aim.[17] This argument is respectable as a matter of history and attractive as a matter of policy. Still, it is hard to read through Senator Sherman's speeches on the Sherman Act and remain surprised that future courts and enforcers could find in them support for more varied and less rigorous interpretations.

Sherman made these varied readings even more likely by the means he chose for enforcing his antitrust legislation. He freely conceded during the Sherman Act debates that he did not know quite what he wanted his act to outlaw: "I admit that it is difficult to define in legal language the precise line between lawful and unlawful combinations." But this was a question, he thought, that must

be left for the courts to determine in each particular case. All that we, as lawmakers, can do is to declare general principles, and we can be assured that the courts will apply them so as to carry out the meaning of the law.[18]

Sherman also made clear that he expected the courts to look for "the meaning of the law" not only in the text of the Sherman Act and the congressional debates surrounding it but also in the existing common law doctrine governing restraint of trade. It is not at all clear that the common law as it existed at the time could really have been used to reach the kind of trusts and cartels that most worried Sherman. But it is clear that Sherman *thought* that the common law provided the requisite principles and that he could therefore leave the content of his law somewhat vague.

Thus Sherman and his fellow congressmen asserted the supremacy of public power over private economic power but drew back from spelling out definite standards by which this private economic power was to be governed. Moreover, they avoided putting any new regulatory authority over the trusts into the hands of an independent rulemaking commission, although the model for this kind of body was already available to them in the form of the Interstate Commerce Commission. They chose the courts—with their ability to discriminate among particular cases, their tendency to incrementalism, and their adversary system—rather than opting for enforcement through general rules handed down by an administrative agency. By their choices, the congressmen set the stage for a protracted case-by-case debate over the meaning of antitrust and guaranteed that the executive branch personnel in charge of antitrust enforcement would be prosecutors advocating their cases before the courts rather than administrative judges mediating among all sides of an antitrust issue. This deliberate decision to leave crucial questions of antitrust policy for the courts to decide was perhaps the single most important influence on the development of our antitrust enforcement apparatus.

Early Enforcement

Responsibility for prosecuting cases under the Sherman Act went to the Justice Department, which acquired still other antitrust statutes to enforce as the years passed. The department was slow in beginning to enforce the Sherman Act, partly because some of the early attorneys general were dubious about the value and the constitutionality of the new law and partly because the department then employed only eighteen attorneys. Given the slow beginning, it is striking that by 1904 Congress had been persuaded to start passing a special appropriation each year for antitrust enforcement and that the department had used the money to hire five full-time antitrust lawyers.[19] The number of cases brought per year began to rise, from an average of fewer than 1.5 in the years 1890 through 1904 to an average of 31 in the years 1910 through 1914.[20]

Beginning in 1915, the Antitrust Division's average case level dropped; it remained at about 11 a year through the 1920s. In the wake of President Franklin D. Roosevelt's decision to protect and even promote industry-wide cooperative arrangements through the National Industrial Recovery Act of 1933, the case level dropped lower still. The trend was reversed abruptly when in 1938, after the NIRA had been declared unconstitutional, Roosevelt decided to reinvigorate antitrust as an alternative means of controlling big business. He named Thurman Arnold assistant attorney general in charge of the Antitrust Division, a post Arnold held until 1943. Arnold increased the number of attorneys in the Division from 59 to 144 in the course of a year, added a small staff of economists for the first time, generated vastly more publicity about the division's activities, and brought the case level up to over 50 per year. Thus, so the story goes, the modern Antitrust Division was born.[21]

There is no doubt that the Antitrust Division grew under Arnold's stewardship. But just as important is the fact that Arnold made few changes in the way the division thought about its mission, defined an antitrust violation, or went about finding one.[22] According to the testimony of some of Arnold's staff, the division they found when they arrived there went about its enforcement duties by responding to complaints, most of them from small businessmen annoyed at their competitors' practices. Arnold did not propose to change this basic method. Instead, he said he wanted two things: more cases and more criminal rather than civil ones.

Arnold made some organizational changes to pursue these goals. First, he instituted a special section to screen complaints so that lawyers would no longer waste so much of their time on wild-goose chases. (It may well be that these fruitless searches—and not just a simple probusiness bias in the White House—had contributed to the decline in the division's case levels during the 1920s). Second, the lawyers would henceforth be aided by economists who would help develop the cases that the lawyers found and suggest other possible avenues of attack against a company under investigation.

Arnold's changes were followed by a swift rise in the division's case levels. But according to some who served with him, his changes were not the primary cause of the increase. The new cases came about, the

Antitrust Division of the Department of Justice

Arnold veterans say, because of increases in the division's size, the additional complaints that came from the new publicity attending its activities, and the sheer hard work that the excitement of serving with Arnold generated. They also came about, as one ex-staffer remembered, because the days of the NIRA had made business careless about concealing its illegal dealings and had actually promoted collusion where none had existed before. "You have to remember," he said, "that those cases were easy. The evidence was just lying around waiting for someone to pick it up. You don't get cases like that anymore."*

Arnold did not change the case–by–case, ad hoc, prosecution-oriented manner in which the lawyers went about deciding how to use their time and their enforcement efforts. He found it there when he arrived, it was still there in his heyday and it remains there today. In 1940 Walton Hamilton and Irene Till made a study of the Antitrust Division for the Temporary National Economic Committee and concluded that one of its crucial problems—and the reason outsiders found it so hard to impose any new policy directions on the agency—was that its professionals were largely attorneys who practiced "The Lawyer's Approach to Antitrust." The character of antitrust investigation, they said,

> is determined by the Division's obligation to prosecute. . . . The Antitrust attorney seizes whatever is helpful, discards whatever might tell against him. . . . He gathers evidence instead of finding facts. . . . The grand total at which he arrives is far more a recitation of wrongdoing than a picture of an industry at work. . . . The attorneys develop zeal in their work, are persuaded of the guilt of the accused, bend every effort that the breach of the law shall be atoned. . . . An Economics Section has been organized but such units tend to be excrescences upon a structure which has made little place for them. They are not easily woven into litigation which is the principal activity of the Division.[23]

By the time of Thurman Arnold, the division had already developed a distinctive character, marked by the prosecutors' zeal, their particularistic approach to enforcement, and their tendency to fashion concepts and doctrines to fit the case at hand rather than the other way around. By this time, the division was already quite stable and resistant to change in this prosecutorial approach. But, as Hamilton and Till suggest, there was another respect in which the organization was quite comfortable with change: it was always ready to take up ideas and arguments to aid its prosecutorial reach. The stability in the organiza-

*All quoted material not otherwise referenced is drawn from interviews conducted by the author.

tion and the instability in the law that it produced mark the division today no less than they did the division that Arnold found and left.

The Division Matures

Thurman Arnold's regime was not the only one that made substantial changes in the division. Another sizable shift occurred during the 1950s. First, in 1955 the Department of Justice instituted its Honors Program for hiring young lawyers. Instead of being hired "off the street," as one division administrator described it, beginning division attorneys now began to arrive through a nationwide hiring system designed to identify bright candidates in the top 10 percent of their law school classes and lure them into the government. Second, and perhaps more important, the division's activities changed somewhat. The Clayton Act was amended in 1950 to bring more mergers within the reach of the antitrust laws, and the division gradually began to use its expanded jurisdiction. In the late 1950s the division also brought some highly publicized price-fixing cases, in one of which business executives were for the first time actually forced to serve jail sentences under the Sherman Act.[24]

These changes left a mark on the division. The young lawyers hired through the Honors Program were told by government recruiters that service in the Antitrust Division offered a chance to gain valuable trial experience. This trial experience was becoming prized on the private market. Business executives were frightened by the increasing antitrust prosecutions of the time and wanted legal counsel. Lawyers who had presumably learned the government's ways by serving in the division were now valuable property.

It was possible to see the effects of the change in the accounts that lawyers of various ages gave an interviewer about why they had joined the Antitrust Division. Lawyers who had joined the division before the mid-fifties gave widely varying reasons for their choice. Some pointed out that the place had been one of the few growth industries for lawyers during the late depression. Some said they'd switched to the division when the World War II agencies for which they had previously worked had been disbanded. Many referred to their choice as "an accident."

In contrast, the younger lawyers gave reasons that were far more uniform. They came to the division for the trial experience and the knowledge of government that they thought the organization would provide. In the main, they intended to go back to the private bar someday. Some had specifically chosen the Antitrust Division over some other places—the Tax Division, for instance—because they thought antitrust more substantively interesting and important. But they did not speak with particular moral or ideological zeal. When they talked about leaving for private practice someday, they emphasized that they did not intend to "sell out" their antitrust beliefs for their clients' money. One young attorney explained what the antitrust defense bar did for businessmen, "Most of the work you do for them will be preventive—telling them what they *can't* do."

It was not surprising, therefore, to learn that what the younger attorneys wanted most out of their time in the division was to learn their craft as antitrust lawyers. They considered this craft inseparable from the art of prosecution. These attorneys would almost invariably explain themselves, "My job is to enforce the antitrust laws." And their hopes for future employment in the private bar did not make them very timid in their idea of what constitutes proper enforcement. On the contrary, they professed to believe that being an energetic prosecutor was the way to build a good reputation with private and government lawyers alike.

Moreover, when they were asked which attorneys in the division they would choose to emulate, the younger lawyers usually came up with one of a small number of division lawyers who presented an especially tough image of what a prosecutor should be. These "stars" were known around the division for the important cases they had tried. They were not part of the administrative hierarchy in the "front office" and were often particularly colorful in expressing their contempt for bureaucratic structures and forms. In fact, they were more colorful in general than most of their colleagues—more aggressive, more talkative, and more entertaining. They took pride in the practical apprenticeships they had served in the division, "carrying the briefcases" of older lawyers who had taught them the trade. They preferred to think of themselves as active and combative types rather than intellectuals prone to see both sides of a question; they seemed proud that once they had taken hold of a case they would sink their teeth into it and, despite the hemming and hawing of the timorous bureaucrats above them, simply not let go. This idea of the tenacious prosecutor, though obviously its effects on division lawyers vary according to temperaments and abilities, can be said to inform in one degree or another nearly all the work of the Antitrust Division.

Suzanne Weaver

Finding a Case

When division lawyers were asked about the day-to-day details of their jobs, they overwhelmingly described their activities as part of the process of pursuing a case or, if they did not already have a case, looking for one. What they were looking for was, in the most general legal terms, evidence of a violation of the Sherman Act or the Clayton Act, the two major antitrust statutes. The Sherman Act, it will be recalled, forbids monopolization of a market, or the attempt to monopolize it, or a conspiracy to monopolize it. The Clayton Act forbids business combinations, including mergers, that may "substantially . . . lessen competition, or . . . tend to create a monopoly." Neither of these formulations even begins to suggest the complexities and ambiguities of the antitrust laws, which keep a sizable section of the American Bar Association busy and well fed. But most of the time, for the Antitrust Division lawyers, such gray areas and borderline questions are academic.

The attorneys sift through several sources of information from day to day for hints of possible violations. They get complaints from citizens and consumers, from businessmen (or their lawyers) upset about competitors' practices, from congressmen helping out constituents, and from other government agencies. They receive reports of merger activity from documents that corporations are legally required to file. The attorneys also follow the business press and have contacts of their own. They believe—rightly—that whatever information comes to the division is handed on to the staff attorneys. They do not think that division higher-ups are keeping anything from them, though they worry about whole categories of violations that they may be missing because "no one will squeal." Most of the time, lawyers said, they never got as far in investigating these things as to worry about the fine distinctions or borderline questions often thrown up by antitrust law, because most of the time the information they got did not have even the remotest possibility of becoming the subject of an antitrust prosecution. "Ninety percent of these things are bummers," one staff attorney summed it up.

Some of what they get is crank mail, in effect. Some complaints are of conduct that, even if true, is simply not an antitrust violation. Sometimes a division attorney writes back for more information and never gets an answer. Sometimes a merger is taking place between companies that are too small to arouse a lawyer's immediate suspicion and have nothing else about them even to suggest the advisability of a second look. Sometimes prior knowledge of an industry in which a merger is taking place tells an attorney that the merger is not anticompetitive.

Lawyers engaged in this kind of search think of their environment as one of information scarcity. An interviewer who kept trying to ask them questions about the kinds of discretion they exercised at this early stage of the prosecution process was almost always greeted by puzzlement and disbelief. They were not acting in behalf of any particular theories of antitrust, they would say. They were not exercising any personal preferences for going hard or easy on one industry or another. They did not go around instituting investigations in "response to pressure" by the politicians above them, whether in the executive branch or in Congress. Indeed, the relationship was better understood the other way around. The attorneys were always in the market for good cases; anybody who had news of one—including a congressman—would receive a more than civil reception.

This disclaimer on the attorneys' part does not fully answer the question of discretion. The division does make choices about where to direct its enforcement resources, if only by its strategy of relying so much on complaints and on published reports and materials that have possible use as part of a case in court. But staff attorneys do not think they are faced with realistic choices as they sort through most of this information. They said they were building their cases where they could find them; the chief constraint they felt was the scarcity of information from which to construct these prosecutions, not the scarcity of resources with which to pursue them.

This picture of staff attorneys governed entirely by their need for information ignores two rather obvious characteristics of the division's environment and behavior. First, in many respects, the antitrust laws are ambiguous; even where they are relatively clear, there will probably be some ambiguity about whether the facts of a particular case bring it within the laws' jurisdiction. Second, the division itself has been instrumental in changing the interpretation of the laws—advancing it, as division personnel would put it—rather continuously over the years. One staff attorney proudly claimed that most of the changes of this sort originate in the minds of the division's lawyers: "Every new idea around here has been discussed up and down these corridors for years." Staff attorneys are not just searching for cases that fit the law, they are also probing for ways to change it.

Most of the time, no such possibility for change presents itself. Therefore it is hardly surprising that the staff attorneys grow eager to pursue openings when they do appear. The eagerness comes from another circumstance as well: once staffers decide to pursue a case and begin collecting the information necessary to make further decisions about actually taking it into the courts, they have committed themselves to a long and tedious process. The work of government is often slow, but antitrust proceedings are famous even in Washington. The division does not keep systematic records of the length of its investigations, but suggestive of the type of work involved in an investigation is the remark of one attorney who described an investigation that had lasted ten months as a "quick" job. Once cases go to trial, of course, the possibilities become even more impressive: the government's case against IBM passed its tenth anniversary at the beginning of 1979, with no end in sight.

Staff attorneys and defense counsel gave several explanations for why the investigative portion of these antitrust proceedings lasts so long. These explanations range from bureaucratic laziness to obstructionism by companies being investigated and the need to persuade slow-witted judges by producing mountains of evidence. But it is agreed that a great part of the reason lies in the law itself and the kind of evidence it requires. A monopolization case may require examination of well over a hundred thousand documents comprising a broad-ranging history of the firm or firms under investigation; even a "simple" merger or price-fixing case may involve a detailed examination of industry history, structure, and pricing patterns.

Attorneys develop a considerable personal and emotional investment in these investigations and are understandably reluctant to see them come to a fruitless end. One lawyer said, "Once you've spent so much time on one of these damn things, you tend to get pretty attached to it." This attachment leads the staff attorneys to persist in an investigation even if violations do not present themselves early on: "We're all looking for the magic document in the last box," one lawyer put it. It also leads them to a considerable amount of innovation. Some of this invention deals with matters of evidence—proving, for example, that parallel price increases by two competitors could not have come about through the normal reaction of one firm to another's action in a competitive market. Some of the innovations involve cases in a new industry or a new geographic location where immunity from the antitrust laws had been thought to apply. But some of them are proposals to change the interpretation of the antitrust laws in significant ways.

A lawyer may look for a way of persuading the court that Company A, which wants to take over Company B, is both a potential purchaser of widgets from Company B and a potential competitor of B's in the widget manufacturing business—and that the merger is illegal for both reasons. The arguments may seem to contradict one another, but the lawyer doesn't want to put all his chances of winning into one legal basket. Or, if there's really not much direct competition between two firms that want to merge, a lawyer may try to invent new meanings for the word—by claiming, for example, that a government-owned utility in one location is actually competing with a utility in a totally different place because one provides "yardstick" competition for the other (that is, a standard for rate-setting bodies in other communities of what constitutes a reasonable price or a reasonable increase). Or a lawyer may even be thinking—as many of them have in the past few years— about new ways to interpret the Sherman Act to get at mergers and combinations that the courts say the Clayton Act permits.

When one looks for patterns in these searches, two appear readily. First, among "conduct" violations—violations stemming from some particular objectionable act that a firm has committed—some attorneys say that certain practices will prod them to special efforts. Boycotts are one example because they are particularly unpalatable to some attorneys in a moral sense: they are flagrant attempts by individuals to use their economic muscle to acquire a kind of personal domination over others. Second, when it comes to "structural" violations—acts or situations that are illegal because they tend to foster too much concentration —attorneys say that when they deal with especially big companies, either in the sense that they dominate a local market or because they are very large in absolute size, they push especially hard to find a cause for prosecution. The effects of this impulse to keep pressing are readily apparent today in the massive and protracted government cases against IBM and AT&T. But, over a longer run, the division's record in pursuing the nation's largest firms has been somewhat more mixed, limited by the staff's tendency to devote its attention to the case immediately at hand whether or not it promises to have particularly large economic effects. Most of the time, one staff attorney put it, "you just don't have time to sit around and think about busting up GM."

Thus, the division's prosecuting attorneys take their cases where they can and are quite willing to push them so that, as one of them put it, "something will come out." A corollary of this proposition is that it is rare to find staff lawyers recommending that a case the division might win should nevertheless not be prosecuted. Some of the lawyers, it is true, reported that some situations "gave them trouble" as they thought about whether to recommend a prosecution. One lawyer mentioned that in a recently discovered "tie-in" (a requirement by a seller that whoever bought its Product A also had to buy its Product B) he felt bad about prosecuting because he thought the effect of the tie-in in this case was to subsidize a medically vital product and keep its price low. Some said they did not like to bring price-fixing cases against small businessmen who operated in particularly precarious circumstances. Some said it was hard for them to decide whether to prosecute mergers—even large ones—when they might create a more formidable competitor to some giant company that dominated a given economic sector. But such considerations are not frequent and they are not consensual: for every attorney who thought such a case should not be prosecuted, there was another who, when given the same facts, said he would recommend that the prosecution go forward. Most doubts of this sort among attorneys investigating a case are resolved in favor of prosecution.

Managing the Lawyers

If this pro-prosecution impulse is so dominant among staff attorneys, it is important to know whether their superiors in the organization temper it in significant ways. The immediate supervisors who can do so are the section chiefs. These managers distribute matters for possible investigation among the lawyers, supervise their investigations and trials, approve or disapprove or amend their briefs and recommendations, help decide about their salaries and promotions, and, in general, mediate between them and the organization's higher echelons.

The section chiefs are usually chosen from among the trial lawyers themselves. They seem to be picked in part for those skills at organization and mediation that are desirable in any administrator. But they also seem, by and large, to be able prosecuting attorneys as well; few of the section chiefs arouse expressions of professional contempt among the attorneys who work for them.

Since all information that comes into the organization is routinely sent to the section chiefs according to the commodities or special activities that each section handles, section chiefs can control the work product of the division by their distribution of preliminary information to the staff lawyers. Usually there is no dispute about the section to which a particular piece of information should go. Where there is an ambiguity, the office of the director of operations, which does the parceling out, will decide on the basis of a section's available personnel or past experience with the topic in question. Sometimes, when the information looks as if it has the makings of a good case, two section chiefs will actually want it enough to stage a small fight over it; then the director of operations' office will settle the dispute. These occasions are rare enough so that it is hard to see any principle except logrolling at work in the office's decisions. Section chiefs express pride in their aggressiveness at getting interesting material to handle; as one of them put it, "I fight to get those good cases for my section." They also express pride in the cases they can drum up on their own through their own contacts and past experience.

On more routine matters, most of the information the section chiefs get is so patently useless for purposes of prosecution that they do not even bother to distribute it to the staff. What looks "good" is sent to a trial attorney with sufficient experience to be trusted with it; what looks remotely useful gets sent out to someone else, more likely a younger lawyer. This pattern does not ensure in advance which matters will finally turn into cases and which will not: a matter going to a young lawyer may not look very big or valuable, but it ends up in the grasp of an attorney with the most incentive to pursue it eagerly in hopes of getting a case of his own.

The section chiefs are reported, by themselves and by their subordinates, to be very liberal about authorizing investigations. Their major function during the course of investigations seems to be counseling and pressing those lawyers who need it with suggestions and directions about looking for possible violations. Something of the same relationship governs their dealings with their staff when the time finally comes to decide whether the section should recommend a prosecution. These matters do not come to a section chief's office unannounced: he probably has been in fairly close touch with an investigation throughout, not just on his own initiative but because his staff attorneys are likely to have found it useful to discuss the case with him and ask his advice on various parts of it.

Usually staff and section chief agree on whether to recommend prosecution. It is rare that the section chiefs want to keep going when their lawyers do not; but in a significant minority of cases, the staff wants to prosecute and the section chief thinks their case is not good enough. Neither section chiefs nor staff reported any particular pattern to the chiefs' doubts, or any reasons that systematically affected the chiefs' thinking, except a relative conservatism on technical legal matters. Usually a section chief seems to try to resolve differences by finding a way to recommend prosecution somehow—perhaps by dropping a defendant or dropping an allegation in the complaint. "We *do* come to a consensus," one section chief explained the process. "You need it to get through the front office." Rarely, the dispute remains unresolved; in such cases a section chief will send the "front office" both his recommendation and the staff dissensions.

The "front office" belongs to the director of operations and his assistants and to the assistant attorney general (AAG) and his assistants and advisory bodies. The director has usually been a career man; his office distributes information to the sections, supervises investigations and trials, and passes on recommendations about prosecution. Describing the director's role in relation to the section chiefs is much the same as describing the section chiefs' relations with the trial lawyers. Both the director's office and the section chiefs report that the office does little preliminary screening of information entering the division; that task is left mainly to the section chiefs. In the same way, division personnel from director of operations to staff attorneys agreed that when a director does not want to bring a case that the staff has recommended, it is almost never because of any systematic bias on policy questions but involves instead matters of craftsmanship and technique. Some staff members professed to find this lack of system maddeningly frustrating. "All ____ kept saying," one lawyer described a fight with the director, "was, 'Show me a case that's ever been brought on that principle.'" Others are more admiring. One attorney explained the director's role, "He can show you where your evidence won't hold up."

Such disagreements occur in a significant minority of cases. But not all of them involve only the choices of prosecuting or not; the participants try to resolve as many as possible by modifying a case still further so that it can go forward in some form. Moreover, the nonsystematic quality of the director's objections means that staff attorneys can't very well censor themselves in anticipation of the director's tastes. In spite of these disagreements, the lawyers keep the initiative in forming the population of cases from which the director must choose.

One director of operations explained that each case he approved left his office as a technically competent piece of work: "Beyond this office, the decisions are made for policy reasons." By "beyond this office," he meant the office of the assistant attorney general. One might well imagine that the AAG and his staff, able to pick and choose from among "good" cases, would try to express through their choices some idea—

whether visionary or corrupt—of what the antitrust laws should be doing. Quite obviously, some of this kind of choice occurs. The division has brought more merger cases, or fewer cases involving vertical integration, or more price-fixing cases under one AAG than with another. Some AAGs have stated explicitly that bringing monopoly cases was too costly in division resources; obviously, some have thought otherwise. But what the AAG can and does do during the review stage should not be exaggerated.

Most of the cases that reach the AAG's office are noncontroversial within the organization. "At *least* 60 percent of these cases," one director of operations described it and others agreed, "the AAG never even *touches.*" Even in the other 40 percent, a good part of the dispute is technical: questions of why the staff is naming a certain defendant or exactly what should be on the list of allegations. Even some of the highly publicized cases the division brings (or does not bring)—cases that provoke wide speculation about the policy and political factors that must have been involved in the decision—are often settled on grounds more narrow and technical than outside observers seem to realize. A typical example occurred in a well-publicized conspiracy case against a group of very large manufacturers. The case as finally brought was civil rather than criminal; the division was widely criticized for laxity in enforcement, and it was rumored that the decision was influenced by partisan politics. But one man who had been in the AAG's office at the time remarked: "*I* was the one who made the recommendation not to bring a criminal case—not any higher-ups. And I would have liked to bring a criminal case, too. But the evidence just wasn't there."

Apart from the technical disputes that occur, very much the same as the kinds of discussion that go on in section chiefs' offices or with the director of operations, there are some broader kinds of differences that an AAG may have with his staff. Unsurprisingly, an AAG may be more sensitive to goals that compete with antitrust enforcement, such as regional employment, national defense, foreign relations, or the performance of the stock market. And outsiders will generally make sure that if the AAG wasn't properly sensitive to begin with, he will be quite aware of their arguments by the time they have finished making their case to him. Some AAGs will overrule their lawyers for reasons that are more idiosyncratic: one is said to have turned down a case in the women's underwear industry because "he said he didn't want to be known as the man who brought the ladies' panties and girdles case." But perhaps the major point to be made from the view of understanding the division's overall performance is that these grounds for debate are comparatively rare. Most of the organization's discussions about whether or not to prosecute—even those held in the AAG's office—take place in terms of considerations that are quite familiar to the staff attorneys and that do not challenge the staff's own methods or goals.

An AAG tends to have his major chance at controlling the Division's output not through the review process, but by innovations that affect where the division will direct its investigative resources in the first place. The foregoing analysis of the staff attorneys' goals would suggest that in some ways the organization would be relatively easy to change. The attorneys would be perfectly amenable to changes, from new areas of jurisdiction to new economic arguments, that will bring new case possibilities within their grasp or increase the chances of quick front-office approval for cases they have found. And, in fact, the rather long list of such changes that the division has undergone in its recent history would seem to bear out such an argument. Thurman Arnold set about redesigning the division's sections; the process has continued since Arnold's time. AAGs have established new sections to deal with regulated industries, with patent problems, and with energy. They have begun antitrust "campaigns" such as attacks on the practice of reciprocity (agreements by two companies to buy and sell from each other on a preferential basis), battles against conglomerate mergers, and a return to a concentration on price-fixing offenses. They have established ancillary methods of investigation, such as economists' price surveys to detect possibilities of price fixing and price-fixing "hot lines" to encourage consumer complaints. The division is quite unresistant to such changes.

The ethos of prosecution that pervades the Antitrust Division also makes its lawyers amenable, as one would expect them to be, to changes in the theories—including economic theories—that underlie their cases, as long as new theories seem to provide ways of reaching objectionable behavior and making cases that were unattainable before. One example of this kind of flexibility occurred during the early 1970s, when the division was faced with a recurring problem in the banking industry. Division lawyers were convinced that many of the mergers occurring in the industry were anticompetitive. It wasn't that the merging banks had been in direct competition with one another; it was that a bank in City A would typically buy a bank in City B instead of moving directly into City B to provide some additional competition. Thus the merger would remove from the climate around City B a "probable entrant" whose presence would have served to keep the City B bank behaving well. The problem was that these banks came under state regulation; and in an antitrust trial, a state regulator could be brought to the stand to say that City A's bank *wasn't* an independent "probable entrant" into City B, because state authorities were unlikely to authorize any such move.

Faced with this problem of evidence, the front office suggested a new tack: the division could argue that in spite of the state regulator's testimony, City A's bank was a "potential competitor" as economic theory defined such a term because no matter what its intentions or those of the regulator, it had the objective characteristics—size, expertise, and such—to be counted as part of City B's economic milieu. The staff lawyers were skeptical about the theory because it was without behavioral evidence. But they accepted it because, as one of them put it, "we couldn't have won on 'probability' anyway." The division brought several cases based on the "potential competition" theory and did not do well with it in the courts. Afterwards the lawyers spoke philosophically of its demise. "Maybe the industry is just too complicated for the theory. After all, there's nothing wrong with the theory, but antitrust law is still based on *facts.*"

Such tolerance has had other examples in the division, from the "aggregate concentration" theory that the organization used in an attempt to fight conglomerate mergers in the early 1970s to changes in direction during the course of its monopolization suits against IBM and AT&T. The lawyers do not stand on personal ceremony or ideological principle in searching for new ways to bring and win cases.

The changes arousing resentment are those that impose limits on the staff's universe of possible cases. This does not happen often: as will be discussed later, an assistant attorney general rarely finds it to his advantage to engage the staff in this kind of struggle. In the late 1960s, though, one assistant attorney general, Donald Turner, a professor at the Harvard Law School, took office with the conviction that the division's ad hoc, prosecution-oriented behavior was producing bad antitrust economics and bad law. He established new positions in the division to help him review cases and find new ones so that the organization could begin concentrating more of its resources on economically significant problems and stop bringing so many cases that wasted effort or established bad precedents. Ultimately he published a set of merger guidelines so that the business and legal worlds could get a clearer idea of the kind of merger the division would consider objectionable: "I didn't want the division to bring every case we *could* win, I wanted us to bring only the cases we *should* win."

After Professor Turner left to return to Harvard, division lawyers looked back bitterly on his attempts to make their product more systematic and predictable. They resented the guidelines: "This can only work against us," one of them explained. "We're bound by the policy; the defendant's not." And they complained about the review process as well. It wasn't that they resented the idea of review in itself; the staff has always been subject to a rather extensive review system. The problem was that this AAG hadn't shared the lawyers' settled conviction that antitrust is a matter of prosecutions, and that they should bring their cases where they could. They spoke with pleasure about how things returned to normal when a new AAG took over. There was a case, one lawyer recalled as an example, in which the front office had wanted to get a ruling from the courts on a question of the relationship between patent law and antitrust. "We had other kinds of evidence, but we never put it in. When it was time to appeal, [the new AAG] was in. He was furious that we had left out evidence; he was a trial lawyer, and he knew you don't go halfway on cases. So we weren't going to bring cases any more just to establish a point of law; we were going to bring them to *win*. That was a big boost to morale."

Though an AAG has broad latitude in directing the division, he will encounter trouble when he tries to make it harder for the lawyers to prosecute. It is not likely that he will be able to impose such change beyond his own tenure. In some cases, he will face even more serious difficulties. The ongoing IBM and AT&T monopolization trials seem to be attended by unusually high turnover among lawyers as they find that the size of the cases prevents them from getting any broad prosecution experience. The prosecutorial style of the division poses these limits to the policy purposes for which the organization can be used.

Outsiders

If this essay had been written five years ago, it would have had to deal at this point with a certain incredulity among a significant part of its audience. The Antitrust Division described so far is an organization slowly but inexorably extending the reach of the antitrust laws through an ongoing series of opportunistically chosen prosecutions. Surely, it would have been said, such an account ignores the most important fact about this country's antitrust experience: the fact that, throughout their administration, the laws have been unable to break up this country's huge industrial wealth. And, the argument would go on, this is no accident. Assistant attorneys general are political appointees, looking to the White House or to powerful businessmen for their next job. Moreover, the White House has political reasons of its own to kill inconvenient prosecutions and to keep the division chronically starved for funds. And if the White House doesn't shortchange the division, the Congress will—by keeping appropriations low, by refusing to put more teeth into the antitrust laws themselves, and by trying to influence individual cases on behalf of powerful constituents. Thus there is a kind of silent conspiracy to keep the division a paper tiger: our antitrust policy is a fine example of the exercises in hypocrisy that have been called "symbolic politics."

Even when this picture enjoyed its greatest currency, it was not very accurate. For one thing, it does not appear that the executive branch exerted much pressure on the division in behalf of any particular policy goals through its power over the division's budget. Department of Justice budget officials lamented their inability to "get control" of the division's budget, which attorneys general treated with special leniency despite the fact that the justifications the division presented were often vague and empty of actual arguments about how expenditures might be related to benefits.

OMB officials in more than one administration testified that they could not seem to get hold of the organization, either. True, it escaped their efforts partly because it was very small in comparison to other budget-cutting opportunities that the federal government presented to an OMB examiner. But it also emerged unscathed because examiners generally approved of the goals of antitrust and because the division itself rarely asked for very big increases. No doubt the division's restraint came in part from obedience to the law of anticipated reactions. But until recently AAGs have felt, as one of them put it, that "I don't really know what we'd *do* with many more men. Besides, they're not even *useful* until they've been trained a couple of years."

Division personnel, Justice Department budget officers, and OMB examiners agreed that one reason the executive branch did not exercise more control over the division budget was that the real power lay in Congress. And it is true that the agency receives an annual grilling from its House appropriations subcommittee. But—again, until recently— the subcommittee did not cut the division's modest requests for budget increases. And, perhaps as important, the subcommittee did not use the hearings to communicate to the division any very specific idea of what the organization should be doing. The committee would ask how many cases had been brought in the past year, how many had been won, how stiff the sentences had been, and how much had been collected in fines and damages. Insofar as these questions gave policy guidance, it was to reinforce the division's tendency to operate in a prosecutorial, case-by-case way. One reason such questions cannot be taken by an AAG as implying any more concrete policy directive than that is that the questions imply contradictory policy goals. "Bring as many cases as you can" entails different decision principles from "Win a high proportion of those cases you *do* bring."[25]

In these hearings, congressmen would occasionally attempt to go further and inquire about particular cases. When they suggested that the division be more aggressive, assistant attorneys general answered that they would try. When congressmen suggested that the division go easier on particular defendants or issues, AAGs would quite bluntly refuse. For instance, there were questions about why the division was prosecuting a farm association that seemed exempt under the antitrust laws, why the division favored deregulation of stock commission rates that may raise prices for small investors, why businessmen feel so harrassed by the division. In these cases, the AAG has invariably and explicitly stated his disagreement with the premise of the question.[26]

The other kind of formal power that Congress holds over the division —the oversight responsibility—has been exercised in a way that was even more supportive of the division. The Senate antitrust subcommittee, the more active of the two oversight committees, frequently has held hearings on various problems of competition in the economy. The division, never averse to getting more information that might be useful to it, has been happy enough with this kind of activity. When it came to particular cases, the subcommittee and its staff maintained a certain distance—not simply, it seems, because it does not look very good to be caught obstructing justice, but because they generally shared the division's notions of what had to be done and how to do it.

But if congressional oversight committees did not want to give the division trouble with its cases, certainly there were others—occupants of the White House, or other members of Congress—who must be presumed to have wished from time to time that the organization would stop making trouble for constituents or contributors. For obvious reasons, it is hard to get a definite answer to the question of outright corruption. The most extensive attempt made to find such an answer remains *The Closed Enterprise System,* a study of U.S. antitrust enforcement published by one of Ralph Nader's study groups in 1971.[27] The study found thirty-two examples of what it thought were attempts at improper influence exercised on the division since the end of World War II.

This is a low figure, especially for an agency dealing with matters that are obscure to the general public but of great moment to the particular businessmen involved. But in addition, many of these attempts were clearly unsuccessful. For example, in the mid-fifties, the study reports, when Representative Emmanuel Celler tried to get the division to act against competitors of one of his law firm's clients, there was an argument in the division not over whether to comply with his request but on whether to ignore him completely or write him back an indignant refusal. Also, many of these attempts were not obviously improper: for instance, congressmen from a given area trying to persuade an attorney general that an antitrust case would mean jobs lost to their constituents. Of the Nader report's thirty-two cases, only a dozen interventions were both successful and tainted by a reasonable possibility that any corruption was involved.

The most recent alleged scandal of this sort—the 1971 attempt by the Nixon administration to prevent the division from carrying forward its cases against conglomerate mergers by ITT—is a case in point. By now there is no real doubt that the White House tried to influence the division on the matter. It is also clear that there was already disagreement within the division over whether the cases would succeed and whether it might not be better to settle. It further appears that White House interest in the matter was not based primarily on considerations of personal or partisan favor, as was alleged in 1972, but on more general views about antitrust policy. The various bodies that investigated the whole cluster of incidents comprising the Watergate scandal concluded that ITT was not a case of corruption in any proper sense of the term, and that there is no real reason to question the verdict.[28]

Perhaps the real question, then, is why the division was being corrupted so little. Part of the answer seems to be found in the nature of antitrust work: division personnel rarely work alone on a matter of any size, and they must frequently provide extensive written justification of their actions. Part probably comes from the fact of competition: for every businessman who is enraged by having to defend himself against an antitrust prosecution, there is another who is absolutely delighted to see him suffering. Part of the division's insulation also comes from the relatively high cost of being found out at trying to influence the division improperly. Trading favors is a bad thing to be caught at in any part of the federal government, and our political mores make it increasingly so; but for an attorney heading a branch of the Justice Department to be accused of obstructing justice is particularly damaging.

A large part of the insulation seems to come from the professional antitrust bar. The division maintains close official relations with the antitrust bar. Division officials routinely speak to its meetings and write for its publications. There are close personal relations as well: division alumni in the private sector keep up with their ex-colleagues in the government. Further, the formalized adversary system of the courts gives division members and private lawyers a close knowledge of each other's doings. "They know what we're doing and we know what they're doing," one division lawyer put it. "We all read the same opinions and the same journals."

This professional community does not exercise its influence simply through pious exhortations. The general opinion it forms of antitrust attorneys in government and out plays a large part in determining how well a lawyer will do in what has become a very lucrative profession. Private attorneys as well as government lawyers approve of colleagues who are vigorous prosecutors. There is no particular mystery in this, since the private antitrust defense bar tends to make money when the government attacks its clients. The close relationship between the private bar and the government obviously imposes limits of its own on how the antitrust laws are enforced; but the relationship also plays a major part in protecting the division from other outside influences.

The assertion that the division has led a relatively sheltered life for a government regulatory agency now meets with less incredulity than it once did; in the past few years, the barriers to effective antitrust prosecution that some saw have been breached one by one. The division has filed some of the big monopolization cases that critics were looking for. The demands of these big cases played a large part in forcing the division to abandon its usual rule and ask for larger budget increases; it has obtained them. The Senate oversight subcommittee has been instrumental in getting passed some of the changes in law that pro-antitrust observers had wanted: penalties have been increased and investigative tools strengthened.

But these changes have not led to a sense of increased power in the organization. On the contrary, the division's success has brought it up against more fundamental challenge from less expected places. The Supreme Court has begun ruling against the organization and its congressional supporters on matters from the rights of franchisers to the question of who has standing to bring price-fixing suits. Part of the reversal doubtless comes from a change in the makeup of the Court itself; part of it seems to come from the fact that the antitrusters are asking for more than they ever have before. But it also seems influenced by another development. At the same time as it is reaching farther than it has in the past, our antitrust administration is falling into a certain disrepute. In the lower courts, the government's major monopolization suits have become palpably monstrous and have thus exposed just how enormous (and dubious) an undertaking real trustbusting might be. Among professionals, it has become impossible to avoid dealing with the view that it would be a kind of madness to pursue the antitrust enterprise any further without doing something to clear up the confusion of goals that has marred the policy in the past and often done actual harm to consumer welfare. This argument is controversial, but there is not much doubt that it is eminently respectable and that it comes from critics who are not motivated mainly by some kind of self-interested desire to defend big business. Antitrust enthusiasts can and do try to ignore it, but they cannot do so in very good conscience.

The Antitrust Division was admirably organized to protect its mixture of antitrust goals in an environment relatively indifferent to them. But it is now becoming successful enough to expose some of the inconsistencies and exaggerations that may be tolerable in a prosecutor but grave when the prosecutor's side of the case threatens to become settled public policy. It would not be surprising if division members came to feel that they had fewer problems in their obscurity than the ones that now attend their growing success.

CHAPTER 5*

Federal Trade

Commission

ROBERT A. KATZMANN

Introduction

Scarcely fifteen years ago, Richard Hofstadter wrote that "the antitrust movement is one of the faded passions of American reform."[1] Yet, he continued in his now classic essay, "the antitrust enterprise has more significance in contemporary society than it had in the days of T. R. or Wilson, or even in the heyday of Thurman Arnold."[2] While public attention has waxed and waned, antitrust has endured. Today, antitrust is once again in the public spotlight. In part, it thrives because the issues which it touches—the extent to which the state should regulate business, the nexus between corporate wealth and political influence, the effect of market concentration on economic problems—are still very much debated. Antitrust is a banner under which many march but for quite different reasons: politicians grappling with inflation; consumer groups convinced that large manufacturers charge supranormal prices; populists fearful that corporate giants corrupt the political process; businessmen threatened by the anticompetitive behavior of others; private attorneys dependent on antitrust practice as a source of income; and economists concerned with the welfare costs of monopoly and the estimated consumer gains from its elimination.

*The material in this chapter is largely adapted from parts of Robert A. Katzmann, *Regulatory Bureaucracy: The Federal Trade Commission and Antitrust Policy* (Cambridge, Mass.: MIT Press, 1980)

Federal Trade Commission

Whatever their policy objectives may be—social, political, economic —these sundry groups closely monitor the activities of those public agencies that largely set antitrust policy. This study endeavors to examine the ways in which one such agency, the Federal Trade Commission (FTC), selects cases for antitrust action.

The FTC, established in 1914, administers both antitrust and trade regulation laws. In recent years, the commission has used its broad powers to launch significant actions against major economic interests; among them the oil, breakfast foods, and document-copying industries. Such efforts have immersed the agency in controversy. In the view of its critics, at least some of the FTC's cases are "anti-business" and injurious to consumer welfare.[3] To others, the agency has not been vigorous enough; in their judgment, we need more antitrust action against large industries.[4] The debate over whether the FTC either does "too much" or "too little" raises the fundamental question of *why* the agency has pursued the kinds of antitrust cases that have characterized its enforcement effort in these past years.

Consideration of the role of the commission as an engine of antitrust policy is particularly appropriate now when politicians from all points on the political spectrum see antitrust enforcement as a major weapon in the battle against inflation. The dramatic increases in the commission's antitrust budget ($30.299 million for fiscal 1979—more than double the amount appropriated by Congress for fiscal 1975) have coincided with the mounting problems of inflation.[5] In a typical budget request, the FTC stated that:

increased commitments of antitrust resources . . . contrary to the rule generally applicable to any government expenditure—*will directly aid in the battle against high* prices.[6]

Not all commentators agree, however, that the commission is, in fact, equipped to deal with complex problems such as inflation.[7] In the aftermath of an organizational crisis in the late sixties when a wide range of persons and groups—including the American Bar Association, Ralph Nader, and President Richard Nixon—severely criticized the commission's performance, the agency engaged in major efforts to improve the quality of its caseload and its decision-making processes. Institutional reforms were implemented and there were high hopes that they would achieve their purposes.

The *Exxon* case, a suit directed against the eight major oil companies, is representative of the agency's recent attempts to pursue the "big" case by attacking structural weaknesses in the market and thereby enhancing consumer welfare. Despite its best efforts, the FTC has encountered severe difficulties in prosecuting such cases. The *Exxon* case, for example, was filed in July 1973; by 1976, some forty attorneys had been assigned to work part- or full-time on the case. Of the original staff, only one lawyer remained on the case in 1976, and only four others were still working in the Bureau of Competition. The average period of involvement of attorneys assigned to the case has been about twelve months; the case is not expected to end in the foreseeable future.[8] The turnover rate among staff attorneys assigned to such vehicles has been so high as to raise doubt about the commission's capacity to handle large structural cases.

The FTC: Its Antitrust Duties and Powers

Among its many antitrust responsibilities, derived principally from the Federal Trade Commission Act[9] and the Clayton Act,[10] the FTC is charged with preventing unfair methods of competition and unfair or deceptive acts or practices in or affecting commerce, and with forestalling mergers or acquisitions that might substantially lessen competition or tend to create a monopoly. Moreover, the commission is to prevent unscrupulous buyers from using their economic power to exact discriminatory prices from suppliers to the disadvantage of less powerful buyers and is to prohibit suppliers from securing an unfair advantage over their competitors by discriminating among buyers.[11] To these various ends, the FTC conducts investigations of alleged violations of the antitrust acts, monitors the implementation of antitrust decrees, investigates the organization, business, conduct, practices, and management of corporations engaged in commerce (except where statutorily exempted), and makes reports and recommendations to Congress.

The FTC has broad powers to fashion appropriate relief if the laws have been violated.[12] The commission may issue a cease-and-desist order prohibiting the continuation of acts judged illegal. It may seek to restore competitive conditions by mandating relief that attacks structural imperfections in the market. For example, the agency can order respondents to dispose of illegally acquired companies or make trademarks, patents, trade secrets, or expertise available to competitors at reasonable royalties—or even without royalties.

The Goals of the FTC's Antitrust Policy

The breadth of the agency's activities is in large part the product of the ambiguous language in the statutes which are the sources of the FTC's authority. What constitutes "unfair methods of competition in commerce and unfair or deceptive acts or practices in commerce" is not self-evident. To state, as does Section 7 of the Clayton Act, that a practice is unlawful when its "effect may be to substantially lessen competition or tend to create a monopoly" says little; the meaning of the phrases "may be," "substantially lessen," and "tend to create" demand definition.

The ambiguous statutory language that is now a source of confusion facilitated the 1914 passage of the Clayton Act and the FTC Act. Imprecise language permitted the legislation to secure needed support from diverse groups, each with differing and sometimes opposing views of the laws' purposes.[13] Some businessmen, for example, pressed for the legislation in the belief that the new regulatory body would restrict economic competition that threatened their interests. They thought the commission would protect business (often large corporations) rather than the consumer. Others, however, felt that the laws would bolster competition and would serve the consumer. Legislation, they argued, was needed to counteract the Supreme Court's 1911 decision that had weakened the Sherman Antitrust Act by holding illegal only "unreasonable" rather than *all* restraints on trade. There were those who believed that new legislation was required to attack monopolies in their incipiency before they could do irrevocable damage; because the Sherman Act apparently could not be invoked until after the monopoly had been created, it was deemed inadequate protection for small businesses unfairly eliminated before the law could be applied. In short, the advocates of the FTC Act and the Clayton Act represented different interests: the consumer, large corporations, and the small businessman.

President Woodrow Wilson, whose support for the measures was important, appeared to accept the many motives and purposes of the actors in the legislative debate. In the end, Congress passed both the FTC Act and the Clayton Act with comfortable majorities.

Today, unclear statutory language exacerbates the problem of determining what end (or ends) the commission should pursue and fuels the debate about the direction of the agency's antitrust policy. Antitrust could serve many purposes, some competing and others complementary. Broadly speaking, those ends are: (1) the achievement of desirable levels of economic performance by individual firms and ultimately by the economy as a whole; (2) the limitation of the power of big business; (3) the maintenance of a "fair" standard of business conduct; and (4) the nurturing of competitive market processes as an end in itself.[14]

Realization of the first goal—the achievement of desirable levels of economic performance—would presumably yield economic growth, full employment, price stability, an equitable distribution of income, efficiency, and progress.[15] Of these results, antitrust is thought to most easily affect efficiency and progressiveness.

The second goal—the limitation of the power of big business—reflects a desire to control unchecked power. This aim arises from a fear of bigness and is based on the assumption that size correlates with power, regardless of whether size is, in fact, synonymous with market control. The proponents of this goal maintain that "great industrial consolidations are inherently undesirable, regardless of their economic results."[16] Many believe that while higher prices may result from the maintenance of inefficient firms or decentralized and fragmented industries, such costs are worth bearing. Populists, in particular, champion the small independent businessman whose existence, they argue, must be preserved, lest large corporations damage the social and political fabric of the nation.

"Fair dealing," essentially a social goal, is concerned not with the existence of power, per se, but with the way in which power is wielded. Those who advocate "fair dealing" place a premium on the individual's opportunity to engage in enterprise and argue that "merit" will be determined in the free market. Fair dealing is a goal worth pursuing, its proponents contend, even if added economic benefit does not result.[17]

A final goal—promotion of competitive processes—views competition as nearly an end in itself, rather than as a means to achieve desired economic objectives. Those who stress this goal argue that self-regulating market processes are preferable to either of two main alternatives: control by government bureaucracy or by private monopolies. If the market is to remain relatively free of government regulation, then some means should be devised to place limits on "unreasonable" market power that stifles structural competition.[18]

The lack of precision in statutory language and the absence of unambiguous directives with respect to policy ends are the sources of wide discretionary authority for the FTC. The extent of this discretion is illustrated by the changes in the commission caseload that have occurred in the last several years. The agency has placed increasing emphasis on "structural" cases that are intended to attack fundamental market imperfections that facilitate anticompetitive activity among the dominant firms in an industry. Such cases, which often require the investment of considerable resources, are intended to yield substantial economic benefits—such as reductions in price levels—to the consuming public. In fiscal 1978, for example, the commission allocated 59 percent of its antitrust budget to what have been described as structural programs having to do with the energy, health care, transportation, chemical, and food industries.[19] The *Exxon* case alone has consumed 12 to 14 percent of recent agency antitrust budgets.[20] Fewer resources have been devoted to simple "conduct" cases (matters which deal with particular business practices such as discriminatory transactions on the seller's side, and not with the underlying structural conditions that might foster anticompetitive behavior), especially those that do not have purely economic objectives. Generally, conduct cases have social and political ends—for example, the preservation of small business. Indicative perhaps of the shifting emphasis in approach to antitrust enforcement has been the decrease in Robinson-Patman actions—cases the effect of which is usually to maintain small, inefficient businesses at the expense of competition. In fiscal 1976 the agency approved only 6 Robinson-Patman investigations; in 1967 the FTC had initiated 173 inquiries.[21]

Explaining Outcomes: The Conventional Wisdom

Many commentators have sought to explain the behavior of government organizations that regulate business. Some theorists maintain that bureaucracies are "rational actors" attempting to maximize organizational self-interest; bureaucrats, they contend, are motivated fundamentally by a desire to maximize budgets or power.[22] Other writers, including such unlikely allies as conservative economists,[23] populists,[24] and radical historians,[25] argue that public agencies serve the very economic interests which they are charged with regulating. One political scientist, writing specifically about the Federal Trade Commission, explains the regulatory body's caseload by focusing upon the statutes which are the sources of the agency's authority. Commission policies, he states, promote both competition and stability because the Federal Trade Commission Act and the Clayton Act enshrine these contradictory impulses.[26]

Economists who have analyzed the Antitrust Division of the Justice Department and the Federal Trade Commission commonly concentrate upon the economic determinants of antitrust activity.[27] They have attempted to explain antitrust cases by industry economic characteristics—the distribution of prosecutions will reflect the industry volume of sales, profitability, concentration, or welfare loss.

In this chapter, I will show that these accounts do not fully explain FTC behavior. The flaws in some of these studies are readily apparent. For instance, the finding that the FTC is inconsistent in its policies because of contradictory purposes embodied in the statutes does not explain how the agency allocates its resources or why the mix of cases has changed over time. This work will suggest that the determinants of antitrust activity are not necessarily or primarily economic. In many situations, in deciding whether to bring a case, the antitrust agencies are more concerned with the probability of success of the case than with its ultimate economic effects. The FTC might decide to prosecute, even though substantial economic benefits are unlikely, because the particular case provides an apt vehicle for establishing an important precedent or because of the presumed deterrence value of prosecutions.[28]

The claims that government serves the economic interests it is supposed to regulate or that agency outcomes reflect the desire of public officials to maximize power, budgets, or convenience tend to be sweeping generalizations often unsupported by evidence. Some assume that "government" is little more than a black box, the policy outcomes of which are entirely a function of the resources or environment of the agency. Others concede that internal processes may be important, but in explaining them assume that all members of the organization have a simple—even identical—set of motives: personal interest, usually portrayed in pecuniary terms. To assess such views, it is important to examine the actual operations of government organizations.[29]

Antitrust Decision-making in the FTC

Organizational arrangements have much to do with determining how power is distributed among participants in the decision-making process, the manner in which information is gathered, the types of data that are collected, the kinds of policy issues which are discussed, the choices which are made, and the way in which decisions are implemented. The various professional norms and personal objectives of the actors—executives, managers, and operators—also affect the decisions of organizations. Moreover, external actors who are obligated to interact with the agency or are touched by its decisions—the president, the Office of Management and Budget, congressional committees, congressmen, public-interest groups, and representatives of private interests—may also influence decisions.

In explaining how the FTC chooses its caseload and why the agency has had problems in prosecuting the "big" structural case, I will argue that in the period studied—1970–76—the caseload of the commission was largely the product of the interaction between two bureaus and the five commissioners.[30] These two bureaus, the Bureau of Competition (the lawyers' unit) and the Bureau of Economics (the economists' unit), were separate and coequal. Each bureau had its own conception of the antitrust goals and cases that the agency should pursue. One bureau competed with the other for commission approval of its viewpoint.

The Bureau of Competition

The Bureau of Competition (the lawyers' unit) is led by a bureau director who is appointed by the chairman, with the approval of a majority of the other commissioners. He directs a staff of some 200 lawyers.[31]

Of all agency decision-makers, with the possible exception of the FTC chairman, the bureau director exerts the most influence. His authority to intervene at every stage of an investigation provides him with many opportunities to affect the course of events. Without the bureau director's approval, resources cannot be allocated to an investigation. An agency official remarked, "The ultimate decision directly or indirectly, is for the bureau director based on the best advice that he can get from the staff."[32] Besides determining whether to open or close an investigation, he can leave his imprint on the caseload by choosing the theory, strategy, and tactics the assistant directors are to follow.

Limitations of time prevent the bureau director from personally overseeing every aspect of each case; he must depend on his assistant directors to supervise most of the investigational activity. Each assistant director directs between twenty and thirty attorneys. His influence results, in part, from his control of data which flow through his office. He reviews "mailbag complaints" (letters from lawyers, businessmen, public-interest groups, and congressmen charging violations of anti-trust laws) that the Office of Evaluation has distributed for examination; he can assess correspondence sent to staff lawyers; he criticizes the work of his lawyers; he edits memoranda directed to the bureau director and commissioners; and he conveys the views of the bureau director to the staff, who in turn communicate through the assistant director to the bureau director. His role extends beyond particular cases; in the process of training young attorneys, he can affect their views about antitrust enforcement. Finally, the bureau director, who needs the cooperation of the assistant directors to achieve his ends, usually considers their opinions and seeks to anticipate their reactions to his policy decisions.

An Office of Evaluation screens incoming correspondence and dis-tributes information to bureau executives. In the period studied, an assistant director for evaluation and four full-time attorneys staffed the office. The assistant director prepares the budget justification, super-vises resource expenditure, and monitors the workload. With the aid of his staff, he drafts comments dealing with proposed and existing legisla-tion and regulations. Moreover, he serves as a liaison with other govern-ment agencies involved in antitrust matters. Finally, he aids the bureau director in generating antitrust initiatives for consideration by the Eval-uation Committee and Merger Screening Committee.

The Office of Evaluation examines "mailbag" correspondence that alleges violations of the antitrust laws. These complaints come from competitors of the firm accused of illegal conduct, financial newspapers, trade journals, congressmen, concerned citizens, and lawyers repre-senting the complainants.[33] If the complaint is related to a current case, then the Office of Evaluation directs it to the appropriate attorney. If a new matter, the Office of Evaluation will review it. The great majority of "mailbag" complaints do not involve antitrust violations; thus, the Office of Evaluation responds by explaining why the FTC cannot take jurisdiction over the matter. But some complaints appear to have sub-stance.

For these, an attorney will conduct a "pre-preliminary" investigation involving several hours of library research. He will check standard public sources in order to learn about such industry indicators as concentration ratios, profitability rates, sales volume, and barriers to entry. If the lawyer determines that competitive conditions may be absent and if the assistant director for evaluation agrees, then the Office of Evaluation will put the matter on the next Evaluation Committee agenda for the bureau director and other officials to determine whether to open an in-depth investigation.

The Office of Evaluation handles merger cases (the bailiwick of the Merger Screening Committee) separately from other antitrust matters. A small group of economists attached to the Office of Evaluation and the Merger Screening Committee gathers information about possible merger cases from five general sources: *The Wall Street Journal,* Standard Corporation Reports, the Standard Industrial Classification system (SIC), *Moody's,* and *Standard and Poor's.* Law firms, representing clients in competition with firms that plan to unite, usually contact the commission about the impending merger. Moreover, the law requires that in some circumstances acquiring firms inform the FTC of planned acquisitions.[34] Each week, the economist who heads the merger study unit compiles the "Merger Information Sheets," "Special Report" forms, and other data that are distributed to the Merger Screening Committee.

Once the Office of Evaluation has completed its preparatory work in merger and other kinds of antitrust cases, the two decision-making bodies that it serves—the Merger Screening Committee and the Evaluation Committee—are ready to deliberate.

The Merger Screening Committee consists of the director of the Bureau of Competition, the assistant director for evaluation, a staff attorney experienced in merger affairs, the assistant director for economic evidence, and the economists of the Merger Screening Unit. As a general rule, the committee will not authorize investigation of a merger that does not meet a minimum figure for industry. For those mergers that are investigated, the lawyers and economists examine certain standard economic features. If the merger would probably create impenetrable barriers to entry (the merged firms could effectively prevent entrants), then the economists and lawyers will recommend a formal investigation or the issuance of a complaint. The application of evaluation criteria will vary depending upon the type of merger: vertical, horizontal, product extension, or market extension.

The Evaluation Committee must approve all investigations. It includes the director of the Bureau of Competition, his assistant directors, the bureau's liaison with the Antitrust Division, the deputy director of the Bureau of Economics, and the assistant director for economic evidence. The last two officials make a special effort to examine all matters which will be discussed at Evaluation Committee deliberations.

The tenor of the meeting largely reflects the personality of the director of the Bureau of Competition who may or may not encourage the participation of assistant directors at Evaluation Committee meetings. Evaluation Committee meetings can be essentially bargaining and strategy sessions in which the bureau director of Competition and the assistant director for Economic Evidence of the Bureau of Economics are the main participants.

The topics of discussion are varied: whether to open a preliminary or formal investigation, whether to ask the commissioners to grant compulsory process or approve an industry-wide investigation, or how to respond to a letter from an influential congressman. Preliminary investigations are "short, informal inquiries, conducted to dispose of relatively minor matters and to determine whether formal 7-digit investigations should be initiated."[35] Preliminary investigations will be initiated "when and only when" research and investigative efforts conducted with regard to such circumstances are expected to exceed an aggregate of sixteen manhours (that is, two man-days).[36] The bureau director may approve the opening of the preliminary investigation only after consultation with officials of the Antitrust Division of the Department of Justice to ensure that the commission and the Antitrust Division do not duplicate each other's work.

Formal investigations (also known as "7-digit" investigations because their file numbers have seven digits) are comprehensive inquiries into possible violations of the laws which the commission is charged with enforcing. These investigations involve a greater expenditure of commission resources than do preliminary investigations. In addition, the authorization of a formal investigation is a procedural prerequisite for a grant by the commissioners of Bureau of Competition requests for the use of compulsory process, special investigatory reports (known as "6(b)" reports), subpoenas, and investigational resolutions.

Policy Choices: The "Reactive" and the "Proactive" Approaches

Because the commission does not have unlimited resources, the Bureau of Competition cannot pursue every apparent infraction; rather, bureau executives must choose among cases. In recommending the issuance of a complaint, they are required by commission law not only to find that "there is reason to believe" that the law has been violated, but also that action would be in the "public interest." There has been much discussion among commission officials and other interested parties as to what kinds of antitrust policies would be in the "public interest"—a term which, being vague, does not mandate that the agency pursue any particular course. In the view of public-interest groups, the commission should devote more of its resources to structural attacks on oligopolies and shared monopolies. However, others (large corporations, for example) believe that such a policy emphasis could injure the economy. In determining what constitutes action in the "public interest," commission officials are setting a course with important implications for public policy.

Debate within the commission about the kinds of cases that would be in the "public interest" has centered on two different conceptions of antitrust policy: a "reactive" and a "proactive" approach. The former approach relies upon the mailbag (that is, upon the letters of complaint that the Bureau of Competition receives) as the source of investigations focusing on illegal practices. The latter perspective is based on the view that the Bureau of Competition should not merely react to the complaints that are directed to the Commission, but should assume the initiative and use its scarce resources selectively to attack abuses in those sectors of the economy that most affect the consumer. The "proactive" perspective leads to a caseload of (often) ambitious and innovative structural matters designed to reduce market power. Quite clearly, the consequences of each approach differ quite dramatically.[37]

Supporters of the "reactive" approach maintain that a decision not to pursue every apparent violation of the law that is reported to Bureau of Competition attorneys, no matter how minor the infraction might seem, is nothing less than an abdication of responsibility. They claim that dependence on the mailbag as a source for antitrust investigations has distinct advantages. The mailbag usually produces "conduct" cases which are easier to prosecute than are complex structural matters, because they focus on the practices of the firms. Thus, all that is essentially needed in court is evidence that the defendants actually engaged in the prohibited acts (for example, price fixing, tying contracts). A big structural case of the proactive kind is far more difficult, so its detractors argue, because it is concerned not so much with the acts themselves as it is with the fundamental economic imperfections (for instance, an anticompetitive market structure on the buying side, the selling side, or both) of which the various aspects of business conduct are merely symptoms. They contend that even if it is conceded that "big" structural cases could have substantial consumer benefit, it cannot be denied that such cases are difficult to prosecute: they are expensive, technically complex, and uncertain of success. (Most innovative structural cases involve legal theories which have yet to be tested in the judiciary.) Attorneys who are convinced that their advancement depends on the securing of trial experience resist assignment to structural matters, since they generally do not reach the courtroom for several years. Those attorneys who are chosen for such cases quickly become disillusioned and try to disengage themselves. As a result, the turnover rate among attorneys on these cases is very high.

Moreover, the proponents of the "reactive" approach are not confident that the supposed economic benefits will flow from the mammoth structural cases. They claim that by the time that the case is finally resolved, market conditions in the particular industry may have changed so dramatically as to render the original remedy inappropriate. Thus the commission may spend years and millions of dollars without achieving substantial results.

Defenders of the "reactive" approach believe that the same problems associated with prosecuting the big structural case beset the commission when pursuing "industry-wide" investigations. The source of such inquiries is not the mailbag, but the Consumer Price Index and other economic surveys. The commission targets for investigation those industries that are highly concentrated. The scope of the investigation is wide: the commission will delve into the practices of numerous firms at all levels of operation. Even firms that have not been the object of consumer and business complaints will be investigated if their market shares and profitability are unusually high. Such investigations are fraught with problems. There is a tendency in industry-wide investigations, so the argument proceeds, to "go on fishing expeditions" in order to uncover violations which will justify the substantial resources devoted to such inquiries. Since Congress (the source of the agency's funding) is thought to measure commission performance in antitrust enforcement largely in terms of the number of cases and investigations that are underway, bureau officials may feel some pressure to "manufacture" cases. Industry-wide investigations pose special risks because they are announced with great fanfare.[38]

The proponents of the reactive approach deny that there is little consumer benefit resulting from conduct cases. For example, predatory or exclusionary practices and merger activity could conceivably change the structure of an industry, transforming a competitive structure into a monopolistic or oligopolistic structure. Thus, by attacking conduct violations, the commission could preserve structural competition. In any event, for most "reactive" approach supporters, the antitrust statutes are concerned primarily with achieving fairness in the marketplace and not consumer benefit. Not surprisingly, many are vigorous advocates of those sections of the Robinson-Patman Act that seek to protect small businesses.

Most of the Bureau of Competition executives—including the director of the bureau—maintain that attention must be given to the planning and evaluation of antitrust efforts. As one official stated:

We simply do not have the resources to fully investigate every possible violation of the law which we learn about. Accordingly, we must constantly make hard choices among alternatives in order to maximize the effect of our enforcement activity.[39]

Advocates of planning in antitrust enforcement are critical of a reactive, ad hoc approach because they believe it wasteful of commission resources. In order to create a balance among the various kinds of antitrust matters and to free the case-selection process of the biases of decision makers, bureau officials created an Evaluation Committee case-selection process in 1972.[40]

Proponents of the proactive approach do not suggest that the mailbag should be ignored; the bureau should closely monitor the mailbag but use it as an "early warning system" (an indicator of possible problem areas). Some reactive cases are valuable, a former bureau director noted, because of their deterrent effect.[41] But, he continued, an enforcement effort which reacts only to specific problems flowing from the mailbag, and which fails to develop broad enforcement plans can only be ineffective.

Advocates of antitrust planning assume that conduct cases have less value to the consumer than do structural prosecutions. Though certain business practices are "unfair" and illegal, they are incapable of altering the structural competition of the industry since they are the products and not the causes of market imperfections that lead to the anticompetitive behavior. While prosecutions would probably succeed in halting the particular practice, they would not deal with the real source of competitive problems (market or financial power) and thus would not restore competition. It may be necessary to analyze the source of power that allows predatory and unfair practices to continue. Having undertaken a structural examination, the staff attorneys may then be able to fashion relief that attacks market power at its root.

165

ROBERT A. KATZMANN

Supporters of the proactive perspective freely admit that big structural cases and industry-wide investigations are more difficult to prosecute than are most conduct violations. Yet the need to attempt such cases is strongly felt among many of the bureau executives. They explain that whether the courts or the commissioners will accept their arguments will never be known unless such cases are attempted.

An analysis of the caseload indicates that the agency has decided to devote more of its resources to what are essentially planned efforts. Reactive cases—especially of the Robinson-Patman variety—command far less attention from the commission than they did a decade ago. Why the commission, given its apparent discretion, does not devote all of its resources to proactive investigations is not immediately obvious. The following sections explain the factors that bear on the case-selection process and thus affect the way in which resources are allocated between proactive and reactive cases. The character of the caseload—the kinds of actions undertaken—can, in some sense, be understood as reflecting the views expressed in the debate between advocates of the two approaches to antitrust enforcement.

Professional Economists and the Caseload: The Impact of the Bureau of Economics

To open an investigation or to recommend that the commissioners issue a complaint, the director of the Bureau of Competition need only decide if there is reason to believe that the law has been violated and that commission action would be in the public interest. In reaching his decision, however, he considers other factors, one variable being the reaction of the Bureau of Economics to his bureau's recommendation. Though the Operating Manual (at least during the period studied) and the Rules and Practices of the Commission did not define a formal role for the Bureau of Economics in the case-selection process (indeed, on no organization chart was there an Evaluation Committee), it is clear that the competition between lawyers and economists often significantly affects and sometimes even determines the definition of antitrust activity. Thus it is important to examine the impact of the Bureau of Economics.

The Bureau of Economics advises the commission on broad policy questions, such as those having to do with suspect business practices and relationships, the evaluation of proposed remedies, and the formulation of legislative recommendations. The Division of Economic Evidence of the Bureau of Economics has a number of opportunities to intervene in the case-selection process: when the director of the Bureau of Competition is deciding whether to open an investigation, he will seek the judgment of the assistant director for economic evidence of the Bureau of Economics; during the course of an investigation, economists, upon the request of the Bureau of Competition, will work with the attorneys; and when the Bureau of Competition has completed its investigation and makes its recommendation to the commissioners, the economists can set forth their own views in support of—or in opposition to—the lawyers' position.

The key member of the Bureau of Economics in the case-selection process is the assistant director for the Division of Economic Evidence. Though formally under the direction of the director and the deputy director of the Bureau of Economics, he is "responsible for *all* economic work of the Commission relating to legal cases involving unlawful corporate mergers and other violations."[42] In addition, he "exercises wide discretion in planning, organizing and directing the economic investigation and analysis of legal cases."[43] He also controls the assignments of cases to the division's forty staff members, guides the staff on matters of policy and economic strategy, and scrutinizes the staff's reports and recommendations in order to insure that they are consistent with agency policy. He is also responsible for training the division staff, evaluating their performance, and recommending promotions. Finally, as the Bureau's spokesman and decision maker in antitrust matters, the assistant director for the Division of Economic Evidence is in frequent contact with the director of the Bureau of Competition.

Nearly all of the more recent economists in the FTC have passed their Ph.D. preliminary examinations;[44] approximately half have completed dissertations. With but a few exceptions, they stated that they did not originally intend to work for the government upon completing their graduate school courses. Their ambition was to become college professors, not government employees. The prospects of academic careers dimmed with the tightening job market. To be sure, there were some economists who were disenchanted with academic life or who simply desired some government experience. For these people, a commission post was a welcome opportunity and not a last resort. For the most part, however, the Division of Economic Evidence economist is on the government payroll because he was unable to secure an attractive academic position.

The staff is drawn from a score of institutions, most of which are generally described as satellites of the University of Chicago, a school whose economists tend to have a deep faith in an unfettered market. In order to qualify for a staff position, the economist has to be well trained in microeconomics. The Bureau of Economics executives prefer the candidate who has mastered some facet of industrial organization or whose specialty is related to commission activities (for example, in the health or energy fields).

Although most of the recent recruits were originally uncertain about their future in government service, few regret having joined the Bureau of Economics. The material benefits the agency provides are far superior to those of academia. Moreover, the typical staff economist has remained with the Bureau of Economics because it satisfies many of his professional interests. For the economist who sought a university life, the Division of Economic Evidence's think-tank environment provides an atmosphere that is conducive to scholarly pursuits.

The assistant director for economic evidence has successfully maintained a high level of morale by fostering an environment which stresses professional competence. He encourages the economists to think of themselves not as subordinates of the attorneys in antitrust cases, but as independent decision-makers. "Attorneys and economists are each housed in separate buildings about a mile and a half apart, and that's the way we want it," commented one economist.

At whatever point they are involved in the decision-making process, the economists who are participants in case selection matters believe that it is the responsibility of their unit to render advice based on economic principles.[45] It is their task to determine whether the business behavior under scrutiny is anticompetitive or otherwise results in a misallocation of resources. What the law says should be of no concern to the Division of Economic Evidence, the assistant director and deputy director of the Bureau of Economics claim.

With the exception of a few veterans, the staff economists expressed their unwillingness to take orders from attorneys or undertake the same kinds of investigative tasks which the attorneys perform: fact finding, data gathering, and the reviewing of company records. Economists are willing to participate in investigations if they are given a role that preserves their sense of autonomy. For example, many economists are willing to formulate questions to be asked of industry officials at investigational hearings and to help compose questionnaires that deal with economic matters. They may find it necessary to become involved in commission investigations because they do not have enough information about the industry or because a deeper understanding of the industry under investigation could aid the economist in designing and evaluating appropriate remedial measures. In some recent significant cases, the economists played a primary role in constructing antitrust relief.

168

Many of the economists in the division—those who have joined the commission since its revitalization—tend to be convinced that without their presence the agency would engage in what they perceive to be a dangerous and relentless assault on American business. (The more senior colleagues have greater sympathy for a governmental role in solving social and economic problems.) "We are saviors of the free market, contending against forces bent on government intervention," exclaimed one typical young economist. For the economists, there is nothing more gratifying than to oppose the Bureau of Competition successfully at the commission table. (The conservative cast of the Division of Economic Evidence may change: Chairman Michael Pertschuk, who took office in 1977, has criticized recent commissions for uncritically accepting the positions of the "Chicago school." How his views will affect recruitment remains to be seen.)

The economists are opposed to most conduct cases, principally because there is often little consumer benefit to be gained from the prosecution of such matters. They also generally disapprove of Bureau of Competition efforts which are directed against vertical and conglomerate mergers, franchise arrangements, tying requirements, (under which the seller of product X compels his purchasers to buy product Y as well, thereby foreclosing competition from other sellers of the tied commodity Y,) and price discrimination cases (Robinson-Patman matters) on the grounds that such actions do little to maintain vigorous competition. Economists particularly dislike the Robinson-Patman Act matters favored by attorneys who support the "reactive" approach.[46] "You could put all pro-Robinson-Patman economists in a Volkswagen and still have room for a chauffeur," commented a Bureau of Economics official.

Given the limited resources of the FTC, the executives of the Bureau of Economics believe that energies should be devoted to those cases that will most benefit consumers. While supporting the structural case and a "proactive" approach to enforcement activity, the assistant director for economic evidence was quick to emphasize that there are only a few areas of the economy which merit commission attention. Along with most of his staff, he was unsympathetic to the notion that governmental solutions to social and economic problems are more effective than reliance upon the market mechanism.

The attorneys in the Bureau of Competition contend that the opposition of the Bureau of Economics to their cases is often unfounded. Several attorneys recounted cases in which intensive fact-finding efforts revealed that the economists had drawn groundless conclusions. Even when they carefully analyze the data which the attorneys have collected, the economists tend to interpret the information in a manner that argues against government action.[47] Thus, the attorneys and economists draw opposite conclusions from the same data. The zones of dispute involve a number of areas: market definitions, concentration ratios, conditions of entry, performance and policy preferences.[48]

Both the economist and the lawyer search for information relating to market power and market performance. Market power can be defined as the "possession by a firm (or group of firms acting jointly) of the ability to behave over fairly long periods of time in a way different from the way a firm in the economist's model of a competitive market facing the same cost and demand conditions would be forced to behave by the pressures of competition."[49] Defining the relevant market is a prerequisite for determining the degree of market concentration.

The staff attorney is inclined to include fewer buyers and sellers in his definition of the relevant market since the higher the concentration ratio, the greater the presumption that the market is not workably competitive. The staff economist is less likely to define the market narrowly or to limit the number of product substitutes (or near substitutes). By including a wider range of substitutes, the concentration ratios of the firms under investigation are thereby reduced.

Economists are more likely than lawyers to find justifications for high concentration, which may result not from anticompetitive behavior, but from a high degree of technical expertise that only a few firms possess, a dying industry that can support only a few firms, high economies of scale, or a young industry that has not yet attracted entry by many companies.

The market power of imperfect competitors may be temporary if other firms can penetrate their markets, take sales away from them, and thereby restore competition.[50] Whether these firms will be able to enter the market depends largely upon the height of the barriers to entry.[51] When lawyers and economists differ about conditions of entry, it is usually the latter who argue that no significant barriers to entry exist that could hinder competition. Because easy entry would make it difficult or impossible for the firms under investigation to impose losses upon consumers, antitrust action in such a situation would yield little or no benefit to the public.

Assessing the workability of competition is not always an easy task for attorney and economist. For any of the measures of unworkable competition—abnormally high profits, excessive selling costs, chronic excess capacity, the absence of progress—the economist and lawyer must make a number of judgments. When are costs "excessive"? When are profits supranormal? When are scales seriously outside the optimal range? What is the optimal range?[52] In making these assessments, the economist is more likely than the staff attorney to argue that workable competition exists.

The economists will oppose the issuance of a complaint, not only when they believe that the attorneys have failed to demonstrate that the market is not functioning properly, but also when they are convinced that antitrust action would interfere with the achievement of policy objectives which they deem desirable. An especially illustrative case involved the linkage of an investigation of natural gas reserves reporting methods and the policy debate about natural gas deregulation.

After a four-and-one-half-year investigation, the Bureau of Competition charged that the American Gas Association and eleven producers had deliberately underreported gas reserves in order to obtain higher wellhead prices from the Federal Power Commission. The bureau urged the commissioners to issue a complaint. The economists, however, who were forceful advocates of natural gas deregulation, argued that commission action would be ill-advised:

If the FTC were to issue a complaint at this point, it would surely cloud the public policy debate on regulation which is presently taking place. Supporters of continued regulation would be able to point to the complaint as proof that the natural gas shortage was a contrivance of the producers. . . . The result might be continued FPC [Federal Power Commission] regulation into the distant future. At a time when the FTC at the insistence of its Chairman is engaging in a thoughtful review of the efficacy of various regulatory institutions, the FTC might be taking steps which would entrench one of those institutions.[53]

Quite naturally, the attorneys do not look favorably upon the economists' opposing positions. They accuse the economists of "God-playing," of making assumptions which have no basis in reality. Stated one Bureau of Competition assistant director: "They're dogmatic, they make all kinds of inferences, but are unwilling to roll up their sleeves and do some investigating to see whether there are facts to support those inferences."* In focusing on economic performance, the assistant directors charge that the Bureau of Economics cares little about the language of congressional intent, judicial opinion, or antitrust laws. The economists are viewed by many as conservative ideologues who are

*All quoted material not otherwise referenced is drawn from interviews conducted by the author.

hostile to government intervention in the economy. Rather than support the Bureau of Competition in its efforts to prosecute violation, the economists are accused of being "case-killers."

In part, disputes between lawyer and economist arise because of legitimate differences about the way in which data should be interpreted. Often, the complexities of the industries under investigation are so enormous that it is difficult to determine the effect that each of a multitude of factors might have on the market. In addition, the standards of reference of the lawyer and economist are not the same: the economist is not concerned with legal criteria when making case-selection recommendations.

More fundamentally, however, disagreements between the Bureau of Competition and the Bureau of Economics exist because lawyers and economists have different professional norms and personal goals. By training, the economist is wary of interference with the market mechanism; as has been noted, he believes his task is to prevent what he perceives to be unwarranted government action. To the extent that he uncritically sanctions such intervention, his professional prestige and career advancement are likely to suffer.

In contrast to the economist, the lawyer, because of his professional training, is prosecution-minded; he believes that his career prospects depend upon his securing trial experience. Thus, the attorney views the economists who oppose cases that could reach the trial stage within a brief period of time as obstacles to the realization of professional rewards.

Ultimately, it is the commissioners who decide whether a complaint should issue, not the Bureau of Economics. Whatever influence that economists have in the case-selection process is largely a function of their ability to secure the support of a majority of the commissioners. The Bureau of Competition is likely to be especially solicitous of the economists' judgment when the Bureau of Economics' recommendations prevail at the commission table; for if the lawyers lose to the economists, then the credibility of bureau executives suffers—hardly a happy effect for attorneys eager to impress their constituency (for example, the private bar). Indeed, the Evaluation Committee was created in part so that Bureau of Competition could learn of the economists' perspectives early in the decision-making process. Should the economists strongly oppose a proposal to open a formal or preliminary investigation, then the lawyers might decide not to pursue the matter, knowing that someday the economists might succeed in dissuading the commissioners from issuing a complaint.

Federal Trade Commission

Executives of the Bureau of Competition also sought the views of the economists because they realized that complex cases that might benefit the consumer could not be prosecuted without substantial economic input. As a result of the regular exchange of ideas between the two bureaus, the economists were able to convince many of the assistant directors of the need for innovative structural cases and planning in antitrust enforcement.

Thus, the increasing emphasis on structural cases is in many ways attributable to the influence of Bureau of Economics' economists who have argued that the commission should shift its attention from conduct actions to matters that could yield substantial economic benefits to the consumer. Moreover, the certainty of an independent evaluation by the Bureau of Economics has forced the Bureau of Competition to give careful thought to the proposals for investigations. Institutionalized conflict between the two bureaus has probably resulted in more enlightened decisions. As Harry Garfield, a former assistant director for evaluation of the Bureau of Competition, stated in 1975:

While there are many instances where there have been disagreements between economists and lawyers, one of the great improvements that has come about at the Commission is the increased cooperation between the two Bureaus. . . . This does not mean, however, that the Bureau of Economics dictates what cases shall be opened or closed or that the analysis of the economists is the whole determinant of such actions. . . . But it is obvious to anyone who has lived with the Commission in recent years that the Bureau of Economics has a profound influence in the ultimate determinations of what cases shall be brought and what matters shall be investigated.[54]

Attorney Tasks, Expertise, and the Case-Selection Process

In the abstract, it would seem that Bureau of Competition executives could easily make case decisions without interference from the staff attorneys. The latter do not have the authority to open investigations, nor do they routinely have access to all the complaints that the Bureau of Competition receives. Even when they learn of a possible violation of the law, staff attorneys are not free to devote time to the matter without an assistant director's approval. It is the Evaluation Office that first sifts information about possible illegal activity, the assistant director who assigns staff to undertake a pre-preliminary investigation, and the bureau director (with the aid of the Evaluation Committee) who decides whether to approve a preliminary or formal investigation or a recommendation that the commission should issue a complaint.

Yet, however much his superiors constrain him, the attorney, because of the limits of his expertise and experience, affects the kinds of enforcement actions that the Bureau of Competition can undertake. The skills and level of expertise demanded of an antitrust lawyer depend on the nature of the case. In the simplest conduct cases, the attorney need only possess a basic understanding of the antitrust laws. In the conventional merger case, he generally need concern himself only with standard economic data and established legal criteria.

The more complex cases—particularly the mammoth structural matters and industry-wide investigations—may present the attorney with great difficulties. He must devote much of his time to gathering data on concentration ratios, profitability, barriers to entry, the structure of the industry and business practices—in short, on all of the key areas involved in antitrust prosecutions. Such information is not always readily available; it may take months or even years of dedicated inquiry. Attorneys make use of a variety of techniques to obtain information: for example, subpoenas, investigational hearings (at which company officials may be called to testify), and questionnaires. The lawyers must have the ability to determine the order in which witnesses should be called at investigational hearings, be crafty interrogators, and be able to orchestrate events in an effort to pressure the companies to respond to agency demands.

Once the attorneys have gathered their data, they must write a memorandum to the assistant director and the bureau director stating their views about the course the bureau should follow. When they are dealing with complex structural investigations, attorneys should have a basic understanding of economics. Their ability to write a sound memorandum depends upon their capacity to relate their information to legal and economic concepts.

Thus, a key resource affecting a decision to open a "big" case is the availability of attorneys who have the requisite experience and expertise. One bureau official commented:

The staff attorney makes or breaks an investigation. Before we can do anything, we have to assess the skills and reactions of the staff. You can't have a caseload consisting totally of complicated matters if you don't have a staff which is sophisticated in gathering data or that doesn't know about the complexities and structural characteristics of an industry. It is *we* who often feel powerless.

To the extent that there is a shortage of attorneys with the skills required to guide an investigation in the precomplaint stages to its completion, the bureau will have difficulty pursuing complex cases.

Case Selection and Organizational Maintenance

The commission has had problems retaining an experienced staff. Judged in terms of turnover rate—a basic measure of the extent to which the executive has managed to secure resources and some degree of contributive effort from staff attorneys over a period of time—the organizational maintenance problems faced by Bureau of Competition officials are severe. Since 1970, the annual turnover rate has ranged from 13 percent to 25 percent; of those attorneys who leave each year, 90 percent have had tenure of four years or less; at the end of fiscal 1976, there were only 20 attorneys of a total of almost 200 whose service dated from 1969. Over 89 percent of all attorneys who joined the commission in the period 1972–75 expected (in July 1976) to leave within two years.[55]

While most of the recent recruits joined the commission because they were interested in antitrust law, only a small minority views the agency as a permanent employer. This minority is sympathetic to populist ideals and believes that the government should curb corporate "power." These attorneys would never consider working for any organization except a governmental agency or a public-interest group. However, the overwhelming majority of Bureau of Competition recruits entered commission service with the intention of leaving within four or five years. For them, government employment offered the opportunity to gain responsibility and experience at a far earlier time in their careers than would have been possible had they first joined a private law firm or corporation.

Above all else, the staff attorney wants to secure trial experience. He is prosecution-minded. He does not believe that he can consider himself to be a consummate lawyer until he has argued a case in a courtroom. The typical staff lawyer is eager for trial work because he thinks that private law firms will not be interested in him unless he has courtroom experience. He has visions of facing the counsel of a distinguished law firm, of impressing him with his wit and expertise, and of ultimately securing employment in the private bar. After gaining experience and obtaining the offer of private employment, he expects to leave the commission. Statistics indicate that those attorneys who joined the FTC with the intention of leaving within a few years have followed to their plans.[56]

For the bureau director who would hope to prosecute protracted structural matters, the high turnover rate poses great obstacles to undertaking ambitious cases. The prosecution of complex matters, requiring years of cooperative effort, is especially difficult when the staff attorneys cannot be induced to remain with the commission for more than a short period of time. As then Director of the Bureau of Competition, Owen Johnson, recently noted:

A lot can be lost, in substance and strategy, each time a new group of attorneys takes over the prosecution of an oligopoly case such as *Cereal* or *Exxon.* We are becoming reconciled to the inevitability of substantial turnover in such litigation. We have noticed that when the case is in its early stages—fighting off motions to dismiss and other "legal" or "jurisdictional" motions—staff morale is usually high and turnover low. Attorneys like these skirmishes. When the case moves into document discovery and depositions, morale drops and staff suffers attrition. *Exxon* is presently in that stage.[57]

As Johnson suggests, the high turnover rate is costly in several respects. Every time a qualified attorney leaves the agency, the commission has lost its investment. The Bureau of Competition must continually devote resources to training new recruits replacing those lawyers who have left the FTC. The brief tenure of most attorneys means that few lawyers have the expertise or experience needed to prosecute complex cases. Those who do acquire the requisite skills do not remain with the FTC for long.

Given the Bureau of Competition's difficulties in retaining its staff, it is understandable that the bureau director will seek to induce lawyers to remain by assigning them to cases that may satisfy their perceived needs.[58] It is perhaps inevitable that the bureau director, regardless of his preference for the large structural case and industry-wide investigations or his desire to secure the goodwill of the Bureau of Economics, will approve the opening of a number of easily prosecuted matters, that conceivably could have little value to the consumer. (To be sure, there are simple conduct matters that *do* yield economic benefits.)

Prosecution of more conventional antitrust cases may also be essential to the meeting of the expectations of those few experienced trial attorneys, without whom the commission would find it difficult to win cases and train young lawyers. In the course of interviewing, it was apparent that the senior men intensely disliked the industry-wide investigations and the more innovative structural cases. Recognizing the aversion of the more experienced attorneys to the ambitious structural matters, an assistant director stated:

If we eliminated the conduct cases, the Robinson-Patman matters and the more conventional merger cases from the menu of cases, we might find ourselves without any experienced trial attorneys. If they left, who would train our newcomers? Who would we rely upon to win cases? As it is, we have a severe shortage of experienced, talented senior men.

The Federal Trade Commission has often been criticized for prosecuting "worthless" cases of little economic value and for not vigorously attacking structural imperfections in the economy. Critics of the commission seem not to realize that the allocation of resources to investigations whose potential value to the consumer is minimal may be an inevitable cost of maintaining and developing the skill of the attorneys.

But assigning attorneys to relatively simple cases that may reach the courtroom is not likely to solve the FTC's chronic turnover problems. Although there is evidence that the morale and turnover problems lessen once the cases reach trial,[59] the rub is that years often pass before the matter moves to the courtroom.[60] By the time the case enters the courtroom (if it does at all), the original team of attorneys (and most probably several other sets of later teams) will almost certainly have left the agency. There does not seem much that the government can do to retain the most promising of the staff short of raising their salaries to the high levels that private firms and corporations offer.

The problems in prosecuting complex cases point to the difficulty of accurately predicting the effects of institutional reform. The shift in emphasis from the "reactive" to the "proactive" approach to antitrust enforcement was engineered by a new FTC leadership of the early 1970s, consisting of dedicated chairmen and bureau executives, who felt strongly that the agency should devote resources to investigations that could benefit the consumer. As I have described elsewhere, FTC officials acted at a time in the early 1970s when the political climate was favorable.[61] The pressure for change came from within and from without the agency; a consensus existed across the political spectrum that the commission of the 1960s had performed poorly. The new leadership proceeded swiftly; they installed mechanisms that centralized control of caseload decisions in the chairmen and top bureau officials and rid the agency of incompetent personnel. For the new administration, for those who wrote the ABA Commission's study of the FTC,[62] as well as for Ralph Nader and his associates whose report[63] called attention to the agency's ills, it seemed clear in 1969 and 1970 that a concerted effort to upgrade the recruitment system would have to be made. They correctly understood that the FTC could not hope to prosecute complex matters without attorneys of high caliber. Most staff attorneys in 1969 did not have the skills to pursue complex structural cases, and many did not have the inclination to investigate any but the simplest conduct cases.

Yet, while the commission of recent years has attracted graduates of the best schools, the difficulties in prosecuting big structural matters remain, largely because of the high turnover rate among its most promising attorneys. Nearly all of those who criticized the commission of the 1960s and offered prescriptions assumed wrongly that the consumer movement would produce enough talented young attorneys in the years ahead to work on the challenging structural cases. Most analysts neglected to consider the possibility that the public-interest fervor of the late 1960s would not continue indefinitely or that the staff lawyer might be concerned not so much with the social or economic benefits of structural litigation as he would be with securing trial experience that would make him attractive to the private bar.[64] At the time, commission critics (both from within and without the agency) did not foresee that by the mid-1970s, the typical young recruit would not join because of a commitment to public service and that he would have every incentive to resist assignment to the complex investigations, which offered little prospect of immediate courtroom exposure. In short, they did not consider how the goals of the personnel within the agency might constrain an organization in the pursuit of objectives, however worthwhile.

The Role of the Commissioners

Ultimately, the five commissioners are charged with making policy. They allocate resources among the various kinds of cases, determine whether a complaint should issue, promulgate rules and guidelines, and review the decisions of administrative law judges. In theory, they are to lead; the bureaus are to respond to the policy directives of the commissioners.

Though each commissioner casts an equal vote in determining whether a complaint should issue, whether compulsory process is in order, if a consent decree settlement is acceptable, the manner in which an appeal should be resolved, or how commission resources should be allocated, the chairman has a far greater impact on the caseload than his colleagues. While, more often than not, the other commissioners find themselves reacting to what the Bureau of Competition and the Bureau of Economics have done, the chairman can make the staff attorneys and economists respond to his policy preferences.

The Role of the Commission Chairman The source of power of the commission chairman lies in Reorganization Plan Number 8 of 1950[65] that vests in the chairman executive and administrative powers to control the appointment of key officials—the executive director, general counsel, secretary, director of policy planning, director of public information, and the directors of the bureaus of Competition, Economics, and Consumer Protection.[66] Though major appointments are subject to full commission approval, there is little doubt among the commissioners that the nominees are the "chairmen's people."

With the exception of the director of the Bureau of Economics, who tends to be a distinguished scholar on a short-term leave from the academic community, the professional prospects of senior officials are likely to be contingent upon their being responsive to the chairman. Recent directors of the Bureau of Economics have been appointed because of their technical expertise and have not been routinely involved in the case-selection process. The economics bureau heads might naturally be reluctant to do anything that would diminish their prestige within the academic community and so are more likely to disagree with the chairman than are the other appointees.

That the chairman can affect the career of the director of the Bureau of Competition, for example, is clear.[67] A bureau director, eager to impress his constituency, seeks to establish a "winning record" at the commission table (that is, to secure complaints from the commissioners in a high percentage of the cases) and to launch significant prosecutions (the "big" cases). He cannot accomplish these objectives without the support of the chairman.

A chairman can have a substantial impact on case selection by involving himself at the earliest stages of the decision-making process when the Evaluation Committee first decides whether to commit resources to an investigation. The chairman, who is deeply involved in developing antitrust policy, uses the bureau director to advance his positions at the bureau level. He can indicate those areas where he thinks resources are warranted and will expect him to act in accordance with his suggestions. His interest in bureau affairs is likely to be especially keen when the case under discussion is of major importance and/or politically controversial. Usually, the chairman will entrust the bureau director with the responsibility of developing specific cases, strategies, and tactics in those program areas which he believes deserve attention. He will also involve officials of the Bureau of Economics when economic advice is needed. Because of the many claims upon his time, the chairman is seldom immersed in routine bureau affairs. For example, while the chairman might very well urge the Bureau of Competition to launch several investigations into the food industry, it is unlikely that he would specify the companies which should be the targets of the inquiry.

The chairman can also dominate the agenda-setting process through his control of the budget. Though a budget cannot become an expression of commission policy until a majority of the commissioners have approved the document, the chairman has a major advantage because he controls the budgetary process through his executive director (the FTC's chief operating officer, charged with exercising executive and administrative supervision over agency bureaus, staffs, and offices). While the chairman can keep abreast of developments throughout the year and can use his executive director and his staff to convey his preferences to the operating bureaus, the other commissioners have merely a short time in July and in September to review the budget.

The Role of the Other Commissioners Constrained as they are, the other commissioners are not without means to make their preferences known. No matter how firmly he may control the staff, the chairman cannot achieve his policy objectives if a majority of the commissioners do not support his position. Thus, in a negative sense, the commissioners can affect the development of policy. Commission decision-making by veto is a poor substitute for active, direct policy-making, and the commissioners interviewed expressed their unhappiness that there are relatively few occasions for them to affect staff behavior in advance of the actual voting.

One such opportunity arises when the commissioner is a "moving commissioner." In order that the administrative process not be clogged by the severe backlog that would result if each commissioner were to examine all cases in detail, the commissioners entrust one of their colleagues—the "moving commissioner"—with the task of thoroughly studying a particular matter upon which they will soon deliberate.

Because the staff attorneys realize that the "moving commissioner" can often affect how the other commission members will vote, they seek his support. It should be noted, however, that even if he is able to exert some control over the staff, a commissioner cannot achieve his policy objectives without the support of at least two colleagues. In fact, there is not much that a commissioner can do to affect the behavior of a fellow decision-maker. If he is an antitrust expert, then, he may, of course, influence their thinking by forcefully presenting his views.

The Criteria for Determining Whether to Vote to Issue a Complaint
In determining whether to vote to issue a complaint, a commissioner must decide that there is reason to believe that the laws have been

violated and that commission action would be in the public interest.[68] Because the "public interest" is not defined in law or statute, the commissioner has the license to consider legal, economic, political, and other factors in reaching his decision. The criteria underlying a commissioner's vote on a particular matter are likely to depend upon the nature of the case. As Commissioner Elizabeth Hanford Dole noted:

There are not set case-selection formulae. . . . I evaluate each case on the basis of the unique fact situation it presents and the probable benefits to competition and consumers from Commission action.[69]

There are several factors which a commissioner may consider when evaluating a complaint recommendation. First, he (or his attorney adviser) will probably ascertain whether successful prosecution of the investigation is likely to yield results which further his policy preference. For example, if he thinks that antitrust enforcement should seek to maintain small business, then he will probably support Robinson-Patman actions. A commissioner who thinks that antitrust policy should serve political or social objectives is less apt to weigh seriously the position of the Bureau of Economics than would a colleague who believes that commission action should promote economic efficiency.

Second, in making his decision about how to vote, the commissioner will probably attempt to judge whether the legal foundation of the case is solid: he will make some prediction regarding the likelihood of the attorneys' satisfying the administrative law judges, the commissioners, and perhaps the federal courts that the laws have been violated.[70]

Third, a politically sensitive commissioner might consider the likely reactions of outside actors—Congress, the media, public-interest groups, the business community—to a decision to prosecute. There are relatively few occasions when the agency must make controversial decisions. Usually, the commission will hesitate to act if there is deep disagreement between the operating bureaus as to what course the agency should follow. Although the commission might attempt to delay reaching a prosecutorial decision until such time when controversy can be avoided or minimized, the agency ultimately has not been deterred from bringing suit against major economic interests.

Outside Actors and Case Selection Decisions

A public bureaucracy does not exist in a political vacuum. People who are touched by commission action or who are obligated by law to interact with it might be keenly interested in agency activities.

The Presidency Although presidents nominate commissioners, they have generally not been deeply involved in the selection process.[71] Usually, they accept the recommendations of their staffs.[72] Recent administrations have not used systematic search-and-evaluation procedures, but have tended to react to campaigns waged by candidates or their supporters. In making appointments, the White House takes into account a number of factors: the candidate's political background, the sources of his support, his policy preferences, and the likely reaction of the Senate to this nomination. Often, the candidate is unfamiliar with the commission's work; in such cases, the backing of an influential politician or group may weigh more heavily than the nominee's fitness for a commissionership.

White House aides tend to be more attentive to the credentials of candidates for the chairmanship than for other commissionerships. Since the agency head can greatly affect the direction of policy, the White House generally seeks to determine whether the would-be chairman's views are consistent with the president's program.

The general lack of presidential involvement in agency affairs is understandable. A chief exeuctive simply does not have the time to immerse himself in the appointment process. The Federal Trade Commission has a small budget. Quite naturally, the president is more likely to devote his attention to the appointment of department and cabinet heads in the executive branch for whose performance he is held accountable.

The commission submits its budget to the Office of Management and Budget (OMB).[73] However, in the period studied, OMB did not try to alter the FTC's caseload. Because the FTC has a small budget and has generally been credited for its commitment to managerial improvement, the OMB spends little time reviewing the commission's antitrust activities. Perhaps, more importantly, recent administrations have called for vigorous antitrust enforcement; therefore, OMB has generally supported commission requests for increased funding as being in accord with the president's program (although the amount approved has tended to be less than the FTC's request).

Congress Without the advice and consent of the Senate, a nominee for a commissionership cannot take his seat. While it might be thought that the Senate would use its confirmation power to affect antitrust policy by approving those who shared a common view about FTC enforcement, the upper chamber has tended to play a passive part in the appointment process. Almost always, nominees are routinely approved.

The Senate Commerce Committee, which examines the qualifications of candidates and makes recommendations to the full Senate, performs its duties in a perfunctory way. Most senators devote little attention to the confirmation process; attendance at hearings is almost always low.[74] At least through the Magnuson chairmanship that ended in 1977, the committee staff did most of the work relating to the screening of nominees. On occasion, the staff did affect the outcome of the appointment process. For example, it made certain that the White House nominated a consumer expert in 1973 to a seat vacated by Mary Gardiner Jones.[75] Moreover, in 1976, the White House withdrew the nomination of Thomas Sowell, a conservative black economist, after the staff indicated that the committee would probably not confirm the candidate for a full term.[76] In the main, however, the committee and staff have rarely sought to block the appointment of a president's nominee; in nearly every instance, committee approval of the nominee has led to his confirmation.

The appropriations committees have several means of affecting commission policy. For example, they could set funding levels for programs or determine the purposes for which the money is to be spent; through nonstatutory techniques, appropriations committees could influence FTC policy.[77] However, in the last few years, at least, the appropriations committees of the House and Senate generally did not use these various means to alter the antitrust caseload of the FTC.[78] To be sure, congressmen raised questions about the progress of major programs and cases; moreover, on occasion, the FTC launched an investigation (the food inquiry, for instance) in response to committee requests. For the most part, however, appropriation subcommittee members tended to be concerned with general matters—for example, the investigational backlog, the staff turnover rate, or the won/lost record of the FTC in the courts—rather than with the substance of the caseload. The House appropriations committee's satisfaction with the FTC's antitrust performance is perhaps best indicated by the consistent increases in agency funding which it recommended.

It would appear, however, that the equable relationship between the agency and the appropriations body is about to change. The subcommittee, unhappy with the Pertschuk administration, urged in fall 1979 that the full committee and House slash the agency's budget and adopt appropriations measures that would effectively halt the FTC's investigations of the petroleum and car manufacturing industries. Given that recent commissions were unquestionably at least as vigorous in their antitrust efforts, the appropriation subcommittee's criticism of the "activism" of the current administration is somewhat puzzling. It may be that the committee and the business community were more comfortable with previous commissions because they justified their antitrust objectives in uncontroversial terms—increasing economic competition and enhancing consumer benefit. In contrast, the present FTC leadership has publicly endorsed the idea that antitrust should be used against large institutions which allegedly exercise undue social and political influence as well as market power, a notion which corporate interests and many congressmen apparently view with alarm.

On the Senate side, the appropriations subcommittee's review of the FTC's antitrust activities was even more perfunctory than the House review during the period studied. Subcommittee hearings usually focused on a few matters raised by senators and upon the area of disagreement between the FTC and the House. The subcommittee served as an appeals forum for the commission when it was dissatisfied with the House's appropriations decision. The Senate annually raised the commission's budget.

Congress could affect the FTC's antitrust policy not only by using its appropriations and confirmation powers but also by means of legislation, hearings, and investigations. The many committees and subcommittees that could interact with the FTC include the House Subcommittee on Oversight and Investigations of the Committee on Interstate and Foreign Commerce, the Subcommittee on Commodities and Services of the House Committee on Small Business, the Ad Hoc Subcommittee on the Robinson-Patman Act, Antitrust and Related Matters of the House Committee on Small Business, the Subcommittee on Monopolies and Commercial Law of the House Judiciary, the Subcommittee on Antitrust and Monopoly of the Senate Judiciary Committee, and the Senate Committee on Interior and Insular Affairs.

The agency's antitrust caseload cannot be explained in terms of congressional efforts to quash investigations.[79] While it is relatively rare for a committee to apply intense pressure on the commission to issue a complaint, there have been notable exceptions. For example, the Senate Interior Committee led by Senator Henry Jackson prodded the agency to issue a complaint in the *Exxon* investigation.[80] The commission does not automatically respond to congressional committee pressure. It did not issue a complaint against natural gas producers following highly publicized hearings of the Moss Subcommittee on Oversight and Investigations of the House Committee on Interstate and Foreign Commerce (indeed, some would argue that the hearings made FTC action less likely);[81] during the Kirkpatrick, Engman, and Collier regimes, the FTC did not alter its policy with respect to the Robinson-Patman Act, despite the efforts of a special subcommittee to induce the agency to issue more complaints;[82] and recently, the FTC declined the request of then chairman of the Senate subcommittee on Antitrust and Monopoly, Senator Edward Kennedy, to investigate a merger case which the Antitrust Division had already examined.[83] To be sure, the commission tends to consider carefully congressional requests for investigations, especially when the committee has jurisdiction over agency activities, if strong sentiment exists within Congress for action or if the congressmen can affect the FTC's future. However, the commission does not automatically affirmatively respond to individual congressmen's requests for action.[84]

Public-interest groups have not been intimately involved in the antitrust case-selection process, in part because precomplaint proceedings are closed to all but agency officials and the relevant parties. Public-interest groups have generally approved of the agency's antitrust policies and have preferred to concentrate on legislative efforts in Congress to strengthen the antitrust laws. While many informed sources believe that private interests intervene improperly in the decision-making process, no solid evidence of such behavior during the period studied was uncovered. In any event, most of these observers are convinced that such impropriety is rare.[85] That private interest groups (such as business associations) have not had much impact on agency deliberations is perhaps indicated by their recent lobbying efforts in Congress, directed towards curbing various antitrust investigations and enacting provisions for the legislative veto of FTC rules. Such activities are not surprising, for as political scientists would predict, interest groups are apt to turn to the legislature when dissatisfied with courts, commissions or the executive.

Conclusion: The Federal Trade Commission, Antitrust and Public Policy

There has been an increasing emphasis within the commission on the "proactive" approach, as exemplified by "planned" efforts in the energy, health, and food areas. Such cases are designed to benefit the consumer. Commission decision-makers still allocate resources to those conduct cases of the reactive kind even if they are unlikely to yield much consumer benefit in order to establish an important legal precedent, to deter businesses that might be tempted to violate sections of the law, and to show Congress that it intends to enforce all laws.

Perhaps more importantly, the director of the Bureau of Competition will authorize the opening of a number of easily prosecuted conduct cases because of considerations of organizational maintenance. Prosecution of such cases is necessary to meet the career expectations of attorneys who value trial experience. Such cases lessen (if only temporarily) the dissatisfaction among those attorneys who are assigned to the mammoth "structural" investigations.

Industry economic characteristics do not by themselves explain the prosecutions the commission has brought.[86] Economists err when they ignore other variables such as professional values and goals; certainly, one cannot explain the FTC's caseload without reference to the interaction between lawyers and economists. Legal precedent, the need to satisfy the professional objectives of staff attorneys, the availability of requisite expertise and the occasional influence of outside actors affect the decision-making calculus of commission officials.

The analysis of commission decision making, as presented in this chapter, is not consonant with the judgment of those scholars, ranging from conservative economist George Stigler to radical historian Gabriel Kolko, who contend that government generally serves the economic interests that it is supposed to regulate.[87] To be sure, there have undoubtedly been instances in which various regulatory bodies have not acted in the public interest. However, sweeping generalizations about agency capture or the causes and effects of regulatory legislation are suspect.[88] With respect to the Federal Trade Commission, the evidence does not support the assumption that the agency was created to serve industry or was later captured by it. As this chapter has attempted to show, moreover, it certainly cannot be stated categorically that the disproportionate possession of resources by various economic interests necessarily results in an inordinate exercise of political power. Clearly, an agency dominated by corporate interests would be unlikely to launch major actions against segments of the petroleum, cereal, or document-copying industries. Even Richard Posner, a proponent of the "economic theory of regulation" which conceives of regulation as a service supplied to effective political interest groups, admits that his view cannot account for the recent activism of the Federal Trade Commission.[89]

186

Moreover, the findings of this study challenge those theorists who argue that bureaucracies rationally attempt to maximize organizational self-interest.[90] Commission officials are not motivated fundamentally by a desire to maximize budgets. While they do seek increases in funding, most expressed concern that a rapid influx of money and attorneys could undermine the agency's efforts to maintain control of caseload decisions—bureau executives might sometimes have to authorize investigations of dubious value simply to provide work for the new attorneys. Moreover, a rapid influx of funds and lawyers could magnify the problems of attorney training and supervision. Finally, most staff attorneys and officials view government service as a brief assignment; they join the commission with the expectation of departing within a few years. Increasing salaries is not likely to induce many to remain with the agency.

Richard Posner argues that the fact that most commissioners do not pursue careers in public service and thus may not be motivated by a desire to increase their government salaries does not invalidate the assumption that they will not do anything in office which could jeopardize future earnings—as members of the private bar.[91] Certainly, recent agency history has failed to confirm Professor Posner's 1969 forecast that the commissioners would not be likely to launch investigations that might earn them the enmity of powerful economic interests.

Perhaps the Federal Trade Commission may be properly understood as an organization which does not proceed in any obvious, maximizing way. Its behavior is not simply that of a rational self-interested actor, seeking to maximize its budget, power, or convenience. Rather, the commission is an agency that has struggled in the last several years to pursue actions in what it perceives to be the public interest, although it has not always been certain as to which policy course would serve that interest.[92] In choosing the caseload, agency policy-makers are constrained by staff attorneys, whose perceived professional objectives must be satisfied to some degree if the organization is to be maintained. The agency operates in a political environment—it must, therefore, not be unmindful of the actors (for example, Congress, the executive) who might attempt to influence antitrust policy. But the agency, while respectful of these elements, does not act as their servant.

PART III

THE

"NEW" REGULATION:

PRODUCTS AND

PROCESSES

CHAPTER 6

Food and Drug Administration

P A U L J. Q U I R K

For many years the federal government has been intervening in the marketplace to ensure the safety and efficacy of prescription drugs. One might ask whether such efforts are potentially useful or even necessary. Don't drug companies have to make drugs as safe and effective as they can just to satisfy their customers? If drugs sometimes cause harm or do not work, does this failure not simply reflect the limits of what the companies can produce at a price consumers can pay?

From the economist's perspective, the principal reason for regulation of prescription drugs is the inevitable ignorance of consumers and physicians. Even for a highly competent physician, drugs are very difficult to evaluate. A drug can appear to be effective simply because of natural recovery, fluctuation in the course of an illness, or placebo effects. Side effects can go undetected or be unconnected to the drug that causes them, especially if their occurrence is delayed or infrequent. The scientific literature on drugs is so complex and voluminous that even academic drug experts can be well informed only in a narrow area of specialization. Moreover, much of this literature exists only because of regulatory requirements for companies to sponsor research. These circumstances strongly suggest that, without government intervention, doctors and patients would have great difficulty selecting drugs intelligently and avoiding those that were (relatively) unsafe or ineffective, and therefore that drug companies would have less than optimal incentives to avoid marketing such products.[1] Nevertheless, there is no guarantee that government intervention will achieve a highly satisfactory solution, or even that it will do more good than harm. It all depends on what intervention is undertaken and on how it is carried out.

This chapter examines the response of the federal government to the problems of drug safety and efficacy. It will consider first the legislative origins of Food and Drug Administration (FDA) authority to regulate drugs and the terms of that authority. A second section describes various influences on the FDA's behavior and the resulting pattern of its decisions. In the third section, the effects of FDA regulation are discussed. Finally, there is a brief consideration of possibilities and prospects for drug regulatory reform.

Throughout the chapter there is a persistent theme: The political circumstances of prescription drug regulation have shaped—and continue to maintain—an inefficient basic statutory structure. Consequently, no matter how skillfully the FDA uses its authority, it provides inadequate consumer protection while imposing excessive burdens on the development of valuable drugs.[2]

The Legislative Politics of Drug Regulation

Current federal regulation of prescription drugs rests primarily on three major pieces of legislation: the Pure Food and Drugs Act of 1906, the Food, Drug, and Cosmetics Act of 1938, and the Drug Amendments of 1962. In tracing the origins of these laws and describing their content, this section will attempt to show how the fundamental structure of contemporary regulation was shaped by the problems in the drug industry, the manner in which reformers interpreted these problems, and the political forces that promoted or resisted regulation.

Though no longer central to the FDA's control of prescription drugs, the Pure Food and Drugs Act of 1906 resulted from a style of regulatory politics that remains conspicuous.[3] By the standards of the drug industry at the turn of the century, today's worst consumer abuses would seem picayune. Patent medicines sold directly to consumers were the most hazardous. Often promoted as "miracle cures" for long and diverse lists of serious diseases, these products were often habit-forming, highly dangerous, or simply worthless. Prescription as well as patent medicines were frequently adulterated.

A movement for reform was championed by the zealous and colorful head of the Agriculture Department's Bureau of Chemistry, Harvey W. Wiley. In 1897 Wiley was instrumental in stimulating the Association of Official Agricultural Chemists to promote a new food and drug law. A few months later, he was the leading spokesman for reform at the National Pure Food and Drug Congress in Washington. Though initially concerned primarily about the bilking of consumers through adulteration of food, Wiley came gradually to be concerned about hazards to consumers' health as well, particularly such hazards posed by patent medicines. Wiley served the cause as its chief strategist, its lobbyist both before Congress and within the executive branch, its arranger of hearings and leading witness, and finally as an effective publicist and solicitor of grass-roots support. Though Wiley himself disdained to exaggerate, sensationalistic press reports of his congressional testimony created a public following for food and drug legislation.

Among the groups supporting the reform effort were the American Medical Association, the American Pharmaceutical Association (representing pharmacists), the Grange, and a variety of women's organizations. The AMA, at the time, represented primarily the more scientifically and professionally oriented physicians, and support for control of medicines served its goal of rooting out medical quackery.

Some of the affected industries reacted positively to Wiley's early initiatives. This should not be too surprising. Consumer protection regulation can benefit an industry by increasing consumer confidence in its products. It particularly benefits larger and more responsible firms. There are often economies of scale in complying with regulatory requirements, which makes it harder for small firms to compete, and regulation hampers less scrupulous competitors. By the spring of 1900, endorsements of a food and drug measure had been obtained from the National Board of Trade, the National Retail Grocers' Association, the National Wholesale Druggists' Association, the National Retail Liquor Dealers' Association, and the Proprietary Association of America (representing patent-medicine manufacturers). As momentum for reform gathered and proposals were broadened, however, industry support tended to dissipate. By 1903 Wiley had begun to give serious attention to the problems of patent medicines and was proposing a new and more inclusive definition of "drugs" for the bill which would cover all patent medicines. Thereafter, although some patent-medicine manufacturers continued to support reform, the bulk of the drug trade, including the Proprietary Association, was steadfastly opposed. The prescription-drug industry evidently did not consider proposed regulation of drugs crucial to its interests, perhaps because its practices were more restrained that those of patent-medicine manufacturers. Thus the prescription-drug industry was not a factor in the politics of the act.

Though initially lacking, public attention and enthusiasm gradually increased in response to an outpouring of muckraking journalism. *The Ladies' Home Journal* published a series of articles revealing the composition of various home remedies that were manifestly useless or dangerous. A general mood of progressivism and skepticism toward business was widespread, as indicated by the publication and popularity of Lincoln Steffens's *The Shame of the Cities*[4] and Ida Tarbell's *The History of the Standard Oil Company.*[5] Most important for the food and drug bill, however, was Upton Sinclair's novel, *The Jungle,* published in 1905, which exposed unsanitary conditions in the meatpacking industry.[6] In addition to having a major impact on public opinion, *The Jungle* impressed President Theodore Roosevelt sufficiently to make him an active sponsor of food and drug reform. The Pure Food and Drugs Act was passed the following year.

The main drug provisions of the act simply prohibited "misbranding" of drug products—that is, the use of false or deceptive labeling claims concerning a product's contents, safety, or therapeutic effect. There was no requirement for a drug actually to be safe or effective, for its safety or effectiveness to be proven, or for prior government approval of a product or of the manufacturer's claims concerning it. The conception underlying the Pure Food and Drugs Act, essentially, was to enable the government to act (after the fact) against blatant, reckless deception.

By the early 1930s, however, the failure of the Pure Food and Drugs Act was manifest.[7] In 1912, in order to accommodate the views of the Supreme Court, Congress had altered the misbranding provision so that it prohibited "false *and fraudulent*" labeling (emphasis added). This meant that, in order to prove a violation, the FDA had to show not only that a labeling claim was false, but also that it had been made with intent to deceive. Furthermore, promotional material other than labeling was not subject to the misbranding provisions. Deceptive promotion of worthless and unsafe drugs remained rampant.

In 1933, with a new administration in control of the executive branch, the FDA persuaded Assistant Secretary of Agriculture Rexford G. Tugwell of the need for a new food and drug law. With President Roosevelt's permission, a bill was written and introduced in Congress. The "Tugwell bill" would have tightened and elaborated the misbranding provisions in several significant ways without changing the basic approach of the 1906 law. A new law was not to be enacted, however, until five years had elapsed, a major scandal had intervened, and the shape of reform had been altered fundamentally.

By 1933 some food and drug industry groups were again receptive in principle to increased regulation. Indeed, the Pharmaceutical Manufacturers' Association (PMA), which represents prescription-drug manufacturers, endorsed FDA regulation of drug advertising. Apparently the PMA was upset by an episode in which one company had dishonestly attacked the reliability of certain products offered by its competitors, which led to considerable adverse publicity. Nevertheless, industry considered the Tugwell bill extremely severe and opposed it virtually in unison.

After 1933 industry support for proposed food and drug measures grew for several reasons. First, seeing the strength of the opposition to the Tugwell bill, the reformers began to compromise their proposals in order to assemble a winning coalition. Weakening amendments were accepted to propitiate not only the food industry but also the broadcast and publishing industries, which were strongly opposed to strict advertising regulation. Second, industry could see that delay was dangerous. Reform sentiment seemed to be growing instead of subsiding; the later legislation came, the more severe it might be. Moreover, federal legislation was needed to stop, by preempting the field, a flood of state laws touching foods and drugs. Finally, the controversy over reform legislation was generating continual bad publicity for the industries involved.

Within a few years, therefore, most of the affected industries and their congressional allies were supporting passage of a food, drug, and cosmetics bill. The long delay before final passage was not due primarily to groups opposed to all reform. Rather, it was caused largely by complex maneuvering by industry to put across weakening amendments and substitute measures, and by reformers' efforts to beat them back. The exception was the patent-medicine industry, which the reformers selected as the industry most needing increased constraint and least deserving conciliation. Some segments of this industry were irreconcilable; others admitted the appropriateness of "reasonable" reform, but never found a bill to their liking.

As prior to the 1906 act, a round of muckraking journalism helped generate public support. The alarmist and moralistic tone of this literature is suggested by titles of popular books, such as *American Chamber of Horrors*[8] (written by the FDA's information officer) and *100,000,000 Guinea Pigs,*[9] and by the latter book's charge that "in the eyes of the law, we are all guinea pigs, and any scoundrel who takes it into his head to enter the drug or food business can experiment on us."[10] Consumers' organizations and the AMA argued emphatically for tough reforms, but these groups were a mixed blessing for the FDA and congressional sponsors of reform bills. Their spokesmen usually denounced as weak any bill that had a hope of passage, and even raised questions about the motives of those who would propose such legislation. As in 1906, the most important organized, nonindustry support was provided by national women's groups, such as the American Association of University Women and the League of Women Voters, who managed to combine reform zeal with political realism.

Despite his initial encouragement, FDR played a limited and ambiguous role in promoting the bill. In addition to his greater attentiveness to issues directly affecting economic recovery, his enthusiasm was lessened by a political falling-out with Senator Royal Copeland, the Senate sponsor of the bill. Finally, enactment of a food and drug bill was complicated by a controversy over whether drug advertising regulation should be handled by the FDA or by the Federal Trade Commission.

Any chance of stalemate was wiped out in late 1937 by a notorious disaster involving the drug, elixir sulfanilamide. The Massengill Company had rushed this new product to market with no prior testing for safety. Unfortunately, for a large proportion of users, the solvent in which the drug was suspended produced excruciating and often fatal toxic side effects almost immediately. By the time the problem was discovered and the drug was recalled, at least 107 deaths were attributable to it. The episode received extensive and long-lasting news coverage, created an intense public demand for reform, and substantially vitiated industry's inclination to haggle over details.

Even more significantly, however, the elixir sulfanilamide disaster led directly to a major revision of the proposed reform bill. Not only was existing law inadequate to protect against such disasters, but even the bills then under consideration could not do so. They did not mandate safety testing to be done prior to marketing a drug or authorize the FDA to do so. The revisions that were quickly incorporated to remedy this defect became the most important part of the bill. New drugs would not be legally marketable until shown safe by "adequate tests" acceptable to the FDA. The agency would also be empowered to remove from the market drugs found hazardous subsequent to marketing.

Food and Drug Administration

Except for some grumbling about the severity of the new provisions, the drug industry made little effort to resist enactment. The final legislative steps were easy. In the House, passage was by unanimous vote. Roosevelt signed the Food, Drug, and Cosmetics Act into law on June 30, 1938.

Two decades later, the reform cycle resumed.[11] The Drug Amendments of 1962 were born in hearings before Senator Estes Kefauver's Subcommittee on Antitrust and Monopoly of the Senate Judiciary Committee. At first Kefauver was interested primarily in prescription-drug prices. His staff had discovered that trade-name products were often sold at prices many times their cost of production. The industry's defense was that large markups were necessitated by costs of research, development, and promotion not included in the calculation of production costs. Kefauver rejected this defense, largely because the industry was exceptionally profitable overall. It evidently did not occur to him that high average profitability might be associated with the high-risk character of the industry, that it might be an expectable consequence of the therapeutic revolution of the previous three decades, or that it might be socially desirable for investment in drug development to offer the possibility of "windfall profits."

The focus of Kefauver's investigation soon expanded. Building on charges suggested in recent hearings headed by Representative John Blatnik, in *Saturday Review* articles by science writer John Lear, and in testimony by medical experts and others before his committee, Kefauver became more concerned about problems relating to health, as opposed to price. Kefauver argued, sometimes with impressive evidence, that prescription drugs were advertised in a misleading manner and that as a result physicians failed to prescribe drugs intelligently; that too many prescription drugs on the market offered no advantages over other products, and tended only to confuse physicians; that the industry spent excessive research resources on "me-too" drugs (minor modifications of patented drugs intended primarily to circumvent patent protection); that fixed-combination prescription drugs encouraged slovenly prescribing, such as prescribing a combination when a single drug would do; and that drugs were often marketed without much evidence of therapeutic efficacy.

Concerning efficacy, FDA Commissioner George Larrick pointed out that FDA routinely considered evidence of efficacy as part of the drug-approval process. Despite the lack of explicit statutory authorization, the FDA felt that unless a drug was effective it could not be considered safe. Nevertheless, evidence of therapeutic efficacy often consisted only of testimonials from practicing physicians who casually tested experimental drugs on their patients and were paid for their efforts. Occasionally, moreover, the FDA could be forced to approve ineffective drugs because it lacked specific authority to reject them.[12]

Kefauver's original bill, introduced in April 1961, contained provisions aimed at lowering drug prices, as well as at improving safety, efficacy, and advertising. The most important price provisions reduced the length of patent protection to be enjoyed by drugs in order to increase price competition in the industry. Owing to vociferous opposition from industry, the AMA, and congressional Republicans and without support from the Kennedy administration, these provisions were deleted in the Judiciary Committee. The other main provisions of the Kefauver bill required that new drugs be proven effective—as well as safe—in order to receive marketing approval, and stipulated that prescription-drug advertising include information on side effects and "contraindications" (conditions in which a drug should not be used).

In responding to these proposals, the PMA was led by the more liberal wing of the drug industry. It opposed the restrictions on advertising, but offered qualified support for the efficacy requirement. Specifically, the PMA supported a proof of efficacy provision on the condition that the standard of proof would require only "substantial evidence" of effectiveness. Thus, "if a number of tests by competent clinicians show that in well-conducted clinical trials a drug produced the claimed effect on their patients," that drug should be approved—even if in other tests it was unsuccessful.[13] This would essentially have formalized the existing practice of relying on casual experimentation by practicing physicians.

But the PMA interpretation did not succeed. In a critical bargaining session with representatives of the administration, the PMA's lawyer (remarkably) accepted a compromise proposal: "substantial evidence" would suffice, but the statute required that this evidence would consist of "adequate and well-controlled investigations, including clinical investigations, by experts qualified by scientific training and experience to evaluate the effectiveness of the drug involved." It seems doubtful that the PMA representative appreciated the power he was handing over to the FDA to demand large and rigorously designed studies to substantiate a drug's efficacy. On its face, and certainly as eventually implemented, this provision went far beyond the spirit of the original drug-industry position.

In a reversal of its historic stance favoring reform, the AMA opposed even the advertising and efficacy requirements of the Kefauver bill. Although a survey of doctors showed widespread discontent with the reliability of prescription-drug advertising, the AMA declared it unreasonable to require advertisers to reveal "the whole truth." Moreover, it opposed any provision for proof of efficacy as a condition for marketing approval. The association argued that drug efficacy varied from patient to patient, and that therefore no determination could be made by government; only the individual physician treating a patient could evaluate drug efficacy for that patient. By thus allying itself with the drug industry and defending the physician's prerogatives against the growth of the FDA's authority, the AMA entered a new era in its politics.[14]

Besides the many medical experts who testified in favor of the Kefauver bill, support was provided by labor unions, health insurance representatives, hospital officials, and consumer groups. The Kennedy administration generally supported Kefauver, except for the patent provisions of his bill, and was even responsible for some strengthening amendments.

Once again, decisive impetus for the passage of legislation was provided by a major scandal—in this case, the thalidomide disaster. In late 1961 a link was established between use of the sedative thalidomide in pregnant women and a gruesome European epidemic of phocomelia (literally, "seal limbs"), a birth defect in which limbs are truncated or missing. Kefauver's staff learned of the episode, held up publicizing it until they believed the drug bill was ready to benefit most, and passed the story to the *Washington Post.* The ensuing national publicity and public horror were then skillfully exploited to generate support for the proposed amendments. The thalidomide episode was politically useful despite the lack of any substantial connection between the disaster and the proposed legislation. Under existing laws, except for limited experimental use, thalidomide had actually been kept off the American market. The disaster occurred almost exclusively in Europe and Canada. But neither public opinion nor politicians were interested in fine distinctions concerning the policy significance of the scandal.

After thalidomide, enactment of Kefauver's bill was virtually a foregone conclusion. The Kennedy administration became consistently supportive of strong legislation, and the drug industry became resigned to its inevitability. After a few final strategic skirmishes, the bill was passed by unanimous votes in both houses of Congress. On October 10 President Kennedy signed the Drug Amendments of 1962 into law.

Results

The central feature of prescription-drug regulation in the United States is premarketing approval by the FDA. In order to market a new drug, a drug company must satisfy the FDA on the product's safety and efficacy for the use or uses intended. The FDA has broad discretion concerning the tests it will require and the standards of safety and efficacy it will apply. After approval, if subsequent evidence casts doubt on a drug's safety or efficacy, the FDA can remove it from the market. Though normally companies need not sponsor postapproval research, they are required to apprise the FDA of any adverse information they receive. The FDA regulates prescription-drug labeling and advertising, including the therapeutic uses recommended, the instructions for these uses, and the side effects, warnings, and contraindications that must be noted. The agency regulates the manufacturing practices and quality controls by which drugs are produced and it determines whether and how a drug sponsor may experiment on humans.

Certain aspects of this regulatory structure warrant special notice and explanation. In relying almost entirely on premarketing testing and control, the statutes forgo the alternative of requiring somewhat less testing prior to any marketing and relying more on systematic learning from experience (involving much larger numbers of patients) after marketing.[15] Particularly if marketing were controlled so that it expanded in stages, the postmarketing approach would offer some of the advantages of incrementalism. This approach probably did not recommend itself because of the grossness of the hazards the premarketing system was designed to prevent. The completely untested Elixir Sulfanilamide was the paradigmatic case. As concerns about safety and efficacy became more refined, further testing requirements were simply added to the premarketing controls.

Despite the serious problem of misprescribing by physicians, discussed below, the FDA is not authorized to control how drugs are actually used (as opposed to the uses for which they are advertised). Indeed, the legislative history indicates explicitly that the agency is not to "interfere with the practice of medicine." Any attempt to give the FDA (or any other agency) regulatory control over the prescribing of drugs undoubtedly would have mobilized the full resources of the AMA and the medical profession in opposition.

The law essentially imposes the full costs of drug testing on the companies whose drugs are involved. As noted below, there are grounds for governmental assumption of some of these costs; but such a measure would have compromised the moral and rhetorical stance of the reform movement. The reformers portrayed themselves as crusaders against the social irresponsibility of the drug industry. This posture was not necessarily unwarranted—gross abuses had indeed occurred. But it constrained the range of solutions that could credibly be advanced. The reformers could not easily have proposed that the burden of responsibility be shared by the public.

The politics of drug legislation in 1906, 1938, and 1962 displayed certain common themes. First, the possibilities for regulatory legislation seem significantly dependent on the overall political climate. All three of the FDA's major laws were enacted during periods of political ferment and governmental activism: the Progressive era, the New Deal, and the 1960s. Second, all three laws benefited greatly from major disasters or other scandals that captured public attention and intensified broadly based support for reform. (Indeed one wonders whether the lesson is that such scandals are generally necessary to the imposition of constraints on powerful industries, or rather that they are generally available.) Third, though industry often supports regulatory legislation —or at least accepts it—this does not mean the legislation is intended to benefit industry at the expense of consumers. Industry motivation is complex. Sometimes regulation that will protect consumers will also help an industry, or part of it. At other times, industry may support reform to prevent the passage of more drastic measures. Interpretation of regulatory legislation requires more sensitivity to the intricacies of industry motivation than is sometimes exercised.[16]

FDA: Administrative Behavior

The Food and Drug Administration is part of the Department of Health, Education, and Welfare. Formally, its statutory authority is granted to the Secretary of HEW, who delegates it to the Commissioner of the FDA. Within the FDA, the drug regulatory responsibilities fall primarily upon the Bureau of Drugs. The determination as to whether new drugs should be permitted on the market is made chiefly by the bureau's Office of New Drug Evaluation (ONDE). ONDE, in turn, has seven divisions, six of which are responsible for reviewing drugs, with each being in charge of specific drug categories. The categories around which the divisions are organized are antiinfective, cardio-renal, surgical-dental, metabolism and endocrine, neuropharmacological, and oncology (cancer) and radiopharmaceutical. Normally, a drug under review will be analyzed by a review team in one of the divisions. The review team consists of a physician who is the team's head, a chemist, a pharmacologist, and often one or more additional specialists, such as a statistician.

In outline, the drug evaluation process follows these steps: A sponsor (usually a drug company), having completed initial screening and animal testing, seeks to undertake human testing of a new drug (or a new use for an old drug). To do so, it must give the FDA an elaborate document with the imposing title, "Notice of Claimed Investigational Exemption for a New Drug" (IND). The exemption claimed allows shipment of the drug in interstate commerce despite its lack of approved status. The IND includes a description of the drug, reports on the animal and other tests which indicate that testing in humans is justified and will be reasonably safe, and detailed plans for the human and further animal testing that will be conducted. Unless the FDA objects within thirty days, the exemption is automatically granted and the contemplated research can begin. As the research is carried on, the FDA is notified of the progress and findings by periodic mandatory reports. Typically there will be revisions or additions to the research plans, often at the suggestion of the FDA's reviewing officers.

When the company believes that the findings are sufficient to demonstrate the safety and efficacy of the drug for its intended use, it submits an application for marketing approval, called a "New Drug Application" (NDA). The FDA then has 180 days in which to act. If it is satisfied that the drug is safe and effective for the proposed use, it will grant marketing approval. Sometimes it will formally deny approval. But more often an unacceptable drug will be terminated by withdrawal of the application. During the 180-day period, the FDA may demand more information—perhaps data from additional or differently designed clinical studies, thereby extending the review process for as much as several years. When approval is imminent, the company and the FDA will negotiate the contents of the "package insert"—the official labeling received by doctors and pharmacists, which is the basis for any legally permissible prescription-drug advertising. The package insert contains a statement of the intended use or uses of the drug; instructions for these uses; contraindications, warnings, and precautions; and a list of side effects. Final approval involves FDA acceptance not only of the evidence on safety and efficacy, but also of the information proposed for the package insert.

After a drug is approved, the company is obliged to notify the FDA of any information it receives indicating unexpected adverse reactions, ineffectiveness, or other problems. The FDA may also receive such information from other sources, such as medical journals or reports to the agency directly from hospitals, doctors, or patients. Based on such information, the agency may take action to remove from the market a drug that has previously been approved, or to change its labeling— adding a warning, listing an additional side effect, or removing an approved use. Finally the agency will monitor the advertising used to promote the drug, making sure that it conforms to the information and recommendations in the package insert.

Dilemmas of Drug Regulation

In order to understand the behavior of the FDA, one must first appreciate the difficulty of the choices it must make. These choices often have the character of a dilemma: no matter how good the analysis is, or how upright the intentions may be, none of the alternatives are even moderately satisfactory. These dilemmas result in part from the state of the art in evaluating and employing drugs and in part from the design of the regulatory structure established by statute.

Much of the difficulty of the FDA's task results from the fact that the statute mainly imposes constraints *prior* to granting permission for a drug to be marketed. This means that decisions are based on evidence limited by the kinds of study that are feasible before marketing. Animal studies, though of some use, are often misleading. For example, if they were subjected to the kinds of animal studies generally used today, both penicillin and aspirin would probably be rejected as unsafe—yet thalidomide's ability to cause birth defects would go undetected.[17]

Testing in humans prior to marketing is limited by the number of patients who can be included in controlled clinical trials within feasible limits of time and cost. Typically a drug will be used in no more than a few thousand patients during clinical trials. This limits the precision with which a drug's efficacy can be evaluated and the frequency of its relatively common side effects can be estimated. And it almost totally undermines the expeditious assessment of side effects that are rare. Chloramphenicol, for example, is now believed to cause fatal bone-marrow poisoning once in roughly 24,000 cases. Since in most of its potential applications there are safer alternatives, this is important to know. Yet tests on even several thousand patients would be unlikely to turn up a single case of this reaction, much less to identify the drug as its cause.[18]

Following approval, the number of patients using a drug may grow rapidly. In some cases, millions of patients will use a drug in its first year or two of marketing. Formally, the FDA has no authority to mandate postapproval monitoring of experience with recently introduced drugs except for reporting adverse experiences voluntarily brought to the company's attention. Though some such voluntary reporting occurs and though there are limited drug-surveillance programs associated primarily with hospitals, the coverage of drug-monitoring programs in the United States is quite selective and uneven. Thus, by the time very large numbers of patients have been exposed to a new drug, no one is really watching. Finally, even if problems are detected, administrative procedures for withdrawing approval are cumbersome and costly. Only when the Secretary of HEW finds an "imminent hazard" to public health (a term that has been interpreted so restrictively that it has been used only once) can a drug be removed prior to a hearing.

This regulatory structure, with its heavy reliance on premarketing testing, gives the FDA grounds for extreme caution in approving new drugs. The evidence available cannot reliably prevent mistakes. Yet a mistaken approval can do widespread harm very quickly, be hard to detect, and—once detected—be hard to correct. In this situation, the agency can and probably must be simultaneously heavy-handed and lax, depending on one's perspective. Even when the evidence indicates that a drug's benefits clearly outweigh its likely risks, the FDA may demand more studies. In all probability, this deprives patients of a valuable drug. Thus it is heavy-handed. Yet, even with the further testing, the evidence may fall short of what we would like to have in order to permit widespread use for an indefinite period. In this way it is also lax.

Further difficulties arise from the fact that, with minor exceptions, the FDA can have research done only by requiring the drug companies to sponsor it. This is a problem for several reasons. First, it imposes all the costs of research on the companies who develop drugs. Though this is appropriate to a certain extent, drug research is partly in the nature of a "public good," in the economist's sense: its benefits are not limited to those who pay for it by purchasing the drug. (Consider, for example, people who conclude from a study *not* to use a certain drug.) Since the company is not paid for all the benefits it produces, it has an incentive to undervalue drug development and thus to do less than the optimal amount.[19] This theoretical concern is supported by evidence that the financial attractiveness of drug development has declined in part because of expanded federal requirements. The FDA must decide either to require all the tests that seem worth the cost of doing them, thereby magnifying the disincentive to develop drugs, or to forgo all but some minimal level of testing. Or it may adopt a compromise. But, once again, it will be both heavy-handed and lax.

Second, since the research is performed or sponsored by the drug companies which have a financial interest in minimizing costs and obtaining favorable results, the FDA must be concerned about whether the research is properly done. Research submitted to the agency is often deficient in scale, design, or execution. Though sometimes due to incompetence, dishonesty, or bias, deficiencies also result inevitably from the complexities of drug investigations and especially the problems of performing controlled experiments on humans. Faced by imperfect research, the FDA must decide whether to reject the research and demand another effort, or to interpret the research in light of its imperfections. For either choice, there are both compelling advantages and disadvantages. If research is rejected for marginal imperfections, even when it strongly supports drug approval, the availability of useful new drugs will be delayed, and the costs of drug development will be increased. But if such research is accepted and relied upon, the evidence supporting drug approvals will be more uncertain and companies will have less reason to strive toward perfection in subsequent research.

Disagreeable choices also arise from the fact that neither the FDA nor any other institution can effectively supervise how drugs are actually prescribed by doctors. The quality of prescribing is often very low.[20] In addition to random carelessness and error, there are many instances where large segments of the medical profession systematically misuse certain drugs: antibiotics are prescribed for the common cold even though they do nothing for it; dangerous and possibly ineffective oral antidiabetic drugs are prescribed for patients who could be treated with insulin; instead of much safer alternatives, the occasionally fatal chloramphenicol is used—six times more often than is appropriate; and so on. Irrational prescribing is directly damaging to public health. But it also poses problems for the FDA.

Frequently the FDA confronts a drug that is useful for a narrowly defined patient population but that if approved (or allowed to remain on the market) would be prescribed excessively and would result in widespread harm. In such cases the agency must either accept the damage from predictable misuse or deprive those patients who could benefit from the drug in question. One example is phenformin, an oral antidiabetic drug whose unique action (among drugs available in the United States) makes it potentially lifesaving for a small number of patients. But it has fatal side effects with significant frequency. For at least fifteen years since its serious hazards were first noticed, phenformin was widely prescribed and put millions of patients at unnecessary risk. In 1978 the FDA withdrew approval of phenformin, designating it an "imminent hazard" to public health. Recognizing its value for certain patients, the FDA attempted to negotiate an arrangement making it available only through rigidly controlled channels on a restricted basis. It is doubtful, however, that such an arrangement can reliably get phenformin to patients who need it and withhold it from those who do not. Moreover, as the AMA pointed out in demanding renewed approval of phenformin, there is no explicit legal authority for distribution of a disapproved drug.

All of these difficulties are exacerbated by the intrinsic ambiguity of decisions on drugs. Difficult value judgments must be made, such as whether a given therapeutic benefit (perhaps relief from mere discomfort) is sufficient to justify a given risk (perhaps a small—but definite—chance of death). Moreover, these benefits and risks are often subject to extreme uncertainty. A handful of persons among hundreds in a large clinical study may die unexpectedly, or cancerous tumors may appear in one animal species tested but not in others. A drug may lower serum cholesterol or blood pressure, but it may take a generation to find out whether these changes enhance health or longevity. The elimination of such uncertainties is made difficult by the costs of research, the lack of suitable methodologies, and the ethical constraints on research involving humans.

In short, given the complexities of drug evaluation and the inefficiencies of the basic regulatory arrangements, FDA decisions will inevitably be attacked as both lax and heavy-handed, with some justification for both views. In attempting to understand how the FDA has responded, we will consider first some conditions and developments internal to the agency, then the agency's relations with a demanding and conflict-ridden environment.

Internal Factors

The FDA has often been criticized for the quality of its decisions and personnel, and for administrative inefficiency and delay. There have been many reasons for such problems. First, the supervision of drug investigations and review of applications for marketing approval for new drugs require an extraordinary amount of information processing. A complete New Drug Application (NDA) may contain up to 200 volumes of information. (Perhaps 30 of these volumes will present significant information in an "expanded summary"; most of the rest will be case reports on individual patients requiring less detailed attention.) Different parts of these submissions are of special interest to different members of the team reviewing the application; but a complete division of issues is impossible, and much mutual consultation is required. The information in an NDA is often in flux; companies respond to requests for more information, additional studies are completed, and so on. Moreover, each medical officer, pharmacologist, and chemist in the Office of New Drug Evaluation is likely to be a member of several different reviewing teams assigned to a number of NDAs and INDs. It is quite easy to lose track of who has certain information, what needs to be done next, and who—if anyone—is doing it.

Second, the FDA has generally had trouble recruiting high-caliber scientific and medical personnel. FDA medical officers do little creative research; instead, they evaluate research submitted by drug companies. Such work, though important, is not attractive to talented research-oriented professionals. Moreover, neither the salary nor the physical working conditions are comparable to those enjoyed by successful physicians in private practice. During the late 1960s, when the agency was expanding rapidly, many of the medical officers recruited were ordinary older practicing physicians, with no particular expertise in drug research. Many of the agency's medical and scientific personnel have been highly competent, but there have been few outstanding individuals. J. Richard Crout, the current director of the Bureau of Drugs, is the first person in that position who came to the agency as an established expert in clinical pharmacology.

In order to make decisions with reasonable speed and accuracy, given the complexity and magnitude of its information-processing requirements, the FDA would need either a great deal of slack resources (i.e., enough extra personnel to reduce the need for close timing and coordination), or a highly sophisticated management control system.[21] Unfortunately, at least until recently, it had neither. Indeed, during the late 1960s and early 1970s, the Bureau of Drugs' line management was in disarray due to a succession of commissioners, a reorganization of the bureau, a move of its offices to Rockville, Maryland, and managerial problems. Morale was at rock bottom. In Dr. Crout's words, which would be amusing if they were not so pathetic:

During his [reform-oriented Commissioner James Goddard] tenure line management tended to break down. Channels of reporting tended to be more personal, that is reporting to Dr. Goddard personally. That, combined with the moves, the reorganization, left line management disastrously weak by the late 1960's. Nobody wanted to be manager. I'll tell you that in my first year at the FDA, and even lasting longer than that into 1972–73, going to certain kinds of meetings was an extraordinarily peculiar kind of exercise. People—and I'm talking about division directors and their staffs—engaged in a kind of behavior that invited insubordination. There were people tittering in corners, throwing spitballs. I'm describing physicians. There were people who slouched down in a chair and did not respond to questions, moaned and groaned with sweeping gestures—a kind of behavior I have not seen in any other institution as a grown man.[22]

One result of these decision-making problems was delay. Though the statute gives the FDA 180 days to act on a completed NDA, this time limit was ordinarily evaded by the agency (mostly by asking the companies for "voluntary" extensions, or declaring the NDA incomplete pending further information); a typical review period was two to three years. In a detailed case study of the FDA's actions on one drug, the HEW Review Panel on New Drug Regulation discovered delays of up to nine months in preparing reviews of company submissions and communicating findings to the company—despite the fact that the drug studied was considered one of a small number of important new chemical entities.[23] The Review Panel also provided an example of delays resulting from the lack of coordination and managerial control:

The processing of the drug Slow-K, which is manufactured by Ciba-Geigy, was delayed for over a year and a half because the Cardio-Renal Division thought it was being handled by the Director of OSE [Office of Scientific Evaluation—the previous name of the Office of New Drug Evaluation], while OSE thought the Division was handling the preparation of evidence for the General Counsel.[24]

The FDA has also been hindered by internal conflict over the appropriate posture of the agency toward the drug industry. A number of medical officers, skeptical of the drug industry, have taken a strongly adversarial stance toward it. In an extreme statement of the adversarial view, one medical officer attacked the common agency practice of offering advice to industry on how to make its submissions acceptable:

That's gamesmanship, the game of schlemiel—to tell drug companies what to do to get approved. It's not up to us to tell them all the details of what should be done. They're the applicant. We're the critic. The game of schlemiel on the part of applicants is the number one game: you lead me by the hand. The number one game of the agency should be "gotcha." You tried to slip one past and I knew where to look for your trick. I called my shots and went there and there it was—GOTCHA![25]

In part, this attitude may result from fear of approving a drug that would have disastrous effects and possibly facing exposure in the press or before Congress. On the other hand, the adversarial attitude also reflects the view that Americans are overmedicated and that the risks and limitations of drug therapy are not generally appreciated. As we shall see below, in discussing the agency's handling of weight-reducing drugs, the views of the dissidents have sometimes had merit.

Especially during the late 1960s and early 1970s, the advocates of an adversarial role had substantial control in a few of the drug-evaluation divisions. In particular they dominated the cardiovascular-renal division, where one of them was the division director. Their effectiveness was enhanced by the weakness of line management. This weakness, in turn, was exacerbated by the dissidents' willingness to take their complaints to Congress, which led to highly publicized hearings in which management was accused of "selling out" to industry. Though not concurring in the dissidents' position, agency management usually did not effectively control or overrule them.

Under Richard Crout's directorship of the Bureau of Drugs in the 1970s, there has been an effort to strengthen the management of the new-drug-evaluation process, both in order to increase its efficiency and to limit the influence of the adversary-minded reviewing officers. A computerized management-information system was installed, which enables the agency to keep track of an IND or NDA, to know what work on company submissions needs to be done and who is responsible for doing it, and to set and enforce deadlines. A drug-classification system has been established to permit the bureau to set priorities so that the processing of important drugs will not be held up unnecessarily by work on less important products. And the scientific data accumulated by the agency is now being committed to the memory of a computer for easier access and cross-referencing.

In order to impose compliance with the leadership's attitudes toward new drugs and the drug industry, a number of changes were made. A new supervisory level—the group leader—was introduced between the individual medical reviewer and the division director. This new level increased the detail with which a particular reviewer's decisions could be scrutinized. There was an expansion of the use of expert advisory committees as a source of recommendations on important decisions.

And there was a greater assertion of authority by the division directors, the associate director for new drug evaluation, and the bureau director; henceforth they would more closely scrutinize and more willingly override the recommendations of subordinate medical officers.

In order to assert control, the Bureau of Drugs sometimes employed deceptive tactics, in particular, transferring troublesome people out of sensitive positions under false pretexts. Occasionally, adversary-minded officials were simply taken off assignments in midstream and even excluded from meetings in which they had an interest. These methods were exposed in hearings before Senator Edward Kennedy's Health Subcommittee in 1974. And the hearings led to a long and controversial investigation by HEW that culminated in the final report of the Review Panel on New Drug Regulation.[26] Though clearing Bureau of Drugs executives of charges of improper motives and undue industry influence, the Review Panel was severely critical of the methods they used to bypass the dissidents. Ostensibly, at least, the bureau is now committed to a policy of greater straightforwardness in dealing with employees whose work is considered unsatisfactory, and of openly documenting decisions to overrule subordinates.

A further internal circumstance that shapes FDA behavior is its domination by members of the medical profession. For over a decade, nearly all of the key line managers in the drug-evaluation process, including all directors of the Bureau of Drugs and all but one commissioner of the agency, have been medical doctors. The reviewing teams are headed by medical officers who are responsible for incorporating the views of the chemists and pharmacologists in their recommendations. The dominance of physicians seems to have at least two important consequences. First, in taking actions that it considers important for public health, the agency has often been willing to ignore or evade the apparent limitations on its legal authority. The agency has attempted to restrict availability of methadone to certain kinds of treatment program, has required prescription drug packages to include labeling to provide extensive medical information to patients, and has required postapproval monitoring and research on some new drugs—all without much support in the words of the statute or the legislative history. An FDA dominated by lawyers might have been somewhat more oriented toward cautiously executing the law. However, this point should not be exaggerated. An aggressive general counsel, Peter Barton Hutt, was instrumental in the agency's expansionism in the early 1970s.

Second, the FDA has traditionally disavowed any concern for the effects of its actions on the economic condition of the drug industry or on the costs of medical care. It has not attempted to use explicit cost-benefit analysis in deciding, for example, what studies should be required to support a new drug application. And, in regard to criticism for creating barriers to drug innovation, the FDA has been more receptive to medical evidence on drugs available abroad than to arguments based on economic models of innovation and measures of "consumer surplus."[27] The agency might have acted differently in these respects if economists had been present and influential. However, this dominance of the medical perspective does not preclude conflict with the medical profession or with parts of it. Doctors in government differ from those in private practice. Indeed, the AMA is often the FDA's staunchest opponent.

External Influences

The impact of external influences on the FDA is a disputed subject: some critics argue that the FDA is subjected to intense pressures primarily by industry;[28] others see the main pressures as favoring tighter regulatory controls.[29] Some features of the FDA's environment support each of these views; it is hard to say which is correct.

Undoubtedly the most significant pressure on the FDA to approve drugs results directly from industry lobbying of the agency. In the drug-evaluation process there are necessarily frequent contacts between agency officials and representatives of drug companies. The issues and information involved are too complex for efficient handling in writing alone. According to FDA medical officers responding to a survey, industry usually behaves itself during such contacts, using factual and reasoned arguments in support of its positions, rather than hard-sell tactics, threats, or bribes.[30] Nevertheless, having frequent contacts with industry representatives, getting to know and perhaps like them personally, and seeing their anxiousness to have drugs approved obviously will tend to create some sympathy for industry viewpoints and interests. Such contacts on a regular basis over a period of years may strongly shape the attitudes of FDA officials. Moreover, there are no regular, direct contacts between reviewing officials and any parties inclined to oppose drug approvals. In addition to its psychological effects, this lobbying imbalance also creates an imbalance of information and analysis —arguments favorable to a drug approval will be discovered and articulately put by company representatives while criticisms must be discovered by the reviewer unassisted.

In addition to this direct lobbying, industry might employ indirect lobbying as well. A company executive might ask the commissioner, the secretary of HEW, a key congressman, or even the president to use his leverage with the Bureau of Drugs to bring about favorable action. Although such political intervention might be hard to observe, it is evidently rare. Very few instances have come to light. The most notable case concerned Panalba—a very popular combination antibiotic that was pronounced ineffective in the review of drugs retroactively subject to the proof-of-efficacy requirement of the 1962 amendments. The Upjohn Company, producers of Panalba, objected to the FDA's decision in May 1969 to decertify the drug by a summary procedure, without a prior hearing, and took its complaint to HEW Secretary Robert Finch. Finch ordered the FDA to grant the prior hearing. However, news of the secretary's intervention immediately leaked to Representative Lawrence Fountain's subcommittee of the Government Operations Committee. The subcommittee staff expressed interest in the matter, and the secretary's order was reversed before it was a day old. Perhaps partly for partisan reasons, Fountain, a Democrat, held hearings on the case which produced publicity embarrassing to the Nixon administration. The Panalba case is the kind of exception that proves the rule: it suggests that attempts to intervene in favor of industry are likely to be politically unrewarding. In interviews with the author, FDA officials have described such political intervention as extremely uncommon.

In some cases, industry can obstruct or at least delay FDA regulatory action by use of administrative and judicial appeals. The effectiveness of these tactics, however, is dependent on the circumstances. The courts generally allow the FDA wide administrative discretion, especially with regard to its scientific and policy judgments on drug safety and efficacy. Judicial limitations on the agency usually concern matters of jurisdiction and procedure. Thus, appeals can be useful to industry primarily to prevent or to delay agency action.

Delay cannot help companies seeking to market a new product, and therefore attempts to secure marketing approval by judicial appeal are rare. Appeals are most useful to industry when the FDA seeks to withdraw an already marketed drug or to change its labeling. Even then, however, a company will not appeal if it believes that the FDA's case is so strong that resisting it would result in bad publicity or that sales would decline anyway. Indeed, most product withdrawals sought by the FDA are accomplished voluntarily.

Some critics have argued that drug companies gain influence with the FDA because officials have often left the agency for jobs in industry.[31] The assumption is that, while they are in the FDA, officials might want to preserve or enhance future opportunities for industry employment and therefore might make more lenient regulatory decisions than they otherwise would. FDA officials do go on to industry jobs with significant frequency—former commissioners Herbert Ley and Charles Edwards, former Bureau of Drugs Director Henry Simmons, and former head of the Office of New Drug Evaluation George Leong all subsequently accepted direct or indirect drug-industry employment. Nevertheless, the contribution of this career pattern to industry influence is evidently very limited.[32] FDA officials believe that industry employment is offered primarily on the basis of experience in the agency and scientific or managerial competence. Only that small fraction of the agency's lower-level officials who take extremely strong antiindustry positions, of a sort considered factually unsupported by most of the agency, are believed to lose opportunities for future industry employment. For the range of policy views covering most of the agency, and all of its high officials, policy is considered irrelevant to such opportunities. In support of this position, some officials point out that both Edwards and Simmons were noted for a tough attitude toward industry, but still were offered industry employment. Thus, even for FDA officials interested in industry employment, the incentives to adopt industry views are negligible as long as they avoid identification as extremists.

On some issues, the main opposition to FDA action is not from the drug industry, but from the medical profession. The FDA has attempted to discourage or prevent certain prescribing practices; it has required "patient labels" for some drugs, which serve to give the patient medical advice; and it has threatened to withdraw drugs whose frequent misuse makes them a public health hazard. The AMA and other medical organizations object strenuously to such efforts, which are perceived as medically and legally unwarranted. They argue that the individual physician can determine patient needs better than a distant and slow-moving bureaucracy such as the FDA, and they argue that Congress intended the FDA to regulate only the production and marketing of drugs—not the practice of medicine. Moreover, the organized medical profession has supported the criticism that burdensome FDA regulation has kept valuable drugs off the American market.

By the mid-1970s, disaffection of the medical profession with the FDA had become quite severe. State and national medical conventions passed resolutions calling for reduction of the agency's authority. On a wide range of issues, the medical profession was acting in concert with the drug industry in pursuit of more lenient regulation.

On rare occasions, the principal resistance to FDA regulation comes from the mass public. The attempted banning of saccharin (a food additive, and thus not strictly our concern here), the attempt to strengthen labeling and dosage restrictions on vitamins and minerals, and the denial of marketing approval to the purported cancer cure, laetrile, have all stimulated intense opposition from a significant segment of public opinion. Apparently, such public opposition occurs when the FDA takes action to prohibit or restrict sale or discourage use of a product that has gained substantial public acceptance. In the cases of saccharin and of vitamins, public opposition was intensified by the presence of obvious disagreement among responsible experts concerning the merits of the FDA's decision. In the case of laetrile, respectable opinion was more unanimously in the FDA's favor, but apparently sympathy for the frustrating and desperate circumstances of cancer victims made many people willing to ignore or disregard the experts.

When FDA actions offend public opinion, other institutions, particularly Congress, are ready to consider reversing them. Congress legislatively reversed the FDA's vitamin and mineral regulations and delayed implementation of the saccharin ban. A bill was introduced, with over one hundred cosponsors in the House, to legalize laetrile by eliminating proof-of-efficacy as a requirement for drug-marketing approval. And a U.S. District Court in Oklahoma enjoined the FDA from interfering with the prescribing or sale of laetrile to patients certified by their doctors to be terminally ill with cancer.

These cases of intense public opposition are significant not only because of the possibility of legislative or judicial reversal, but also because they threaten the agency's political support and its access to needed resources. Some analysts have argued that regulatory agencies must avoid doing serious harm to regulated industry interests in order to assure survival and to permit growth.[33] They have budgetary incentives to adopt policies favored by industry. In interviews designed to test this hypothesis, however, FDA officials perceived no threats to the agency budget resulting from actions opposed by industry alone or by industry along with the medical profession.[34] Except for some issues on which agency decisions affect agriculture, the only actions seen as bearing a risk of budgetary damage were those that led to *public* protest and opposition. Thus the agency has strong incentives to minimize the number of decisions likely to generate mass resistance.

The drug industry might learn to exploit this FDA vulnerability by using tactics designed to stimulate public protest. Bureau of Drugs Director Richard Crout argues that industry has attempted to hasten approval of new drugs by applying for approval early, before acceptable evidence of safety and efficacy has been assembled, and then generating stories suggesting that the FDA is sitting on an application for a valuable new drug. This criticism leads to intense pressure on the agency to approve the drug from patients wishing to use it, their families, and their doctors. One such example is sodium valproate, a promising drug for children's epilepsy that was available abroad for several years but was not available in the United States until intense public and congressional pressure provoked accelerated FDA approval. From another perspective, this tactic is helpful rather than harmful if it serves as a means of alerting the public to the damage that can be done by excessive testing requirements and unnecessary delays.

Counteracting any pressures in favor of swift or lax drug approvals are important forces tending to produce strict or even burdensome regulation. Consumer groups such as the Ralph Nader–affiliated Health Research Group and the Consumer Federation of America actively promote stricter regulatory standards and criticize FDA decisions that they consider weak or irresponsible. Although the financial resources and personnel of these organizations are completely eclipsed by the resources that the drug industry is able to devote to regulatory affairs, consumer groups have certain advantages over industry. Their news releases make good copy and are often picked up by the press, they have a generally favorable public image and can often count on rallying significant public support for their actions, and they have powerful allies in Congress (and, during the Carter administration, in the White House).[35] Their resource limitations are partly compensated for by the willingness of some FDA officials, who are critical of the agency's leadership, to supply them with information and tips about potentially controversial issues.

The positions consumer groups advocate do not necessarily represent the objective interests of consumers. Because they must gain publicity and persuade the public of their importance in order to remain in business,[36] such groups have reason to exaggerate industry's irresponsibility and to depict the FDA as completely "captured" by the industry. This enables them to assume the role of lone protector of the public interest. The demands of this role lead consumer groups to argue consistently for more and tougher regulatory control and therefore to ignore or deny the costs of regulation.

Probably the most important pressures on the FDA to regulate strictly result from congressional oversight. For two decades a number of congressmen—especially Senators Estes Kefauver, Gaylord Nelson, and Edward Kennedy and Representatives Lawrence Fountain and Paul Rogers—have headed almost continuous investigations of the FDA and the drug industry. These investigations have often gained national attention and have helped the congressmen involved rise in prominence. With rare exceptions, these congressional hearings have criticized FDA decisions and enforcement as lax, have attributed this laxness (directly or by implication) to agency subservience to industry, and have demanded tougher regulation. According to then-Commissioner Alexander Schmidt, testifying before Congress in 1974:

By far the greatest pressure that the Bureau of Drugs or the Food and Drug Administration receives with respect to the new drug approval process is brought to bear through Congressional hearings. In all our history, we are unable to find one instance where a Congressional hearing investigated the failure of FDA to approve a new drug . . . the message conveyed by this situation could not be clearer. . . . Until perspective is brought to the legislative oversight function, the pressure from Congress for FDA to disapprove new drugs will continue to be felt, and could be a major factor in health care in this country.[37]

Congressional oversight of drug regulation is affected by some of the same biases that influence consumer groups, for similar reasons. Thus, in 1973 and 1974, Senators Nelson and Kennedy tended to dismiss all evidence that high regulatory barriers were creating a significant disincentive to new drug development and keeping useful drugs, available abroad, off the American market.[38] In part, such behavior simply reflects the necessity for congressmen to decide who will be their friends, and who their enemies—an attitude of judicious moderation is likely to gain the support of no one.

The importance of these congressional pressures is worth examining: Schmidt's estimate, suggesting their preeminent effectiveness, need not be taken at face value. Interestingly, FDA officials do not consider consumer-oriented congressional criticism of the FDA threatening to the agency's budgetary stability and growth.[39] It is not the appropriations committees that make this criticism; nor are they perceived as being negatively influenced by it. More to the point, criticism often has the effect of supporting FDA claims for more resources and authority. Accordingly, the congressmen who are most critical are those who most support strengthening the agency. In short, it is not clear that consumerist congressional pressures carry with them any credible threat of sanctions—at least of the kinds usually supporting congressional influence with administrators. There are, however, other reasons why the FDA might respond to them, including the need to protect the president from adverse publicity, to maintain agency morale and reputation, and to avoid painful accusations and conflict.

The FDA operates quite independently of HEW and the presidential administration. Presidential influence has probably occurred in recent years primarily through appointments of high-level FDA officials, especially commissioners. And, at least since the mid-1960s, these appointments have supported strong regulation. Dr. James Goddard dramatically changed the tone of the agency when he became commissioner in 1966. Under previous commissioner George Larrick, the FDA had been quite passive; the drug industry had praised Larrick's spirit of cooperation. Goddard, however, spoke very critically in public about the drug industry, began the enormous task of subjecting thousands of pre-1962 drug products to an efficacy review, and took effective action to require balanced presentation of information in prescription drug advertising.

Even under Republican administrations there was no return to passivity. Under Charles Edwards, who served from 1969 to 1973, the FDA tightened advertising regulations, imposed patient labeling requirements for oral contraceptives, began to make strong and explicit criticisms of careless prescribing on the part of doctors, and defended stringent testing requirements against the evidence of a drug lag. Donald Kennedy, who headed the FDA for the first part of the Carter administration, has outspokenly rejected claims of excessive regulation. Moreover, judging from interviews with high officials beneath the level of commissioner in 1976, support for strong regulation has apparently been prevalent among individuals selected for these positions also.[40] Thus administration influence, operating primarily through the selection of personnel, has also tended to counteract the influence of industry. It seems that presidents, both Democratic and Republican, find it politically advisable to support an activist FDA. Given the degree of congressional and public attention the agency receives, that is not surprising.

Finally, the FDA may find it difficult not to be extremely cautious in approving new drugs because the consequences of a seriously mistaken approval would be so much more visible than those of unnecessary obstruction and delay. The error would be directly traceable to the FDA, and even to the particular officials who were responsible for approval. On the other hand, when approval of a valuable drug is delayed (at least until recently), the general public and the medical profession ordinarily know little about it. And nothing is known about the benefits of drugs that, because of discouragingly high costs of drug development, are never even developed. Under such circumstances, the prudent course for the FDA is to delay and strive for maximum certainty.

It is important to notice that the balance of external forces impinging on the FDA is not a constant. It fluctuates with events, with the rise and decline of social movements and political organizations, with experience of the impact of previous regulatory decisions, and with broad changes of public attitude. Prior to the late 1950s, consumer-oriented pressure on the FDA was minimal. By the mid-1960s, however, the situation had changed dramatically. The thalidomide disaster, though largely avoided in the United States, had demonstrated the risks associated with prescription drugs and the inability or unwillingness of the drug industry to control itself adequately. And the consumer movement was underway. (Ralph Nader first captured national attention in 1965, with the publication of *Unsafe at Any Speed*[41]; by the early 1970s, he was the operational or symbolic head of nineteen consumer-oriented organizations with a combined budget of $2.5 million.) The peak period for demands on the FDA to deal strictly with the drug industry was probably from the late 1960s to the early 1970s. After that, though the consumer movement did not disappear, new developments strengthened its opposition. Among these was the increasing evidence that stringent regulatory requirements were having important undesirable consequences (even for those whose sole concern was public health). In 1972–73, many commentators began to point to a serious decline in the discovery and introduction of valuable new drugs, apparently due in substantial part to increased regulatory burdens.[42] Added to this was an apparent trend in elite (and possibly public) opinion against big government in general and against "excessive regulation" in particular. The mood of the late 1970s was certainly more favorable to industry than that of the late 1960s. But it was far from as favorable as that of the 1950s. And by the 1970s an elaborate regulatory mechanism was in place and well established politically.

There are significant pressures on the FDA to regulate both strictly and leniently. Since we are unable to measure the force of the various pressures quantitatively, any assessment of their net effect would be subject to challenge. We can, however, say that the belief that the FDA is dominated by pressures from industry—as well as the belief that it is lacking any strong incentives to approve drugs—are equally wrong. It is also clear that the FDA's political environment allows for—and indeed probably causes—noticeable fluctuation in the orientation of the agency over time.

Food and Drug Administration

FDA's Regulatory Performance

We have discussed the problems the FDA faces in regulating prescription drugs and some other factors that influence its behavior. It remains to examine the agency's response—the principal policies and patterns of action that characterize its regulatory performance.

Drug Testing Since 1962, testing procedures for new drugs have become quite elaborate. The details vary considerably depending on the type of drug, the kinds of hazard that seem most likely, the results of early tests, and so on. But, in general terms, from its initial discovery or invention until its approval for marketing (if it is approved), a drug undergoes the following lengthy and rigorous program of investigations: (a) a preliminary assessment of therapeutic potential primarily by small-scale animal studies; (b) short-term toxicity studies in animals to gauge the safety of initial testing in humans; (c) brief and closely supervised testing on small numbers of healthy human subjects, primarily to confirm animal findings on short-term toxicity; (d) three-month animal studies, primarily to estimate the safety of longer-term studies on humans; (e) two phases of clinical trials, involving perhaps a few thousand individuals in need of the treatment the drug is supposed to provide, in order to confirm clinical efficacy, develop further evidence on hazards, and determine appropriate dosages and other aspects of treatment; and, finally, (f) two-year animal studies to assess hazards possibly resulting from long-term treatment. The FDA has strictly interpreted the statutory requirement that clinical investigations intended to establish efficacy be "adequate and well-controlled." Except where it would be infeasible, these investigations are expected to employ the elaborate "double-blind" design, which controls against placebo effects and investigator bias. Mere testimonial evidence from doctors who have used a drug is given virtually no credence. After a full program of tests has been completed and an application for marketing approval (NDA) submitted, the agency may demand still more tests if it believes that significant questions remain.

During the 1970s, the FDA has shown a desire both to limit the barriers to drug innovation and to improve the evidence available for its decisions. The reduction of barriers is exemplified by the agency's willingness, announced for the first time in 1973, to accept foreign data and to give it limited weight in the drug-evaluation process. This move was intended to reduce the need for duplication of studies already conducted abroad, while maintaining an emphasis primarily on domestic studies subject to the FDA's scrutiny and control. Similarly, since 1974 the FDA has resisted (by not responding to) a petition by the Health Research Group asking the agency to require completion of two-year carcinogenicity testing prior to any exposure of humans to investigational drugs. These positions apparently represent the agency's response to increased concern that regulation may discourage or delay new-drug development.

During the same period, however, the FDA has also sought various improvements in the quality of drug information. First, responding to congressional exposure of rampant carelessness and even dishonesty in research submitted by drug companies, the FDA has increased its monitoring of the actual conduct and reporting of drug research. Second, with increasing frequency since about 1970, the agency has approved some drugs on the condition that the sponsoring company conduct postapproval research and surveillance on experience with the drug. This mitigates the problem of the limited number of patients involved in preapproval studies. But in the absence of explicit statutory authority to require postapproval studies, this policy development remains somewhat tenuous. Finally, the FDA has discussed the possibility of adopting the concept of "the developing NDA," in which the agency would enter earlier and in more detail into the planning of research for specific new drugs. The drug industry argues that this would create additional delays, would remove needed flexibility, and would represent governmental intrusion in the scientific process. From the agency's perspective, this move would help avoid the dilemma of whether to accept imperfectly designed research. Thus, despite some effort to reduce barriers to drug innovation, a trend toward insistence on more and better research has continued.

Decision Making on INDs and NDAs   In its decisions on particular INDs (applications to begin testing in humans) and NDAs (applications for marketing approval), the FDA has been somewhat inconsistent. While at times the agency has been severe to a point most critics would consider unreasonable, at other times drugs have been approved with rather weak justification.

A study of FDA decisions on INDs was sponsored by the Review Panel on New Drug Regulation.[43] The panel, which was indisputably consumer-oriented, assembled a group of nationally recognized experts in pharmacology and toxicology and divided them into teams of two. Thirty IND submissions on which the agency had acted either positively or negatively were chosen at random and distributed to the expert teams for their review and evaluation. The results are interesting. In fifteen of the thirty cases, both experts agreed with the FDA's decision. In ten, the two experts disagreed with each other about whether the agency's decision was appropriate. And, in five, both disagreed with the agency. Of these five, where the agency seems most likely to have been in error, three were decisions to approve, two to deny.

Three conclusions are suggested by these findings: First, IND decisions are often ambiguous. Half of the randomly chosen cases occasioned some disagreement. Second, the FDA's judgments were apparently no less defensible than those of the experts. In the fifteen cases where there was disagreement, the FDA's judgment stood alone five times, and either of the two experts was alone ten times—the same proportion. The experts were no more inclined to agree with each other than with the agency. Third, there is no evidence of FDA bias (as compared to the experts) toward either accepting or rejecting industry requests. Where both experts disagreed with the FDA, IND status was denied almost as often as it was granted.

A rough sense of the FDA's orientation toward drug approvals is provided by a study of 324 INDs for new chemical entities submitted between 1963 and 1967.[44] Such a submission indicates that a sponsor has findings from in vitro (artificial environment) and animal studies that it considers sufficiently favorable to warrant the initiation of studies involving humans. As of April 1974, 86 percent of the 324 drugs had been discontinued. Only 7 percent had been approved for marketing, and another 7 percent were still pending. Clearly, the scrutiny exercised by the FDA (plus the policing that the companies employ voluntarily) was eliminating a large majority of the initially promising new chemical entities. On the other hand, most drugs for which the drug companies actually request marketing approval are eventually approved. This should not be surprising, however, since it may suggest only that industry is able to anticipate the FDA's decisions and that it avoids submitting NDAs for products unlikely to be approved. Unfortunately, evidence of this sort is of only limited value in assessing the FDA's performance: we do not know what proportion of INDs or NDAs should be approved; thus we have no standard for evaluation.

Another perspective on the FDA's performance on INDs and NDAs is provided by comparing the number of new drugs approved in the United States and in certain other countries. Such comparisons will be considered more broadly below, but one such comparison—already referred to in part—shows that the FDA has sometimes been extremely cautious in its new-drug evaluations. As bureau director Crout himself pointed out, "The [Cardiovascular-Renal] Division approved no new chemical entities during the period from 1968 to 1972, an experience which contrasted with the experience of every other modern nation."[45] In 1970–71 this division attempted to deny marketing approval for antihypertensive drugs until it was demonstrated by long-term, controlled clinical studies that chemically lowering blood pressure actually reduces disease or delays death. This policy would have ignored the strong correlational evidence of adverse effects of high blood pressure and would have delayed the introduction of these agents for several years. Though the Cardio-Renal Division was not typical of the FDA during this period, and indeed its performance reflected the lack of centralized control of the Bureau, we shall see that the FDA issued few approvals compared to other nations across the whole range of drugs during the late 1960s and early 1970s. In the middle 1970s, however, its approvals became relatively more frequent, particularly in the cardio-renal area.

The FDA's occasional approval of drugs that are at best marginal is illustrated by its handling of amphetamines intended for use in weight reduction in the early 1970s. Amphetamines are dangerous drugs— habit-forming, subject to abuse, and capable of producing serious adverse effects from prolonged or excessive use. However, they also have some appetite-suppressing effect, and by the late 1960s the FDA was considering several applications to market amphetamines for weight reduction. Clinical studies were able to define the effectiveness of amphetamines for this purpose quite precisely. Compared to the control groups, overweight patients lost more weight when dieting was combined with use of these drugs. But the difference lasted only several weeks, and only amounted to about half a pound per patient per week; then a tolerance developed, and appetite suppression was lost entirely. Despite considerable criticism and resistance within the agency, Dr. Crout approved the drugs involved. His rationale was that, in order to be considered effective under the law, a drug's superiority to placebos had merely to be *statistically* significant, and need not also be *clinically* significant. (Studies had to show definitely that there was some weight-reduction effect, but that effect was not required to be large enough to offer appreciable value in treatment.) This legal interpretation had no apparent basis in the words or legislative history of the statute and ran counter to the agency's usual posture of balancing efficacy against risk. In 1979, the FDA gave notice that it intended to withdraw approval of amphetamines for weight reduction.

Food and Drug Administration

Similarly, in a decision that was reversed without going into effect, in 1973 the FDA decided to approve Depo-Provera, the first long-lasting injectable contraceptive. Despite a significant increased risk of serious side effects compared to oral contraceptives, the FDA argued that Depo-Provera was appropriate for patients who could not safely use pills or other methods of birth control. However, intense congressional criticism forced the FDA to reconsider the matter, and approval of Depo-Provera was ultimately refused. Agency officials now reject the suitability of Depo-Provera for any significant group of American women.

Two points about these apparently lenient drug-approval decisions need to be kept in mind. First, since one decision has been reversed and the other may be, these cases are probably at or near the limit of what the FDA has been willing to approve. Second, in both cases, the FDA's decision to approve was somewhat supportable on the merits, not strictly indefensible. Thus, although the FDA appears to have occasionally approved drugs on rather shaky grounds, the agency has not approved drugs in reckless or obvious disregard of its responsibility to protect the public.

Decisions on whether to remove drugs from the market would seem to raise issues essentially similar to those on whether to permit marketing in the first place. But the FDA acts far less aggressively on removals than on initial approvals; thus, it is generally easy to keep a drug on the market, once it has been approved. This is the result of several factors. There is a paucity of information about experience with marketed drugs. The greater visibility of a decision to withdraw—compared to a decision to withhold approval—makes it more embarrassing for the agency if the drug ultimately warrants approval. And the drug companies have substantial opportunities to appeal withdrawal decisions; these actions tie up agency resources. Moreover, the importance of appeals has been exaggerated by the nearly complete disuse of the statutory "imminent hazard" standard for immediate suspension of marketing approval. (This disuse may result from the fact that a finding by the secretary of HEW is required to invoke the clause.)

A recent illustration of the resulting disproportion in FDA aggressiveness is provided by Naprosyn. Despite the discovery that the drug's long-term animal toxicity study had been clearly invalid, the FDA acted to withdraw the drug only after a long delay. Without an apparently valid long-term toxicity study, initial approval would not even have been considered. The FDA did manage to remove over six hundred drugs from the market as a result of the Drug Efficacy Study, which applied the proof of efficacy requirement to drugs marketed before the 1962 amendments. The Drug Efficacy Study actions, however, involved special circumstances. For many of these drugs, no evidence of significant efficacy had been submitted; thus, the case for withdrawal was clear. Moreover, because of the large number of such drugs, the FDA established, and the courts upheld, a special simplified administrative process that facilitated action. Nevertheless, the implementation of the Drug Efficacy Study stretched over several years.

Attempts to Influence Prescribing A number of FDA policies and activities are intended primarily to influence how prescription drugs are actually utilized. Among such activities, the agency's regulation of drug labeling and advertising are the most clearly authorized by the words and history of the statute. During the Larrick regime, FDA control of drug promotion was quite limited; a major theme of the Kefauver hearings was the prevalence of distortion and withholding of negative information in the promotion of prescription drugs. But James Goddard made reform of drug promotion a major priority when he became commissioner in 1966. Strict regulations were issued requiring that advertising include a statement of a drug's side effects, contraindications, and appropriate precautions and warnings; that its effectiveness be described in a "fair summary"; that all information be presented "in fair balance"; and that promotional claims be restricted to those approved in the drug's official labeling. Goddard also initiated the practice of forcing companies that had used misleading advertising to send "Dear Doctor letters" to all physicians, correcting the false impressions they had given.

Subsequent commissioners have carried forward Goddard's insistence on full disclosure and fair balance in advertising. Nevertheless, the FDA has not made advertising an optimal source of drug information for physicians. Information on side effects is essentially a list of effects believed to have occurred, with little or no indication of their frequency. And labeling and advertising contain little comparative information about the safety or efficacy of competing drugs.

Moreover, FDA action to change drug labeling and advertising in response to new adverse information tends to be painfully slow. Sometimes this is due to litigation. For example, a suit by a committee of diabetes practitioners has kept the FDA from incorporating a warning in the labeling of certain oral antidiabetic drugs, despite reports since 1971 that these drugs double the risk of fatal heart disease. Other delays have been caused by organizational inefficiency and resource shortages.

Food and Drug Administration

For example, delays of several years in the relabeling of thyroid drugs and digoxin (a drug used principally for heart disease) to warn against their use for obesity were evidently due to unwieldy bureaucratic procedures, the pressures of other work, and inadequate communication of priorities.

In addition to controlling labeling and advertising, the FDA sometimes directly publicizes findings about appropriate drug use, especially through its *Drug Bulletin* which is mailed to all physicians. On rare occasions, the agency has attempted to alter patterns of utilization through releases to the mass media. But the effectiveness of FDA publicity is much in doubt. Recently, the FDA attempted to stop the prescribing of estrogen-progesterone compounds for prevention of miscarriage and other problems in pregnancy. Despite newspaper publicity and a mailed notice to physicians describing serious hazards of such use, over half a million prescriptions for these drugs were written for pregnant women in the following year. This was only 10 percent fewer prescriptions than in 1974, when uses in pregnant women were still approved.

During the 1970s, beginning with Charles Edwards's term as commissioner, the FDA has attempted to invent more effective methods for gaining control of prescribing practices. The most ambitious effort concerned use of the narcotic substitute methadone and was motivated by the special susceptibility of that drug to abuse. The FDA ordered the restriction of methadone distribution to treatment centers that registered with the agency and met its standards of practitioner qualifications and treatment methods. Furthermore, practitioners in these programs were required to comply with the FDA's detailed set of instructions concerning proper administration of methadone. This procedure would have represented the FDA's most direct involvement in the regulation of medical practice. But the agency's authority to add such restrictions to the distribution of an approved drug was not upheld in court.

An apparently more viable FDA innovation is patient labeling. The FDA requires that packaging for certain prescription drugs include medical information and instructions to be given to the patient upon purchase. Patient labels were first introduced in 1972 for oral contraceptives in order to provide warnings about possible adverse reactions, to point out danger signs to watch for, and to indicate circumstances under which the drugs should not be used. Subsequently, patient-labeling requirements were proposed or adopted for a few other drugs. For example, estrogen was given a patient-label warning against its use for

225

long-term mitigation of symptoms of menopause. Patient labeling may be the FDA's most effective method for controlling prescribing practices. In effect, labeling enforces the FDA's conception of appropriate therapy by warning the patient against any deviations from it. Presumably, doctors will be reluctant to ignore advice given in this form. However, its usefulness is clearly limited to discouraging certain practices that can easily and accurately be defined for patients. It cannot force doctors to become more sophisticated and discriminating across the whole range of complex problems involved in drug utilization.

The Effects of Regulation

Some critics argue that, on balance, regulation has hurt medical care by inhibiting the development and introduction of valuable new drugs; others contend that such obstruction has been minimal and is easily justified by the added protection from inferior medicines afforded by strict regulation. The issues in this debate are far too complex for adequate summary here.[46] I will only indicate, and briefly defend, a few conclusions that seem warranted.

The severity of FDA regulation has sometimes deprived American patients and physicians of valuable new drugs that were available in other countries and would otherwise presumably have been available in the United States. From 1962 to 1976, more than three times as many new chemical entities were introduced in Great Britain, but not in America, than vice versa. Quite possibly, much of this difference represents the FDA's exclusion of less desirable drugs. But even if one examines only drugs that ultimately became available in both countries, a substantial "drug lag" is evident. For eighty-two drugs that became available in both countries during the decade 1962–1971, the average drug was introduced almost nine months earlier in Britain than in the United States.[47] A survey of British academic medical experts in 1972 found that in several broad therapeutic areas, drugs that were available in Britain but not here were considered to be highly useful and important.[48]

By 1976 the differences in availability of effective therapy between the two countries had narrowed considerably, but the United States still appeared to be "substantially behind" in drugs for treatment of cardiovascular disease, peptic ulcer, and nervous-system diseases, including depression, epilepsy, and migraine.[49] For drugs of genuine importance, the health costs of such a lag may be extraordinary. For example, practolol is a cardiovascular drug available in Great Britain but (as of 1978) not in the United States. According to Wardell, clinical trials indicate that practolol reduces the mortality of myocardial infarction (heart attack) patients in the two years following release from the hospital by 40 percent. He estimates that in the United States the availability of practolol for these patients could save 10,000 lives per year, with side effects that would be trivial by comparison. Whatever the actual merits of practolol, the potential significance of a drug lag is clear.[50]

Regulation has apparently reduced the financial capacity and incentive for drug companies to attempt drug development and therefore has reduced the rate of new-drug development in the United States. In large part, the therapeutic losses here involve not drugs developed abroad, but drugs never developed anywhere that otherwise would have been developed in the United States.

Figure 6–1, which is reproduced from Sam Peltzman's elaborate cost-benefit analysis of FDA regulation,[51] shows the dramatic decline in introduction of new chemical entities in the United States. An important ambiguity in the interpretation of the data arises, however, from the fact that the decline in NCEs had begun by 1960, prior to the enactment of the 1962 amendments and the subsequent phased-in tightening of regulation. Defenders of the FDA interpret this fact as strongly supporting the view that the decline in drug innovation is due primarily to nonregulatory changes, such as the exhaustion of easy opportunities for therapeutic advancement. Based on the previous behavior of the industry, however, Peltzman believes that the post-1957 drop-off was predictable, but that if not for increased regulation, NCE introduction would have rebounded substantially by 1964 and remained high until at least 1971—which it did not. Specifically, Peltzman demonstrates that, from 1948 to 1962, NCE introduction is highly correlated with the growth rate in the demand for drugs (as indicated by the growth in the number of prescriptions) two years previously. After 1962, the year of the enactment of stricter legislation, the number of NCEs falls dramatically below the level expected based on previous demand. Thus most of the reduction in NCE introduction during the 1960s is still arguably attributable to regulation.

In view of the strong correlation between demand and NCE introduction up to 1962, Peltzman's argument must be taken seriously. But

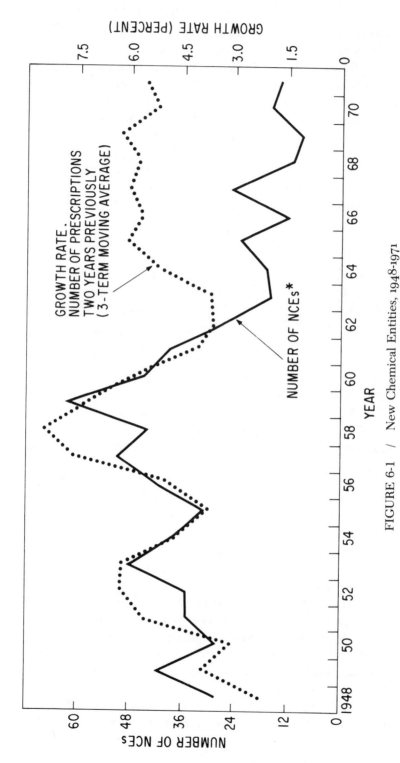

FIGURE 6-1 / New Chemical Entities, 1948-1971

SOURCE: Sam Peltzman, *Regulation of Pharmaceutical Innovation* (Washington, D.C.: American Enterprise Institute, 1974), p. 15. *The term "new chemical entity" (NCE) refers to a new drug having chemical content or structure significantly different from previous products. An NCE is thus considered a genuine innovation, though it need not be an important one.

it should not be considered conclusive. First, the hypothesis that drug innovation is simply responsive to demand offends common sense. It requires us to believe that innovation is not affected by the state of medical knowledge or by differences in the intrinsic difficulty of various advances. In any case, Peltzman does not test whether in the 1960s there were changes in the scientific or medical situation that contributed to the declining rate of drug innovation. The fact that drug innovation slowed in other countries as well as the United States during this decade supports the suspicion of nonregulatory factors. But it remains true that the United States underwent a sharper downturn than did the other drug-developing countries.

Corroborating evidence of a disincentive effect is available in data on drug R&D costs, financial returns, and investment patterns.[52] According to estimates in an industry-sponsored study, between 1960 and 1973 the development costs per NCE rose 1,015 percent, exclusive of inflation. Some of these increases were due to improvements in scientific standards and methods, concerns about carcinogenicity and birth defects, attempts to treat more difficult diseases, and other factors largely independent of regulation. But, by estimates of two separate investigators, about half of the increases since 1962 had regulatory origins.[53] Even though the overall profitability of the drug industry remained high, one financial analysis suggests that rates of return on new R&D investment have fallen sharply since 1960.[54] Indeed, by 1973 it appeared that investment in drug development would be less remunerative than alternative investment strategies open to the industry. Cost increases due to regulation would appear to contribute substantially to this deteriorating financial situation. Finally, by the early 1970s, there was evidence of declining investment in pharmaceutical innovation in the United States. Much of this investment was being shifted to overseas subsidiaries. There its benefits for American consumers would be more indirect, delayed, and uncertain, though not totally lost.

Thus several types of data converge to suggest that FDA regulation has discouraged drug innovation in the 1960s and 1970s. Presumably cost increases would have especially serious implications for the development of drugs for rare diseases because of their limited sales potential. It has even been argued that there is little disincentive affecting development of genuinely new products for common untreatable diseases.[55] But this argument is dubious. While it is true that such drugs are enormously profitable to their successful discoverers, their development is also extremely difficult and risky. Indeed, drug companies have long been criticized for their limited involvement in truly innovative research. Increased costs of drug development due to regulation must inevitably exacerbate this situation. Moreover, development of highly innovative products may be too risky if the investment is not cushioned by a large volume of reliably profitable projects of minor importance. Given primarily private financing of drug development, it may therefore be important to preserve the possibility and profitability of such minor projects—even if the resulting products are redundant and more distracting than medically advantageous.

On the positive side, FDA regulation has undoubtedly produced significant benefits by raising the standards of safety and efficacy for drugs on the American market. In a few instances, these benefits are readily visible. For example, during the 1960s there was a striking increase in deaths from asthma in England, Ireland, Australia, and several other countries. In England and Wales, by the peak of the epidemic in 1966, there had been a sevenfold increase in mortality from asthma in only seven years. This accounted for 7 percent of all deaths in persons ten to fourteen years old. The United States and Canada were spared these additional deaths. Apparently, the deaths (or many of them) were caused by a type of pressurized aerosol mist not approved for marketing by the FDA. For the most part, however, the benefits of FDA regulation are subtle and hard to observe, resulting primarily from exclusion of *marginally* unsafe or ineffective drugs that would otherwise be marketed.

Thus it is difficult to estimate the overall benefits of FDA regulation of prescription drugs, in either health or dollar terms, or to compare these benefits with the costs discussed above. (In addition, the cost-benefit balance would depend on the baseline—or alternative arrangement—to which FDA regulation is compared.) Nevertheless, a few attempts at an overall assessment have been made.

Peltzman's economic analysis suggests that the consumer surplus (a measure of the benefits derived from a consumer product) from prescription drugs has declined as a result of regulatory changes since 1962, implying that the costs have exceeded the benefits.[56] The amount of the loss is estimated at $250–$350 million per year, or about 6 percent of total sales. However, Peltzman's consumer surplus estimates are subject to serious question. First, they depend on his conclusion that the decline in drug innovation is mainly due to regulation; this, as we have seen, is questionable. Second, they depend on Peltzman's argument, based on their relative success in the market, that post-1962 drugs are not significantly better than pre-1962 drugs, and that therefore the reduced number of post-1962 drugs is not offset by improvements in their quality. However, to use market success as the measure of quality is to assume that doctors and consumers are able to evaluate drug quality with reasonable precision. This is just what proponents of regulation deny, with occasionally striking evidence. Peltzman's claim, therefore, that regulatory changes since 1962 have imposed costs that are greater than their benefits is inconclusive.

Wardell compared the effects of FDA regulation to those of the looser British system of prescription drug controls and found the British system more favorable.[57] As noted previously, the British system makes new drugs available more quickly and in larger numbers. Based on his survey of the medical literature, Wardell finds no evidence of significant numbers of especially unsafe or ineffective British drugs, and concludes that British patients have not been exposed more than Americans to harm from such drugs. This approach, unlike Peltzman's, had the advantage of observing medical effects fairly directly, rather than through the uncertain lens of market success. Unfortunately, it is impossible through such literature–review techniques to measure the relevant costs and benefits comprehensively and systematically. For example, it is possible that many drugs in widespread use in Britain are marginally less safe or effective than drugs used in America. Harmful effects from such drugs would be hard to identify, but might be important in the aggregate.

Though the evidence on their comparative effects is inconclusive, the British system probably is superior to the American. Premarketing testing requirements and approval procedures are less burdensome in the British system, but they are supported by more effective postmarketing surveillance and stronger controls over the manner in which drugs are used. As we have seen, it is the American system's nearly exclusive emphasis on premarketing controls that both forces the FDA to impose burdensome constraint and yet weakens its protection of the public.

In sum, FDA regulation of prescription drugs seems to have had both costs and benefits. It has delayed and discouraged the introduction of useful new medicines. But it has probably also eliminated large numbers of relatively unsafe or ineffective drugs that consumers are better off without and has certainly prevented several drug catastrophes. Since neither the costs nor the benefits can be measured precisely, the balance between them is uncertain. Thus Peltzman's claim that the Drug Amendments of 1962 did more harm than good must be judged inconclusive. Wardell's finding that the British system of controls is superior overall to the American also is inconclusive on the evidence. But it gains credibility from the manifest inefficiency of the American system's almost total reliance on premarketing clearance. None of this, of course, necessarily casts blame on the FDA. Rather, if the analysis presented above is correct, a tendency toward burdensome and yet inadequate regulation is thrust upon the agency by the basic regulatory structure.

Regulatory Change

We have seen that the regulatory framework for prescription drugs established by Congress creates intractable policy dilemmas for the FDA, compelling the agency both to impose heavy burdens on the drug development process and to provide inadequate protection from inferior drugs. Consequently, the benefits of regulation have been balanced (or even overbalanced) by heavy costs. This situation benefits neither industry nor consumers. One would imagine, therefore, that Congress would quickly change it to the satisfaction of all concerned. But, in fact, Congress seems reluctant to adopt the implied changes. The limitations on feasible reform, and the reasons for them, reveal important features of regulatory politics generally.

In recent years a number of bills have been introduced in Congress to change various aspects of prescription-drug regulation, the FDA, and the drug industry. In 1977 the Carter administration adopted the issue of drug regulatory "reform" and proposed a major revision of the Food, Drug, and Cosmetics Act. The administration bill was formulated after extensive consultation with key members of Congress, especially Senator Kennedy and Representative Rogers, and representatives of the drug industry, consumer groups, the medical profession, and other interest groups. As discussions were being held in both houses in the summer of 1978, it was generally expected that the Drug Regulation Reform Act would be enacted, if not shortly after the election recess, then early in the subsequent Congress. Though these optimistic expectations proved unfounded, the bill was important for what it indicated about the limits of reform.

In relation to the analysis presented in this chapter, the Drug Regulation Reform bill contained some significant improvements over existing legislation. It gave the FDA strong and explicit authority to require postmarketing surveillance and research on approved drugs. This procedure would allow exploitation of the experience with a drug in many thousands of patients for the purpose of evaluating its safety and efficacy and would remove some of the burden of protecting the public from the premarketing clearance process. In addition, the bill marginally strengthened the FDA's authority to remove drugs from the market prior to a hearing.

However, the bill also had crucial shortcomings. First, though intended to enhance the FDA's control of prescribing, its provisions for doing so were awkward and weak. The most broadly relevant provisions simply made explicit the agency's authority to impose patient labeling and instructed the agency to do so routinely. As noted above, however, patient labeling can militate against only rather gross and easily described forms of misprescribing.

In addition, the bill gave the FDA authority to restrict distribution of a drug in various ways—for example, by limiting its use to hospital settings or to physicians having specific training or experience. As a means for controlling prescribing, however, such restrictions would be of limited value. Use of these restrictions would be confined to very special cases where, without them, a drug would not be sufficiently safe to warrant approval. Furthermore, these restrictions are an extremely crude way to control drug use: for example, limiting access to a drug to certain classes of physicians obviously guarantees neither that the right patients will receive it nor that the wrong ones will not.

Second, the bill provided for no general reductions in premarketing test requirements. It did mandate some reduction in the agency's supervision of the earliest stages of research (which are intended only to determine whether a project should proceed) as well as a reduction in the amount of long-range research planning required before initiation of preliminary research in humans. These are useful but very modest steps to facilitate drug development and seem to have no significant costs to regulatory objectives. Premarketing testing requirements would be significantly reduced only under extreme circumstances to hasten the availability of "breakthrough drugs." Given a finding of sufficient urgency, the FDA would be able to provisionally approve drugs of major therapeutic importance; some of the usual premarketing tests would then be conducted after marketing had begun.

The bill could have reduced elaborate premarketing test requirements in exchange for more effective and less obstructive postmarketing surveillance. But it did not. As the administration's literature explaining the bill emphasized, the strengthening of postmarketing surveillance was not to replace any significant premarketing testing—it was to be *added* to such testing.[58] Such redundancy—though desirable in the absence of regard for costs—would not come cheaply. Some studies utilizing postmarketing surveillance have cost from $7 to $40 million. Clearly, the addition of surveillance requirements without compensating decreases in other requirements could have a serious impact on the already shaky financial picture for new-drug development.

Finally, the reform bill had no provisions to significantly improve the rewards for new-drug development—not even for development of genuinely new and useful products as opposed to merely imitative ones. A variety of subsidies, tax credits, or amendments to the patent laws could have been fit to these purposes. But there is no evidence of such provisions even being considered.[59]

In short, where there is an apparent need for increased regulatory constraint (postmarketing surveillance, summary removal from the market, and control of prescribing), the reformers sought to meet it (though the controls on prescribing were quite limited). But where there is a strong argument for reduction of constraints (elaborate premarketing testing requirements), or enhancement of rewards (patent, tax, or subsidy provisions), the reformers turned a deaf ear. One can state a surprisingly simple rule: Increasing regulatory constraints and burdens is politically acceptable; reducing constraints or increasing financial rewards is not—even as part of a larger strategy to enhance consumer protection while simultaneously facilitating and encouraging innovation. The only exceptions were the willingness to simplify the investigational drug procedures—at virtually no cost to regulatory objectives—and the special provisions for breakthrough drugs—whose delayed availability causes clearly identifiable harm.

What accounts for this inability to adopt or even consider reform measures apparently advantageous both to industry and to consumers? We saw above how the current regulatory structure, with its inordinate reliance on premarketing testing and its imposition of costs entirely on industry, was shaped by the political circumstances under which it developed. Similar political circumstances continue to operate and tend to maintain these features.

It is politically difficult to strengthen controls over drug prescribing simply because the politically powerful medical profession fervently opposes it. The AMA already objects to FDA infringement on the physician's discretion. Any highly effective governmental or professional control of prescribing would be even more strenuously resisted.[60]

Food and Drug Administration

It is also politically difficult for liberal and consumer-oriented politicians to support reduction of constraints on the drug industry or enhancement of its rewards for drug development. Such politicians typically adopt a crusading, adversarial posture toward the industry. To an extent, this posture may be justified by the behavior of the industry. But it also serves political functions. Drug regulation has no natural constituency of well-organized groups with strong economic incentives to provide support. Thus, if effective regulatory measures are to be enacted, broadly based popular support must be elicited. Moralistic criticism and the creation of a palpable villain in the drug industry are ideally suited to this purpose.[61] Moreover, consumer-oriented politicians gain publicity and electoral advantage by cultivating an image of "standing up to the special interests." Consequently, drug regulatory politics is characterized by rigid ideological cleavages and an atmosphere of zero-sum conflict between the critics and the defenders of the industry. A consumer-oriented politician proposing reductions in premarketing testing or increases in patent protection would be attacked for "selling out" and would suffer politically.

Fundamental change toward a more efficient regulatory structure for prescription drugs must await answers to two political questions: How can we mitigate or overcome the resistance of the medical profession to measures impinging on its professional autonomy? And how can we make politically effective a more calculating stance toward the drug industry—one that sets aside moralistic rhetoric and punitive policies, and attempts carefully to manipulate the industry's performance by an appropriate combination of constraints, punishments, and rewards?

CHAPTER 7

Occupational Safety and Health Administration

STEVEN KELMAN

Industry abounds with hazards which may cause traumatic injury.[1] Factories are filled with machinery capable of sawing, cutting, flattening, bending, or grinding hard material—and any soft human tissue that gets in its way. There are heavy objects which must be picked up and transported by ropes or chains (which may snap), by conveyors (off which the objects may tumble), or by human muscle-power (which may fail). People who work from heights may fall. There is hot or caustic material with which workers may come in contact, and electric current which can electrocute. If attention is not paid to plant housekeeping, floors may get wet or cluttered, and people may slip.[2]

In 1972, the first full year for which the Occupational Safety and Health Administration collected statistics, there were 5.7 million on-the-job accidents in the private sector. The majority of these were just cuts and bruises, but still there were 1.7 million accidents which caused workers to miss at least one day of work.[3] In the private sector as a whole, more than three out of every hundred workers suffered an injury which caused them to lose at least a day's work. (In construction, it was about six out of a hundred.)[4] The average lost worktime for lost workday injuries was 15 days.[5] That same year, there were about 11,000 on-the-job fatalities.[6] To put the toll in perspective, we might note that

236

Occupational Safety and Health Administration

some 50,000 people a year are killed in highway accidents—that is, about five times as many as die in job accidents.[7]

Workplace health hazards involve exposure to chemicals or to physical agents (such as noise or radiation). It is sometimes pointed out, particularly by those who for one reason or another wish us to abandon the fear and trembling many of us feel when exposed to the word "chemical," that not only our bodies, but everything around us, is composed of chemicals. (We need the chemical element oxygen in order to live.) Furthermore, although most of the products the chemical industry produces are not found in nature, it would be wrong to draw a simple distinction between harmless "natural" chemicals and harmful "artificial" ones. The Greeks did not need a chemical industry to find a substance with which to poison Socrates. Indeed, some of the most serious and pervasive workplace health hazards come from exposure to dusts of naturally occurring minerals or metals (asbestos, silica, lead, arsenic).

If everything around us is a chemical, why should we be especially concerned about the products and byproducts of the chemical industry which multiply around us? The key is the concept of dose-response. In large enough doses, any chemical—table salt, water, milk—will harm the body. We need worry about our exposure to a dose of any chemical (whether table salt or trichloroethylene) which elicits a toxic response. Special concern about exposure to chemicals which many workers are exposed to in industry arises because the risk of their being exposed to toxic doses of such chemicals is greater than the risk of such exposures to salt or water.

Conversely, below certain doses, humans will survive contact with cyanide gas or hemlock, and not be the worse for wear. The dose of a chemical below which no toxic response is produced is called a "threshold" or "no-effect" dose. In occupational health, the no-effect dose for a chemical, below which worker exposure is regarded as safe, is called a "threshold limit value."[8]

Information on the extent of occupational disease resulting from chemical exposure is scanty at best, because disease resulting from chronic exposures occurs, by definition, long after initial exposure, and because occupational diseases frequently produce symptoms similar to nonoccupational diseases. One cannot readily distinguish occupationally caused cancer or bronchitis from nonoccupationally caused versions of the same diseases. Certain symptoms produced by overexposure to chemicals (such as headaches, dizziness, or stomach pains) are extremely diffuse and may have countless causes.

Nevertheless, it is probably true that occupational illnesses kill a good many more people each year than the number killed in on-the-job accidents. Nicholas Ashford reports that "epidemiological analyses of excess mortality among workers in several industries suggest that as many as 100,000 deaths occur each year as a result of occupational disease," alt ough Ashford goes on to say that it is impossible to know if the figure is that high.[9] In a survey prepared for the National Institute for Occupational Safety and Health, approximately one thousand employees were selected at random from firms in industrial classifications where there are typically exposures to hazardous chemicals. It was found that 31 percent of the medical conditions found in the group— and almost all the workers surveyed suffered from one or more conditions—probably were related to occupational exposures to chemicals or to noise, and another 10 percent might have been.[10] (These high figures were for workers in industries where chemical exposure was expected.)

There are no good estimates of the total number of workers exposed to harmful doses of different chemicals. Thousands of chemicals are produced and used in the United States; studies of those who work with a given chemical have typically found several thousand workers exposed, sometimes several tens of thousands, rarely more. Thus, when decisions are made about regulating a given chemical, the number of workers (and firms) directly affected by the decision is typically not large. But compliance with health regulations generally costs a good deal more money than compliance with safety regulations.

The Passage of the Occupational Safety and Health Act of 1970

The machines and chemicals that accompanied the Industrial Revolution created concern about work-related accidents and injuries. Occupational safety laws, albeit primitive, were among the first protective laws passed in America. In 1867 a Massachusetts law created a Department of Factory Inspection, and an 1877 law in the same state required that spinning machinery be guarded. By the turn of the century, most of the industrialized states had some sort of occupational safety legislation.[11] But legislation remained mostly at the state level, with little

Occupational Safety and Health Administration

federal involvement except for some research efforts and programs for some limited categories of workers.

In 1967 the Department of Labor included a federal occupational safety and health bill in a package of legislative proposals sent to the White House.[12] Neither the proposal nor the inclusion of a call for new legislation which followed in President Lyndon Johnson's 1968 Manpower Message seemed to arise out of any extensive interest-group pressure (from trade unions, for instance).

Instead, the process was rather idiosyncratic. The brother of Robert Hardesty, one of President Johnson's speechwriters, worked at the Bureau of Occupational Safety and Health in HEW, a small office which did research on occupational safety and health problems (but had no regulatory authority). The result of some brother-to-brother lobbying was that Robert Hardesty occasionally inserted references to the importance of occupational safety and health in various presidential speeches. Meanwhile, there had been reports in 1967 of a high incidence of lung cancer among uranium miners. Esther Peterson, one of the assistant secretaries in the Labor Department, visited some of the mines and spoke with miners and their families. She was deeply touched personally and took the issue up with the Secretary of Labor.[13] Labor Department executives were looking for new programs to propose for the agency to administer. Thanks to the references to occupational safety and health in the presidential speeches (which suggested presidential interest in—and thus likely approval of—a proposal in this regard that Labor developed) and to the newfound interest of Assistant Secretary Peterson, some kind of federal occupational safety and health legislation seemed like a good choice for such a program. The Labor Department thus prepared a draft of a federal occupational safety and health bill and included it in a package of legislative ideas sent to the president in late 1967. The White House bit, although hardly after any great pressure from the Labor Department. "We didn't know, frankly, till several days before the Message that the President had decided to make occupational safety and health a principal element in his program this year," Secretary of Labor Williard Wirtz said later.[14]

This brief account of the emergence within the executive branch of a proposal for a federal occupational safety and health regulatory presence illustrates issues of concern to students of the "agenda formation" process—that is, how issues come to be considered in the political system. Participants in the political system define their roles in different ways: within Congress, for instance, Fenno distinguishes among congressmen who emphasize constituent service, influence among fellow congressmen, and formation of public policy.[15] Walker notes that a significant portion of the "discretionary agenda" of Congress (that is, consideration of bills other than periodic budget and authorization requests) responds to initiatives by congressmen who consciously search for new issues in which to become involved.[16]

The important point is that there are participants in the political system—within the executive branch as well as Congress—who are searching for "good causes" to push. This makes them receptive to certain kinds of stimuli. Which stimulus turns out to get the attention of the person looking for "good causes" is often as much a matter of happenstance as anything else. There is no "deep" reason why the particular issue, and not some other one, comes to be the object of the governmental participant's attention; the search for "good causes" is conducted to find a cause that is "good enough" to promote—not necessarily the ideal cause.[17] This is what appeared to have happened within the Labor Department in 1967. Assistant Secretary Peterson happened to become interested in the plight of uranium miners; some positive references to the necessity of federal action happened to have been placed in some presidential speeches. So Secretary of Labor Wirtz chose the issue as a "good cause" for the department to promote. To the extent that increasing numbers of governmental participants become interested in searching for "good causes" on their own, rather than leaving such initiatives to central executive- or legislative-branch leadership, the importance of this model of the agenda-formation process increases. The increase in congressional staff, and in policy-planning staffs in executive-branch agencies, allows congressmen or cabinet secretaries more easily to transform wishes into policy-initiating activity.

The administration's occupational safety and health bill was introduced into Congress on the heels of President Johnson's 1968 message, and hearings were held in both House and Senate committees that year. Although there had been minimal interest-group involvement before the introduction of the administration bill, the hearings produced a relatively uncomplicated confrontation between trade unions and business groups. Representatives for seven international unions testified in favor of the proposed legislation, as did George Meany, speaking for the AFL-CIO. Representatives of both the U.S. Chamber of Commerce and the National Association of Manufacturers argued that legislation was unnecessary: that the safety and health situation was not as bad as critics argued, that most accidents were due to human error or negligence, and that industry was already doing everything it could.[18]

Occupational Safety and Health Administration

Introduction of administration legislation obviously does not assure its passage, and other events during the dramatic year 1968 (LBJ's withdrawal from the presidential race, the assassinations of Martin Luther King and Robert F. Kennedy, the events at the Chicago Democratic Convention) overwhelmed occupational safety and health. Neither the Senate nor the House committee reported out a bill.

In 1969 the Democrats in Congress who had introduced the original legislation reintroduced their bill. This time, however, the new Nixon administration introduced a bill of its own. According to Page and O'Brien, a Republican occupational safety and health law was regarded within the White House as a demonstration of concern for "the silent majority" and "hard hats" in a political context where strategists hoped to wean blue-collar workers away from a Democratic party increasingly associated with hippies and antiwar protesters.[19] Furthermore, in November 1968, a mine disaster in Farmington, West Virginia, took seventy-eight lives, and this accident gave impetus to the occupational safety and health legislation that had already been introduced. (Note the importance of timing here: if there is not already a proposal on the table, or supporters able to generate a proposal very quickly, the momentum from a dramatic event can be lost quickly.) The Republican bill differed in several ways from the Democratic one, including the organizational form of the regulation-issuing authority (an independent commission instead of the Department of Labor) and the ease with which penalties for violating the regulations could be set.

The introduction of the Republican bill had two important effects. First, it made the passage of *some* bill much more likely. After the introduction of the Republican bill, the business organizations which in 1968 had opposed any legislation came out in favor of the new administration bill. Second, its introduction increased trade-union commitment to the original bill, which now became a partisan vehicle for lambasting a Republican administration. When the Republican bill was introduced in 1969, "union officials took the position that they would prefer no bill at all to the 'abomination' concocted by the Nixon administration."[20]

In 1969 and 1970, occupational safety and health legislation became an important priority for AFL-CIO lobbyists. Meanwhile, during 1970, Republican members of the subcommittee of the House Education and Labor Committee considering the bill boycotted subcommittee sessions to prevent the Democratic bill from being reported out, and a quorum on the committee was achieved only when the chairman of the full committee came in his ex officio capacity to the subcommittee vote.[21] (The bill was reported out of the subcommittee 9–0.) There were fights on both the Senate and House floors regarding the major points of contention between the two bills. The votes were highly partisan: to cite one representative example, an amendment modifying provisions that would allow an inspector to close down a firm in a case of imminent danger was rejected in the Senate 40–42, with Republicans voting 30–5 in favor, northern Democrats 0–32 against.[22] However, when the bill came for final votes after the amendment process, the results were lopsided: the Occupational Safety and Health Act passed the House 384–5 and the Senate 83–3. The final bill passed by Congress reflected the Democratic far more than the Republican version. The administration had committed itself to some new federal legislation, and was hesitant about opposing "safety," so President Nixon, on December 29, 1970, signed the bill into law.

Three broad questions about the legislative history of the law creating OSHA should be raised. First, to what extent did the businesses to be regulated themselves seek the creation of the agency? The answer is rather clear: to no extent. The legislation originated in the Labor Department and the White House, and its major advocates were trade unions representing the workers to be protected.

Second, to what extent were "Naderism" and "environmentalism" important factors in the passage of the legislation? This answer is somewhat more difficult. At neither the 1968 or 1969 hearings did Ralph Nader testify, and environmentalism did not emerge as a politically potent phenomenon until the spring of 1970. Nader did, however, testify at length and with gusto at the last set of hearings, conducted by the Senate Labor and Public Welfare Committee in late 1969 and early 1970. ("I am grateful to testify regarding the domestic form of violence known as occupational casualties and diseases," Nader began his testimony.)[23] Furthermore, traditional "public interest" health groups, such as the American Public Health Association, testified for the bill from 1968. By the time the final battle over the bill took place in 1970, Nader operatives were involved. And the activist mood of the time, which saw the passage of other pieces of safety legislation, certainly aided the unions in gaining support for new federal legislation. After passage of the tough highway safety legislation in 1966, spearheaded by Nader, general-purpose "public interest advocates" were encouraged to choose safety as an area where chances of success looked good. Furthermore, the auto safety legislation could be cited as a precedent by proponents of legislation in other safety-related areas.[24]

Finally, to what extent were participants in the process aware that "health" rather than "safety" would gradually come to be a major focus of agency mission and agency conflicts? The impression here is that concern over industrial accidents, rather than exposure to chemicals, dominated—though not overwhelmingly. Of the union representatives testifying at the 1968 hearings, two stressed safety concerns, two stressed health concerns, and four stressed both about equally. However, it should be noted that George Meany's testimony concentrated on health problems almost exclusively. "Every year," stated Meany, "thousands of workers die slow, often agonizing deaths from the effects of coal dust, asbestos, beryllium, lead, cotton dust, carbon monoxide, cancer-causing chemicals, dyes, radiation, pesticides, and exotic fuels. Others suffer long illnesses. Thousands suffer from employment in artificially created harmful environments."[25]

Agency Tasks

The Occupational Safety and Health Administration (OSHA) is an agency within the Department of Labor, headed by an Assistant Secretary of Labor for Occupational Safety and Health (one of the seven assistant secretaries in the department) appointed by the president.

Broadly, OSHA undertakes two types of tasks. First, it promulgates regulations regarding workplace conditions deemed related to employee safety and health. These regulations state, for example, that machine parts must be guarded, floors must be kept uncluttered, stairways must have handrails, and employees may be exposed to no more than a certain concentration of harmful chemicals. Second, OSHA inspects workplaces to determine compliance with the regulations. These two tasks define the essential organizational division within the agency. OSHA's Washington headquarters is the locus of standards development, while OSHA's eighty-nine area offices are the loci of compliance activities. "Washington" and "the field" are not two airtight compartments. Field offices are asked to comment on proposed regulations from an enforcement point of view, and headquarters maintains an elaborate system for controlling the behavior of field inspectors.

In determining the content of regulations, OSHA must decide how far it wishes to require reductions of risk to which workers are exposed. Each reduction of risk costs money, and successive reductions cost successively larger amounts of money. The statute establishing OSHA gives the agency power to promulgate regulations requiring employers to eliminate specific conditions judged unsafe or unhealthy. These regulations have the force of law, yet they are not adopted by the legislature, but by administrative agencies consisting entirely of appointed officials. Furthermore, the statute gives the agency considerable discretion about the content of the regulations. OSHA's goal is stated in the statute in extremely general terms: "to assure so far as possible every working man and woman in the Nation safe and healthful working conditions."[26] The statutory language on safety regulations gives no guidance at all about the level of protection regulations should mandate. For health regulations, the language is a bit more specific, but not much. OSHA

shall set the standard which most adequately assures, to the extent feasible, on the basis of the best available evidence, that no employee will suffer material impairment of health or functional capacity even if such employee has regular exposure to the hazard dealt with by such standard for the period of his working life.[27]

What makes the waters murky here is the statement "to the extent feasible," since people will disagree as to what is feasible. In particular, there is disagreement about how much a regulation need cost before it becomes "infeasible." Agency decision makers are thus left with little guidance and much discretion.

OSHA promulgates regulations after a process that is Byzantine in its complexity. Normally, the first stage of OSHA rulemaking, especially for health regulations, is for the National Institute for Occupational Safety and Health to submit to OSHA a "criteria document" containing a summary of existing literature and recommendations for a regulation. (The National Institute is a research organization that is not part of OSHA—or even of the Department of Labor—but of HEW.) The OSHA legislation also authorizes nongovernmental parties (in practice, labor unions) to petition OSHA to issue a temporary standard in emergency situations.[28]

The second stage of OSHA rulemaking is frequently the appointment of an advisory committee, authorized but not required by the statute.[29] An advisory committee consists of equal numbers of representatives of labor and business, as well as a number of "public" representatives. Advisory committees meet informally. Members sit at the same table and talk directly with each other. However, advisory committees also take testimony from interested outside parties. The Federal Advisory

Occupational Safety and Health Administration

Committee Act requires that all meetings be open to the public and that verbatim transcripts be made. At the end of its deliberations, the advisory committee produces a text of a recommended regulation which it transmits to OSHA.

Next, OSHA publishes a proposed regulation in the *Federal Register.* The proposal represents the result of an initial consideration of the technical evidence and of the deliberations of the advisory committee by a project manager within the Office of Standards Development specially assigned to the regulation in question, the chief of the Office of Standards Development, and the assistant secretary.

The National Environmental Policy Act and executive orders from Presidents Gerald Ford and Jimmy Carter on inflationary impact statements impose additional procedural requirements on OSHA. For each proposed regulation, OSHA is required to draft an environmental impact statement discussing the effect that the proposal would have on the external environment. Furthermore, every proposed regulation with a significant economic impact must be accompanied by an inflationary impact statement that discusses (and quantifies so far as possible) the costs and benefits of the contemplated action.

Next, at public hearings on proposed OSHA regulations, any interested parties—national or local organizations, business firms, even single individuals—may present oral or written testimony before the administrative law judge who presides. A good deal of the testimony is presented by organizations. The AFL-CIO has its own small health and safety staff, and many individual unions have at least one employee working on these questions. The National Association of Manufacturers and Chamber of Commerce have one person each working on occupational safety and health, but these organizations have played a modest role in most OSHA rulemaking proceedings. Trade associations representing the political interests of business firms in a given industry are more important. Another frequent organizational participant in OSHA public hearings is the Health Research Group, a Nader organization.

Most hearings also feature testimony from businessmen operating the processes being regulated and from individual workers exposed to the hazards, including fingerless machine operators and cancer victims who have had parts of lungs, throats, or other organs removed. At one hearing, representatives of the Communist party testified; at others, promoters of assorted devices and processes, hoping to have their inventions written into OSHA regulations, have appeared.

After the public hearing, additional time is made available for submitting "posthearing comments" by anyone who wishes. Frequently lawyers submit full-blown legal briefs, resembling briefs submitted to a court. Then the OSHA project manager must go through the entire record—all the written comments, oral submissions, and exhibits. The record is usually so extensive that it is impossible for anyone higher up in OSHA to look at anything but the highlights.

When the final regulation is published in the *Federal Register,* both the Administrative Procedure Act and the OSHA legislation require that it be accompanied by a "statement of reasons" explaining why each provision was adopted and answering arguments against it made in the course of rulemaking.[30] OSHA decisions may then be challenged in court.

One result of the tortuous OSHA administrative procedures is that the agency has promulgated extremely few regulations by this process. The vast majority of regulations OSHA enforces are those adopted during the agency's first month of existence from previously existing consensus standards and federal standards. During its first two years of existence, OSHA was directed by the statute to "promulgate as an occupational safety or health standard any national consensus standard, and any established Federal standard" without going through any of the rulemaking procedures described previously.[31]

Most of the new regulations OSHA has promulgated through normal rulemaking procedures have been on exposure to chemicals. A list of some 400 threshold-limit values for maximum exposure to chemicals was part of the initial package OSHA adopted in 1971. Regulations developed since then have lowered maximum exposure limits and added requirements for periodic medical examinations to detect evidence of disease among exposed workers, for employer monitoring of exposure levels, and for warning signs. In 1972 OSHA promulgated one health regulation (asbestos); in 1973 no regulations were promulgated; in 1974 two (fourteen carcinogens and vinyl chloride); in 1975 none; in 1976 one (coke oven emissions); in 1977 none; in 1978 six (arsenic, benzene, cotton dust, lead, acrylonitrile, and DBCP, a pesticide which causes sterility in males). As can be seen, the pace of promulgation of health regulations increased dramatically in 1978.

OSHA's other main task is to induce compliance by firms. Every firm with one or more employees, from a giant steel mill to the legendary "mom and pop" grocery store (where "mom" is the employee), is subject to occupational safety and health legislation. No fewer than four million firms are covered.

Furthermore, OSHA regulations are voluminous. Early on in OSHA's history, one senator gathered all of them, including those referenced but not printed in the *Federal Register,* and showed his astounded colleagues that they formed a stack some six feet high. To be sure, only a minute fraction of this stack is likely to be applicable to a given employer, but finding out *which* fraction is part of the problem.

Employers must also figure out what they are supposed to do to comply. Unfortunately, this is rarely as easy as knowing what is expected in order to comply with a simple command such as "Thou shalt not kill." OSHA regulations are necessarily filled with engineering formulas and complex instructions. In many cases, the employers need not worry about any of these; they simply buy equipment which is labeled, "Meets Government Safety Standards." Frequently, however, this is not possible. In the case of threshold limit values for chemicals, it may be difficult to know even what chemicals to look for. A substance may, for instance, be produced as an intermediary during a chemical reaction. Special inquiries to the manufacturer must often be made to determine the composition of trade-name products.

Finally, compliance is often no one-shot matter; it requires constant vigilance. Compliance with threshold-limit values cannot be a one-time proposition because equipment must be maintained at regular intervals. Closed chemical systems must be checked for leaks. Respirator filters must be replaced frequently so they do not become clogged. And a good number of regulations involve conditions that frequently change. Slippery or cluttered floors may be clean today and messy tomorrow. Flammable, solvent-soaked rags may be placed in the proper containers today, but tomorrow be left out near a worker lighting a cigarette.

Even firms that seek voluntarily to comply with government regulations face the problem of finding out about applicable regulations and what they need do to comply. In firms that normally would not comply voluntarily, OSHA's task becomes that much more difficult. To induce compliance among such firms, OSHA inspectors visit plants to detect noncompliance and assess penalties for violations.

OSHA has approximately 2,800 inspectors, including those operating under OSHA state plans. Critics look at the enormous numbers of workplaces covered by legislation, and then at the number of inspectors, and conclude that agency monitoring of employer performance is impossible because inspectors will never get out to most workplaces. Robert Stewart Smith wrote in a widely quoted passage that "the typical establishment will see an OSHA inspector about as often as we see Halley's comet."[32] Such statements are amusing but misleading. Quantitatively, the vast majority of workplaces are stores and offices. Each year OSHA inspectors visit a small fraction of *workplaces* covered by the Act, but a much larger proportion of *employees* covered.

The problem with monitoring employer performance is not that the inspector never comes, but that once is not enough. No inspector can be expert on the characteristics of all kinds of operations he encounters —not to mention the special features of individual firms. Thus, a firm's inspection is no proof that all hazards have been uncovered. Add to this the fact that compliance is often not a one-time activity.

Inspectors seek out violations during a "walkaround" on the firm's premises, accompanied by company and worker representatives. Once violations are uncovered, penalties are meted out. Two key elements of the OSHA enforcement system are the routine imposition of monetary fines without trial and the levying of these fines the first time an inspector discovers a violation, whether or not the violation is subsequently corrected (so-called "first-instance sanctions"). If OSHA had to put an employer on trial before penalties could be imposed, such imposition would become relatively uncommon, since trials consume many resources. To make the imposition of fines a significant element of an enforcement program, a way must be found to routinize the punishment. Thus the statute allows inspectors to impose fines.[33]

Explaining Why the Agency Acts as It Does: Setting Regulations

In determining the content of regulations, OSHA decision makers have usually chosen more protective over less protective alternatives— especially in some of the more dramatic decisions the agency has made. These include the 1974 decision to require an extremely low exposure limit (1 part per million or ppm) for the carcinogen vinyl chloride, despite predictions that the industry would be shut down because of inability to comply; the 1976 decision on the eve of an election, where President Ford had denounced excessive regulatory costs, to establish strict emissions limitations for coke-oven batteries in steel plants, despite criticisms that the cost-per-life-saved of the regulations far exceeded similar costs in other government programs; and the 1978 decision to back strict exposure limits for textile workers exposed to cotton dust in the face of strong opposition from Carter administration inflation fighters.

Most OSHA rulemaking decisions involve technical matters, and the vocabulary is rife with unfamiliar words. By looking at the state of expert knowledge in the area of getting threshold-limit values for chemicals, for example, we can see the limits of the role that expertise can play in determining safety and health rulemaking decisions.

The quality of the knowledge available on risks and costs in the area of occupational safety and health is surprisingly—indeed, shockingly— poor. Estimates of the costs of achieving various levels of protection have varied widely in every OSHA rulemaking proceeding.

The same problem exists for the scientific evidence. These days, most social scientists are trained to seek inspiration from the natural sciences and the canons of the scientific method. Social scientists frequently feel frustrated at the difficulties involved in applying the methods of the natural sciences to the testing of social science hypotheses. It would gratify some social scientists—and shock others—to learn just how frequently the application of the scientific method in the natural sciences runs into the same problems.

Establishing a dose-response curve is essential for setting threshold-limit values for chemicals. But many problems exist in getting human data to establish such points.[34] Lacking such data, judgments on dose-response curves are usually based on animal experimentation. Animals studies are expensive, and tests for chronic effects have not been done for most chemicals to which workers are exposed. In addition to discouraging testing altogether, the high cost has promoted the development of testing protocols using only small numbers of test animals in order to save money.

A typical carcinogenicity study on rats will involve 60 animals in the experimental group and 120 in the control group.[35] In order to elicit statistically significant effects from small test populations, large doses of the carcinogen are then administered to the animals. If one exposed a small group of animals to the dose to which humans are exposed, it is unlikely that any test animal would develop cancer from the exposure unless the carcinogen was extremely potent. By massively increasing the dose, experimenters increase the risk to a point where possible carcinogenic effect may be observed in even a small test group. This has occasioned some ridicule—particularly from industry spokesmen, who have argued that one would have to drink hundreds of bottles of diet soda a day (or whatever) in order to be exposed to the doses being fed the test animals in carcinogenicity tests. It is not correct, as is often alleged, that any chemical is carcinogenic if administered in high enough doses; results for most chemicals tested for carcinogenicity by these methods have been negative. However, it is possible, for those carcinogens which can be detoxified by metabolism, that large doses may overwhelm the organism's capability for dealing with them, and thus produce inaccurate results.

Finally, even when animal testing is done, there remains the question of extrapolating the results to humans. Extrapolations are always guesses. And even if we assume that animal evidence is *qualitatively* applicable to humans, we have no way—*quantitatively*—to extrapolate animal dose-response curves to human dose-response curves. We do not know whether 100 ppm for a rat is equal to 100 ppm for a human.

But even if we had data filling in points on the dose-response curve, decisions on the stringency of occupational safety and health regulations could still not be based simply on scientific expertise. Expert knowledge may tell us how many injuries, illnesses, or deaths will result from different levels of protection and what these levels of protection will cost. But even if we have that information, we still must make a value judgment about how great a degree of protection to mandate. To say that we wish to mandate "complete safety" is itself a value judgment, since mandating lesser safety would cost less money and would thus free resources for other uses.

The evidence suggests that the most important factor explaining OSHA decisions on the content of regulations has been the pro-protection values of agency officials, derived from the ideology of the safety and health professional and the organizational mission of OSHA.

Most OSHA officials either come from the occupational safety and health professions (safety engineering or industrial hygiene) or take courses in these fields after going to work for the agencies. Members of these professions share a body of knowledge. Like members of many professions, they also tend to share certain values or orientations which comprise a professional ideology. For occupational safety and health professionals, these are pro-protection values. They tend to believe that workers ought to be protected from hazards to life and limb and that larger reductions of risk are preferable to smaller reductions (without much consideration of cost).

Like most ideologies, that of occupational safety and health professionals may be adopted for a variety of reasons. It is plausible to believe that, as a group, individuals attracted to work involving a strong component of service to others tend to be people for whom "doing good" is

Occupational Safety and Health Administration

relatively important. The first page of the National Safety Council's manual for safety engineers states solemnly that industrial accidents must be prevented because "needless destruction of life and health is a moral evil" and that "failure to take necessary precautions against predictable accidents involves moral responsibility for those accidents."[36] I have frequently been struck by hearing safety professionals utter expressions such as "We killed ten workers when that scaffold collapsed" rather than saying, impersonally, "Ten workers were killed." One frequently encounters safety people who report having lost relatives in industrial accidents—possibly a major influence in their choice of profession.

Pro-protection values also clearly serve the interests of the profession. The more safety and health protection workers are afforded, the more important safety and health professionals become.

One of the clearest examples of how the ideology of the occupational safety and health profession affects OSHA rulemaking decisions is the agency's insistence—so irrational to most businessmen (and some others as well)—on requiring engineering controls rather than personal protective equipment for the abatement of health hazards. This OSHA policy has been one of the agency's most controversial. Reducing exposure to health hazards (such as noise or chemicals) by engineering controls is often horrendously expensive, especially when the new controls must be fitted onto existing machines at existing plants with fixed layouts. By contrast, personal protective equipment—ear plugs, earmuffs, and respirators—costs a tiny fraction of what engineering controls cost.

There are reasons to be critical of reliance on personal protective equipment in dealing with health hazards. Take noise. The first objection to earmuffs and ear plugs is that workers do not like to wear them. Although in some cases the discomfort disappears with use, it is universally agreed that hearing protection, worn for an entire day, produces feelings of confinement and isolation, that workers get sweaty behind the ears, and that many get headaches or ear infections. And, since the factory noise level remains unchanged, workers still have as much difficulty speaking with each other over the din as they had previously. This objection to personal protection is that it puts the burden of compliance on the employee rather than the employer.

The second objection relates to OSHA's ability to enforce a regulation. Once engineering controls have been installed, the problem is basically solved. OSHA inspectors can observe whether the controls have quieted the workplace down to the threshold-limit value and thereby establish compliance or noncompliance. Establishing compliance with a noise regulation by means of personal hearing protection is well-nigh impossible, since workers may wear their earmuffs the day the inspector comes but not wear them the next day. And it is very difficult for the inspector to establish whether personal protection, even if used, has been fitted properly. It is difficult to fit ear protection well, and even a good fit can come undone if workers chew gum or tobacco. Poorly fitted hearing protection does not protect.

These arguments apply a fortiori to the use of respirators for reducing chemical exposures. Present respirators make speech communication extremely difficult, limit the field of vision, cause skin irritation, and produce heat stress. It is difficult to maintain proper facial fit. Above all, people simply cannot breathe well enough with existing respirators for them to be worn for a whole day when work is at all strenuous.

Reasons of public policy aside, however, if business critics of OSHA's stance on personal protection had read the textbooks used to train their own safety and health professionals, the reason for the attitude of OSHA officials would have become clear. The view that hazards should be corrected by means other than personal protective equipment is a dictum of these professions. Nearly every textbook on safety engineering or industrial hygiene is replete with warnings against reliance on personal protective equipment.[37]

Safety and health professionals defend their opposition to personal protective equipment with the substantive reasons cited above. But the textbooks imply that relying on personal protective equipment is seen as a confession of failure, a betrayal of the can-do approach of the engineer, a renunciation of pluck and determination, and a yielding to laziness and defeat. "Personal protective devices have one serious drawback," *Fundamentals of Industrial Hygiene* states. "They do nothing to reduce or eliminate the hazard."[38] Personal protective equipment is visualized as a paste-over, a Band-Aid—indeed, a sort of industrial Potemkin village, a pleasing facade masking actual failure. As much as it may be unpleasant to the workers, personal protective equipment is insulting to the engineer.

Reliance on engineering controls rather than personal protective equipment also enhances the role of the safety and health professional in the corporate organization. If hazards are to be dealt with by passing out safety shoes, hard hats, earmuffs, and space suits, then the safety or health professional need not be present when facilities are being designed. Company designers may wreak whatever safety and health havoc they wish; the safety engineer or industrial hygienist need only appear later to plaster on some personal protective equipment so employees don't suffer injury. On the other hand, an engineering-controls approach encourages participation by safety and health professionals during the planning stage and upgrades their role within the organization.

The pro-protection values of OSHA officials arise predominantly, I believe, from the ideology of the occupational safety and health professions. But these values serve important purposes for the agency as well. As James Q. Wilson writes:

Few organizations . . . can tolerate having more than a single governing ethos: the need for morale, for a sense of mission and of distinctive competence, and for standard operating procedures means that competing norms will be suppressed, ignored, or isolated.[39]

Wilson summarizes a great deal of importance in that one sentence. Morale and a sense of mission are important if an organization is, by its own lights, to function successfully and to recruit good people. The statutory mission of OSHA is to protect workers. An attraction of working for government is that one may show that one is more concerned about "nonmaterial" things like health and safety than about money. (An attitude survey of top agency officials in the American civil service found that these officials tended to view people outside the government as "materialistic, less educated, and less intelligent; 'they sell their souls.' "[40]) An excessive concern by OSHA officials for the cost implications of regulations would counteract that source of organizational pride.

An important alternative explanation remains: what about "political" factors in OSHA decisions about the content of regulations? During most of OSHA's existence, the president, who appoints OSHA's boss and who is the chief officer of the executive branch, has been uneasy at the least and openly critical at the most about the pro-protection slant of OSHA regulatory decisions. And business organizations have conducted a loud campaign against OSHA almost since the agency's inception.

Despite its legal authority and political influence, the White House has had great difficulty in influencing OSHA decisions. The barriers to greater White House influence over decisions made by OSHA and other agencies include lack of time, agency hostility, a desire to get and keep high-quality political appointees, and hesitancy about becoming involved in difficult decisions.

Here I will discuss the first two of these problems.[41] The most important barrier to White House influence over agency decision making is the fact that time is finite. Although the capacity of the president himself and of the "institutionalized presidency" (the White House Staff and the Office of Management and Budget) to work endless hours is legendary, it is far outstripped by the stupendous number of important issues with which agencies deal. The size of the institutionalized presidency keeps growing, but the tasks for government grow even faster, and they continue to overwhelm the president's aides. Clearly, there are decisions made by government agencies whose content is determined—or at least influenced—by the White House. This may be so in the case of the most important decisions agencies make. But, as far as I can determine, there were no instances of presidential involvement in any OSHA rulemaking decisions before 1978. Lack of time also means that intervention, when and if it comes, tends to come late in a drawn-out decision-making process and to be based on fragments of information rather than lengthy consideration that agency officials have given the question. It is "crisis-oriented." Thus it is often poorly timed and poorly justified.

Lack of time is only the first barrier to White House control of agency decision making. Although we may look at White House involvement as an attempt to assert democratic accountability over discretion granted to nonelected bureaucrats, the fact is that many actors in the political system—including, not surprisingly, most agency officials—regard such White House control as illegitimate. Agency officials view themselves as experts on the subjects with which they deal and see political intervention in their decision making as "political" in the negative sense—that is, as an attempt to change a decision in response to "special-interest" maneuvering.

The fact that intervention, when it does occur, is typically poorly timed and poorly justified, contributes to the view that what is involved is "political interference." Furthermore, the pressure-cooker atmosphere in the White House, and the many matters staffers must attend to, contribute to a perception of staffers by agency people as arrogant, ignorant, and not worth heeding.[42]

As for pressure by business organizations against protective OSHA decisions, labor unions have pressured OSHA to make decisions as protective as possible. Has this pressure been as "strong" as business pressure on the other side? Such questions are difficult to answer except as some way of measuring the strength of political pressure. In my own work comparing the content of decisions about regulations by OSHA and its Swedish counterpart, I found that in two countries where the relative political strength of business and labor is rather different, agency decisions were nonetheless rather similar in content.[43] This suggests that, at least in an environment where an agency hears from more than one organized interest group, the values of agency officials appear to be more important in determining the content of decisions than interest-group pressures. Perhaps this conclusion applies only to agencies where there are multiple interest groups on different sides; it may be difficult for agency officials to weigh the groups' relative strengths exactly, and officials' values in such an environment may be allowed relatively free rein. Perhaps the conclusion applies more broadly, which suggests the difficulties of making bureaucratic discretion accountable in the political system.

Explaining Why the Agency Acts as It Does: Enforcement

One of the main issues in the congressional battles over federal occupational safety and health legislation in 1969 and 1970 involved the enforcement methods of the agency. The Republican bills allowed penalties to be meted out only after a lengthy judicial procedure on a case-by-case basis and permitted fines only in cases of willful violations of the regulations.[44] Essentially, the Republican bills continued the approach of earlier state legislation, where "voluntary compliance" by employers was sought and penalties almost never imposed. The Democratic bills included provisions for first-instance sanctions, routinely imposed, and these were embodied in the final law.

The decision to use the first-instance-sanction approach was based on a view among occupational safety and health workers that the attempts by state occupational safety and health agencies to induce compliance without routine imposition of penalties had not worked and that stronger methods were needed. The feeling was that, absent fear of punishment, large numbers of employers would simply ignore the regulations. In a survey of American and Swedish occupational safety and health inspectors, at one end of a seven-point scale was placed the statement: "Most employers are law-abiding, and try to follow the standards simply because a government agency has issued them." At the other end was the statement: "Without the penalty-imposing powers

TABLE 7–1

*Evaluation by American and Swedish Inspectors
of Employer Law-Abidingness*

		U.S. Inspectors	Swedish Inspectors
Most employers	1–2	9%	18%
law-abiding	3	6	26
	4	8	22
Many employers would	5	21	20
ignore standards	6–7	56	15
		(N=78)	(N=76)

SOURCE: Survey of sample of American and Swedish inspectors, 1975. See Steven Kelman, "Regulating Job Safety and Health; A Comparison of U.S. Occupational Safety and Health Administration and the Swedish Worker Protection Board" (Ph.D. diss., Harvard University, 1978) p. 574, and, generally, ch. 6.

they have, many employers would simply ignore the standards." Table 7–1 below displays the results, which indicate that American inspectors have little faith in the automatic acceptance of the law, while Swedish inspectors are more sanguine. The Swedish results do not show inspectors to be certain of automatic compliance: Over half the inspectors rate most employers at the middle of the scale or worse. But it is the overwhelming vote of no-confidence that American inspectors give employers which stands out. Inspectors do not determine occupational safety and health policy; their attitudes are presented here because they illustrate views which probably represent those of people active in the area.

Controversies over OSHA

Few of the agencies formed during the binge of regulatory agency creation in the late 1960s and early 1970s have been as controversial as OSHA. However, the specific controversies, of which there have been many, should be seen in the light of structural factors in the agency's environment which promote political confrontation. First, with OSHA, unlike many regulatory agencies, both costs and benefits are concentrated, and there are two well-organized groups—business and unions—facing each other. In *Political Organizations,* James Q. Wilson argues we may better understand the variations in the ways societies deal with

Occupational Safety and Health Administration

different policy areas by looking at the distribution of costs and benefits in the area in question. Policy areas, Wilson argues, can be classified based on "whether the costs and benefits are widely distributed or narrowly concentrated from the point of view of those who bear the costs or enjoy the benefits." Wilson elaborates:

A cost may be widely distributed (as with the general tax burden, generally rising crime rates, the widespread practice of some objectionable act such as the sale of obscene literature) or it may be narrowly concentrated (as with a fee or impost paid by a particular industry or locality or a highway construction program that destroys a particular community). Similarly, a benefit may be widely distributed (as with social security and unemployment compensation payments or national defense) or narrowly concentrated (such as a subsidy paid to a particular industry or occupation, a tariff on a particular product, prestige conferred on a person or group, or a license to operate a television station).[45]

Classically, it has been easier to organize people who are to receive concentrated benefits or pay concentrated costs than people who are to receive dispersed benefits or pay dispersed costs. Thus, in policy areas characterized by a disparity in the concentration of costs and benefits, there has tended to arise a situation with a well-organized group on one side of the issue and a dispersed, relatively unorganized "public" on the other side.

Under such conditions, where politicians or agency officials face only one organized group, cozy relationships frequently evolve. Wilson notes that policy areas involving concentrated benefits and dispersed costs facilitate the emergence of voluntary associations that enter into a symbiotic relationship with the agency administering the program, while programs imposing concentrated costs and granting dispersed benefits tend to fall victim to "capture." In occupational safety and health rulemaking, *two* groups, and not just one, are organized. In such cases, Wilson's prediction is that such programs "generate continuing organized conflict."[46] OSHA certainly fulfills the prediction. (The rulemaking procedures used, with their emphasis on adversary trial–like confrontation, do nothing to encourage agreement.[47]) Furthermore, OSHA's reliance on fines as a means to induce compliance with its regulations—adopted out of a view that compliance couldn't be achieved any other way—has created resentment (the way punishment generally does). In a democracy, the resentful may—and do—act politically against the object of their resentment.

Through 1976 OSHA was in the unenviable position of being attacked by both labor and business. Labor criticized OSHA for not making rules fast enough and not being serious enough about enforcement. Both union spokesmen and representatives for the (Naderite) Health Research Group expressed alarm at the succession of dramatic revelations of occupational health hazards—the deaths from a rare form of liver cancer from workers exposed to vinyl chloride, the cancer epidemic among the millions of workers exposed to asbestos—and deplored the slow pace of standards development. Union spokesmen also criticized the small number of inspectors, the "piddling" fines levied against firms, and what they perceived as successful White House "sabotage" of the OSHA program during the Nixon and Ford years. A secret memo written by Assistant Secretary of Labor George Guenther, the first head of OSHA, to White House political operatives as part of the 1972 "responsiveness program" by the White House was (incorrectly, I believe) interpreted by union spokesmen, when released two years later, as "proof" that President Nixon had exchanged lax OSHA activity for campaign contributions.[48]

With the appointment by President Carter of Eula Bingham, a cancer researcher with close ties to the trade union movement, as head of OSHA, and with the increasing political hostility to government regulation, the stance of the unions toward OSHA shifted, starting in 1977 from criticism to support. Indeed, after union defeats on labor law reform and other union issues during the 1977–78 session of Congress, defending OSHA against attack began to assume an increasingly prominent place in union political activity. In September 1978 the AFL-CIO held a national conference on occupational safety and health attended by 1,200 delegates and addressed by George Meany. The *AFL-CIO News*—which began during 1978 to devote substantially increased space to occupational safety and health issues—reported on the conference with a banner headline: "Moves to Undercut OSHA Threaten Workers' Safety."[49]

For business, OSHA has been a four-letter word. Business organizations have forcefully taken their criticisms of the agency out of the executive branch to both Congress and the courts.

Business has criticized the content of OSHA regulations. For a long time, the bulk of this criticism was directed at "Mickey Mouse standards" said to impose silly burdens unrelated to improving safety or health. OSHA regulations were lambasted for requiring split toilet seats, forbidding ice in drinking water, and specifying heights for guardrails in construction sites. There was criticism of pages and pages of requirements on ladder design.

Many of the "Mickey Mouse" requirements appeared during the

Occupational Safety and Health Administration

wholesale adoption of earlier voluntary standards by OSHA in 1971. Some of these requirements were outdated; others bore little relation to safety. Many of these requirements were repealed early on in OSHA's history (although criticisms alleging their continued presence continued to appear long after their revocation); most of the others were, if cited at all by inspectors during inspections, classified as *de minimis* (trifling) violations, not subject to fines and not requiring correction. In 1978, in one move, OSHA repealed about a thousand passages of regulations deemed unrelated to safety protection.[50]

Such criticisms made good newspaper copy, thus temporarily deflecting attention from the more serious grounds for controversy over what OSHA was doing in the regulation-setting area. In 1977 and 1978, as OSHA moved to deflect those criticisms, business organizations began increasingly to turn their attention to the enormous compliance costs that many OSHA health regulations were imposing. OSHA regulations were attacked for being an important contributor to inflation, for inhibiting productivity growth in the economy (by forcing capital investment into safety and health, rather than machines that could produce more goods), and for discouraging innovation (by raising the costs of doing business, thus inhibiting people entering business).[51]

Business organizations have challenged every OSHA health regulation in court, with the exception of the asbestos regulation adopted in 1972. The courts have generally backed OSHA decisions. In a decision on an industry challenge to OSHA's 1974 vinyl chloride regulation, the court decision endorsed OSHA's requirement that industry go beyond the bounds of what was currently technologically feasible. "In the area of safety, we wish to emphasize, the Secretary is not restricted by the status quo. He may raise standards which require improvements in existing technologies."[52]

In 1978, for the first time, a judicial challenge to an OSHA regulation was successful. The Fifth Circuit in New Orleans vacated OSHA's regulation on benzene (an industrial solvent linked with blood diseases, including leukemia) that reduced the threshold limit value from 10 to 1 ppm.[53] The court argued that OSHA had failed to show that this new threshold-limit value would produce incremental health benefits over the previous standard. The test the court decision applied to OSHA regulations was that the agency determine both the benefits and the costs:

Although the agency does not have to conduct an elaborate cost-benefit analysis, it does have to determine whether the benefits expected from the standard bear a reasonable relationship to the costs imposed by the standard.[54]

The court in *American Petroleum Institute* v. *OSHA* recognized that its decision contradicted earlier decisions in other circuits on OSHA regulations. OSHA appealed the decision to the Supreme Court. As of this writing, the court is expected to decide imminently.

There have been congressional attempts to challenge OSHA regulations. A rider which would have delayed OSHA's cotton-dust regulation by at least one year passed the Senate in 1978, but was removed in conference. Bills have been introduced to require OSHA to prepare cost-benefit analyses of regulations.

But the main congressional activities regarding OSHA—not surprising, since they represent less technical issues and involve statutory language—have been in the enforcement area. Within one year of the effective date of the OSHA law, members of Congress, inundated by protest mail, had introduced some one hundred bills to amend or even repeal the law. A large proportion of the bitterness to be found in the record of various congressional oversight hearings on OSHA has had to do with how OSHA regulations were enforced. Letters to congressmen complained that businessmen were being "treated like criminals," subjected to punishment where the OSHA inspector was "both judge and jury," and made the victims of "harassment." Some typical complaints:

A few years ago this type of harassment by the mobsters was considered illegal. Today the U.S. government does it, and it is legal.[55]

Please compare the penalty of up to $10,000 fine PER violation of the act with those extended to draft card burners, flag defilement, establishment vandals and other gross disrespecters of property rights and government. As a small businessman, my fate is much worse than theirs.[56]

As early as 1972, the House passed an amendment that would remove firms with less than fifteen employees from OSHA coverage. It did not pass the Senate. In 1973, however, a similar amendment passed Congress but was vetoed because President Nixon vetoed the Labor-HEW appropriations bill to which the amendment was attached. In 1974 an amendment exempting firms with fewer than twenty-five employees was passed by the House but rejected by the Senate.[57]

Until 1976 OSHA had thus narrowly avoided any change in its enforcement methods. But the precariousness of OSHA's perch was demonstrated by the results of a seemingly trivial event in the summer of 1976 involving *Safety with Beef Cattle,* an informational pamphlet OSHA had just issued. As part of a program to prepare informational booklets on job hazards for distribution to workers, OSHA had contracted with Purdue

Occupational Safety and Health Administration

University to prepare a series of booklets for farmworkers. Some of the brochures were to be written in simplified "Basic English" for farmworkers whose native language was not English and who came from countries where farmworkers receive little education. The booklets were not intended for general distribution to, say, Kansas wheat farmers. Instead, the idea was that OSHA inspectors would hand them out appropriately during inspections. The very first booklet in the series, *Safety with Beef Cattle*, was written in Basic English. However, so as not to offend recipients, this fact was not stated on the brochure itself.

Instead, it ended up offending everyone else. To someone not aware of its background, the booklet appeared paternalistic, patronizing, and downright insulting: one passage warned farmworkers to be careful lest they slip on manure, another cautioned that "you can get sick from working with beef cattle," and went on to cite a list of infectious diseases. Upon the issuance of the booklet, outraged newspaper editorials followed almost immediately, starting in small-town newspapers but soon spreading like a prairie fire to a number of big-city papers and even national columnists.

The flap occurred just as Congress was debating the year's Labor-HEW appropriation; the coincidence proved to be more than OSHA's standing on Capitol Hill could bear. Congress came out with two amendments to the year's OSHA appropriations, one of which exempted from OSHA coverage farms with fewer than ten employees. The other prohibited the imposition of fines for mild violations if there were fewer than ten such violations in a citation. These were amendments to the appropriations bill and not to the legislation itself, and thus applied only for a year, but they have been renewed since.

There have also been court challenges to OSHA enforcement methods, two of which reached the Supreme Court. In one case, the court ruled against a contention that imposition of fines by OSHA violated the constitutional right to a jury trial.[58] In another case, the court ruled that employers had a right to require that OSHA inspectors produce warrants before inspecting a firm. But the court decision established liberal criteria for granting such warrants, and the decision does not appear to be having much effect on OSHA inspection activities.[59]

In 1975 and 1976 President Ford made a number of statements critical of "overregulation" in general and OSHA in particular. Economists in the Council of Economic Advisers and the Council on Wage and Price Stability, both part of the Executive Office of the President, attempted to intervene in a number of OSHA rulemaking proceedings—always without success.

These efforts continued under the Carter administration, with the White House economists again spearheading the attack. The economists, like OSHA regulators, are motivated in significant measure by a professional ideology. The norms of the economics profession predispose its members to be relatively sanguine about market outcomes, wary about government intervention, and quick to note that "there's no such thing as a free lunch" (whether the good being purchased is oranges or health). However, the economists' concerns have dovetailed recently with the growing criticism of regulation and the increasing concern about inflation in 1978 and after.

There were two battles between White House economists and OSHA during 1978. The most dramatic involved efforts to get OSHA to relax its cotton-dust standard, and, in particular, to allow firms to comply with the regulation by handing out respirators rather than installing engineering controls. After losing an argument with OSHA, the White House economists, headed by Charles Schultze, chairman of the Council of Economic Advisers, went directly to the president to get him to overrule OSHA's decision. This was apparently the first time a decision on an OSHA regulation had ever come to the president. Carter first acceded to the economists' call, but then, after protests from George Meany and a group of congressmen, and a White House meeting between the president, Schultze, Secretary of Labor Roy Marshall and OSHA Assistant Secretary Bingham, Carter backed away and generally supported OSHA.[60]

The second battle, involving the regulatory agencies in general and not just OSHA, occurred over a suggestion by White House economists that a provision for White House vetoes of proposed regulations be included in the president's 1978 anti–inflation plan. What emerged instead was a council of regulatory agency heads which, an account in *Business Week* noted, "could make matters worse, not better" by bringing regulators together to share information and develop a common strategy.[61]

The experience during the first two years of the Carter administration provides further support for the view that White House control over OSHA decision making is very difficult to exercise. Compared to the situation under the Ford administration, White House *surveillance* of OSHA has definitely increased. There is now a Regulatory Analysis Review Group, headed by White House economists, that analyzes major OSHA proposals. Carter himself was involved in a major decision. But as surveillance increases, so does resistance. Suspicion of White House "dictation" has been reflected in legal claims by OSHA advocates that participation by White House officials, beyond comments made part of the public record, violates principles of American administrative law (because private comments are "ex parte" communications).[62] This issue will probably go to the courts; meanwhile, news of "secret" meetings by White House staffers with agency officials over a regulatory decision can still generate newspaper headlines, with intimations of "scandal."

Despite all this, it is an open question how long OSHA can continue to resist greater political direction by the president, especially if current antiregulation political trends continue. The most dramatic step a president could take to make OSHA responsive to his political views would be to appoint a head of the agency (say, an economist) who is strongly committed to changing agency decisions on regulations. This would probably hurt morale among OSHA employees tremendously—but, perhaps such an administrator, or such a president, wouldn't care. One important lesson of the controversies over OSHA rulemaking is the enormous difficulty that elected officials have influencing agency behavior.

Conclusion: OSHA—The Policy Issues

What effects has OSHA had on occupational accidents and ill health? And what has it cost? Robert S. Smith made a study of OSHA's impact through 1973 on the injury rate in those especially hazardous industries selected for targeted inspection. He found no effect.[63]

John Mendeloff, looking at manufacturing as a whole, produced an estimate that OSHA reduced injuries about 3 to 5 percent through 1975.[64] The number of "applicable" workplace deaths (i.e., excluding auto accidents to and from work, and heart attacks), he concluded, declined by about 10 percent.[65] Mendeloff concluded that the types of injuries subject to prevention through safety standards—machine accidents, falls from heights, electrocutions, roll-over accidents from earthmoving equipment—did indeed fall rather dramatically, but that such accidents account for only a small percentage of the total, leading to the conclusion that OSHA may have proved effective at doing the little bit it could in the safety area.[66] There have been no attempts to estimate the impact of OSHA on the reduction of occupational disease; for reasons noted earlier, such an impact, if it exists, will show itself only in the future.

Weidenbaum estimated 1976 compliance costs for OSHA regulations at approximately $3.2 billion.[67] This was considerably less than the costs estimated for compliance with EPA regulations, or the costs that economic studies have imputed to the regulation of entry and prices in the airline and trucking industries. The contribution of OSHA compliance costs to the *overall inflation rate* is negligible, even if $3.2 billion is a lot of money. Capital costs for meeting earlier OSHA regulations are likely to tail off as time passes, but the costs of complying with new health regulations will add new regulatory costs associated with OSHA.

Scholarly critics of OSHA have made three sorts of arguments: (1) advocates of government regulation underestimate the extent to which the unregulated market can successfully deal with providing appropriate levels of safety and health protection; (2) many OSHA health regulations cost far more per life saved than other government lifesaving programs; and (3) government intervention, to the extent it occurs, should move away from promulgation of specific standards and toward using taxes as a more economically efficient way to produce a given result.[68]

If two jobs are alike in all other respects, and differ only in their risk, we would expect that an employer would have to pay a potential employee more to take the second than the first job. This observation is the basis for the view that market transactions between employers and workers could provide a means for supplying appropriate levels of occupational safety and health protection without governmental intervention. Employers would provide increasing levels of protection up to the point where the marginal cost of additional protection is greater than the marginal increase in wages which the employer would have to pay to attract workers at a certain level of riskiness. (To illustrate with a simple example, it would be much cheaper for an employer to set up scaffolds with wide working surfaces and guardrails for work at great heights than to have employees work at such heights on thin boards and pay them the wages they would demand for such extremely risky work.) Economists have made some studies to test empirically the presence of wage premiums for risky work. While the results are varying, they tend to show that some premiums do exist.

Supporters of these arguments concede that there are "market imperfections" which prevent perfect market function. In particular, they recognize that worker information about health hazards is likely to be

Occupational Safety and Health Administration

poor. (The studies on wage premiums all relate to jobs with accident—rather than health—hazards.) Some critics suggest that government action in regard to occupational safety and health ought therefore be directed primarily where, in this view, the problems lie. Instead of promulgating regulations, the government should limit itself to informing workers about hazards and let the workers choose how to react.

Those critics who accept the argument that OSHA ought to go beyond an information-dissemination role and set health regulations have nonetheless argued that OSHA does not give careful enough attention to whether the benefits of the level of protection OSHA mandates outweigh the costs. Some would argue that if the justification for OSHA regulation is conventional market failure, the stringency of the regulations should reflect what the market outcome would have been if the market had been perfect. The benefits of a given reduction in risk could be measured by what workers would have been willing to pay to achieve such a reduction in risk had there been no market failure. (Measures of willingness to pay are then sought in wage premium data, or other kinds of data.) The costs would be compliance costs for that reduction in risk. According to this analysis, the optimum level of protection an OSHA regulation should mandate is that at which the benefits exceed the costs by the greatest amount. By this standard, critics argue, OSHA regulation has mandated excessive levels of protection. If we compare the cost per life saved of various OSHA health regulations, it often appears high compared with costs in other government lifesaving programs.

These criticisms raise fundamental and difficult philosophical questions about what constitutes good public policy. The counterargument to the criticism would begin by questioning the moral status of the marketplace exchange between employers and employees accepting hazardous employment. Even absent imperfect information, the limited opportunities for choice available to many of the people who take relatively unattractive jobs (some of which are low paid and others of which are hazardous, and therefore a bit higher paid) make it impossible to conclude that if there are risk premiums for hazardous work, government intervention is unnecessary.[69]

The argument that a policy should not be undertaken unless the benefits outweigh the costs seems self-evident until it is subject to further analysis. We do not condone rape even if it can be demonstrated that the rapist derives enormous pleasure from his actions while the victim suffers only in small ways. We undertake no cost-benefit analyses of the effects of freedom of speech or trial by jury before allowing them to continue. We often endow people with rights—based on some conception of justice, fairness, or human dignity—without asking whether the person granted the rights would be "willing to pay" as much for the right as it costs society to provide it for him. It is in this sense that supporters of occupational safety and health regulation speak about a "right to a healthy workplace."[70]

Many of the benefits of social regulation have no ready dollar value because they are not traded on markets. To economists, this is an unfortunate obstacle to analysis—and economists are forever trying to come up with measures of people's "willingness to pay" for clean-smelling air, living in a quiet environment, recreational benefits, or reduced risks of premature death. But there is a counterargument: no dollar value is assigned to those benefits because they are special. Most reasonable people agree that there is a place for markets in society, but most reasonable people also agree that market relationships have their costs as well. Dealings in the market can promote certain undesirable personal attitudes and interpersonal relationships. Even the economists are few (although there are some!) who would wish market relationships to dominate within families, or among friends. An obsession with the calculating mindset of market relationships and cost-benefit analyses would itself remove something of what is special about the social regulatory agencies as expressions of a desire to keep market relationships in their place.

Still, there is a point at which even the advocate of such a view would have to say "stop"—that we cannot guarantee a right to a healthy workplace if it would cost half the GNP to save one life. Rights are not absolute. Thus the difficult decisions remain. Regulatory decisions made by OSHA involve issues of life and of health, and thus are inevitably among the most emotion-laden issues governments deal with. The interest groups contending over government occupational safety and health policy, organized labor and business, are the best organized in society, which makes these questions among the most difficult to resolve politically. And the achievement of compliance with OSHA regulations, once issued, by the millions of firms subject to them exemplifies the most difficult implementation problems governments face. For these reasons, the experience with OSHA gives us a good, if larger-than-life, view of the most difficult problems of policymaking in American society today—and tracking OSHA's future provides a good way of tracking how government is dealing with some of the harder domestic policy issues it faces.

CHAPTER 8

Environmental Protection Agency

ALFRED MARCUS

The creation of the Environmental Protection Agency (EPA) in 1970 and the passage shortly thereafter of statutes giving the new agency broad powers to reduce pollution were political moves informed by a theory of how to best prevent a regulatory agency from being "captured" by industry or afflicted with bureaucratic sloth. When the White House, with congressional approval, merged fifteen existing programs managed by five different departments or councils, it brought into being an organization headed by a single administrator—not a commission—and charged with regulating virtually all sources of pollution rather than a single industry.[1] It was thought that fixing responsibility in one person and equipping him with authority over many different industries would minimize the chances that the EPA would become the tool of any single source of influence. When President Richard M. Nixon issued the executive order creating the EPA, he directed it to deal with the environment "as a single interrelated system," not only because that was the "rational" way to proceed, but also because it was the prudent way.[2]

Even more important than these organizational arrangements were the provisions of the new statutes. Congress sought to reduce the risk that the agency would abuse its discretionary authority by placing sharp limits on that authority. The EPA was required to achieve specific air and water quality goals within a fixed—and short—period of time. The 1970 Clean Air Act required that EPA achieve healthy air by 1975, and the 1972 Federal Water Pollution Control Act (FWPCA) required that EPA eliminate discharges into the nation's waterways by 1985.[3]

The contrast with older regulatory agencies is clear.[4] The Federal Trade Commission (FTC) does not have an explicit deadline to eliminate unfair methods of competition, nor is that goal given a clear definition. The Antitrust Division of the Justice Department was not given a timetable to end combinations in restraint of trade, nor was it provided with any legislative determination of what that objective requires. In contrast, the EPA has been delegated clear goals and given specific timetables to achieve them.

The creation of an agency with statutes possessing these attributes was an experiment in regulatory reform that had been called for many times by scholars who criticized the vague language of the older regulatory statutes.[5] They felt Congress was at fault for delegating authority to regulatory agencies without clear standards of implementation or unambiguous statements of means and purposes. It said to the bureaucracy, "Here is the problem—deal with it."[6] When Congress passed the 1970 clean air and 1972 clean water acts, it was sensitive to this criticism and was less willing to relinquish control over regulatory policy to the bureaucracy.

The creation of an agency with these attributes tests the theory that the bureaucracy needs clear instructions from Congress to eliminate sloth and to avoid "capture." This account of an experiment in delegating clear legal authority to a regulatory agency will describe the circumstances under which this departure in regulatory policy originated. It will enumerate the tasks the agency had to perform, discuss the controversies that arose in the course of carrying out these tasks, and assess the impact that the media, professional norms, the courts, and interest groups had on the efforts to achieve stated goals within an explicit timetable.

In 1977 Congress significantly modified EPA's original statutes, amending both the 1970 Clean Air Act and the 1972 Federal Water Pollution Control Act.[7] This chapter also summarizes these changes in environmental law.

The Passage of Pollution-Control Laws in 1970 and 1972

The passage of pollution-control laws in 1970 and 1972 with clear goals and timetables to achieve them was a policy innovation. Like other innovations, it had "inventors," "transferrers," and "adopters."[8] A group of professors, fearful of the influence that industry could exert on government, formulated the notion that vague regulatory statutes encouraged industrial control of regulatory agencies. Marver Bernstein, one of these professors, suggested in 1955 that vague statutory language was a cause of the "capture" of regulatory agencies by business.[9] Drawing upon existing legal literature about delegation of authority to regulatory agencies, he argued that the character of the law affected an agency's relationship to the businesses it tried to control: the vaguer the laws that the agency administered, the less likely that the agency would be independent of the businesses it was supposed to govern.

Bernstein's theory of regulation was based on a biological model of agency growth, development, and decay.[10] Although his "life cycle" theory of regulatory behavior is somewhat obscure and complex, its essence can be summarized. Regulatory agencies pass through stages that lead them from the vigor of "youth" to the debilitation of "old age." After jubilant beginnings with high expectations and massive political support, they decline and perform inadequately. Once the original public that supports passage of their legislation has lost interest, vague statutes give regulated industries the chance to control the law's interpretation and administration.

The remedy for agency decline attributable to vague and ill-informed legislation is statutes drafted by Congress that have clear goals and explicit means of implementation. Statutes of this character institutionalize and make binding the sentiments of the public originally mobilized for the purpose of passing the legislation. Armed with strict legal authority that stands as a monument to the sentiments of this once-aroused public, a regulatory agency is less likely to languish, even if its activities no longer command general interest or attention.

The "life cycle" theory of regulation proposed by Bernstein was restated and elaborated by Theodore Lowi. In 1969, the year before EPA's birth, Lowi brought together much of the scholarly criticism about vague legislation in a chapter in his book *The End of Liberalism.* [11] Lowi relied heavily on the works of law school professor Kenneth Culp Davis and former FCC commissioner (and later federal judge) Henry J. Friendly.[12] These authors stressed the evils of undefined discretion in government agencies. Lowi developed a general argument that the growth of broadly delegated legislative authority and increased bureaucratic discretion had led to a perversion of liberalism—what he called "interest-group liberalism"—and a reduction of the power of popular majorities.

The insights of Lowi, Bernstein, and the other scholars were incorporated into political science textbooks[13] to such an extent that it would have been hard for an undergraduate interested in government and attending a liberal arts college in the 1960s to have avoided contact with them.

This scholarly notion, however widely dispersed among college graduates, may not have been adopted by Congress had it not been for the work of middlemen who transmitted the notion to politicians. Without middlemen, the professors' theory might have remained on the library shelves. In the language of the innovation literature, the middlemen "transferred" the professors' idea, if to "transfer" means not only to publicize, but also to apply pressure needed to get the idea adopted.

The "transferrers" of the idea that vague legislation contributed to inadequate regulatory performance were members of a Ralph Nader organization, The Center for the Study of Responsive Law. This group had two task forces: one on air and one on water-pollution policy. The former, led by John Esposito, published *Vanishing Air* in 1970; the latter, led by David Zwick and Marcy Benstock, published *Water Wasteland* in 1971.[14] In the period when Congress was considering amending pollution control laws these task forces published books critical of Congress's prior work.

The people who participated in compiling these volumes generally were graduates of liberal arts colleges in the 1960s. Many had majored in the social sciences and had become lawyers or law students.* The Naderites wrote detailed case studies of bureaucratic efforts to implement earlier air- and water-pollution-control laws in which they demonstrated that poorly conceived, politically compromised legislation led to regulatory imcompetence. They recommended the adoption

---

*It is likely that during the course of their studies they came across the theory that since vague regulatory legislation caused regulatory failures, loose statutes had to be tightened to limit bureaucratic discretion. If they had not come upon this notion during the course of their studies, they surely encountered it while working for Nader.

of strict new statutes that eliminated the possibility of delay and forced the bureaucracy to achieve goals by specific dates.

Although the substance and specific recommendations of the Nader reports were important, the timing and staging of their appearance were also significant. Their appearance after the 1970 "Earthday" celebration, in the midst of a general public debate about environmental degradation, had an impact on a central figure in Congress's deliberations: Senator Edmund Muskie, a Democrat from Maine, who was chairman of the Subcommittee on Air and Water Pollution of the Senate Committee on Public Works.

The appearance of *Vanishing Air* in May 1970, after the "Earthday" demonstration of April, demonstrates how a timely accusation can evoke a commitment to a particular posture from an elected official.[15] The report accused Muskie of not taking a "tough" stand against private industry, and the media gave this criticism of a potential presidential candidate extensive coverage. The stories stressed the task force's charge that Muskie had "sold out" to political expediency and industry interests. Muskie was indignant. At a press conference the day after the report appeared, he maintained that his subcommittee had not acted "for the dark, secret, conspiratorial reasons" suggested by the Nader report. He criticized those who adopted a tactic of "excessive confrontation" and promised to strengthen the air-pollution law before the end of the year. According to Charles O. Jones's account of the incident, "the overall effect put Muskie in the position of having to do something extraordinary in order to recapture his [pollution-control] leadership."[16]

In assessing the influence of "public interest" leaders like Nader, James Q. Wilson has argued that a "symbiotic political relationship" existed between some of these activists and subcommittee chairmen who were interested in gaining national prominence.[17] He gave the example of auto-safety legislation, where Senator Abraham Ribicoff and his Senate Subcommittee on Executive Reorganization of the Senate Committee on Government Operations worked together with Nader against the auto manufacturers. While this theory of a symbiotic relationship between a congressional committee and a public-interest representative may apply to the passage of various consumer laws, it does not fit the case of the 1970 clean-air amendments. In this instance, Senator Muskie's subcommittee on air and water pollution and the Nader task force were antagonists, not collaborators. In the case of the 1970 and 1972 pollution-control laws, the influence of the public-interest leaders rested on their ability to embarrass a key senator.[18]

The Nader task force attacked an individual who ordinarily was considered their friend. Attacking a friend was more effective than attacking a known enemy because it had greater shock value and invited more media coverage. As Richard Leone comments, "Public interest groups are dependent on shock techniques. . . . Extra headlines are brought about only by controversy and response."[19] Since the media tend to "view public affairs as a species of athletic contest," a "bit of theatrics" was involved in the way "public interest" leaders aroused "public indignation."[20]

With public concern over air and water pollution rising, Muskie's expertise and experience in the area of pollution control made him an attractive contender for the presidency. He was a speaker at the April "Earthday" rallies and generally was respected within the ranks of the environmental movement. Because of the national exposure he gained as vice-presidential candidate in 1968, he was a front runner among Democratic contenders and his activities were scrutinized carefully by influential reporters who covered national issues.

In 1970, when Senator Muskie adopted the view that strict statutes with specific goals and timetables were needed, he was a target vulnerable to attack by public-interest leaders not only because he was being mentioned as a Democratic presidential candidate, but also because the 1967 Air Quality Act, which his subcommittee drafted, had not been administered successfully.[21]

The 1967 Air Quality Act was not working, in part because of its complicated provisions.[22] It was based on a regional approach. From the time that the National Air Pollution Control Administration (a predecessor of the EPA) issued "criteria documents" for a specific pollutant, the states had ninety days to file a letter of intent stating that they would establish standards for the pollutant. These criteria documents were scientific descriptions of the health effects that would occur when the ambient air level of a pollutant exceeded a certain figure. There was no timetable in the law for the publication of the criteria documents, however, and as of March 1, 1970—more than two years after the act had been passed—no criteria documents had been issued and no state had established a full set of standards or adopted an implementation plan to control any pollutant.[23]

Without the accusations of the Nader reports, Muskie might have acted anyway—the mood of the times, House criticism of existing laws, and presidential proposals to increase federal authority over pollution might have forced Muskie to examine the statutes. But had there been no Nader reports, Muskie's examination would not have had the same magnitude. Before the reports were published, Muskie planned to make adjustments in the old *regional* air- and water-quality schemes. After they appeared, he accepted the concept of *national* standards. He tried to devise tough laws that would produce quick and dramatic progress by applying pressure on the bureaucracy and on industry.

The policy recommendations of Muskie's subcommittee received almost unanimous endorsement from Congress. Time and again, by extraordinary majorities, both houses passed legislation with explicit goals and timetables. President Nixon's Special Message on the Environment called for national air-quality standards and federal effluent guidelines for water polluters. By a 374–1 vote, the House passed an air-pollution bill that followed the general outline of the president's proposals,[24] but after the Nader task force published the report that questioned Muskie's air-pollution record, the senator's subcommittee drafted an air-pollution bill that exceeded both the House and administration proposals in stringency. The new bill called for air-quality standards based on health-and-welfare criteria that ignored economic cost or technological feasibility, state implementation plans that would achieve national air-quality standards by 1975, reductions in automobile pollutant emissions of 90 percent by 1975, and adoption of traffic control plans that would eliminate automobile use in some parts of the cities. The Senate *unanimously* endorsed this bill on September 21, 1970.[25]

In October 1971 Muskie's subcommittee drafted a 120-page water-pollution bill that declared it to be national policy to eliminate the discharge of *all* pollutants into the nation's waterways by 1985. The Senate passed this bill 86–0.[26] The House-Senate conferees agreed that polluters should achieve the best practicable technology (BPT) by 1977 and the best available technology (BAT) by 1983. Alarmed by the impact that the bill might have on the nation's economy, Nixon vetoed the bill; but the bill became law when the Senate voted 52–12 and the House 247–23 to override the president's veto.[27]

The policy innovation in the 1970 and 1972 pollution-control statutes was the use of deadlines, specific goals, and a plan of implementation. The "inventor" of this notion was a group of academics; the "transferrers" were public-interest activists; and the "adopter" was Senator Muskie and Congress. David Vogel suggests that groups similar to the one responsible for EPA's statutes be looked at in the following light.[28] Like business and labor, they attempt to achieve some sign, such as subsidy or promotion, of semiofficial incorporation into the existing system. In this instance, by creating strict statutes with timetables and standards of implementation, the group responsible for EPA's statutes became the semiofficial guardian of a plan to make rapid pollution-control progress in a short period of time.

The Tasks of EPA

Under the 1970 Clean Air Act, EPA had the following tasks to perform in order to achieve healthy air by 1975:[29]

1.   Thirty days after the passage of the act, propose national ambient air quality standards to protect public health (primary standards) and welfare (secondary standards).

2.   Approve state implementation plans that prescribed specific emission limitations for types of polluters within a year after the proposal of the air-quality standards. (The state plans had to meet the health standard by 1975. To meet this goal, the states had the authority to use transportation control measures, if necessary.)

3.   Set emission levels for new and modified stationary sources of pollution, for pollutants which EPA considered toxic, and for motor vehicles. (The motor vehicle standards mandated by Congress called for 90 percent reductions in auto emissions in five years. The manufacturers, however, could appeal and request a one-year extension.)

Under the 1972 Federal Water Pollution Control Act (FWPCA) EPA had to perform the following tasks:[30]

1.   Within one year after the act was passed, promulgate effluent guidelines that designated allowable discharges for various industrial categories (such as cement manufacturers, beet-sugar processors, petroleum refiners, etc.). The effluent guidelines specified the meaning of the 1977 best practicable technology (BPT) goal and the 1983 best available technology (BAT) goal.

2.   Within two years after the act was passed, issue permits to individual manufacturers that would achieve BPT and BAT in the time allowed.

The general rules contained in the guidelines would state the minimum standard that an entire industry had to achieve, while the permit would specify a limitation figure for a particular source. The permit

Environmental Protection Agency

writer would have guidelines to support the numbers he demanded from industry, and there would be less room for negotiation on a case-by-case basis.

The 1970 Clean Air Act and the 1972 water-pollution-control act were not the only pieces of legislation EPA had to administer. It inherited a solid waste, a pesticide, and a radiation program. Its responsibilities in the solid wastes and pesticides area were expanded by Congress in 1970, when EPA received new solid-waste authority, and in 1972, when EPA received new pesticides authority.[31] Congress also created entirely new programs for EPA to administer. In 1972 it passed a noise bill, in 1974 a drinking-water act, and in 1976 a toxic-substances act.[32]

In addition, EPA had major research responsibilities. Of its nearly $2.5 billion budget in 1972, over $2.2 billion was appropriated to air- and water-pollution control. But the second biggest appropriation was research, which received nearly $.7 billion.[33]

EPA was created by a Reorganization Plan that consolidated several existing agencies. Under Reorganization Plan No. 3 of 1970, the Environmental Protection Agency, which began operations on December 2, 1970, brought together close to 6,000 employees from 15 government programs located in 3 departments (HEW, Agriculture and Interior). Many of these employees were scattered throughout the United States in laboratories and regional offices. The two biggest organizational components were the Federal Water Quality Administration (FWQA) with 2,700 employees from the Department of Interior and the National Air Pollution Control Administration (NAPCA) with 1,150 employees from the Department of Health, Education and Welfare. The smaller organizational units included: from HEW—the Bureau of Water Hygiene, the Bureau of Solid Waste Management, the Office of Pesticides, and the Bureau of Radiological Health; from Agriculture—Pesticides Regulation; and from Interior—the Pesticides, Wildlife and Fish Office.

The activities of this new agency with its diverse inheritance were numerous and fragmented.* This was not what the White House intended. In his Message Relative to the Reorganization, President Nixon called for a system of comprehensive waste management to be achieved by centralized administration:

Despite its complexity, for pollution control purposes the environment must be perceived as a single interrelated system . . . a single source may pollute the air with smoke and chemicals, the land with solid wastes, and a river or lake with

*A large part of the authority for carrying out these programs was delegated to regional offices and state and local governments.

chemicals and other wastes. Control of the air pollution may produce more solid wastes which then pollutes the land or water. Control of the water may convert it into solid wastes which must be disposed of on land. . . . A far more effective approach to pollution control would: identify pollutants—trace them through the entire ecological chain, observing and recording changes in form as they occur—determine the total exposure of man and his environment—examine interactions among forms of pollution and—identify where in the ecological chain interdiction would be more appropriate.[34]

William Ruckelshaus, the first administrator of EPA, tried to carry out what Nixon intended by developing a "functional" plan for organizing the new agency. This plan called for amalgamating EPA's programs into functional administrative offices, such as planning and management, standards and compliance, and research and monitoring.

Before EPA's creation, consultant Alain Enthoven, helped devise the "functional" strategy.[35] Enthoven, a former Defense Department official, applied that department's program planning experiments to EPA's organizational design.[36] Just as Defense Department budget categories were broken down into functional units (such as strategic retaliation, general purpose, and air defense), so EPA's organizational division would be broken down into "functional" units (such as abatement, monitoring, research, and standard setting). Just as Defense Department mission-based categories were intended to do away with artificial bureaucratic distinctions and eliminate duplication and waste in order to achieve greater integration of operations, so EPA's mission-based divisions were supposed to eliminate archaic bureaucratic distinctions and promote cost-effectiveness in order to achieve better coordination. Enthoven's plan for functional management argued forcefully for eliminating EPA's "programmatic" inheritance—that is, the distinct air-pollution-control, water-quality, solid-waste, radiation, and pesticides pieces that EPA inherited. Enthoven felt that EPA should carry out President Nixon's expressed intent and deal with the environment as an interrelated system.

But the functional plan was not effected.[37] Only one administrative office, the Office of Planning and Management, adhered strictly to the scheme. Other offices, such as Research and Development and Enforcement, roughly corresponded to the scheme but were divided into units that carried out different parts of diverse statutes. Air-pollution specialists pursued their activities in offices different from water-pollution specialists and had little contact with them. Similarly, solid-wastes specialists had little communication with pesticide employees. Comprehensive environmental management—the president's official reason for EPA's birth—was a distant aspiration, not a concrete reality.

A major reason for the failure to adopt the functional plan was legislative—there was no statutory basis for comprehensive management. The air- and water-pollution programs had different legal foundations. According to the Clean Air Act, air-quality goals were based on health-and-welfare criteria; according to the federal water-pollution act, discharge limitations were based on technological considerations. The federal government established air-quality goals, but state governments set pollutant-discharge limitations. The federal government set water-discharge limitations, while states established water-quality goals. The two programs had different operating procedures. Dialogue between them was rare, and employees generally did not switch from program to program. In air pollution, the major concern was health hazards caused by pollutants in the air. In water pollution, the major problem was technological: how to remove organic waste material from the water. The tasks of the program were so different as to preclude cooperation and the development of a common method or strategy or implementation.

The president's plan for comprehensive management could not have been carried out as long as EPA was divided into programs with separate requirements. Moynihan distinguishes between program and policy: "Programs relate to a single part of the system; policy seeks to respond to the system in its entirety."[38] Comprehensiveness was an effort to elevate pollution control activities from the level of program to the level of policy. Nixon's message on the reorganization tried to have EPA respond to the "system in its entirety":

... we need to know more about the total environment—land, water, and air ... only by reorganizing ... can we effectively ensure the protection, development, and enhancement of the total environment. . . .[39]

But the president's message did not take into account the fact that agency bureaucrats had no reason to be concerned about the "total environment." Their task was to carry out specific statutory requirements.

ALFRED MARCUS

Controversial Issues in Implementation

The political and administrative problem of ensuring that bureaucratic behavior would conform to some definition of the public interests
was far more complex than first supposed. The fear of "industry capture" and the desire to "compel" technological advancement led to
statutory language that created—or failed to anticipate—a host of other
issues. To be sure, there was little sign that the EPA was being "captured," but abundant evidence that it was not going to achieve its stated
goals. To see why this was the case, we must examine some of the
economic, technological, administrative, and political problems faced
by the agency—problems made worse, in many cases, by the nondiscre-
tionary language and explicit timetables of the pollution control legislation. The environmentalists and the Naderites did not take into account
the existence of competing priorities, nor did they anticipate public
opposition to the scheme of committing administrators to specific goals.
The controversial issues that arose as EPA tried to implement the 1970
and 1972 pollution-control acts centered around issues of feasibility.

Economic Feasibility

It is a truism that making rapid progress in a short period of time costs
a lot of money. The 1970 and 1972 pollution-control acts, however, did
not require or perhaps even allow EPA to take pollution-control costs
directly into account. If EPA adhered strictly to the language of the
1970 Clean Air Act, it would disregard economic factors and judge
emission-reduction requirements entirely on the basis of health-and-
welfare criteria. In order to compel EPA to take economic considerations into account, three administrations, both Republican and Democratic, tried to impose various economic restrictions on the
promulgation of environmental regulations. Two kinds of economic
considerations became important—the cost-benefit ratio of pollution-
control systems and the effect of antipollution expenditures on the
economy as a whole.

Evaluations of pollution-control costs exist but are uneven in quality,
while evaluations of benefits are hard to come by.[40] Cost studies are
done more frequently than benefit studies, but the accuracy and reliability of the former are difficult to assess because economists use different methods to reach their conclusions. With these qualifications in

278

Environmental Protection Agency

mind, the findings of a few studies will be noted. One estimate by the Council of Environmental Quality (CEQ) has pollution control costing each person living in the United States $47 in 1974 and $187 in 1977.[41] The CEQ estimates that these costs will continue to rise to 2.5 percent of gross median family income before they start to decline again in the mid-1980s.

Robert Dorfman has shown that rich people pay more for pollution control than poor people.[42] Using 1976 figures, he demonstrated that families with incomes over $11,410 paid an average of $549 a year for pollution control, while families earning less than $5,701 per year paid an average of $121 a year. But Dorfman argues, using a 1969 opinion survey about willingness to pay, that rich people generally would be willing to spend more for pollution control than poor people. The rich spent $59 *less* than they were willing to pay, while the poor spent $61 *more* than they were willing to pay.

The costs of reduction escalate as the amount of pollution control increases. After studying EPA and CEQ statistics, Paul McCracken concludes that the twenty-five-year-costs to reach a 95 percent effluent reduction would be around $119 billion, while the cost of achieving the remaining reduction to achieve "zero discharge" would amount to $200 billion.[43] The last 5 percent of reduction is the most costly to achieve. Achieving "zero discharge" would involve spending at least $81 billion more than achieving 95 percent reduction.

Benefit studies appear less frequently than cost studies because measuring benefits is generally more difficult.[44] The most sensitive problem is expression of the value of human life and health in monetary terms. In spite of this difficulty, studies that estimate benefits and compare them with the costs have been undertaken. In a 1977 study, Lave and Seskin concluded that the benefits of controlling stationary-source air-pollution emissions outweigh the costs, while the costs of controlling motor-vehicle emissions outweigh the benefits. (Lave and Seskin's findings can be compared with an earlier NAS (National Academy of Sciences) study that concluded that the cost to achieve motor-vehicle standards would be between $5 billion and $11 billion, while the benefits would be between $3.6 billion to $14.3 billion.[45]) According to Lave and Seskin, the stationary-source program will show a net benefit of $6.5 billion (in 1973 dollars), while the motor-vehicle program will show a net loss of $6.0 billion (in 1973 dollars).[46] To Lave and Seskin, these statistics indicate that stationary-sources goals have been appropriately set while the motor-vehicle goals should be reconsidered.

Macroeconomic indicators measure the effects that pollution-control expenditures have on growth, inflation, and unemployment. The 1970 and 1972 pollution-control laws require that new pollution sources must achieve higher pollution-control standards than old ones. Some critics have charged that this requirement tends to dampen economic progress and that the "significant deterioration" and "non-attainment" provisions of the 1970 Clean Air Act hinder economic expansion.* Government-sponsored macroeconomic studies, however, suggest that on the whole, pollution-control expenditures stimulate economic growth, not retard it.[47] Some 20,000 employees have been put out of work because of plant closings, but over 600,000 are employed in various pollution-related activities.[48] The additional inflation attributable to pollution control is between 0.3 and 0.5 percent. Some industries, such as the electric utilities, face severe capital shortages. Specific individuals, plants, and locales suffer and inflation rises, but the overall macroeconomic impact appears to be positive.

Technological Feasibility

Air-pollution standards, based solely on health-and-welfare criteria, were designed to force technological change. But legal requirements alone will not compel rapid technological innovation. As a result, serious technological obstacles plagued efforts to reduce emissions from major sources such as steel mills, power-generating plants, and motor vehicles.

Steel mills, power-generating plants, and motor vehicles are the most significant air-pollution sources in terms of total emissions.[49] They contribute more tons of air pollution than any other three sources combined. For steel mills, controlling fugitive (nonsmokestack) emissions at coke plants has been the most pressing problem. EPA advocated practices such as "pushing control" technology, "stage control," and other techniques that the steel industry was reluctant to accept.[50]

In response to EPA air-quality goals, power companies started switching to cleaner fuels such as natural gas, higher-grade oil, and low-sulfur coal. But these fuels became costly and scarce during the energy "crisis" precipitated by the oil embargo and the quadrupling of OPEC oil prices. This led President Nixon in his 1974 energy message to propose that air-quality standards be lowered temporarily to enable power com-

---

*The "significant deterioration" provision is interpreted by the courts to mean that new sources cannot locate in particular areas where air quality is pristine. The "non-attainment" provisions do not allow new air pollution in areas that are below national health standards. By not allowing new sources in areas with pristine air and by not allowing new sources in areas with dirty air, "significant deterioration" and "non-attainment" provisions can hinder economic expansion.

panies to switch to coal.[51] In 1974 Congress passed an amendment to the Clean Air Act—the Energy Supply and Environmental Coordination Act—that prohibited conversion from coal to natural gas or oil and ordered plants that had converted to the cleaner fuels to switch back to the dirtier one.[52]

Although they could be granted an extension until 1979, the power companies that converted to coal still had to meet primary air-quality health standards. To do this, they had to install flue gas desulfurization (FGD) equipment, which they were reluctant to do. EPA found FGD to be economically and technologically sound, but the power companies argued that it was too costly and fuel consuming.[53] They maintained that they should be allowed to build tall stacks and employ intermittent controls instead of installing FGDs.

With the Arab boycott and the sudden rise in oil prices, the trade-off between clean air and gas mileage also came under scrutiny. In his January 1974 energy message, President Nixon proposed that interim 1975–76 auto emissions standards be extended until 1977 so that auto manufacturers could concentrate on improving fuel economy.[54] There was some dispute, however, over the relative fuel penalty of emission reductions.[55] The auto makers had taken a number of steps that reduced fuel economy of 1973–74 autos about 10 percent over that of 1970 autos—6 percent for compacts and 15 percent for standard and luxury autos. A large percentage of the loss in 1973 and 1974 fuel economy was due to the use of retarded spark timing to control hydrocarbons and carbon monoxide and the installation of exhaust gas recirculation to control nitrogen oxides. In 1975 the automakers were slated to install catalytic converters in new cars to reduce exhaust emissions. Catalytic converters were devices attached to a car's tailpipe which removed hydrocarbons, carbon monoxide, and nitrogen oxides from the exhaust system. Top EPA officials were convinced that the converters would entail virtually no fuel penalty, that in fact by switching to them instead of employing other techniques that reduced gasoline mileage, the auto companies would actually improve fuel efficiency at the same time as they reduced pollution.[56]

The relationship between the catalytic converter and decreased fuel efficiency was questionable. In addition, there were more fundamental causes for added fuel consumption beside the catalytic converter. Heavier automobiles were the most important factor. There was also a substantial fuel penalty for air conditioners (9 to 20 percent) and for automatic transmissions (approximately 7 percent). However, Congress, in response to the energy crisis of 1973 singled out auto-pollution standards. It passed the Energy Supply and Environmental Coordination Act which extended the auto-emission-reduction deadline, as President Nixon suggested. Davies and Davies maintain that

The power companies, the automobile industry, and the coal and oil companies saw the energy crisis as an opportunity to weaken the provisions of the Clean Act.[57]

However, there was a technological problem associated with the catalytic converter that was unrelated to fuel economy. The converter emitted sulfuric acid, and therefore was itself a health hazard.

"Acid emissions" were brought to EPA's attention by the Ford Motor Company, which first identified the problem in February of 1973. The issue remained dormant until the fall of that year, when John Moran, an EPA scientist in North Carolina, held an unauthorized press conference which alerted the public to the "danger."[58] A January 30, 1975, EPA report on the "acid" problem concluded that the health risks from sulfuric acid emissions would exceed the benefits from reduced auto emissions after four model years.[59]

Several studies criticized the original EPA report.[60] An environmental consulting firm hired by the EPA and the trade association for the catalyst manufacturers found that EPA overestimated sulfate exposure levels by between 200 and 500 percent. The California Air Resources Board rejected the EPA analysis and decided to adhere to a stricter timetable. In response to this criticism, EPA reevaluated the earlier report. The reevaluation estimated that exposure to sulfuric acid would be more than one-third less than the original report estimated. However, the reevaluation still concluded that the dangers from sulfur emissions would exceed benefits from reducing other pollutants after twelve model years.

Administrative Feasibility

Two administrative problems in trying to achieve air and water pollution control goals by a specific date also deserve mention: the lack of time to gather and evaluate information and the need for public support.

In May 1972, before the passage of the 1972 Federal Water Pollution Control Act, the water program office of EPA created an effluent-guidelines division to gather the information needed to implement the proposed legislation. The only regulations similar to effluent guidelines that the agency had produced were a handful of new-source air-pollution standards. It lacked experience in directly regulating industry's emissions or effluents. As of October 1, 1973, the day they were due, not one effluent guideline had been promulgated.

One reason for delay was the time required to collect and evaluate information. Most of what the effluent-guidelines division knew about industrial practices was general and was based on outdated or second-hand descriptions. Members of the division therefore had to visit plants throughout the country and acquire additional information from scientific and engineering associations. The information showed that for most industrial categories, no single plant has yet developed the best practicable or best available technology (BPT or BAT), but that each plant might have some special feature that functioned well. In order to ascertain what an industry could achieve, the agency had to bring together the best features of plants operating under different circumstances throughout the country. The task of assembling this information was immense and could not be completed in a single year, as the law required.

The effluent-guidelines division hired private contractors to help it complete the guidelines.[61] The contractors had to establish the state of the art in industries with which they often did business, and therefore were carefully monitored by EPA officials. The division checked to see if the contractors sampled the right proportion of plants, if they handled the data properly, and if they examined all the factors involved. This took time. Moreover, many firms were reluctant to hand over data to contractors they knew were working for the EPA. When a company resisted, the data had to be discovered in public records, or the firm had to be served an administrative order requiring that it produce the information. In either case, there was more delay. The contractors were given nine months to develop the reports, but some took as long as two or three years to complete them.

The effluent-guidelines division, staffed mostly by engineers, was reluctant to make recommendations without complete reports. Hesitant about making decisions when it lacked reliable information, EPA missed the one-year statutory deadline for promulgating guidelines. Meanwhile, the enforcement office, staffed mostly by lawyers, was still trying to meet the two-year deadline for permits. It issued them before guidelines were even proposed. In many instances, permits contradicted ultimate guideline figures. Industries, confused by the contradictory signals they received from different EPA offices, challenged both guidelines and permits in judicial proceedings. They used one EPA figure to refute the other.

Other administrative problems affected EPA's ability to win public support. In 1973 EPA administrator William Ruckelshaus extended the 90 percent auto-emission deadline for one year. The Energy Supply and Environmental Coordination Act extended the deadline another year and gave EPA the right to extend it for still another year if petitioned by the auto manufacturers. Yet, even after these extensions, the 1975 healthy-air goal could be achieved on a nationwide basis only if transportation control measures were introduced in major metropolitan areas.

The 1970 Clean Air Act granted EPA the authority to use transportation control to achieve air-quality goals. This provision, however, was broad and meaningless as written; EPA did not know what Congress intended. The agency therefore listed what it considered the alternatives.[62] They included bicycle paths, parking restrictions, auto-free zones, gas rationing, gas taxes, mass-transit construction, bus lanes, car pooling, and inspection-maintenance programs. Some of these alternatives were not viable for political reasons. Few politicians could afford to support gas rationing or increased gasoline taxes and expect to be reelected. Some of the alternatives were not viable for economic reasons. The construction of additional mass-transit systems was too expensive for most cities to undertake. Moreover, there was not enough open space where new systems could be built.

No matter how transportation control was defined, it required a significant decrease in the use of private automobiles in large urban areas. The most notorious example, the California plan for the city of Los Angeles, required gasoline rationing.[63] Rationing, the only way to achieve the necessary 82 percent reduction in gasoline use during the high smog period between May to November, involved issuing gasoline coupons and limiting the amount of gasoline produced for or shipped to the state. Neither the politicians nor the public reacted favorably to a plan that would drastically curtail driving.[64] Former EPA Assistant Administrator for Enforcement and Deputy Administrator John Quarles, writes:

The public reaction was one of utter disbelief. It seemed incredible that the Environmental Protection Agency could propose a virtual shutdown of the auto transportation system in a major United States city.[65]

The plan for New York City, approved by EPA, included higher tolls on the bridges coming into the city and bans on taxi cruising; the city was not willing to put it into effect. The plan for Pittsburgh called for exclusive bus lanes, staggered work hours, bridge tolls, increased parking fees, and emergency procedures to limit the number of autos in the central business district; it, too, was attacked by local officials.[66]

Resistance to transportation plans was exacerbated because many of them were made in Washington by national authorities not familiar with local conditions. Local businessmen complained that inner cities would experience greater decline because of traffic restrictions. Taxi drivers and highway construction workers felt that their livelihood was threatened. Citizens failed to support experimental bus lanes and new public transportation routes. Most of these groups and individuals believed that healthy air did not merit fundamental changes in driving habits or in the average citizen's "longstanding and intimate relations to private automobiles."[67]

The innovators who influenced EPA's legislation overshot their mark, for the law appeared to go beyond what was feasible. Any given feasibility problem may not have been enough to retard achievement of statutory commands, but the cumulative effect of all the economic, technological, administrative, and political problems set back goal achievement dramatically. Trying to implement the plan for rapid progress uncovered an almost obvious inadequacy in the original theory about the need for clear statutes. Explicit goals and dates of achievement were not sufficient to ensure goal accomplishment. Goals and timetables that were explicit without also being achievable and defensible were declarations of intention without real credibility.

The Media, Professional Norms, the Courts, and Interest Groups

Two limits on the EPA's regulatory efforts have been noted. First, its explicit legal authority was so narrow that it stood in the way of efforts to manage the environment comprehensively. Second, that authority did not require (or, in some cases, even permit) EPA to take into account questions of economic, technological, or administrative feasibility. There was conflict between what the language of the law prescribed and what the country, business, and the EPA were able to accomplish. One consequence of not having the right to view the environment comprehensively was that the agency could not consider options that may have been less costly and more feasible than the ones Congress required. And if the agency could not affect feasibility, it lost credibility. Goals, which seemed fixed and permanent, became flexible. They were bent when the occasion arose, as it did for instance, during the energy "crisis," leading some to suppose that the agency was "caving in" to pressure.

But other factors besides explicit legal authority influenced the achievement of pollution-control goals. In addition to being bound by the laws that they administer, bureaucrats are also influenced by the media, professional values, the courts, and interest groups.

The Media

The media gave extensive coverage to the critical comments the Nader task force made about Muskie. They thereby influenced the passage of the 1970 and 1972 pollution-control bills. Their coverage of William Ruckelshaus's nomination as EPA administrator also affected agency behavior. When President Nixon chose Ruckelshaus, a relatively obscure Justice Department official under John Mitchell, to head the agency, they publicized the charge of an Indiana conservationist that Ruckelshaus was an "environmental Carswell," a nominee with no credentials.[68] At televised nomination hearings, Ruckelshaus promised to enforce pollution-control laws vigorously.[69] One week after the agency started operations, he sued Atlanta, Detroit, and Cleveland.[70] To attract media attention, he made the announcement at the National League of Cities Convention in Atlanta. In the agency's first two months, Ruckelshaus's EPA brought five times as many enforcement actions as all its predecessors had initiated in any two-month period.[71]

Ruckelshaus worried about the environmentalists' tendency to represent public officials as either friends or enemies of polluters. By questioning the agency's willingness to prosecute, he feared they would undermine public confidence in the agency. According to John Quarles, an assistant administrator under Ruckelshaus, EPA's first administrator

did not seek support for his, actions in the established structures of political power. He turned instead directly to the press and to public opinion, often in conflict with those very structures. In so doing, he tied the fortunes of EPA to public opinion as the only base for EPA's political support. . . .[72]

In order to establish credibility with the general public, Ruckelshaus believed that the agency needed to cultivate a reputation for being a vigorous enforcer of pollution-control laws.

Environmental Protection Agency

Ruckelshaus was concerned that without favorable attention from the media, EPA would be more closely tied to the White House and therefore be less able to pursue an independent policy. The president communicated to Ruckelshaus that he thought the environmental issue faddish, and the White House threatened to keep close tabs on the appointments Ruckelshaus made and the regulations his agency issued. For instance, the Office of Management and Budget in 1970 demanded that the states balance costs against benefits when drafting air-pollution implementation plans.[73] The media, on the other hand, had been instrumental in making pollution control an issue. In the late 1960s the networks, journals like *Time* and *Newsweek,* and dailies like the *New York Times* and the *Washington Post* focused on crises such as the 1969 Santa Barbara oil spill and demonstrations such as "Earthday," which aroused public concern about environmental hazards.

Ruckelshaus used television and the national press to put distance between the agency and the White House. The attention the media gave the agency helped sustain the image of independence. In the short run, this image had a positive affect on the effort to achieve goals within statutory limitations. It energized the inherited bureaucracy, which was accustomed to operating at lower departmental levels, where media attention was not common. Once aroused, however, media-generated enthusiasm among EPA bureaucrats was not sustained. As time passed, issues that were perceived as competing priorities attracted media attention. Media coverage of the "energy crisis," inflation, and unemployment dampened efforts to achieve progress in the time period set by Congress. The media reinforced the notion (perhaps sensible) that environmental goals, energy goals, and economic goals could not be achieved simultaneously.

In addition, media influence was limited because lawsuits and adverse publicity against firms that violated the law did not always force these firms to comply. Companies that did not sell directly to consumers were not usually concerned about the bad publicity. Moreover, the media did not cover enforcement activity closely after the series of initial suits was brought. Only the *Wall Street Journal* regularly reported the progress of court cases. Since companies did not have to make expenditures for pollution control as long as cases stood before the courts, corporate attorneys had no incentive to move cases along quickly. In the long run, generating adverse publicity against offenders did not help to achieve statutory objectives in the time allowed.

Professional Norms

Lawyers, economists, and research scientists played prominent roles in the effort to achieve statutory goals in the period specified by law. Ruckelshaus, a former Justice Department official accustomed to managing attorneys, brought many young and ambitious lawyers into the agency. He gave them responsibility for enforcement. The earlier pollution-control authorities had almost no lawyers on their staffs. Composed almost entirely of research scientists, they had the reputation of being able "to study a problem to death," not the reputation of being able to solve a problem quickly. Ruckelshaus stressed EPA's enforcement duties as opposed to its research responsibilities.

At first, these lawyers were on the offensive. They revived the 1899 Refuse Act as a water-pollution enforcement tool. Under the provisions of this act, all discharges into navigable waters were subject to the conditions of a permit. While the Refuse Act was in effect, the lawyers referred 371 enforcement actions to the Justice Department for prosecution.[74] They brought criminal actions against Allied Chemical, FMC, Gulf Oil, Cities Service, Jones and Laughlin, Minnesota Mining and Manufacturing, Mobil Oil, Republic Steel, Texaco, and U.S. Steel. In all, they brought 169 criminal actions, 106 civil actions, and 96 actions for failure to apply for a permit.

However, court cases took a long time to complete and often did not result in compliance. As time passed, EPA attorneys increasingly found themselves on the defensive. The permits issued under the FWPCA were contested by over 2,000 industries in adjudicatory proceedings.[75] One of the issues raised was the conflict between guidelines and permits. Were limitations in permits binding if they derived from more stringent "interim" guidelines? In addition, industry brought more than 150 lawsuits against the effluent guidelines themselves. Du Pont prepared its case while the agency was still developing the guideline for the chemical industry. It brought suit on the day the guideline for this industry was promulgated.*

*The case of the corn millers against EPA is a good example of a suit brought against the guidelines. EPA had changed the original effluent guidelines figure in response to industry comments and it felt that it was being lenient and flexible when the original regulation was issued. Therefore, agency lawyers were surprised when a petition of challenge was filed in the Eighth Circuit Court of Appeals. The legal brief submitted on behalf of the dry millers by the Corn Refiner's Association and a few of the producers brought out the standard issue in almost all industry suits. The dry millers claimed that EPA did not have the statutory jurisdiction to set specific numerical requirements. Guidelines should have been interpreted to mean a range of figures and not a single number, and EPA should have allowed the permit writer to set limitations only for a particular plant.[76]

Environmental Protection Agency

Almost all the effluent guidelines EPA issued were challenged by industry lawyers on the basis of EPA's interpretation of the law. They asserted that EPA had no statutory authority to prescribe a single number. "Guidelines" meant the agency had to establish a range of figures. Whether a particular guideline was sustained depended less on the capability of EPA attorneys and more on the inclinations of the particular court and judge involved.

The issue of whether guidelines meant a single figure or a range of numbers was resolved only in February 1977 when the Supreme Court decided in EPA's favor in the du Pont case.[77] In the year that EPA had to achieve the goals of the best practicable technology, the Supreme Court sanctioned the administrative framework for achieving that goal —five years after Congress had established it.

Economists

Unlike EPA lawyers, who were wed to decisive action and legal standards, the economists who worked for the agency were engaged in efforts to realize economic well-being. They communicated the notions of scarcity and choice—not all goals could be achieved simultaneously, and choices had to be made among competing goals.

Most economists were hired to work in the Office of Planning and Evaluation. This office, first led by Robert Sansom, a former aide to Henry Kissinger, functioned as staff to the administrator. Sansom chaired a regulatory review committee, and his office gathered data about the economic costs of regulations.

The agency created the Office of Planning and Evaluation and developed a regulatory review process because the administrator needed cost information to justify agency decisions to the White House. In order to compel EPA to take cost factors into account, OMB Director George P. Schultz had informed Ruckelshaus on May 21, 1971, that EPA regulations had to be cleared by OMB, other relevant agencies, and the Commerce Department before they could be promulgated. Before the Office of Planning and Evaluation and the regulatory review process existed, Ruckelshaus had trouble refuting challenges to EPA regulations made by Commerce Department economists. He needed EPA economists to gather information and run a regulatory review process that would internalize the debate taking place outside the agency. By trying to internalize this debate, Ruckelshaus hoped to recapture the autonomy EPA was losing to the White House and the Commerce Department.

The regulatory review process tried to bring internal agency differences about regulations into the open.[78] If agreement was impossible, the administrator would be given alternatives and the evidence needed to weigh them. If there were two or three ways of addressing a particular problem, he could pick the least costly alternative. The economists in EPA, while a small proportion of total employees and having entered the agency later than the attorneys, ran the regulatory decision-making process. From their position as managers of regulatory decision making, they had the agency examine alternatives and they recommended what they calculated as least costly options.

The regulatory review process made a difference in the case of air-pollution regulations issued under the 1970 Clean Air Act. But in 1972, when Congress passed the new water-pollution-control bill, EPA decided to abandon the review process for the water-pollution regulations that had to be issued under this act. Too many of them had to be issued in too short a time for the steering committee to maintain intensive economic review.

Under the 1972 Water Pollution Control Act, EPA had to control pollution from over 200,000 industrial sources. To regulate 200,000 industrial polluters required information about the discharges, manufacturing processes, and technical options of diverse firms operating in different circumstances throughout the country. Water polluters were divided by the EPA into more than 30 categories and 250 subcategories on the basis of product, age and size of plant, and manufacturing process. They manufactured everything from asbestos and beet sugar to steam electricity and textiles. The task of regulating 200,000 diverse polluters overloaded the bureaucracy in general and the economists in particular with more work than they could handle. It frustrated the efforts of the economists who were not able to take responsibility for the drafting of these new water-pollution regulations.

Research Scientists

There were two groups of research scientists in the EPA—the public health specialists and the engineers.[79] The health scientists generally belonged to organizations (such as the American Public Health Association, the National Environmental Health Association, and the National Tuberculosis and Respiratory Disease Association) that advocated a strong health basis for standard setting and enforcement. They performed research on pollution hazards. The engineers, on the other hand, built and tested technology. The sanitary engineers, who usually belonged to the Conference of State Sanitary Engineers, perfected water waste-treatment plants, while the automotive engineers, who usually belonged to the Society of Automotive Engineers, tried to perfect devices such as the catalytic converter.

There was a difference in time horizons between research scientists and engineers, on the one hand, and lawyers and economists, on the other. Unlike lawyers and economists, who had immediate regulatory and enforcement responsibilities, research scientists and engineers had more distant goals and aspirations. Most believed that as environmental science and technology was undeveloped, their purpose was to do "pure," "state of the art" research and make a contribution to knowledge. They were wedded to their academic disciplines, in touch with the work done by their colleagues in universities, and less constrained by statutory timetables than lawyers or economists.

While lawyers and economists had to apply existing knowledge to regulatory decision making and enforcement, research scientists and engineers wanted to do long-term work that might produce significant breakthroughs. Health and ecological research took a great deal of time to complete. EPA researchers measured actual discharges and emissions, wanted to gauge human health effects in both the short (three to ten years) and long (twenty to forty years) run, and hoped to trace impact through the ecosystem for number of generations. For example, a predecessor to the EPA began a program on eutrophication* in the early 1960s that started to yield *preliminary* results only in 1976.

Developing and demonstrating technology also took years to finish. First the basic technological theory had to be tried on a small scale. A larger project was initiated only if a pilot plant could be perfected. A full-scale demonstration was started only if a larger project proved feasible. Six months to a year could be spent on a pilot plant, two years on a larger project, and up to four years on a full-scale demonstration. Research required time, money, and patience.

From the perspective of the research scientists and engineers, the deadlines in the 1970 and 1972 pollution control acts were unrealistic. Spread out in labs throughout the United States and communicating with other agencies' employees mostly through the mail, these researchers did not feel a responsibility to meet congressional goals and deadlines. In 1974 the Task Force to Define an Office of Research and Development (headed by the director of EPA's Cincinnati lab, Andrew W. Breidenbach) concluded:

---

*Eutrophication occurs when there is an abundance of nitrogen in a body of water. This encourages the growth of algae, and leads to the decomposition of this algae and oxygen in the lake. With less oxygen in the lake, it is more difficult for fish and other animals to survive.

Past experience with the Office of Research and Development has resulted in the rest of the Agency viewing the Office of Research and Development as an independent self-serving operation rather than as an integral part of the Agency.[80]

The Breidenbach report explained that research scientists did not have the time to service the needs of lawyers and economists for information relevant to regulatory decision making and enforcement. It suggested that EPA was two agencies: one dedicated to research and the other to regulation.

In addition to their responsibility to EPA statutes, the agency's professionals dealt with their counterparts outside the agency. The research scientists within the agency were judged by the standards applied to and by their academic counterparts outside the agency. The agency's lawyers contended with corporate attorneys; its economists coped with economists in the Commerce Department. The outward-looking character of these professional groups made them less than obedient servants to congressionally established deadlines.

The Courts

The discretionary behavior of the bureaucracy, already limited by Congress, was further checked by the courts. The courts restricted EPA's freedom by deciding issues on a case-by-case basis. From an administrative perspective, they interpreted the law by using different principles at different moments.

Exercising authority granted him by the 1970 Clean Air Act, Ruckelshaus, for the purpose of expediting matters, wanted to grant citizens and localities a two-year extension on transportation controls while denying the auto companies an extension on the 90 percent reduction in five years. Ruckelshaus acted as though he believed that the auto companies were more capable than states and cities of achieving what the law required. Moreover, public resistance to transportation control would be a heavier political burden for the EPA to bear than opposition from the auto manufacturers.

But the courts did not permit EPA to make this trade-off. They forced Ruckelshaus to reconsider his denial of the auto companies' request for an extension of the original 90 percent reduction in five years. A 1972 National Academy of Sciences (NAS) study claimed that the 90 percent reduction in five years was unfeasible.[81] When Ruckelshaus refused to grant an extension, even after NAS reported its results, the manufacturers appealed to the U.S. Court of Appeals for the District of Columbia.[82]

The court ordered a reconsideration. The presiding judge stated in a lengthy opinion that economic factors had to be given greater weight.[83] Responding to the court's order, Ruckelshaus promulgated less stringent interim standards for auto pollutants in California.

The court did not allow Ruckelshaus the right to refuse the automobile companies' request for an extension. It then compelled Ruckelshaus to impose unpopular transportation-control requirements. No matter how transportation control was defined, it required a significant decrease in the use of automobiles in most large urban areas. Owing to the political costs of stopping citizens from driving, Ruckelshaus felt that the states should be granted additional time to devise traffic-control measures. Therefore, on May 31, 1972, he granted seventeen of the most urbanized states a two-year transportation-control-plan extension.[84]

The municipalities of Riverside and San Bernardino then sued EPA in the U.S. District Court because Ruckelshaus had granted their state additional time.[85] A court order directed the agency to propose by January 1973 a transportation-control plan that would meet the statutory requirements for California. The National Resources Defense Council (NRDC) also sued to overturn the extension in the other forty-nine states. On January 31, 1973, the Court of Appeals for the District of Columbia ruled in favor of the NRDC stating that the administrator had not shown sufficient cause why the two-year extension of transportation control had been granted. The judge gave the states only a few months to submit plans to control traffic.

In these air-pollution examples, the courts interfered with the administrator's efforts to carry out what he believed was a reasonable implementation strategy. They did not give him the right to make a trade-off he thought necessary for the purpose of administration. The courts also interfered with agency efforts to carry out its water-pollution implementation strategy. On December 23, 1970, the White House announced the establishment of a permit program based on the 1899 Refuse Act. By July 1971, 23,000 applications had been filed and a few permits issued. This effort, however, was brought to a standstill by a court order. A district court decision in Ohio ruled that the permit program was subject to the requirements of the 1970 National Environmental Policy Act.[86] EPA was overwhelmed by the prospect of drafting environmental-impact statements for over 50,000 permits. Because of the burden it imposed on the agency, the court decision delayed the carrying out of the permit program for a little over a year.[87]

The district court prohibited EPA from using the Refuse Act to carry out the permit program, but the authority to run such a program as well as the authority to issue effluent guidelines were contained in the FWPCA. Under this act, EPA had to produce effluent guidelines for over 30 categories and 250 subcategories of industry by October 1973. It was crucial that the guidelines appear on time because they were supposed to be the basis for permits that had to be issued polluters by December 1974. As of October 1, 1973, however, no effluent guideline has been promulgated. The National Resources Defense Council had to sue EPA before it released the guideline figures. Again, court interference changed the way EPA administered the law —in this instance, speeding up what would have taken the agency longer to accomplish.

Nothing would be wrong with the courts compelling EPA to achieve statutory deadlines if EPA bureaucrats had the time to gather and analyze the information needed to issue these guidelines. But the courts ignored EPA bureaucrats' engagement in the lengthy analysis needed to determine best practicable and best achievable technology. They compelled the agency to issue guidelines before adequate information had been collected and evaluated.

In both these air- and water-pollution examples, EPA's ability to devise and carry out implementation policies as it saw fit was restricted by the courts. The Court of Appeals of the District of Columbia forced Ruckelshaus to reconsider the first auto-extension decision, but it also sustained a National Resources Defense Council suit that led to the adoption of transportation-control plans. The district court prevented EPA from using a permit system prior to the passage of the water-pollution-control act; but once the act was passed, they forced EPA to issue effluent guidelines according to a timetable.

Interest Groups

The EPA was designed to represent environmentalists. Roy Ash, head of a presidential council on reorganization, wanted to create a new Department of Natural Resources instead of another independent regulatory agency. His theory was to unite competing interests in a single department and thereby reduce the number of secretaries reporting directly to the president. Ash reasoned that departments containing competing interests would be more loyal to the White House than to their constituencies.[88]

The staff of the council which Ash headed wanted to create an independent agency. It opposed combining pollution control and natural resource programs in one department because it feared that such an agency might be dominated by groups interested in economic develop-

Environmental Protection Agency

ment.* The staff view was that competing interests should be represented by separate structures in the federal government. Industry already was represented by several administrative bodies. Fairness dictated that those who favored environmental protection should also have a supportive agency.

EPA was created according to the principles of the staff and not those of Ash. It did not, however, represent environmentalists exclusively. A modicum of cooperation between industry and the EPA was necessary to keep the routine of the regulatory process running smoothly. EPA depended on industry to provide information, ideas, and a rapid flow of communication. In addition, Ruckelshaus felt that to prove its integrity, EPA had to demonstrate independence from both factions. He therefore consciously sought to antagonize both industry and environmentalists. Russell Train, the second administrator, describes how EPA became positioned between the parties:

> If a decision doesn't go as far as our environmental friends would like, it is immediately called a sellout. If the decision goes against industry, we're accused of giving in to environmental emotionalism.[89]

In some instances, environmentalists accused EPA of "dragging its feet because of political cowardice or sloth."[90] In other cases, regulated firms complained that controls were "excessive, non-productive, conflicting, or too subject to change."[91] Standing between industry and environmentalists, the agency tried to achieve a reputation for fairness and impartiality.

The "significant deterioration" issue is a case in which the EPA used its position between interests to play the role of mediator. Environmentalists held that air quality should not be allowed to decline in areas that already exceeded national health standards. Industry, however, claimed that if air quality were not allowed to deteriorate in these areas, there would be little room left for industrial expansion. In 1974 the Supreme Court decided in favor of the environmentalists. It forbade any "significant deterioration" in air quality in regions that *exceeded* national health standards. In response to the Supreme Court decision, industry tried to get Congress to eliminate the "significant deterioration" ruling by amending the Clean Air Act.

EPA constructed a compromise to appease both parties[92] by interpreting the Supreme Court ruling to mean that there could be different categories of air use: in one category, air that exceeded national health

---

*The "fox" as the staff put it, had to be keep out of the "chicken coop."

standards would have to be maintained at existing levels; in another category, air that exceeded national health standards would be allowed to deteriorate; and in a third category, where air was below national standards, new pollution would not be permitted. This compromise tried to save "significant deterioration" while at the same time permitting industrial expansion. This case, where EPA played the role of mediator, is fairly typical of the agency's attempt to position itself between contending interests, rather than supporting one side or the other.

Interest Groups and the 1977 Amendments

The EPA had two organized sectors with which it had to contend—environmentalists and industry. James Q. Wilson argues that when two organized sectors strive under conditions where one's gain is the other's loss, it is not likely that the agency in question will be "captured" or permanently controlled by a single interest.[93] Instead, "if favoritism develops, it will represent an unstable equilibrium of forces, and the balance will shift from time to time."[94] In the case of the EPA, the balance shifted from environmentalists in the 1970–1972 period, when Congress passed EPA's original legislation, to industry in 1977, when Congress amended the earlier laws.

In 1977 amendments were adopted that modified, eliminated, or revised the original deadlines in the 1970 and 1972 acts.[95] The amendments created six major changes:

1. The 1977 air-pollution amendment postponed the "healthy" air goals (that had to be achieved by 1975, under the 1970 act) to 1982, and in some instances to 1987. States had to submit revised implementation plans that would achieve air-quality goals by 1982. For areas heavily affected by auto emissions, states had until 1987 to achieve air-quality goals.

2. The 1977 air-pollution amendment extended the deadline for 90 percent reduction in automobile emissions, originally set for 1975 and subsequently postponed to 1978, to 1980 for unburned hydrocarbons and to 1981 for carbon monoxide. The administrator of EPA again was given discretionary authority to delay the achievement of auto pollution reduction objectives further, but only for carbon monoxide and nitrogen oxides, not for unburned hydrocarbons. The administrator could delay the 1981 carbon monoxide and nitrogen oxides standards for up to two years, if by taking into account factors such as cost, drivability, fuel economy, and impacts on health, he determined that required technology was not available.

3. The 1977 air-pollution amendments required that EPA give variances for technological innovation. The agency also had to file economic-impact and employment-impact statements with all new regulations. In addition, the governor of any state could suspend transportation control measures that required gas rationing, reductions in on-street parking, or bridge tolls.

4. The 1977 water-pollution amendments gave industries that acted in "good faith," but did not meet the 1977 best practicable technology (BPT) deadlines, additional time to meet this standard. These industries had until April 1, 1979, instead of July 1, 1977.

5. The 1977 water-pollution amendments postponed and modified the best available technology (BAT) requirement that industry was supposed to achieve by 1983.* Instead of BAT, BCPCT—"the Best Conventional Pollution Control Technology"—had to be achieved.† BCPCT gave EPA flexibility to set standards less stringent than BAT when the costs of employing BAT exceeded benefits. Industrial discharges now had to meet BCPCT by 1984, instead of BAT by 1983.

6. The 1977 amendments retained the goal of "zero-discharge" into navigable waters by 1985, but the practical implications of retaining this goal were few. The extension of the BPT objective and the modification of the BAT objective eliminated the connection between "zero-discharge" and a specific abatement program. The 1977 amendments, while not directly changing the zero-discharge goal, effectively abandoned it for the 1980s.[96]

In the 1970–77 period, industry manifested opposition to the deadlines in the 1970 and 1972 acts. As this chapter has shown, industry challenged EPA's interpretation of the law in the courts. Spokesmen for water polluters testified before Congress that "zero-discharge" was neither possible nor desirable.[97] The auto companies threatened to stop production if Congress did not extend the 90 percent reduction requirement.[98] Industry, the courts, White House proposals, and the knowledge Congress gained about feasibility problems led to modifications in the earlier statutory framework. The agency, which had been designed to represent environmentalists, was compelled under the new amendments to consider industry's position.

Economic, technological, and administrative obstacles prevented the

---

*They retained the strict standard for toxic pollutants but modified it for conventional pollutants. Conventional pollutants are solids, BOD ("Biochemical oxygen-demanding" pollutants), pH, and fecal coliform.
†According to the conferees, "best conventional pollution control technology" was at least as stringent as best practicable pollution control technology, but not more stringent than best available technology.

agency from achieving statutory goals according to the original timetable established by Congress. These obstacles, however, were not the only ones EPA faced in its efforts to make rapid progress in a short time. The media, professional norms, the courts, and interest groups influenced the agency's ability to achieve goals by statutory deadlines. The media generated enthusiasm for pollution control, but this enthusiasm waned when energy and economic issues captured media attention. The values of professional groups transcended loyalty to the EPA and diluted the commitment of the groups to congressional goals and timetables. The courts interfered with EPA efforts to carry out what the agency considered reasonable implementation strategies. EPA tried to stand between environmentalists and industry, rather than exclusively representing one party. By revising EPA's laws in 1977, Congress readjusted EPA's position between interest groups. It preferred industrialists, while originally the agency's structure and statutes had favored environmentalists. Political feasibility, defined in terms of factors such as the media, professional norms, the courts, and the conflict between interest groups was as much a problem in achieving goals by statutory deadlines as economic, technological, and administrative problems.

Conclusion

In general, Congress can take three approaches when it drafts regulatory statutes and delegates authority to agencies.[99] With the older commissions, it drafted vague legislation with general goals but no specific instructions on how or when to achieve these goals. In these instances, Congress, in effect, said to the bureaucracy: "Here is the problem—deal with it" or even "Discover the problem and deal with it." A second alternative is for Congress to draft, as it did with the EPA, clear statutes with specific goals, timetables, and instructions. However, there is a third alternative, which has not been tried on a widespread basis. Congress can abandon these legal-administrative approaches and adopt instead a market-incentive approach which does not necessarily involve an orientation toward goal achievement.

Legal-administrative approaches try to command private economic behavior. The market-incentive approach, in contrast, decentralizes decision making.[100] It relies upon individual firms who are supposed to possess the information needed for making optimum cost-benefit and efficiency trade-offs. Individual decisions in response to market incentives lead to choices between environmental control, energy use, and economic growth that EPA found so difficult to make. The "hidden hand" of the market, rather than the "heavy hand" of legal and administrative dictation, allocates resources among competing ends. If there is any dominant innovative idea about regulation that academics —particularly economists—promote today, it is the notion that a market-incentive approach should replace legal-administrative methods.

EPA's authority under the 1977 pollution-control amendments mixed aspects of both the legal-administrative and the market-incentive approaches. Original timetables were extended, but not eliminated. The credibility of these deadlines, however, was damaged by the extensions. A precedent for delay was established. Once delayed, timetables could be delayed again and again. They lost legitimacy. Exceptions, conditions, and special categories in the 1977 amendments again gave the bureaucracy authority to put off achievement of objectives. They brought EPA closer to the vague "let the bureaucracy decide" method. They qualified—but they did not eliminate—the basic goal and timetable approach.

The 1977 amendments, by creating a limited market for emission rights in "non-attainment" areas, also introduced a version of the market-incentive method.[101] This policy evolved gradually. A Supreme Court decision under the 1970 Clean Air Act prohibited construction of new industrial sources of pollution in regions where air quality was below national standards.* This decision had the effect of severely limiting economic growth in these "non-attainment" areas. In 1976 EPA began to allow growth of new sources in "non-attainment" regions if deterioration in air quality caused by the new sources was more than "offset" by emission reduction in other facilities. For example, EPA allowed Standard Oil of Ohio (SOHIO) to build a pipeline terminal near Long Beach, California, only when SOHIO bought another nearby polluting facility and closed it down. In essence, the oil company purchased the emission rights of the facility it closed. Under the 1977 amendments, EPA obtained authority to set up a limited market for trading in emission rights in "non-attainment" areas.†

*Even if from a "cost-benefit" perspective, a further deterioration in air quality was justified.

†This market exists under the 1977 amendments until 1979. In 1979 attainment areas without state implementation plans that ensure attainment of air-quality objectives by 1982 face a ban on new sources of emission. In effect, their industrial growth is restricted.

The offset policy is not a major breakthrough with respect to the use of the market-incentive approach. EPA was and remains an experiment in regulation reform relying on timetables that require it to achieve specific goals by fixed dates. Its authority to use the market-incentive approach is limited. When Congress drafted the 1977 amendments, it considered pollution-tax and effluent-charge schemes, the most commonly discussed market-incentive systems. (Congressional Research Service prepared an 869-page collection of articles, probably the most comprehensive ever assembled on the subject of incentives pollution taxes, effluent charges, and the like: 835 pages were devoted to a discussion of incentives, charges, and pollution taxes; 34 pages were devoted to sanctions and penalties.[102]) But the 1977 amendments did not adopt any of these systems. Instead the penalty provision in the 1970 Clean Air Act was changed. A firm no longer could avoid paying for the costs of pollution control by delaying in court. It now would be assessed a fine equivalent to the amount it could save by judicial delay.[103] In 1977 Congress altered this fining mechanism, but it did not grant EPA the right to use incentives such as pollution taxes or charges.

A pure market-incentive scheme was not adopted because it encountered political obstacles. Senator Muskie opposed taxes or charges because, as some suggested, their "adoption would imply a failure in the legislation he shepherded through the Congress."[104] The Treasury Department and powerful members of Congress balked at the use of taxes for regulatory rather than revenue purposes. Environmentalists opposed charges or taxes because they did not trust the government to set the price for pollution high enough to improve environmental quality. Finally, industry also opposed taxes and charges because it was afraid that the government would set the price for pollution too high. Lacking strong support from any group and without significant support from the public or leadership from the White House, effluent-charge and pollution-tax proposals were doomed politically.

Meanwhile, EPA could claim that the use of explicit goals and timetables achieved some results.[105] By 1977 over 90 percent of the nation's water polluters had achieved best practicable technology according to the schedule established by Congress. In 1975, 75 percent of the major stationary sources of air pollution complied with state implementation plan requirements. In addition, sulfur dioxide emissions were down 25 percent, and particulate emissions were reduced 14 percent. New car emissions, while not meeting the 90 percent reduction requirement, had been lowered by 67 percent. In the year Congress intended "clean air" for the nation, more than 30 percent of the nation's 247 air-quality-control regions met clean air goals.*

The progress made under the 1970 and 1972 acts did not meet the expectations initially written into law, but this progress was substantial, especially given the rapid changes in the economy and perceived inadequacy of the nation's energy supply. Specific goals and deadlines had some advantages. They aroused the bureaucracy to action and were an effective bargaining ploy, a legal "weapon" that the bureaucracy used against industry. They played an affirmative role in getting the bureaucracy and industry to act; without these strict standards and timetables, action may have been slower or may not have taken place. Was it worth the price, was it worth the $187 that each citizen had to pay for pollution control in 1977? Was it worth the administrative bother, the antagonism between government and business and between government and ordinary citizens that developed? These are questions that this chapter cannot answer. What can be said is that though not a panacea, specific goals and timetables at least were partially effective in achieving what Congress intended.

Clear standards were catalysts of change, not final determinants. When clear standards are set, it is probable that some change will follow, but the degree of this change depends on many factors. The perceived benefit of this change must exceed the perceived cost. A proven technology must be available. Extraordinary events, such as an energy crisis, must not intervene. Bureaucrats must be able to carry out what the law dictates. Citizens must be willing to accept alterations in life-style and habit that clear standards require. The media, professional norms, the courts, and interest groups must support the proposed change for an extended period.

This chapter has identified major limitations to the use of clear statutory authority—inflexibility in the face of changing circumstances, narrow definition of goals, and the absence of serious effort to consider potential economic technological, administrative, and political problems. It has shown that energy and economic problems intervened, that bureaucrats did not have the legal right to consider alternatives from a policy framework that stood above specific programmatic responsibilities, and that feasibility was an issue that Congress ignored. These

*More than 60 percent did not largely because noncomplying sources were difficult-to-control major emitters—like motor vehicles, steel mills, and utilities. One of the unanswered questions in regulatory administration is whether legal-administrative means as employed by the EPA, market-incentive methods as have yet to be tried, or some combination of the two approaches would be more effective in terms of achieving goals and reconciling their achievement with other objectives.

limitations were traced back to the 1970–1972 period when Congress, in response to the prevailing political atmosphere, drafted and passed pollution-control legislation by overwhelming majorities without considering feasibility.

The limits of the theory of strict standards included basic economic conditions such as growth, employment, and the role of inflation; emergencies, such as the energy crisis, that provided a sense of overwhelming necessity and allowed for revisions in clean-air goals; the relative lack of reliable scientific knowledge about the side effects and implications of a technology like the catalytic converter; the difficulties of administration, of getting bureaucrats to cooperate to achieve common goals; and popular attitudes, habits, and ideals—the fact that laws and decisions that called for the use of transportation control strayed too far from common expectations.

Such writers as Roscoe Pound have noted that with "the ascendance of social interests over parochial interests," law becomes increasingly socialized, subordinating individually held rights to consideration of the general welfare.[106] Legislatures delegate power to administrative agencies which become vehicles for social change. The failure of a program like Prohibition, however, illustrates that agencies of social change have to depend on group norms as much as on formal legal statutes. In the case of the EPA, clear statutes with goals and timetables helped the agency achieve substantial progress in eliminating pollution, but there were limitations to what these laws could accomplish. They were of limited influence in achieving pollution-control goals because such factors as technology, costs, the media, professional norms, judicial opinions, and interest-group pressures also influenced agency behavior.

Given these limitations, to what extent and under what circumstances is "the clear standard" theory correct? It is correct to the extent that goals are defined broadly enough to allow for flexibility in the face of changing circumstances. It is also correct to the extent that Congress tries to anticipate potential economic, technological, administrative, and political difficulties before establishing goals and timetables. If Congress does not take potential consequences seriously, if it makes no effort to anticipate the feasibility of the goals and timetables it establishes, then unrealistic standards will be implemented and public confidence in the ability of government to achieve what it intends will diminish. However, if Congress spends time gathering information and considering feasibility and shies away from decisive action, then public impatience with its ability to confront serious problems will develop. Thus Congress must make feasibility studies within practical time limits; it must then establish clear standards and timetables that are flexible enough that they can be modified as experience grows and more information is collected.

This experiment in clearly delegating authority to a regulatory agency proves that Congress must assess the feasibility of the goals it establishes and allow for flexibility in the face of changing circumstances. More flexible standards do not signify inevitable "capture" by industry. Standards have to be flexible enough to respond to the exigencies of new information and circumstances whether it supports the position of industry or of the environmentalists. Ultimately, all policy is made under conditions of some uncertainty. Given this uncertainty, it would be a mistake not to set goals and timetables; but given this uncertainty, it would be equally mistaken to set goals and timetables too rigidly to preclude their further modification. If policy makers cannot predict precisely the problems that a program with clear standards and timetables is likely to encounter, then they should at least frame goals and timetables in such a way that these goals and timetables can be revised through legitimate legal channels.

CHAPTER 9

Office for Civil Rights

JEREMY RABKIN

It is hard to find anyone who will defend the record of HEW's Office for Civil Rights (OCR) over the past decade; it is equally hard to find any agreement on the nature of its faults.* Many critics see OCR as a hotbed of regulatory zealots obsessed with vast social engineering schemes that bear little relation to their actual statutory mandates. To its constituents, on the other hand, OCR is a lumbering bureaucracy, addressing its obligations in the most timid, half-hearted, and ineffectual manner. Confronted with such mildly conflicting characterizations, a sophisticated newspaper reader might be inclined to suppose that the truth is somewhere in between. The truth is actually much more interesting: both those who fault the agency for its excesses and those who fault it for its deficiencies can, in fact, cite a great deal in OCR's record to substantiate their opposing criticisms.

Charges of bureaucratic zealotry are sure to return at some point to the agency's notorious ruling in the summer of 1976 that separate father-son and mother-daughter school banquets constituted an illegal form of sex discrimination. OCR's regulations offer numerous other examples of "non-discrimination" requirements carried to an absurd

*That portion of OCR's operations dealing with educational institutions—the bulk of OCR's work, in fact—was scheduled for transfer to the new Department of Education at the end of 1979. By itself this will probably mean little more than a change in name.

extreme.[1] Criticism may shift abruptly from sarcasm to indignation, though, when the subject is OCR's efforts to impose "forced busing" for school integration purposes, its reliance on statistical indications of discrimination (and corresponding inclination toward "numerical remedies"—"quotas," to the critics), or its avowed indifference to the cost or disruption imposed by many of its "affirmative" requirements. And charges that the agency has, in its activist zeal, distorted its statutory mandates can find official confirmation in a string of district court decisions striking down different aspects of OCR's regulations for exceeding their authorized reach.

But if the federal courts are to be accepted as a neutral umpire, judicial rulings supply even more powerful support to the counter claims of OCR's constituents. Beginning in 1970, the agency was subjected to a series of suits by civil rights groups charging deficient enforcement of its regulations and the plaintiffs prevailed in every case—even though legal challenges of this kind were virtually unprecedented in federal administrative law before the 1970s. OCR officials themselves concede that, for all the sound and fury generated by their efforts over the last decade, OCR has managed to impose significant changes in no more than a relative handful of institutions outside the South. Yet before 1972, when its staff was one-fifth as large as it is today, OCR successfully enforced racial integration on the vast majority of southern school districts.

The reason such apparently conflicting lines of criticism can be so readily sustained is that they have, for the most part, focused on different sides of OCR's regulatory operation. Those who fault the agency's excessive zeal generally point to the ambitious reach of its formal regulations and official statements of policy—often without noticing that it has rarely enforced those demanding standards in practice. Conversely, OCR's constituents have directed the bulk of their criticism at this undeniably poor enforcement record—though often without sufficient recognition of the vastly greater enforcement burdens posed by its complex new requirements, compared with the school desegregation effort in the South during the 1960s.

If this accounts for the apparent contradictions in the bill of particulars against OCR, it still leaves one to wonder how the agency let itself fall into an operating pattern that was bound to infuriate political factions on all sides. One can say that both sides of the indictment suggest an agency with an unsettled sense of its own basic mission or at least an agency that has formulated its goals unrealistically. But this hardly explains why, through almost a decade of debilitating and demoralizing controversy, OCR failed to redefine its basic mission in terms consistent with its capacities—as organization theory would suggest—or in terms that might earn approval of its performance at least in some quarters —as the conventional theories of bureaucratic politics would assume. Or, one can pose the problem in a more general political context: If OCR's constituents were able to win such far-reaching regulatory requirements on paper, why were they unable to secure effective enforcement? If contrary political pressures have hobbled the agency's enforcement, why did they not prevent the agency from issuing unenforceable regulatory standards in the first place? And finally, one may wonder how an agency with an enforcement mandate in the area of "civil rights"—a term which once suggested clear and inviolable constitutional guarantees—could ever have been left with so much confusion and uncertainty about its operating goals.

In fact, it is the peculiar character of "civil rights" regulation which probably offers the most useful key to understanding OCR's plight. For "civil rights" does indeed carry a special mystique, which has greatly inhibited open political bargaining over the proper scope or direction of OCR's activity. OCR's statutory mandates are nonetheless extremely loose and ambiguous and, like any substantial regulatory mandate, carry the authority to impose considerable cost and disruption on regulated interests. Thus while facing many of the same challenges as other regulatory agencies, OCR has had to operate under an unusual handicap: given the antipolitical atmosphere surrounding "civil rights" enforcement, OCR has had great difficulty building political support for realistic operating goals and still more difficulty adapting its operating patterns into politically sustainable routines. In this situation, the inherent weaknesses in OCR's enforcement machinery—and there are several—have grown from awkward challenges to pathological problems.

This is not to say that OCR's poor performance was simply foreordained in all respects by the special circumstances of its "civil rights" operating environment. But in retrospect it is striking how many of its problems were already prefigured in the way Congress formulated its basic mandates—a legislative approach which left the agency wide open to pressures to expand its rules far beyond its limited enforcement capacities.

Office for Civil Rights

The Statutory Framework

Notwithstanding its official title, HEW's Office for Civil Rights does not have the full panoply of civil rights concerns characteristic of the U.S. Commission on Civil Rights (a monitoring and advisory body) or the Civil Rights Division of the Justice Department (the federal government's principal litigation agency for civil rights offenses). OCR's statutory mandates, in fact, bear only limited and indirect relation to "civil rights," as normally conceived.

Title VI of the Civil Rights Act of 1964, the earliest and still (by volume of cases, at least) the most important of OCR's statutory mandates, served as the model for all subsequent enforcement mandates accorded to the agency. Its sole substantive prohibition provides: "No person in the United States shall, on the basis of race, color, or national origin, be excluded from participation in, be denied the benefits of, or be subjected to discrimination under, any program or activity receiving federal financial assistance." Subsequently, in Title IX of the Education Amendments of 1972, Congress used the same phrases to enact a ban on sex discrimination in federally assisted programs—though, because the measure was embedded in an aid to education bill, its substantive prohibition was limited to "any *education* program or activity." Congress then borrowed the same language (without the restriction to "education" programs) for Section 504 of the Rehabilitation Act of 1973, a measure prohibiting discrimination against the handicapped in "any program or activity receiving federal financial assistance."

The Office for Civil Rights has the responsibility for enforcing these measures against all recipients of federal grants channelled through the Department of Health, Education and Welfare.[2] These include virtually all public school systems in the country, virtually all institutions of higher education, as well as most hospitals, nursing homes, state and local service agencies. But until recently OCR's enforcement activities have concentrated for the most part on educational institutions.[3] It is this sphere of enforcement that has stirred the most controversy for the agency and gathered the most public attention.

OCR is authorized, under all three statutes, to enforce compliance by ordering termination of HEW funding to any recipient institution that refuses to correct its discriminatory practices. But that is the agency's sole sanction, and its responsibility ends once the sanction has been invoked. All three statutes also allow enforcement "by any other means authorized by law" (meaning a court action by the Justice Department), but the Department of Justice's Civil Rights Division, with its limited staff and wide range of other responsibilities, has been unable or unwilling to take on more than a small number of such cases over the years. Technically, then, the only "right" OCR protects is the right not to be discriminated against in the use of federal funds. Once an institution has been deprived of federal funding, OCR itself has no authority to help individuals or groups still victimized by that institution, even if its discriminatory actions are plainly illegal (under another statute) or (in the case of state institutions) plainly unconstitutional. The victims must go to another federal agency or directly to the courts for relief.

The "rights" protected by OCR are, in some ways, even more limited and ambiguous than the preceding formula suggests. Racial discrimination in the disbursement of federal funds to individuals (through Social Security payments or any of the existing array of special purpose loan programs) would clearly be unconstitutional, but is excluded from OCR's enforcement authority by a series of exemptions appended to all three statutes.[4] On the other hand, the statutes undoubtedly go further in their prohibitions, in some respects, than the Constitution requires. Federal courts had pronounced against federal funding of completely segregated institutions, on constitutional grounds, before the enactment of Title VI.[5] But it remains unclear from the existing precedents whether the federal government may be permitted under the Constitution to fund a nondiscriminatory element of an institution's programs, when the institution practices discrimination elsewhere.[6] And there is no clear line of cases establishing that sex discrimination and discrimination against the handicapped have the same sensitive constitutional status as race discrimination, even though the statutes treat them as equivalent.[7] Nor do the statutes explicitly incorporate constitutional standards to define discrimination (their prohibitions are not necessarily limited, that is, to practices that would be unconstitutional if maintained directly by the federal government, itself).

If the "civil rights" dimension of OCR's mandate is ambiguous, it is clear at all events that its fund-withholding authority affords the agency broad regulatory leverage in some of the most sensitive sectors of American society. During the congressional debates on the 1964 Civil Rights Act, many Title VI proponents insisted that the measure should not be viewed as a regulatory scheme at all. "It is simply," as Senator Kuchel (R-Cal) put it, "the exercise of the unquestioned power of the federal government to fix the terms on which federal funds shall be dispersed (and) . . . no recipient is required to accept federal aid."[8] But many federal regulatory programs, stretching back to the agricultural support system enacted by the early New Deal, operate entirely through the mechanism of conditional funding in otherwise voluntary programs. Fear of a dramatic increase in federal control over local schools had, in fact, led to the defeat of every major aid to education measure (usually including a nondiscrimination provision) that came before Congress in the 1950s and early 1960s.[9]

As late as the spring of 1963, President Kennedy rejected the pleas of the Civil Rights Commission that he issue an executive order forbidding federal funds to segregated facilities, warning that "it would probably be unwise to give the President . . . that kind of power because it would start in one state and for one reason or another it might be moved to a state which was not measuring up as the President would like to see it measure up in one way or another."[10] Only two months later, though, a brutal assault on civil rights marchers by local police in Birmingham, Alabama, shocked the nation from its ambivalence and spurred the Kennedy Administration to propose a sweeping series of new civil rights measures to Congress, including a bill authorizing the cut-off of federal funds to segregated institutions. In the ensuring clamor for strong federal action on civil rights, reenforced by an emotional "March on Washington" in the summer of 1963, the House Judiciary Committee recast the administration's proposal for discretionary withholding authority to a mandatory enforcement provision.[11]

By the time the civil rights bill reached the Senate at the beginning of 1964, its leading proponents urged that the funding provision (Title VI) ought to be the least controversial element of the entire legislative package. "If anyone can be against that," Hubert Humphrey exclaimed in his first speech to the Senate on behalf of Title VI, "he can be against Mother's Day. How can anyone justify discrimination in the use of Federal funds and Federal programs?"[12] Senator Ribicoff, in a statement typifying both the political complacency and the moral passion expressed by many advocates of the measure in both houses of Congress, declared:

> . . . of all the provisions of the Civil Rights bill, none rests on so simple and so sound a principle as does Title VI. That principle is that taxpayers' money, which is collected without discrimination, shall be spent without discrimination. This principle requires no argument. It is based on simple justice. It is based on ordinary decency. It is consistent with, if not required by, the U.S. Constitution. . . . This is a principle on which 100 Senators and indeed every American can and do agree.[13]

Southern opponents of the civil rights bill did indeed direct more of their outrage to the dramatic extensions of federal authority provided in Title VII of the civil rights bill (a ban on racial discrimination in private employment) and Title II (banning racial discrimination in hotels, restaurants, and other "public accomodations").[14] But many expressed equal alarm at the new powers accorded to the federal government by Title VI, for in threatening termination of funding by the direct action of executive branch agencies—rather than relying on enforcement through the federal courts, as did all other provisions of the bill—it opened the way, in their view, to federal interventions in an arbitrary manner and for more extreme ends. Senator Talmadge echoed the view of many southern representatives in his bitter reversal of Ribicoff's assurance: "Of all the unwise and vicious parts of this so-called civil rights bill, in my judgment Title VI is the worst."[15] The most elequent formulation of southern concern about Title VI was provided by Senator Russell of Georgia, who characterized the measure as "the realization of a bureaucrat's prayers":

The main target of the bill is supposed to be a terrible dragon called discrimination. Discrimination is a word with many fine shades of meaning and not all of them are completely evil. There is no attempt whatever in any title of the bill to define what is meant by the offense of discrimination. That definition is nowhere in the context, in the intent or in the purpose or even in the preface of the bill. That is done in order to leave the definition not to the law; not to the Congress; not, except in some very rare occasions to the courts; but to leave the definition up to anyone of an army of bigoted bureaucrats who would be sure to be employed to administer the new law.[16]

Such forebodings did not deter Congress from enacting the measure. Near the end of the Senate debate, in fact, a motion to delete Title VI from the civil rights bill was defeated by a substantially greater majority (69–25) than that which later voted to enact the 1964 civil rights package as a whole. But this resounding support for Title VI hardly indicated a firm congressional resolve to accept continued disruptions in the flow of authorized federal funding programs. Undoubtedly congressional willingness to endorse the basic principle of nondiscrimination in federal funding reflected, in large part, a belief that it would seldom be necessary actually to cut off funds. Briefing papers prepared for the bill's defenders by the Justice Department indicated that the Johnson Administration would, in fact, rely primarily on formal litigation and thus Senator Ribicoff could assure his colleagues that "it would be a rare case when funds would actually be cut off."[17] Confirming this view,

Sentator Humphrey noted that "immediate cut-offs of Federal funds would defeat important objectives of Federal legislation without commensurate gains in eliminating racial discrimination or segregation. Therefore, the desire and objective is to seek compliance with this important title [VI] without exercising the [funding termination] provisions."[18]

What made such assurances persuasive were the number of safeguard provisions written into Title VI to hedge the funding sanction. Rather than placing enforcement authority in a specialized civil rights agency, which might have been expected to take a doctrinaire approach to its mandate, Title VI directed each of the various federal funding agencies to adopt their own implementing regulations and specifically cautioned that these be "consistent with achievement of the objectives of the [funding] statutes" administered by the agency. It also took the unusual step of stipulating that these regulations, in each case, must be approved by the president before going into effect. It required that no enforcement action be taken until the agency had "determined that compliance cannot be secured by voluntary means." Then, after providing opportunity for a formal administrative hearing to the noncompliant recipient, it still required that the funding agency take no action on the funds in question until it had waited thirty days after notifying "the committees of the House and Senate having legislative jurisdiction over the program or activity involved" with "a full written report of the circumstances and the grounds for such action." Even then, Title VI expressly provided for judicial review of the agency's action.

The Senate added a further safeguard to allay fears that large scale cutoffs of funding might be used to increase the financial pressure or the political leverage on isolated offenders: A so-called "pinpoint" provision was inserted into the enforcement section to specify that "termination or refusal [of funding] shall be limited . . . in its effect to the particular program or part thereof in which such non-compliance has been found." The Senate also added a separate provision expressly exempting employment practices from Title VI coverage ("except where a primary objective of the Federal financial assistance is to provide employment"), thereby making explicit the assurance of the measure's defenders that Title VI would not normally affect employment practices since employees are not generally regarded as "participants" in a program nor as the intended "beneficiaries" of any federal funding the program may receive.

With all of this, Senator Humphrey could assure his colleagues near the end of the debate: "We have written into [Title VI] every precaution and every safeguard that I could think of. The only thing left would be to declare that Federal funds should be used in a discriminatory way."[19] A safeguard notably lacking, in fact, was the one demanded by Senator Russell: a clear definition of the term "discrimination" or any real guidance to the funding agencies (apart from the employment exemption) on how to interpret the pregnant phrases of the substantive prohibition in Title VI. Southern protests on this point were ignored, however, presumably because the various procedural safeguards inspired so much confidence and because the northern majority did not wish to provoke discord in its own ranks or appear to demean the grand declaration of principle in Title VI by tacking on to it a host of petty qualifications and exceptions. Proponents of the measure in both houses of Congress were profuse in their assurances that Title VI would not allow bureaucrats to impose extensive busing plans to achieve racial balance in the schools, to impose statistical quotas in school admissions or employment, or to pursue any other such extreme policies.[20] Humphrey's defense of Title VI assumed that its provisions would require no more than the courts had interpreted the Constitution to require. In 1964 federal courts in the South were still evaluating desegregation plans on the modest standard of "all deliberate speed" announced by the Supreme Court ten years before. (And the courts in the North had given no indication that segregated school patterns there might also be subject to constitutional attack.) Leaving things at the level of grand principle seemed safe.

The practical expectations for administrative activity under Title VI were actually so modest that Humphrey could ridicule warnings "that the [civil rights] bill would produce a gigantic Federal bureaucracy, when in fact it will result in creating about four hundred permanent new Federal jobs"—an estimate that was meant to accommodate the entire staff of the newly created Equal Employment Opportunity Commission and all new personnel at the Justice Department as well as the officials charged with enforcing Title VI in each separate funding agency.[21] The estimate, in fact, rested on the assumption that Title VI compliance would be enforced for the most part by existing staffs of the funding agencies in the course of their routine monitoring and accounting activities.

Yet events quickly belied almost all of these assurances. While the leading congressional proponents of Title VI were undoubtedly sincere in their modest characterization of the measure's significance, their forecasts proved to be wildly off the mark, at least regarding enforcement by HEW, the largest disburser of federal funds and the agency that was to handle the most publicized and most controversial matter (i.e., education) under Title VI. Within a year after the Civil Rights Act had been signed into law, HEW's Title VI enforcement staff was bringing powerful financial pressure to bear on southern school districts in a manner that by-passed all of the elaborate safeguard provisions in Title VI. Within two years it was requiring statistical indications of effective school integration and within four years was requiring busing. Within six years it was interpreting Title VI to require special remedial language programs for students with English language difficulties. And, of course, by then there were more than Humphrey's estimated 400 permanent personnel in HEW's Office for Civil Rights alone. Yet it was also very largely through the administrative enforcement actions of this agency that by 1972 there was more actual integration in the school districts of the South, according to government statistics, than in those of any other region of the country—a truly remarkable achievement which was itself surely contrary to the expectations of most of those who complacently voted to make Title VI part of the Civil Rights Act in 1964.

The unexpected power of Title VI did not induce Congress to hesitate much, however, before enacting in the early 1970s a parallel measure against sex discrimination, when the women's rights issue achieved national prominence. In the same year that it voted to propose the Equal Rights Amendment to the Constitution, Congress passed Title IX of the Education Amendments of 1972, prohibiting federal financial assistance to any education program or activity that engaged in sex discrimination.

It was originally proposed as a direct amendment to Title VI, one of a number of measures against sex discrimination put forward by Congresswoman Edith Green's Special Subcommittee on Education in 1970. The Green subcommittee had taken up a number of suggestions for extending federal protections against sex discrimination advocated by the report of a presidential task force on women's rights in 1970. But the task force had not mentioned the possibility of amending Title VI, and the hearings conducted by Congresswoman Green in 1970 treated the issue of sex discrimination in universities only in rather general terms, without focusing on the need for, or the appropriateness of, a broad-gauged fund-withholding measure. No further hearings were ever held, though, on the provision that became Title IX.

All of the different sex discrimination measures were to be included in the massive aid-to-education measure being prepared by the Green subcommittee at the same time. While many of the other measures were eventually removed for independent consideration elsewhere, the withholding measure remained a part of the large and complex education bill during its long development in the House over the next two years.[22] Recast as a parallel statute (rather than a direct amendment to Title VI), it was eventually approved by voice vote in both houses of Congress, along with the expansion of federal education subsidies enacted in the spring of 1972.

Intense lobbying by women's groups undoubtedly had something to do with the relative ease with which Title IX was enacted. Its inclusion in a major education funding bill also smoothed its way, since controversy over other portions of the bill tended to limit close scrutiny of Title IX.[23] But probably most crucial to the measure's easy success was the skill of its sponsors in preempting obvious points of concern with special exemptions written into the legislation. In the Senate, Birch Bayh, the measure's principal sponsor, introduced a version that provided complete exemptions for the military academies, for schools run by religious organizations ("if application of this subsection would not be consistent with the religious tenets of such organization") and for *admissions* policy (not for internal operation, that is) of all academic elementary and secondary schools. While the House had narrowly passed an exemption for all undergraduate college admissions (proposed as a floor amendment by Republican critics), Bayh countered with an exemption only for private colleges and traditionally single-sex public colleges. Bayh's version prevailed with little controversy on all these points.[24]

The House's principal contribution to minimizing controversy was a provision stating that the prohibition on discrimination should not be construed "to require any educational institution to grant preferential or disparate treatment to the members of one sex" on account of any statistical imbalances in the sex of program participants. Although this was intended to allay widely expressed fears that sexual quotas would be imposed under Title IX, even women's groups supporting hiring quotas in other contexts had no trouble accepting this language. The Equal Employment Opportunity Commission had already been imposing racial and sexual quotas for some years, notwithstanding a similar ban on action against "imbalance" in Title VII of the 1964 Civil Rights Act. The EEOC circumvented this by maintaining that it could act against "discrimination" as proved by imbalance figures and then impose employment quotas to remedy discrimination rather than "mere" imbalance. And the Title IX provision went even further than the "imbalance" provision in Title VII by explicitly authorizing statistical evidence to be considered in Title IX enforcement proceedings. Still this was little noted at the time and Title IX received little national attention. President Nixon's formal statement on signing the act criticized several features of it but made no reference at all to the sex discrimination provisions of Title IX.[25]

The absence of serious controversy at the time did not mean that Congress was clear about what it expected from Title IX, however. For the most part, congressional debate rarely descended from broad generalizations and pious invocations of the need to assure fair treatment to women. There was no serious effort to review enforcement experience with Title VI for clues as to the problems that might emerge from a similar ban on sex discrimination. Nor, on the other hand, was there any serious effort to consider whether sex discrimination might raise rather different problems or issues than race discrimination or the extent to which separate facilities for men and women should be treated in the same way as racial segregation under Title VI.[26] Congress, in short, simply handed over to HEW an extremely broad mandate in a very sensitive area, with a legislative history affording virtually no more guidance to HEW officials than the ambiguous terms of the statute itself.

The relative ease with which Title IX moved through Congress might suggest that Congress had grown to be quite comfortable with fund withholding as an enforcement device and equally comfortable with delegating broad authority to administrative agencies to define nondiscrimination provisions according to their own judgment. Notwithstanding the precedents, however, one cannot fail to be astonished at the cavalier manner in which Congress tossed off a comparable provision, prohibiting discrimination against the handicapped in federally assisted programs, the year after it enacted Title IX.

Several bills to amend Title VI to cover the physically handicapped had been submitted both in the House and the Senate in 1971, but none even reached the stage of committee hearings. In 1973, a separate provision was added to a large, complex bill designed to provide federal aid for vocational training of the handicapped. Enacted as Section 504 of the Rehabilitation Act of 1973, it consisted of one sentence, borrowing the language of the substantive prohibition in Title VI: "No otherwise qualified handicapped individual in the United States shall, solely by reason of his handicap, be excluded from participation in, be denied the benefits of, or be subjected to discrimination under, any program or activity receiving Federal financial assistance." There is no indication in the statute about how, or indeed whether, it is to be enforced. There was no separate debate on Section 504 and the committee reports on the Rehabilitation Act make no effort to explain congressional intent with respect to enforcement. Needless to say, there had been no hearings on the need for, or the feasibility of, such a provision.

Given virtually no information on what the costs or consequences of such a requirement might turn out to be, Congress might have hesitated to direct its administrative enforcement. But the truth, undoubtedly, is that Congress had no clearer notion of what the absence of enforcement provisions for Section 504 might signify than of what was meant by the substantive discrimination ban itself. It has been claimed that proponents of the measure deliberately omitted any enforcement provisions to avoid arousing opposition to a vast new regulatory scheme.[27] At all events, when Congress enacted the Rehabilitation Act Amendments of 1974, proponents of Section 504 managed to have a paragraph included in the committee reports stating that, of course, Congress expected Section 504 to be enforced in just the same way as Title VI—but somehow statutory enforcement provisions were never submitted for an actual vote of the whole Congress. The House report blandly noted that it expected to see implementing regulations drawn up for enforcement purposes that same year.[28]

But if this did not exactly clarify administrative enforcement authority, still less did it provide guidance on what was to be enforced. For the wording of Section 504 left its nondiscrimination provision not merely ambiguous, but on its face absurd: As HEW later pointed out, the requirement that an "otherwise qualified" individual not be discriminated against "solely by reason of his handicap" would, if taken literally, entitle a blind man to demand employment as a bus driver so long as he was "otherwise qualified." Obviously, that is not what Congress intended, but it did not trouble itself to specify the sort of program it did expect to emerge from its expression of good intentions toward the handicapped.

In the end, Congress did not even have to trouble itself to devise suitable enforcement provisions for the sweeping regulations that eventually did emerge from HEW. In the spring of 1976, responding to pressure from organizations of the handicapped, President Gerald Ford issued an executive order providing the same terms for enforcement of Section 504 regulations as those that had been enacted for Title VI and Title IX.[29] But the executive order gave no more guidance to regulation-writers on the meaning of the substantive prohibition in Section 504 than did the statute itself. That was left to the suggestions of the handicapped and the ingenuity of HEW to figure out.

All of these statutes were undoubtedly motivated by a desire on the part of Congress to assure better treatment of particular groups in

American society, not merely to protect the federal government from the charge of maintaining unconstitutional funding arrangements. But the sweeping language of the statutes affords few hints about how much, or how little, Congress was actually prepared to see demanded of recipients of federal funding in the name of fair treatment of minorities, women, and the handicapped. What does seem clear, though, from the elaborate safeguard provisions in the statutes, is that Congress was not prepared to see enforcement of fair treatment in a manner that produced continual disruptions in the flow of authorized federal funding programs.

Interpreting the Statutes

The Department of Health, Education and Welfare had virtually no experience with civil rights enforcement when it first assumed its responsibilities under Title VI. President Johnson pressed HEW for quick action, however, after the Civil Rights Act had been signed into law, and the department was able to present implementing regulations for his approval only six months later. The regulations were prepared by a small group of HEW officials who consulted closely with White House staffers and attorneys at the Justice Department, but rebuffed all inquiries and offers of assistance from civil rights leaders.[30] The regulations which emerged from this first effort to interpret Title VI, though, were brief and largely procedural in character—plainly leaving most issues to be elaborated in the course of subsequent enforcement activities.

The department's approach to the drafting of regulations for Title IX and Section 504 in the early 1970s was quite different. In developing these later regulations, the department solicited extensive public comment and reaction from affected interests. The drafting process in each case stretched to more than three years. Yet this contrast does not really reflect HEW's greater confidence in identifying or defining race discrimination compared with sex discrimination or discrimination against the handicapped. For the later regulations actually attempted a far more detailed and comprehensive exposition of nondiscrimination requirements than the original Title VI regulations.

Paradoxically, the narrower scope of the first regulations may have reflected HEW's greater sense of urgency about getting enforcement under way (though it no doubt also reflected a natural sense of caution in setting up a very new sort of program). Unlike the later statutes, the 1964 Civil Rights Act marked the culmination of intense national debate on the propriety of federal action, a debate focused largely on the highly visible "problem" of segregation in the South. Action against the dual school systems of the South was a clear and urgent priority for HEW. Defining other areas of coverage could wait. There was no equally looming target for enforcement under Title IX or Section 504, however, and certainly no broad public demand for action. It is not surprising, then, that the Nixon and Ford administrations, which had not initiated either legislative measure, failed to impress their HEW Secretaries with the urgency of issuing interpretive regulations for these hard-to-interpret laws. The lack of urgency did not translate into a modest assessment of what was needed, however, for by then the evolution of Title VI enforcement had accustomed the department to a very broad view of its "civil rights" responsibilities.

At the outset, though, there was not even a separate enforcement agency within HEW. Congress seemed to expect that Title VI could be enforced in the course of normal grant processing activities and did not appropriate funds for a separate enforcement staff. But the Commissioner of Education at the time started with a very activist approach to Title VI, setting in motion a highly controversial enforcement operation which could not long coexist with the tradition-bound routines of the Office of Education. By the summer of 1965, there were 135 Office of Education officials (borrowed at first from other assignments) working full-time at Title VI enforcement and rapidly developing a sense of their own bureaucratic mission, distinct from that of the Office of Education as a whole. This group was the administrative nucleus of HEW's Office for Civil Rights, organized as a separate unit in 1965 in large part to rescue the Office of Education from the continual controversy generated by Title VI enforcement.[31] And while later regulations were still issued in the name of the entire department (as the funding agency involved), OCR played the central role in their development and acquired full responsibility for interpretive guidelines.[32]

HEW was dragged into the central role in the federal government's school desegregation effort (despite the general expectation in Congress that the Justice Department would carry the primary enforcement burden) by two early decisions in 1965 of Francis Keppel, the Commissioner of Education. Soon after HEW's Title VI regulations went into effect, Keppel announced that he would defer new grant applications from any southern school district that had not committed itself to an acceptable desegregation plan. And he backed up this decision by refusing to accept the paper assurances of prior desegregation that flowed in at the beginning from school districts in Georgia, Arkansas, and elsewhere. Both of these decisions might be regarded as circumventing the system of safeguards which Congress had so carefully written into the body of Title VI, since they assumed system-wide rather than program-by-program noncompliance and, in effect, applied sanctions without due process.

It is a fair measure of the South's political isolation by 1965 (and of the Johnson Administration's determination to act against segregation) that this activist approach could be sustained long enough to have a powerful effect. In fact, late in 1965 when the Commissioner of Education was rash enough to order new funds to the Chicago school system deferred (pending investigation of complaints from civil rights leaders there), a direct appeal from Mayor Daley to President Johnson brought an immediate restoration of the funds, a quick close to the Title VI investigation in Chicago—and an early retirement for Commissioner Keppel.[33] In response to protests from the Illinois delegation in Congress, HEW agreed not to defer new funds in the future until specific, formal charges of Title VI violations were brought against a school district. But through the spring and summer of 1965 (when schools suddenly stood to lose considerable grants, newly available under the Elementary and Secondary Education Act of 1965), the deferral tactic forced most southern school districts to commit themselves to HEW-approved desegregation plans.

The plans were judged by standards set out in OE Guidelines which sought to synthesize the existing precedents from court orders in (constitutionally based) desegregation suits. But in 1966, the Title VI enforcement staff issued new guidelines which actually moved some steps in front of the existing constitutional precedents by requiring statistical indications of actual integration. The new approach suited the administrative imperatives of a still relatively small enforcement staff, although The Washington-based Equal Educational Opportunities Program simply did not have the resources to investigate all the numerous complaints it received charging that southern school officials were nullifying "freedom of choice" desegregation plans (acceptable under the 1965 Guidelines) by threatening or harassing black students who sought to exercise their "choice" to attend schools formerly reserved for whites. President Johnson and his new HEW secretary, John Gardner, sought to calm outraged southern leaders by denying that the new requirements involved quotas, portraying the integration standards (20 percent of black students in formerly all-white schools) as mere administrative indicators to trigger further investigation.[34]

But in 1966 HEW did begin its systematic surveys of the racial composition of southern schools, and while the new guidelines were applied very cautiously at first, in ensuing years, with support from the courts, HEW continually tightened integration requirements for Title VI compliance.[35] By 1970, official policy demanded a level of integration sufficient to satisfy the Supreme Court's 1969 demand for the elimination of "all vestiges of dual school systems": segregated school districts would be required to maintain approximately the same proportion of black students in each school as in the school district as a whole, with no more than a maximum 20 percent deviation in any one school permitted, except in unusual circumstances.

By 1972 this phase of Title VI enforcement had been so successful that HEW figures indicated more integration in the school districts of the South than in those of any region of the country. The magnitude of this achievement—and its emphatic endorsement by the federal courts—undoubtedly influenced OCR officials to apply activist, result-oriented approaches in other areas as well. But the scale of OCR's enforcement operation in the South also prompted a sympathetic hearing for the complaints of southern politicians that their region was being unfairly singled out.

Over the protests of HEW officials, still preoccupied with the southern desegregation drive, Congress in 1968 attached a rider to the HEW appropriations bill requiring OCR to apply the same rules and standards throughout the country and later that year passed another rider requiring the agency to maintain at least as many investigators in the northern and western states as in the South.[36] Though the latter provision was effectively circumvented while the southern desegregation drive continued, the earlier requirement encouraged OCR to elaborate new policy guidelines for Title VI much before it was prepared to investigate systematically—let alone intensively enforce—these new compliance standards. By the time OCR began to prepare implementing regulations for Title IX and Section 504 in the mid-70s, then, it had already extended its regulatory reach under Title VI rather dramatically on paper—though without having acquired a great deal of enforcement experience with many of these new issues. And the regulations eventually issued for the new statutes started at once at the ambitious level that Title VI requirements attained after several years of elaboration.

The resulting code of prohibitions and requirements is too extensive to summarize in a brief space and would be too tedious to recount at any length. But before examining the causes or consequences of this regulatory expansion, it may be useful to sketch some of its principal features. It is worth noting, in particular, the extent to which the regulations actually have carried OCR's enforcement jurisdiction (and its attendant enforcement burdens) beyond the obvious or necessary reach of the statutes. It is also important to recognize that this attempt to cover so many institutional practices with formal rules has not, in fact, always produced greater clarity about compliance requirements. Indeed, in some areas an activist approach to regulation writing has actually added conflict and confusion to compliance standards.

In the first place, OCR's regulations have taken up virtually all the slack left by the statutory ambiguities in its *institutional* jurisdiction. The statutes, it should be recalled, give the agency enforcement authority over "any program or activity receiving federal financial assistance." But they do not define the crucial phrase "program or activity" and the legislative histories are ambiguous on the point. Can an entire college or school district be understood as a "program"—or does the term refer to any discrete operating unit which might be separately assisted by a federal subsidy (a laboratory for science instruction, for example, or a foreign language department)? Although a number of district court rulings have suggested that a narrower interpretation is more appropriate, HEW defined the relevant "program" in the broadest possible terms from the beginning.[37]

The question did not, in any case, have much practical significance in the early desegregation effort, since the dual school systems of the South could not usually integrate the particular school activities receiving federal funds without desegregating the entire system. But this approach later allowed OCR—in spite of the pinpoint provisions in the statutes—to regulate school activities that did not receive direct federal assistance, even where basic desegregation was no longer the issue. By the early 1970s it was, for example, announcing policies on school disciplinary practices and imposing requirements on the manner in which schools communicated with the parents of enrolled students.[38]

The Title IX regulations illustrate the full potential of this approach. Although the statute prohibits sex discrimination only in an *"education program or activity,"* the regulations treat every type of activity that may occur within schools—whether or not its immediate purpose is educational—on the premise that the college or school district as a whole is the relevant "education program." Thus the regulations cover, among other things, health care facilities and insurance plans, student housing, extracurricular activities, and disciplinary procedures. Indeed, the regulations even reach beyond the schools themselves: One provision forbids colleges or school districts to assist "any agency, organization or person which discriminates on the basis of sex in providing aid, benefit or service to students or employees." The Section 504 regulations naturally wound up with an equally comprehensive scope, since the statute does not in this case restrict its prohibition to "education" programs.

The various regulations greatly expanded OCR's institutional jurisdiction in another way by interpreting the statutes to cover the employment practices of federally assisted "programs." Title VI included a provision which expressly exempted employment practices from its coverage, confirming the original presumption that employees of a federally-assisted program would not be considered "beneficiaries" or "participants" of the program for the purposes of its nondiscrimination requirement. But HEW early on asserted authority to order integration of teaching staffs under Title VI, on the theory that this was necessary to assure nondiscriminatory treatment of students, the actual program "participants" or "beneficiaries." It was not an implausible theory in the Deep South, where the refusal of school officials to establish integrated faculties served as a reminder of the traditional dual system.[39]

Any connection with the quality of service to students, however, became rather attenuated in later years as the employment requirements were further extended. Interpretive guidelines issued in 1968 extended the original rationale to prohibit racial discrimination in "recruiting, hiring, assigning, promoting, paying, demoting and dismissing . . . professional staff." An OCR policy memorandum issued on 14 January 1971 required that the ratio of black teachers to white teachers in each school approximate the ratio in the school district as a whole— whether or not the school district had a past history of segregation or discrimination. The same memorandum also warned school districts that racially disproportionate hiring, promotion, or dismissal records in faculty employment would justify an inference of unlawful discrimination. OCR thus took on responsibility for wide-ranging reviews of employment practices, paralleling the activities of the Equal Employment Opportunity Commission.[40]

The pattern was extended still further under the later statutes. Neither Title IX nor Section 504 includes an explicit provision exempting employment practices from coverage, but their legislative histories do not indicate that this omission was actually intended to bring employees of federally-assisted programs under the legal protections accorded to program "participants." Several U.S. district courts have indeed held in recent years that the statutes afford no general jurisdiction over employment practices.[41] Nonetheless, OCR took the absence of any explicit provision to the contrary as a license to impose elaborate nondiscrimination requirements under the new statutes covering every aspect of employment from recruitment and hiring procedures to sick leave and pension policies. By treating employees themselves as "program" participants, the new regulations could also assert jurisdiction over employees of every category, not just teachers or others who directly served the principal beneficiaries of the programs. Notwithstanding the restriction to "education" programs in the statute, the Title IX regulations thus purport to cover every school employee from cafeteria worker to sports director. And the 504 regulations are, of course, equally comprehensive in this regard.

It was not, though, the expansion of OCR's jurisdiction in these ways, but the manner in which it handled its expanded jurisdiction—the activist character of the "non-discrimination" requirements it imposed —that finally added the most to its enforcement burdens and difficulties. The early transformation of the school desegregation drive in the South set the pattern for later requirements. What had begun as an effort to assure neutral or color-blind school enrollment policies soon aimed at achieving predefined levels of integration in southern schools. New Title VI guidelines issued in 1968 warned northern school districts against taking any action which had the *effect* of increasing racial imbalance in their schools—whatever the intent—by the pattern of new school construction, the granting of student transfers out of certain schools, or by the class assignment of pupils. The agency began making systematic surveys of the racial composition of northern and western school districts, starting with the 1967–68 school year. And OCR for some years claimed authority to order systematic integration of northern school districts where at least some increases in *de facto* segregation could be traced to the actions of school officials. By the early 1970s, OCR was challenging admission standards for elite high schools and placement criteria for in-school tracking systems which had the *effect* of increasing segregation.

If these Title VI policies have received strong support from constitutional decisions of the courts,[42] the same cannot be said for the aggressively integrationist approach of the Title IX regulations. However the courts or the public may feel about a "separate but equal" standard where sex is concerned,[43] the Title IX regulations forbid schools to maintain separation of the sexes in any classes or activities (including physical education, home economics, and vocational or technical training courses). Exemptions are permitted only for sex education courses and sports in which "the purpose or major activity . . . involves bodily contact." Single sex situations are also permitted in athletics and choral groups, when the single sex pattern results from grouping on the basis of relevant individual ability (But OCR is the final arbiter of what constitutes relevant ability: Thus it subsequently forbade separate boy/-girl choirs in elementary schools on the ground that there was no relevant difference between prepubescent male and female voices). On the other hand, schools are responsible for ensuring that enrollment in elective courses is not disproportionately of one sex as "the result of discrimination on the basis of sex in counseling or appraisal materials or by counselors." In 1976, OCR began collecting data on the sexual (as well as racial and ethnic) breakdown of student enrollments in major academic fields *within* colleges and universities, and the regulations make it plain that the burden is on the colleges to explain any statistical discrepancies that appear.[44]

The statistical, result-oriented approach has been carried wholesale into admissions practices of higher education institutions and employment practices generally. The Title VI requirement, that schools not maintain teacher employment standards that have the statistical *effect* of disqualifying minority candidates more than whites, is applied to hiring and promotion standards for all employees in the regulations against sex discrimination. Similarly, colleges or graduate programs are forbidden to maintain admissions criteria or recruitment policies that have the *effect* of excluding candidates of one race or sex more than those of the other. Both the Title VI and Title IX regulations, in fact, require schools to take "affirmative action" to remedy the effects of past discrimination in admissions and authorize schools to take such action even where racial or sexual imbalances are not the result of discriminatory policies. ("In such circumstances, [a school] may properly give special consideration to race, color, or national origin to make the benefits of its program more widely available to such groups, not then being adequately served," goes the Title VI version.) Given the overall statistical approach to discrimination, the burden is plainly on the schools to show that they are doing enough.[45]

The Section 504 regulations go very much further, though, in demanding "special consideration" for the handicapped. Employment tests and criteria must be specially tailored "so as best to ensure" that any applicant with a handicap that "impairs sensory, manual or speaking skills" can still reveal his true aptitude or job skills. They also demand that employers consider what "reasonable accommodation" could be made to an applicant's "known physical or mental limitation" before judging his qualification for employment. "Accommodation" includes such things as "job restructuring," "modified work schedules," "acquisition or modification of equipment or devices" and "the provision of readers or interpreters"—and they must be made, unless "the recipient can demonstrate that the accommodation would impose an undue hardship on the operation of its program." "Undue hardship" is not defined beyond noting that it will be determined by considering such factors as the type and size of the recipient's operation and the "nature and cost of the accommodation needed."[46]

Even more extensive accommodations must be made for students with personal handicaps. Admissions tests and graduation requirements must be specifically tailored to the individual handicapped applicant. Schools must assure that every "aid, benefit or service" they provide is "as effective" for handicapped students "as that afforded others." Special services must thus be provided for students with hearing impairments ("interpreters or other effective methods of making orally delivered materials available"), visual impairments (taped texts and reading assistants for library work), manual incapacities (specially adapted classroom equipment), and so on. Educational institutions must also make all necessary architectural changes (construction of wheelchair ramps, elevators, and so on) to comply with a requirement that by 1980 every course offering or other institutional activity be "readily accessible to handicapped persons."[47]

While no one has claimed that such accommodations are undesirable, recent estimates have put the total cost of mandated architectural changes in institutions of higher education alone at well over half a billion dollars.[48] But HEW has insisted that it has, in general, no responsibility to consider costs. An official "analysis" published along with the 504 regulations states explicitly that the entire code (with two narrow exceptions) "does not take into account the cost or difficulty of eliminating discrimination in establishing the standards for what constitutes discrimination. . . . The Department agrees in principle with the concept that cost or difficulty are appropriate considerations, not in determining what constitutes discrimination, but in fashioning a remedy if a recipient has been found to be discriminating."[49] Following the open-ended provision in the Title VI and Title IX regulations, however, the 504 regulations state only that institutions found to be discriminating under its standards "shall take such remedial action as the (OCR) Director deems necessary to overcome the effects of discrimination"—without limiting what remedies OCR may impose.

The notion that "non-discrimination" can require elaborate special accommodations (to ensure "equally effective" services) had actually been pioneered by OCR some years earlier in relation to students with English language difficulties. There is no indication in the legislative history of Title VI that its prohibition of discrimination on the basis of "national origin" (in addition to "race" and "color") was intended as more than a bar against discriminatory treatment of people with foreign accents or exotic surnames. An OCR policy memorandum of 25 May 1970 warned school officials, though, that they would be found in noncompliance with Title VI if they could not show that they were taking active steps to remedy language deficiencies of "national origin-minority group students." Schools were forbidden to maintain testing, counseling, or class assignment practices which put children on a lower track because of deficiencies in English rather than basic intelligence.

Eventually, under this policy, schools were not only required to make an elaborate "educational diagnosis" of all students with English language difficulties, but also required to provide them instruction in their native language (and with "culturally suitable" materials) if necessary to maintain their academic progress. OCR cooperated with the U.S. Office of Education to set up special advisory centers around the country to assist schools in establishing new bilingual–bicultural remedial programs, which OE experts proceeded to elaborate in considerable detail. The effectiveness of these programs is actually a matter of some controversy, for while several studies have cast doubt on their benefits, no comprehensive and systematic comparison of educational performance under such programs and possible alternatives has yet appeared.[50] Nonetheless, OCR policy essentially requires school districts to adopt certain specified approaches unless a school district can demonstrate that its alternative provisions are "equally effective"—a rather formidable challenge, given the prevailing uncertainly about how effective OCR's favored approaches may be.[51]

The bilingual education requirements also seem to conflict, at least potentially, with another Title VI requirement that OCR began to elaborate in the mid-1970s. Responding, it seems, to the frustrations of imposing complete integration on urban school districts in the north, OCR, after 1972, began to demand that school systems at least assure equal per capita spending for students of each racial and ethnic group within the area.[52] Neither intent to discriminate nor the actual effects of unequal expenditure totals (which necessarily aggregate hundreds of disparate budget items) were acknowledged as relevant to determination of Title VI compliance under this policy. Nor did OCR officially recognize exemptions for bilingual education programs or other extenuating circumstances. On the other hand, many civil rights advocates have criticized the bilingual education requirements for raising potential conflicts with OCR's wider requirements for racial and ethnic integration.[53]

But the bilingual education program is by no means the only OCR requirement subject to ambiguities. For example, OCR officially maintains that Title VI protects whites and Title IX protects males from discrimination. There are presumably limits to the sort of "special accommodation" schools may make to minorities and women, then, before they run afoul of these guarantees against "reverse discrimination." But OCR has never clarified what these limits are.[54] Similarly the regulations provide exceptions to the "no adverse impact" rule on admissions or employment criteria, where a particular standard is proven to be "job-related" or "educationally necessary" and no reasonable alternatives are available. But OCR has never clarified how narrowly or severely these exceptions will be regarded. In the same way, again, escape clauses for overly burdensome accommodations to the handicapped do not spell out the circumstances under which normal standards may be relaxed or how far they may be relaxed. And finally there are many areas where regulations emphatically assert jurisdiction (as when the Title IX regulations demand "equal opportunity" for women in intercollegiate sports, including revenue-producing sports) without clarifying what will actually be required to satisfy nondiscrimination standards.[55]

In general, then, the implementing regulations make clear that virtually no area of institutional activity is considered beyond the potential reach of OCR's enforcement. But the regulations are less concerned to clarify minimum obligations than to afford maximum leverage for OCR's enforcement effort. Enforced to their fullest potential, the regulations would seem to require major exertions from almost every school and college in America, aimed at an unprecedented standard of systematic, intergroup equity. That an undertaking of such extraordinary dimensions has not really been carried through should not be surprising. That it has not settled back to more modest requirements for routine enforcement may seem much more surprising—until one understands how the regulations achieved such ambitious scope to begin with.

Explaining the Expansion of Regulatory Requirements

What accounts for this continuing expansion of regulatory authority, in the face of long-established traditions of local autonomy in education? The political party occupying the White House (and controlling top appointments at HEW) does not seem to have affected this tendency from one regulation to the next. Nor do changes in the administrative context of the drafting process seem to have made much of a difference. The formal regulations for Title IX and Section 504, though they required direct presidential approval, were certainly no less far-reaching than various Title VI guidelines and policy memoranda which did not. HEW Secretary Joseph Califano, a Democrat, was active in reviewing the final draft of the Section 504 regulations before their publication, but the result was not significantly different from the draft versions published during the tenure of his Republican predecessor, David Mathews, who remained much more remote from the actual drafting process.[56] Nor were the bilingual-bicultural education requirements initiated during the Nixon administration notably less "activist" or obtrusive or ground breaking–in their way, than the Section 504 regulations adopted under the Carter administration.

Purely legal arguments are equally unsatisfactory in explaining this regulatory expansion, though they have been advanced often enough by HEW officials. Secretary Caspar Weinberger, for example, defended the comprehensive scope of the Title IX regulations (promulgated during his tenure in office) on the grounds that Congress had really left the department no choice.[57] It had directed HEW to promulgate implementing regulations to enforce the general prohibitions in Title IX, but had not, he insisted, authorized HEW to make exceptions to this mandate (apart from those specifically enacted into law). But Weinberger himself decided to make an exception of textbook and curriculum content, without any explicit statutory authorization for doing so. Over the heated protest of women's groups, he decided to exclude from the final version of the regulations a draft provision dealing with sex-stereotyping in elementary and secondary school textbooks.[58] He could equally well have insisted on a narrow interpretation of the statute to exclude regulatory coverage of extracurricular activities, housing, health care services, or, for that matter, all regulation of employment practices.

Moreover, even if the statute were understood to direct HEW coverage of every conceivable school activity, it certainly did not direct more intrusive approaches (such as requiring coeducational gym classes) or expressly authorize more tempered approaches (such as permitting separation of the sexes for sex education classes). Here too, the department acted as if it were free to pick and choose its "legal obligations." The question, then, is why HEW so often *chose* to address issues that were certain to embroil it in controversy and so often *chose* to assert jurisdictions that were sure to overtax OCR's already hard-pressed enforcement resources?

Many people assume the true explanation is simply that HEW bowed to the pressure of new constituency groups in its regulatory initiatives of the 1970s. It is quite true that women's groups and organizations of the handicapped had become as active and well-organized in Washington as traditional civil rights groups by the early 1970s. While the Title IX and Section 504 regulations were being drafted, they followed the process closely, sending in hundreds of carefully-prepared written comments, urging the need for additional or stronger provisions.[59] (To this day, the most detailed and comprehensive public record of OCR policy rulings under the Title IX regulations is not a government publication but the newsletter of the National Organization of Women (NOW), Project on Equal Educational Resources). The new constituency groups were also adept at applying pressure to speed up the lagging drafting process. In 1974, women's groups succeeded in getting a rider attached to the HEW appropriations bill demanding issuance of draft Title IX regulations that same year. Two years later, organizations representing the handicapped won a federal court order making the same demand for Section 504 regulations.[60] And in the spring of 1977, handicapped groups organized sit-ins at HEW offices in San Francisco and Washington (with activists in wheelchairs adding a melodramatic touch) to force immediate issuance of 504 regulations in final form.

Yet constituency pressures can hardly explain why OCR agreed to regulatory requirements that it was subsequently unable to enforce—to the predictable outrage of its constituents. Cynics may be inclined to see in this a calculated strategy:[61] HEW could appease the demands of minorities, women, and the handicapped with far-reaching paper requirements, while avoiding the political costs by providing only token enforcement afterwards. But such a strategy could not explain OCR's continued refusal to extend northern desegregation requirements beyond the existing constitutional precedents, as traditional civil rights groups and even the U.S. Commission on Civil Rights repeatedly urged.[62] Nor would it explain a number of compromises in the Title IX regulations which angered some women's groups so much that they seriously considered testifying against the regulations in a congressional hearing.[63]

The notion of a calculated appeasement strategy is even more inconsistent with OCR's willingness to enter controversial new fields of regulation without (and at times against) the urgings of its traditional constituency groups. OCR began to elaborate its bilingual education requirements, for example, at a time when there was little well-organized or strongly directed pressure on the agency to do so.[64] Similarly, in one published proposal for the 504 regulations, HEW offered the suggestion that homosexuals ought to be included within the nondiscrimination protections of Section 504. The department subsequently retracted that proposal, acknowledging the storm of protest it provoked from the handicapped (in the traditional sense). But the final regulations did include drug addicts and alcoholics within the protected class, over the strong objections of organizations representing the blind or those confined to wheelchairs.[65]

If neither the "letter of the law" nor the standard patterns of constituency brokering can adequately explain the evolution of OCR's regulatory requirements, it would still be a mistake to discount these explanations altogether—and still more of a mistake to regard them as mutually exclusive. For at the heart of OCR's regulatory dilemma is the difficulty of establishing independent criteria to assess the "civil rights" claims of its various constituents. In a number of areas, OCR's requirements pose complex policy issues, quite apart from their associated costs. It remains unclear, for example, whether bilingual education, extensive busing for integration, or the sexual integration of athletics programs will, on balance, be effective in assisting the intended beneficiaries—partly because there is so much dispute about how "effectiveness" ought to be measured or defined in regard to such programs. But when policy issues are posed as essentially legal matters of right or entitlement, questions about effectiveness tend to recede into the background: Thus, by the late 1970s proponents of busing frequently disparaged social science studies suggesting its minimal effect on the educational achievement of minority students, urging that integration ought to be pursued as a constitutional imperative, regardless of its immediate consequences.

The civil rights perspective introduces still more difficulty when the issue is not the intrinsic benefit of a particular requirement but whether the burdens it imposes on affected institutions (in dollars, disruption, or simple loss of autonomy) are an acceptable price for that benefit. Where a judgment is called for, the civil rights perspective seems to preclude the weighing of countervailing claims. The Supreme Court has declared on several occasions that where constitutional obligations are at issue, cost or convenience cannot be considered in determining individual rights.[66] And indeed most Americans probably take it for granted that, by definition, the acknowledgment of one person's "right" cannot be made conditional on the interests or attitudes of others.

It may be true that the statutes do not direct OCR to make federal funding contingent on the vindication of every plausible constitutional claim, and it is certainly clear that many of OCR's regulatory requirements go well beyond established constitutional obligations (particularly where the rights of women, the handicapped, or foreign language minorities are concerned). But it is obviously to the advantage of OCR's constituents to invest every claim with the moral aura of a constitutional right. And in retrospect it is not surprising that it has been so difficult for the agency to resist this approach.

Title VI, after all, was passed in the context of a surging national concern to wipe out a particular constitutional and moral offense, segregation in the South. But Congress itself adopted the wording of Title VI for the later statutes, even though discrimination against women or the handicapped does not have the same constitutional status as race discrimination. Congress, itself, had established the Equal Employment Opportunity Commission in the Civil Rights Act of 1964, even though there is no constitutional bar to race discrimination in private employment, and Congress strengthened the commission's powers in 1972 even though the EEOC had already embarked on an extremely expansive and ambitious approach to its "civil rights" mandate. Moreover, through the late 1960s and early 1970s lower federal courts on their own displayed a readiness to adopt expansive interpretations of constitutional and statutory guarantees to vindicate the "civil rights" claims of minorities in areas outside the original concern for segregation in pupil assignment patterns. Given the prevailing atmosphere of civil rights activity, then, an agency with "civil rights" in its official title could not readily resist the pleas of its constituents to extend its own regulations to incorporate the most advanced rulings of other federal authorities that might be applied (if only by analogy) to its own statutory mandates.[67]

But the process of incorporating diverse precedents into general rules imparted an additional expansionary dynamic. When a court or an agency decides a particular case, it need not explore all the logical implications that seem to follow from the principle of the decision. Later cases may indeed spell out those apparent implications but they may instead articulate countervailing principles (or stress distinguishing circumstances in the first case) that limit the reach of the original principle. The burden of decision, at any rate, is spread out over time and often over different judges (whether administrative or judicial) as well. But an agency attempting to formulate general rules in advance faces an immense burden of decisions all at once. It was one thing, for example, for OCR to charge particular Texas school districts in the late 1960s with discrimination ("on the basis of national origin") because they had left otherwise capable Chicano children to vegetate in classes for the mentally-retarded simply because of their difficulties with the English language. It was quite a different matter to formulate general rules spelling out the remedial obligations that every school district would have to meet to avoid such charges. It was one thing for the EEOC, with its jurisdiction limited to employment, to propound rules protecting female employees from dismissal or forced leave simply because of pregnancy. It was quite a different thing for OCR to apply these "precedents" to its own jurisdiction over sex discrimination in schools: should the Title IX regulations modify the EEOC principle (because younger students lack sufficient maturity to decide on their own what is best for them? because schools have a responsibility to consider the emotional or educational impact on other students which private employers do not have in regard to adult employees?)—and, if so, to what extent?

For the most part, OCR responded to such challenges by refusing to make balancing or limiting judgments about the "civil rights" principles it had to work with: Regulations and guidelines on most issues either followed various precedents to their furthest plausible reach or suggested possible limits in only the vaguest terms. The agency generally proceeded, in other words, as if it had far less policy discretion in its rule-making than it actually did. And, paradoxical as it may sound, this probably struck agency officials as the safest course. OCR refused to take a more cautious or modest approach to the "civil rights" claims of women or the handicapped than it had toward those of racial minorities when Congress had not distinguished them in the statutes. So, in the same way, it usually refused to weigh countervailing considerations in applying ambiguous precedents or abstract principles to the broad subjects of its regulations, just as Congress had sidestepped consideration of complicating issues when it enacted such broadly worded statutes in the first place. Congress found it politically convenient to legis-late in sweeping generalities (a principle which "requires no argument . . . based on simple justice . . . on ordinary decency"), ignoring all the detailed policy questions that could not be settled without painful, protracted deliberation and the onerous political challenge of mediat-ing opposing interests or legitate competing viewpoints. Had OCR acknowledged the full range of discretion left to its rule-making author-ity (including the discretion to require less or to remain silent in many areas), it would have had to take on the very responsibility for political balancing that Congress had so determinedly shunned.

This is not to say that OCR officials would otherwise have been reluc-tant to extend "civil rights" requirements in so many directions: It is rare for people to seek responsible positions in such an agency if they do not already have considerable enthusiasm for its mission. (The three-year delays in getting out regulations for Title IX and Section 504 suggest, however, that top officials may not have been so enthusiastic about the agency's new mandates as they were about its traditional mission.) But it is noteworthy that successive secretaries of HEW, whose cabinet rank and resulting high visibility should have made them much more sensitive to the need for political balancing, also were quite com-fortable with the rather uncompromising "civil rights" perspective of the regulation-writers in OCR.[68] On the other hand, having rejected the propriety of political balancing, HEW could not even plead ad-ministrative exigency (point, that is, to OCR's limited enforcement resources) as a legitimate reason for narrowing the "civil rights" claims of the new constituencies: Women's groups and the handicapped were quite alert to the consideration that HEW regulations would very much strengthen their hands in private litigation (or in exerting psychological or moral pressure before resorting to the courts) regardless of OCR's own enforcement performance.[69]

That HEW let itself be swept into activist interpretations of the stat-utes, time after time, is even more understandable when one considers how little it has since been checked in this course by the political branches. President Ford signed the Title IX regulations without trying to introduce any significant modifications in their scope.[70] Nor did Presi-dent Carter interfere with the development of the Section 504 regula-tions. Congressman Vanik, the original sponsor of Section 504, admitted after the regulations went into effect that he had never anticipated such a costly and ambitious regulatory program would emerge from his bill;[71] nonetheless he did not propose any legislative action to correct the misunderstanding. Indeed, appropriations for programs to assist the handicapped have been extended several times since Congress enacted Section 504, but hearings have never been held on the HEW regulations in this area and there has been no legislative initiative from any quarter to limit their requirements.[72] Congresswoman Green, the original sponsor of Title IX in the House, subsequently expressed outrage at the statistical approach to discrimination envisioned in the regulations. She did lend her support to an unsuccessful floor amendment to an HEW appropriations bill in 1974, that would have prohibited HEW from requiring schools to maintain racial and sexual data on employees and students.[73] But she never sought to organize hearings on the Title IX regulations as a whole and never proposed any separate modification of the sex discrimination regulations themselves. Similarly, since enacting the Bilingual Education Act in 1968, Congress has several times appropriated money for schools wishing to establish bilingual-bicultural education programs but has never bothered to clarify whether these programs should be mandatory, as OCR regulations essentially require.[74]

The Title IX regulations are the only part of OCR's code that have been scrutinized in a formal oversight hearing and even that episode ended rather farcically. In 1974, Congress enacted a provision making all new regulations in the area of education subject to veto by concurrent resolution within forty-five days of promulgation, if judged by Congress to exceed their statutory mandate. On this basis, Congressman James O'Hara (D-Mich.), chairman of the House Postsecondary Education Subcommittee, conducted hearings on the Title IX regulations after they were signed by President Ford in June 1975. But the veto resolution O'Hara proposed, after a week of impassioned testimony on both sides, was absurdly narrow in focus: It said nothing about the disputed coverage of employment, nothing about coverage of noneducational activities, and nothing, in fact, about any substantive requirement in controversy. It charged only that HEW had exceeded its statutory authority in three procedural requirements, which O'Hara himself conceded were unobjectionable in themselves.[75] While O'Hara pushed the resolution through his own subcommittee, the House Education and Labor Committee as a whole, subjected to intense lobbying by women's groups, managed to avoid taking a stand on the resolution until after the deadline for action had passed.

Efforts to restrict or modify the coverage of athletics in the Title IX regulations (through floor amendments to HEW appropriations bills) have succeeded in passing one house of Congress, only to be derailed by parliamentary maneuvers or greater resistance on the other side of the Capitol. The only amendments to Title IX actually enacted have been extremely narrow exemptions, supported in each case by early champions of the broad measure—and accepted by women's groups—to forestall greater limitations. In 1976, for example, Congress overturned OCR policy rulings by expressly authorizing separate father-son and mother-daughter school events as well as school cooperation with the Boys' State and Girls' State programs of the American Legion.[76] But a series of other proposed exemptions, many dealing with intercollegiate athletics, have failed to get out of committee and no proposal for modifying the regulations has ever received formal committee hearings. Yet this meager record represents more oversight activity than any of the regulations under OCR's other mandates has received.

Lax Congressional oversight is hardly unique to civil rights regulation, of course. Nor, for that matter, are broad delegations of regulatory authority unique to this area. But buck-passing must be particularly tempting in such an emotionally charged political environment, where policy decisions usually turn not on questions of instrumental effectiveness (which might be experimentally determined), but on abstract notions of fairness.[77] And when particular OCR decisions provoke a great public outcry, it is all too easy for politicians to blame the bureaucrats —after the fact. OCR's ruling on mother-daughter and father-son banquets, for example, was unusual only in that it happened to be picked up by the wire services and then received front-page coverage in the *Washington Post:* It was, in fact, perfectly consistent with the approach to sex discrimination adopted throughout the Title IX regulations. Yet the ruling was heatedly denounced by President Ford, who had himself signed the regulations that had made such a ruling almost inevitable. And his denunciation was quickly seconded by a number of Congressional liberals, who had made no complaint about the scope of the regulations prior to that ruling.[78]

The intense and skillful lobbying efforts of OCR's constituents contribute to the reluctance of elected officials to make more far-reaching decisions on basic policy in this area.[79] But the political strength of these groups undoubtedly reflects not only their vote-marshaling capacity, but the moral prestige of their cause. As one congressional aide put it, "The older members (of Congress) remember the great civil rights struggles of the 1960s and even now can't bring themselves to vote with the other side. A lot of the issues are also very complicated, so if you don't want to be accused of being against civil rights, you just stay out of it."*

*All quoted material not otherwise referenced is drawn from interviews conducted by the author.

The moral prestige of "civil rights" also seems to have disarmed educational institutions in coming to terms with OCR's regulations. As a senior official at the American Council on Education (an umbrella organization for a wide range of Washington lobbying groups involved with higher education) explained: "This is socially oriented regulation and we don't want to look like we're opposed to it." Indeed, it is hard to find any organization representing educational interests in Washington that does not claim to support OCR's regulatory activity in principle. A spokesman for the National School Board Association insisted, "We generally support OCR. For example, we believe there should be a firm federal policy against discrimination." It is certainly more than lip service. The Association of American Colleges and the American Council on Education have separate offices promoting broader opportunities for women in higher education. ACE, in cooperation with other organizations, has also made extensive efforts to clarify and disseminate Section 504 requirements to institutions of higher education.[80] But schools and colleges have found many of OCR's particular requirements unreasonably costly, arbitrary, or inflexible, and their Washington representatives have complained that OCR gives little consideration to the comments or suggestions they have offered on proposed regulations. "We always got the idea that OCR's mind was made up, that it was single-mindedly bent on its course, even when its requirements were simplistic or unrealistic," explained an official of the National Association of Secondary School Principals.

The general inability of education interests to modify or moderate OCR regulations doubtless has something to do with the great diversity of American education. Schools with different types of programs, different financial resources, or different local traditions often have varied considerably in their complaints about the regulations and, as one education lobbyist put it, "it's hard to get schools active at the same time or agreed on anything but the lowest common denominator."

It is also true that educational institutions have a great many other regulatory and legislative concerns in Washington—OCR hardly stands in the same relation to them as the Interstate Commerce Commission does to the trucking industry, for example—while the organizations representing OCR's constituents can concentrate most of their energy and passion on the programs of this one agency.[81] Moreover, in the absence of vigorous enforcement, schools have not felt quite so much urgency about modifying OCR's formal requirements as they might have otherwise. But for all that, it is still rather surprising that no major educational organization has ever publicly lobbied in Congress for modifications of OCR's regulations. In the end, it is hard to explain this reticence without recognizing the reluctance of educational institutions to pit their historic claims to independence against the moralistic rhetoric of OCR's constituents.

In the one area where Congress has placed significant limitations on OCR's regulatory authority, it was, in fact, responding to pressure that derived from far beyond educational institutions themselves. Intense public resentment of "forced busing" moved Congress in 1972, and again in 1974, to enact legislation to discourage desegregation remedies deviating from neighborhood school assignments. In truth, it is unclear whether Congress really could prevent the courts from ordering busing remedies on a constitutional basis, but the language of the 1974 measure was strong enough for OCR officials to announce that their hands were tied by it.[82] Still, in 1975 and again in 1976, Congress passed amendments to the annual HEW-Labor Appropriations bill that forbade use of federal funds, directly or indirectly, to require the transportation of any student to a school other than the one nearest to his home. When Secretary Califano announced, early in 1977, that these amendments would be interpreted to allow some scope to HEW enforcement of desegregation plans involving busing, Congress promptly passed a new amendment designed to close any remaining legal loopholes and enforce its categorical opposition to "forced busing." OCR has not, in fact, imposed a busing plan on any school district since 1974.[83]

The entire episode offers dramatic proof—if proof were really needed—that Congress is perfectly capable of altering OCR's regulatory requirements if it is really determined to do so. The various antibusing amendments over the years were denounced with more fury and more moral passion than any of the changes ever proposed in OCR's statutory mandates and were resisted by congressional liberals with all the parliamentary skill at their command. It is notable, moreover, that in curtailing OCR's authority to impose integration remedies, Congress acted against one of the few OCR jurisdictions in which enforcement standards could actually rely on direct constitutional precedents. In other areas, though, where OCR requirements derive almost entirely from the agency's own interpretation of congressional mandates, Congress has never been determined enough to force significant changes. But, in other areas, where there is not the same intense public feeling, Congress has never been pushed so hard to act.[84]

In a number of respects, then, one can say that the expansion of OCR's regulatory requirements (and the wide berth given to OCR's interpretive authority during the process) has represented a triumph of the civil rights ideology over routine politics. But, as OCR's own experience suggests, the "rights" ideology is not a very useful guide for establishing an effective enforcement program.

Enforcement Dilemmas

OCR's enforcement record in the 1970s offers a study in contrasts with the achievements of its early years. Widely regarded in the 1960s as an activist agency in the forefront of social change, by the mid-1970s, OCR was being denounced by its constituents for betraying its basic missions. Yet the institutions regulated by OCR hardly regarded it with the smug satisfaction one might expect from a secure interest group surveying a tamed or "captured" agency. And certainly no outside observer could recognize in OCR a "mature" agency, entering the "accommodationist phase" of its "bureaucratic life cycle." The truth seems to be that OCR's effectiveness deteriorated throughout the 1970s not because it abandoned its mission but because it was unable, or unwilling, to readjust its enforcement operations to the very different circumstances it faced in the 1970s.

There can be no doubt that OCR's performance as an enforcement agency did deteriorate sharply. OCR's enforcement of school desegregation in the South during the 1960s made it, in Gary Orfield's apt phrase, "an engine of social revolution." By 1972, the HEW schools survey revealed, only 8.7 percent of black students in the states of the "Old Confederacy" were still attending all (90 percent or more) black schools; the figure had been 68 percent when the Johnson administration left office four years earlier and was estimated at higher than 98 percent when the Civil Rights Act was enacted four years before that.[85] Though some school districts in the South were integrated by federal courts in suits brought by the Justice Department or private litigants, the overwhelming majority were integrated through the enforcement efforts of HEW's Office for Civil Rights. Over 3,000 school districts were affected, most of them bitterly opposed to change at the outset. It was, by any reckoning, an extremely impressive enforcement achievement.

The Office for Civil Rights tripled its staff between 1970 and 1977 and its annual budget appropriations grew sixfold.[86] With all these added resources the agency achieved relatively little. Even before Congress sought to restrict HEW's authority to impose busing remedies, OCR's own enforcement actions had produced an extensive integration plan in only one major city outside the South.[87] Where it took only seven years to integrate almost the entire South, seven years after the 25 May 1970 memorandum OCR had approved the mandated bilingual education plans in barely one-third of the 334 school districts with greater than 5 percent concentrations of "national origin–minority" children.[88] Though OCR was required to devote equal resources to enforcement outside the South after 1968, it had managed to investigate Title VI compliance in only 84 school districts in the rest of the country by 1974. Moreover, it had obtained some form of relief (by its own efforts) in only 12 of these districts, though most of the investigations had been started years before.[89] By the end of 1977, almost three years after the Title IX regulations were finally promulgated, the agency had initiated "comprehensive" Title IX compliance reviews in only 42 of the nation's 16,000 school districts and had resolved barely a handful of the violations uncovered in these reviews.[90] By that time it had investigated and resolved only 179 individual complaints of sex discrimination, barely one-fifth of the total it had received over the previous four years. By the end of 1978, fewer than 50 school districts and 25 colleges had been reviewed for general compliance with the Section 504 regulations.[91]

Civil rights leaders often charged that this dramatic drop in OCR's effectiveness was attributable to a "civil rights retreat" by the Nixon administration, engineered solely for partisan gain. Later, with women's groups and organizations of the handicapped joining in the chorus, they faulted the Ford administration for "lack of commitment to civil rights." There is some plausibility to this thesis. During the 1968 presidential campaign, candidate Nixon did, in fact, urge a more moderate pace in federal enforcement of school desegregation. In its first year in office, the Nixon administration did make several gestures that seemed designed to placate southern resentment of federal desegregation efforts. And President Ford certainly did not voice support for civil rights enforcement as frequently or emphatically as President Johnson had during his term in office.[92]

But partisan politics cannot really account for OCR's difficulties. The greatest progress toward school integration in the South (at least in statistical terms) took place during the first Nixon administration. By the summer of 1970, the White House was actually pressing OCR to complete the politically awkward business of southern school integration as quickly as possible.[93] Moreover, "lack of commitment to civil rights enforcement" did not prevent the two Republican administrations from approving dramatic extensions of OCR's formal regulatory requirements. Nor did it prevent their budget offices from recommending substantial increases in OCR's budget and personnel allocations in every year after 1970. And while OCR's performance has improved in some respects since the advent of the Carter administration, many of the operational problems of the mid-1970s remain.

A more adequate understanding of OCR's problems must begin with a recognition that the school desegregation effort in the South was, in many respects, a more manageable undertaking than the enforcement challenges it undertook later on. In the first place, during its early years, OCR had no need to deliberate about appropriate enforcement priorities. Its goal was sharply defined by public expectations and the overriding logic of events. Almost all of its enforcement effort went into ensuring integrated enrollment patterns in southern schools, following through on the same great undertaking set in motion by the Office of Education in 1965. Though Title VI guidelines and policy statements began to cover other school practices even in the 1960s (such as the treatment of teachers), OCR did not have to justify its decision to make integration of students its overriding priority. Even the pace of change and the appropriate standards of compliance in this area were settled for the agency by highly publicized court decisions in the late 1960s and early 1970s. Outside the South, however, as OCR's regulatory requirements proliferated, and as later on new statutory mandates were added to its responsibilities, determining suitable enforcement priorities became a very real problem.

What is more, enforcing school integration in the South was not really very difficult in administrative terms, compared with later challenges. The persistence of unlawful segregation in southern schools was so taken for granted that Title VI enforcement officials did not even bother to conduct on-site investigations before rejecting the assurances of desegregation sent in from many southern school districts at the beginning. In later years, racial enrollment data made it quite easy to monitor compliance with integration requirements. In northern school districts, however, where segregated enrollment patterns were not illegal unless they could be shown to follow from official policy decisions (in the drawing of attendance zones, siting of new schools, and so on), very extensive research was necessary (reviewing thousands of separate administrative decisions, going back many years) before OCR could order any remedial action at all. Elaborate statistical evidence was often needed to prove charges of employment discrimination or unequal services: indeed, such evidence was required to support almost any charge dealing with the discriminatory *effects* of seemingly equal treatment. Similarly, compliance with later regulatory provisions relating to internal school operations usually could not be monitored without detailed on-site investigation.

But equally crucial to the dramatic achievements of the southern desegregation effort was the fact that this operation had broad political support at the beginning and continued to have high visibility even when political support declined somewhat later on. In 1965, political support was so intense that the Commissioner of Education for a time could get away with deferring new grants to southern school districts without even allowing them a formal administrative hearing. School districts that did not respond to this financial pressure by committing themselves to desegregation offered ready opportunities to demonstrate the credibility of the complete funding cutoff as a sanction. In 1965 neither Congress nor the White House, after all, could afford to intervene on behalf of rural school officials still crying "Segregation Forever!".

In fact, only the most openly recalcitrant or defiant school districts were actually brought to formal enforcement proceedings after 1965, and OCR officials subsequently admitted that enforcement of the 1966 guidelines relied at first largely on bluff.[94] The bluff gained in credibility, though, as the courts began to show equal or greater impatience with the slow pace of school integration. Eventually, federal district courts issued desegregation orders reaching every school district in all the southern states, warning that districts that did not submit acceptable plans on schedule would be forced to reassign students in midterm, despite any public disorder or administrative chaos that might result. In 1969 the Fifth Circuit Court of Appeals refused the request of Justice Department attorneys for further delays in the desegregation of various Mississippi school districts, and the Supreme Court itself declared that "all vestiges of dual [i.c., segregated] school systems" in the South must be "eliminated at once." By that stage, the vast majority of politicians and school officials in the South, even most of those who had been belligerent at the outset, seem to have concluded that further resistance could only forestall the inevitable by a short time. If negotiations with HEW were broken off, civil rights groups or the Justice Department could quickly secure specific court–ordered integration plans. Once local officials did agree to cooperate with OCR, though, working out a satisfactory plan of integrated school assignments was usually a relatively mechanical task.[95]

Outside the South, where school districts had no history of explicit, officially-sanctioned segregation, there was never the same momentum for change. For if civil rights violations in northern school districts were harder to prove (for civil rights groups or Justice Department attorneys, as much as for HEW investigators under Title VI), they were also far less evident to the general public. Northern school officials who denied OCR's charges or resisted its compliance demands could not be so readily depicted as racist scofflaws, and certainly in the larger cities of the North, they could never be so politically isolated as were the school authorities OCR faced in its early days in the South. But precisely in these circumstances, where effective sanctions were most essential, the only real sanction that OCR itself could bring to bear—the funding cutoff—was least available.

As everyone in the original congressional debates on Title VI had conceded, funding terminations punish the innocent along with the guilty, penalizing needy students, for example, along with intransigent school officials. And funding terminations are particularly embarrassing to congressmen, who are, after all, elected to look after local interests at the federal level. The embarrassment is particularly acute where school funds are concerned, since schools are such a vital and closely followed community service. Thus, while enactment of the Elementary and Secondary Education Act of 1965 and the Higher Education Act of 1965 (massive federal aid-to-education measures which have been continued and expanded ever since) enormously increased the power of the funding sanction for HEW, this simultaneously increased the political costs of invoking it. It was with these political costs in mind, of course, that Congress sought to hedge the funding sanction with so many safeguards. OCR's broad interpretation of the pinpoint provision, while greatly expanding its jurisdiction, compounds the political costs by tending to place all federal funds to a college or school district equally at risk in an enforcement proceeding. The less substantial (or publicly evident) the violation, though, the harder it is politically to invoke such an awesome sanction. (School officials sometimes refer to the funding cutoff as the "atomic bomb": like the genuine article, it is capable of inflicting so much damage that it intimidates the prospective user at least as much as the potential victim.)

While civil rights groups bitterly denounced the Nixon administration's publicly stated reluctance to invoke fund cutoffs, it thus seems doubtful that any administration could have tolerated a significant number of funding withdrawals after OCR's enforcement moved beyond rural southern school districts, whose resistance to any form of desegregation was readily associated in the public mind with redneck sheriffs and hooded Klansmen. In fact, the number of Title VI cases brought by OCR to administrative proceedings, preliminary to fund cutoffs, actually declined at first under the present Democratic administration from the number initiated in the last years of the Ford administration—and is still nowhere near the high number of proceedings launched in the first two years of the Nixon administration.[96] Notwithstanding frequent claims by Secretary Califano and his top OCR appointees that they would reverse the "timid" and "half-hearted" enforcement record of their predecessors, Carter's is actually the first administration since the enactment of Title VI in which no school district or college has actually had federal funds withdrawn.

If funding termination has become a less credible sanction in the enforcement conditions of the 1970s, however, its deficiencies as a deterrent are perhaps even more fundamental. One of OCR's greatest problems in securing general compliance with its regulations is that it has no way to punish recipients for past violations.[97] If investigation discloses that a college or school district is out of compliance with some requirements, it only need agree to comply from then on to avoid a loss of funds, or any other penalty. Under the circumstances, institutions have little incentive to comply with any requirements that are especially costly, unpopular, or inconvenient—and many of OCR's requirements fit these categories for many institutions. Moreover, in contrast to desegregation in the South, these later requirements are less systematically enforced by OCR, receive far less attention in the news media, and are less frequently attacked by the Justice Department or by private litigants. Thus, school and college administrators rarely develop the sense of resignation and fatalistic acceptance that eventually brought most southern school districts into compliance with integration requirements. Accordingly, schools and colleges have shown an increasing readiness to protract negotiations and fight their cases, often with the assistance of high-priced, sophisticated legal counsel, rather than simply give in to OCR's initial demands.[98] On the other hand, even on less costly compliance demands, they have often shown little inclination to initiate substantial changes before coming under direct OCR supervision (fewer than 20 percent of districts investigated for compliance with bilingual education requirements, for example, had taken all mandated measures on their own).[99]

Any enforcement agency in these circumstances would be in danger of dissipating its resources in a vast number of inconclusive contests, churning a sea of violations without really forcing the waters to recede.

And that is essentially what has happened to OCR. To ensure compliance with its more detailed or complex requirements, it has been obliged to undertake more thorough on-site investigations of regulated institutions. In practice, regional investigators have often tried to secure improvements or changes even before issuing a formal "letter of findings" citing specific violations. In larger cases, however, attorneys for the HEW General Counsel's Office or higher OCR officials at headquarters have often refused to approve proposed letters of findings, instructing regional investigators to go back for more court-worthy, more systematic, or more up-to-date evidence before making formal charges of noncompliance.[100] Thus there have usually been long delays (in which preliminary compliance negotiations and further investigations may continue simultaneously) even before OCR issues formal charges. Then there may be further long delays while the agency seeks to negotiate a voluntary settlement, to avoid recourse to a formal proceeding and eventual termination of funding. Given the ambiguity or vagueness surrounding many of the agency's regulatory provisions, the whole process can take on the aspect of an extended bargaining session, with OCR officials sometimes seeking "remedies" for more violations than they can yet prove and in later stages often accepting somewhat less extensive "remedies" than they might be able to impose through a formal proceeding.[101] In the mid-1970s, this approach stretched the average time needed to settle a school district review to more than thirty-two months.[102] And, often enough, the changes finally produced were quite limited.

If many of OCR's enforcement problems were unavoidable, its general ineffectiveness over the present decade undoubtedly is much more a result of the way it has managed its available resources. There is no question that OCR has been extremely ill-managed throughout the 1970s. Confusion and misunderstanding have repeatedly developed between headquarters and regional offices over what to look for in an investigation, how and when to make formal charges, what to settle for in compliance negotiations, and when to resort to termination proceedings. The inevitable result has been tremendous amounts of wasted motion.

Top officials at OCR have claimed that investigators (and their managers in the regional offices) are not sufficiently qualified for the sophisticated enforcement challenges faced by the agency. There is undoubtedly more to the claim than simple scapegoating. Although OCR personnel must meet qualifications laid down by the Civil Service Commission, they are classified as "equal opportunity specialists"; government employees in this category are not required to pass normal civil service entrance examinations nor to possess any well-defined technical skills.[103] Many came to the agency from a background in private or voluntary civil rights organizations, which often prepared them with more moral passion than technical expertise.

On the other hand, numerous outside studies have found that regional offices were not getting adequate guidance or instruction in the first place, nor were higher officials at headquarters always well informed about the manner in which investigations or compliance negotiations were being conducted by the regional offices.[104] As recently as the spring of 1977, a report by the General Accounting Office faulted the agency for, among other things, lack of a comprehensive and reliable management information system, lack of uniform policy guidelines and compliance standards, failure to determine job skills and knowledge required for effective staff performance, absence of uniform criteria for allocating staff resources among enforcement activities, and limited communication between headquarters and regional offices.[105] Two incidents may put these rather abstract formulas in better perspective. In the fall of 1977, Senator Daniel P. Moynihan requested figures on the number of individual complaints received and the number settled by OCR's various regional offices under each of its statutory jurisdictions. A personal reply from HEW Secretary Califano admitted that the figures could not be supplied at the time.[106] Early in 1978, the Civil Rights Commission requested data on the results of district-wide reviews conducted under Title VI during 1977. It was informed that "reliable summary data do not exist for that time period."[107]

Without this kind of basic data it is, of course, virtually impossible to make meaningful plans or establish sensible enforcement priorities. But it has been characteristic of OCR over the years to seek ambitious settlements in particular cases, at the expense of broader efforts to assure at least minimal compliance everywhere else. Thus, in the mid-1970s it devoted much effort to negotiating elaborate bilingual–bicultural plans with a small number of Texas school districts—covering use of bilingual teachers, appropriate textbooks, and so on—while as late as 1977, the agency had not forced most school districts with large concentrations of "national-origin minority" children even to identify the extent of their language problems. OCR continues to investigate the (potentially illegal) sources of de facto segregation in northern school districts, despite the legislative and political constraints making it unlikely the agency can ever impose significant changes in this area even if it does acquire enough evidence in these difficult investigations to support charges. On the other hand, in the years since Title IX and Section 504 regulations went into effect, OCR has conducted detailed investigations of a tiny fraction of the nation's schools and colleges, while more than 98 percent of them have not even received spot checks for compliance.

Perhaps the best example of the pattern is the massive investigation that OCR launched in 1973 to determine "equality of educational services" in New York City, the nation's largest public school system. Calling for data collection "on a scale that would have been unimaginable before computerization,"[108] OCR's study of expenditure patterns, in-school tracking systems, and many other school operations in New York consumed more than three years of effort on the part of its New York regional office—during which time it could devote only peripheral attention to possible civil rights violations in all other school districts of New York and New Jersey. And after all this effort, OCR in the end backed away from its threat to cut off funds to financially stricken New York, settling for only minor changes in the city's pattern of student services.[109]

It is fair to say, then, that OCR has been mismanaged in larger strategic terms as much as in smaller aspects of its operating routine. The enforcement challenges of the 1970s required a careful assessment of priorities and a disciplined concentration on feasible undertakings, if its limited resources were to have any significant impact. OCR did neither. Why did it not redefine the sprawling mandate implied by its regulations into a set of manageable enforcement goals? Why did it not concentrate its resources on those discrimination issues where it had the political strength to force changes or where its regional personnel had the capacity to conduct investigations at the required level of sophistication? One is tempted to say that the agency simply tried to act on the principle that "civil rights cannot be compromised" and therefore refused to acknowledge that hard choices would have to be made and systematically imposed on regional investigators. But there are a number of reasons why this has been peculiarly difficult for OCR's leadership.

With one exception, all of OCR's directors have been lawyers and none had had previous experience administering a large organization before coming to OCR. Perhaps they were conditioned by the tradition of civil rights litigation to pursue dramatic, attention-getting precedents rather than wider compliance with more modest standards. For a variety of reasons they may also have seen more political potential in such demonstrations of toughness or commitment.[110] Even when directors have made efforts to improve routine management, though, a continuing series of crises has distracted their attention and disrupted their plans. Periodic reorganizations, designed to give regional offices more autonomy, have been overturned by publicized foul-ups or unanticipated confrontations, leading directors to reclaim more decision-making authority into their own hands to protect themselves—with bottlenecks and confusion the inevitable result.

In the same way, the continuing atmosphere of crisis and controversy surrounding OCR's operations has made the agency's leadership almost pathologically cautious about clarifying particular requirements. For more than two years after the blow-up over the father-son banquet ruling, for example, OCR headquarters officials hesitated to make any basic policy rulings to clarify Title IX requirements, with the result that several hundred unresolved sex discrimination complaints accumulated with regional offices, for want of clear guidance on how to settle them.[111] On the other hand, OCR's constituents protested vehemently on several occasions when the agency sought to restrict its enforcement responsibilities, as when it suggested in 1975 that it would no longer accept responsibility for investigating each individual discrimination complaint it received.[112] Some OCR officials have claimed that fear of antagonizing constituent groups has made headquarters reluctant to clarify for regional offices the appropriate scope of individual investigations or the sorts of issues that are not worth pursuing in practice, whatever their status in official regulations.[113] Yet while denouncing the agency's poor performance in existing operations, OCR's constituents have not hesitated to urge additional enforcement initiatives on the agency—often with considerable success.[114] And while deploring OCR's reluctance to cut off funds, they have invariably opposed HEW suggestions that some OCR enforcement responsibilities be given to other agencies.

But the underlying problem in establishing priorities (and the appropriate operating routines to sustain them) is comparable to OCR's underlying problem in promulgating formal requirements. There is no obvious formula for weighing the relative benefits of particular enforcement objectives, even if OCR had more reliable data on their relative "costs" in terms of requisite enforcement resources. How is the agency to determine, for example, whether assuring women "equal opportunity" in college athletics is more or less urgent than assuring blind students the assistance they need for a college education: Even the certain knowledge that more women than blind students would be served by the same amount of effort would not really clarify the appropriate balance of enforcement resources between them. In the same way, it is easy to criticize OCR in retrospect for devoting such extensive resources to initiatives that brought little change in the end, but it is extremely difficult to determine the appropriate balance of effort between enforcement initiatives offering at least a small chance of very significant changes and others that promise only modest changes, though with much more assurance of attaining them. In contrast to the situation in the 1960s, public expectations do not establish any clear priority for enforcement objectives and the traditions of the agency itself—which may simplify decisions for regulatory officials in other programs—are obviously not very relevant to the bewildering novelties of recent years.

Yet in this inherently perplexing situation, where there is no escape from hard political decisions, OCR has been given almost no direction from the political authorities in the federal government. Just as they have in regard to OCR's elaboration of formal requirements, Congress and the White House have essentially remained aloof from OCR's struggle to determine enforcement priorities and procedures, leaving the agency to follow its own impulses (however misguided) or to heed the clamor of constituency groups (however unrealistic). Nor have political authorities called the agency to account for its ineffectualness, despite clear signs of mismanagement by the mid-1970s. OMB has routinely recommended, and Congress has routinely approved, increases in OCR's budget allocations throughout the 1970s and no OCR director has been forced from his position since 1970. As one OMB official explained, "We never had any real leverage on OCR, because it was so politically dangerous to interfere. Anyway, they knew we could never cut the budget of a civil rights agency or even hold it level because dollars are so much cheaper to any administration than bad public relations." The implicit signal they received from higher authorities, top OCR officials assert, was simply to avoid excessive controversy whatever else they did. Even this mandate has been difficult to follow, given conflicting pressures on the agency and the difficulty of anticipating points of controversy when instructing regional investigators. But it has contributed to the suspicions and defensiveness of constituency groups about changes in OCR policy, and this doubtless reenforces the reluctance of political authorities to get involved.

The most powerful efforts by constituency groups to reform OCR enforcement operations have been exerted, in fact, not through the political process but through the courts. Whether judicial interventions have, on balance, enhanced OCR's effectiveness or simply exacerbated its inherent enforcement difficulties remains in considerable doubt, however.

The first suit against the agency actually attacked a rather clear cut policy decision by OCR, rather than general mismanagement. *Adams* v. *Richardson,* a class action launched by the NAACP Legal Defense Fund in 1970 (in the name of a black Mississippi student named Kenneth Adams), originally cited the agency for failure to invoke its funding sanction against southern school districts with more than 20 percent racial imbalance.[115] And in most of the hundred-odd school districts involved, OCR was, without doubt, avoiding enforcement actions which would have required it to impose extensive busing—a practice repeatedly denounced by the Nixon administration. OCR lost the suit and lost again in its appeal to the D.C. Court of Appeals.[116] The Court of Appeals was particularly emphatic in dismissing OCR's claim to the "prosecutorial discretion" normally accorded enforcement agencies, stressing that OCR's enforcement obligation was greater than that of the Justice Department because in OCR's case failure to enforce meant violations would not only persist but continue to be subsidized with federal funds. But the same rationale allowed the *Adams* plaintiffs to return in later years with requests for more relief in areas where mismanagement and limited resources, more than deliberate policy, accounted for the agency's failures. Thus what began as a suit against then-HEW Secretary Elliot Richardson has subsequently borne the name of each of his successors. In 1976, the *Adams* suit was formally joined with separate suits by the Mexican-American Legal Defense Fund and the Women's Equity Action League to assure their respective constituencies a share in the relief orders.[117] And though the *Adams* litigation covered OCR's enforcement only in seventeen southern and border states with a history of *de jure* segregation, a parallel suit launched by civil rights groups in the north brought a court order in 1976 governing its Title VI enforcement in the remaining states of the union.[118]

What has all this litigation accomplished? It did force the agency to settle some outstanding cases within a specified period, though civil rights groups have claimed that in many cases it settled more quickly by compromising more with the school districts involved than it should have.[119] The court orders have been entirely procedural, setting time limits but not substantive standards for settling cases and nowhere have civil rights groups actually returned to court to contest the terms on which OCR settled. OCR has not always met the time frames imposed on it for closing investigations,[120] but these obligations have produced a speed up in its reviews, as well as a narrowing of their reach in many instances.[121] At the end of 1977, the new leadership at OCR negotiated a new settlement with all the different plaintiffs, committing the agency to conduct a specified number of reviews under various jurisdictions in the coming years, but leaving the agency considerable discretion in choosing which issues to address.[122] Though OCR's monitoring and reporting of enforcement activities have improved in the last two years, it has not yet released enough data for anyone to attempt to judge how —not to say, how well—it has been ordering enforcement priorities on a case by case basis.[123]

The clearest effect of the suits has been to shift the bulk of OCR's enforcement activity from compliance reviews initiated by the agency to investigation of outside complaints. The regulations essentially do not distinguish between individual complaints (which need not be submitted by the victims themselves or actually be limited to individual violations) and other indications of discrimination (such as statistical survey results): "prompt investigations" are promised for everything. But the agency has traditionally been reluctant to devote extensive resources to following up individual complaints, fearing that this would dissipate its strength on smaller issues and shift excessive enforcement resources to more sophisticated discrimination victims (such as women in college employment), at the expense of needier constituencies (such as Mexican-American children in the Southwest) who might be too helpless even to file complaints. But an early phase of the *Adams* suit forced the agency to address its growing backlog of race discrimination complaints in the South, and in 1976, in response to further litigation, it agreed to process all new complaints on precise time schedules.[124] Here again there have been substantial improvements in the last two years in the rate at which complaints are processed but OCR's reporting system is not yet sophisticated enough to provide a very clear picture of what has been achieved in complaints recorded as "settled." Regional investigators have been pressured to increase their "productivity" in complaint handling, but have been given little guidance from headquarters about how this should be done, apart from warnings not to broaden investigations beyond the specific terms of the complaint (as was frequently done in the past).[125] Thus OCR recently reported that the average number of complaints settled by each regional investigator had increased threefold in the course of 1978, but it has not yet determined whether more people have been affected or more significant changes secured through these (presumably) less thorough and (undoubtedly) less far-ranging investigations.

350

What is plain is that the complaint investigation process has forced the agency to address a large number of issues it might have preferred to avoid. In December 1978, Secretary Califano announced that OCR would drop a large number of backlogged complaints dealing with discriminatory hair length or dress code requirements, by amending the Title IX regulations to put such questions outside OCR's jurisdiction. On the other hand, Califano announced on the same day that OCR was preparing to interpret the Title IX requirement for "equal opportunity" in athletics as obliging schools and colleges at least to assure equal per capita expenditures on men's and women's sports programs. This formula may have offered a quick index of compliance for regional investigators, but it provoked a storm of protest from colleges and universities—and from sports fans across the country who feared the requirement's effect on favored teams. The department assumed a brave pose of deliberation for a full year before finally giving in: in December 1979, Califano's successor, Patricia Harris, announced that HEW would only insist on equal per capita expenditures in the awarding of athletic scholarships, leaving the proviso of the Title IX regulations for "equivalent opportunity" in athletics otherwise about as vague as before. As if to reassure women's groups of its essential fairness, however, the department prefaced this prudent retreat with the announcement two weeks earlier that it would, after all, enforce its previous ban on discriminatory dress codes. Whatever this compromise may have done for OCR's public image, however, it did little to reduce the burden on its regional investigators to process complaints within tight timeframes—and it did still less to advance headquarters officials toward the sort of clear-cut policy rulings that would make this possible. Thus, the pressure to meet court-ordered timetables, both in OCR-initiated reviews and in individual complaint investigations, should produce more hard thinking about appropriate enforcement priorities in the years to come.

In a sense that is when the politics of OCR's regulation will come into the open. The suits against the department have helped OCR to claim larger personnel authorizations, and for fiscal 1979 it finally sought and received budgeting for an extra 895 investigators (nearly doubling its staff) to keep up with its complaint processing obligations. But it is safe to say that OCR will never have the administrative or political resources to enforce all of its present regulations to their fullest extent. In any case, it seems most unlikely that it will ever be politically acceptable for OCR to cut off federal funding to more than a very small number of institutions in order to enforce compliance.

Under the circumstances, OCR cannot enforce more stringent requirements than most institutions are prepared to accept without much of a fight. For the enforcement challenge is no longer one of breaking down a principled resistance to any change, as in the segregated South in the 1960s. For the most part, it is the challenge rather of prodding institutions, most of which feel an undoubted sympathy and sense of obligation toward fairness requirements, to devote more resources, more attention and more allowance for inconvenient or disruptive change to the concerns of minorities, women, and the handicapped. But there are limits to what can be expected of most institutions, even with some degree of pressure. By refusing to consider these limits in promulgating its regulations (or in setting its official enforcement standards and priorities) OCR committed itself to far more than it was able to deliver. Even the pressure of court orders cannot force the agency to do what it is unable to do, though it may be useful in forcing it to face up to its limitations and start making hard decisions about where its limited resources can be used to best effect. If OCR remains unwilling, or unable, to bargain seriously with regulated interests in setting official, national compliance standards, however, it will be forced to continue making compromises in the negotiation of settlements on a case by case basis. That will probably be to the detriment of its constituents' interests and almost certainly to the detriment of the agency's own public prestige and internal morale.

OCR's constituents, and agency officials themselves, have been extremely resistant to the notion that formal requirements should be subject to open political bargaining, and certainly congressmen up until now have not forced the agency to undertake such bargaining nor have they undertaken it on OCR's behalf. In the last analysis, what has blocked bargaining over official compliance standards for OCR is the notion that "civil rights cannot be compromised," that "civil rights" like constitutional guarantees, must stand as an outer boundary on the free play of political preferences, not a subject for their determination. That may not be a particularly appropriate philosophy where the "rights" in question imply affirmative (and often quite costly and burdensome) obligations, not mere prohibitions. It is certainly a difficult philosophy to sustain when the sanction to enforce those "rights" remains so precariously dependent on the willingness of Congress to accept disruptions in its funding programs.

But in a larger sense, too, it may be inherently unrealistic in applying the rhetoric of courts to a complex scheme of social regulation. For ultimately the limits on politics can only be determined by political means. Even in the name of "civil rights" it is impossible to force more change than dominant political interests are prepared to accept (and that is why the Supreme Court's ruling against segregation in 1954 had only limited impact on the South for ten years, until a majority of the country determined to see it enforced). In any country where dominant feeling could not be given political effect, special protection for minorities might not be necessary—but no one's rights could then be very secure.

PART IV

CONCLUSIONS

CHAPTER 10

The Politics of Regulation

JAMES Q. WILSON

The principal argument of this book is that there *is* a politics of regulation. To citizens, such a statement will appear self-evident, even trivial; to scholars studying the subject, it is controversial.

Most Marxists, for example, would disagree. To them, politics is but a reflection of the underlying economic order. The bourgeoisie, and especially the large corporations, will acquire and use the power of the state to protect and enhance their interests. The claim that governmental authority can be used to control corporate power would strike the traditional Marxist as an absurdity; it would be tantamount to saying that the height of the mercury in a thermometer controlled the temperature in a room. Some Neo-Marxists are attempting to develop a theory of the state that allows for the possibility that political power can be assembled and used independently of economic power, but even they would find it most unlikely that this independence would be exhibited with respect to economic regulation.

But many non-Marxist scholars also doubt that the government will regulate an industry over the objections or against the interests of business. This view, held chiefly but not solely by certain economists, does not arise out of any conviction that the historically formed interests of the dominant social class always find expression in the prevailing political structure, but rather out of the assumption that individual behavior can best be understood by assuming that it is rationally self-interested. Indeed, most economists find the Marxist argument murky and unconvincing precisely because it lacks any psychological theory that would explain how class position determines individual behavior.

The Economic Perspective

Such economists as George Stigler have offered a theory to explain why, as a rule, "regulation is acquired by the industry and is designed and operated primarily for its benefit."[1] All firms seek to maximize profits, and profits can be increased if competition is reduced or governmental subsidies are obtained. Though firms will not refuse subsidies if they are offered, subsidies have the disadvantage of increasing profitability without necessarily restricting entry into the industry. The prospect of these benefits will encourage new companies to form, increase competition, and thus reduce each firms share of the subsidies.

Far better are government regulations that restrict entry by requiring a firm or a member of an occupation to be licensed. By creating such political barriers to entry, the per-firm or per-person profits of truck operators, airline companies, dry cleaners, beauticians, doctors, lawyers, broadcasters, and other protected enterprises are increased. "We propose [a] general hypothesis," Stigler writes: "Every industry or occupation that has enough political power to utilize the state will seek to control entry."[2]

A firm is able to use state power to its advantage for two reasons. First, the firms in any given industry are fewer in number than the persons outside the industry that must bear the cost of any restrictions on entry. Therefore, the firms seeking political protection find it easier to organize to wield political influence: since the per capita gains to them are likely to be high, they have an incentive to combine their efforts to achieve their collective ends. In all likelihood, the more numerous (and more diverse) individuals or firms who will bear the burdens of reduced competition will pay only a small per capita cost—the price to the typical consumer of reduced competition among taxicabs, dry cleaners, airlines, television stations, or lawyers will be either trivial or unnoticed. This fact, together with the large and diverse nature of the group to be organized, will inhibit or prevent altogether collective political action. Hence, the beneficiaries of regulation have a lopsided advantage in the exercise of influence.

But even if a group has a strong incentive to organize, it must still acquire and use influence. Stigler's second assumption is that government officials, like business executives or consumers, are rationally self-interested. They will seek to maximize their votes (if they are elected officials) or their wealth (if they are appointed officials) or both. Regulated firms can supply these resources by providing campaign contributions and political advertising to elected officials and by supplying lucrative opportunities for postgovernment employment to appointed ones; they may also offer cash bribes. But it is not necessary to suppose that firms provide cash payoffs to get their way. If they can influence—by propaganda or campaign contributions—the electoral prospects of politicians, then these politicians, once in office, can see to it that their bureaucratic subordinates, the regulatory officials, are selected and instructed so that they serve the interests of the regulated firms.

Not long after Professor Stigler's article appeared, political events took a turn that is not easily explained by the theory that government regulations will serve producers at the expense of consumers by restricting competition. The oil-import quota that had once provided a substantial benefit to certain oil companies was virtually eliminated. In 1976, the Civil Aeronautics Board became increasingly receptive to the entry of new air carriers on certain routes and to discount fares, a change to which most airlines objected. In 1978, Congress passed a law that requires the CAB to allow price competition and will, indeed, phase the CAB out of existence by the early 1980s. Greater competitiveness was allowed in setting interest rates paid to bank depositors and brokerage commissions to be charged by members of stock exchanges. The Interstate Commerce Commission announced that it intended to reduce substantially the authority of private trucking organizations (called "rate bureaus") to fix prices charged for goods shipped on certain truck lines. Restrictions on advertising and fee competition that had been maintained by professional groups, such as bar associations and medical societies, were undercut by court decisions.[3]

Public utility commissions in various states began considering proposals to give specially low rates to certain residential users—over the objections of electric utilities and industrial consumers of electricity. The California PUC approved such a "lifeline" rate and put it into effect. The Federal Communications Commission authorized certain firms to compete with the American Telephone and Telegraph Company by selling telephones and other devices to be attached to AT&T lines. Similarly, the FCC began to move in the direction of easing restrictions that had inhibited the growth of cable television as a competitor of over-the-air broadcasting and proposed the relaxation of controls on radio broadcasters. New regulations increasing the cost of doing business were imposed by the Environmental Protection Agency, the Occupational Safety and Health Administration, and the Food and Drug Administration. And perhaps most dramatic of all, farmers, long thought to be politically the most advantaged of all occupations, were unable to get the government to provide price supports at 100 percent of parity even though many of them held a noisy and disruptive demonstration in Washington, D.C.

These changes were not predicted by the Stigler theory and could be explained by it only with great difficulty. But the problem was not simply that of a few economists; scarcely any political scientist was prepared for the events of recent years. Theodore J. Lowi had described government-business relations as a "new feudalism," a form of "interest-group liberalism" that was immune to planned change, or perhaps to any change at all.[4] Murray Edelman had dismissed attempts at government regulation of business as a charade—"symbolic politics" —that soothes consumers by supplying them with a pleasant myth rather than tangible benefits.[5] Marver H. Bernstein had pictured regulatory agencies as having a life cycle that began with youthful enthusiasm for the task of consumer protection, only to end in a senile old age in which the agency becomes, at best, a protector of the status quo and at worst the captive of the regulated industry.[6]

Though each of the theories had some distinctive features, they tended to share a common perspective: that economic groups control a disproportionate share of political resources and that these resources can be used to control the behavior of administrative agencies. Thus all of them were implicitly if not explicitly theories about politics generally, and not simply about regulatory politics. They were statements about what factors motivated persons holding public office and thus about how the behavior of such persons would change with changes in the value of the relevant incentives.

In 1976 Sam Peltzman made this general theory explicit by trying to account for the fact that government, on occasion, seemed able to act contrary to the preferences of organized economic interests. Whereas Stigler had dwelt on the incentives for firms and occupations to attempt to exercise political influence (thereby explaining the demand for government regulation), Peltzman looked more closely at the motives of government officials and the incentives to which they might respond (thus accounting for the supply of government regulation). Peltzman suggested that government officials are vote maximizers who arbitrate among competing interests that seek to use government to redistribute resources. Under differing conditions of supply and demand, either producer or consumer interests may become more vocal and influential. Accordingly, politicians will favor one or another interest as economic circumstances give greater urgency to the needs of one or the other. Because interests compete, politicians must reach compromises that permit large, politically heterogeneous coalitions to be formed in support of a policy.[7] Neither adversary party gets all it wants; each is optimally disgruntled.

The virtues of the economic perspective on regulation are clear. It cuts away the naïve assumption, sometimes to be found in the minds of unreflective proponents of regulation, that government officials, unlike businessmen or consumers, are selfless, altruistic individuals. They, too, respond to rewards. We want to understand these rewards in order to predict how they will behave as regulators. Moreover, the economic perspective is a powerful analytical tool; provided the facts are consistent with the model, it offers an elegant and parsimonious way of explaining a great deal of human behavior.

Evaluating Economic Assumptions

But are the facts consistent with the model? In one sense, the model is self-evidently true: almost all behavior serves personal "interests," somehow defined, and thus is self-interested. But that is a circular and nearly useless interpretation of the theory. In another sense, the model is clearly true some of the time. Very few firms and very few individuals will refuse to accept a government subsidy if it is offered them. Virtually every effort to weaken or eliminate occupational licensing rules has been resisted by the licensed occupation. Nearly every move to restore price competition or ease barriers to entry has been fought by the industry that has been the beneficiary of price-fixing or entry-restricting regulation. Other things being equal, politicians will prefer more votes to fewer and bureaucrats will choose higher salaries over lower ones.

361

To say that firms prefer higher profits, politicians more votes, and bureaucrats larger incomes is to make an important but incomplete assertion. If we wish to explain public policy by reference to such preferences, we must be able to say more—to show that policies are made so that profit-seeking firms can affect the votes won by vote-hungry politicians who will in turn constrain the behavior of money-hungry (or power-hungry, or status-hungry) bureaucrats, whose behavior will in turn affect the profitability of firms. It is a long and complex causal chain.

From the examples already mentioned, it is not clear that the theory is useful in all or most cases. If it is not, it may be because politics differs from economics in three important respects.

First, politics concerns preferences that do not always have a common monetary measuring rod. In an economic market, we seek to maximize our "utility," a goal that substantively can be almost anything but in practice involves things that have, or can easily be given, money values. We may wish to be saints or sinners, to feed the poor or to indulge our basest appetites; but so long as we do these things by consuming more of something when its (money) price goes down and consuming less of it when its (money) price goes up, the economist is indifferent to our ultimate purposes.

In nonmarket relationships, such as in voluntary associations or in legislatures, we may also behave in a rationally self-interested manner —but we do so in a setting that does not usually permit monetary (or quantitative) values to be assigned to our competing preferences in any nonarbitrary way. As voters, bureaucrats, or legislators, we may wish to regulate nuclear energy, provide more jobs for the unemployed, reduce the foreign trade deficit, curb inflation, and minimize the cost of government; but we have no way of expressing our choices among these partially competing goals in nonarbitrary, quantitative terms. Indeed, if we are typical citizens or canny legislators, we will deny that any choices among these things need be made at all: We want each one, and will vote accordingly as each issue arises. Unlike the economic market, where the observer can make the radical but reasonable assumption that each person has the same motive (rational wealth-maximization), in the political arena the observer can note only that each participant wants different things, and sometimes several different things simultaneously, and that each participant assigns a different but impossible-to-quantify value to each goal.[8]

Second, political action requires assembling majority coalitions to make decisions that bind everyone whether or not he belongs to that coalition. When we make purchases in a market, we commit only ourselves, and we consume as much or as little of a given product as we wish. When we participate in making decisions in the political arena, we are implicitly committing others as well as ourselves, and we are "consuming" not only a known product (such as the candidate for whom we vote) but also a large number of unknown products (all the policies the winning candidate will help enact). We vote for Lyndon Johnson because he promises not to send troops to fight in Southeast Asia—and he sends troops to fight there anyway. We vote for Richard Nixon because he is tough on communists—and then he recognizes Red China.

The third and most important difference between economics and politics is that whereas economics is based on the assumption that preferences are given, politics must take into account the efforts made to change preferences. Consumers have "revealed preferences," the origin or value of which is of little importance. *What* people want is thought to arise from outside the market—to be "exogenous." Only *how much* they purchase is affected by the market. But much, if not most, of politics consists of efforts to change wants by arguments, persuasion, threats, bluffs, and education. *What* people want—or believe they want—is the essence of politics. Government does not ordinarily operate merely by changing the relative price of clean air, racial segregation, or an interventionist foreign policy; government (or persons competing to be its leaders) tries to make people want more clean air, favor racial integration, and support (or oppose) an activist policy abroad.

Both economics and politics deal with problems of scarcity and conflicting preferences. Both deal with persons who ordinarily act rationally. But politics differs from economics in that it manages conflict by forming heterogeneous coalitions out of persons with changeable and incommensurable preferences in order to make binding decisions for everyone. Political science is an effort to make statements about the formation of preferences and nonmarket methods of managing conflict among those preferences; as a discipline, it will be as inelegant, disorderly, and changeable as its subject matter.

If various economic theories of regulation have failed to account for regulatory behavior that is inconsistent with the notion of producer dominance, it may be because insufficient attention has been given to one or more of the three difficulties listed above: understanding motives, accounting for changing preferences, or recognizing the need for heterogenous coalitions.

363

James Q. Wilson

The Origins of Regulation

The formative experiences of the regulatory agencies described in this book do not allow for a single explanation. The Civil Aeronautics Board (CAB) was created to help business, but the Occupational Safety and Health Administration (OSHA) was formed over the objections of business. The laws administered by the Environmental Protection Agency (EPA) were enacted over the opposition of these segments of the economy to be regulated, and one law was passed over the veto of a conservative president. The Shipping Act which was to be administered by what later became known as the Federal Maritime Commission (FMC) was passed over the opposition of the shipowners whom it was to regulate, but with the support of shippers it was supposed to help. The Civil Rights Act of 1964 that forms the basis for the Office for Civil Rights (OCR) was passed as a result of a broad popular movement, not to provide competitive advantages for the organizations—schools and colleges—that were to be regulated by OCR. Though the Sherman Antitrust Act did not have to overcome well-organized business opposition, neither was the chief impetus for its passage the demand of business. There is much evidence of Progressive and antibusiness sentiment behind the Sherman Act and little or no evidence of industrial skulduggery.

Some regulatory laws did receive support from part or all of the relevant sector of business. The bill creating the Federal Trade Commission (FTC) was supported by some firms that hoped it would restrict the predatory practices of their competitors and by other—usually smaller—firms that found the Sherman Act inadequate as protection against large industrial trusts. But proconsumer sentiment was very much a part of the coalition that supported the bill.

The movement for state regulation of electric utilities was championed by certain utility magnates, notably Samuel Insull, but it seems unlikely that these state public utility commissions (PUCs) would have come into being without the additional support of Progressive politicians such as Charles Evans Hughes and Robert La Follette. It was a curious coalition: utility executives who feared municipal ownership even by honest regimes joined by Progressives who feared municipal ownership or regulation by dishonest machines.

The Civil Aeronautics Board (CAB) was created explicitly to help the

364

domestic airline industry by regulating—that is, restricting—competition, but this objective was not achieved by stealth or subterfuge: There had been over a dozen congressional investigations of the airline industry in the years preceding the passage of the law in 1938 and widespread expressions of public interest in seeing the fledgling airlines grow.

The pharmaceutical manufacturers supported the 1906 Food and Drug Act, in part because it was only a labeling requirement and in part, no doubt, because it would hurt the makers of patent medicines. But the pharmaceutical industry would almost surely have opposed the far tougher 1938 law that required testing for safety had not the sulfanilamide disaster made any opposition politically suicidal. It is not clear whether the Pharmaceutical Manufacturers' Association knew what it was letting itself in for when it failed to oppose the 1962 drug amendments (that required testing for efficacy as well as safety); since then, they have clearly come to regret it.

What is striking about the origins of the regulatory programs studied in this book is that in almost every case, the initial law was supported by a rather broadly based coalition. Sometimes industry was eagerly and happily a part of that coalition (as with the CAB and the PUCs), sometimes it was a reluctant partner (as with the 1938 and 1962 drug amendments), and sometimes it was an outright opponent (as with much of the environmental and occupational safety legislation). The same pattern seems to be true for major regulatory laws studied by others. The act creating the Interstate Commerce Commission, for example, provided something for almost everybody: for railroaders, a ban on paying rebates to big shippers; for shippers, a ban on price discrimination against short-haul traffic. Even so, most railroad executives opposed the bill in its final form.[9]

Large coalitions are so often formed to support new governmental policies because in politics, unlike in the market, decisions must have justifications. Proponents who have a stake in the outcome must make an argument to convince people who do not have a stake, or have a different one. The argument may be good or bad and the symbols to which it appeals may change over time, but the argument must persuade. If probusiness values are widely shared, an argument to regulate business is hard to make. One must therefore either include provisions in the bill that will moderate business opposition (as with the 1906 drug laws) or hope for a crisis or scandal that will evoke antibusiness sentiments (as with the 1938 and 1962 drug law amendments).

In recent decades, the perceived legitimacy of business enterprise has declined (corporations, especially oil companies, command scarcely more public confidence than does organized labor or Congress—i.e., hardly any) and thus the concessions that must be made to business interests are fewer and the need for a crisis or scandal is diminished.[10] But even in the heyday of Horatio Alger and popular sermons on the virtues of wealth, there was enough antibusiness opinion fomented by the Grangers and the muckrakers to make it difficult for any federal regulatory law to be purely business-serving. If business influence was to be truly successful, it would have to keep a regulatory proposal from being placed on the political agenda in the first place—something which no doubt occurred, but this meant that business thereby forfeited the opportunity to use regulation to maximize profits.

But though broad coalitions were formed in almost every instance of regulatory legislation, it would be foolish to claim that this is evidence of the public-serving quality of the regulation or to deny that in many cases business proponents of the regulations exercised decisive influence. To understand the origins of regulation, we must distinguish between cases in which business influence is likely to be strong and those in which it is likely to be weaker or more easily countered. In short, it is necessary to have a theory that helps us explain the kinds of coalitions likely to be formed and the arguments that will have to be made to create them.

Elsewhere I have suggested that policy proposals, especially those involving economic stakes, can be classified in terms of the perceived distribution of their costs and benefits.[11] These costs and benefits may be monetary or nonmonetary, and the value assigned to them, as well as beliefs about the likelihood of their materializing, can change. Indeed, changes in the perceptions of these costs and benefits, at least among political elites, have become so common and have had such profound effects in recent years that special attention will be devoted to the phenomenon later in this chapter.

The political significance of costs and benefits arises out of their distribution as well as their magnitude. To simplify the analysis, I will emphasize the distributional effect. Magnitudes are certainly important (politics is replete with discussions of "windfall profits," "tax burdens," and "unmet needs"), but the incidence of these magnitudes is especially relevant to political action. As we shall see, the distribution of consequences affects the incentive to form political organizations and to engage in collective action. Moreover, perceptions of the fairness and unfairness of a policy profoundly affect the extent to which it is regarded as legitimate and thus the difficulty (or cost) of finding persuasive justifications for that policy.

The Politics of Regulation

A substantial body of psychological data supports the view that people are quite sensitive to the perceived equity of any allocation of rewards.[12] They judge equity by comparing the ratio of burdens and benefits they must bear with the ratio of burdens and benefits others similarly situated must bear: what A gets in return for his efforts should be comparable to what B gets in return for his. People like legislators, whose consent is necessary for the adoption of a proposed regulatory policy, will feel uncomfortable or even angry if the policy seems inequitable. The supporters of such a policy must respond by either modifying its terms, changing the perception of its effects, justifying those effects, or inducing (perhaps corruptly) others to ignore those effects. In the private market, equity issues are resolved largely by changing prices. In the political process, there is either no "price" that can be altered (shall A or B receive the television license?) or the participants in the decision will refuse to allow the matter to be judged simply as a transaction that has no third-party effects.

Costs and benefits may be widely distributed or narrowly concentrated. Income and social security taxes are widely distributed; subsidies to a particular industry or regulations imposing costs on an industry that cannot be fully passed through to consumers are narrowly concentrated. Though there are many intermediate cases, four political situations can be distinguished by considering all combinations of the dichotomous cases.

When both costs and benefits are widely distributed, we expect to find *majoritarian* politics. All or most of society expects to gain; all or most of society expects to pay. Interest groups have little incentive to form around such issues because no small, definable segment of society (an industry, an occupation, a locality) can expect to capture a disproportionate share of the benefits or avoid a disproportionate share of the burdens. Not all measures that seem to offer a net gain to popular majorities are passed: proposals must first get onto the political agenda, people must agree that it is legitimate for the government to take action, and ideological objections to the propriety or feasibility of the measures must be overcome. All these issues had to be dealt with in the case of such conspicuously majoritarian policies as the Social Security Act of 1935 and the proposal to maintain a large standing army just before and just after World War II.

The passage of the Sherman Antitrust Act, and perhaps also of the Federal Trade Commission Act, arose out of circumstances that approximate those of majoritarian politics. No single industry was to be regulated; the nature and scope of the proposed regulations were left quite vague; any given firm could imagine ways in which these laws might help them (in dealing with an "unscrupulous" competitor, for example). But though there was no determined industry opposition, neither was there strong business support. The measures could not be passed until popular sentiment supported them (Grangers and muckrakers had first to persuade people that a problem existed and that there was a gain to be had) and elite opinion was convinced that it was legitimate for the federal government to pass such laws. (Prevailing Supreme Court decisions gave no assurance ahead of time that these measures would be constitutionally permissible and, as it turned out, the reach of the Sherman Act was sharply restricted by subsequent Court rulings.)

When both costs and benefits are narrowly concentrated, conditions are ripe for *interest-group politics.* A subsidy or regulation will often benefit a relatively small group at the expense of another comparable small group. Each side has a strong incentive to organize and exercise political influence. The public does not believe it will be much affected one way or another; though it may sympathize more with one side than the other, its voice is likely to be heard in only weak or general terms. The passage of the Commerce Act in 1886 resulted from interest-group politics as each affected party—long-haul and short-haul railroads, farm groups, oil companies, and businessmen representing various port cities —contended over how, if at all, railroad rates should be regulated. Much labor legislation—the Wagner Act, the Taft-Hartley Act, the Landrum-Griffin Act, the proposed labor law reform act of 1978—is also a product of interest-group politics.

The Shipping Act of 1916 pitted those who shipped goods by sea against those who operated the ships; by and large, the former won. Steamship lines had been engaged in price fixing by means of cartels. The issue was whether the cartels should be put out of business as a violation of the antitrust act (as they almost surely were) or regulated in the interests of the shippers. Congress chose the latter course of action, allowing the rate-fixing cartels to remain, but not, it would seem, because the carriers demanded it. The shippers, in whose interests the rates would presumably be regulated, favored the continuation of the cartels because they feared that competition would drive all marginal carriers out of business until only a single monopoly carrier remained. The legalization of the cartels pleased the carriers even if they opposed the rate-fixing powers given to what later was called the Federal Maritime Commission. As with most examples of interest-group politics, there was something in the final legislation to please each affected party.

The Politics of Regulation

When the benefits of a prospective policy are concentrated but the costs widely distributed, *client politics* is likely to result. Some small, easily organized group will benefit and thus has a powerful incentive to organize and lobby; the costs of the benefit are distributed at a low per capita rate over a large number of people, and hence they have little incentive to organize in opposition—if, indeed, they even hear of the policy. As we shall see, however, an important organizational change has occurred that has altered the normal advantage enjoyed by the client group in these circumstances—the emergence of "watchdog" or "public interest" associations that have devised ways of maintaining themselves without having to recruit and organize the people who will be affected by a policy. Absent such watchdog organizations, however, client politics produces regulatory legislation that most nearly approximates the producer-dominance model. Countless industries and occupations have come to enjoy subsidies and regulations that, in effect, spare them the full rigors of economic competition.

The Civil Aeronautics Board arose from circumstances conducive to client politics and, after its formation, the CAB operated in a manner most solicitous of the health of the domestic aviation industry. Public utility commissions were created in part at the urging of electric utility executives; though one cannot be certain, the desires of these industry spokesmen may well have been the most important source of the PUC movement. But, as we have already seen, neither the CAB nor the PUCs conform exactly to the model of client politics. There was much public discussion of the matter, nonbusiness groups were important parts of the supportive coalition, and public-serving arguments were made and taken seriously. These circumstances are somewhat different from those normally associated with client politics: backstairs intrigue, quiet lobbying, and quick passage with a minimum of public discussion. (One thinks of the shadowy maneuvering by which various milk-producer organizations and their political allies have sometimes managed to get higher milk price supports.)[13]

Given the evidence in this book, we cannot say whether the political sources of the CAB and the PUCs were anomalous or are typical of policies having this pattern of costs and benefits. Perhaps more representative cases of client politics would be found in the origins of less conspicuous regulatory programs, such as state laws that license (and protect) occupations. Or perhaps the popular image of client politics is more commonly to be found where the government is supplying a cash subsidy to an industry or occupation. After all, in the case of the CAB and the PUCs, we are dealing with laws explicitly stating that an industry is to be regulated *in the public interest.* We may, in hindsight, dismiss such language as vague or even meaningless, but it was not meaningless at the time such laws were passed. If someone proposes, sincerely or hypocritically, to use the law to make behavior conform to general standards of rightness or justice, then one is obliged to devise more elaborate justifications—and thereby mobilize a more extensive coalition—than if one gives money away because somebody "needs" it.

Finally, a policy may be proposed that will confer general (though perhaps small) benefits at a cost to be borne chiefly by a small segment of society. When this is attempted, we are witnessing *entrepreneurial politics.* Antipollution and auto-safety bills were proposed to make air cleaner or cars safer for everyone at an expense that was imposed, at least initially, on particular segments of industry. Since the incentive to organize is strong for opponents of the policy but weak for the beneficiaries, and since the political system provides many points at which opposition can be registered, it may seem astonishing that regulatory legislation of this sort is ever passed. It is, and with growing frequency in recent years—but it requires the efforts of a skilled entrepreneur who can mobilize latent public sentiment (by revealing a scandal or capitalizing on a crisis), put the opponents of the plan publicly on the defensive (by accusing them of deforming babies or killing motorists), and associate the legislation with widely shared values (clean air, pure water, health, and safety). The entrepreneur serves as the vicarious representative of groups not directly part of the legislative process. Ralph Nader was such an entrepreneur, and the Auto Safety Act of 1966 was one result. Policy entrepreneurs are found not only in the politics of business regulation. Howard Jarvis was an entrepreneur who helped pass Proposition 13 in California; Joseph R. McCarthy was an entrepreneur when he galvanized large parts of the public into an anticommunism crusade.

Policy entrepreneurs and their allies inside the government were in large measure responsible for the laws enforced by the Environmental Protection Agency. Nader worked both with and against Senator Edmund Muskie to obtain a stringent clean-air act, just as he had earlier worked with Senator Abraham Ribicoff to obtain an auto-safety act. Dr. Harvey Wiley mobilized support for the 1906 Food and Drug Act and his cause was powerfully aided by the publication of Upton Sinclair's *The Jungle* in 1905. Thirty years later, the appearance of *American Chamber of Horrors* by Ruth Lamb and and *100,000,000 Guinea Pigs* by F. J. Schlink and Arthur Kallet helped prepare the way for the 1938 drug laws. Senator Estes Kefauver and his staff skillfully laid the groundwork for the 1962 drug amendments by feeding to the press stories about the harmful effects of certain prescription drugs.

Occasionally, the work of a policy entrepreneur is made easier by a scandal or crisis, such as that involving Elixir of Sulfanilamide in 1937 and thalidomide in 1961. We conjecture that such crises are most important when the regulated industry is associated in the popular mind with positive values, such as free enterprise, the accomplishments of technology, or the virtues of limited government. The need for a crisis declines as the value of these symbols—or the ability of business to attach itself to these symbols—declines. No crisis in auto fatalities preceded the Auto Safety Act; no grim industrial accident preceded the Occupational Safety and Health Act; no tragic deaths from air or water pollution preceded the various environmental protection laws.

Indeed, the passage of one regulatory law can prepare the way for another if the legislators believe the experience rewarding. The popularity of the Auto Safety Bill made it easier—that is, politically more attractive—to support the OSHAct, so much so that the policy entrepreneur in this case was only a little-known assistant secretary of labor who had become interested in the problems of uranium miners. (To be sure, his cause was powerfully aided by the support of organized labor; the OSHAct campaign has features of both interest group as well as entrepreneurial politics.)

Entrepreneurial politics depends heavily on the attitudes of third parties. The reaction of the regulated industry is predictably hostile (though in the case of the 1962 drug amendments, the more liberal spokesmen for the pharmaceutical companies were willing to accept the efficacy standard); the reaction of the public that is to benefit may be hard to discern or evident only in general terms ("do something about this problem"). Third parties are those members of various political elites—the media, influential writers, congressional committee staff members, the heads of voluntary associations, political activists—not affected by the policy whose political response to the entrepreneur's campaign is important. Reverend Martin Luther King, Jr. was such an entrepreneur when he led his small but dedicated band of civil-rights followers into confrontations with the police in Selma and Birmingham. The vivid scenes of police violence that followed had a galvanic effect on key third parties, and, to a degree, on the public at large. The 1965 Civil Rights Act was the result.[14]

In sum, the politics of regulation follows different patterns, mobilizes different actors, and has different consequences depending, among other things, on the perceived distribution of costs and benefits of the proposed policy. In some of these political patterns, the economic interests of the key actors are both plain and decisive—for example, in most forms of client and interest-group politics. In others, economic interests are either not apparent (at least among the proponents) or are not of decisive importance—for example, in many instances of entrepreneurial politics. In still other cases, such as certain examples of majoritarian politics, the material interests of affected parties may be plain but not decisive or too dependent on future events to be known at all. Any theory that fails to account for these and other variations in regulatory policies is defective.

A complete theory of regulatory politics—indeed, a complete theory of politics generally—requires that attention be paid to beliefs as well as interests. Only by the most extraordinary theoretical contortions can one explain the Auto Safety Act, the 1964 Civil Rights Act, the OSHAct, or most environmental protection laws by reference to the economic stakes involved. And even when these stakes are important, as they were in the case of electric utility regulation, the need for assembling a majority legislative coalition requires that arguments be made that appeal to the beliefs (as well as interests) of broader constituencies.

The Behavior of Regulatory Agencies

Anyone who purports to explain the behavior of regulatory agencies must first make clear what behavior is worth explaining. By carefully selecting certain examples and ignoring others, the behavior of many of the regulatory agencies reviewed in this book can be made to appear industry-serving in the narrow sense. Until recently, the CAB refused to allow any new airline to provide scheduled service on major routes, thereby shielding established trunk carriers from increased competition. The FMC routinely approved the rate schedules of the shipping companies. The FDA, at least during the 1950s, was lenient in approving new drug applications from pharmaceutical companies. For many years, the FTC devoted much of its effort to prosecuting minor violations of the Robinson-Patman Act, to the advantage of certain small business firms.

But a fuller list suggests that industry-serving behavior is only part of the story. The CAB may have helped the established major air carriers as a group, but its actions often penalized individual carriers by causing long delays or adverse decisions in specific route and tariff applications. And by the late-1970s, the CAB was moving toward deregulation in a manner that, at least initially, caused great alarm among the carriers.

The FDA was energized in the mid-1960s by a series of new appointments and new laws that, by the 1970s, had moved the pharmaceutical industry and many physicians to complain bitterly of costly delays in the introduction of new drugs.

The FTC, after a major reorganization (under a Republican president) began to bring large "structural" cases against such firms as Exxon and the leading cereal manufacturers; at the same time, the Antitrust Division was attempting to expand the reach of the antitrust law by questioning the formation of conglomerates.

The California Public Utilities Commission adopted a "lifeline" electric rate over the objections of Pacific Gas & Electric, and the New York Public Service Commission adopted a modified form of peak-load pricing over the objections of many of that state's largest electric power users.

These particular instances might be dismissed as exceptions to the normal pattern of industry service by regulatory agencies, but a fair reading of the case studies in this book suggests that they are a good deal more than that—they are the leading edge of either a broad shift in, or a previously undiscussed dimension of, bureaucratic behavior. To be sure, such examples cannot be found in every agency: the FMC continues to approve carrier rate requests without blinking an eye, except when the carrier types its requests on the wrong paper or with incorrect margins. But what might be exceptions in these "old" or "traditional" regulatory agencies is clearly the norm in the "new" agencies. EPA and OSHA have, in general, chosen stricter and more costly standards over more lenient, less expensive ones. And though the Office for Civil Rights (OCR) has not pleased civil rights organizations, neither has it endeared itself to schools and colleges. If it has been "captured" by anyone, it has been by a federal district court.

In short, the behavior to be explained is complex and changing; it cannot easily be summarized as serving the interests of either the regulated sector or the public at large. To account for this, I suggest we view these agencies as coalitions of diverse participants who have somewhat different motives.[15] In some cases, the maintenance of the regulatory organization is only weakly affected by these differences (the members of the FMC are sufficiently like-minded to create few internal strains);

373

in other cases, profound differences of opinion and interest make agency maintenance difficult. This coalition must be held together in a political environment that provides a changing pattern of rewards to each coalition member. In the remainder of this section, I will discuss the principal members of these coalitions and their motives; in the next section, I will take up the effect of the political and economic environment on how these motives are satisfied.

To simplify, government agencies have at least three kinds of employees who can be defined in terms of their motives. The first are the *careerists:* employees who identify their careers and rewards with the agency. They do not expect to move on to other jobs outside the agency or otherwise to receive significant rewards from external constituencies. The maintenance of the agency and of their position in it is of paramount concern.

The second are the *politicians:* employees who see themselves as having a future in elective or appointive office outside the agency. They hope to move on to better or more important undertakings. They may wish to run for Congress, become the vice-president for public relations of a large firm, enter the cabinet or subcabinet, or join the campaign staff of a promising presidential contender. The maintenance and enhancement of their careers outside the agency is of paramount importance.

The third are the *professionals:* employees who receive rewards (in status if not in money) from organized members of similar occupations elsewhere. They may hope to move on to better jobs elsewhere, but access to those jobs depends on their display of professionally approved behavior and technical competence. They may also be content to remain in the agency, but they value the continued approval of fellow professionals outside the agency, or the self-respect that comes from behaving in accordance with internalized professional norms. The maintenance of this professional esteem is of major importance to these employees.[16]

These are obviously analytical distinctions; any given agency member may combine two or more motives. And no motive corresponds exactly to any given organizational position. However, we would expect to find politicians heavily represented among commissioners and agency executives, especially those whose appointment requires legislative confirmation; we would expect careerists to be found in all ranks, but perhaps especially in the ranks of middle-level managers; we would expect professionals, to the extent they exist in the agency at all, to be found among rank-and-file operators, especially if they have taken jobs in government to prepare themselves for more attractive careers elsewhere.[17]

In virtually every agency discussed in this book, we find a coalition of differently motivated participants. (The FMC may be the conspicuous exception; it consists almost entirely of careerists.) Tension and change in the agency involve competition among these variously motivated members.

Careerists

Careerists (and politicians facing a political environment that provides no rewards for making controversial changes in an agency) will develop, by experience and judgment, a view of what constitutes the essential maintenance problem of the agency. Every agency requires budgets, personnel, and political support, but in most agencies these things are available more or less routinely. Budgets and personnel are rarely cut; they usually grow incrementally (or, when the agency is new or in the spotlight, rapidly). Few officials need fear for their jobs and their salaries are determined by government-wide laws and regulations rather than by the size, rate of growth, or "success" (if such a quality can even be measured) of the organization.[18] What *can* threaten the position, comfort, and prospects of a careerist is a crisis or scandal.

Many of the agencies here studied seem to have developed a shared view as to what constitutes a serious crisis. For the CAB and for the FMC, it was the possibility of a bankrupt major carrier. Agencies could explain away an unpopular rate or route decisions, they could ignore (up to a point) the anticompetitive results of these decisions, but they could not explain away the government allowing or forcing an airline or shipping company into economic collapse. The reason was clear: Congress said, implicitly if not explicitly, in the laws creating the CAB and the FMC, that they were to preserve, protect, and enhance the carriers.

For the EPA, FDA, and OSHA, a major scandal would be a dramatic loss of life or catastrophic injury among people nominally protected by the decisions of the agency. No arguments about the need to protect public health or to encourage pharmaceutical innovation have had a fraction of the impact on FDA as have the sulfanilamide and thalidomide scandals. In regulating pesticides, EPA is keenly aware that if a product it has registered is later shown to produce cancer on a large scale, the agency will be crucified and the careers of all concerned blighted, if not destroyed. The FDA is under a legal obligation to permit *no* carcinogenic additives in any food or drug (except tobacco). Indeed, fear of cancer (along, perhaps, with fear of deformed babies) has become the litmus test of any decision by these agencies. Whatever its incidence, whatever its harm compared to other illnesses or injuries, cancer has acquired a position in the public mind—and thus in political discourse—that subordinates almost every other consideration to its prevention. (The tolerance of cancer-inducing tobacco products is the conspicuous exception: here public opinion is divided—or, in an economist's language, people compare costs and benefits.)

Government agencies are more risk averse than imperialistic.[19] They prefer security to rapid growth, autonomy to competition, stability to change. Exceptions exist, but they tend to be found among agencies with specially benign environments—strong public support and popular leadership. Much of what otherwise might seem puzzling about these agencies becomes clearer once we understand how they define the nature and source of potential threats to their security and support —in short, once they determine what constitutes a threatening crisis.

When the EPA was formed under the leadership of William Ruckelshaus, it gave almost no serious consideration to relying on effluent charges to reduce air and water pollution. Instead, Ruckelshaus immediately brought suit against several cities and large firms for violating antidischarge rules and activated machinery to ban discharges above some minimal amount. In the precarious early months of the EPA, when environmentalists were expressing skepticism about the Nixon administration's commitment to environmental programs, any sign that EPA was even considering effluent charges would have immediately been interpreted as an indication that the agency proposed to "sell licenses to pollute." Such a charge, however misleading, would have dealt a serious blow to the EPA's need to find some political breathing room. Similarly, the maintenance needs of the FDA since the mid-1960s have been such that any public espousal of cost-benefit or cost-risk analysis of programs designed to protect health and safety would have provoked the damaging criticism that the agency was trying to "put a price on a human life."

Caught as it is between organized labor and organized business, OSHA has an especially difficult maintenance problem. The debate over the costs and effectiveness of its major regulatory policies—concerning vinyl chloride or coke-oven emissions, for example,—is limited to a relatively small circle of activists. Nevertheless, each side in that debate knows that a much larger public, and thus many more congressmen, can be activated if OSHA can be shown to be doing something foolish, however unimportant. Hence OSHA finds itself constantly defending its decision to issue orders requiring the installment of split toilet seats or to publish booklets in Basic English warning farmers to avoid slipping on manure. Ridicule is a powerful weapon, and OSHA has moved rather quickly to get rid of minor regulations that might stimulate such ridicule and to minimize the enforcement of those questionable ones that remain.

So also with OCR: the efforts it has made to constrain the hiring policies of private universities raise fundamental questions of public power and public purpose, but these questions are discussed only among a handful of specialists and in ways that elicit little, if any, congressional attention. But let it ban father-son banquets in high schools or all-girl basketball teams in Iowa, and the popular and congressional outrage is overpowering.

In short, agencies quickly learn what forces in their environment are capable of using catastrophe or absurdity as effective political weapons, and they work hard to minimize the chances that they will be vulnerable to such attacks.

That agencies are risk averse does not mean they are timid. Quite the contrary: their desire for autonomy, for a stable environment, and for freedom for blame gives these agencies a strong incentive to make rules and to exercise authority in all aspects of their mission. No agency wishes to be accused of "doing nothing" with respect to a real or imagined problem; hence every agency proliferates rules to cover all possible contingencies. The process is known familiarly in the bureaucracy as "covering your flanks." The more diverse the organized constituencies with which an agency must deal, the more flanks there are to be covered. Furthermore, regulations tend to multiply owing to the unanticipated consequences of any given regulation. James W. McKie has called this the "tar-baby effect."[20] For example, a PUC may set the rate of return that an electric utility may earn only to discover that this rate diminishes the incentive the utility managers have to be efficient. As a result, the PUC must devise new rules to insure that levels of service to politically important consumers do not deteriorate.[21] The more visible the agency, the greater the demands on it, and thus the more rules it must produce to assure its security and survival. The CAB became the inevitable locus of a variety of demands regarding air service, especially demands from small communities that feared they would be abandoned by the airlines if not for CAB-enforced service requirements. Finally, considerations of equity require that benefits given to one group be extended to others who can argue that they are similarly situated.

Critics of regulatory agencies notice this proliferation of rules and suppose that it is the result of the "imperialistic" or expansionist instincts of bureaucratic organizations. Though there are such examples, I am struck more by the defensive, threat-avoiding, scandal-minimizing instincts of these agencies.

Politicians

When appointment to a top position in a regulatory agency is seen as a political dead end—as a reward for an elderly defeated congressman or as a place in which to "bury" an untalented political hack with a powerful sponsor—the agency will be led by executives who act like careerists. They will have no incentive to make changes or play a visible role. Reappointment comes from avoiding enemies, not from winning friends. The confirmation hearings of appointees to the FMC, as described by Edward Mansfield, vividly illustrate this strategy.

At one time, many if not all federal regulatory commissions may have followed this pattern. Perhaps it was because these commissions became, after their formative years had passed, dumping grounds for people who had to be "taken care of" that scholars such as Marver Bernstein began to formulate life-cycle theories of regulatory politics. It did not take a close student of Shakespeare's "Ages of Man" to recognize senescence when he saw it. Even today, many state public utility commissions still are of this character. When an agency's top posts are filled with old people on their way down and young people going nowhere—when, in short, there are neither political nor professional rewards available to incumbents—we are naturally tempted to speculate about the availability of economic rewards. In these circumstances, we might assume that politicians would cater to industry in exchange for lucrative positions after government service or material favors (or perhaps merely esteem) while still in that service. The examples uncovered in the occasional congressional inquiries into these matters are evidence that such speculation is not unfounded.[22]

What is striking about the contemporary period is the extent to which service in regulatory agencies is now seen as providing future political rewards. William Ruckelshaus headed EPA at a time when he probably thought of himself as having a substantial political career ahead of him and, indeed, he later became deputy attorney general and acting director of the FBI. When Leonard Ross became a member of the California Public Utilities Commission, he was thinking of a larger, future political role and acting in ways designed to increase—not minimize—his public visibility. John Robson and later Alfred Kahn did not take up the chairmanship of the CAB out of a desire for pleasant obscurity or free trips to airline resorts. The selection of first Miles Kirkpatrick (by President Nixon) and then Michael Pertschuk (by President Carter) to be chairman of the FTC is hardly consistent with the view of that agency as a political graveyard: Kirkpatrick was a distinguished lawyer with an active career still ahead of him, Pertschuk an experienced congressional staff member with a good deal of energy.

As Douglas Anderson suggests, a "political market" has arisen in regulatory agencies that is as strong—or stronger—than the economic market. Why this political market should have emerged is a large question on which we shall touch in the next section, but it clearly has much to do with the arrival of a political elite that has absorbed the neopopulist outlook fostered by the 1960s: the suspicion of institutions, the criticism of business enterprise, the interest in speaking on behalf (or so they think) of unorganized consumers, and the conviction that such an outlook is not only morally correct but politically useful. They would appear to be right: President Carter evidently thought so when he appointed scores of environmentalists and consumer advocates to key administrative posts, much as Governor Jerry Brown in California and Governor Michael Dukakis in Massachusetts had done before him. That Carter, Brown, and Dukakis were viewed, by liberal activists, as "conservative" politicians reinforces my point: even officeholders criticized as illiberal believed that energetic advocates of regulation made desirable political appointees.

Professionals

Some regulatory agencies have tasks that only professionals—that is, people trained and certified by some external institution—can perform, or perform well. Lawyers are the most numerous of these professionals but economists, engineers, physicians, and public health specialists are increasingly common. The extent to which someone acts as a professional as opposed to a careerist depends on the extent to which he or she receives important rewards, intangible as well as tangible, from professional colleagues outside the government agency. Not all occupations conventionally called professions—and not all members of a given profession—are alike in this regard. Physicists may accept the standards and seek the esteem of fellow physicists more than lawyers crave the good opinion of fellow lawyers. But some lawyers, especially those seeking careers with the more prestigious law firms, will be highly sensitive to their reputation in the profession. And, in varying degrees, almost every member of a profession will have learned distinctive ways of thinking about policy problems.

379

JAMES Q. WILSON

The role of lawyers in the FTC and the Antitrust Division is crucial. They define their task as that of responding to complaints alleging violations of a statute, investigating the complaint, and initiating a prosecution if the law and facts warrant it. They are accustomed to thinking in terms of two-party adversary proceedings conducted by advocates who use all the evidence that supports their respective case and ignore or downplay evidence that weakens it. The benefits of a legal victory are measured in terms of the gain to the party whose rights were secured and to the law whose supremacy was vindicated.[23] This leads lawyers, in both the FTC and the Antitrust Division, to favor a "reactive," answer-the-mail approach to the enforcement of the antitrust laws. Reinforcing this tendency is the ambition among younger attorneys—who are a majority of all the attorneys in these agencies—to find cases that can be investigated and prosecuted in a reasonably brief period of time with maximum display of legal acumen. The lawyers' opportunities to prove their legal talent in the courtroom or in consent-decree negotiations substantially enhance their market value to prospective private employers such as law firms and corporations.

This professional orientation has two policy consequences. First, antitrust lawyers have a strong incentive to investigate thoroughly and prosecute vigorously. The more lucrative the opportunities for postgovernment employment, the stronger the incentive. Private law firms and corporations hire the ablest antitrust lawyers; the ablest lawyers are the ones who have *defeated* the private law firms and corporations. The chapters by Robert Katzmann and Suzanne Weaver leave little doubt as to the importance of this consideration; the high turnover rate among government antitrust lawyers confirms the point.

Second, antitrust lawyers have an incentive to prefer simple cases in which one party alleges that the other party engaged in conduct explicitly prohibited by law. These "conduct" cases are numerous; to the complaining party, they are important. To an economist, however, they may have only a small social benefit and may be less valuable than cases that prosecute firms, or combinations of firms, that by their size and structure dominate an industry. The lawyers disagree with this view: they claim that tackling complex "structural" cases is an exercise in futility—there is no guarantee the court will sustain the charges, the legal precedents are often shaky, the economic evidence is typically controversial, and, in any event, the cases drag on for years. Whoever is right about the social merits and demerits of these two kinds of cases, one fact is indisputable: no lawyer relishes the idea of burrowing through the files of an IBM for ten years or so, hoping eventually to get

The Politics of Regulation

a chance to appear in court. As a result, lawyers tend to walk away from these cases.

The FTC has organized the competition between economists and lawyers into rival bureaus (the Bureau of Competition and the Bureau of Economics). When Donald Turner was the assistant attorney general in charge of the Antitrust Division, the Division also tried to incorporate economic considerations into the case-selection process, but with only limited success. Even that success evaporated with the return of Turner to the Harvard Law School. The FTC caseload has shifted toward structural cases and away from smaller conduct cases as a result of the influence of the Bureau of Economics and the support it has received from several recent FTC chairmen. It would be impossible to explain this shift by claiming changes in the "economic pressures" or "client demands" confronting the FTC.

The outlook and influence of lawyers also help explain the early strategy of the EPA. Alfred Marcus notes the extent to which lawyers came to dominate the EPA because they were skilled at issuing orders and filing lawsuits, methods the first administrator saw as important if the EPA was to gain visibility and public support. But these orders and suits were often based on incomplete or questionable evidence. Economists in the agency criticized some rules for being too costly or conferring too few benefits; scientists in the agency attacked them for being half-baked. As outside groups—other government agencies and private interests—hired economists and scientists to challenge EPA decisions, the power of economists and scientists within EPA grew. Which profession dominated EPA's decision making—lawyers, economists, or scientists—had an important effect on the kinds of decisions it made.

Physicians and medical scientists brought to the FDA a distinctive orientation. Paul Quirk notes that the key FDA professionals have had little interest in economic analyses and have favored an aggressive expansion of the agency's legal authority.

So also in OSHA. Businessmen and economists bitterly complain of that agency's preference for "engineering" rather than "personal equipment" solutions to such problems as noxious fumes or industrial noise. Rebuilding a foundry to reduce noise levels is exceptionally expensive; giving ear plugs to foundry workers is much cheaper. Still OSHA has maintained its commitment to engineering solutions. Part of the reason is that this attitude accords with the preferences of organized labor, which objects to personal equipment as inconvenient, easily misused, and inadequate.

But labor's demands alone do not explain OSHA's actions; after all,

OSHA can choose between competing demands, each forcefully presented. OSHA's choice reflects in addition the preferences of the public-health specialists who occupy the key decision posts in the agency. As Steven Kelman suggests, they have been trained to believe in engineering solutions; only such solutions, the textbooks argue, address the causes of the problem. Personal protective equipment deals only with "symptoms"; it is a "Band-Aid." Industrial hygienists are trained to "eliminate hazards," not to engage in cost-benefit analysis. To the extent that public-health specialists dominate OSHA, they will come to play a larger role in corporations regulated by OSHA. As Harold L. Wilensky observed long ago, political rivals hire rival professional and intellectual specialists.[24] But this may have unanticipated consequences, for the employer cannot easily limit the professional to being merely a rhetorical advocate; the professional is likely to start influencing the employer's own decisions as well.

So far we have seen instances of professional norms leading agencies to regulate more aggressively than they otherwise might. But such norms can have the opposite effect as well. Engineers dominate the staffs of public utility commissions, such as those in New York and California. Engineers define their job as achieving efficiency; as staff members of the California PUC, they took efficiency to mean setting electric rates to encourage the most efficient production of electricity. This, in turn, meant the engineers generally favored lower rates for large (usually industrial and commercial) users, either to encourage maximum sales (and thus achieve economies of scale) or to discourage large users from shifting to alternative energy sources (and thus avoid excess capacity). "Lifeline" rate proposals—giving free or below-cost electricity to small residential users—was contrary to this way of thinking and vigorously (though, in California, unsuccessfully) opposed by the engineers as "welfare" or a "free lunch."

In some cases, professional norms were decisive; in other instances, they were only a constraining factor. In almost all the cases reviewed in this book, however, they had to be weighed. Any such norm can be overcome, but the cost—in energy, persistence, conflict, and staff turnover—can be high, as Donald Turner discovered in the Antitrust Division and as Michael Pertschuk may yet discover at the FTC.

The Politics of Regulation

The Regulatory Environment

The political environment within which regulatory agencies operate affects their behavior. That unsurprising fact becomes more interesting —or more sinister—if only one feature of the environment is emphasized at the expense of others. Some critics draw attention to the activities of corporations, others to the rise of Ralph Nader. Both of these parties are important, but so are several others.

Technology and Economy

Some changes in regulatory practice can be explained simply by reference to important changes in the underlying technology of an industry or in its price structure. Electric rate regulation was not a political issue so long as the utility industry was able to reduce or maintain the price of electricity by taking advantage of economies of scale and installing new, more efficient generating equipment. State PUCs had scarcely anything to do: if rates were steady or falling, the most that would be expected of the PUCs would be to nod approvingly (perhaps after a suitable delay). It may have been this fact that led to the 1962 discovery by George Stigler and Claire Friedland that electric utility regulation had no discernible effect on rates.[25] Though later studies modified this conclusion, no one suggested the PUC's had a dramatic effect on rates.

Sharp increases in oil prices, the absence of feasible new ideas in generating technology, and the exhaustion of available economies of scale put an end to this golden age. Rates began moving up inexorably, with the Arab oil embargo and the subsequent imposition of "fuel adjustment charges" on consumers' bills dramatizing the change. Now there was something to fight about. But even here, the economic changes *alone* did not alter the politics of regulation; electricity consumers, numerous and unorganized, rarely raised the issue spontaneously. As Anderson makes clear, liberal and environmental activists found the issue and exploited it.

The shift in medical practice toward increasing reliance on drugs created potential problems of safety and efficacy that had not existed before on quite the same scale or with quite the same degree of scientific uncertainty. It was easy to regulate useless patent medicine containing opium; it was something else again to decide how, if at all, to regulate the marketing and use of drugs that have beneficial effects for some patients, harmful effects for others, and unknown effects for still others. Even if the FDA had not been hit with scandals in the 1960s, it would have been on the firing line: as Paul Quirk notes, the agency has had to reconcile competing interests under conditions of risk and uncertainty.

Politics and Ideas

By far the largest number of regulatory issues discussed in this book arose not because of a fundamental shift in technology or prices, but because perceptions about what constituted a problem changed. As we have already seen, OSHA was created because the rate of industrial accidents became an issue even though that rate had been generally declining. EPA was born not because scores of people were dying from pollution, but because the *potential* (and possibly large) effects of pollution had become a matter of concern. The movement to deregulate domestic aviation and trucking arose not because the airlines or trucking companies had changed, but because the beliefs of key political participants had changed.

The effect of the political environment will depend in part on the configuration of forces confronting the agency. Earlier we saw how the creation of an agency was affected by the perceived distribution of costs and benefits of the regulatory policy. Where benefits remain concentrated and costs widely distributed, the pattern of client politics will persist. The FMC is in this position and thus receives unambiguous and consistent cues from its political environment, cues that provide little incentive for change. The merchant carriers benefit from its action; those who bear the costs of these benefits have little interest in organizing. This may seem strange, since presumably the shippers would want to keep costs down and thus would press the FMC to lower rates. But, as Mansfield indicates, for many firms the price of ocean shipping is a very small part of the cost of doing business. Moreover, the largest shippers can often negotiate, on an item-by-item basis, attractive rates with individual carriers and do not need FMC help. Indeed, since a negotiated low rate will benefit only themselves and not their competitors, they prefer to avoid appeals to the FMC. Small shippers that cannot obtain such favorable rates are too numerous to organize and in any event often deal with freight forwarders who charge a commission based on the rates paid that gives these middlemen no incentive to shop around for low rates. Similarly, for decades, the CAB dealt with a generally supportive client, encountering demands for change only during those periods when low-fare unscheduled air carriers were trying to initiate scheduled service on major routes.

Some regulatory agencies must deal with competing demands—that is, with interest-group politics—because their policies produce both concentrated costs and concentrated benefits. The National Labor Relations Board has always been in this situation; so has OSHA. But because the NLRB is a commission, the direction—prolabor or probusiness—in which it tilts can be altered rather easily by changing the political composition of the board. Changing the posture of OSHA, on the other hand, requires changing a single visible administrator and his key deputies, a move which has struck most presidents as politically too costly.

But the distribution of costs and benefits, and their effects on the distribution of political influence, do not alone account for the kinds of cues regulatory agencies receive from their environment. We have seen the CAB and the FDA change its policies over objections of their clients, the airlines and the pharmaceutical industry. HEW's Office for Civil Rights has continually expanded its regulations even though we would have expected schools and colleges, with their strong links to HEW and Congress, to be able to resist such encroachments. The National Highway Traffic Safety Administration has not become the pawn of the automobile manufacturers even though NHTSA closely regulates that highly concentrated industry. EPA has had to deal with as many complaints and lawsuits from environmentalists as from industry, despite the economic and political advantages industry presumably enjoys.

These apparent anomalies can all be explained: the cost of obtaining effective access to the political process has been lowered dramatically in the last decade or two. Once national interest groups could exist only if they had corporate sponsors or a mass membership; today "public interest" lobbies can be sustained by the availability of foundation grants and the use of computerized direct-mail fund drives. As Jeffrey M. Berry has found, many of these new lobbying groups have no "members" at all, but depend on the Ford Foundation or similar sponsors or on their ability to generate (as does Common Cause) a large income from mail solicitations of persons who are members in name only.[26] Though such groups rarely have the legal staffs or war chests of a well-heeled business lobby, they have at least two offsetting advantages. First, they can enter the federal courts to challenge agency decisions rather easily because the rules governing standing have been liberalized and because in many cases (such as suits involving civil rights or the EPA) the plaintiffs may be reimbursed for their costs if they win. Second, the public-interest lobbies have many friends in the national media who are happy to cover their activities and publicize their complaints. Ralph Nader and his successors have been good copy for many reporters, especially for those who bring an antibusiness attitude to their jobs.

The cost of effective political access has also been lowered by the existence within government, especially in Congress, of people who are sympathetic to consumerist and environmental organizations. President Carter's appointments of these people to executive branch positions has already been mentioned; equally important is the rapid expansion of the size of congressional staffs and the recruitment to many of these staffs of persons who derive either satisfaction for themselves or political rewards for their superiors from their ability to mount investigations or draft legislation in the regulatory area.

It would be misleading, however, to label these young staffers, in many cases the product of the political turmoil at elite colleges and law schools in the 1960s, as "proregulation." No doubt many such activists share the general public distrust of corporations (and of institutions generally). But in addition they have views about specific political strategies and policy tools. In his study of the EPA, Marcus notes the extent to which congressional staffers and often younger congressmen have opinions about regulation quite different from those held by their predecessors. A student in college or law school in the 1930s and 1940s would probably have been taught that government regulation of entry into and the prices charged by an industry was desirable and that the commission form of regulation was optimal. James Landis's book on regulation was a root-and-branch defense of the desirability and feasibility of applying neutral administrative expertise to the management of economic enterprise.[27]

By contrast, in the 1960s, college and law school students were exposed to books and articles written by people disillusioned with the regulatory commission, though not with the idea of regulation. Scarcely any student majoring in political science could have avoided hearing that regulatory agencies were "captured" by industry and that commissions went through a "life cycle" that led inevitably to senility or dependence. A bright student would also have heard economists say that regulation of entry and rates, as practiced by the ICC and the CAB, imposed costs on the consumer by keeping prices at above-market levels. At the same time, they would learn from each other, if not from their professors, that the environment was being degraded and the consumer "ripped off." These students would later enter government service carrying with them the political residue of these intellectual arguments: agencies should be reorganized to prevent their capture, regulation of entry and rates is of questionable value, and regulating the nature and quality of the product and the conditions of the workplace will produce substantial benefits.

The executive order creating EPA and the laws that EPA was to administer were drafted with just such views in mind. The result was a series of new agencies headed by single administrators (rather than commissions), committed to regulating quality rather than price, and governed by standards and deadlines affording minimal opportunity for the exercise of discretion. One additional proposal that supposedly would have further reduced the presumed threat of capture was the consumer advocacy agency, but Congress was not persuaded. Finally, key congressional staff members, such as those serving Senator Edward M. Kennedy, began pressing for deregulation of rates and entry.

In short, the political environment of the regulatory agencies changed significantly in a short time. These changes had many sources, but one common characteristic: they reveal the extent to which intellectual descriptions (and criticisms) of institutional arrangements come to have practical consequences. Any generalization about how government works is vulnerable to the behavior of persons who have learned that generalization and wish to repeal it.

Institutions

The political changes I have described may strike some readers as rather fuzzy shifts in mood that are not likely to have the impact of dollars and votes. It would certainly be absurd to argue that politicians have no interest in reelection, bureaucrats no interest in advancement, and corporations no interest in profits. Nor do I argue this: there are clearly examples of these motives shaping the regulatory process. But the impact of these motives is constrained not only by the interests of professionals, the mobilization of opponents, and the intellectual baggage of public officials, but also by the uncertain connections between votes and dollars.

It is difficult to be certain about the relationship between campaign contributions, electoral success, and bureaucratic policy: these matters are not always open to scrutiny, and we cannot be certain whether the publicized cases of influence peddling are typical or exceptional. That there has been an incentive for regulated industries to supply campaign contributions, however, is beyond dispute. Long before the government began overtly subsidizing presidential campaigns, it had passed a number of de facto "campaign finance" bills—all those laws that made the profits of an industry or occupation dependent on the discretionary authority of government officials. The list of firms that made illegal (and legal) contributions to President Nixon's reelection effort in 1972 reads like a Who's Who of regulated industries—airlines, milk producers, truckers, bankers.

What is less clear is what these companies got for their money. The milk producers received higher government-fixed prices; beyond that, the facts are uncertain. The EPA remained aggressively committed to strict environmental standards, even though Maurice Stans, a Nixon fundraiser, used the example of EPA as a reason that corporations ought to give to the president's war chest. (We suspect that a vigorous EPA was more valuable to Nixon than a passive one. There is a fine line between bribery and extortion.) Marcus finds that the White House made an effort to curb EPA, but that it was largely unsuccessful. In 1974 conservative businessmen also gave (now in legal ways) to the Republican party, partly perhaps in response to President Gerald Ford's scathing criticism of OSHA, but if so it was to little avail—Kelman finds OSHA as tough-minded after the president's criticisms as before them. It is hard to imagine what feelings gripped the hearts of airline executives when, after giving lavishly to politicians of both parties, they saw first John Robson and then Alfred Kahn push them in the direction of price competition; however, we can safely assume that gratitude was not one of those emotions.

What is striking about the case studies in this book is that, though written by people expecting to find external meddling in the affairs of these agencies, so little actual meddling was discovered. Nonetheless, on reflection, the explanation becomes obvious.

By and large, the policies of regulatory commissions are not under the close scrutiny or careful control of either the White House or of Congress simply because what these agencies do has little or no political significance for either of these institutions. Votes are won or lost by grand issues (war and peace), by pocketbook issues (inflation, unemployment), or by personal style and party identification. There are scarcely any votes to be had from regulating or deregulating an industry (unless there has been a major scandal) or from intervening in specific regulatory issues. If an outraged constituent demands intervention, a politician can always promise to "look into" the matter and make a pro forma inquiry. If nothing happens as a result, it is, of course, because of "arrogant" or "unreasonable" bureaucrats. They could try to do more than this, and sometimes congressmen and other politicians have—but they run the risk of exposure (and possibly indictment) if they are caught taking money or selling influence. Even a small chance of such a penalty makes the likely benefit—a few votes, a few thousand dollars—seem rather unappealing to most legislators.

The appropriations committees of Congress, which have the greatest potential impact on regulatory agency policy, have largely ignored policy questions when marking up budget requests. Such interest as is shown in policy matters has been evinced by the legislative committees, and usually only a few of them. The House Merchant Marine and Fisheries Committee has watched the FMC with benign neglect, at best; the Senate Commerce Committee staunchly supported the CAB for years. Policy change comes when an "outsider" committee horns in on the act, as when Estes Kefauver's investigating committee looked at the drug industry or Edward Kennedy's Subcommittee on Administrative Practice and Procedure took an interest in airline and truck deregulation.

When it proposes appointments to the regulatory agencies, the White House would presumably take a considerable interest in the policy views of its nominees. Here, surely, the ruling party can affect, at little cost, the posture of the agencies. No doubt the White House is generally aware of whether a candidate is probusiness or a consumer activist, a liberal or a conservative. The Carter White House could not have been unaware of Michael Pertschuk's attitudes toward big business or Alfred Kahn's view of rate regulation. But we are equally struck by the shallowness of the White House assessment of the policy views of most nominees. No one seems to care what an FMC commissioner thinks; John Robson was appointed to the CAB because President Ford had confidence in him, but at the time neither Robson nor Ford had a well-worked-out view on airline regulation; when Mort Corn was selected to run OSHA, the White House seemed not to know that he was likely to persist in the very policies President Ford had been condemning; the various heads of the Antitrust Division have been lawyers whose general policies have been similar whatever the political coloration of the White House.

Organized groups no doubt affect the appointment process (though we gathered no information on that). Industry lobbies to have one of its number put on a particular commission; Ralph Nader makes clear to whom he will object; public-interest organizations and professional societies form a complex Washington network of information and candidacies. But, as with the selection of federal judges, the need to please a constituency, to satisfy the obligations of senatorial courtesy, and to take care of a political supporter combine to produce nominees who are, except in the unusual case, known by their general inclinations but not by their specific policy preferences.

In short, the relationship between electoral needs and policy outcomes is problematic because of the many diverse persons whose actions must be coordinated, the uneven but generally low political payoffs of any given policy, and the difficulty of predicting action from professed beliefs.

This very diffusion of political supervision of regulatory agencies has facilitated a striking growth in judicial supervision of them. The courts provide a ready and willing forum in which contending interests may struggle over the justification and interpretation of specific rules and practices, matters that ordinarily are of little interest to congressional committees or the White House except when dramatic events (or rivalry between two or more congressional committees) bring an issue to the fore. It is possible, of course, to devise a "maximizing" or "capture" model of judicial behavior, but thus far none seems especially useful or persuasive. Judges, like professors, have the occupational security that permits them to indulge, to an even greater degree than most political actors, in the explication and application of ideas. And though both industry and its critics grumble about the burdens of litigation, especially when a decision goes against them, one suspects that each finds court appeals of regulatory decisions an economical way to advance or protect its interests—lawyers may be expensive, but they are cheaper, and the outcome of their actions is more predictable, than is the case with efforts to change the ideological composition of Congress, or even of one of its committees.

Court supervision has its costs for the public at large as well as the participants. Decisions are made on a case-by-case basis, rather than by the development of policies. Uncertainty about the consequences of any action or rule is increased. All parties to a dispute have an incentive to stake out extreme positions so as to widen the area in which a final settlement may be reached. There is little sense of finality about an agency decision and this may weaken the agency's incentive to take seriously its responsibilities. Judges ordinarily have little expertise in the substance of an issue but may be nonetheless prepared to act as if they did. Not all persons affected by a decision will be represented in court; other than by further court appeals, there may be no feasible way of challenging judge-made policy.

Conclusion

Having set out to correct what we regard as an overly simple theory about regulatory politics, we may appear to have gone to the opposite extreme and left matters in such a complex—not to say confused—state as to preclude saying anything at all about the subject. If so, we should correct these appearances; continuities, if not cosmic generalizations, are evident to us.

One point involves the largely unsupervised nature of most regulatory activity. Whoever first wished to see regulation carried on by quasi-independent agencies and commissions has had his boldest dreams come true. The organizations studied for this book operate with substantial autonomy, at least with respect to congressional or executive direction. There is supposed to be an "iron triangle" of influence linking each agency, congressional committee, and interest group into a tight and predictable pattern of action, but we have not seen many of these triangles. Those we have seen appear to be made of metal far more malleable than iron. There is no distinctive pattern of influence at all in the case of the FTC and the Antitrust Division; the relationship is more bilateral than triangular in the case of OCR rulemaking (the agency and civil rights organizations) and quadrilateral in the case of EPA, OSHA, and FDA (agency, committee, pro-industry group, and anti-industry group).

The White House repeatedly tries to tidy up these relationships and bring the regulatory agencies under closer supervision, but the history of these attempts is one of dashed hopes and wasted energies. The Hoover Commission, the Ash Commission, President Carter's reorganization project—all have struggled in vain to produce more than cosmetic changes. As this is being written, the Regulatory Analysis Review Group (RARG) has been formed, made up primarily of members of the Council of Economic Advisers, the Office of Management and Budget, and the Council on Wage and Price Stability, and charged by Carter with getting regulatory agencies to pay more attention to the costs (as well as the benefits) of their rules, thereby implementing a presidential order to choose the least burdensome way of achieving regulatory goals. RARG is viewed with suspicion by the regulatory agencies, which have reacted by forming a Regulatory Council, made up of the heads of thirty-five such agencies, to compete with RARG. RARG has pressed the agencies to make some changes; the council has attempted to defend the agencies' turf; the outcome of these initiatives remains in doubt.

A second generalization is the absence of good evidence that there is a clear statutory solution to the problems that beset these agencies. A generation taught to fear the capture of agencies with broad administrative discretion has attempted to write into law strict standards, enforce tight deadlines, and guarantee frequent court review. The auto-emission standards, the Delaney amendment banning carcinogens, the clean-water requirements, the administrative development of numerical "goals" and "targets" for civil-rights compliance—all are animated by a desire to minimize discretion.

But the effort to forestall one problem creates others. Agencies may no longer be captured (it is not clear they ever were), but costs and benefits are no longer compared, and competing values are no longer weighed. Or rather they are weighed, but by judges, rather than administrators. Friedrich Engels's hope that the government of persons would give way to the administration of things remains as chimerical in a welfare state as in a socialist one. Perhaps "juridical democracy," to use Lowi's phrase, is possible in a regime with a limited government and minimal public intervention in the market, but it is unrealistic to suppose that unambiguous legislative standards (or sunset laws, or bureaucratic accountability) can be achieved when the government plays a large role in human affairs. The larger the role of government, the more diverse the range of interests which it must reconcile and thus the greater the scope of administrative discretion—de facto if not de jure. This may be a good thing or a bad thing; but given an activist government, it is very nearly an inevitable one.

A third conclusion is that much of what appears to be the result of bureaucratic ineptitude, agency imperialism, or political meddling is the result of the sheer magnitude of many regulatory tasks. Improving the quality of our air and water, making the workplace safer, guaranteeing that only efficacious drugs are used, regulating the price of natural gas, assuring that educational programs have no discriminatory effects —all these and many other laudatory goals impose simply staggering workloads on the responsible agencies.

Decades will pass before EPA can hope to have carefully reviewed all of the thousands of pesticides and other toxic chemicals and for it to have found, much less controlled, all effluent discharges. OSHA devotes 80 percent of its staff to inspecting workplaces, but manages, with the best efforts and intentions, to inspect only about 2 percent of all such places each year.[28] The more careful the FDA is to protect users against dangerous drugs, the slower will be the rate at which new—and potentially useful—drugs reach persons they may benefit. OCR can make life miserable for college administrators by demanding vast amounts of paperwork on hiring practices, but in fact OCR would have to be many times its present size if it were realistically to hope to alter in a systematic manner the employment patterns of the thousands of (highly decentralized) colleges in this country. If the FMC really tried to set shipping rates on a case-by-case basis (instead of routinely approving everything that is filed on the proper form), it would drown in its own paperwork. This aspect of regulatory politics is not much appreciated by the supporters of regulation. As Peter H. Schuck, former Washington counsel for *Consumers Union*, has noted, the advocates of regulation tend to believe that motives and intentions are more important than results, and that implementation problems are matters of mere detail and goodwill.[29]

Fourth, "regulatory politics" is not an especially useful category of analysis because it encompasses forms of political action that have little in common other than the fact that some agency issues or applies a rule. A single-explanation theory of regulatory politics is about as helpful as a single explanation of politics generally, or of disease. Distinctions must be made, differences examined. These differences are not endless or random. Here, an attempt has been made to bring them into a manageable compass by drawing attention to the distribution of costs and benefits (giving rise to entrepreneurial, client, majoritarian, and interest-group politics), the differing motives of bureaucratic actors, and the changing technology and economics of industries.

Last, we must be struck at every turn by the importance of ideas. Regulation itself is such an idea; deregulation is another. The targets of antitrust investigations are selected in large part because of the ideas of lawyers and economists; the value of regulation by command-and-control as opposed to regulation by the alteration of market incentives requires an assessment of two competing ideas. What Harold Demsetz said about the Antitrust Division and the FTC might be said as well about almost any agency that is not wholly under the control of external forces or its own weighty traditions: the "combination of unsatisfactory theory and the absence of 'captors' encourages [the agencies] to be overly influenced by the scribbling of academics."[30] To the extent an agency can choose, its choices will be importantly shaped by what its executives learned in college a decade or two earlier.

Among the more important parts of this new learning have been the teaching of economists about the costs and benefits of regulation. The very influence of this teaching itself suggests that ideas as well as interests play a role in shaping policies. It would be a pity if an excessive devotion to the assumption of utility maximization as an *explanation* of behavior led scholars to ignore the intellectual impact of the efficiency test as a basis for *evaluating* behavior. Moreover, a preoccupation with the political role of material interests, while useful under many circumstances, can detract attention from the greater challenges to liberty and economic growth raised by the ideas of those groups in our society—bureaucrats, professionals, academics, the media—whose political position depends on controlling resources other than wealth and whose motives are more complex than wealth maximization.

NOTES

Introduction

1. *Federalist,* No. 51.
2. Theodore J. Lowi, *The End of Liberalism* (New York: W. W. Norton, 1969).

Chapter 1

1. William E. Mosher and Finla Crawford, *Public Utility Regulation* (New York: Harper, 1933), p. 551: "with unvarying consistency and stubborness, all the political influence at [the utilities'] command has been mustered, in the first instance, to oppose the establishment of regulatory bodies and later the extension of the powers of such bodies, when once established." See also Merle Fainsod, Lincoln Gordon, and Joseph C. Palamountain, Jr., *Government and the American Economy,* 3d edition (New York: W. W. Norton, 1959), p. 317.
2. Gabriel Kolko argues that railroads sought federal regulation to get out from under the yoke of state regulation. Exactly the opposite is true of electric utilities, which consider state regulation to be preferable to federal or local control. See his *Railroads and Regulations, 1877–1916* (Princeton: Princeton University Press, 1965).
3. Forrest McDonald, *Insull* (Chicago: The University of Chicago Press, 1962), p. 55.
4. Ibid., pp. 84–90.
5. Ibid.
6. National Electric Light Association, *Proceedings* (New York: National Electric Light Association, 1898), pp. 14–29. (Hereafter, *Proceedings.*)
7. Ibid., pp. 27–28.
8. Not all of Insull's fellow committee members supported his views. Edgar Davis later expressed hostility toward the idea of government regulation in his presidential address before the NELA Convention in 1905: "The one great and constant menace to the industry is unwise, burdensome and restrictive legislation by the municipality and the state. . . . The power to regulate contains the germ of the danger of confiscation, in whole or in part."

See *Proceedings* (1905), pp. 6–7.
9. McDonald, *Insull,* p. 117.
10. The prestige of the committee was attested to by the conventions's presiding officer, who remarked, not altogether gratuitously, "It has been said that our public policy committee is the strongest committee that has ever been formed on behalf of any association, and I do not think anyone will be inclined to differ with that opinion." See *Proceedings,* 1(1907), p. 517.
11. Ibid., Appendix A, p. 10.
12. Ibid., p. 9.
13. Ibid., pp. 20–21.
14. Ibid., p. 12.
15. Ibid., pp. 11–12.
16. Ibid., p. 16.
17. Ibid., p. 27.
18. Ibid., p. 30.
19. Ibid., p. 4.
20. Forrest McDonald, *Let There Be Light* (Madison, Wisconsin: American History Research Center, 1957), p. 118.
21. Mansel Griffiths Blackford, "Businessmen and the Regulation of Railroads and Public Utilities in California During the Progressive Era," *Business History Review* XLIV (1970): 313.
22. *Proceedings of the Annual Convention of the Pacific Coast Gas Association,* 1909, p. 23 in Blackford, "Business and Regulations."
23. Proceedings of the Annual Convention of the Pacific Coast Gas Association, 1910, p. 506 in Blackford, "Businessmen and the Regulation of Railroads. . . ."

Notes

24. *San Francisco Examiner,* 8 December 1911, cited in Blackford, "Businessmen and Regulation," p. 314.

25. *Pacific Gas and Electric Magazine,* March 1912, p. 385, cited in Blackford, "Businessmen and Regulation," p. 315. This is not to suggest that all industry executives supported regulation or viewed it as the only alternative to public ownership; they did not. In 1908 Dudley Farrand, the president of the NELA national convention, expressed his concern that the movement for regulation might go too far and unnecessarily restrict the industry's autonomy:

The interests that we represent have been subjected to an agitation having an indefinable source but extending practically all over the country. This agitation, wearing the cloak of reform, has for its objective the creation and establishment of a multiplicity of commissions, national, state and municipal, and seeks not only a reasonable regulation and control, as stated in some of the arguments in favor of the movement, but it actually prevents progress by unreasonable interference with private interests, stifles individual initiative, and in many instances favors acts that are no less than actual confiscation.

Farrand counseled his fellow executives to "feel free to protest . . . and to defeat the enactment of measures designed for political purposes and tending to undermine the very foundations of our investments." There were, of course, utility managers who agreed with and followed this strategy. See *Proceedings,* 1(1908), p. 3.

26. For a history of the NCF, see Gordon Maurice Jensen, "The National Civic Federation: American Business in an Age of Social Change and Social Reform, 1900–1910" (Ph.D. diss., Princeton University, 1956). It is always difficult to assess the importance of one particular organization to the success of legislation as complex as the laws which created state utility commissions but Shelby B. Schurtz, a contemporary critic of the utilities and of state regulation, was moved to say:

The most potent influence in the passage of all of the recent public utility legislation has been the National Civic Federation. . . .

See Shelby B. Schurtz, "The State Public Service Commission Idea," an address presented before the convention of The League of Michigan Municipalities, July 26, 1917. A copy of this address is shelved at Baker Library, Graduate School of Business Administration, Harvard University.

27. National Civic Federation, *Municipal and Private Operation of Public Utilities,* vol. 1, part 1 (New York: National Civic Federation, 1907), p. 12.

28. Ibid., p. 23.

29. Ibid.

30. This point was argued by Edgar and Walton Clark, but it found expression elsewhere in the report as well. See Ibid., pp. 25–26, 40–42, 309.

31. Ibid., pp. 25, 100.

32. Ibid.

33. Ibid. The corporations were as much the victim as the source of municipal corruption, in the view of Walter L. Fisher, author of the committee's summary report on the state of the American city, and onetime president of the Municipal Voter's League of Chicago. Therein lay the basis for agreement with the utilities on the principle of regulation:

It is . . . claimed and . . . sometimes true that the political activity of the public service corporation, after it has been granted . . . a franchise . . . is due to necessity for self protection against unreasonable attacks by public officials inspired by corrupt or demagogic motives. To remove such justification where it exists and to render public regulation intelligent and fair as well as effective, is one of the results hoped for from the creation of . . . expert commissions under legislation such as . . . the public utility statute in New York.

See Ibid., p. 40.

34. John R. Commons, *Myself* (New York: Macmillan, 1934), pp. 111–20. Despite Commons's strong statement of support for the NCF, it would be just as much in error to suggest that all "civic reformers" were in favor of state regulation as to suggest that all

heads of public utilities were. In the large cities of Illinois, Ohio, Michigan, and Minnesota, especially, "home rule" advocates were in large part "good government" reformers. In 1915 Charles Merriam, professor of political science at the University of Chicago and a onetime candidate for mayor, argued:

It is difficult in any state to make the choice of a utilities commission an effective issue in the selection of a governor, and it is precisely for this reason that public utility interests, as a rule, prefer that type of regulation. Upon this point they are certainly "wiser in their day and generation than the children of light." I know that the public service corporations of Chicago will never be as effectively regulated in the public interest by the state, as they will by the city of Chicago, and I have reason to believe that the same situation is found in many other large cities. In my opinion the cry that "politics" will interfere with adequate municipal regulation is in itself one of the cleverest pieces of "politics" in the long history of clever utility corporation tactics.

Charles E. Merriam, "The Case for Home Rule," *Annals of the American Academy of Political and Social Science,* LVII (January 1915): 174. The "home rule" movement was so successful in Minnesota that it was 1975 before a state commission gained jurisdiction over electric utility rates in the state. For an early history of the home rule movement in Minnesota, see Stiles P. Jones, "What Certain Cities Have Accomplished Without State Regulation," *Annals of the American Academy of Political and Social Science,* LVIII (January 1915): 72–82.

35. La Follette was a United States senator in 1907 when the Wisconsin law was passed, but the crucial political contest that cleared the way for its passage came two years earlier, when he was governor.

36. Mosher and Crawford, Public Utility Regulation, p. 23.

37. Merlo J. Pusey, *Charles Evans Hughes* vol. 1, (New York: Macmillan, 1951), p. 134.

38. *New York Evening Mail* 1 April 1905, cited in Pusey, *Hughes,* p. 135.

39. *New York World* 14 May 1908, depicted in Pusey, *Hughes,* p. 231.

40. New York World 25 March 1905, in Pusey, *Hughes,* p. 136.

41. Ibid., pp. 138–39.

42. *Committee Report,* p. 94, quoted in Pusey, *Hughes.*

43. See Henry Bruère, "Public Utility Regulation in New York," and Horatio M. Pollock, "The Public Service Commissions of the State of New York," in *Annals of the American Academy of Political and Social Science,* XXXI (May 1908): 542, 653.

44. See David J. Danelski and Joseph S. Tulchin, eds., *The Autobiographical Notes of Charles Evans Hughes* (Cambridge Mass.: Harvard University Press, 1973), p. 206.

45. See John R. Commons, "The Wisconsin Public Utilities Law," *Review of Reviews,* XXVI (1907): 221–24.

46. Schurtz, "State Public Service Commission Idea," p. 6.

47. Supporters of regulation are fond of saying that it serves as a substitute for competitive markets. While regulation is clearly an alternative to the free market, it is not the market's substitute. On this point see the unpublished manuscript of Professor Stephen Breyer: "The Reform of Economic Regulation" (Cambridge: Harvard Law School, 1978). For an early conceptualization of regulation as a substitute for competition see Alex Dow, *Some Public Service Papers,* 1892–1927 (Detroit, 1927), p. 204.

48. See Alfred E. Kahn, *The Economics of Regulation: Principles and Institutions* vol. 1 (New York: John Wiley 1970), pp. 54–57.

49. See Paul L. Joskow, *A Behavioral Theory of Public Utility Regulation* (New Haven: unpublished Ph.D. diss., Yale University, 1972), pp. 17–81 for a detailed description of these three phases in New York. It should be noted that state utility commissions and their staffs vary in size, in mode of selection, in jurisdiction, in statutory authority, and in the pay they receive. But this variation is deceptively complex. In fact, most state commissions can be classified as either "leaders" or "followers." Almost always, important regulatory innovations are implemented first in the states which have the largest staffs and most resources: New York, California, and Wisconsin. Other states adopt a "wait and see" attitude, preferring to observe which innovations are successful in the big states before they adopt similar procedures of their own. Over time despite the wide degree of variation in the institutional details of regulation, the rate-making procedures of most states

Notes

come to resemble closely those of the leaders. One consequence is that differences among states are most striking during the early stages of regulatory change. For details of state utility commission organization see National Association of Regulatory Utility Commissioners (NARUC), *1974 Annual Report on Utility and Carrier Regulation* (Washington, D.C.: NARUC, 1976).

50. The decision to institute formal rate proceedings is an important one. The commissioners and staff obviously like rate reductions. Yet, during the ten-year period from 1960 to 1970, when rate reductions were possible, only two formal proceedings aimed at lowering rates were instigated by the New York Public Service Commission, while there were a number of voluntary reductions. Of these, one appears to have been more the cause of political pressure by the mayor of Rochester than the commission's concern over excessive profits. Joskow, *Behavioral Theory,* pp. 32–34.

During the 1960s, the New York commission clearly seems to have favored the role of negotiator to that of advocate. There are a number of possible reasons for this paucity of commission-instigated proceedings. One: the commission may have felt that only one or two proceedings were necessary to convince other utilities to file voluntary reductions rather than wait for the commission to order a hearing—sort of a "station the highway cop in full view" strategy. Two: the commission could have felt that a small, quick reduction was preferable to a larger and later one because of the cost in time and resources necessary to pursue a formal proceeding. Since rates—once established—are presumed to be reasonable, the burden of proof is on the party that proposes a change in rates. When utilities file for an increase, they have to prepare the affirmative case; but if the commission decides to seek a decrease, the staff has to develop the case. These cases are long and complex. From 1969 to 1974 the average rate case took eleven months in New York; a year and a half in California. NARUC, *1974 Annual Report,* pp. 548–49.

A third—and more likely—reason is that there was simply no great popular demand for rate reductions during that time period. The real price of electricity was falling, so consumers were satisfied. Rather than incur the wrath of utilities, commissions decided to avoid controversy and negotiate. They certainly were not overworked in those years. From 1960 to 1967 the New York commission issued only seven opinions in rate cases compared to twenty-five in the four-year period 1968–1971. Joskow, *Behavioral Theory,* p. 203.

51. For the details of cost of service rate making see Charles F. Phillips, Jr., *The Economics of Regulation* rev. ed. (Homewood: Richard D. Irwin, 1969).

52. The basic formula for setting rates can thus be expressed:

$$RR = OC + D + T + (RB)r$$

where
$$RR = \text{revenue requirement}$$
$$OC = \text{operating costs}$$
$$D = \text{depreciation}$$
$$T = \text{taxes}$$
$$RB = \text{rate base}$$
$$r = \text{overall rate of return}$$

53. Alfred E. Kahn, "Remarks at the New York Society of Security Analysts," December 18, 1974, p. 2. A copy of this address is on file at the State of New York Public Service Commission.

54. See Kahn, *Economics of Regulation,* pp. 87–103.

55. Clair Wilcox and William G. Shepherd, *Public Policies Toward Business,* 5th ed. (Homewood: Richard D. Irwin, 1975), p. 408.

56. McDonald, *Insull,* pp. 67–69.

57. It is generally conceded that industrial users have a more elastic demand for electricity generated by utilities than do residential customers because they have the option of generating their own power. Residential customers, meanwhile, have a greater elasticity of demand for electric space heating than for lighting. Instead of electricity, householders can use oil or gas to heat their homes; few, however, would use candles or gas lamps in place of electric lighting. By providing a quantity discount, utilities charge those customers less who are more likely to shift from electricity when its price rises.

58. See, for example, William G. Shepherd and Thomas G. Gies, *Utility Regulation:*

New Directions in Theory and Practice (New York: Random House, 1966), pp. 277–78.

59. In the following section, I am indebted to Professor Paul L. Joskow of the Massachusetts Institute of Technology, for helpful comments and for his paper, "Electric Utility Rate Structures in the United States: Some Recent Developments," presented at the Seventh Michigan Conference on Public Utility Economics (April 1977).

60. This quote comes from an interview conducted by the author in June 1977 and reported in Douglas Delano Anderson, "Regulatory Politics and Electrical Utilities" (Ph.D. diss., Harvard University), 1978, p. 133. For this and succeeding quotes based on the above research, I shall use the designation: "DDA interview."

61. DDA interview, June 1977.

62. Kahn, "Remarks."

63. *Business Week,* 25 May 1974, pp. 111–12.

64. See Edward Berlin, Charles J. Cicchetti, and William J. Gillen, *Perspective on Power* (Cambridge Mass.: Ballinger, 1975), pp. 1–11.

65. Joskow, *Behavioral Theory.*

66. Phyllis Peterson and George C. Lodge, "Consolidated Edison (B)" (Harvard Business School: Case 9-375-130).

67. DDA interview, June 1977.

68. *Business Week,* May 25, 1974.

69. *Electrical World,* 15 November 1977, p. 9.

70. *Wall Street Journal,* 25 May 1978, p. 48.

71. The "turbulence" in a regulator's world which resulted from these structural changes is perhaps reflected by the fact that in 1978 there were only 30 regulators nationwide with ten or more years of experience compared with 55 ten years earlier. See *Wall Street Journal,* 23 May 1978, p. 48.

72. A "generic rate proceeding" is one which examines rate-making principles outside of the confines of any utility's specific rate case.

73. For an analysis of the distributional effects of various lifeline proposals see Joe D. Pace, "Lifeline Rates: Will They Do the Job?" *Public Power* (November–December, 1975), pp. 21–30.

74. *Wall Street Journal,* 28 January 1978, p. 14.

75. DDA interview, August 1976.

76. See *Los Angeles Times,* 22 December 1974, part I, pp. 1, 3, 27–28.

77. Ibid., part II, p. 1.

78. DDA interview, August 1977.

79. Ibid.

80. Ibid.

81. Mike Miller, "The Electricity and Gas for People Campaign, 'E&GP': An Analytic History," unpublished paper (San Francisco: Citizens Action League), p. 6.

82. DDA interview, August 1977.

83. Ibid.

84. *San Francisco Examiner,* 3 February 1974.

85. Letter on file with the author.

86. DDA interview, August 1977.

87. DDA interview, August 1977.

88. Letter on file at the California Public Utilities Commission (hereafter, CPUC).

89. Ibid.

90. See Cherry's statements in the reporter's transcript of hearings in CPUC Case 9804, April 10, 1975, pp. 351–58.

91. *Los Angeles Times,* 27 March 1975.

92. Letter on file at the CPUC.

93. California Assembly Bill No. 167, 1975.

94. CPUC, "Application of Pacific Gas and Electric Company," Decision No. 84902, 16 September 1975.

95. CPUC, "First Interim Opinion, Preliminary Considerations," (Case 9988: Decision No. 86087, 13 July 1976).

96. A copy of this report is on file at the CPUC.

97. This report was prepared by PG&E for CPUC President Robert Batinovich and shared with the author by Batinovich.

Notes

98. State of New York Public Service Commission (hereafter, NYSPSC), "Opinion and Order Determining Relevance of Marginal Costs to Electric Rate Structures" (Case 26806: Opinion No. 76–15, 10 August 1976), pp. 31, 34.

99. NYSPSC, "Opinion and Order Requiring the Establishment of Time-of-Day Rates for Large Commercial and Industrial Customers" (Case 26887: Order No. 76-26, 16 December 1976).

100. Chairman Kahn's appointment was effective July 1, 1974, but he was not fully "on board" at the commission until September.

101. See Kahn, *Economics of Regulation, op. cit.*

102. Public Service Commission of Wisconsin, "Application of Madison Gas and Electric Company for Authority to Increase Its Electric and Gas Rates," 2-U-7423, 8 August 1974, p. 49.

103. DDA interview, June 1977.

104. DDA interview, June 1977.

105. National Economic Research Associates (NERA) had previously presented testimony in Wisconsin and was headed at the time by Irwin Stelzer, who studied with Kahn at Cornell University.

106. NYSPSC, Opinion No. 76–15, pp. 4–6.

107. DDA interview with Edward Berlin, June 1977.

108. See J. W. Wilson and Associates, *Elasticity of Demand: Topic 2* (Washington, D.C.: Electric Utility Rate Design Study, 10 February 1977).

109. See Robert H. Frank, "Lifeline Proposals and Economic Efficiency Requirements," *Public Utilities Fortnightly,* 26 May 1977, pp. 11–15.

110. DDA interview, June 1977.

111. DDA interview, June 1977.

112. For a discussion of the problem of the shifting peak, see Kahn, *Economics of Regulation,* pp. 91–94.

113. NYSPSC, Case 26887, Opinion No. 76–26.

114. DDA telephone interview, September 1978.

Chapter 2

1. *Congressional Quarterly,* 14 February 1977, p. 1064.

2. Carl C. Davis, "Federal Maritime Commission" (briefing paper prepared for the Carter Administration—no date), p. 2.

3. Richard J. Daschbach, FMC Speech No. 77–17, 17 November 1977, p. 1.

4. *Congressional Record,* vol. 53, 16 May 1916, p. 8077.

5. House of Representatives, Committee on Merchant Marine and Fisheries, *Report on Steamship Agreements and Affiliations,* 63rd Cong. 2nd sess. (Washington: U.S. Government Printing Office, 1914), pp. 311, 417. (Hereinafter cited as *Alexander Report.*)

6. House of Representatives, Committee on Merchant Marine and Fisheries, *Investigation of Shipping Combinations,* 62nd Cong., 3rd sess. (Washington: U.S. Government Printing Office, 1913), p. 1407.

7. *Alexander Report,* p. 295.

8. Daniel Marx, Jr., *International Shipping Cartels* (Princeton: Princeton University Press, 1953), pp. 19–21.

9. Esra Bennathan and A. A. Walters, "Shipping Conferences: An Economic Analysis," *Journal of Maritime Law and Commerce,* 4 (October 1972): p. 97. For an even tidier demolition of the "natural monopoly" argument, see U.S. Department of Justice, *The Regulated Ocean Shipping Industry* (Washington: U.S. Government Printing Office, 1977), Appendix J.

The key fallacy of the "natural monopoly" argument is the confusion of marginal cost and variable cost. When a ship is filled to capacity with cargo, the marginal cost of adding one more crate is very high; in this situation a carrier who prices according to marginal cost will obviously not lose money in the long run.

10. *Alexander Report,* p. 416.

11. *Investigation of Shipping Combinations,* p. 1293.

12. Ibid., pp. 1404–5.

13. *Alexander Report,* p. 304.

14. *Investigation of Shipping Combinations,* p. 1428.

15. *Alexander Report,* pp. 419–20.

16. James S. Gordon, "Shipping Regulation and the Federal Maritime Commission," *University of Chicago Law Review,* 37 (Fall 1969): p. 126.

17. Manuel Llorca, "Antitrust Exemption of Shipping Conferences," *Journal of Maritime Law and Commerce,* 6 (January 1975): p. 292. See also Andreas Lowenfeld, "To Have One's Cake . . .," *Journal of Maritime Law and Commerce,* 1 (October 1969): p. 23.

18. *New York Times,* 15 August 1916, p. 2; *Congressional Record,* vol. 53, 14 August 1916, pp. 12553, 12574.

19. See Paul Zeis, *American Shipping Policy* (Princeton: Princeton University Press, 1938), p. 91. *New York Times,* 20 August 1916, p. 9; 19 April 1916, p. 7; 21 April 1916, p. 10.

20. James Q. Wilson, *Political Organizations* (New York: Basic Books, 1973), p. 335. See also Wilson, "The Rise of the Bureaucratic State," *The Public Interest,* Fall 1975, p. 97.

21. *Nation,* 9 March 1916, pp. 294–95; *Washington Post,* 9 July 1916, p. 2.

22. Samuel A. Lawrence, *United States Merchant Shipping Policies and Politics* (Washington: Brookings Institution, 1966), p. 38.

23. Documentation on the dramatic rise in freight rates is provided in: House of Representatives, Committee on Merchant Marine and Fisheries, *Creating a Shipping Board, a Naval Auxiliary, a Merchant Marine, and Regulating Carriers by Water Engaged in the Foreign and Interstate Commerce of the United States,* 64th Cong. 1st sess. Rept no. 659 (Washington: U.S. Government Printing Office, 1916), pp. 43–69.

The samples of crisis rhetoric are taken from: *New York Times,* 10 April 1916, p. 10; *New York Times,* 24 August 1916, p. 8; *Congressional Record,* vol. 53, 14 August 1916, p. 12576.

24. *Journal of Political Economy,* p. 24 (December 1916): 1013.

25. Technically, tariff-filing was not incorporated into the Shipping Act until 1916, but the FMC's predecessors had issued rules requiring conferences (but not independents) to keep their rates on file with the agency. These rules did not contain any thirty-day notice provision for rate increases.

26. House of Representatives, Committee on the Judiciary, *The Ocean Freight Industry,* 87th Cong., 2nd sess. (Washington: U.S. Government Printing Office, 1960), p. 359.

27. U.S. Federal Maritime Commission, *Annual Report, Fiscal Year 1976* (Washington: U.S. Government Printing Office, 1976), p. 22.

28. 46 CFR 536.6 (c). These statistics are based on FMC internal memoranda summarizing tariff rejections by the section of the CFR violated.

29. Mark Green, ed., *The Monopoly Makers, Ralph Nader's Study Group Report on Regulation and Competition* (New York: Grossman, 1973), pp. 133–34.

30. U.S. Department of Justice, *The Regulated Ocean Shipping Industry,* p. 47.

31. Green, *The Monopoly Makers,* pp. 133–34.

32. People who doubt this version of how rates are made should read Lowenfeld, "To Have One's Cake . . . ," pp. 32–33.

33. See James Gordon, "Shipping Regulation and the Federal Maritime Commission," p. 125. See also George F. Galland, "Steamship Tariffs in Foreign Commerce," *Tulane Law Review,* 35 (December 1960): p. 145: "While the power has been claimed, it has never been exercised." The Office of General Counsel maintains today that the FMC has this power. As one official put it, "If the rates seem to be too high, the commission could break up the conference."

34. Federal Maritime Commission, et al., v. Aktiebolaget Svenska Amerika Linien, et al., 390 U.S. 238 (1968).

35. Comments of Continental North Atlantic Westbound Freight Conference, et al., in FMC Docket 76–63, p. 5.

36. Ibid., p. 2.

37. Statement of Justification filed on behalf of Agreement No. 9474–3, 1 March 1977.

38. U.S. Department of Justice, *The Regulated Ocean Shipping Industry,* p. 155.

39. Maritime Space Enclosures, Inc., v. Federal Maritime Commission, 420 F.2d 577 (D.C. Cir 1969). In general, an agreement is considered to have "a significant impact on commerce" if it is a *per se* violation of the antitrust laws. See House of Representatives, Committee on Merchant Marine and Fisheries, *Federal Maritime Commission Oversight,* 95th Cong., 2nd sess. (Washington: U.S. Government Printing Office, 1978), p. 449.

Notes

40. This table is based on the FMC's docket listings. Domestic commerce agreements are not included.

41. See Orders of Investigation for Agreement Nos. 10041–4 and 10044–3.

42. Motion for Reconsideration of Order of Investigation and Hearing in FMC Docket 77–44.

43. *Seatrade*, September 1977, p. 85.

44. Almarin Phillips, ed., *Promoting Competition in Regulated Markets* (Washington: The Brookings Institution, 1975), pp. 133–34.

45. U.S. Department of Justice, *The Regulated Ocean Shipping Industry*, pp. 190–215. One further note on economic impact: The FMC, unlike the ICC, for example, has no direct authority to restrict entry. On first glance, this apparent gap in the regulatory scheme would seem to pose a threat to conferences' monopoly power. However, conferences are permitted, under section 14(b) of the Shipping Act, to offer lower rates to shippers who sign a so-called dual rate contract, which binds the shipper to do business only with conference members. Most observers agree that this powerful tying device is indeed a "barrier to entry."

46. U.S. Senate, Committee on Governmental Affairs, *Study on Federal Regulation, Volume I*, 95th Cong., 1st sess. (Washington: U.S. Government Printing Office, 1977), pp. 287–88.

47. U.S. Senate, Committee on Commerce, *Nominations*, 92nd Cong. 2nd sess. (Washington: U.S. Government Printing Office, 1972), p. 3.

48. U.S. Senate, Committee on Commerce, *Nominations*, 90th Cong. 1st sess. (Washington: U.S. Government Printing Office, 1967), p. 43.

49. *Federal Maritime Commission Oversight*, pp. 391–92.

50. *Study on Federal Regulation, Volume I*, pp. 98–99.

51. Davis, "The Federal Maritime Commission," p. 7.

52. *Federal Maritime Commission Oversight*, p. 380.

53. Joint Economic Committee, *Discriminatory Ocean Freight Rates*, 89th Cong., 2nd sess. (Washington: U.S. Government Printing Office, 1965), p. 22.

54. Bennathan and Walters, "Shipping Conferences," p. 114.

55. University of Wales Institute of Science and Technology, Department of Maritime Studies, *Liner Shipping in the U.S. Trades*, a study commissioned by the Council of European and Japanese National Shipowners' Association, April 1978, p. 264. See also Lawrence, *United States Merchant Shipping Policies and Politics*, p. 12: "Shipment costs are only a small portion of the cargoes' delivered value."

56. U.S. Federal Maritime Commission, *Hawaiian Trade Study: An Economic Analysis* (Washington: U.S. Government Printing Office, 1978), pp. 335–37; Federal Maritime Commission, *Puerto Rican–Virgin Islands Trade Study* (Washington: U.S. Government Printing Office, 1970), p. 234.

57. University of Wales Institute of Science and Technology, *Liner Shipping in the U.S. Trades*, p. 268.

58. House of Representatives, Committee on Merchant Marine and Fisheries, *Third Flag*, 94th Cong., 1st sess. (Washington: U.S. Government Printing Office, 1975), pp. 285–88. See also the *Wall Street Journal* editorial, "The Pacific Red Herring," included in the testimony at pp. 157–58.

59. *Nominations*, 1972, p. 3.

60. *Study on Federal Regulation, Volume I*, p. 287.

61. Harold Seidman, *Politics, Position and Power* (New York: Oxford University Press, 1975), p. 38.

62. Richard F. Fenno, Jr., *Congressmen in Committees* (Boston: Little, Brown, 1973), p. 1.

63. Lawrence, *United States Merchant Shipping Policies*, p. 298.

64. The Ralph Nader Congress Project, *The Commerce Committees* (New York: Grossman, 1975), p. 280. David E. Price is the author of the chapter on merchant marine programs.

65. Lawrence, *United States Merchant Shipping Policies*, p. 248.

66. Wilson, *Political Organizations*, p. 335.

67. Zeis, *American Shipping Policy*, pp. 114, 168–69.

68. The Merchant Marine Act of 1920 provided indirect aids to the shipping industry–

for example, the president was authorized to terminate any treaties restricting the right of the United States government to impose discriminatory duties on imports arriving in foreign vessels. Also, the preamble to the act stated that the purpose of the legislation was "to provide for the protection and maintenance of the American merchant marine." This was in contrast to the Shipping Act of 1916, which had a goal of "meet[ing] the requirements of the commerce of the United States." Although comprehensive subsidies were not introduced for another sixteen years, the 1920 act represented a turningpoint in United States policy. (See Lawrence, *United States Merchant Shipping Policies*, p. 41.)

Chapter 3

The author is grateful to Martha Derthick, John T. Golden, R. Tenney Johnson, James C. Miller III, Roy Pulsifier, and Cheryl D. Stein for their helpful criticisms and suggestions.

1. Public Law 95–504; U.S. *Statutes at Large* 92:1705, (1978).

2. Other regulatory agencies have disappeared, but through reorganization or through expiration of a temporary mandate rather than through a congressional vote to deregulate.

3. Between 1974 and 1978, the CAB's members were as follows:

Name	Month Entered Office	Month Left Office
G. Joseph Minetti	June 1956	August 1978
Whitney Gillilland	November 1959	April 1975
Robert D. Timm	January 1971	March 1976
(chairman March 2, 1973 to December 31, 1974)		
Lee R. West	November 1973	June 1978
(acting chairman May 1, 1977 to June 10, 1977)		
Richard J. O'Melia	November 1973	—
(acting chairman January 1, 1975 to April 21, 1975)		
John E. Robson	April 1975	April 1977
(chairman April 21, 1975 to April 30, 1977)		
R. Tenney Johnson	March 1976	June 1977
Alfred E. Kahn	June 1977	October 1978
(chairman June 10, 1977 to October 25, 1978)		
Elizabeth E. Bailey	August 1977	—
Gloria Schaffer	September 1978	—
Marvin S. Cohen	October 1978	—
(chairman October 25, 1978 to present)		

The Airline Deregulation Act received final approval from both houses of Congress on October 14, 1978 and was signed by President Carter on October 24. (See note 195 for a brief legislative history of the act.) September 1, 1978 (the day after Joseph Minetti left office) was the first day that members appointed during or before 1973 were outnumbered by those appointed after 1973. (The Board's members then were Richard O'Melia, Alfred Kahn, and Elizabeth Bailey.) September 26, 1978 (when Gloria Schaffer was sworn into office) was the first day that members appointed after 1973 held more than two seats on the Board.

4. For a prominent example of an economist urging that "command-and-control" regulation be replaced by market-oriented regulation, see Charles L. Schultze, *The Public Use of Private Interest* (Washington, D.C.: Brookings Institution, 1977).

5. At President Ford's September 1974 "Summit Conference on Inflation," twenty-one of the twenty-three economists present endorsed a list of proposals that included abolition of CAB price floors and reduction of CAB controls on entry. The common purpose of the

Notes

proposals was to curtail government programs that raise prices. The two economists who declined to endorse the list contended that enactment of the proposals would not significantly reduce inflation (rather than that the proposals would be harmful). *The Economists' Conference on Inflation* (Washington, D.C.: U.S. Government Printing Office, 1974), vol. 1, pp. 11–13; and *The Conference on Inflation* (Washington, D.C.: U.S. Government Printing Office, 1974), p. 484.

For a concise discussion of this and other indications of an economist's consensus favoring airline deregulation, see United States, Committee on the Judiciary, Subcommittee on Administrative Practice and Procedure, *Hearings on Oversight of Civil Aeronautics Board Practices and Procedures,* 94th Cong., 1st sess., 1975, vol. 1, pp. 75–76.

6. Other major responsibilities of the CAB have included: (1) ruling on airline requests for antitrust immunity to engage in mergers or pooling agreements (Federal Aviation Act of 1958, U.S. *Statutes at Large* 72:731 (1958), Sections 408 and 412); (2) administering the subsidy program for air service to small communities (Federal Aviation Act, Section 406); and (3) in a consumer-protection role, preventing carriers from engaging in "unfair or deceptive practices or unfair methods of competition" (Federal Aviation Act, Section 411).

7. Federal Aviation Act of 1958 (hereafter referred to as "Act"), Sections 401 and 416.

8. Act, Sections 404 and 1002(d)–(h). The CAB has been empowered to disallow fares on either of two grounds: (1) that the fares are not "just and reasonable" (specifically, that they are too high to be reasonable to consumers or are too low to secure a reasonable profit or to allow competing carriers to secure a reasonable profit); or (2) that the fares are discriminatory (specifically, that they give "undue or unreasonable preference or advantage" to some "person, point, locality, or description of traffic" and thereby make others the victims of "undue or unreasonable prejudice or disadvantage").

9. Act, Section 401(j).

10. William A. Jordan, "Airline Capacity Agreements: Correcting a Regulatory Imperfection," *Journal of Air Law and Commerce,* 39 (spring 1973): 179–213.

11. Act, Section 401(e)(4).

12. Measured as the rate of return on investment, the airline industry's profits under CAB regulation characteristically have been mediocre or low relative to profits secured by other American industries—even though consumer demand for air service has grown rapidly. During the thirty-year period from 1947 through 1976, the CAB-certificated airlines' overall rate of return on investment was above 10.0 percent during only six years, between 5.0 and 9.9 percent sixteen years, and below 5.0 percent eight years. The airlines' highest rate for any year between 1947 and 1966 was 13.0 percent; and between 1967 and 1976, 9.6 percent.

This lackluster profit record developed in spite of the fact that consumer demand sustained a dramatic boom in traffic. Between 1947 and 1976, the traffic carried by the certificated airlines grew from 7.9 million revenue passenger–miles to 179.0 million—thus becoming more than twenty times greater in thirty years. Traffic growth was not only large but also reasonably steady: the annual rate of growth was below 5.0 percent during only six of the thirty years and exceeded 15.0 percent during twelve years. Data taken or calculated from Civil Aeronautics Board, *Handbook of Airline Statistics,* 1973 ed. (Washington, D.C.: Civil Aeronautics Board, 1973), pp. 23, 76 (part II, tables 15 and 68); Civil Aeronautics Board, *Supplement to the Handbook of Airline Statistics,* 1973–1974 (Washington, D.C.: Civil Aeronautics Board, 1975), pp. 7, 105 (part III; and part VI, table 1); and Civil Aeronautics Board, *Supplement to the Handbook of Airline Statistics,* 1975–1976 (Washington, D.C.: Civil Aeronautics Board, 1977), pp. 7, 97 (part III; and part VI, table 1).

13. U.S. *Statutes at Large* 52:973 (1938). Originally, the agency was established as the Civil Aeronautics Authority. It was renamed the Civil Aeronautics Board in 1940, when President Roosevelt issued Reorganization Plan No. 4, which reorganized the administration of regulatory functions created by the Civil Aeronautics Act. This act was superseded by the Federal Aviation Act of 1958 [(U.S. *Statutes at Large* 72:731 (1958)], which removed safety regulation from the CAB (transfering it to what is now the Federal Aviation Administration) but left intact the Board's responsibilities for economic regulation.

14. Act, Sections 101(b) and 101(f).

15. Between October 1, 1977 and September 30, 1978, CAB-certificated carriers had total operating revenues of $22.3 billion, of which $71.4 million was subsidy. Civil Aeronautics Board, "Air Carrier Financial Statistics," September 1978, p. 1.

16. The revenue figure for 1938 is drawn from *Annual Report of the Civil Aeronautics Board*, 1941 (Washington, D.C.: U.S. Government Printing Office, 1941), p. 47. Domestic passenger revenues for 1978 were $15.5 billion. Civil Aeronautics Board, "Air Carrier Financial Statistics," December 1978, p. 2. In May 1978, the consumer price index was 4.42 times what it was in 1938. U.S. Bureau of the Census, *Statistical Abstract of the United States* (Washington, D.C.: U.S. Government Printing Office 1957), p. 328 (which shows the 1950 CPI to be 1.7 times the 1938 CPI); and 1978 ed., p. 490 (which shows the May 1978 CPI to be 2.6 times the 1950 CPI). Thus, in 1938 dollars, the airlines' domestic passenger revenues in 1978 were $15.5 billion / 4.42 = $3.51 billion. $23.4 million / $3.51 billion = 0.67 percent.

17. A "revenue passenger-mile" is one fare-paying passenger carried one mile. The 1938 figure is from Civil Aeronautics Board, *Handbook of Airline Statistics* (Washington, D.C.: Civil Aeronautics Board), p. 23 (part II, table 15). The airlines carried 227 billion revenue passenger-miles in 1978. Civil Aeronautics Board, "Air Carrier Traffic Statistics," December 1978, p. 1. 533 million / 227 billion = 0.23 percent.

18. U.S. *Statutes at Large* 43:805 (1925).

19. Robert E. Cushman, *The Independent Regulatory Commissions* (New York: Oxford University Press, 1941), pp. 391–392.

20. These percentages are calculated from information in *Annual Report of the Civil Aeronautics Board*, 1941, p. 47.

21. Federal regulation of airline safety began under the Air Commerce Act of 1926, U.S. *Statutes at Large* 44:568 (1926).

22. For more detailed information on this period, see United States, Senate Committee on the Judiciary, Subcommittee on Administrative Practice and Procedure, Committee Print: *Civil Aeronautics Board Practices and Procedures*, 94th Cong., 1st sess., 1975 pp. 200–206; and Francis A. Spencer, *Air Mail Payment and the Government* (Washington, D.C.: Brookings Institution, 1941), pp. 40–75.

23. U.S. *Statutes at Large* 48:933 (1934).

24. Cushman, *Independent Regulatory Commissions*, p. 393; *CAB Practices and Procedures*, pp. 206–207.

25. Cushman, *Independent Regulatory Commissions*, pp. 393–394; *CAB Practices and Procedures*, p. 208.

26. Cushman, *Independent Regulatory Commissions*, pp. 393–401.

27. For examples of proregulation presentations, see statements by Joseph Eastman, Edgar Gorrell, and Senator Patrick McCarran in United States, House Committee on Interstate and Foreign Commerce, *Hearings on H.R. 5234 and H.R. 4652: Aviation*, 75th Cong., 1st sess., 1937; and United States, Senate Committee on Interstate Commerce, *Hearings on S. 2 and S. 1760: Regulation of Transportation of Passengers and Property by Aircraft*, 75th Cong., 1st sess., 1937. A concise review of arguments made in favor of airline regulation is contained in *CAB Practices and Procedures*, pp. 208–212.

28. During May 1938 debates in the House on airline regulation, Representative Lea contended that the airline industry had reached the threshold of financial self-sufficiency and that the main problem keeping air service from being profitable was competition:

". . . aviation today faces a crucial test that is new and distressing. Aviation has about reached the point where it is self-supporting. It is today self-supporting under favorable conditions of volume and security of traffic. It has reached the stage where there is an invitation to cutthroat and destructive competition which, unless prevented, is going to impede aviation for a good many years to come." *Congressional Record* 83:6406 (May 7, 1938).

29. Spencer, *Air Mail Payment*, pp. 91–92.

30. *CAB Practices and Procedures*, p. 210.

31. Claude E. Puffer, *Air Transportation* (Philadelphia: The Blakiston Company, 1941), pp. 245–246.

32. *Annual Report of the Civil Aeronautics Board*, 1941, pp. 47–48. The airlines flew 48.3 million plane-miles in 1935 and 70.7 million in 1938; their capacity was 447 million

Notes

available seat-miles in 1935 and 905 million in 1938; and their passenger traffic was 222 million revenue passenger-miles in 1935 and 444 million in 1938.

33. *Hearings on H.R. 5234 and H.R. 4652: Aviation,* p. 81.

34. *Hearings on S. 2 and S. 1760: Regulation of Transportation of Passengers and Property by Aircraft,* pp. 79, 91, 96–98, 118–124.

35. During hearings in spring 1938 on airline regulation, Representative Carl Mapes contended that the Post Office and the Department of Commerce had indeed opposed airline-regulation proposals mostly if not entirely because of organizational jealousy. United States, House Committee on Interstate and Foreign Commerce, *Hearings on 9738: To Create a Civil Aeronautics Authority,* 75th Cong., 3rd sess., 1938 pp. 134–135. Perhaps realizing the futility of opposing regulation and almost certainly being pressured by President Roosevelt (who had never wavered from his desire for economic regulation of the airlines), the Post Office and the Department of Commerce had both withdrawn— or at least softened—their opposition to airline-regulation legislation. See comments by Clinton Hester, ibid.

36. Cushman, *Independent Regulatory Commission,* p. 401; *Congressional Record* 83:-8869, 8963, 9616 (June 1938). The Senate passed S. 3845—an extensively amended version of the "McCarran bill"—on May 16, 1938. *Congressional Record* 83:6879. The House passed H.R. 9738—the "Lea bill"—on May 18. (It submitted H.R. 9738 to the Senate as a substitute version of S. 3845.) Ibid., p. 7104. The conference version of S. 3845 was reported on June 7. Ibid., pp. 8354, 8456. It was approved by the House on June 11 and by the Senate on June 13. Ibid., pp. 8869, 8963. All of the votes were unrecorded. Insofar as only weak opposition to the legislation presented itself in congressional debates and elsewhere in 1938, it is reasonable to infer that all of those unrecorded votes were overwhelmingly favorable. In any case, if the congressional debates that preceded the votes are any indication, very few of the congressmen who voted "no" did so because they opposed the concept of competition–limiting regulation.

37. Act, Section 406(b)(3).

38. Civil Aeronautics Act, Section 401(e)(1), U.S. *Statutes at Large* 52:988 (1938). This provision gave automatic grandfather authority to applicants that operated as air carriers "continuously" from May 14, 1938, until the effective date of the act, which turned out to be August 22, 1938.

39. More specifically, Roosevelt believed that deregulation of the railroads would incite rates war and bankruptcies like those that occurred in the railroad industry in the late nineteenth century.

40. *New York Times,* 18 September 1932, pp. 1, 32.

41. One of the most prominent of the blue-ribbon panels that endorsed the concept expanding transportation regulation to equalize it was the National Transportation Committee, which was formed on October 1933 at the behest of a group of savings banks, insurance companies, and colleges. The committee's membership included former president Coolidge and its research staff was drawn from the Brookings Institution. The committee's conclusions are presented in detail in Harold Moulton et al., *The American Transportation Problem* (Washington, D.C.: Brookings Institution, 1933).

42. A survey of the literature in economics journals and law journals of the 1930s suggests that virtually no one prominent in academic circles opposed extension of federal economic regulation to all modes of transportation. Debates centered on the details involved in a proper system of comprehensive regulation, not on whether regulation should be extended in the first place. For example, see writings by William C. Cunningham, D. Phillip Locklin, Harold Moulton, Leo Scharfman, and G. Lloyd Wilson.

43. Act, Section 102.

44. Act, Section 401(d)(1).

45. Act, Section 1002(e).

46. American Export Airlines, Certificate of Public Convenience and Necessity, 2 *CAB Reports* 16 (1940); and All American Airlines, Certificate of Public Convenience and Necessity, 2 *CAB Reports* 133 (1940). Both cases are described by John H. Frederick, *Commercial Air Transportation,* 5th ed. (Homewood, Ill.: Richard D. Irwin, Inc., 1961), p. 149.

47. Delta Air Corporation, et al., 2 *CAB Reports* 447 (1941), as cited by Frederick, *Commercial Air Transportation,* p. 150.

Notes

48. CAB Economic Regulation 292.1, made effective August 22, 1938, and described by Frederick *Commercial Air Transportation,* pp. 181–182; and by Lucile Sheppard Keyes, *Federal Control of Entry into Air Transportation* (Cambridge, Mass.: Harvard University Press, 1951), pp. 177–178.

49. Richard E. Caves, *Air Transport and Its Regulators* (Cambridge, Mass.: Harvard University Press, 1962), p. 171; and Keyes, *Federal Control of Entry* p. 178.

50. Caves, *Air Transport,* pp. 172, 370; and *CAB Practices and Procedures,* p. 240.

51. As of 1949, the CAB defined large irregulars as nonscheduled carriers utilizing individual aircraft having gross take-off weights of over 12,500 pounds or maintaining aircraft fleets having aggregate gross take-off weights of over 25,000 pounds; the CAB classified all other nonscheduled carriers as "small irregulars." Frederick, *Commercial Air Transportation,* p. 182.

52. For detailed accounts of the CAB's actions to restrict the nonscheduled carriers' operating exemption, see Keyes, *Federal Control Entry,* pp. 192–198; and United States, House Committee on the Judiciary, Antitrust Subcommittee, *Report Pursuant to H.R. 107: The Airlines Industry, H.R. 1328,* 85th Cong., 1st sess., 1957 excerpted in *CAB Practices and Procedures,* pp. 231–243.

53. *CAB Practices and Procedures,* pp. 244–246; and Frederick, *Commercial Air Transportation,* pp. 187–191. The CAB's certification of the supplementals was disallowed in April 1960 by the U.S. Court of Appeals for the D.C. Circuit and then reinstated on a temporary basis by legislation Congress passed in July 1960 and on a permanent basis by legislation Congress passed in July 1962.

54. Information supplied by Civil Aeronautics Board to Senate Subcommittee on Administrative Practice and Procedure, in United States, Senate Committee on the Judiciary, Subcommittee on Administrative Practice and Procedure, *Hearings on Civil Aeronautics Board Practices and Procedures,* 94th Cong., 1st sess., 1975, vol. 1 of Appendix, pp. 334–347.

55. The CAB's insistence on confining new entrants to peripheral specialty services is reflected by the names given to the various classifications of air carriers:
—trunk air carriers (American, Continental, Delta, Eastern, Northwest, TWA, United, and the other airlines that were certificated in 1938 under the "grandfather" clause of the Civil Aeronautics Act and that have always devoted most if not all of their operations to routes between major cities—in other words, to "trunkline" routes);
—local-service air carriers (Allegheny, Frontier, Ozark, Piedmont, and the other airlines that were certificated in the 1940s and early 1950s to provide scheduled passenger service on a subsidized basis to lightly traveled routes that trunk carriers wanted to abandon or that had never received scheduled air service);
—Alaskan air carriers and Hawaiian air carriers (airlines certificated to provide scheduled passenger service within Alaska or within Hawaii);
—all-cargo air carriers (carriers lacking any authority to carry fare-paying passengers); and
—air taxis and commuter air carriers (airlines operating small aircraft whose seating capacity and take-off weights are low enough to qualify for an automatic exemption from CAB regulation).
After 1965, as the CAB allowed local-service carriers to serve an increasing number of major routes in competition with the trunk carriers, the functional distinction between the two carrier classifications began to blur. However, until the late 1970s, when the CAB adopted a deregulationist route policy, the Board persisted in refusing to allow *newly* certificated airlines to enter routes served by the trunk carriers—or even by the local-service carriers. Ibid., pp. 331–332.

56. 14 *CAB Reports* 720 (1951).

57. An additional seventeen irregular carriers also filed applications, but the high legal costs involved in pressing their applications and the low likelihood of success caused all of them to drop out of the case before the Board rendered its final decision. Caves, *Air Transport,* p. 173.

58. Ibid.

59. For a description of this pressure, see Ibid, pp. 271–287.

60. *CAB Practices and Procedures,* pp. 220–225, 227; and George C. Eads, *The Local Service Airline Experiment* (Washington, D.C.: Brookings Institution, 1972), pp. 42, 97–104.

Notes

61. Between 1938 and 1974, the CAB aroused only two major congressional bursts of criticism for being unduly anticompetitive: one came in the early 1950s from the Senate Select Committee on Small Business, chaired by Senator John Sparkman; the other came in the late 1950s from the House Antitrust Subcommittee, chaired by Representative Emanuel Celler. Both committees held extensive hearings examining burdens imposed by the CAB on the irregular carriers and also issued reports recommending procompetitive changes in CAB policy. (See United States, Senate Select Committee on Small Business, *Hearings on the Role of Irregular Airlines in the United States Air Transportation Industry*, 82nd Cong., 1st sess., 1951; Senate Select Committee on Small Business, *Hearings on the Future of Irregular Airlines in the United States Air Transportation Industry*, 83rd Cong., 1st sess., 1953; Senate Select Committee on Small Business, Senate Report 822: *The Future of Irregular Airlines in United States Air Transportation*, 83rd Cong., 1st sess., 1953; House Committee on the Judiciary, Antitrust Subcommittee, *Hearings on Monopoly Problems in Regulated Industries—Airlines*, 84th Cong., 2d sess., 1956; and House Committee on the Judiciary, Antitrust Subcommittee, *Report Pursuant to H.R. 107: The Airlines Industry, H.R. 1328*, 85th Cong., 1st sess., 1957.

It is arguable that both committees, especially the Small Business Committee, were more alarmed about CAB regulation having put irregulars out of business than about CAB regulation having passed up opportunities to promote low-fare service. Indeed, if not for the post-World War II growth of the irregulars and the CAB's apparent high-handedness in restricting them, the CAB even during the 1950s might not have faced any serious challenges to the anticompetitiveness of its policies.

62. See note 13.

63. The Administrative Procedure Act of 1946 (U.S. *Statutes at Large* 60:237) and subsequent amendments to it have established procedural requirements applying generally to federal regulatory agencies.

64. See *CAB Practices and Procedures*, pp. 249–250; Caves, *Air Transport*, pp. 144–151; and Civil Aeronautics Board, Bureau of Operating Rights, *The Domestic Route System: Analysis and Policy Recommendations* (a staff study), October 1974, pp. 33–37. (*The Domestic Route System* is reprinted in *Hearings on Civil Aeronautics Board Practices and Procedures*, vol. 4 of Appendix, pp. 2235 ff.)

65. See Caves *Air Transport*, pp. 271–287.

66. For example, see U.S. Commission on Organization of the Executive Branch of the Government, *The Hoover Commission Report on Organization of the Executive Branch of the Government* (New York: McGraw-Hill, 1949), pp. 429–439; James M. Landis, *Report on Regulatory Agencies to the President-elect*, released as a committee print by the U.S. Senate Committee on the Judiciary, 86th Cong., 2nd sess., 1960; and U.S. President's Advisory Council on Executive Organization (commonly called the Ash Council after its chairman, Roy L. Ash), *A New Regulatory Framework: Report on Selected Independent Regulatory Agencies* (Washington, D.C.: U.S. Government Printing Office, 1971).

67. See note 61.

68. The leading proderegulation works published before the mid–1960s on CAB policy were Caves and Keyes, both cited above.

69. William A. Jordan, *Airline Regulation in America: Effects and Imperfections* (Baltimore: The Johns Hopkins Press, 1970), pp. 279–281, 285.

70. Michael E. Levine, "Is Regulation Necessary? California Air Transportation and National Regulatory Policy," *Yale Law Journal*, 74 (1964–1965): 1433.

71. *CAB Practices and Procedures*, p. 41.

72. Simat, Helliesen, and Eichner, Inc., *An Analysis of the Intrastate Air Carrier Regulatory Forum*, January 1976 (prepared for the U.S. Department of Transportation, Washington, D.C.), vol. 1, Appendix Exhibit 1.

73. *CAB Practices and Procedures*, p. 41.

74. Simat et al., *An Analysis* vol. 2, p. II–96.

75. PSA put 158 seats in each of its Boeing 727–200 aircraft, while CAB-certificated carriers put an average of 125 seats in each of the same aircraft. *CAB Practices and Procedures*, p. 45, 45n. Southwest's seating configurations tended to be as dense as PSA's.

76. Simat et al., *An Analysis*, vol. 2, p. V–14.

77. *CAB Practices and Procedures*, p. 44.

78. Simat et al., *An Analysis*, vol. 1, pp. 4–5. The intrastate airlines' use in some cities of airports more convenient to travelers than those used by CAB-certificated carriers no doubt contributed to the increase.

79. Ibid., vol. 1, pp. 6–7; vol. 2, pp. VI–20, VI–21.

80. George W. Douglas and James C. Miller III, *Economic Regulation of Domestic Air Transport: Theory and Policy* (Washington, D.C.: Brookings Institution, 1972), pp. 39–57. and testimony by Alfred E. Kahn in United States, Senate Committee on the Judiciary, Subcommittee on Administrative Practice and Procedure, *Hearings on Oversight of Civil Aeronautics Board Practices and Procedures*, 94th Cong., 1st sess., 1975, vol. 1, pp. 90–91.

81. Of course, the primary incentive for any profit–oriented firm to reduce its prices (or to improve quality without charging extra for it) is to gain an edge on its rivals and thereby to attract enough new business to increase profits. And a firm's profits benefit most from a price reduction during the period before the firm's competitors respond with reductions of their own; thereafter, the firm's profits might well be lower than they were originally. The fewer firms there are in a particular market, the faster a price reduction by one firm becomes a market-wide reduction and thereby loses its profit-boosting capability. (After all, the fewer firms there are, the faster consumers can find out which firm in the industry gives them the most for their money and the faster they will flock to that firm—and the easier it is for the various firms to keep track of changes in each other's marketing practices and of the need for changes in their own practices.)

Therefore, the competitiveness of markets inhabited by only a few firms is likely to depend on how easily new firms can enter. If there is a high probability of new firms entering whenever the incumbent firms' prices rise "too high," then the incumbents will be compelled by the *threat* of entry to keep their prices competitively low; on the other hand, if there are impenetrable barriers to entry—barriers stemming from regulation or other factors—the few firms, realizing the futility of trying to underprice each other, could be expected to abstain from price competition.

82. More specifically, the capital costs associated with starting an airline (for example, costs of buying aircraft and maintenance equipment and of securing access to airport facilities) need not be large; and economies of scale are slight enough that per–unit operating costs will not necessarily be much higher for small carriers just starting business than for large, well-established carriers in the same market. Thus, new airlines that operate efficiently should have a reasonable chance of competing successfully against previously existing carriers.

For detailed discussions of barriers to entry in the airline industry, see Caves, *Air Transport*, pp. 55–97; and *Report of the CAB Special Staff on Regulatory Reform*, pp. 98–124.

83. See, for example, the CAB's decisions on the *Transcontinental Coach-Type Service Case*, 14 *CAB Reports* 720 (1951); and *Milwaukee-Chicago-New York Restrictions, Reopened*, 18 *CAB Reports* 586 (1954).

84. In 1972, as part of the Domestic Passenger-Fare Investigation, the CAB formally adopted the procedure of evaluating proposed discounts using a "profit-impact test"—a procedure that the Board previously had invoked on an ad hoc basis in rate cases. Under this procedure, the Board automatically disapproved the discount unless the carrier proposing the discount could convince the Board that the discount would not endanger either its own profits or those of the carriers' competitors. CAB Order 72–12–18, December 5, 1972, reprinted in Civil Aeronautics Board, *Domestic Passenger-Fare Investigation, January 1970 to December 1974* (Washington, D.C.: U.S. Government Printing Office), pp. 226, 235, 253.

85. *The Domestic Route System*, p. 52; and Lucile S. Keyes, "A Survey of Route Entry Awards by the CAB, 1969–1974," in *Hearings on Civil Aeronautics Board Practices and Procedures*, vol. 4 of Appendix, pp. 2563–2564.

86. *Report of the CAB Special Staff on Regulatory Reform*, pp. 93–95.

87. For a summary of CAB-approved mergers of scheduled passenger airlines, see *CAB Practices and Procedures*, pp. 222, 252.

88. *Report of the CAB Special Staff on Regulatory Reform*, p. 149.

89. The average fare per mile (commonly called the "yield" per revenue passenger-mile) charged by CAB-certificated airlines for scheduled service was 5.50 cents in 1938, 6.30 cents in 1948, 5.80 cents in 1958, and 5.46 cents in 1968. Civil Aeronautics Board,

Notes

Reports to Congress, fiscal year 1977 and transitional quarter (Washington, D.C.: U.S. Government Printing Office, 1978), p. 140 (table 17). During the twenty-four-year period from 1947 through 1970, the real fare (the average fare per mile divided by the Consumer Price Index) fell during nineteen years and rose during only five. None of the yearly increases was greater than 5.4 percent. Civil Aeronautics Board, *The Domestic Route System*, Appendix A, table 16.

90. Until 1978, most congressmen viewed abolition of CAB restraints on competition as infeasible if not irresponsible. Hence, debates on reducing CAB regulation commonly focused not on "airline deregulation" but on "aviation regulatory reform," which connoted a moderate reduction stopping far short of full-fledged deregulation. It is notable that no prominent regulation-reducing bill before 1978 had the word "deregulation" in its title. Proposals preceding the Airline Deregulation Act of 1978, which Congress ultimately passed, bore such titles as "Aviation Act" (of 1975, S. 2551), "Air Transportation Act" (of 1976, S. 3364), "Air Transportation Regulatory Reform Act (of 1977, S. 689; then of 1978, S. 2493), and "Air Service Improvement Act" (of 1977, H.R. 8813).

91. *Report of the CAB Special Staff on Regulatory Reform*, p. 64.

92. The annual rates of traffic growth were as follows: 1965–1966, 17.4 percent; 1966–1967, 16.3 percent; and 1967–1968, 23.6 percent. *Handbook of Airline Statistics*, 1973 ed., p. 24 (part II, table 16). The annual rates of return on investment for domestic operations were as follows: in 1965, 11.8 percent; 1966, 10.3 percent; 1967, 8.2 percent; 1968, 4.8 percent. Ibid, p. 76 (part II, table 68); and *Supplement to the Handbook of Airline Statistics*, 1973–1974, p. 105 (part VI, table 1).

93. *CAB Practices and Procedures*, p. 250.

94. The average rate of return on investment for the CAB-certificated carriers' domestic operations was 10.3 percent in 1966 and 8.2 percent in 1967. The rate dropped to 4.8 percent in 1968. It fell a bit further in 1969—to 4.2 percent—and then plummeted to 2.0 percent in 1970. *Supplement to the Handbook of Airline Statistics*, 1973–1974, p. 105 (part VI, table 1).

95. CAB Order 73–11–101, "Dismissal of Stale Route Applications," November 21, 1973. Also see motion of World Airways for an expedited hearing, pp. 1–2, in CAB docket 27693.

96. *The Domestic Route System*, pp. i–ii; and Civil Aeronautics Board, memorandum from Director, Bureau of Operating Rights, to the CAB, October 2, 1972, re future of the Board's route program (notation #3320), in *Hearings on Oversight of CAB Practices and Procedures*, vol. 4 of Appendix, pp. 2490–2494.

97. Douglas and Miller, *Economic Regulation*, pp. 129–133.

98. The CAB's motives for conducting the DPFI were not only substantive but also procedural. In 1969, a group of congressmen headed by Representative John E. Moss brought suit against the CAB, attacking the CAB's lack of a clearly defined pricing policy and challenging a recent CAB-approved fare increase for having been unduly arbitrary and having involved excessive contact between Board members and airline representatives. Aside from finding ways of alleviating the airlines' profit squeeze without large fare increases, the CAB's main purpose for performing the DPFI was to establish a pricing formula that would make CAB decisions on fare levels more objective and automatic and less vulnerable to criticisms like those from the Moss group.

Commencing the DPFI in January 1970 (CAB Order 70–1–147), the CAB may have been anticipating the court's adverse ruling in the Moss case. In July 1970, the U.S. Court of Appeals for the District of Columbia reprimanded the CAB for its "intimation . . . that its responsibilities to the carriers are more important than its responsibilities to the public." Citing procedural improprieties, the court disallowed the Moss-challenged fare increase pending a complete reexamination by the CAB of the need for an increase. Moss v. CAB, 430 F.2d 891 (1970).

99. CAB Order 71–4–54, April 9, 1971, reprinted in Civil Aeronautics Board, *Domestic Passenger-Fare Investigation, January 1970 to December 1974* (Washington, D.C.: U.S. Government Printing Office), pp. 451–476. *(Domestic Passenger-Fare Investigation* is hereafter referred to as *"DPFI."*) The 55-percent standard applied to the so-called trunklines (defined in note 55), who account for more than 90 percent of the airline industry's revenue passenger-miles. The CAB through Order 71–1–54 also imposed a 44.4–percent load–factor standard on the local-service carriers, but it revoked that standard in 1974.

CAB Order 74–3–81, March 18, 1974, in *DPFI,* pp. 510–513. For a general discussion of the DPFI, see *Report of the CAB Special Staff on Regulatory Reform,* pp. 65–76.

100. CAB Order 72–12–18, December 5, 1972, in *DPFI,* pp. 226–266.

101. CAB Order 74–3–82, March 18, 1974, in *DPFI,* pp. 759–847.

102. After falling to 2.0 percent in 1970, the average rate of return on investment for CAB-certificated carriers' domestic operations rose to 4.3 percent in 1971, to 6.1 percent in 1972, to 6.3 percent in 1973, and to 9.1 percent in 1974. *Supplement to the Handbook of Airline Statistics,* 1973–1974, p. 105 (part VI, table 1).

103. Jordan, "Airline Capacity Agreements: Correcting a Regulatory Perfection."

104. Douglas and Miller, *Economic Regulation,* p. 133.

105. *CAB Practices and Procedures,* p. 113.

106. See, for example, Albert Karr, "Timm for a Change," *Wall Street Journal,* 7 August 1973, p. 36.

107. Donald Simon, "Senator Kennedy and the Civil Aeronautics Board" (prepared as case study C94–77–157 for the Kennedy School of Government at Harvard University, 1977), part I, pp. 15–16.

108. Ibid., pp. 16–20; and Stephen Breyer, memorandum to Senator Edward Kennedy, May 20, 1974.

109. *Los Angeles Times,* 13 July 1974, sect. III, p. 8, col. 5; and *Washington Post,* 16 July 1974, sect. D, p. 7, col. 2.

110. *New York Times,* 16 August 1974, p. 58, col. 1.

111. United States, Senate Committee on the Judiciary, Subcommittee on Administrative Practice and Procedure, Committee Print: *Procedures Relating to Minimum Charter Air Fares,* 93rd Cong. 2nd sess., 1974, pp. 8–9, 17. Senator Kennedy's Subcommittee on Administrative Practice and Procedure held oversight hearings in November 1974 on the proposed rate floor.

112. Representative Staggers, continuing to criticize Chairman Timm, held hearings to investigate whether the CAB had committed any improprieties in enacting the November fare increase. United States, House Committee on Interstate and Foreign Commerce, Special Subcommittee on Investigations, *Hearings on Policies and Procedures of the CAB: Ratemaking,* 93rd Cong., 2nd sess., 1974.

113. That report is *CAB Practices and Procedures.*

114. The Subcommittee on Administrative Practice and Procedure asked the various airlines to submit lists of the routes that they considered unprofitable and therefore would probably abandon in the event of deregulation. Analyzing these lists, the subcommittee found that airlines served only a small number of routes that were genuinely unprofitable and that could by any stretch of the imagination be considered cross-subsidized. See *CAB Practices and Procedures,* pp. 66–68.

115. See, for example, Caves, *Air Transport,* pp. 435–436; Eads, *The Local Service,* pp. 169–170; and *CAB Practices and Procedures,* p. 65.

116. See the Annual Report of the Council of Economic Advisers, in *Economic Report of the President* (Washington, D.C.: U.S. Government Printing Office 1970) p. 109; 1971 ed., pp. 128–129; and 1975 ed., pp. 154–155.

117. Simon, "Senator Kennedy and the CAB", part II, pp. 3–6, 12–16.

118. See polling data cited in "The Coming of the Tax Revolt," *Public Opinion,* 1 (July–August 1978): 30–31.

119. See note 5.

120. President Gerald Ford, economic message to Congress, October 8, 1974, in *Weekly Compilation of Presidential Documents* 10 (October 1974): 1241–1242. This address was well-known as the "WIN" speech ("Whip Inflation Now").

121. *Hearings on Oversight of Civil Aeronautics Board Practices and Procedures,* vol. 1, pp. 4–5.

122. *National Journal,* vol. 7, 27 December 1975, p. 1768; and *Aviation Daily,* vol. 222 11 December 1975, p. 217. Timm submitted his resignation December 10, 1975, but remained at the Board until March 1976, when his successor was sworn in.

123. See note 3.

124. Civil Aeronautics Board, memorandum from the comptroller (Raymond Kurlander) to the secretary and managing director (Edwin Z. Holland), December 30, 1974, re CAB Select Committee on Regulatory Reform.

Notes

125. Civil Aeronautics Board, memorandum from Robert Timm to Richard O'Melia, January 15, 1975, re Committee on Regulation.

126. Although many observers have claimed that President Ford appointed Robson with a "mission" to turn the CAB into a proponent of deregulation, Robson insists that he arrived at the Board with no strong disposition one way or the other on deregulation. He says that he took office only with an open mind toward change.

127. *National Journal,* vol. 7, 15 November 1975, p. 1563; and CAB Press Briefing, July 7, 1975. The study, entitled "A Proposed Means of Evaluating the Consequences of Changed Approaches to Economic Regulation of the Domestic Commercial Air Transportation System," was prepared by Harbridge House, Boston.

128. The experiment probably would not have produced dependable information because, among other reasons, airlines anxious to discredit the concept of deregulation would have had a strong incentive to try to manipulate the experiment's outcome—for example, by setting prices below cost in order to demonstrate the destructiveness of unregulated competition. Moreover, letting airlines freely enter, exit, and set prices on even a limited number of routes probably would have violated the CAB's statutory responsibilities for due process in handling applications and challenges to applications.

129. *Report of the CAB Special Staff on Regulatory Reform,* Executive Summary, pp. 1–2.

130. Indeed, the aviation subcommittees in both the Senate and the House held hearings on the Ford Administration proposal in spring 1976.

131. The task force and the steering committee both resoundingly rejected Chairman Robson's proposal for a deregulation experiment. CAB Press Release 76–4, 9 January 1976; and *Aviation Daily* vol. 223, 13 January 1976, p.60. Robson officially withdrew the proposal on January 11, 1976. *Aviation Daily* vol. 223, 12 January 1976, p. 50.

132. Minetti and West often complained that Robson was trying to assert "one-man rule," unilaterally developing initiatives such as the proposed deregulation experiment and announcing them to the public before consulting with other Board members. See, for example, Lee R. West (Address to the Association of Local Transport Airlines, Minneapolis, Minn., May 20, 1977) pp. 1–5 of mimeographed text. Friction between West and Minetti, on one hand, and Robson and a few of his top aides, on the other, was substantial and was widely recognized by CAB observers. See, for example, *Aviation Daily* vol. 224, 26 March 1976, p. 153.

133. The Ford Administration introduced the Aviation Act of 1975 (S. 2551) in October 1975; Kennedy introduced the Air Transportation Act of 1976 (S. 3364) in May 1976. Kennedy's bill was cosponsored by Senators James Buckley (Conservative, New York), Philip Hart (Democrat, Michigan), and Hugh Scott (Republican, Pennsylvania).

134. The chairman of the House Aviation Subcommittee (which is part of the House Committee on Public Works and Transportation) was Representative Glenn Anderson (Democrat, California). Anderson's subcommittee had only recently been created by a committee reorganization in the House (jurisdiction over aviation previously had been vested in a subcommittee of the House Committee on Foreign and Interstate Commerce), so few observers would even make predictions about how Anderson and his subcommittee would treat airline deregulation.

135. Financial-survival arguments had for years been advanced in favor of reducing federal controls on pricing and routes in the railroad industry, but not in the airline industry. When proponents of aviation regulatory reform began invoking such arguments to make their case, they portrayed reform as necessary to prevent the airline industry from "going the way of the railroads."

136. United States, Committee on Commerce, Subcommittee on Aviation, *Hearings on S. 2551, S. 3364, and S. 3536: Regulatory Reform in Air Transportation,* 94th Cong., 2nd sess., 1976, p. 348.

137. Ibid., pp. 348–349. Because of the ever-present pressure on regulators not to approve large or frequent price increases—a pressure that by the mid-1970s had grown especially strong with respect to the CAB—airlines could not expect fare increases to save them from the predicted profit squeeze.

138. Ibid., pp. 349–350.

139. Ibid., pp. 350–351.

140. Between 1972 and 1975, Senator Cannon advanced proposals to liberalize operating

guidelines for low-cost charter air service—including charter flights to Las Vegas, in Cannon's home state. (Specifically, the proposals would have liberalized rules for "Inclusive Tour Charters.") As Senator Cannon noted in an April 1977 speech deriding airlines for reactionary opposition to aviation regulatory reform, many airlines assailed Cannon's relatively minor charter-liberalization proposals with the same fervor that they later exhibited in attacking deregulation. For example, at May 1973 hearings on the charter bills, Paul Ignatius, President of the Air Transport Association, testified that

"Both bills permit unrestricted entry by any carrier into any market, causing a fundamental shift in the nature of the system which we believe would be bad for the public, bad for both scheduled and supplemental air carriers, harmful to shippers, and detrimental to the smooth working of the American economy.... *Enactment of such legislation could spell the beginning of the end of the Nation's air transportation system as we know it today.*" [Emphasis added.]

In August 1975, the CAB enacted the same charter-liberalization measure that was contained in one of the bills Ignatius so vehemently attacked (see note 148 on One-stop-inclusive Tour Charters). Insofar as the measure had hardly appeared to "spell the beginning of the end" for the nation's airlines, Cannon saw good reason to distrust airlines' dire forebodings about deregulation. Senator Howard Cannon, speech at the Aero Club, Washington, D.C., April 26, 1977, mimeographed text, pp. 4–5.

141. Senator Howard Cannon, speech at the Aero Club, Washington, D.C., June 22, 1976, mimeographed text, pp. 1–3.

142. Ibid., pp. 6–7.

143. See note 90.

144. See Cannon, Speech at the Aero Club, April 26, 1977, pp. 10–11; Lee West, address to the Association of Local Transport Airlines, May 20, 1977, pp. 6–8; West, quoted in *Aviation Daily* vol. 238, 3 July 1978, pp. 2–3; and statement of G. Joseph Minetti, in United States, Senate Committee on Commerce, Science, and Transportation, Subcommittee on Aviation, *Hearings on S. 292 and S. 689: Regulatory Reform in Air Transportation*, 95th Cong., 1st sess., 1977, part I, p. 139. Between 1976 and 1978, Richard O'Melia not only opposed the idea of total deregulation but was also the CAB's least procompetitive member. As CAB policies became increasingly procompetitive and then deregulationist in 1977 and 1978, O'Melia with increasing frequency dissented against Board decisions or, when he agreed with decisions but disliked their deregulatory implications, filed concurring opinions advising the Board to be more cautious on removing restraints on competition. See, for example, statements he filed to accompany CAB Order 78-4-121, April 19, 1978; Order 78-7-40, July 12, 1978; and Order 78-9-96, September 21, 1978.

145. Richard O'Melia, testimony presented February 18, 1975, in *Hearings on Oversight of CAB Practices and Procedures*, vol. 1, pp. 649–650.

146. CAB Press Release 75-69, April 11, 1975, announcing proposals for One-stop-inclusive Tour Charters.

147. CAB Order 75-7-98, July 21, 1975; and CAB Press Release 75-116, July 21, 1975.

148. CAB Press Release 75-127, August 8, 1975; and *Federal Register* 40 (August 14, 1975): 34089–34105. This action established a new form of CAB-approved charter: the One-stop-inclusive Tour Charter (commonly known as the "OTC").

149. CAB Order 77-1-94, January 14, 1977.

150. CAB Order 76-12-149, December 28, 1976.

151. CAB Order 77-6-68, *Laker Airways Limited—"Skytrain Service,"* June 6, 1977. This recommendation was approved by President Carter on June 13. (CAB directives affecting international air service are subject to presidential approval.)

152. *Federal Register* 41 (September 8, 1976): 37763–37775, announcing new rules approved by the CAB on September 1, 1976. These rules allowed a new type of charter: the Advance Booking Charter (commonly known as the "ABC").

153. CAB Order 77-2-133, February 25, 1977.

154. CAB Order 77-3-80, March 15, 1977. The other two airlines were TWA and United. Both argued that the CAB should not approve Super Savers but also promised to match American's discounts if it did. *Wall Street Journal*, 11 February 1977.

155. In addition to winning back passengers it had been losing to charter carriers,

Notes

American had a second motive for introducing Super Savers: an ardent opponent of deregulation, it hoped to convince Congress that regulatory reform was unnecessary for competition to intensify and low-fare service to expand in the airline industry. It is probably no coincidence that American unveiled its Super-Saver proposal during the same week (in early February) that Senators Cannon and Kennedy introduced a new regulatory reform bill and that Senator Cannon announced he would hold hearings in March on reform.

The travel requirements for Super-Saver passengers included making reservations at least thirty days in advance of departure and staying at the destination for seven to forty-five days before returning.

156. See note 144.

157. As of 1977, congressmen tended to be so skeptical toward deregulation that for Kahn to have publicly endorsed rapid and complete deregulation would have been worse than futile; it would have been self-defeating. To have a chance of converting opponents of deregulation into supporters of it, Kahn needed to convince them that he was open-minded and reasonable in wanting deregulation. In particular, he had to convince them that he was sensitive to financial problems carriers might suffer and to service problems small communities might encounter during any transition to deregulation. As of 1977, he could do so and still endorse deregulation only by confining his endorsement to *cautious, gradual* deregulation; if he had endorsed rapid deregulation, he would have been widely criticized in Congress as a closed-minded, "ivory tower" economist blind to the problems of applying deregulation theory to the real world. It is significant that, when Kahn publicly explained why in 1977 he supported gradual rather than rapid deregulation, he mentioned not only economic considerations but also tactical ones:

"My original attitude [favoring gradualism] was based, first, on simple intellectual caution [about dangers of economic dislocations]; second, on a *desire not to discredit deregulation by showing an insensitivity to the fears of both Congress and the financial community* about what a sudden total immersion in the waters of competition might do to the financial health of the industry . . ." [Emphasis added.]

Alfred E. Kahn, "Applications of Economics to an Imperfect World" (Paper presented to the American Economic Association, Chicago, August 26, 1978), p. 11 of mimeographed text. Also see Kahn, "Deregulation of Air Transportation: Getting from Here to There" (Paper presented at the Northwestern University Transportation Center, Chicago, November 6, 1977), pp. 8–9 of mimeographed text.

158. For example, to the position of director of the Bureau of Pricing and Domestic Aviation, Kahn appointed Michael Levine, a proderegulation law professor who in 1965 had written a major article attacking CAB regulation (see note 70). Other proderegulation appointments included Philip Bakes, who became CAB general counsel after working for airline deregulation on behalf of Senator Kennedy; and Donald Farmer, who became director of the Bureau of International Aviation after working for deregulation on behalf of the Antitrust Division of the Department of Justice.

159. See Kahn, "Getting from Here to There," pp. 8–9; and Kahn, "Applications of Economics to an Imperfect World," pp. 11–12.

160. In March 1978, Super Savers became available on all of the routes of all of the CAB-certificated scheduled airlines. While Super Savers spread, so did numerous other discounts offered by various airlines. For a summary of discount fares initiated on domestic routes in 1977 and 1978, see Elizabeth E. Bailey, "History and Recent Experience with Low Fare Policies in Domestic U.S. Air Transportation and Their Relevance Internationally" (Speech presented to the Symposium on International Civil Aviation Policy, Kingston, Jamaica, January 31, 1979), appendix to mimeographed text.

161. See CAB docket 31363, *North Atlantic Standby, Budget, and Super-Apex Fares;* and the *Official Airline Guide* (which is published semi-monthly and lists schedules and fares for all airlines).

162. The CAB-certificated scheduled airlines' traffic in 1977 was 193 million revenue passenger-miles, 8.0 percent above the previous record, which was set in 1976; their traffic during the fourth quarter of 1977 was 12.2 percent greater than during the corresponding portion of 1976. Their average revenue-passenger load factor during the fourth quarter

of 1977 was 57.4 percent, or 2.8 percentage points above the load factor for the fourth quarter of 1976. "Air Carrier Traffic Statistics," December 1977, p. 1; and *Handbook of Airline Statistics,* 1973 ed., p. 23 (part II, table 15).

The CAB-certificated scheduled airlines' operating profits for 1977 were $908 million, representing a 12.6 percent increase over profits of the previous year and breaking the previous record of $775 million, set in 1966. "Air Carrier Financial Statistics," December 1977, p. 1; *Handbook of Airline Statistics,* 1973 ed., p. 72 (part II, table 64); *Supplement to the Handbook of Airline Statistics,* 1973–1974, p. 45 (part IV); and *Supplement to the Handbook of Airline Statistics,* 1975–1976, p. 41 (part IV).

163. The "Peanuts" fare and other discounts that were free of advance-reservation requirements and length-of-stay guidelines were restricted to flights offered at particular off-peak times—typically late at night or early in the morning.

164. CAB Order 77–12–50, *Chicago-Albany/Syracuse-Boston Competitive Service Investigation,* December 9, 1978, p. 3.

165. See, for example, CAB Order 78–1–116, *Phoenix-Des Moines/Milwaukee Route Proceeding,* January 26, 1978, pp. 25–29.

166. CAB-certificated scheduled airlines earned operating profits of $103 million during the first quarter of 1978, up from the $8 million loss sustained in the first quarter of 1977; $450 million during the second quarter of 1978, up from the $245 million profit of the second quarter of 1977; and $705 million during the third quarter of 1978, up from $459 million. "Air Carrier Financial Statistics," at p. 1 of the March 1978, June 1978, and September 1978 editions.

167. The most prominent of these airlines were Continental and American. Their objection to gradual deregulation was that it could push them into a route squeeze, with other carriers being given permission to enter their markets but with their being unable to obtain permission to expand elsewhere. *Aviation Daily,* vol. 236, 9 March 1978, p. 51 and vol. 236, 13 March 1978, p. 68.

168. Kahn demonstrated an exceptional ability to explain economic concepts (particularly those arguing for airline deregulation) in simple, straightforward terms easy for noneconomists to understand. Furthermore, Kahn's sharp wit made his discussions interesting even to persons who are generally bored by economics.

169. This requirement is the "Ashbacker Doctrine."

170. Civil Aeronautics Board, "Disposition of Route Authority Applications, January 1965–December 1974," in *Hearings on Oversight of CAB Practices and Procedures,* vol. 1 of Appendix, pp. 379–385. See also "The Report of the Civil Aeronautics Board Advisory Committee on Procedural Reform," December 31, 1975, pp. 5–6.

171. Kahn, Speech to the New York Society of Security Analysts, New York City, February 2, 1978, mimeographed text, p. 6.

172. CAB Press Release 78–66, April 14, 1978; CAB Order 78–4–121, April 19, 1978.

173. CAB Press Release 78–79, April 24, 1978.

174. CAB Order 78–7–40, July 12, 1978.

175. *Aviation Daily,* vol. 237, 23 June 1978, p. 306.

176. See the statement of the House and Senate managers of the bill, in United States House of Representatives, *Conference Report on S. 2493: Airline Deregulation Act of 1978,* House Report 95–1779, 95th Cong., 2nd sess., 1978, p. 56.

177. CAB Press Release 78–38, March 14, 1978, announcing proposals for creation of the "Public Charter"; and *Federal Register* 43 (March 17, 1978): 11215–11226.

178. *Federal Register* 43 (August 18, 1978): 36604–36618, announcing August 14 adoption of proposals for the "Public Charter."

179. CAB Press Release 78–66, April 14, 1978; and *Federal Register* 43 (April 19, 1978): 16503–16512. Since the early 1970s, the CAB had set standard fares using the DPFI (Domestic Passenger-Fare Investigation) formula described on page 99.

180. *Federal Register* 43 (September 5, 1978): 39522–39536, announcing August 25 adoption of pricing-flexibility policy made effective on September 5.

181. CAB Order 76–1–88, January 23, 1976. As the Board itself noted, the rejection of World's application was based on purely legal grounds and did not reflect on the substantive merits of the application. In a statement issued the same day as the order, the Board recommended that Congress reexamine the legal barrier to airlines being certificated both as scheduled carriers and as supplemental carriers.

Notes

182. World Airways, Inc. v. CAB, 547 F.2d 695 (D.C. Circuit, 1976).

183. At Board meetings in 1978, Kahn frequently expressed the attitude that, since the Board could count on the courts to disallow any illegal actions, it should not let legal uncertainty make it timid in departing from precedent; when economically desirable policies are of debatable legality, the Board should go ahead with them rather than holding back (except, of course, when the policies are unquestionably illegal). Board member Elizabeth Bailey shared that attitude.

184. In the Senate, a regulatory-reform bill had been reported by the Commerce Committee on February 6, 1978 (pursuant to an October 1977 vote of the committee) and was scheduled to be voted upon that spring. The bill, which was generally considered likely to pass, would have significantly reduced the CAB's powers to restrain competition but would have stopped far short of full-fledged deregulation. (See United States, Senate Committee on Commerce, Science, and Transportation, *Report on S. 2493: Amending the Federal Aviation Act of 1958*, Senate Report 95–631, 95th Cong., 2nd sess., 1978).

In the House, the issue of airline deregulation was still in committee, and many observers considered the odds of a significant regulation-reducing bill being reported—much less approved by the whole House—to be only about 50–50. As in the Senate, no bill providing for full-fledged deregulation had received serious consideration.

185. *Hearings on Regulatory Reform in Air Transportation* (1976), pp. 532, 534; and *Hearings on Regulatory Reform in Air Transportation* (1977), pp. 412–414.

The three other CAB-certificated airlines besides United supporting reform as of February 1978 were Frontier, Hughes Airwest, and Pan American.

186. For statements of the various airlines' positions on deregulation, see transcripts from the five rounds of congressional hearings held on the topic between 1976 and 1978. The Aviation Subcommittee of the Senate Committee on Commerce, Science, and Transportation held two sets of hearings: *Hearings on S. 2551, S. 3364, and S. 3536: Regulatory Reform in Air Transportation*, 94th Cong., 2nd sess., 1976; and *Hearings on S. 292 and S. 689: Regulatory Reform in Air Transportation*, 4 vols., 95th Cong., 1st sess., 1977. The Aviation Subcommittee of the House Committee on Public Works and Transportation held three sets of hearings: *Hearings on Reform of the Economic Regulation of Air Carriers*, 94th Cong., 2nd sess., 1976; *Hearings on H.R. 8813: Aviation Regulatory Reform*, 2 vols., 95th Cong., 1st sess., 1977; and *Hearings on H.R. 11145: Aviation Regulatory Reform*, 95th Cong., 2nd sess., 1978.

187. In terms of discount fares, traffic, load factors, and profits, the airline boom intensified markedly between spring and fall 1978—in other words, roughly between the time the CAB launched its deregulatory policy of multiple permissive entry and proposed giving airlines blanket approval for 50-percent price reductions to the time Congress passed the Airline Deregulation Act.

After spreading to a number of major markets in 1977, discount fares proliferated dramatically during the spring and summer of 1978. For example, in March 1978 the CAB-certificated carriers began offering Super Savers on all of their routes rather than on just a small proportion of them. See note 160.

During each month from March through October of 1978, traffic (in revenue passenger-miles) was between 14 and 22 percent greater than it was during the same month in 1977. During the period from June through September of 1978, traffic was more than 20 percent greater than it was during the corresponding portion of 1977. "Air Carrier Traffic Statistics," March–October 1978 editions, p. 1.

This surge in traffic enabled airlines to achieve substantial increases in load factors. Between March and September of 1978, average revenue-passenger load factors on CAB-certificated carriers scheduled flights during each month were 4.3 to 10.0 percentage points higher than they were a year earlier. In August, the load factor reached 71.1 percent. "Air Carrier Traffic Statistics," March–October 1978 edition, p. 1.

Airline profits for April through June 1978 were $450 million, or over 80 percent higher than the $245 million earned between April and June 1977. Profits for July–September were $705 million, or more than 50 percent greater than the $459 million earned during July–September 1977—and also greater than the airlines' *annual* operating profits for *every* previous year except 1966, 1967, 1974, 1976, and 1977. "Air Carrier Financial Statistics," p. 1 of the June 1978 and September 1978 editions; *Handbook of Airline Statistics*, 1973, p. 72 (part II, table 64); *Supplement to the Handbook of Airline*

Statistics, 1973–1974, p. 45 (part IV); and *Supplement to the Handbook of Airline Statistics,* 1975–1976, p. 41 (part IV).

188. This estimate is based on the average time needed for cases to reach decision after filing and on the lack of pressing circumstances (for example, the impending bankruptcy of an airline ostensibly threatened by the CAB's policies) that might have induced the court to issue a temporary injunction against the CAB before rendering the final decision. Addressing Delta's challenge against the CAB's multiple-permissive-entry policy, the U.S. Court of Appeals for the District of Columbia Circuit turned down Delta's request for an injunction. *National Journal* 10 (August 26, 1978): 1358.

189. As of early 1977, major moneylenders (specifically, banks and insurance companies) had regarded the airline industry as a dismally poor credit risk. (See testimony by Frederick W. Bradley, Jr., of Citibank and by William McCurdy of the Equitable Life Assurance Society, in *Hearings on Regulatory Reform in Air Transportation* (1977), part 2, pp. 687, 692–693. The industry's credit rating markedly improved during the 1977–1978 upswing in airline profits, but nonetheless continued to be significantly poorer than it would have been if not for the persisting uncertainty about what Congress would ultimately decide to do on deregulation.

190. *Aviation Daily* vol. 236, March 8, 1978, p. 41 and vol. 236 (March 20, 1978), p. 108.

191. Compare these new positions with Western's and Braniff's previous positions. For example, see *Hearings on Regulatory Reform in Air Transportation* (1977), part 2, pp. 517 ff.; and part 3, pp. 1191 ff.

192. *Aviation Daily* vol. 237, May 19, 1978, p. 113.

193. In particular, American favored giving the CAB power to impose capacity controls for the purpose of raising airlines' load factors. *Hearings on Regulatory Reform in Air Transportation* (1977), part 3, pp. 1394 ff.

194. *Aviation Daily,* vol. 237, June 16, 1978, p. 266.

195. The Senate passed S. 2493—an amended version of the "Cannon–Kennedy bill"—on April 19, 1978, by a vote of 83 to 9. *Congressional Record* 124:S5900. The House passed H.R. 12611 on September 21, 1978, by a vote of 363 to 8. Ibid., 124:H10331. (The House submitted H.R. 12611 to the Senate as an amended version of S. 2493.) The conference version of S. 2493 was reported October 12, 1978 and passed both the Senate (by a vote of 82 to 4) and the House (356 to 6) on October 14. Ibid., 124:H12636, S18800, H13449.

196. Airline Deregulation Act, Section 40, U.S. *Statutes at Large* 92:1744–1745 (1978).

Chapter 4

1. For varying versions of this thesis, see Samuel P. Huntington, "The Marasmus of the ICC: The Commission, the Railroads and the Public Interest," *Yale Law Journal,* LI, no. 4 (April 1952): 467–509; Marver Bernstein, *Regulating Business by Independent Commission* (Princeton: Princeton University Press, 1955); J. Murray Edelman, *The Symbolic Uses of Politics* (Urbana, Ill.: University of Illinois Press, 1964); Gabriel Kolko, *Railroads and Regulation, 1877–1916* (Princeton: Princeton University Press, 1965); and Kolko, *The Triumph of Conservatism* (Glencoe, Ill.: The Free Press of Glencoe, 1963).

2. 15 U.S.C. secs. 1–7 (Supp. I 1975).

3. 15 U.S.C. secs. 12–27, 44; 29 U.S.C. 52–3.

4. See, for example, Mark J. Green, ed., *The Closed Enterprise System* (Washington, D.C.: Center for the Study of Responsive Law, 1971), and Simon Lazarus, *The Genteel Populists* (New York: Holt, Rinehart & Winston, 1974).

5. *Report to the President and the Attorney General of the National Commission to Review the Antitrust Laws* (GPO, 1979).

6. See Brunswick Corp. v. Pueblo Bowl-O-Mat, 429 U.S. 477; Continental TV v. GTE Sylvania, 433 U.S. 36; Illinois Brick Co. v. Illinois, 431 U.S. 720.

7. See Robert H. Bork, *The Antitrust Paradox* (New York: Basic Books, 1978).

8. The chief sources for this account are William Letwin, "Congress and the Sherman Antitrust Law," *The University of Chicago Law Review,* XXIII, no. 1 (Autumn 1955): 221–56; Letwin, *Law and Economic Policy in America* (Edinburgh: Edinburgh University Press, 1966); and Hans B. Thorelli, *The Federal Antitrust Policy* (Baltimore: Johns Hopkins University Press, 1954).

Notes

9. For an account, see Solon J. Buck, *The Granger Movement* (Cambridge, Mass.: Harvard University Press, 1913).

10. See Henry George, *Progress and Poverty* (New York: Modern Library, 1938), and Edward Bellamy, *Looking Backward, 2000–1887* (Cambridge, Mass.: Harvard University Press, 1967).

11. See especially Thorelli, *Federal Antitrust Policy*, p. 110, and Letwin, *Law and Economic Policy*, p. 76.

12. Letwin, "Congress and the Sherman Act," p. 254.

13. This speech is reproduced in Thorelli, *Federal Antitrust Policy*, p. 180.

14. Ibid., pp. 180–81.

15. See John Sherman, *Recollections of 40 Years in the House, Senate, and Cabinet: An Autobiography* (Chicago: The Werner Company, 1895), II:1010, and Theodore Elijah Burton, *John Sherman* (Boston: Houghton Mifflin, 1906), p. 360.

16. *Report to the President*, p. 162.

17. Robert Bork, "Legislative Intent and the Policy of the Sherman Act," *Journal of Law and Economics*, IX (October 1966): 7–48.

18. Thorelli, *Federal Antitrust Policy*, p. 184.

19. Letwin, *Law and Economic Policy in America*, p. 183.

20. Richard Posner, *Antitrust Law: An Economic Perspective* (Chicago: University of Chicago Press, 1976), p. 25.

21. Corwin D. Edwards, "Thurman Arnold and the Antitrust Laws," *Political Science Quarterly*, LVIII, no. 3 (September 1943):338–55.

22. Edward P. Hodges, "Complaints of Antitrust Violations and Their Investigation: The Work of the Complaints Section of the Antitrust Division", *Law and Contemporary Problems*, VII, no. 1 (Winter 1940): pp. 90–95; Charles L. Terrel, "Processes in the Investigation of Complaints," *Law and Contemporary Problems*, VII, no. 1 (Winter 1940): 99–103.

23. Walton Hamilton and Irene Till, *Antitrust in Action*, Monograph no. 16 of the U.S. Temporary National Economic Commission, Investigation of Concentration of Economic Power (Washington, D.C.: U.S. Government Printing Office, 1940), pp. 27–30.

24. John Herling, *The Great Price Conspiracy* (Washington, D.C.: Luce, 1962).

25. U.S. Congress, House, Committee on Appropriations: Departments of State, Justice, Commerce, and the Judiciary, and Related Agency Appropriations, *Hearings*, 84th Cong., 1st sess., to 94th Cong., 1st sess.

26. *Hearings*, 91st Cong., 1st sess., 1969, pp. 784–85; 91st Cong., 2d sess., 1970, pp. 555, 561; 92d Cong., 1st sess., 1971, p. 1222.

27. Mark Green, ed., *The Closed Enterprise System* (New York: Barron, 1971).

28. The account of these hearings is given in: Robert M. Goolrick, *Public Policy Toward Corporate Growth: The ITT Merger Cases* (Port Washington, N.Y.: Kennikat Press, 1978).

Chapter 5

1. Richard Hofstadter, "What Happened to the Antitrust Movement?," in *The Paranoid Style in American Politics and Other Essays* (New York: Vintage Books, 1965), p. 188.

2. Ibid., p. 189.

3. For an argument that antitrust activity against concentrated industries is misplaced, see J. Fred Weston, "Statement of J. Fred Weston," in U.S., Congress, Senate Committee on the Judiciary, Subcommittee on Antitrust and Monopoly, *Hearings on Oversight of Antitrust Enforcement* (hereafter *Oversight Hearings*), 95th Cong., 1st sess., 1977, pp. 558–65, 569–71; see also Yale Brozen, "Antitrust Witch Hunt," *National Review* 30 (24 November 1978): 1470–77.

4. Mark Green, Beverly C. Moore, Jr., and Bruce Wasserstein, *The Closed Enterprise System: Ralph Nader's Study Group on Antitrust Enforcement* (New York: Grossman Publishers, 1972); compare this book with Richard Posner's "Antitrust Policy and the Consumer Movement," *Antitrust Bulletin* 15 (1970): 361. In contrast to Green, Posner holds that attempts to press antitrust into the service of the consumer movement are essentially opportunistic.

5. U.S. Congress, House, Committee on Appropriations, *Hearings on Department of State, Justice and Commerce, the Judiciary and Related Agencies, Fiscal Year 1976*, part 7, 94th Cong., 1st sess., 1975, p. 7; U.S. Congress, Senate, Committee on Appropriations,

Notes

Report No. 95–1043, 95th Cong., 2d sess., 1978, pp. 72–73; House Committee on Appropriations, *Report No. 95–1565*, 2d sess., 1978, pp. 23–24.

6. U.S. Congress, House, Committee on Appropriations, *Hearings, Fiscal Year 1976*, p. 7 (emphasis added).

7. Dean Ernest Gellhorn, "Statement of Ernest Gellhorn," *Oversight Hearings*, pp. 617–31.

8. U.S. Congress, House Committee on Foreign and Interstate Commerce, Subcommittee on Oversight and Investigations, *Hearings on Regulatory Reform*, vol. IV, 94th Cong., 2d sess., 1976, p. 625.

9. 38 Stat. 717 (1914), as amended, 15 U.S.C.A., sections 41–58 (1976).

10. 38 Stat. 730 (1914), as amended, 15 U.S.C.A., sections 12–27 (1976). Besides exercising jurisdiction in cases arising under the Federal Trade Commission Act (FTCA) and the Clayton Act, the Federal Trade Commission has authority over some cases that might be considered Sherman Act (and therefore Department of Justice) matters. The courts have ruled that conduct violative of that act is also an "unfair method of competition" and is thus subject to commission action under Section 5 of the FTCA.

11. 49 Stat. 1526 (1936), 15 U.S.C., section 13 (1976). For historical background on the Robinson-Patman Act, see Joseph C. Palamountain, Jr., *The Politics of Distribution* (Cambridge, Mass.: Harvard University Press, 1962), and Merle Fainsod, Lincoln Gordon, and Joseph Palamountain, Jr., *Government and the Economy* (New York: Norton, 1959).

12. In affecting the behavior of business, the five commissioners need not resort to adjudicatory proceedings. The agency's methods include trade practice conferences, the issuance of guides, and advisory opinions. These means are seldom used in antitrust proceedings. See, e.g., Earl Kintner, *An Antitrust Primer*, 2nd ed. (New York: Macmillan, 1973), pp. 143–147.

Should the agency decide that a complaint may be in order—that is, that the Commission, upon the recommendations of staff attorneys and (sometimes) economists, should prosecute—then the respondent can indicate its willingness to sign a consent order, a formal document by which the business or company certifies that the challenged practices will be discontinued. The consent order is negotiated with various members of the staff. If the Commission rejects the consent settlement, the matter is adjudicated through the normal processes. A hearing is held before an administrative law judge. His "initial decision," delivered upon the conclusion of the hearings, becomes the Commission's final order unless appealed within thirty days. In reviewing an appeal, the commissioners may affirm, modify, or reverse the judge's decision. The Commission's decision is appealable in federal court.

13. The conclusion that the FTC Act and the Clayton Act were the resultants of a diverse coalition of groups and person is in contrast both to those who contend that the laws enacted to bolster large corporations eager to extinguish competition or that the legislation was designed to defeat those large business interests seeking to increase their power. For the latter perspective, see, for example, Harold U. Faulkner, *The Decline of Laissez-Faire* (New York: Holt, Rinehart & Winston, 1951); for the revisionist view, see, for example, Gabriel Kolko, *The Triumph of Conservatism* (New York: Free Press, 1963). The legislative debates surrounding the acts can be found in *Congressional Record*, vol. LI (63rd Cong. 2d sess. 1914). For a fine summary of the events, see Alan Stone, *Economic Regulation and the Public Interest: The Federal Trade Commission in Theory and Practice* (Ithaca N.Y.: Cornell University Press, 1977), pp. 26–51. See also G. Cullom Davis, "The Transformation of the FTC, 1914–1929," *Mississippi Valley Historical Review* 49 (1962): 437–445; George Rublee, "The Original Plan and Early History of the Federal Trade Commission," *Academy of Political Science Proceedings*, 11 (1926): 666–672; Gerald Leinwand, "A History of the United States Federal Bureau of Corporations" (Ph.D. diss., N.Y.U., 1962); James C. Lang, "The Legislative History of the Federal Trade Commission Act," *Washburn Law Journal* 13 (1974): 6–25; Arthur S. Link, *Wilson: The New Freedom* (Princeton: Princeton University Press, 1956); Gerard C. Henderson, *The Federal Trade Commission* (New Haven: Yale University Press, 1924); Thomas C. Blaisdell, Jr., *The Federal Trade Commission* (New York: AMS Press, 1967); and Douglas Walter Jaenicke, "Herbert Croly, Progressive Ideology, and the FTC Act," *Political Science Quarterly* 93 (Fall, 1978): 471–495.

14. Pp. 181–182 of this section benefit much from Carl Kaysen and Donald F. Turner's

Notes

Antitrust Policy: An Economic and Legal Analysis (Cambridge, Mass.: Harvard University Press, 1959), pp. 11–18.

15. Ibid., p. 11.

16. U.S. v. Aluminum Company of America, 148 F.2d 416 (2d Cir. 1945).

17. A striking example of the triumph of the idea of the dispersal of power over that of economic benefit is the opinion of Chief Justice Warren in *Brown Shoe:*

We cannot fail to recognize Congress' desire to promote competition through the protection of viable, small, locally owned businesses. Congress appreciated that occasional higher costs and prices might result from the maintenance of fragmented industries and markets. It resolved these competing considerations in favor of decentralization. We must give effect to that decision.

Brown Shoe Co. v. *United States,* 370 U.S. 297 at 344 (1962).

18. The proposed Hart Industrial Reorganization Act was a deconcentration measure. See Harvey J. Goldschmid, H. Michael Mann, and J. Fred Weston (eds.), *Industrial Concentration: The New Learning* (Boston: Little, Brown and Co., 1974), chapter 7, pp. 339–426.

19. U.S. Congress, Senate Appropriations Committee, Subcommittee on State, Justice and Commerce, The Judiciary and Related Agencies, *Justifications, Fiscal Year 1978,* 95th Cong., 1st sess., 1977, p. 339.

20. Ibid., p. 344.

21. U.S. Congress, Ad Hoc Subcommittee on Antitrust, the Robinson-Patman Act and Related Matters of the House Committee on Small Business, *Hearings on Recent Efforts to Amend or Repeal the Robinson-Patman Act—Part 2,* 94th Cong., 1st sess., 1975, pp. 186–91. Also, Richard A. Posner, *The Robinson-Patman Act: Federal Regulation of Price Differences* (Washington, D.C.: American Enterprise Institute, 1976).

22. See William A. Niskanen, Jr., *Bureaucracy and Representative Government* (Chicago: Aldine Press, 1971); George Stigler, "The Process of Economic Regulation," *The Antitrust Bulletin* 17 (1972): 207–35; Richard Posner, "The Federal Trade Commission," *University of Chicago Review* 39 (1969): 47–89.

23. See, e.g., George Stigler, "The Theory of Economic Regulation," *Bell Journal of Economics and Management Science* 2 (1971): 3–21.

24. See Ralph Nader's introduction to Green, Moore and Wasserstein, *Closed Enterprise System,* p. viii.

25. Gabriel Kolko, *Railroad and Regulation 1877–1916* (Princeton: Princeton University Press, 1966), and Kolko, *Triumph of Conservatism* (New York: Free Press of Glencoe, 1963).

26. Alan Stone, *Economic Regulation and the Public Interest* (Ithaca, N.Y.: Cornell University Press, 1977). Stone argues that the public-ownership model should be used because other modes of business control—free-market, atomistic restructuring of industry, restructuring of industry at a lower level of oligopoly, full-scale public utility—are not viable. However, he does not, in my judgment, explain in adequate detail the distinctive merits of the public-ownership model.

27. Long, Schramm, and Tollison concluded that economic variables account for variations in the Department of Justice cases across industries. The most prominent determinant of case-bringing activity, they inferred, is that of industry sales. Variables more closely measuring performance—concentration, aggregate welfare losses, and profit rate on sales—play a secondary role. William F. Long, Richard Schramm, and Robert Tollison, "The Economic Determinants of Antitrust Activity," *Journal of Law and Economics* 16 (1973): 351–64. Long et al. drew upon data collected by Richard Posner ("A Statistical Study of Antitrust Enforcement," *Journal of Law and Economics* 13 [1970]: 365–426).

Siegfried, using different statistical measures, disputed the findings of Long, Schramm, and Tollison. He found that economic variables have little influence on the case-selection process. John J. Siegfried, "The Determinants of Antitrust Activity," *Journal of Law and Economics* 18 (1975): 559–74.

In another study, economist Peter Asch, employing still different statistical techniques, concluded (after surveying Federal Trade Commission and Department of Justice cases) that even statistically significant relationships between industry characteristics and antitrust cases do not indicate that the criteria underlying case selection can be inferred unambiguously. Moreover, "even if clearer inferences could be drawn, it might not be possible to proceed to very specific conclusions about policy effects." Peter Asch, "The Determinants and Effects of Antitrust Activity," *Journal of Law and Economics* 18 (1975): 575–81.

28. "Repeat players," those that are frequently in court, may seek a victory in a small case because the precedent set may have favorable implications for subsequent major prosecutions. See Marc Galanter, "Why the 'Haves' Come Out Ahead: Speculations on the Limits of Legal Change," *Law and Society Review* 9 (Fall 1974): 95–160.

29. One work that does so is political scientist Suzanne Weaver's *Decision to Prosecute: Organization and Public Policy in the Antitrust Division* (Cambridge, Mass.: Massachusetts Institute of Technology Press, 1977).

30. The data in this chapter were gathered between 1975 and 1978. Most of the interviews were conducted in the summer of 1975; in subsequent years, follow-up interviews were conducted to secure current information. Information is partly based upon over 100 in-depth interviews with commissioners (those in office in 1975), agency lawyers, economists, bureau heads, the agency secretary, administrative law judges, congressional staff, members of the private bar, and agency observers. I scheduled all interviews; on average each interview lasted two hours. Thousands of pages of documentary material were examined, many secured through the Freedom of Information Act. The commission, in the exercise of its discretion, granted access to many documents having to do with caseload data. Memoranda of the Bureau of Economics and the Bureau of Competition with respect to the issuance of complaints or the closing of cases indicate the different vantage points of lawyer and economist. In accordance with the terms of the grant of access, I will not state the names of cases, corporations, or individuals mentioned in the memoranda.

31. Information supplied by Harry Jordan, administrative officer of the FTC, January 1978.

32. Statement of Harry Garfield, U.S. Congress, House Committee on Small Business, Ad Hoc Subcommittee on Antitrust, Robinson-Patman Act and Related Matters, *Recent Efforts to Amend or Repeal the Robinson-Patman Act,* part 2, 94th Cong., 1st sess., 1975, p. 160.

33. See statement of Daniel Schwartz, U.S. Congress, House Committee on Small Business, Ad Hoc Subcommittee on Antitrust, the Robinson-Patman Act and Related Matters, *Recent Efforts to Amend or Repeal the Robinson-Patman Act,* part 3, 94th Cong., 2d sess., 1976, p. 8. In calendar year 1975, the Bureau of Competition received 2,069 complaints.

34. The Hart-Scott-Rodino Antitrust Improvements Act of 1976 (PL 94–435), 15 U.S.C. 13n, Title II, formally institutionalized the commission's premerger notification procedures which had been in existence for some time.

35. *Operating Manual of the Federal Trade Commission* (1975), chap. 1, p. 8.

36. Ibid., chap. 2, p. 1.

37. The terms "proactive" and "reactive" were used by Albert J. Reiss, Jr., in his book, *The Police and the Public* (New Haven: Yale University Press, 1971). I think these terms provide useful handles for grasping two kinds of mentalities or styles of decision making. I do not mean, however, to apply them too tightly or to imply that they represent "pure" types. The "proactive" approach involves planning and generally yields structural vehicles (for example, oligopoly cases) designed to attack market power. Yet not all structural matters—for example, standard merger cases that the commission has prosecuted for years—are products of the proactive approach (that is, involve extensive planning, cost/benefit analysis, etc.).

Generally speaking, when the term "structural" is used in connection with the proactive approach, I am referring to the mammoth, innovative investigations (for instance, *Exxon* or the *Cereal* case). Moreover, it should be noted in the course of an investigation of the proactive type, attorneys may uncover apparent conduct violations which they may pursue.

Finally, although the conduct cases that are the products of the "reactive" approach generally do not have economic ends, the prosecution of some of those matters could benefit consumers.

Notes

38. A public agency's announcement of its plans may not only heighten expectations among supporters of the organization's objectives but also invite opposition, which may seek to thwart the agency. See Edward C. Banfield, "Ends and Means in Planning," in *Concepts and Issues in Administrative Behavior*, Sidney Mailick and E. Van Ness, eds. (Englewood Cliffs, N.J.: Prentice-Hall, 1962), pp. 70–80.

39. James T. Halverson, "F.T.C. and the Food Industries—1974's Major Antitrust Emphasis," before the Eighth Annual Antitrust Institute of the Ohio State Bar Association, Antitrust Law Section, October 18, 1974, p. 1.

40. Statement of Harry Garfield, *Hearings on Recent Efforts to Amend or Repeal the Robinson-Patman Act*, part 2, p. 160.

41. Halverson, "F.T.C. and the Food Industries," p. 3.

42. "Position Description" of Assistant Bureau Director for Economic Evidence, 1975, p. 1. Michael Glassman, a University of Chicago trained economist, was a staff economist and later assistant director for economic evidence during the period in which the economists gained influence in the case-selection process. An aggressive and articulate leader, Glassman set the independent path which the economists have followed. In 1977 Glassman left the commission to become a private consultant.

43. Ibid., p. 2.

44. Data in this paragraph furnished by Deputy Director James M. Folsom, August 1976.

45. For a discussion of the role of the economist in the policy-making process, see Joseph Pechman, "Making Economic Policy: The Role of the Economist," in *Handbook of Political Science*, Fred Greenstein and Nelson W. Polsby, eds. vol. 6 (Reading, Mass.: Addison-Wesley Publishing Co., 1975), pp. 23–79; Robert Lekachman, *Economists at Bay: Why the Experts Will Never Solve Your Problems* (New York: McGraw-Hill, 1976); Harold Demsetz, "Economics as a Guide to Antitrust Regulation," *Journal of Law and Economics* 19, no. 2 (1976): 371–84; and Kenneth W. Dam, "Comment," *Journal of Law and Economics* 19, no. 2 (1976): 385–389.

46. See statement of Frederic M. Scherer before the Ad Hoc Subcommittee on Antitrust, the Robinson-Patman Act and Related Matters of the House Committee on Small Business, *Recent Efforts to Amend or Repeal the Robinson-Patman Act*, part 2, 94th Cong., 1st sess., 1975, p. 145.

47. Cf. Robert L. Heilbroner, "Economics as a Value-Free Science," *Social Research*, Spring 1973, pp. 129–43; Robert M. Solow, "Science and Ideology in Economics," *Public Interest*, No. 21 (Fall 1970), pp. 99–107.

48. The nature of the disagreements between economist and lawyer is discussed in detail in Robert A. Katzmann, *Regulatory Bureaucracy: The Federal Trade Commission and Antitrust Policy* (Cambridge, Mass.: MIT Press, 1980), pp. 39–54. There are many works dealing with the economics of antitrust law; for example: Carl Kaysen and Donald Turner, *Antitrust Policy: An Economics and Legal Analysis* (Cambridge, Mass.: Harvard University Press, 1959); Carl Kaysen, *United States v. United Shoe Machinery Corporation: An Economic Analysis of an Antitrust Case* (Cambridge, Mass.: Harvard University Press, 1950); Ernest Gellhorn, *Antitrust Law and Economics in a Nutshell* (St. Paul, Minn.: West Publishing Company, 1976); Frederic M. Scherer, *Industrial Performance and Market Structure* (Chicago: Rand-McNally, 1970); Phillip Areeda, *Antitrust Analysis, Problems, Text, Cases*, 2d ed. (Boston: Little, Brown, 1974); and Richard Posner, *Antitrust Law: An Economic Perspective* (Chicago: University of Chicago Press, 1976).

49. Kaysen, *U.S. v. United Shoe Machinery Corporation*, p. 16.

50. Areeda, *Antitrust Analysis*, pp. 18–23; Kaysen and Turner, *Antitrust Policy*, pp. 71–75; Scherer, *Industrial Market Structure*, pp. 96–97, 341–45.

51. Areeda, *Antitrust Analysis*, p. 38.

52. Joe Bain, "Workable Competition in Oligopoly: The Theoretical Considerations and Some Empirical Evidence," *American Economic Review* 40 (1950): 37.

53. Memorandum to the Commission from F. M. Scherer, Director, James M. Folsom, Deputy Director, and Michael L. Glassman, Assistant Director for Economic Evidence, Bureau of Economics, Regarding American Gas Association, reprinted in House Committee on Interstate and Foreign Commerce, *Hearings Before the Subcommittee on Oversight and Investigations on Natural Gas Supplies*, vol. I, part 1, 94th Cong., 1st sess., 1975, p. 615.

Notes

54. Statement of Harry Garfield, *Hearings on Recent Efforts to Amend or Repeal the Robinson-Patman Act,* part 2, p. 160.

55. These statistics were provided by the Office of the Executive Director. See also Meredith Associates, Inc., *Report to the Chairman, Federal Trade Commission, Attorney and Attorney Manager Recruitment, Selection and Retention,* July 15, 1976, pp. 12–14. The Meredith Associates *Report* is essentially a statistical survey with little analysis.

56. Meredith Associates, *Report,* p. 13.

57. *Oversight Hearings,* p. 359. In *Kellogg Company, et al.* (D. 8883)—popularly known as the *Cereal* case—the commission charged that four major manufacturers of "ready-to-eat" (RTE) breakfast foods had maintained a shared monopoly and noncompetitive market structure through restrictive retail shelf-space tactics, the proliferation of brands and trademark promotion, the artificial differentiation of products, unfair methods in product promotion and advertising, and through the acquisition of companies. Although the commission issued its complaint in 1972, the *Cereal* case, which relies heavily on an innovative "shared monopoly" theory, has yet to be resolved.

58. For a discussion of organizational maintenance and incentives, see James Q. Wilson, *Political Organizations* (New York: Basic Books, 1973), chap. 3, pp. 30–55.

59. *Oversight Hearings,* p. 359.

60. Such has been the fate of *Exxon* and *Cereal.* See *National Journal,* vol. 9 (9 January 1977): 1071–75.

61. The uses and limits of reorganization are discussed at greater length in Katzmann, *Regulatory Bureaucracy,* chap. 8, pp. 112–133.

62. *Report of the ABA Commission to Study the Federal Trade Commission* (Chicago, 1969).

63. Edward Cox, R. Fellmuth, and John E. Schulz, *The Consumer and the Federal Trade Commission* (New York: Richard W. Baron Publishing Co., 1969), pp. 172–73.

64. Richard Posner correctly perceived that the staff attorneys would seek trial experience above all else. He was wrong in believing that the commissioners would not bring actions against major economic interests. Posner, "The Federal Trade Commission," pp. 85–87.

65. 64 Stat. 1264 (1950).

66. I have discussed the commission form of governance in detail elsewhere. See Katzmann, *Regulatory Bureaucracy,* chap. 7, pp. 86–111.

On the subject of political statecraft in the bureaucracy, see also Hugh Heclo, *A Government of Strangers: Executive Politics in Washington* (Washington, D.C.: Brookings, 1977), and Marver H. Bernstein, *The Job of the Federal Executive* (Washington, D.C.: Brookings Institution, 1958).

67. A bureau director who does not intend to seek employment in the private bar may care little about losing influence within the agency; at least in recent years, however, bureau directors have joined private firms which deal with the commission.

68. Analyzing how the commission weighs these various criteria is not a simple task for the observer, principally because the complaint itself reveals little about the thought processes of the commissioner. It merely identifies the respondents, states the alleged violations of law, outlines the effects of the possible violations, and sometimes includes a notice of contemplated relief. However, on the basis of analysis of agency budgets, interviews with the decision makers, and examination of their public testimony, some remarks can be made about the factors which the commissioners consider in their deliberations.

69. Statement of Commissioner Elizabeth Hanford Dole, *Hearings on Recent Efforts to Amend or Repeal the Robinson-Patman Act,* part 3, p. 81.

70. In reaching such legal judgments, a commissioner has the aid of three attorney advisers—personal staff members knowledgeable about FTC activities. Often the attorney adviser plays an indispensable role, especially since most commissioners are not antitrust experts when they assume office. By my calculations, the average tenure of a commissioner in the period 1961–76 has been 5.1 years—less than a single term. Of those commissioners sitting in 1972, only Paul Rand Dixon remains. Quite obviously, the inexperience of the commissioners could contribute to the difficulties in making informed judgments about complex problems.

71. For a thorough discussion of the White House appointment process with respect to

Notes

the Federal Trade Commission, see James M. Graham and Victor H. Kramer, *Appointments to the Regulatory Agencies*, printed for the use of the Committee on Commerce, U.S. Senate, 94th Cong. 2d sess., 1976.

72. Richard Cohen, "Making a Point on Appointments," *National Journal*, 9 (19 February 1977): 291.

73. Executive Office of the President, Office of Management and Budget, *Preparation and Submission of Budget Estimates, Circular No. A–11*, June 1975, p. 5.

74. At the 1976 confirmation hearings of Calvin Collier (whom President Ford nominated to be chairman), for example, only Senators Frank Moss (Democrat–Utah) and James B. Pearson (Republican–Kansas) were present. U.S. Congress, Senate Committee on Commerce, *Hearings on the Nomination of Calvin Collier to be Chairman, Federal Trade Commission*, 94th Cong., 2d sess., 1976, p. 83. Similarly, Stephen Nye had to confront only two senators at his confirmation hearings: Senator Moss and John Tunney (Nye's home-state senator). Senate Committee on Commerce, *Nye Hearing*, 93d Cong., 2d sess., 1974, p. 108.

75. See Magnuson's preface to Graham and Kramer, *Appointments to the Regulatory Agencies*, p. vi.

76. *Antitrust Trade and Regulation Report* (hereafter *ATRR*), No. 758, 4/6/77, p. AA-2; *ATRR*, No. 765, 3/25/76, pp. A-30-A-31; *ATRR*, No. 775, 8/3/76, p. A-5.

77. Professor Arthur Maass develops this point in a Harvard University lecture course.

78. There have been a number of House appropriations subcommittees which have successively had jurisdiction over commission matters. These subcommittees are the Subcommittee on Independent Offices and the Department of Housing and Urban Development; Subcommittee on Agriculture, Environmental and Consumer Protection; and the Subcommittee on State, Justice, Commerce, the Judiciary and Related Agencies. Of these, at least until 1979, only the Subcommittee on Agriculture, Environmental and Consumer Protection, chaired by Jamie Whitten (Democrat–Mississippi), actively monitored the antitrust affairs of the commission. Whether a subcommittee is active tends to depend upon the interest and style of the chairman.

79. My concern here is with the attempts of congressional committees to affect caseload decisions. Certainly congressional committees might affect agency activities more generally through legislation. One such example of legislation that originated in the Senate Judiciary Subcommittee on Antitrust and Monopoly and the House Judiciary Subcommittee on Monopolies and Commercial Law is the Antitrust Improvements Act of 1976 (90 Stat. 1383) which required in part that the commission and the Antitrust Division formulate rules and forms for premerger notification. See *National Journal*, no. 39 (September 25, 1976): 1353–55.

80. *ATRR*, No. 617, 6/12/73, pp. A-4, A-5; *ATRR*, No. 618, 6/19/73, p. A-8; *ATRR*, No. 621, 7/10/73, p. A-12; *ATRR*, No. 623, 7/24/73, p. A-1.

81. *ATRR*, No. 725, 8/5/75, p. A-4.

82. See statement of vice-chairman James M. Hanley (Democrat–New York). U.S. Congress, House Committee on Small Business, Ad Hoc Subcommittee on Antitrust, the Robinson-Patman Act and Related Matters, *Hearings on Recent Efforts to Amend or Repeal the Robinson-Patman Act, Part 2*, 94th Cong., 1st sess., 1975, p. 131.

83. *New York Times*, 22 November 1978, Section D, p. 3, col. 1.

84. For an example of the way in which the FTC handles requests of individual congressmen, see U.S. Congress, House Committee on Appropriations, Subcommittee on State, Justice, Commerce, the Judiciary and Related Agencies, *Hearings, Part 7*, 94th Cong., 1st sess., 1975, pp. 409–10.

85. The focus here is on efforts of attorneys and business interests to influence the commission directly. Certainly, private attorneys and business interests do not limit their efforts to the commission itself in attempts to affect the course of antitrust policy. For example, the private bar sought to pressure the commission to increase its Robinson-Patman caseload by working with a specially created Ad Hoc Subcommittee of the House Small Business Committee. In another instance, the "Business Roundtable"—an umbrella for leading corporate organizations—lobbied vigorously (but unsuccessfully) against the Antitrust Improvements Act of 1976. A business interest which believes that the commission is hostile to its interests may attempt to pull an end-run around the agency. For example, the soft-drink industry promoted a bill in Congress which was intended to

exempt from antitrust prosecutions those soft-drink manufacturers who allocate exclusive sales territories among their bottlers. The bill had as its purpose the rescission of antitrust actions, brought by the commission in 1971 against seven major companies, which annually sell $8 billion of soft drinks. See *National Journal*, 8 (28 August 1976): 1223.

86. See Long, Schramm, and Tollison, "The Economic Determinants of Antitrust Activity," and Siegfried, "The Determinants and Effects of Antitrust Activity."

87. Stigler, "The Theory of Economic Regulation"; George Stigler, "The Process of Economic Regulation," *The Antitrust Bulletin* 17 (1972): 207; Kolko, *Railroads and Regulations 1877–1916*, and *The Triumph of Conservatism;* Samuel Huntington, "The Marasmus of the ICC: The Commission, the Railroads and the Public Interest," *Yale Law Journal* 61 (1952): 467; see also Ralph Nader's introduction in Green, *The Closed Enterprise System*, p. viii.

88. James Q. Wilson, "The Politics of Regulation," in James McKie (ed.), *Social Responsibility and the Business Predicament* (Washington, D.C.: Brookings Institution, 1974), pp. 138–39.

89. Richard A. Posner, "Theories of Economic Regulation," *The Bell Journal of Economics and Management Science* 5 (1974): 353.

90. Niskanen, *Bureaucracy and Representative Government*, and Stigler, "The Process of Economic Regulation," pp. 230–32.

91. Posner, "The Federal Trade Commission," p. 86.

92. Elsewhere, I have discussed in depth the role of the FTC as a protector of competition, the various proposals designed to remedy the agency's problems in prosecuting the big structural cases, the FTC's relationship with the Antitrust Division, and have examined whether legal processes are fit to deal with economic matters. See Katzmann, *Regulatory Bureaucracy*, chap. 10, pp. 185–213.

Chapter 6

1. This deficiency of incentives probably pertains mostly to drugs that are marginally less safe and effective than competitive treatments. Catastrophically harmful drugs may produce costly damage suits that drug companies certainly wish to avoid, and may hurt a company's reputation and thus its sales of other products. The argument of this paragraph appeals to the economist's notion of "market failure" resulting from inadequate information. For a detailed treatment of this and other forms of market failure, see Charles L. Schultze, *The Public Use of Private Interest* (Washington, D.C.: Brookings Institution, 1977), pp. 28–46.

2. The concept of efficiency I employ here is not merely the minimization of budgetary or other costs, or the smoothness or rapidity of decision making. Rather, it refers to the ratio of benefits to costs associated with a program, including those not readily measurable in monetary terms. For this context, the principal benefits presumably are the health gains from protection from inferior drugs and the principal costs are losses of effective therapy resulting from any delay or discouragement of drug development or exclusion of useful drugs. Thus drug regulation is inefficient if the health benefits it achieves could be obtained with fewer health costs or if more benefits could be achieved for the same cost.

3. For a more detailed treatment of the 1906 act, see Oscar E. Anderson, Jr., *The Health of a Nation: Harvey W. Wiley and the Fight for Pure Food* (Chicago: University of Chicago Press, 1958), chs. 7–8. For a general treatment of consumer protection legislation and administration, see Mark V. Nadel, *The Politics of Consumer Protection* (Indianapolis: Bobbs-Merrill, 1971). See also James Harvey Young, *The Medical Messiahs* (Princeton, N.J.: Princeton University Press, 1967).

4. Lincoln Steffens, *The Shame of the Cities* (New York: Hill and Wang, 1963).

5. Ida Tarbell, *The History of the Standard Oil Company*, vols. 1 and 2 (New York: Macmillan, 1925).

6. Upton Sinclair, *The Jungle* (New York: New American Library, 1973).

7. The history of the Food, Drug and Cosmetics Act has been chronicled in one of the best studies of a single piece of legislation, Charles O. Jackson, *Food and Drug Legislation in the New Deal* (Princeton: Princeton University Press, 1970).

8. Ruth Lamb, *American Chamber of Horrors* (New York: Farrar and Rinehart Inc., 1936).

Notes

9. F. J. Schlink and Arthur Kallet, *100,000,000 Guinea Pigs* (New York: Vanguard Press, 1933).

10. Quoted in Jackson, *Food and Drug Legislation,* p. 17.

11. A good, though rather one-sided, journalistic account of the 1962 Drug Amendments is provided by Richard Harris, *The Real Voice* (New York: Macmillan, 1964).

12. See the testimony of FDA Commissioner George Larrick in *Drug Industry Antitrust Act,* Hearings Before the Subcommittee on Antitrust and Monopoly of the Committee on the Judiciary, U.S. Senate, 87th Cong., 1st sess., part I, pp. 426–27.

13. Ibid., part IV, pp. 1997–99.

14. As late as 1954, the AMA had specifically endorsed regulation to ensure drug efficacy. By 1959, however, its position had shifted. According to one commentator, this was part of a broad shift to the right in the association's position on medical issues resulting from the increasing prosperity of the medical profession, conflict between the profession and government on certain antitrust issues, and the controversy over Medicare. See Harry F. Dowling, "The American Medical Association's Policy on Drugs in Recent Decades," in *Safeguarding the Public: Historical Aspects of Medicinal Drug Control,* John B. Blake, ed., (Baltimore: Johns Hopkins Press, 1970), pp. 123–31.

15. For an analysis of problems of evidence facing the FDA that suggests increased emphasis on postapproval monitoring, and reduced reliance on premarketing controls, see William M. Wardell and Louis Lasagna, *Regulation and Drug Development* (Washington, D.C.: American Enterprise Institute, 1975), esp. chs. 5 and 13.

16. See, for example, the influential studies of the progressive period by Gabriel Kolko: *The Triumph of Conservatism* (New York: Glencoe Free Press, 1963), and *Railroads and Regulation, 1877–1916* (Princeton: Princeton University Press, 1965).

17. See Wardell and Lasagna, *Regulation and Drug Development,* chs. 2–3 and 12.

18. If only one or a few cases of bone-marrow disease occurred, one could not with reasonable confidence rule out the possibility that they occurred purely by chance—i.e., by the accidental inclusion of patients who were about to get the disease anyway—rather than because of the drug. In order to rule out this possibility, the number of occurrences must significantly exceed the maximum number that could reasonably be expected to occur by chance. Thus the patient population tested must be large enough to experience such a number of excess occurrences. In the case of chloramphenicol and bone-marrow disease, the number of patients required might be in the hundreds of thousands (depending on the frequency of the disease in the general population and the amount of certainty needed). Even for a side effect occurring once in every 100 patients exposed to a drug, several thousand patients might be required to establish the causal connection. For a detailed explanation of these matters, consult the exposition of hypothesis testing in any elementary statistics textbook, such as Hubert Blalock, *Social Statistics,* 2d ed. (New York: McGraw-Hill, 1972), part Three.

19. A naïve rebuttal would assert that the drug companies cover such costs simply by raising prices and passing them on to consumers (and thus often to government health programs or insurance companies). In fact, price increases that fully cover cost increases are not generally possible. New drug products often compete against old drugs which are not affected by increasing costs for drug development. For new drugs having no competition, the companies would charge profit-maximizing prices even if development costs did not rise; when they do rise, therefore, no further price increases will be helpful.

20. For a summary of frequent types of misprescribing, see Milton Silverman and Philip R. Lee, *Pills, Profits and Politics* (Berkeley, Calif.: University of California Press, 1974), esp. ch. 12. The authors argue that improved prescribing is far more important to public health than improving regulation of drug production and marketing.

21. For a discussion of alternatives available to organizations facing complex tasks, see Jay R. Galbraith, *Organization Design* (Reading, Mass.: Addison-Wesley, 1977), esp. chs. 6–8.

22. Quoted in Rita Ricardo Campbell, *Drug Lag: Federal Government Decision Making* (Stanford, Calif.: Hoover Institution Press, 1976), pp. 29–30.

23. Review Panel on New Drug Regulation, "Interim Report: IND/NDA Case Study —Tolmetin," in *Interim Reports,* vol. 2, (Washington, D.C.: HEW, 31 May 1977).

24. Review Panel on New Drug Regulation, *Investigation of Allegations Relating to the*

Bureau of Drugs, Food and Drug Administration (Washington, D.C.: HEW, April 1977), p. 475.

25. Ibid., p. 179.

26. The chairman of the panel was Norman Dorsen, a law professor at New York University. The panel also sponsored a wide-ranging set of studies on FDA decision making, the effects of regulation, needed legislative amendments, and so on, which are printed in the panels *Interim Reports*, vols. 1–3 (Washington, D.C.: HEW, 1977).

27. "Consumer surplus" is the amount, in dollar terms, by which consumers are better off for having purchased a given product. It is the value of the product less the amount paid for it. The measure of consumer surplus is derived from the demand curve for the product involved, which, in turn, is estimated from data on variations in its price and the quantity sold. Although consumer surplus attempts to measure health and other benefits of drugs as reflected in consumer preferences, it is very indirect and dependent on economic techniques and theories.

28. See, for example, Morton Mintz, *The Therapeutic Nightmare* (Boston: Houghton Mifflin, 1965).

29. See Henry G. Grabowski, *Drug Regulation and Innovation: Empirical Evidence and Policy Options* (Washington, D.C.: American Enterprise Institute, 1976), esp. pp. 1–8 (by Yale Brozen); and Wardell and Lasagna, *Regulation and Drug Development*, ch. 10. For indirect evidence that industry influence is limited, see Robert S. Friedman, "Representation in Regulatory Decision Making: Scientific, Industrial, and Consumer Inputs to the F.D.A.," *Public Administration Review* (May/June 1978), pp. 205–14.

30. Review Panel on New Drug Regulation, "Interim Report: FDA's Relationships and Communications with the Pharmaceutical Industry," in *Interim Reports*, vol. 1, (Washington, D.C.: HEW, 31 May 1977).

31. This argument is made by scholars and consumer advocates in reference to regulatory agencies in general. See, for example, Louis Kohlmeier, *The Regulators* (New York: Harper & Row, 1969), p. 77; Roger G. Noll et al., *Economic Aspects of Television Regulation* (Washington, D.C.: Brookings Institution, 1973), pp. 123–24; Common Cause, *Serving Two Masters: A Common Cause Study of Conflicts of Interest in the Executive Branch* (Washington, D.C.: Common Cause, 1976).

32. Paul J. Quirk, *Corporate Influence and Regulatory Policy* (Princeton, N.J.: Princeton University Press, forthcoming), ch. 5. The other agencies included in this research were the Federal Trade Commission, the Civil Aeronautics Board, and the National Highway Traffic Safety Administration.

33. See, for example, Marver Bernstein, *Regulating Business by Independent Regulatory Commission* (Princeton: Princeton University Press, 1955), ch. 3; Roger G. Noll, "The Behavior of Regulatory Agencies," *Review of Social Economy* 19 (March 1971): 15–19; and Noll et al., *Economic Aspects of Television Regulation*, pp. 120–26.

34. Quirk, "Corporate Influence and Regulatory Policy," ch. 4.

35. President Carter has supported several major legislative initiatives favored by consumer groups, including creation of a consumer protection agency, deregulation of the airlines, and deregulation of the trucking industry. He has also appointed a number of former consumer activists to important offices, including Joan Claybrook as Administrator of the National Highway Traffic Safety Administration and Michael Pertschuk as chairman of the Federal Trade Commission.

36. For an extended discussion of voluntary associations stressing the importance of organizational maintenance and enhancement needs in shaping their behavior, see James Q. Wilson, *Political Organizations* (New York: Basic Books, 1973).

37. U.S. Senate, *Regulation of New Drug R&D by the Food and Drug Administration.* Hearings before the Committee on Labor and Public Welfare and the Committee on the Judiciary, 93d Cong., 2d sess., 1974, p. 207.

38. See David Seidman, "The Politics of Policy Analysis: Protection and Overprotection in Drug Regulation," *Regulation* (July/August, 1977), pp. 23–37.

39. Quirk, "Corporate Influence and Regulatory Policy," pp. 131–32.

40. Ibid., ch. 3.

41. Ralph Nader, *Unsafe at Any Speed* (New York: Grossman, 1965).

42. For a more detailed account of the emergence of this criticism, and discussion of how the agency and its political supporters responded to it, see Campbell, *Drug Lag;* and

Notes

David Seidman, "The Politics of Policy Analysis: Protection or Overprotection in Drug Regulation," *Regulation* (July/August 1977), pp. 22–37.

43. Review Panel on New Drug Regulation, "Interim Report: FDA's Review of Initial IND Submissions: A Study of the Process for Resolving Internal Differences and an Evaluation of Scientific Judgments," in *Interim Reports*, vol. 2, (Washington, D.C.: HEW 31 May 1977).

44. Louis Lasagna and William Wardell, "An Analysis of Drug Development Involving New Chemical Entities Sponsored by U.S.-Owned Companies, 1962–74." Paper presented at the Conference on Drug Development and Marketing, American Enterprise Institute for Public Policy Research, Washington, D.C., July 25–26, 1974, summarized in David Schwartzman, *Innovation in the Pharamceutical Industry* (Baltimore: Johns Hopkins University Press, 1976), pp. 60–62.

45. Quoted in Review Panel on New Drug Regulation, *Investigation of Allegations*, p. 183.

46. The debate has become extraordinarily complex. For a detailed and balanced review of the economic literature, see Review Panel on New Drug Regulation, "Staff Paper: Economic Effect of New Drug Regulation in the United States," in *Interim Reports*, vol. 1, Washington, D.C.: HEW, 31 May 1977 (prepared by Charles F. Stone).

47. William M. Wardell, "A Close Inspection of the 'Calm Look,'" *Journal of the American Medical Association*, 239 (12 May 1978): 2004–11; Cf. Donald Kennedy, "A Calm Look at 'Drug Lag,'" *Journal of the American Medical Association*, 239 (30 January 1978): 423–26.

48. Wardell and Lasagna, *Regulation and Drug Development*, ch. 8.

49. Wardell, "A Close Inspection of the 'Calm Look,'" p. 2008.

50. Ibid., pp. 2009–10. Recent evidence of serious adverse reactions affecting the eyes, skin, and surroundings of the intestinal tract have led Britain to restrict use of practolol to hospitals; for discussion of these adverse reactions see, J. T. Nichols, "The Practolol Syndrome: A Retrospective Analysis," *Medico-Pharmaceutical Forum*, Publication No. 7, 7 December, 1977, pp. 4–11.

51. Sam Peltzman, *Regulation of Pharmaceutical Innovation* (Washington, D.C.: American Enterprise Institute, 1974).

52. See Robert B. Helms, ed., *Drug Development and Marketing* (Washington, D.C.: American Enterprise Institute, 1975), Part Two; and Schwartzman, *Innovation in the Pharmaceutical Industry*, esp. chap. 7.

53. Schwartzman, *Innovation*, pp. 69–70.

54. Ibid., chap. 7; David Schwartzman, "Pharmaceutical R&D Expenditures and Rates of Return," in Helms, *Drug Development*, pp. 63–80. Note that concern about returns on new drug development are not refuted simply because the drug industry as a whole remains quite profitable. If its profits result mainly from drugs developed in the past and current development appears unprofitable, the industry may continue to be profitable overall but make fewer new advances. Compare, however, more favorable trends noted in *FDC Reports*, April 2, 1979.

55. Frederic M. Scherer, "Comment," in Helms, *Drug Development*, pp. 121–23.

56. Peltzman, *Regulation of Pharmaceutical Innovation*.

57. William M. Wardell and Louis Lasagna, *Regulation and Drug Development*, chaps. 7, 8.

58. Department of Health, Education and Welfare, *Drug Regulation Reform Act of 1978: The Administration Proposal, Section-by-Section Analysis* (Washington, D.C.: Government Printing Office, 1978), pp. 24–25.

59. This judgment is based primarily on interviews, conducted in Washington in August 1978, with several congressional staff and executive branch officials involved in formulating and promoting the Carter administration bill. In addition, I examined transcripts of oral statements and written submissions by various interested parties presented at a series of HEW hearings on drug regulatory reform held in late 1978.

60. In addition, designing effective prescribing controls poses serious technical, as opposed to political, problems. Appropriate prescribing practices may be difficult to define precisely enough for purposes of law enforcement, and regulatory agencies may lag behind the medical profession in the recognition of innovative practices. Nevertheless, some controls would almost certainly be both useful and technically feasible. At a

minimum, for example, the FDA might be authorized to designate certain readily definable and clearly inappropriate practices (e.g., the use of antibiotics for the common cold, or the use of oral antidiabetic drugs for patients capable of receiving insulin) as presumptive medical malpractice. More subtle prescribing errors can perhaps best be addressed by mandating more detailed and stringent peer review. For an extended treatment of strategies and problems of controlling drug utilization, see William M. Wardell, ed., *Controlling the Use of Therapeutic Drugs: An International Comparison* (Washington, D.C.: American Enterprise Institute, 1978).

61. Cf. James Q. Wilson, "The Politics of Regulation," in James W. McKie, ed., *Social Responsibility and the Business Predicament* (Washington, D.C.: Brookings Institution, 1974), pp. 135–68.

Chapter 7

I am grateful to David Bussard and Karla K. Grinnell for helpful research assistance.

1. Much of the material in this essay is adapted from Steven Kelman, "Regulating Job Safety and Health: A Comparison of the U.S. Occupational Safety and Health Administration and the Swedish Worker Protection Board" (Ph.D. diss. Harvard University, 1978). A revised version will appear as *Comparing Countries, Comparing Policies: A Study of Occupational Safety and Health Regulations in the United States and Sweden* (Cambridge: MIT Press, 1980).

2. For an exhaustive discussion of the types of hazards in various industrial operations, see National Safety Council, *Accident Prevention Manual for Industrial Operations*, 7th ed. (Chicago: National Safety Council, 1974).

3. Bureau of Labor Statistics, *Occupational Injuries and Illnesses in the United States, by Industry, 1972* (Washington, D.C.: Government Printing Office, 1974), p. 3.

4. Ibid., p. 16.

5. Ibid.

6. Ibid., p. 3. This figure includes deaths among workers not regulated by OSHA, such as miners, government employees, and the self-employed.

7. See National Safety Council, *Accident Facts* (Chicago: National Safety Council, 1977), p. 3.

8. For a political scientist to attempt a bibliography on a field as broad as toxicology would be as ill-advised as for a toxicologist to attempt one on political science. The following books are helpful: Ted A. Loomis, *Essentials of Toxicology*, 2d ed. (Philadelphia: Lea and Febiger, 1974); National Institute for Occupational Safety and Health, *The Industrial Environment—Its Evaluation and Control* (Washington, D.C.: Government Printing Office, 1973); National Academy of Sciences, *Principles for Evaluating Chemicals in the Environment* (Washington, D.C.: National Academy of Sciences, 1975) and *Decision Making for Regulating Chemicals in the Environment* (Washington, D.C.: National Academy of Sciences, 1975).

9. Nicholas A. Ashford, *Crisis in the Workplace* (Cambridge, Mass.: MIT Press, 1976), p. 93.

10. David P. Discher et al., *Pilot Study for Development of an Occupational Disease Surveillance Method* (Washington D.C.: National Institute for Occupational Safety and Health, 1975), p. 41. Medical "conditions" are different from acute illnesses such as infections or strokes.

11. Ashford, *Crisis*, pp. 47–50.

12. Joseph A. Page and Mary-Win O'Brien, *Bitter Wages* (New York: Grossman, 1973), p. 139. Much of the account that follows is based on material from chaps. 7–8 of this work.

13. Ibid., pp. 137–39.

14. Quoted in Ibid., p. 140.

15. Richard F. Fenno, Jr., *Congressmen in Committees* (Boston: Little, Brown 1973).

16. Jack L. Walker, "Setting the Agenda in the United States Senate," *British Journal of Political Science*, 7 (October 1977), pp. 423–445.

17. The behavior is thus "satisficing" rather than maximizing. See Herbert Simon, *Administrative Behavior* (New York: The Free Press, 1975), ch. 5.

18. See the testimony for the Chamber of Commerce by Sharp Queever, *Occupational Safety and Health Act of 1968* (Hearings before the Select Subcommittee on Labor of the

Notes

House Committee on Education and Labor, 90th Cong., 2d sess., February 1–March 14, 1968), pp. 186–232. Information on the groups testifying and the general content of their testimony comes from these hearings. Four industry-specific trade associations also testified against federal legislation. The witness for the Manufacturing Chemists Association was less critical than the other industry witnesses. See testimony of John O. Lyons, Ibid., pp. 232–47.

19. Page and O'Brien, *Bitter Wages,* p. 144.
20. Ibid.
21. Ibid., pp. 170–71.
22. *Congressional Quarterly Reports,* 20 November 1970, p. 2813. This account cites several other amendments and the votes on them.
23. Testimony of Ralph Nader, *Occupational Safety and Health Act, 1970* (Hearings before the Subcommittee on Labor, Senate Labor and Public Welfare Committee, 91st Cong., 2d sess., September 1969–April 1970), p. 625. Nader's entire testimony appears in pp. 625–57.
24. These points are made in Walker, "Setting the Agenda," p. 436.
25. *Occupational Safety 1968 Hearings,* p. 704.
26. OSHAct, Section 2(b).
27. Ibid., Section 6(b)(5).
28. Ibid., Section 6(c)(1).
29. Ibid., Section 6(b)(1).
30. Ibid., Section 6(e).
31. Ibid., Section 6(a).
32. Robert S. Smith, *The Occupational Safety and Health Act* (Washington, D.C.: American Enterprise Institute, 1976), p. 62.
33. The idea that an inspector can act as "prosecutor, judge, and jury" by both inspecting and imposing fines is contrary to most people's sense of justice, and therefore the OSHAct constructs an elegant fiction, namely, that OSHA may only "propose" penalties. The OSHAct established a quasi-judicial body, independent of the Agency, called the Occupational Safety and Health Review Commission, and technically only the commission can impose penalties. If the employer is cited by OSHA for a violation and OSHA "proposes" penalties, these penalties "shall be deemed a final order of the Commission" if they are not appealed (OSHAct, Section 10(a)). For this reason, fines are always referred to in OSHA jargon as "proposed penalties." The term "fines" will nevertheless be used here.
34. See Kelman, *Regulating Job Safety,* pp. 270–72 for a brief discussion.
35. Loomis, *Essentials of Toxicology,* p. 189.
36. National Safety Council, *Accident Prevention,* p. 2.
37. See, for instance, Harry F. Schulte, "Personal Protective Devices," in NIOSH, *Environment,* p. 519; National Safety Council, *Accident Prevention,* p. 105; Julian B. Olishifski and Frank E. McElroy, *Industrial Hygiene* (Chicago: National Safety Council, 1971) pp. 66, 101, 126–27; and Vaughn Hill, "Control of Noise Exposure," NIOSH, *Environment,* p. 533.
38. Olishifski and McElroy, *Industrial Hygiene,* p. 499.
39. James Q. Wilson, "The Politics of Regulation," in James McKie, ed., *The Social Responsibility of Business* (Washington D.C.: The Brookings Institution, 1973), p. 162.
40. W. Lloyd Warner et al., *The American Federal Executive* (New Haven: Yale University Press, 1963), p. 230. See also David Truman, *The Governmental Process* (New York: Alfred A. Knopf, 1951), pp. 446–50.
41. These questions are discussed in greater detail in Kelman, *Regulating Job Safety,* pp. 294–326.
42. See Thomas E. Cronin, " 'Everybody Believes in Democracy Until He Gets to the White House': An Examination of White House–Departmental Relations," in *Perspectives on the Presidency,* ed. Aaron Wildavsky, (Boston: Little, Brown, 1975).
43. See Kelman, *Regulating Job Safety,* chs. 3–4.
44. Page and O'Brien, *Bitter Wages,* p. 173.
45. James Q. Wilson, *Political Organizations* (New York: Basic Books, 1973), pp. 331–332.
46. Ibid., pp. 334–35.

47. This is the subject of Kelman, *Regulating Job Safety*, ch. 5.

48. For an account, see Ibid., pp. 310–14.

49. John R. Ovavec, "Moves to Undercut OSHA Threaten Workers' Safety," *AFL-CIO News*, 23 (September 16, 1978). The AFL-CIO has also upgraded its safety and health staff.

50. Some of the criticisms on "Mickey Mouse" regulations were based on misunderstandings or misinterpretations. No individual employer had to worry about the details in OSHA ladder regulations; he could simply buy a ladder labeled, "meets OSHA requirements." OSHA requirements on guardrails stated recommended heights as approximate; the brunt of the requirement was to require the *presence* of guardrails, not to prescribe their height.

51. A pioneering presentation of these views is Murray L. Weidenbaum, *Government-Mandated Price Increases* (Washington D.C.: American Enterprise Institute, 1975). For a representative business leader's views, see Willard C. Butcher, "The Stifling Costs of Regulation," *Business Week*, 6 November 1978).

52. Society of Plastics Industry v. OSHA, 509 F.2d 1301 (C.A. 2, 1975) cert. denied, 421 U.S. 922 (1975).

53. American Petroleum Institute v. OSHA.

54. Ibid.

55. U.S. House of Representatives, Hearings Before the Select Subcommittee on Labor of the Committee on Education and Labor, House of Representatives, *Occupational Safety and Health Act of 1970 Oversight and Proposed Amendments*, 93d Cong., 2d sess., March—November 1974, p. 44.

56. U.S. House of Representatives, Hearings Before the Select Subcommittee on Labor of the Committee on Education and Labor, House of Representatives, *Occupational Safety and Health Act of 1970 Oversight and Proposed Amendments*, 92d Cong., 2d sess., March 1972, p. 173.

57. For information on the fate of these various bills, I am grateful to Mike Goldberg of the Senate Subcommittee on Labor for assistance.

58. *Atlas Roofing Co.* v. *Occupational Safety and Health Review Commission*, 430 U.S. 442 (1977).

59. Marshall v. Barlow's Inc., 436 U.S. 307 (1978).

60. For an account of these events, see "A Cloud of Cotton Dust Tests Carter's Loyalties," *Business Week*, 12 June 1978; Philip Shabecoff, "Carter, in Shift, Backs Stiff Cotton Dust Rules," *New York Times*, 8 June 1978; and Urban C. Lehner, "Work-Safety and Anti-Inflation Agencies Split Over Drive to Cut Regulatory Costs," *Wall Street Journal*, 3 August 1978.

61. "A Flawed Program to Curb Regulators," *Business Week*, 20 November 1978. See also Helen Dewar, "Regulatory Curbs Weighed in Anti-Inflation Plan," *Washington Post*, 18 October 1978.

62. An "ex parte" communication is one in which a contending party communicates with an agency official privately, without opportunity for cross-examination or questioning by opposing contending parties. For a presentation of the attack by regulatory agency defenders on this point, see Robert Rauch, "Legal Restrictions on Presidential Interference in EPA Rulemaking," mimeographed (Washington, D.C.: Environmental Defense Fund, 1978).

63. Robert Stewart Smith, "The Estimated Impact on Injuries of OSHA's Target Industry Program" (Paper presented to Department of Labor Conference on Evaluating OSHA, Annapolis, Md., 1975).

64. John Mendeloff, *Regulating Safety* (Cambridge, Mass.: MIT Press, 1979), p. 117.

65. John Mendeloff "Costs and Consequences: A Political and Economic Analysis of the Federal Occupational Safety and Health Program" (Ph.D. diss., Univ. of California at Berkeley, 1977), p. 328.

66. Ibid., pp. 106–15.

67. Murray Weidenbaum, "The Cost of Federal Regulation of Economic Activity" (Washington, D.C.: American Enterprise Institute, 1978), p. 4. Actually this is an estimate for total business investment in occupational safety and health, rather than an estimate of incremental compliance costs of OSHA regulations. It would thus be methodologically inappropriate to use this number as a numerator to estimate the cost per accident or cost

Notes

per life saved from OSHA, even if plausible numbers were available for OSHA's impact on occupational health.

68. Two presentations of this critique are Robert S. Smith, *The Occupational Safety and Health Administration,* and Albert L. Nichols and Richard Zeckhauser, "Government Comes to the Workplace: An Assessment of OSHA," *The Public Interest* (Fall 1977). For reasons of space, and because the idea has not made much headway in political debates over OSHA, I will not deal with the third argument here. See Steven Kelman, *Economic Incentives and Environmental Policy: Politics, Ideology, and Philosophy* (manuscript).

69. See Robert L. Hale, "Bargaining, Duress, and Economic Liberty," *Columbia Law Review,* 43 (1943).

70. For discussions of these questions, see Charles Fried, *Right and Wrong* (Cambridge, Mass.: Harvard University Press, 1978) and Ronald Dworkin, *Taking Rights Seriously* (Cambridge, Mass.: Harvard University Press, 1977), chs. 6–7. See also Steven Kelman, "Regulation That Works," *New Republic,* 25 November 1978.

Chapter 8

1. See "William D. Ruckelshaus and the Environmental Protection Agency" in *Public Management: Text and Cases,* eds. Joseph L. Bower and Charles J. Christenson, (Homewood, Ill: Richard D. Irwin, 1978), p. 102.

2. See "Message of the President Relative to Reorganization Plans Nos. 3 and 4 of 1970." (July 9, 1970); found in *Environmental Quality: The First Annual Report of the Council on Environmental Quality* (Washington, D.C.: Government Printing Office, 1970), pp. 294–300.

3. Clean Air Amendments of 1970, Pub. L. No. 91–604, 84 Stat. 1676 (1970) (amending the Clean Air Act, 42 U.S.C. Sec. 1857 *et seq.* (1970)), the Federal Water Pollution Control Act Amendments of 1972, Pub. L. No. 92–500, 85 Stat. 816 (1972) (codified at 33 U.S.S. Sec. 1251 *et seq.* (Supp. V. 1975)).

4. A distinction between "old" and "new" regulation, similar to the distinction made here between old and new agencies, can be found in William Lilley and James Miller, "The New 'Social Regulation,'" *The Public Interest,* 47 (Spring 1977): 49–62. A good source of information mostly about "old style" agencies is Clair Wilcox and William G. Shepherd, *Public Policies Toward Business* (Homewood, Ill: Richard D. Irwin, 1975). Murray Weidenbaum closely examines the costs of the "New Social Regulation" in his book *Business, Government, and the Public* (Englewood Cliffs, N.J.: Prentice-Hall, 1977).

5. See Roger Noll, *Reforming Regulation: An Evaluation of the Ash Council Proposals* (Washington, D.C.: The Brookings Institution, 1971).

6. See Theodore Lowi, *The End of Liberalism* (New York: W. W. Norton, 1969), p. 126. Lowi derives this notion about delegation primarily from the legal scholar Kenneth Culp Davis. See Kenneth Culp Davis, *Administrative Law Treatise* (St. Paul: West Publishing Company, 1958), especially pp. 9–53 and 144ff. of the 1965 *Supplement.* See also Kenneth Culp Davis, *Discretionary Justice: A Preliminary Inquiry* (Urbana, Ill: University of Illinois Press, 1977) and Henry J. Friendly, *The Federal Administrative Agencies* (Cambridge, Mass.: Harvard University Press, 1962).

7. Clean Air Amendments of 1977, Pub. L. No. 95–95, 91 Stat. 685 (1977). The entire act has been recodified in 42 U.S.C. Secs. 7401–4642 (1976); Clean Water Act of 1977, Pub. L. No. 95–217, 91 Stat. 1566–1611 (1977).

8. See Kenneth E. Warner, "The Need for Some Innovative Concepts of Innovation: An Examination of Research on the Diffusion of Innovations" *Policy Sciences* 5 (1974): 433–51; Lawrence Mohr, "Determinants of Innovation in Organization" *American Political Science Review* 63 (March 1969): 111–26.

9. Marver Bernstein, *Regulating Business By Independent Commission* (Princeton N.J.: Princeton University Press, 1955), pp. 263–67; Merle Fainsod, "The Nature of the Regulatory Process" in *Public Policy 1940,* eds. C. J. Friedrich and E. S. Mason, (Cambridge, Mass.: Harvard University Press, 1940) pp. 297–323; and Samuel P. Huntington, *Clientalism: A Study in Administrative Politics* (Cambridge, Mass.: Harvard University Government Department, 1950).

10. See Barry Mitnick, "A Critique of Life Cycle Theories of Regulation," working paper (Ohio State University, College of Administrative Science, 1978).

11. Lowi, *End of Liberalism,* pp. 125–56.

12. See note 6 for Davis and Friendly references.

13. For instance, see Robert Carr et al., *American Democracy in Theory and Practice* (New York: Rinehart and Co., 1956) and Kenneth Prewitt and Sidney Verba, *An Introduction to American Government* (New York: Harper & Row, 1974). Also note the comments Paul H. Weaver makes in "Regulation, Social Policy, and Class Conflict" *The Public Interest* 50 (Winter 1978): 45–47.

14. John C. Esposito, *Vanishing Air* (New York: Grossman Publishers, 1970) and David Zwick and Marcy Benstock, *Water Wasteland* (New York: Grossman Publishers, 1971).

15. Accounts of the passage of the 1970 Clean Air Act can be found in the following sources: Charles O. Jones, *Clean Air: The Policies and Politics of Pollution Control* (Pittsburgh: University of Pittsburgh Press, 1975), pp. 175–210; Elias Zuckerman, "Senator Muskie and the 1970 Amendments to the Clean Air Act," (Cambridge, Mass.: Harvard University Kennedy School of Government, 1976); J. Clarence Davies and Barbara Davies, *The Politics of Pollution* (Indianapolis: Bobbs-Merrill, 1975), pp. 52–56; and Henry D. Jacoby et al., *Clearing the Air: Federal Policy on Automotive Emissions Control* (Cambridge, Mass.: Ballinger Publishing Co., 1973), pp. 9–15. See also James Q. Wilson, "The Politics of Regulation" in *Social Responsibility and the Business Predicament,* ed. James W. McKie, (Washington, D.C.: Brookings Institution, 1974), pp. 151–52. Charles McCarry has written a lively biography of Nader: *Citizen Nader* (New York: Saturday Review Press, 1972).

16. Jones, *Clean Air,* p. 192. Also see Jacoby et al., *Clearing the Air,* p. 11.

17. McKie, p. 145.

18. See Simon Lazarus, *The Genteel Populists* (New York: Holt, Rinehart, and Winston, 1974), p. 158.

19. See Richard C. Leone, "Public Interest Advocacy and the Regulatory Process," in *The Government as Regulator,* ed. Marver H. Bernstein (Philadelphia: The American Academy of Political and Social Science, 1972), p. 55.

20. Ibid., p. 53 and Lazarus, *Genteel Populists,* p. 79.

21. See Davies and Davies, *Politics of Pollution,* pp. 49–52 for a description of the 1967 Air Quality Act.

22. See John T. Middleton, "Summary of the Air Quality Act of 1967," *Arizona Law Review* (1968) and Sidney Edelman, "Air Pollution Abatement Procedures Under the Clean Air Act," *Arizona Law Review* (1968) reprinted in James E. Krier, ed., *Environmental Law and Policy* (Indianapolis: Bobbs-Merrill, 1971), pp. 304–07 and pp. 321–26.

23. Esposito, *Vanishing Air,* pp. 161 and 158.

24. Davies and Davies, *Politics of Pollution,* p. 54.

25. Ibid., p. 55.

26. Ibid., p. 41.

27. Ibid., p. 45.

28. David Vogel, "Promoting Pluralism: The Public Interest Movement and the American Reform Tradition" (Paper prepared for delivery at the 1978 Annual Meeting of the American Political Science Association, . . .)

29. This list of tasks EPA had to perform under the 1970 act is selective. It does not include all agency's responsibilities. It is a broad outline of tasks that is appropriate for the purposes of this study. See note 6 for the citation of the 1970 Clean Air Act.

30. Again, the list of tasks is selective and is made for the purpose of this study. For example, the sewage waste-treatment program—a major funding program with respect to local governments—is not mentioned because it is an instance where the government is "regulating itself" and not regulating business per se. See note 3 for the citation of the 1972 FWPCA.

31. Resource Recovery Act of 1970, October 26, 1970, Pub. L. 91–512, 84 Stat. 1227. Federal Environmental Pesticides Control Act of 1972, October 21, 1972, Pub. L. 92–516, 86 Stat. 973.

32. Noise Control Act of 1972, October 27, 1972, Pub. L. 92–574, 86 Stat. 1234. The Safe Drinking Water Act, December 16, 1974, 42 U.S.C. Sections 300 (f) *et seq.,* Pub. L. 93–523. See "Toxic Substances Control Act," *Environmental News* (New England Regional Office, December 1976), pp. 13–17. Also see Office of Toxic Substances, "A Framework for the Control of Toxic Substances," (Washington, D.C.: EPA, April 1975) and Office of Toxic

Notes

Substances, "Draft Economic Impact Assessment for the Proposed Toxic Substances Control Act," (Washington, D.C.: EPA, June 1975).

33. *U.S. Budget, Fiscal Year 1972.*

34. Message of the President found in *Environmental Quality*, p. 295, see note 2.

35. See Alain Enthoven, "A Functional Organization and Financial Plan for the Environmental Protection Administration" (memo dated October 5, 1970). Douglas Costle, present EPA administrator, also played a role in devising this strategy. See William Ahern, Jr., "Organizing for Pollution Control: The Beginnings of the Environmental Protection Agency, 1970–1971," (Cambridge, Mass.: Harvard University Kennedy School of Government, 1973).

36. See Alain C. Enthoven and K. Wayne Smith, *How Much is Enough: Shaping the Defense Program 1961–1969* (New York: Harper & Row, 1971).

37. See Alfred A. Marcus, "What Does Reorganization Accomplish?—The Case of the EPA" (working paper, University of Pittsburgh Graduate School of Business), p. 10.

38. See Daniel P. Moynihan, "Policy vs. Program in the 1970's," *Coping: Essays on the Practice of Government,* (New York: Random House, 1973), p. 273.

39. Message of the President found in *Environmental Quality*, p. 294. See note 2.

40. This is the conclusion of the Council on Environmental Quality in its 1977 annual report. See *Environmental Quality: The Eighth Annual Report on the Council on Environmental Quality.* (Washington, D.C.: Government Printing Office, 1978). In 1977 CEQ decided not to include benefit studies in its discussion of environmental economics.

41. *Environmental Quality: The Sixth Annual Report of the Council on Environmental Quality,* p. 533; and *Environmental Quality: The Eighth Annual Report on the Council on Environmental Quality,* p. 323.

42. Robert Dorfman, "Benefits and Costs of Environmental Programs" *Society* (March/April 1977) pp. 63–66. See also Nancy Dorfman and Arthur Snow, "Who Will Pay for Pollution Control?" *National Tax Journal* 28 (March 1975): 101–15.

43. Paul McCracken, chairman, Council of Economic Advisers, Russell Train, chairman, CEQ, and William Ruckelshaus, administrator, EPA, in remarks about the Senate bill before the House Public Works Committee, *Hearings on H. R. 11896, H. R. 11895 to Amend the Federal Water Pollution Control Act* (Washington, D.C.: Government Printing Office, Dec. 7, 1971), p. 213.

44. *Environmental Quality: The Eighth Annual Report,* pp. 321–35.

45. National Academy of Sciences, *Air Quality and Automobile Emission Control, the Cost and Benefits of Automobile Emission Control—A Report by the Coordinating Committee on Air Quality Studies,* vol. 4, prepared for the Committee on Public Works, U. S. Senate, pursuant to S. Res. 135, approved August 3, 1973 (Washington, D.C.: Government Printing Office, 1974), p. 78, Tables 2–14 and p. 417, Tables 6–7.

46. Lester Lave and Eugene Seskin, *The Costs and Benefits of Air Pollution Control* (Washington, D.C.: Resources for the Future, 1977).

47. *Environmental Quality: The Sixth Annual Report of the Council of Environmental Quality,* pp. 533–44.

48. The eighth annual report estimates that there were 677,900 people employed directly for pollution abatement in 1974, p. 332.

49. See Alfred Marcus, " 'Command and Control': An Assessment of Smokestack Emission Regulation," (working paper University of Pittsburgh Graduate School of Business) p. 17.

50. Coal is cooked in a coke oven at 1900° F for 16 to 20 hours to produce blast furnace coke. Pushing control technology tries to reduce the fumes that escape when the coke is pushed out of the oven. After it is cooked, the coke is conveyed to a quench station where 20,000 gallons of water or more are sprayed to cool it. Stage control tries to reduce the fumes that are released when the coke is conveyed to the quench station. See *Progress in the Prevention and Control of Air Pollution in 1977* (Washington, D.C.: U.S. Senate Committee on Environmental and Public Works, 1978), p. 90.

51. See "President Nixon's Statement and Message on Energy" in *Environmental Quality: The Fifth Annual Report of the Council on Environmental Quality,* pp. 545–64.

52. Energy Supply and Environmental Coordination Act of 1974, P. L. No. 93–319, Section 3, 88 Stat. 248 (1974) (Codified at 42 U.S.C. Section 1847 C–10 (Supp. V 1975)).

53. See *Progress in the Prevention of Air Pollution.* Annual reports 1974, 1976, 1977 (U.S.

Notes

Senate Committee on Environmental and Public Works). See also Ronald H. White *The Price of Power Update: Electric Utilities and the Environment* (New York: Council on Economic Priorities, 1977), pp. 41–46. For an update of this issue, see Dick Kirschten, "The New Clear Air Regs—More at Stake than Breathing," *National Journal Reports* (9/2/78), pp. 1392–96.

54. "President Nixon's Statement and Message on Energy" in *Environmental Quality.*

55. See "A Report on Automotive Fuel Efficiency," (Washington, D.C.: EPA, February 1974).

56. John Quarles, *Cleaning Up America* (Boston: Houghton Mifflin, 1976), p. 194.

57. Davies and Davies, *Politics of Pollution,* p. 56.

58. Quarles, *Cleaning Up America,* p. 30.

59. Theodore Bogosian, "Automobile Emissions Control: The Sulfate Problem (A)," (Cambridge, Mass.: Harvard University Kennedy School of Government, 1975), p. 15.

60. Ibid., pp. 3–9.

61. See Effluent Limitations Guidelines: Contractor Information," (EPA, March 14, 1973).

62. See "Transportation Controls to Reduce Automobile Use and Improve Air Quality in Cities," (Washington, D.C.: EPA, November 1974).

63. Jones, *Clean Air,* p. 270.

64. Ibid.

65. Quarles, *Cleaning Up America,* p. 202.

66. Jones, *Clean Air,* p. 270.

67. Quarles, *Cleaning Up America,* pp. 203–04.

68. Gregory Mills, "William Ruckelshaus and the EPA," (Cambridge, Mass.: Harvard University Kennedy School of Government, 1974).

69. *Nomination of William Ruckelshaus* (Senate Public Works Committee, December 1 and 2, 1970).

70. See Quarles, *Cleaning Up America,* pp. 37–58; and Peggy Wiehl, "William D. Ruckelshaus and the Environmental Protection Agency" (Cambridge, Mass.: Harvard University Kennedy School of Government, 1974).

71. U.S. EPA, *The First Two Years: A Review of EPA's Enforcement Program* (Washington, D.C.: EPA, February 1973).

72. Quarles, *Cleaning Up America,* p. 36.

73. See the "Schultz Memorandum" (Washington, D.C.: Office of Management and Budget, October 5, 1971).

74. Davies and Davies, *Politics of Pollution,* p. 209.

75. *Environmental Quality: The Sixth Annual Report,* pp. 60–68.

76. See CPC International, Inc., et al., Petitioners, v. Russell E. Train, et al., Respondents, *Brief for the Respondents on Demand* (U.S. Court of Appeals for the Eighth Circuit). See also Development Document for Effluent Limitations Guidelines, *Grain Processing: Segment of the Grain Mills* (Washington, D.C.: EPA, March 1974).

77. Du Pont v. Train, U.S. Supreme Court, No. 75–978, decided February 23, 1977.

78. Codified in December, 1971 under the title EPA Order 1000.6.

79. William R. Ahern, Jr., "Organizing for Pollution Control," pp. 69–70.

80. Andrew W. Breidenbach, Chairman, "Report of the Task Force to Define an Office of Research and Development Planning Process: Executive Summary," (Washington, D.C. EPA: October 3, 1974).

81. See Jones, *Clean Air,* p. 255 and Committee on Motor Vehicle Emissions, "Semi-Annual Report," (Washington, D.C.: National Academy of Science, January 1, 1972), pp. 39, 49. Reprinted in the Senate hearings, pt. 3, pp. 1153–1237.

82. See R. Kaspar, "Auto Emission Standards Suspension," in NAS, *Decision Making in the EPA* (Committee on Environmental Decision Making, 1976). See also "Hearings on Motor Vehicle Pollution Control," (EPA, May 6–7, 1971).

83. Quarles, *Cleaning Up America,* p. 189.

84. See Jones, *Clean Air,* p. 269.

85. Quarles, *Cleaning Up America,* p. 201.

86. Kalur v. Resor. See "The National Water Permit Program," (Washington, D.C.: EPA, June 1, 1973), pp. 1–4.

87. Quarles, *Cleaning Up America,* p. 110.

Notes

88. Richard Nathan, "The Administrative Presidency," *The Public Interest* (Summer 1976), pp. 42–45. See also Richard Nathan, *The Plot That Failed: Nixon and the Administrative Presidency* (New York: John Wiley, 1975).

89. Gladwin Hill, "EPA Turns from Cures to Prevention," *New York Times* 2 December 1975, pp. 1, 23.

90. Ibid.

91. Ibid.

92. James E. Anderson, David Brady, and Charles Bullock, *Public Policy and Politics in America* (North Scituate, Mass.: Duxbury Press, 1978), pp. 79–80. *Environmental Quality: The Eighth Annual Report*, pp. 23–24.

93. McKie, *Social Responsibility*, p. 159.

94. Ibid.

95. This account of the 1977 amendments is derived primarily from Christopher Davis, Jeffrey Kurtock, James P. Leape, and Frank Magill, "The Clean Air Act Amendments of 1977: Away from Technology Forcing?" *Harvard Environmental Law Review* 2 (1977): 1–103 and James Voytko, Kurt M. Hunaker, and Richard Lazarus, "The Clean Water Act and Related Developments in the Federal Water Pollution Control Program During 1977," *Harvard Environmental Law Review* 2 (1977): 103–99. See also *Environmental Quality: The Eighth Annual Report*, pp. 22–27 and Edmund Muskie, "The Meaning of the 1977 Clean Water Act" *EPA Journal*, 4 (July/August 1978): pp. 4, 36.

96. See Voytko, "Clean Water Act," p. 126.

97. Ibid., p. 125.

98. See Bernard Asbell, "The Outlawing of Next Year's Cars," *New York Times Magazine*, 21 November 1976, p. 41.

99. See Barry M. Mitnick, "Organizing Regulation: Considerations in Regulation by Incentive and by Directive," (working paper, College of Administrative Sciences, The Ohio State University, March 1977).

100. Charles L. Schultze, "The Public Use of Private Interest," *Regulation* (Sept/Oct. 1977) pp. 10–14. See also Allen V. Kneese and Charles L. Schultze, *Pollution, Prices and Public Policy* (Washington, D.C.: Brookings Institution, 1975) or Larry S. Ruff, "The Economic Common Sense of Pollution" *The Public Interest* (Spring 1970) pp. 69–85. Ruff's article and many others on tax and charge systems to reduce pollution are contained in a congressional report. See Environment and Natural Resources Policy Divisions of the Congressional Research Service, *Pollution Taxes, Effluent Charges, and Other Alternatives for Pollution Control* (Washington, D.C.: U.S. Senate Committee on Environment and Public Works, 1977).

101. See Bruce Yandle, "The Emerging Market in Air Pollution Rights," *Regulation* (July/August 1978), pp. 21–30.

102. Ibid.

103. The new penalty provision is called "The Connecticut Plan" because it was first tried in the state of Connecticut when present EPA administrator Douglas Costle was director of environmental affairs in that state. For a technical discussion of this penalty provision, its origin, and proposed functioning, see Davis, Kurtock et al., "Clean Air Act Amendments," pp. 78–83.

104. Anderson et al., *Public Policy and Politics*, p. 89.

105. *Environmental Quality: The Sixth Annual Report of the Council on Environmental Quality*, p. 45.

106. Quoted by Edwin M. Schur in *Law and Society: A Sociological View* (New York: Random House, 1968), p. 121.

Chapter 9

1. The Title IX regulations against sex discrimination are rich in examples. Schools are not only forbidden to employ discriminatory recruiting practices in general, for instance, but are specifically admonished never to use "any announcement, bulletin, catalog or application form [which] suggests by text or illustration [!] that such recipient treats applicants, students, employees differently on the basis of sex." Some pass beyond the unnecessary to the unintelligible: "A recipient [institution] may make preemployment inquiry as to the sex of an applicant for employment, but only if such inquiry is made

equally of such applicants of both sexes." What colors such picayune requirements with more than literary interest is that OCR has pledged itself to provide a "prompt investigation" of all individual complaints it receives. With the dissemination of its regulations through constituency groups, even quite marginal provisions have a way of bringing forth indignant complaints about local violations. Thus the agency received more than fifty complaints against the retention of differing dress codes for boys and girls in public schools, in violation of a requirement in the Title IX regulations.

2. In addition to the three statutory mandates discussed in this chapter, OCR also has enforcement jurisdiction under the Age Discrimination Act of 1975. Regulations for that statute only went into effect in June 1979, however, and there has thus far been no actual enforcement by the agency. Other statutory jurisdictions—dealing with sex discrimination in medical training programs and discrimination against alcoholics and drug addicts in hospital admissions—have been superceded by the broader grants of authority in Title IX and Section 504. OCR is also responsible for determining the eligibility of school districts for federal grants under the Emergency School Aid Act (ESAA) of 1972, which provides financial assistance for the implementation of desegregation plans. No school district can apply for the money unless it has already developed a desegregation plan—usually pursuant to court orders—and OCR's role is limited to certifying the adequacy of the plans under the standards enunciated by the courts. The only major enforcement field unmentioned in this study, then, is Executive Order 11246, prohibiting discrimination and requiring affirmative action in employment practices (on behalf of women and minorities) by government contractors. From 1968 until 1978, OCR was responsible for enforcing its provisions against contractors doing business with HEW—chiefly construction companies and universities. In the fall of 1978, President Carter ordered enforcement activities under this program consolidated in the Labor Department's Office of Federal Contract Compliance Programs, thus removing OCR from any further involvement. Regulations and policy guidelines for the Executive Order program had all along been promulgated by the Labor Department. It may be worth mentioning, though, that the pattern of enforcement by OCR, while it retained this jurisdiction, was very similar to that described in Part IV of this study: No university ever lost its eligibility for federal contracts (the only real sanction under the program) in all the years of OCR's enforcement; the vast majority of university contractors did not even receive spot checks of minimal compliance with the program's requirements, and OCR instead expended almost all of its effort negotiating extremely elaborate and ambitious affirmative action plans with a small number of prestige universities.

3. Shortly before the creation of OCR, HEW officials put intense effort into ensuring that hospitals in the South would no longer segregate patients by race. Because desegregation in this area was less resisted than in education (and because HEW never demanded precise statistical indications of effective integration) the effort was completed in only two years, in time to qualify hospitals for the new system of federal payments under Medicare. Until recently, more than three-fourths of OCR's enforcement personnel were assigned to investigate education institutions, however, the majority of them concentrating on elementary and secondary schools.

4. The provision states: "Nothing in this title shall add to or detract from any existing authority with respect to any program or activity under which Federal financial assistance is extended by way of a contract or insurance of guaranty." Individuals are, of course, free to contest alleged discriminatory practices in such programs through private (constitutionally-based) litigation. But the presence of this exemption in the statutes strengthens the presumption that they are primarily intended to authorize a scheme of regulation, rather than merely to ensure the constitutional purity of federal funding arrangements.

5. The leading case is Simkins v. Moses H. Cone Memorial Hospital (323 F.2d 959) which overturned the provision explicitly authorizing operation of "separate-but-equal" facilities under the Hill-Burton hospital grant program. The case plainly established that the federal government may not directly authorize funding of segregated institutions, but it leaves unclear whether the federal government has an independent obligation under the Constitution to determine that grants are not being used to subsidize discrimination, even where this is no part of federal intentions.

6. The leading case is still probably Burton v. Wilmington Parking Authority (365 U.S.

Notes

715) in which the Supreme Court affirmed that "private conduct abridging individual rights does no violence to the Equal Protection Clause [of the Fourteenth Amendment] unless to some significant extent the state in any of its manifestations has been found to have become involved in it. . . . Only by sifting facts and weighing circumstances can the non-obvious involvement of the State in private conduct be attributed its true significance." Although *Burton* dealt with state funding of private institutions, the Court has found the federal government to have equivalent obligations under the due process clause of the Fifth Amendment. (Bolling v. Sharpe, 347 U.S. 497).

7. The Supreme Court has struck down a number of legislative provisions in the course of the present decade on the grounds that they unconstitutionally discriminate on the basis of sex. But a majority of the Court has never held that classifications based on sex are inherently "suspect" and demanding of "strict scrutiny" by the courts, as they traditionally have been for race (see, e.g., Frontiero v. Richardson, 411 U.S. 677).

8. The unedited version of the debates on the 1964 Civil Rights Act runs to several thousand pages in the *Congressional Record*. I have therefore relied on an edited version of the debates which pares them down to several hundred pages by omitting filibustering speeches, extensive insertions into the record and so on. It is found in the Statutory History of the United States, Part II of the volumes on "Civil Rights," edited by Benjamin Schwartz (New York: Chelsea House, 1970). Kuchel's statement appears on p. 1249.

9. Gary Orfield, *The Reconstruction of Southern Education* (New York: Wiley, 1969), p. 25.

10. John Fitzgerald Kennedy, *The Public Papers of the President,* 1963, p. 333.

11. An extensive account of the legislative development of Title VI is provided in Orfield, *Reconstruction,* pp. 33–47.

12. *Statutory History,* p. 1420.

13. Ibid., p. 1281.

14. Orfield, *Reconstruction,* pp. 39–41.

15. *Statutory History,* p. 1420.

16. Ibid., pp. 1147–48.

17. Ibid., p. 1285.

18. Ibid., p. 1221.

19. Ibid., p. 1326.

20. See, for example, the exchange between Senator Humphrey and Senator Robert Byrd at Ibid., pp. 1343–46.

21. Ibid., p. 1236.

22. In separate actions the same year, Congress amended Title VII of the 1964 Civil Rights Act so that its prohibitions on sex discrimination would extend to the employment practices of educational institutions and it amended the Civil Rights Act of 1957 to direct the U.S. Commission on Civil Rights to monitor sex discrimination (along with the original charge to study race discrimination) throughout American society. A provision tacked to the end of Title IX itself amended Title IV of the 1964 Civil Rights Act to allow the attorney general to intervene in sex discrimination cases against public educational institutions (as well as in the race discrimination cases originally authorized). The same provision also amended the Equal Pay Act of 1965 to extend to educational institutions its ban on sex discrimination in employment compensation (which is enforced by the Wages and Hours Division of the Labor Department).

23. A great deal of the debate focused on efforts to attach a limitation on "forced busing" to the education bill. Ironically, it was to avoid opening the busing controversy that Congresswoman Green had agreed not to submit the sex discrimination provision as a direct amendment to Title VI. Whether Title IX would have emerged in different form had it been tied directly to the much scrutinized—and endlessly redrafted—busing provision in the overall bill is difficult to judge. At all events, education lobbyists, particularly those representing higher education, were preoccupied with an ongoing controversy over the proper scale and conditions of federal student aid, a major element of the 1972 bill.

24. A relatively detailed account of the legislative development of Title IX is provided in Andrew Fishel and Janice Pottker, *National Politics and Sex Discrimination in Education* (Lexington Mass.: Lexington Books, 1977), pp. 95–105.

25. President Nixon's official statement on signing the 1972 Education Amendments was

entirely taken up with expressions of disapproval for congressional action on the student aid question and for the congressional compromise on busing. Richard M. Nixon, *The Public Papers of the President*, 1972, p. 642.

26. In explaining his desire to include an exemption for admissions practices of elementary and secondary schools, Senator Bayh noted, "no one even knows how many single sex schools exist on the elementary and secondary levels or what special qualities of the schools might argue for a continued single sex status." (*Congressional Record*, vol. 118, 28 February 1972 p. 5804.) But the same point could easily be made about many areas of educational practice that were covered by the statute. The willingness of Congress to make exemptions at all confirms that Congress itself did not view sex discrimination as entirely analogous to race discrimination: it had not been willing to accept any institutional exemptions from its sweeping prohibition of race discrimination in Title VI. But after implicitly acknowledging that sex discrimination was not quite comparable to race discrimination, Congress did not pause to consider how the differences should be handled where Title IX did accord jurisdiction.

27. This was, at all events, widely suspected within HEW—and is certainly a plausible interpretation.

28. Conference Report, H.R. Report No. 93–1457, 1974, p. 27.

29. Executive Order 11914 of 26 April 1976 also specified that the implementing regulations for Section 504 developed by HEW would serve as the model for regulations to be adopted subsequently by all other departments and agencies with enforcement responsibilities. HEW had already begun work on the regulations, however, before the executive order clarified its enforcement authority.

30. Orfield, *Reconstruction*, pp. 122–23

31. Ibid, pp. 324, 328.

32. But as regulations issued in the name of the entire department, the formal regulations for Title IX and Section 504 had to be cleared through each major "program operating unit" in the department. According to Gwendolyn Gregory and John Wodatch (OCR officials, respectively chairing ad hoc drafting committees for Title IX and Section 504 regulations), OCR was often pressed to take stronger stands by the other units, which did not have enforcement responsibility. Personal interviews, July 1976 (Gregory), October 1976 and July 1978 (Wodatch).

33. An extensive account of the whole affair is provided in Orfield, *Reconstruction*, pp. 151–208. Orfield insists that Keppel had decided to leave the government even before the Chicago debacle, but he acknowledges—what is doubtless more important in political terms—that Congress and the public perceived Keppel's departure as a delayed result of Mayor Daley's highly publicized complaint.

34. Orfield, *Reconstruction*, pp. 144–47.

35. The courts assisted in two important respects. In 1967 the Fifth Circuit Court of Appeals held that HEW guidelines should be accorded great weight in the elaboration of desegregation remedies by district courts in formal litigation. In the same year, the Fifth Circuit also ruled that freedom of choice plans were unacceptable unless they produced substantial integration in practice and the judgment was confirmed by the Supreme Court the following year. OCR's definition of substantial integration thereafter followed the standards (and deadlines) established by a succession of cases before the Supreme Court culminating in *Swann* v. *Charlotte-Mecklenburg Board of Education*, 402 U.S.1 (1971).

36. Eventually codified, after reenactment, at 42 *U.S. Code*, sec. 2000d(6).

37. See Taylor v. Finch, 414 F. 2d 1073 (1969).

38. In 1975 OCR required all elementary and secondary schools to maintain records on the number of students of each race that were suspended, expelled, or subject to lesser disciplinary measures each year. Policy statements indicated that the agency would view disproportionate racial patterns as evidence of discrimination and would not require proof of conscious discriminatory intent to charge violations of Title VI on this ground. (See "Student Discipline", "*HEW Fact Sheet*," September 1975). In a memorandum of May 1970 on "national origin-minority students" OCR admonished school districts that parents who did not speak English must be supplied with school communications in a language they did understand.

39. Federal courts have ordered the integration of teaching staffs as part of desegrega-

tion orders in constitutionally-based suits. See, e.g., Singleton v. Jackson Municipal Separate Schools 419 F. 2d 1211 (1970).

40. A striking example: In 1976 OCR charged the New York City school system with violating Title VI because it had, for a broad category of teachers, demanded higher standards of qualification than New York State generally. This effort to raise the standard of professional competence among the city's teachers could not be allowed, OCR maintained, because the higher standards had the effect of disqualifying black applicants for teaching jobs disproportionately more than whites. Letter from OCR Director Martin Gerry to New York Schools Chancellor Irving Anker, 9 November 1976.

41. For example, Romeo Community Schools v. U.S. Dept. of HEW, 438 F. Supp. 1021.

42. For example, Hobson v. Hanson, 269 F. Supp. 401, 408 F. 2d 175 (D.C. Cir. 1969).

43. See, e.g., Kahn v. Shevin 416 U.S. 351.

44. According to Burton Taylor, formerly director of OCR's Higher Education Division and currently director of the agency's Policy Planning Division, the agency might consider imposing some sort of quota arrangement to redress a marked and persistent imbalance in the participation of male and female students in particular areas of study —"but only as a last resort." (Personal interview, July 1976)

45. Whether or not the regulations would support a formal proceeding on the basis of mere statistical imbalance remains to be seen. But statistical evidence is used to select schools for investigation (where the investigation is not triggered by direct complaints) and the usual aim of these investigations is not to sustain formal charges but to get the school to sign a consent decree, agreeing to take affirmative action to remedy the imbalance. And such consent agreements need not include an admission by the school of actual violations of the regulations.

46. Though OCR itself has issued no further policy clarifications on this point, the first ruling by the Supreme Court on this statute suggests that the ultimate definition of "undue hardship" may be crucial to the viability of HEW's regulations. In June 1979, the Court ruled that Section 504 was intended to prohibit overt discrimination against the handicapped but not to require costly affirmative action on their behalf (Southeastern Community College v. Davis, No. 78-711 (11 June 1979). It remains to be seen whether this decision will lead lower courts to strike down entire sections of the HEW regulations or merely to insist on their being interpreted leniently.

47. The regulations do not require *every* building to be made accessible to wheel-chair bound students, but do require that at least one section of every course offering or program be situated in an accessible building. The pleas of several colleges to allow pooling of courses or programs with other colleges in the area to meet this requirement were dismissed entirely by the regulation-writers, however.

48. *Chronicle of Higher Education,* 14 May 1979.

49. *Federal Register,* vol. 41, no. 138 (16 July 1976), p. 29550.

50. Noel Epstein, *Language, Ethnicity and the Schools: Policy Alternatives for Bilingual-Bicultural Education* (Washington, D.C.: George Washington University Press, 1977), pp. 14–15. Most of HEW's requirements in this area were elaborated after the 1974 decision of the Supreme Court in Lau v. Nichols (414 U.S. 564) in which the court upheld the claim of Chinese immigrants in San Francisco for some form of compensatory instruction for children in the public schools with English language difficulties. The Court refused to reach the constitutional claims of the plaintiffs, merely deferring to HEW's authority to interpret the requirements of Title VI (though OCR had not investigated this particular case or involved itself in the litigation). Where the court held that the school system was obliged to provide *some* form of compensatory action, but refused to lay down general rules about what would be most appropriate for particular cases, HEW has subsequently shown far less restraint.

51. Gary Orfield, who has generally been sympathetic to activist interpretations of civil rights requirements, characterized HEW policy in this area as "predicated on sweeping assumptions new to civil rights enforcement—that the schools had an obligation to assure equal results for each major racial or linguistic minority and that HEW knew what educational practices would best assure this." Gary Orfield, *Must We Bus?* (Washington, D.C.: Brookings, 1978), p. 303.

52. OCR Memorandum on "Equal Educational Services," July 1976. According to Orfield, where district courts have ordered equalization of spending on constitutional

grounds this "has frequently meant the unpredictable shifting of teachers and other resources, making any kind of planning exceedingly difficult, disrupting the organizational structure of individual schools and requiring small schools that lose students to double up classes or even grades and narrow the range of their curricula." Ibid., p. 300.

53. Epstein, *Language, Ethnicity and the Schools*, pp. 57–60, 87–88.

54. A policy statement on the legal limitations on affirmative action in educational admissions was drawn up by OCR officials in the summer of 1976, in response to repeated inquiries about the agency's stand on the "reverse discrimination" issue. But Secretary Mathews refused to approve the statement for publication at the time, and under the new administration thereafter HEW officials took no public action to fill the policy void in this area. Ironically, the *Bakke* case—for however much guidance it may have provided—reached the Supreme Court only because OCR regional officials were so slow in pursuing Allan Bakke's complaint to them about the admissions practices of the University of California's Davis Medical School. There is no evidence that OCR's sluggishness in investigating Bakke's charges of "reverse discrimination" was calculated or deliberate—the agency has been notoriously slow in investigating straightforward discrimination complaints, as well—but the delay did drive Bakke to seek a policy ruling from the federal courts instead.

55. Rather than equal aggregate expenditures on sexually integrated teams, the regulations only required an overall athletic program reflecting the "interests and abilities" of students of each sex—leaving it unclear how or by whom those "interests and abilities" were to be determined.

56. Interview with John Wodatch, director of special programs, OCR (responsible for coordinating the drafting process for Section 504 regulations), July 1978.

57. Department of Health, Education, and Welfare, Transcript of Press Briefing by Secretary Caspar Weinberger, 18 June 1974 (announcing draft version of Title IX regulations).

58. Statement of Caspar Weinberger, secretary of Health, Education, and Welfare, 3 June 1975 (at a press briefing to announce the final version of Title IX regulations).

59. Interviews with Gwendolyn Gregory (special assistant to the director, OCR, 1974–76, responsible for coordinating the drafting of Title IX regulations) and John Wodatch. See also summaries of comments received on Title IX regulations (*Federal Register*, vol. 40, no. 108, pp. 24128–136) and Section 504 regulations (*Federal Register*, vol. 41, no. 138, pp. 29548–60 and vol. 42, no. 86, pp. 22678–97).

60. Cherry v. Mathews, No. 76–0255 (District Court of the District of Columbia).

61. See, for example, Murray Edelman, *The Symbolic Uses of Politics* (Urbana, Ill.: Univ. of Illinois Press, 1964).

62. United States Commission on Civil Rights, *The Federal Civil Rights Enforcement Effort-1974*, vol III (January 1975), pp. 48–49.

63. Fishel and Pottker, pp. 121–22. This surely reflected the ambition of the women's groups more than the modesty of the regulations. Their "major" complaints focused on the absence of any provision relating to sex stereotyping in textbooks, the vagueness of the "equal opportunity" in sports requirements and the failure to mandate a certain accounting method in employee insurance policies. See Holly Knox, "A Feminist Looks at the Title IX Regulations," distributed by the Project on Equal Education Rights, National Organization of Women.

64. Personal interviews (July 1976) with Martin Gerry, deputy director of OCR between 1970 and 1975 and with Peter Holmes (August 1976), deputy director of OCR between 1971 and 1974.

65. *Federal Register*, vol. 41, no. 138, pp. 29548–49. Also vol. 42, no. 86, p. 22685: "The most common recommendation was that only 'traditional' handicaps be covered. The Department continues to believe, however, that it has no flexibility within the statutory definition to limit the term to persons who have those severe, permanent, or progressive conditions that are most commonly regarded as handicaps. . . . the definition also includes some persons who might not ordinarily be considered handicapped, such as persons with disfiguring scars, as well as persons who have no physical or mental impairment but are treated by a recipient as if they were handicapped." By this line of reasoning, it was not, in fact, illogical to include homosexuals under the protections of the statute and the department did not offer a new principle to explain the announced exclusion.

Notes

66. See, for example, Watson v. City of Memphis, 373 U.S. 526 at 537.

67. The Equal Employment Opportunity Commission had pioneered the "no adverse (or disproportionate) impact" rule on employment criteria before 1970, for example, and also pioneered the notion that the failure to accommodate pregnant employees constituted a form of sex discrimination. Similarly, many elements of the Section 504 regulations were modeled on requirements issued by the Department of Labor in 1975 to implement a parallel statute requiring government contractors to take affirmative action on behalf of the handicapped.

68. Secretary Weinberger's personal decision to exclude textbook stereotyping from the Title IX regulations was the rare exception—which doubtless reflected his judgment that the possibility of First Amendment difficulties (a nonpolitical rationale) could be invoked to justify the exception in this case. It is noteworthy in this connection that First Amendment considerations did not prevent OCR from elaborating (during Weinberger's tenure) policy guidelines regarding the treatment of "national origin-minorities" in elementary and secondary school curricula and textbooks.

69. There has, in fact, been much uncertainty about whether these statutes actually establish a private right of action, since they are phrased as admonitions to federal agencies rather than guarantees to private individuals. As late as 1978, Justice White challenged the right of Allan Bakke to bring a private action under Title VI and several lower courts ruled that Title IX afforded no private right of action. The latter judgments were overturned by the Supreme Court in May 1979 (Cannon v. University of Chicago, No. 77–926), however, and several weeks later the Court assumed the existence of a private right of action under Section 504 as well (Southeastern Community College v. Davis, No. 78–711). But HEW all along seems to have accepted the notion that its regulations could be enforced by private suits: see, for example, the matter-of-fact reference to this in a draft version of the Section 504 regulations, *Federal Register*, vol. 41, no. 138, p. 29552. This is particularly noteworthy, since federal enforcement agencies generally have opposed private enforcement actions on the ground that they complicate regulatory management (by introducing conflicting legal precedents).

70. According to Robert Goldwin, former dean of St. Johns College and a White House special assistant in 1975, several White House staffers did stress that the Title IX regulations could pose substantial difficulties and burdens for many colleges, particularly in connection with their athletic programs. Other advisers, however, pointed out that Ford's refusal to sign the regulations (three years after the enactment of the statute) was sure to outrage women's groups and that such outrage was sure to be remembered in the upcoming election year. One need not be particularly cynical to assume that this consideration weighed significantly in President Ford's decision to sign the regulations as he received them, rather than send them back to HEW for substantial revisions, thereby ensuring still further delays before they could finally go into effect.

71. Representative Vanik's statement was cited in a column by Neil Pierce, which appeared in the *Washington Post* on Friday, 29 December 1978. It was confirmed for me subsequently in a personal interview with Maggie Morrison, a legislative assistant to the Congressman.

72. One partial exception to this statement may be cited: in 1978 Congress amended the Rehabilitation Act to authorize special financial assistance to institutions for some portion of the expenses they incurred in complying with Section 504 requirements. But no money was actually appropriated, or distributed, for this purpose.

73. Fishel and Pottker, p. 114

74. Epstein, *Language, Ethnicity and the Schools*, p. 14

75. The resolution condemned requirements in the resolution for (1) a comprehensive self-evaluation of discriminatory practices to be undertaken by all institutions and maintained on file for OCR inspection; (2) establishment of internal grievance procedures for handling discrimination complaints; and (3) an explanation to HEW of the specific religious tenet by which religiously-affiliated institutions claimed exemption from the regulations (under the statutory exemption provided for such institutions). All of these requirements, in fact, paralleled requirements that had already been imposed under Title VI. If their flaw, as O'Hara claimed, was that they went beyond elaborating prohibitions to requiring positive actions, there were certainly many other "affirmative" requirements

in the regulations—far more controversial politically—which could be struck down on the same argument. O'Hara did not reach for those, however.

76. Another amendment, adopted in 1976 without debate, exempted scholarships given as awards in beauty pageant contests: Senator Thurmond (R–SC) obviously had a particular, cherished local institution in mind. An amendment adopted in 1974, at the behest of Senator Bayh, exempted social fraternities and sororities but was carefully drafted to apply only to their admissions practices and only to purely social organizations (i.e., not to any group with a professional, scholarly or honorary significance).

77. This is not to say that minds might not be changed by a careful study of the circumstances surrounding a particular issue and the immediate, foreseeable consequences of a decision one way or the other. But schools usually have reasons for wanting to do things their own way, so that even where a proposed new policy seems to have clear advantages for a particular group, the decision to impose the new policy on everyone requires a careful balancing of competing values.

78. Senator Hubert Humphrey, for example, sent a long and eloquent letter to the OCR director in July 1976, denouncing the agency's ban on separate "father-son dinners" as arrogant meddling in purely local affairs. But Humphrey had never previously criticized the Title IX regulations that allowed this.

79. For example, in April 1975 the House of Representatives voted by an overwhelming margin of 253–145 to amend Title IX to exempt campus honorary societies and to permit separation of the sexes in physical education classes at the elementary and secondary level (contrary to HEW's regulations). But the House reversed itself in July, agreeing to drop the Title IX amendment from the education funding bill to which it had been attached, when the Senate failed to include the amendment in its version of the funding bill. In the days before its second vote on the amendment, the House was subjected to what Representative Robert Casey (D–Tex.), the original sponsor of the amendment, called "the heaviest lobbying I've ever seen around here." According to the *Washington Post* (19 July 1975), the women lobbyists were "roaming the corridors, handing out literature, pursuing House members onto elevators, meeting in hallways and cafeterias to map tactics . . . to press their case on Capitol Hill. . . . Hundreds of women volunteers augmented lobbying efforts of representatives of the League of Women Voters, American Association of University Women, National Organization for Women, Women's Equity Action League, Women's Lobby and other groups."

80. ACE's most ambitious effort, undertaken in collaboration with several other organizations representing higher education, was the publication of the HEITH Report (the so-called "Yellow Book") to guide colleges on 504 compliance requirements. Advice and consultation has also been made available on this subject by the National Association of College and University Business Officers.

81. The asymmetry can be exaggerated, since minorities, women, and the handicapped are all affected by the activities of other federal agencies—many others, in fact, also have civil rights responsibilities of one kind or another. But expanding opportunities in education has been one of the top priorities for all these groups (or at least, for the political activists representing them) and so disproportionate attention has been given to the activities of OCR.

82. An account of the episode is provided in Orfield, *Must We Bus?*, pp. 312–14.

83. Ibid., p. 284. OCR may still try to negotiate busing plans by threatening to refer recalcitrant school districts to the Justice Department for action in the courts. After three years of investigation and many months of fruitless negotiation, this was the course OCR finally took with the Chicago school district in the fall of 1979—with results that are still quite uncertain.

84. The new policy on Title IX athletic provisions that was proposed in December 1978 may have provided another exception. An informal coalition of some 300 colleges and universities was formed to protest the new policy on the grounds that it would pose intolerable financial burdens on schools and could threaten the continuation of high level intercollegiate competition in such sports as football and basketball. Their intense lobbying activity, joined to earlier efforts by the National Collegiate Athletic Association, doubtless contributed significantly to HEW's reluctance to finalize the new policy—for fear of a congressional reversal.

85. More detailed statistical indications of this progress are provided in "Title VI of the

Notes

Civil Rights Act of 1964—Ten Years Later, An Anniversary Report," U.S. Department of Health, Education, and Welfare, Office of the Secretary, July 1974.

86. Hearings, HEW-Labor Subcommittee, House Appropriations Committee, "Departments of Labor and HEW Appropriations for 1979," Part 6, p. 1346.

87. Orfield, *Must We Bus?*, p. 284.

88. Figures supplied by Juan Trevino, *"Lau* unit" of Enforcement and Compliance Division, OCR, personal interview, February 1979.

89. Center for National Policy Review (School of Law, Catholic University, Washington, D.C.), *Justice Delayed and Denied, HEW and Northern School Desegregation,* (1974) pp. 45–53.

90. Project on Equal Education Rights, NOW Legal Defense and Education Fund, *Stalled at the Start, Government Action on Sex Bias in Schools* (1978), pp. 28–29.

91. Estimates supplied by Clark Leming, program analyst, OCR.

92. For an account stressing the absence of civil rights leadership under the Republican administrations, see Orfield, *Must We Bus?;* also Leon Panetta and Peter Gall, *Bring Us Together: The Nixon Administration and the Civil Rights Retreat* (1971).

93. Interview with Martin Gerry, December 1978.

94. Orfield, *Reconstruction,* pp. 126, 252, 262, 332.

95. Gerry and Holmes interviews.

96. Figures supplied by Richard Slippen, director, Title VI Reviewing Authority, HEW.

97. Technically, a recipient institution that is found to have violated any of the regulations might be sued for breach of contract and be assessed for penalties in this connection, regardless of subsequent conduct. But such a suit has never been attempted by HEW, evidently for political reasons.

98. Interviews with Cynthia Brown, deputy director, OCR (December 1978) and Arlene Pacht, Office of General Counsel, HEW (February 1979).

99. Figures supplied by Juan Trevino.

100. *Justice Delayed,* pp. 56, 78. That such patterns have continued, if in less severe form, was confirmed in interviews with Arlene Pacht, Office of General Counsel (February 1979) and Robert Sermier, Office of the Assistant Secretary for Management and Budget, HEW (February 1979).

101. Gerry, Holmes, Sermier interviews.

102. *Justice Delayed,* p. 53.

103. Interview with Jim O'Connell, Bureau of Policies and Standards, U.S. Civil Service Commission, August 1976. See "Position Classification Standard for Equal Opportunity Series, GS–160," U.S. Civil Service Commission, TS-10, May 1972.

104. Gerry, Holmes, Taylor interviews.

105. GAO Report No. HRD–77–78, 30 March 1977.

106. The letter from Secretary Califano to Senator Moynihan is dated 7 November 1977.

107. U.S. Commission on Civil Rights, *Desegregation of the Nation's Public Schools: A Status Report,* (February 1979) p. 17

108. The phrase is Gary Orfield's, *Must We Bus?*, p. 300.

109. An elaborate agreement on *employment* policy—requiring assignment of teachers to particular schools on the basis of race—was finally negotiated between OCR and the New York City school authorities, only to be subsequently overturned by successful court challenge from the teachers union. Negotiations for a new agreement are still underway.

110. According to Martin Gerry, then deputy director of OCR, the agency began to investigate de facto segregation in Boston in the early 1970s, for example, to respond to complaints in Congress from southern representatives that OCR was overly preoccupied with segregation in their own region (personal interview, February 1979). But in more general terms, it is worth noting that private civil rights organizations, like the NAACP Legal Defense Fund, have tended to concentrate their efforts on large, attention-getting "precedent" cases.

111. *Stalled at the Start,* p. 36.

112. The agency issued a proposed set of new "consolidated procedural rules" in the *Federal Register* in June of 1975, explaining that it would no longer commit itself to investigate every individual discrimination complaint it received so that OCR would "be free to adjust [enforcement] priorities to meet shifting needs." The response from constituent groups was uniformly and intensely hostile. In the face of this reaction, the

proposed new rules were withdrawn and the following March the HEW Secretary announced that OCR would find ways to investigate all discrimination complaints in a "timely manner." Nonetheless, it remains the consensus among OCR officials that the investigation of individual complaints is a far less productive use of investigative resources than larger compliance reviews initiated by the agency, itself. Yet to fulfill this commitment, the agency had to devote almost 90 percent of its investigative effort in the education area to the following up of individual complaints during 1977 and 1978.

113. For example, OCR's "Manual for Investigation of Allegations of Employment Discrimination at Institutions of Higher Education," issued to regional investigators in the fall of 1975, describes the "no adverse impact" rule on employment eligibility criteria in such a way (citing numerous precedents from industrial employment cases) as to suggest that OCR investigators should challenge Ph.D. requirements that prevent minorities from getting a "proportionate" share of jobs on university faculties. Though regional investigators have apparently questioned Ph.D. requirements in a few instances, OCR has never pursued a case based squarely on this issue—and seems most unlikely to, given the predictable response from the higher education community. According to Barry Anderson, then chief of the policy planning unit in OCR's Higher Education Division, the agency feared to clarify its stand on this issue in the Manual, lest this provoke the wrath of constituency groups (personal interview, July 1976).

114. OCR's policy statements and direct investigations of race discrimination in student disciplinary practices, starting in 1976, constitute one example. Another is the agency's attention to sex discrimination in vocational education schools starting the same year.

115. Adams v. Richardson, 351 F. Supp. 636 (D.C.D.C. 1972).

116. Adams v. Richardson, 480 F. 2nd 852 (D.C.Circ. 1973).

117. Adams v. Mathews, 536 F. 2nd 417 (D.C.Circ. 1976); Adams v. Mathews, No. 3095 (D.C.D.C. Mar. 30, 1976). The handicapped were finally brought in too, in Adams v. Califano, No. 3095-70 (D.C.D.C. 29 Dec. 1977).

118. Brown v. Weinberger, No. 75-1068 (D.C.D.C., 20 July 1976).

119. Orfield, *Must We Bus?*, pp. 294–96.

120. See Adams v. Mathews, No. 3095-70 (D.C.D.C., 14 June 1976) and similar claims in Adams v. Califano, No. 3095-70 (D.C.D.C, 26 Oct. 1977).

121. Sermier interview (February 1979)—Mr. Sermier was one of the senior members of a study team commissioned by Secretary Califano to study ways of speeding up OCR's complaint processing operations. Also, John Hodgdon, director of Management Information Division, OCR (personal interview, November 1978).

122. Adams v. Califano, No. 3095-70 (D.C.D.C. Dec. 29, 1977).

123. According to Mr. Hodgdon, the agency is trying to develop a uniform system of impact or productivity criteria so that the results of different reviews (or complaint investigations) can be readily tabulated and compared. At present it is still difficult to get much of an overview of what regional investigators are achieving, since OCR's reporting system only breaks down investigations by statutory jurisdiction (Title VI, Title IX, etc.) with only a few gross subdivisions ("employment" vs. "student services" or race-related vs. language-related)—so that it is virtually impossible to know the kinds of issues routinely addressed. Similarly, the reporting system does not distinguish the kinds of changes introduced by complaints or reviews reported as "settled, with changes."

124. In Adams v. Mathews, No. 3095-70 (D.C.D.C. July 1975), OCR was ordered for the first time to address individual complaints within specified time-frames, but the order applied only to race-related complaints in the 17 southern and border states involved in the *Adams* litigation. After women's groups and Mexican-American groups were allowed by the courts to intervene in *Adams,* OCR was forced to negotiate complaint investigation time-frames for sex discrimination and bilingual cases in those states too. The settlement with these provisions was entered by the D.C. district court on June 14, 1976, as an order modifying its previous orders in *Adams.* Though the court order in *Brown* did not specifically require it, OCR announced in July 1976 that, for the sake of uniformity, it would follow the complaint procedures agreed to in *Adams* throughout the country.

125. Hodgdon, Sermier interviews.

Notes

Chapter 10

1. George J. Stigler, "The Theory of Economic Regulation," *Bell Journal of Economics and Management Science*, 2 (Spring 1971): 3.

2. Ibid., p. 5.

3. Goldfarb v. Virginia State Bar, 421 U.S. 773 (1975); Virginia State Board of Pharmacy v. Virginia Citizens Consumer Council, 425 U.S. 748 (1976); Bates v. State Bar of Arizona, 433 U.S. 350 (1977).

4. Theodore J. Lowi, *The End of Liberalism* (New York: Norton, 1969), chaps. 3–4.

5. Murray Edelman, *The Symbolic Uses of Politics* (Urbana, Ill.: University of Illinois Press, 1964).

6. Marver H. Bernstein, *Regulating Business by Independent Commission* (Princeton, N.J.: Princeton University Press, 1955), pp. 74–95.

7. Sam Peltzman, "Toward a More General Theory of Regulation," *Journal of Law and Economics*, 19 (August 1976): 211–40.

8. The argument is more fully developed in James Q. Wilson, *Political Organizations* (New York: Basic Books, 1973), chap. 2. It was first suggested to me by Edward C. Banfield; of late, a distinguished professor of economics has made the same point in explaining the limitations of economic analysis: Ronald H. Coase, "Economics and Contiguous Disciplines," *Journal of Legal Studies*, 7 (June 1978): 201–11.

9. John A. Garraty, *The New Commonwealth, 1877–1890* (New York: Harper & Row, 1968); Edward A. Purcell, Jr., "Ideas and Interests: Businessmen and the Interstate Commerce Act," *Journal of American History*, 54 (December 1967): 561–78; Robert W. Harbeson, "Railroads and Regulation, 1877–1916: Conspiracy or Public Interest?" *Journal of Economic History*, 27 (June 1967): 230–42. These findings demolish, in my opinion, the essential argument of Gabriel Kolko, *Railroads and Regulation, 1877–1916* (Princeton, N.J.: Princeton University Press, 1965).

10. See the Harris Survey, March 1976. Only 17 percent of the persons interviewed had a "great deal of confidence" in the people in charge of major companies; only 9 percent had confidence in Congress.

11. Wilson, *Political Organizations*, chap. 16, presents an early version of this theory; the full version, with examples drawn from many policy areas, is James Q. Wilson, *American Government: Institutions and Policies* (Lexington, Mass.: D.C. Heath, 1980), pt. IV.

12. Elaine Walster et al., *Equity: Theory and Research* (Boston: Allyn and Bacon, 1978).

13. Paul W. MacAvoy, ed., *Federal Milk Marketing Orders and Price Supports* (Washington, D.C.: American Enterprise Institute, 1977).

14. David J. Garrow, *Protest at Selma* (New Haven, Conn.: Yale University Press, 1978).

15. My argument follows Richard M. Cyert and James G. March, *A Behavioral Theory of the Firm* (Englewood Cliffs, N.J.: Prentice-Hall, 1963).

16. Classifying organizational members by their motives is an inelegant way to theorize, but almost everybody who has tried to explain differences in bureaucratic behavior has had to do so. My formulation derives from a pioneering but almost forgotten essay by Leonard Reissman, "A Study of Role Conceptions in Bureaucracy," *Social Forces*, 27 (1949): 305–10.

17. Distinctions among executives, managers, and operators are set forth in James Q. Wilson, *The Investigators: Managing FBI and Narcotics Agents* (New York: Basic Books, 1978).

18. That personal rewards and organizational growth are often unrelated in government is but one of the problems with William A. Niskanen's effort to produce an "economic" theory of bureaucracy in his *Bureaucracy and Representative Government* (Chicago: Aldine-Atherton, 1971).

19. Wilson, *The Investigators*, chap. 6, and Marc Tipermas, "Jurisdictionalism: The Politics of Executive Reorganization" (Ph.D. diss., Department of Government, Harvard University, 1976).

20. James W. McKie, "Regulation and the Free Market: The Problem of Boundaries," *Bell Journal of Economics and Management Science*, vol. 1 (Spring 1970): 9.

21. James Q. Wilson, "The Politics of Regulation," in *Social Responsibility and the*

Notes

Business Predicament, ed. James W. McKie (Washington, D.C.: Brookings Institution, 1974), pp. 153–54.

22. Bernard Schwartz, *The Professor and the Commissions* (New York: Alfred A. Knopf, 1953).

23. Abram Chayes, "The Role of the Judge in Public Law Litigation," *Harvard Law Review,* 89 (1976): 1281–1316.

24. Harold L. Wilensky, *Intellectuals in Labor Unions: Organizational Pressures on Professional Roles* (New York: Free Press, 1956).

25. George J. Stigler and Claire Friedland, "What Can Regulators Regulate? The Case of Electricity," *Journal of Law and Economics,* 5 (October 1962): 1–16. But compare the evidence of a regulatory effect in Louis De Alessi, "An Economic Analysis of Government Ownership and Regulation," *Public Choice,* 19 (Fall 1974): 1–42.

26. Jeffrey M. Berry, *Lobbying for the People* (Princeton, N.J.: Princeton University Press, 1977), chap. 3.

27. James Landis, *The Administrative Process* (New Haven, Conn.: Yale University Press, 1938).

28. Peter H. Schuck, "Regulation: Asking the Right Questions," *National Journal,* April 28, 1979, p. 712.

29. Ibid., p. 717.

30. Harold Demsetz, "Economics as a Guide to Antitrust Regulation," *Journal of Law and Economics,* 19 (August 1976): 383.

CONTRIBUTORS'
BIOGRAPHIES

DOUGLAS D. ANDERSON is an Assistant Professor at the Harvard Graduate School of Business where he teaches courses in business and government relations and international political economy. In addition he is studying economic policy-making in the Federal Republic of Germany.

BRADLEY BEHRMAN was graduated from Harvard College in June 1978 and subsequently worked as a research assistant at the Civil Aeronautics Board, the American Enterprise Institute, and the Brookings Institution. He entered Harvard Law School in September 1979.

ROBERT A. KATZMANN was graduated from Columbia College and received his A.M. and Ph.D. from the Government Department of Harvard University. He is a J.D. candidate at the Yale Law School where he is an articles and book review editor of the *Yale Law Journal.* He is the author of *Regulatory Bureaucracy: The Federal Trade Commission and Antitrust Policy* (MIT Press, 1980).

STEVEN KELMAN is an Assistant Professor at the Kennedy School of Government at Harvard University. He is the author of the recently published *Improving Doctor Performance* and has written widely on issues regarding safety, health, and environmental regulation. His study *Comparing Countries, Comparing Policies: A Study of Occupational and Health Regulations in the United States and Sweden* will be published in 1980 by the MIT Press.

EDWARD MANSFIELD is a law student at Yale University. He was graduated from Harvard College in 1979. This chapter is based upon his senior honor thesis: "The Theory and Practice of Utility: A Study of the Federal Maritime Commission."

ALFRED MARCUS is a policy analyst at the Battelle Human Affairs Research Center in Seattle, Washington. His book on the EPA, *Promise and Performance: Choosing and Implementing an Environmental Policy* has been published by Greenwood Press. He has written many other articles about the politics of pollution control and government regulation.

PAUL J. QUIRK is a research associate at the Brookings Institution and an assistant professor of political science at The Ohio State University (presently on leave). His dissertation on corporate influence and regulatory policy will be published by the Princeton University Press. His current research (in collaboration with Martha Derthick) is on the politics of deregulation.

JEREMY RABKIN is a graduate student in the Department of Government at Harvard University where he is completing a doctoral dissertation on judicially imposed limitations on the enforcement discretion of federal regulatory agencies, with special attention to the Office for Civil Rights. He is a graduate of Cornell University.

Contributor's Biographies

SUZANNE WEAVER is an editorial writer for the *Wall Street Journal.* She is the author of *Decision To Prosecute: Organization and Public Policy in the Anti-Trust Division* (MIT Press, 1977) and with Daniel P. Moynihan, *A Dangerous Place* (Atlantic Monthly Press, 1978).

JAMES Q. WILSON is the Henry Lee Shattuck Professor of Government at Harvard University. He is the author of, among other books, *Political Organizations* (Basic Books, 1973), *The Investigators: Managing FBI and Narcotics Agents* (Basic Books, 1978), and *American Government: Institutions and Policies* (D.C. Health, 1980).

NAME INDEX

SUBJECT INDEX